The Dialectic of Capital, Volume 1

Historical Materialism Book Series

The Historical Materialism Book Series is a major publishing initiative of the radical left. The capitalist crisis of the twenty-first century has been met by a resurgence of interest in critical Marxist theory. At the same time, the publishing institutions committed to Marxism have contracted markedly since the high point of the 1970s. The Historical Materialism Book Series is dedicated to addressing this situation by making available important works of Marxist theory. The aim of the series is to publish important theoretical contributions as the basis for vigorous intellectual debate and exchange on the left.

The peer-reviewed series publishes original monographs, translated texts, and reprints of classics across the bounds of academic disciplinary agendas and across the divisions of the left. The series is particularly concerned to encourage the internationalization of Marxist debate and aims to translate significant studies from beyond the English-speaking world.

For a full list of titles in the Historical Materialism Book Series
available in paperback from Haymarket Books, visit:
https://www.haymarketbooks.org/series_collections/1-historical-materialism

The Dialectic of Capital

A Study of the Inner Logic of Capitalism

Volume 1

*Introduction, the Doctrine of Circulation,
and the Doctrine of Production*

Thomas T. Sekine

Haymarket Books
Chicago, IL

First published in 2021 by Brill Academic Publishers, The Netherlands
© 2021 Koninklijke Brill NV, Leiden, The Netherlands

Published in paperback in 2021 by
Haymarket Books
P.O. Box 180165
Chicago, IL 60618
773-583-7884
www.haymarketbooks.org

ISBN: 978-1-64259-591-8

Distributed to the trade in the US through Consortium Book Sales and
Distribution (www.cbsd.com) and internationally through Ingram
Publisher Services International (www.ingramcontent.com).

This book was published with the generous support of Lannan
Foundation and Wallace Action Fund.

Special discounts are available for bulk purchases by organizations and
institutions. Please call 773-583-7884 or email info@haymarketbooks.org
for more information.

Cover art and design by David Mabb. Cover art is a detail of *Long Live
the New! no. 35*, Kazimir Malevich drawing on Morris & Co. design, paint
and wallpaper on canvas (2016).

Printed in the United States.

10 9 8 7 6 5 4 3 2 1

Library of Congress Cataloging-in-Publication data is available.

To my father
with filial affection

Contents

Preface to this Edition

Marx has been widely known and understood as an outstanding social thinker and revolutionist, and many volumes of work have been devoted to eternalising him in this regard. Yet it is not so well known and understood that Marx was, at the same time, an exceptionally penetrating and dependable economist whose theoretical acumen arguably surpassed that of Adam Smith and David Ricardo. This important fact in the *Dogmengeschichte* of economics has been carefully hidden and buried for years by the still dominant liberal ideology, which inspires and nurtures 'mainstream, bourgeois economics', bidding it to never stop singing the anachronistic hymn of the eternity of capitalism, which is understood to constitute the economic base (or substructure) of modern society. In partial proof of this contention, as yet no systematic work that reproduces and restates the full splendour of Marx's economic theory as perceived in a contemporary light (that is to say, as remoulded with updated analytical techniques) has been attempted. Marx's economic theory, which was expounded 150 years ago, expressly intending to 'lay bare the law of motion of modern society', has been left to sink into oblivion on the dusty shelves of some obscure archives. The sole exception to the rule has been Kôzô Uno's priceless effort towards the dialectic of capital. Unfortunately, however, Uno wrote all his works in Japanese – a peripheral language that has yet to become international. He also abided by the old method of using numerical examples to illustrate the theory rather than rigorously prove the scope of its general applicability. When Western Marxists (in co-operation with neoclassical *marxisants*) surmounted these limitations, however, their dilettantish approach of picking and choosing topical subjects at random in Marx's economics altogether lacked the systematic approach that an objective exposition of what constitutes the capitalist mode of production (that is, the *definition of capitalism by capital itself*) required. This book intends to fill that gap - that persistent lacuna in the history of economics - the reclaiming of which has long been overdue.

This book was written about three decades ago when I was still in the prime of my career. While working on it, I was somehow under the impression that a university press would undertake its publication as soon as the manuscript was completed. However, I was rudely informed at the last moment that some committee or other of the press had decided against it. Was this because the manuscript was too long and heavy, or did the theme of the book appear too unfamiliar to the potential reader? There was and remains no way of knowing. But if the committee was not wholly made up of blind souls, it may have perceived a potential danger of this book to both bourgeois economics and conventional Marxism – two professions well attuned to contemporary society as its, respectively, major and minor ideologies with which to stabilise or appease its superstructure, while preserving the appearance of vigorous academic freedom. In re-reading the book after so many years, I have that impression rather strongly, since human beings often make a 'right' decision without knowing why. In any case, I then chose to privately publish the book in Japan – volume one in 1984 and volume two in 1986 – in a limited number of copies for circulation primarily among my personal acquaintances. I, therefore, inserted the epithet 'preliminary edition' on the title page in parentheses. Yet over time the presence of the book began to be known more broadly than I had expected, especially after its shortened version, *An Outline of the Dialectic of Capital*, was published in 1997. Around the turn of the millennium, then, I was pleased to be told by Jim Kincaid and Sebastian Budgen that the possibility existed for this book to be published in a typeset edition. While being grateful to them, I was also rather hesitant, partly because I was still in active teaching and did not believe I could allocate enough time for an overhauling of the manuscript.

Now, several years into my retirement, I have more free time at my disposal than before. Yet the insidious advance of my age makes it impossible to produce a fully renovated version of this book. For one thing, I am no longer quite as mathematically alert as I used to be, so that it is possible for me to overlook many technical errors that ought to be corrected on this occasion. The only reason I decided to hazard such a risk, however, is that technical lapses can always be corrected without necessarily affecting the overall tenor of the arguments, which make up the real content of this book. Therefore, in preparing this new edition, I have adopted and abided by the policy of minimal corrections and alterations of the original text, the overall appearance of which I have wished to preserve. Thus, for example, I decided to maintain my original spelling (such as '-ise' and '-isation') and wording (such as 'commoditise' and 'commoditisation', instead of 'commodify' and 'commodification', which have since become the more common usage). I did not change the old-fashioned 'mankind' to the gender-neutral 'humankind'. I even retained the appellative 'political economy' in the sense of non-bourgeois economics, although today I would prefer to go back to the word 'economics' in its place, since I have little intention of meddling with political elements in my economic discourse. I have, however, rephrased a number of sentences and added a few more, where appropriate, hoping to make the text more easily readable. My old friend, Professor John R. Bell, has as always offered to me invaluable help in this regard, which I wish to acknowledge with my heartfelt thanks. In order to 'electronify' the manuscript for this edition, the originally typewritten text had to be scanned, page by page, first into PDF files, which were then converted into a Word document. For volume one, Joe Wheeler very generously offered to undertake that thankless task. For volume two, my wife Kazuko Sekine, and my daughter Reiko Salib, have most diligently applied themselves to the drudgery (or what is perhaps better described as *corvée abrutissante*). Furthermore, the 'figures and charts' that abound in some chapters of this book had to be redone to satisfy the typesetter. My son Kevin Sekine offered me his skills in order to meet this challenge. To the selfless assistance of all these persons, I am most deeply indebted.

At the present time, the world economy seems to be irrevocably sliding into a deflationary spiral, which will eventually lead to a 'great depression', comparable in its severity to the one experienced in the dark years of the 1930s. As it becomes clear that no 'policy recommendation' proffered by mainstream bourgeois economics would prove effective in reversing or even arresting that ominous fall from grace, the bankruptcy of that ideologically motivated teaching will become apparent. No new 'model' inspired by the liberal creed that irredeemably postulates the permanence of capitalism as a pre-established harmony can possibly furnish an effective measure to hold it back from disintegration when its time expires. To understand why this is so, a Copernican revolution in economics will be necessary. This book, despite the many flaws that may remain, will offer a base upon which to build a new approach to economics, transforming it from wishful thinking to true knowledge.

•••

After the above was written seven years ago, the works to republish this old volume in the present form were interrupted for a long while, before being suddenly resumed last year. Already in the twilight years of my life, I am not certain if I could do all I needed this time to bring this old manuscript fully up-to-date so as to serve, and appeal to, the new generation of readers interested in the economics of this kind. Traditionally, economics never directly studied "capitalism" as such, which it left in the background more or less as Providence that would realize itself automatically, if only left to itself uninterfered with. It was only Marx, who wanted to "lay bare the inner logic of the capitalist mode of production in its whole. Whereas most Marxists devoted themselves in revolutionary actions, whereby to replace "capitalism" with a "socialism", Kôzô Uno (1897–1997) persisted in completing Marx's unfinished work to eventually disclose the full inner logic of capitalism. My work on "the dialectic of capital" consciously abides by his tradition. For the preparation of this new edition, I am most deeply indebted for advice and help overall to my old friend Professor John R. Bell, especially in the preparation of the index to this book. I would also like to thank Professor Takashi Satô of Ritsumeikan University, for advising me specifically in mathematical matters.

Thomas T. Sekine, September 2019

Postscriptum

Since the above was written in 2012, a long interruption somehow intervened before the present work was abruptly resumed early in 2018. By that time, however, due to the aging of the author, the work of finalizing the text of this book could no longer proceed as vigorously and speedily as before. He is grateful to the present staff of the publisher for patiently helping him to keep alert to details and subtleties, which otherwise might have escaped his attention. He is also grateful especially to Professor Satoh Takashi of Ritsumeikan University, who kindly guided him in regard to the proof of the inequalities (76), appearing in B (b)(β) of Chapter 7, The Theory of Profit. Apart from the valuable help in such specific points, the author is also most deeply indebted to the constant moral support and encouragement lavished on him by his old friends, Professors R. Albritton, John R. Bell and Richard Westra as well as by Mr. Ken Kubota, without which this book would not have been made available in this form. Professor Bell, in particular and among other things, produced the original version of the Subject Index to this book, relieving the author from the chore to which he is no longer fit.

The only regret that the author must admit at this point is that the original text of this book was written in the 1980s, when the so-called "gender-neutral style of writing" was not quite as widely in practice as it is today. Ideally, he would have liked to change his archaic style to the new one in this edition. But that would have taken much more time and effort than he could afford at this point. He is, therefore, obliged to maintain that archaic style reluctantly, unless a chance arrives for a new edition of this book, while he is still alive.

April 2020

Preface to the First Edition

The study of Marxian political economy in the West seems to have gained momentum in recent years, as if to presage the impending collapse of bourgeois social science. This tendency is, of course, both reassuring and gratifying. Yet many theoretical studies in this direction still concentrate on such specific issues as Marx's value-and-price theory, crisis theory, reproduction theory, and so on, without paying sufficient attention to the manner in which they might all be integrated in a total system. These studies often imply that the nature of Marxian economic doctrine as a whole could be surmised simply from the conventional understandings of Marxism. Radically different from such approaches is that of Kôzô Uno. The latter advances the idea that the Marxian economic doctrine as a whole constitutes a self-contained system, no part of which can be adequately comprehended in isolation from the rest, and that the logical synthesis of this system (which I call the 'dialectic of capital') should precede not only Marxism, but the very concept of capitalism that it intends to criticise. In the introduction to this book, I shall elaborate on the methodology of Uno's political economy. In view of its radical departure from conventional Marxism, Uno's contribution reveals a new direction in which future scholarly works in the Marxian tradition may be developed more fruitfully.

The 1980 publication in English of Uno's *Principles of Political Economy* should, therefore, lend significant impetus to Western studies in Marxism. Yet the extraordinary conciseness of its style makes it difficult for anyone to immediately grasp the meaning of Uno's thought. While using the text of the *Principles* in seminar discussions at York University over several years, I was frequently obliged to produce explanatory notes of my own to supplement it. The present volume has developed from the pile of such notes, originally intended to merely elaborate on and amplify Uno's text. Yet as *The Dialectic of Capital* grew into an independent book, it was inevitable that my exposition would diverge somewhat from Uno's. Just as Uno himself, while intending to be faithful to Marx's thought, did not hesitate to depart from Marx's text, I too felt free to reproduce Uno's thought in my own language, without being unduly constrained by the text of his writings. For this, Uno would not blame me, since it was he who taught me that what is to be learned is the thought itself, and not the text that (more or less imperfectly) expresses it.

However, I am convinced that this book contains nothing fundamentally opposed to or incompatible with Uno's thought. I have tried to be 'innovative' only in two respects, both of which are matters of expository technique. First, I have explicitly brought out the correspondence between the dialectic of capital and Hegel's logic – a correspondence Uno chose to hold implicit. The purpose is not only to make evident that there is no oriental mysticism involved in Uno's reasoning, but also to draw on existing Hegel scholarship in the West. Secondly, I have freely resorted to the mathematical method of economic analysis where appropriate, although Uno (like Marx) held fast to the more traditional arithmetical method. There will be little objection nowadays to the use of mathematics in the formulation of economic theory. However, I must stress here that the formally logical argument must always be assigned its proper place in the total structure of the dialectic. Since the dialectic is not an axiomatic method, it is impossible for the economic theory to be stated entirely in mathematical terms. In this book, the use of mathematics is concentrated particularly in Chapter 7 (which will feature in Volume Two), where the theories of price and profit are studied.

From what has been said above, it should be clear that there is nothing ambiguous about the purpose of this book. It intends to expose the core of Uno's paradigm, which is not yet well known in the West. This book does not intend to make incremental contributions to current debates on various aspects of Marxian economic theory. It is true that it makes its own contributions to the transformation problem, the falling rate of profit, the reproduction-schemes, and other popular topics. However, I would ask the reader to appraise them in the context of the dialectic of capital, rather than to immediately try to relate them to current debates. Indeed, similar conclusions of the dialectic and Western Marxism, respectively, may have been reached from altogether different perspectives. For this reason, I have intentionally kept references to the current literature to an unavoidable minimum. But this must not be taken to mean that the dialectic refuses to learn from ongoing theoretical debates or shirks productive controversies with other approaches. The dialectic of capital welcomes criticisms, provided that they are offered with an awareness of the whole of its scope.

The idea of this book has developed from my teaching and research at York University over many years, during which I benefited from the active support and sympathetic understanding of my colleagues and students. I am especially grateful to Professor Robert R. Albritton, whose friendship and encouragement have been invaluable in the preparation of this book, and with whom I have shared a number of first-rate graduate students. The three most promising of them, Messrs. John R. Bell, Colin Duncan, and Brian MacLean, have gone out of their way in assisting me to edit the text of this book. No word can suffice to express my gratitude for their kindness and devotion. On technical matters, I have been the fortunate recipient of much willingly proffered advice. I am particularly indebted to Professor Wahidul Haque of the University of Toronto, who went through the whole of an earlier version of the text and brought to my attention many slips, which would otherwise have gone uncorrected. I am also grateful to Professor Yoriaki Fujimori of Josai University, Japan, who kindly advised me on many mathematical parts of this book. However, none of these persons is responsible for whatever errors that might still remain. Parts of this book were previously published as articles in *Science and Society* and *York Studies in Political Economy.* I am grateful to the editors of these journals for their permission to reproduce the same contents in this volume.

In view of the difficulty in publishing a book of this size on a commercial basis, this word-processed edition has been prepared as research material at York University in a limited number of copies, pending formal publication. Much of the work in this connection has been carried out during my absence from York University by the Secretarial Services of its Faculty of Arts, under the guidance of Professor Albritton. My thanks are due to Professor Albritton and Mrs. Doris Rippington, the director of Secretarial Services. I would also like to thank a number of people who cheerfully and competently typed and retyped parts of this voluminous manuscript in the past several years.

Thomas T. Sekine, June 1983
Mitaka, Tokyo

Introduction

A   Marxism, Ideology and Science

(a)   *Marxism as an Ideology*

(α) The professed aim of Marxism is to dislodge the existing regime of capitalism and to establish in its place an alternative regime of socialism. Understood in this way, Marxism is no more than one of many alternative socialist ideologies. I understand an ideology to be, in the first instance, a set of value judgements, more or less clearly formulated, that calls for a definite form of social action, or 'practice', as the latter is frequently called. A 'definite form of social action' includes consistent inaction, which amounts to a conscious or unconscious acceptance of the *status quo*. A vision, or *Anschauung* (outlook), that implies a definite form of social action may also be considered synonymous with an ideology. Manifold shades of ideology exist in all societies, ranging from the ultra-reactionary to the recklessly radical. As a rule, the more decisive the social action called for by an ideology, the more clearly it is formulated and the more vigorously it is advocated. A large segment of the population, however, often remains complacent with the existing principles and values of social life, adopting a neutral or centre-of-the-road ideology. Such an ideology tends to be inconspicuous and unsystematic, for there is little need to reassert social values that are already accepted.

Conversely, every consistent social action – whether conscious or unconscious – implies some ideology, that is to say, a preconceived idea as to what society ought to be like. The 'ought' is a matter of practical wisdom and cannot be logically deduced from an objective knowledge of the facts. An ideology that subjectively interprets facts defines the ought of social action. Facts can be perceived either correctly or incorrectly. Knowledge can be established as either true or false. However, an ideology cannot be scientifically right or wrong, true or false; rather, it is only individually acceptable or unacceptable, and hence socially effective or ineffective. An ideology consists of practical decisions and moral judgements arising from the subjective priorities of the individual or a group of individuals. Thus, whenever an ideology is in the ascendant, it is so by sheer force of persuasion, which need not necessarily satisfy any criterion of objective truth. An ideology becomes stronger as it forces its way to widespread acceptance and allegiance. In order to achieve their aim, socialists too must vigorously pursue an ideological campaign and win mass support. For this reason, they must form political parties to rally for concrete actions.

If all forms of social action are thus explicitly or implicitly motivated by an ideology, it does not follow that the study of society cannot hope to be objective, or that social science necessarily retains ideological biases. Since 'science' means objective knowledge, social science that is not objective is a contradiction in terms. The totality of social actions motivated by different ideologies constitutes a social process. Social science worthy of its name must explain the social process objectively, that is to say, free from subjective interpretations, wishful thinking and value judgements; in short, free from ideological biases. If no social process could be objectively studied, social science would clearly be an impossibility. But if there is one social process susceptible of objective explanation, it is in principle possible to establish the whole edifice of social science on the knowledge of that process. The purpose of this Introduction is to show that the capitalist mode of production is the only social process susceptible to objective analysis.

Marxists invariably call for a 'unity of theory and practice', but it is not clear what exactly is meant by 'theory' in this oft-repeated phrase. If by 'theory' they simply mean a vision (*Anschauung*) that calls for a particular type of social action, that is, an ideology, the unity of theory and practice is a pure pleonasm. For an idea of society that does not involve a practice – passive or active – is not an ideology. If by 'theory' they mean a natural-scientific conjecture or hypothesis, and by 'practice' its empirical test by experiments or observations, then the phrase is a commonplace reassertion of empiricism. If by 'theory' they mean a revolutionary or other strategy, and by 'practice' its trial-and-error application, then the phrase merely advises a pragmatic approach to everyday life. According to the conventional interpretation, the 'unity of theory and practice' appears to mean all of these, in which case the slogan amounts to little more than a glorious pontification of conventional wisdom.

I believe that a more sensible interpretation of the phrase is possible. If 'theory' means an objective knowledge of society, and 'practice' means a particular type of social action, then the unification of the two is possible only by means of an ideology, which is not in this case a blind ideology that ignores the objective knowledge of society, but an enlightened one that presupposes it and specifies a particular type of social action in its light. It makes sense to characterise an 'enlightened' ideology as an ethical converter or transformer of the objective knowledge of society (theory) into a specific form of social action (practice). Even this type of ideology involves ethical judgements and cannot be logically deduced from theory. But since 'theory' in the sense of objective knowledge does not by itself uniquely determine a specific practice, an ideology has an active role to play in unifying them. If that interpretation is accepted, Marxism can be described as both an enlightened ideology that unifies the objective knowledge of capitalism, and a revolutionary practice that aims to achieve socialism.

Marxism, in this sense, clearly differs from other socialist ideologies in explicitly recognising an objective knowledge of capitalist society prior to itself. Marx often criticised utopian socialists for lacking a scientific conception of capitalism, and claimed that his own brand of socialism, unlike any other, stood on the scientific analysis of capitalism. Quite apart from what the scientific knowledge of capitalist society might consist in, Marx clearly intended to differentiate his 'enlightened' ideology from those less sophisticated kinds entertained by the utopian socialists. The utopians were directly moved by the distress of the working class – an empirically observed fact – holding capitalism responsible for it. But their theories of capitalism were purely *ad hoc*, unsystematic and naïve. Marx was not satisfied with the fragile foundation of utopian socialism, and sought an objective account of the capitalist mode of production. He believed that true socialism – although itself an ideology involving moral judgements – must at least begin with an objective comprehension of the laws of the existing regime. It is this fact that unambiguously demonstrates the greatness of Marx.

(β) Marxism, for this reason, has come to be called 'scientific' socialism, in contrast to utopian socialism. But this expression is misleading. It is not Marxist socialism itself that is scientific, for Marxism, like any other brand of socialism, is an ideology, and as such cannot be scientific or objective. What is scientifically defensible is the knowledge of capitalist society, which Marxism recognises as prior to itself. The confusion of prominent Marxists – including Engels, Lenin, and perhaps even at times Marx himself – with regard to this fundamental point has obscured the distinguishing feature of Marxism from other socialist ideologies. The facile idea that Marxism by itself constitutes a science has misled many of its adherents into a false conviction of infallibility, which has in turn rendered them less tolerant, and more dogmatic and abrasive, than other socialists. The popular conception that Marxism is a secular religion stems, not without reason, from the inordinate self-righteousness and inflexibility of convinced Marxists.

The disastrous confusion is nowhere more apparent than in the orthodox Marxist claim of 'partisan science'. Marxists are, of course, entirely justified in denouncing the ideological biases of bourgeois social science, insofar as the latter represents capitalist society one-sidedly, namely, from the point of view of the capitalists. The image of capitalist society, when viewed by the workers, may indeed be quite different. For example, from the point of view of the workers, capitalism may not appear to be the paradise of Pareto-optimality that standard textbooks of economics never cease to inculcate. Instead, it may appear to be a dismal world of alienation, class hostilities and exploitation. From this, however, it does not follow that the negative view of capitalist society is necessarily less fallible than the apologetic one. Both are one-sided and contain ideological biases. If several blind men touch different parts of an elephant, it is only to be expected that they will come to widely divergent conclusions. To claim that the revolutionary proletariat, to which history assigns a progressive mission, is necessarily equipped with a God-given clairvoyance is merely to confuse ideology with objective knowledge.

In order for the knowledge of capitalist society to be objective it must surely be intersubjective, that is to say, it must be convincing regardless of one's ideology. This means that capitalism must be understood not in its partial aspects from the differing viewpoints of the capitalists, the workers, or any other sectional interests, but rather as a total social process viewed from all angles. The objective knowledge of capitalist society must, in other words, transcend all ideologies, including socialist ideologies. An *ad hoc* theory of capitalism or an ideologically motivated interpretation of some of its empirical phenomena certainly does not satisfy this condition of objectivity.

(γ) I have so far defined social practice in its narrower sense, without including in it the pursuit of social-scientific knowledge. But if the latter is also included as a special form of practice, as is sometimes advised, then it becomes quite logical to conclude that a motivating ideology or 'vision' should precede it as well. In that case, I shall call such an ideology 'passive' or 'implicit' and distinguish it from the 'active' ideology, which I have already described as an ethical converter. Indeed, the history of political economy shows that the frontier of knowledge was always opened when a new critical ideology challenged the existing outlook on society, motivating further enquiries. Since society can be studied only by man who lives in society, his pursuit of social scientific knowledge implies his desire to situate himself objectively in society. It is the self-consciousness of the questioning person that in the form of a passive ideology motivates the advancement of social-scientific knowledge.

The present view thus requires a differentiation of ideology into the passive part that precedes objective knowledge, and the active part that follows it. The usual neglect of this differentiation stems from the failure to give objective knowledge its proper place. Indeed, if the knowledge of society is either absent or scanty, a passive ideology may immediately link with an active ideology. This is the case, for example, with utopian socialism, which produced no recognisable knowledge capable of mediating the passive and the active part of its ideology. Such an ideology is frail and can never mobilise a significant social force, which might determine the course of history. It remains an ever-present noise in society, with varying audibility, depending on contingent circumstances. In contrast, a great ideology that spawns social progress makes some contributions to social-scientific knowledge. Such contributions cannot be altogether ignored, even if they are one-sided or narrowly restricted in scope.

Consider the history of liberal ideology. By being a critic of mercantilism, the then dominant ideology, Adam Smith could descry what remained beyond the scope of traditional knowledge, namely, the fact that capital unfolds its full potential in a regime of free competition. Instead of merely resorting to political polemics, Smith sought to demonstrate this fact objectively, and in so doing produced the first systematic treatise of economic theory, for that was the surest way to discredit mercantilism. Indeed, a critical ideology confronting a powerful opponent cannot help invoking objective truth, if that is at all possible. However, when liberalism itself became the dominant ideology – when capitalism was materialising the golden age of free trade – it provided political economy with no new insight. It served solely as an active dogma in support of the existing regime and against the rising tide of socialism. Classical political economy, on which liberalism as an active ideology continued to feed, lost its original inspiration and respect for truth, and degenerated into a lifeless catechism. Indeed, knowledge once appropriated by an active ideology cannot remain free and objective. For an active ideology only makes use of established knowledge for a definite purpose; it is not interested in the objectivity of the knowledge itself.

Returning to Marxism, I now intend to represent its structure schematically as in Chart 0.1. Marx was a socialist before being an economist. It was his socialism that guided him to the study of political economy. But as a passive ideology, his socialism at that point was quite open, inasmuch as it merely criticised the existing regime of capitalism as being incompatible with human existence. The vaguely understood impermanence of capitalism was, however, not enough for Marx to stipulate an active ideology. He needed an objective critique of the capitalist mode of production before he could convert his passive

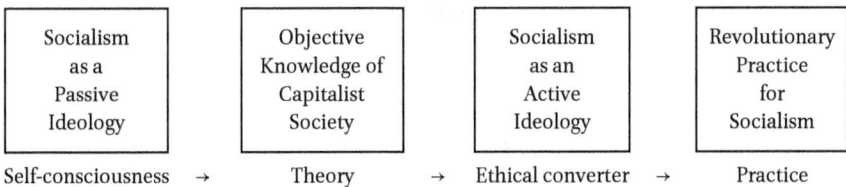

Socialism as a Passive Ideology	Objective Knowledge of Capitalist Society	Socialism as an Active Ideology	Revolutionary Practice for Socialism
Self-consciousness →	Theory →	Ethical converter →	Practice

CHART 0.1

ideology into an active one. It was this that rendered Marxism an enlightened and powerful ideology.

However, this does not mean that Marxism is a 'correct' ideology. Rather, it only means that it is a 'strong' ideology. Whether or not a Marxist practice is the only or the most effective way to overcome capitalism and to replace it with socialism is always open to question, for it necessarily depends on the concrete conditions that prevail at a particular moment in a particular place. However, as an active ideology, Marxism too prohibits the questioning of its own judgment. This unavoidable single-mindedness of an ideology, if uncontrolled, can easily paralyse the objectivity of the knowledge of capitalism that originally inspired it, for unlike a *passive* ideology, which is open to objective knowledge, an *active* ideology is necessarily closed with respect to its interpretation. It is this point that must be clearly borne in mind in the following evaluation of the threefold doctrinal contents of Marxism.

(b)   The Three Elements of Marxist Knowledge

(α) Conventional Marxism advances the following three forms of knowledge, all of which it claims to be scientific: (1) dialectical materialism, or the dialectic of nature; (2) historical materialism, or the dialectic of history; and (3) the political economy of capitalism, or the dialectic of capital. I will argue, however, that only the last can be defended as objective knowledge.

Having been trained in the tradition of German-idealist philosophy, Marx maintained a lifelong admiration of Hegel, whose dialectic was a method of logically synthesising a metaphysical (philosophical) system. Marx, however, believed that Hegel's dialectic could be disengaged from idealism and made consistent with materialism. In 1873, in the afterword to the Second Edition of *Capital*, Volume I, Marx wrote:

> The mystification which dialectic suffers in Hegel's hands, by no means prevents him from being the first to present its general form of working in a comprehensive and conscious manner. With him it is standing on its head. It must be turned right side up again, if you would discover the rational kernel within the mystical shell.[1]

From this it is apparent that Marxist knowledge intends to ground itself on a materialistic transposition of Hegel's dialectic. Of the three forms of the presumed materialistic dialectic, however, Marx is mainly responsible for the last

---

1   Marx 1967, *Capital*, Volume I, p. 20.

two; the first and the most general form, dialectical materialism, is generally understood to be the work of Engels and Lenin.

Believing that 'nature is the proof of dialectics', Engels sought to confirm in some nineteenth-century discoveries of the natural sciences the manifestations of so-called dialectical laws. One of the most striking consequences of these discoveries, as Engels saw it, was the realisation that 'nature does not just exist, but comes into being and passes away'.[2] To Engels, this meant that the decisive mode of thought in the natural sciences should be dialectical, for only the dialectic could clarify 'the evolutionary processes occurring in nature, interconnections in general, and transitions from one field of investigation to another'.[3] It is true that the empirical sciences must begin with given facts, not with thoughts – as in the case of Hegel;[4] but 'laws of thought and laws of nature are necessarily in agreement with one another'.[5] The 'tremendous mass of positive materials for knowledge' thus far accumulated by the natural sciences was in need of systematic investigations for which 'theoretical thinking' was indispensable, and to develop the capacity for theoretical thinking 'there is as yet no other means than the study of previous philosophy'.[6] Indeed, 'the investigation of the forms of thought, the thought determinations, is very profitable and necessary, and since Aristotle this has been systematically undertaken only by Hegel'.[7]

Thus, Engels hoped to systematise the interconnections of natural phenomena by means of the dialectic, and to establish the proof of dialectical materialism in place of Hegel's *Naturphilosophie*. However, Engels's own book, *Dialectics of Nature* (written circa 1880 and published posthumously in 1925) shows that his aim was frustrated by the 'relative character of knowledge', that is, by the fact that the scientific conception of nature necessarily remains relative to (and dependent on) the current state of knowledge, the 'falsification' of which is imminent with every progress of science. Dialectic, as I intend to show in this Introduction, is a method of total knowledge, and cannot account for samples of tentative knowledge. Since no 'final' discovery of nature can ever be made, and since the knowledge of nature must always consist of *so-far-so-good hypotheses*, 'the interconnexions of natural phenomena' cannot be synthesised or systematised dialectically. Engels himself may have realised this limitation, for he did not continue to work on that book after the death of Marx in 1883.

---

2 Engels 1969, p. 38.
3 Engels 1969, p. 59.
4 Engels 1969, p. 64.
5 Engels 1969, p. 299.
6 Engels 1969, p. 58.
7 Engels 1969, p. 318.

Not only did Engels lose his reliable mentor, but also by the end of the 1880s the state of the so-called 'crisis of physics' was clearly looming on the horizon.

Engels's book contains a short article called 'Dialectics' written in 1879, with the subtitle: 'The general nature of dialectics to be developed as the science of inter-connections, in contrast to metaphysics'. Regardless of what he meant by 'the science of inter-connections', however, such a 'science' is not developed in that article, nor is it developed anywhere else in Engels's writings. The article merely contains a brief exposition of the three so-called laws of the dialectic: the transformation of quantity into quality; the interpenetration of opposites; and the negation of the negation. Much is also made of these laws in Engels's *Anti-Dühring* and elsewhere. Yet a mere assertion of such laws, illustrated by trivial examples, cannot possibly explain the dialectic of nature, or that of the universe, any more than the hackneyed triad of 'thesis, antithesis and synthesis' can. Lenin's *Materialism and Empirio-Criticism* of 1908, which was written without the knowledge of *Dialectics of Nature*, competently reproduces many of Engels's ideas, but apart from some polemical passages of interest, it adds little to *the three laws* of the dialectic. Lenin also fails to prove that the dialectic governs nature or the universe, and none of his followers has had any success either. Thus, dialectical materialism remains the unfulfilled dream of conventional Marxists; it has never been demonstrated as objective or scientific knowledge.

(β) Many Marxists rightly criticise Engels's rather formalistic approach, and try to discover a more authentic version of the materialistic dialectic in Marx's historical materialism, otherwise known as the 'materialistic conception of history'. This second example of Marxian dialectic was formulated by Marx himself as the 'guiding thread' to the study of political economy when, in his youth, he criticised Hegel's philosophy of law. According to Marx's Preface to *A Contribution to the Critique of Political Economy*, it consists of the three main principles or propositions:

1. *The principle of substructure*: the material base (or *substructure*) of any society consists of its *production-relations*, namely, the interrelations of men, organised in the activity of producing use-values. That economic substructure determines, but is not determined by, the ideological *superstructure* or the conscious elements of society.
2. *The principle of correspondence*: a definite set of production-relations depends upon and corresponds with a particular level of development of *productive forces* available to society. Thus, if productive powers develop beyond a certain limit, the existing set of production-relations invariably breaks up in order to be replaced by a new set of production-relations.

3. *The principle of class antagonism*: the history of mankind from its be-
    ginning to the age of capitalism is a history of *class struggles*. Bourgeois
    society is the last class-antagonistic society, and ends the *pre-history of
    humanity*.

These principles are said to apply universally to the history of human societies up to and including modern bourgeois society, although perhaps excluding
some prehistoric, classless societies.

   These propositions, however, cannot be objectively or scientifically confirmed, not even as empirically testable hypotheses. For example, how can one
conclusively test that the economic is prior to the ideological in the constitution of any society? Max Weber's proposition that the Protestant ethic gave
rise to capitalism is at least as empirically plausible as the counter-proposition
that capitalism promotes the Protestant ethic. In ascertaining the correspondence between production-relations and productive powers, how should one
determine the level of technological development? The capitalist mode of production alone appears to correspond with such vastly different technological
stages as the seventeenth-century manufacture of wool in England and the
present-day application of electronics and nuclear energy to industry. Is it possible to convincingly argue that bourgeois society is the last class antagonistic
society by pointing to the accomplishments of present-day Communist nations, or should one withhold judgement (perhaps forever) until a truly classless society evolves in history? Even if there existed some universal knowledge
of history in the light of which these propositions were subjectively deemed
fair enough interpretations, that would not establish the truth and objectivity
of these propositions. Only charlatans would vouch for the veracity of such
sweeping generalisations.

   It is quite obvious that Marx did not intend the three propositions of historical materialism to be 'empirically testable' hypotheses. Had that been the
case, he would no doubt have searched the history of mankind for instances of
their verification or falsification, which he did not. Instead of embarking first
on detailed historical investigations, he turned instead to the study of political
economy. This implies that these universal propositions are not meant to be
directly tested as true or false, but merely to be formulated as general ideological *hypotheses*. Indeed, if they were by themselves true, why would they not
be sufficient? There would be no need to appeal to political economy merely
to reaffirm already authenticated truth in the narrower context of bourgeois
society. This important point is often overlooked by those Marxists who exploit
the inevitable ambiguities of the statements of historical materialism and sally
forth with arbitrary interpretations. Whatever 'creative' interpretations may
be advanced, the fact remains that these unproven propositions of historical

materialism cannot by themselves constitute an objective knowledge of human history. They are, at most, general 'ideological hypotheses' whose contribution to real knowledge is, in the first instance, limited to being a 'guiding principle' to it.

In this book, however, it will be shown that the propositions of historical materialism are not irrelevant to the political economy of capitalism. Although these propositions are not demonstrable *in toto*, they can be shown to be true, insofar as they pertain to capitalist society, the only society susceptible to objective analysis. Indeed, the logical self-containedness of the dialectic of capital (which is to be demonstrated in this book) implies that the *substructure* of capitalist society hangs together without depending on any element of its ideological *superstructure*. The fact that capital introduces a new technology whenever the existing value relation reaches a stalemate indicates a particular mode of operation of the principle of correspondence within capitalism. Finally, capitalist society forms its class relations by means of purely commodity-economic necessities, and not by the direct application of extra-economic forces; in other words, it not only disavows its own class divisions at an ideological level, but also implicitly aspires to a classless society. The propositions of historical materialism are, therefore, not empty generalisations from history. These propositions can be shown to be true, albeit in specific senses, as fundamental characteristics of capitalist society. Because of this fact historical materialism also offers an important working hypothesis in the evaluation of pre-capitalist societies, just as 'the anatomy of man is a key to the anatomy of the ape'.[8] Historical materialism is thus double-edged. On the one hand, it is a guiding principle for the study of political economy, and on the other, it is a working hypothesis for the study of history in the light of political economy.

(γ) The third component of Marxist doctrine – the political economy of capitalism – has a much more restricted scope. It does not interpret the whole universe, nature, or history, but only examines capitalist society, a historically unique and transient institution. To the study of this much less grandiose subject matter, Marx's *Capital* devotes nearly two-thousand pages, in three volumes, and develops detailed economic arguments in the scientific tradition of classical political economy, while exhaustively criticising prior doctrines related to the subject matter. Consequently, the dialectic of capital does not consist of a mere triplet of general laws or principles; instead it forms a self-contained logical system. This fact cannot be underestimated, for it means that the transposition of Hegel's dialectic from idealism to materialism is not merely

---

8   Marx 1970, *A Contribution to the Critique of Political Economy*, p. 211.

intended, but is in essence accomplished in *Capital*. Thus, if a materialistic dialectic that is supposed to generate objective and scientific knowledge is to be found anywhere in Marxism, *Capital* is the only place to find it. The exposition of the dialectic of capital is by no means perfect, even in *Capital*, which in fact contains many unconvincing and even misleading arguments, if not outright errors. However, such shortcomings can be, in principle, corrected in the well-posed context of *Capital*. There is no doubt that Marx has laid the foundation of the *dialectic of capital*, which can be made fully defensible as the objective knowledge of capitalist society.

An important question naturally arises: why only in political economy, the express purpose of which is the clarification of the laws of motion of capitalism (in the sense of the capitalist mode of production), could a materialistic dialectic be accomplished in an essentially correct form? The answer may be found in one of Hegel's most celebrated metaphors, namely, that 'the owl of Minerva spreads its wings only with the falling of the dusk'. These cryptic words are preceded by the following explanation:

> One word more about giving instruction as to what the world ought to be. Philosophy in any case always comes on the scene too late to give it. As the thought of the world, it appears only when actuality is already there cut and dried after its process of formation has been completed. The teaching of the concept, which is also history's inescapable lesson is that it is only when actuality is mature that the ideal apprehends this same real world in its substance and builds it up for itself into the shape of an intellectual realm. When philosophy paints its grey in grey, then has the shape of life grown old. By philosophy's grey in grey it cannot be rejuvenated but only understood.[9]

Since the dialectic is a method for the total comprehension of an evolutionary (historical) process, it is impossible to 'know' the full nature of the process before it reaches a certain level of maturity, that is to say, before it itself exhibits its own formative logic. The only reason that Hegel was successful in building his system of philosophy dialectically was that, at the time of his writing, the age of philosophy as a system of metaphysical knowledge was ending, and was destined to be superseded by the age of science. It is, therefore, correctly said that philosophy came to an end with Hegel.

Neither can political economy, which studies the historical institution of capitalism, form a self-contained system of knowledge prior to its own maturity.

---

9   Hegel 1967, pp. 12–3.

The history of economic doctrines demonstrates that the mercantilists never grasped a global concept of capitalist society, and that even their classical critics who envisaged the golden age of free trade did not recognise capitalism as a historically transient institution. It was the distinguishing trait of Marx's approach to political economy to view capitalism as a historical institution. Such a critical outlook, which enabled Marx to evaluate capitalism as a total social process, was in effect socialism in an implicit form (a passive ideology, as described in the previous section). It naturally called for a historical approach to political economy, but Marx's success in arriving at the dialectical synthesis of capitalism would have been limited if capitalism in history had not itself reached its maturity by the time of the writing of *Capital*. Marx, who undertook his economic studies during the 1850s and 1860s in England, had the remarkable opportunity of combining his philosophical insight with the direct observation of capitalism in the process of self-synthesis. Yet the fact that Marx's death occurred before the conclusive evolution of imperialism, the last stage of capitalist development, meant that he did not and could not clearly distinguish the logical constituents of capitalism from their empirical contingencies. Thus, *Capital* discusses both the inner logic of capitalism and its historically particular manifestations as if they were one and the same thing. To that extent, *Capital* falls short of presenting a pure dialectic of capital in strict correspondence with Hegel's metaphysical logic. In the stage of imperialism, in which the inner logic of capitalism appears only with predictable distortions, not only is the end of the institution clearly foreseen, but also the theoretical necessity of separating the logical from the contingent becomes unavoidable. Only with the realisation of this necessity can the dialectic of capital be completed.

Kôzô Uno was undoubtedly the first to realise this fact consciously. He did not wholly accept *Capital* as it was written, but rather searched for the *dialectic of capital* as it should be written. Many Marxists would still consider it a blasphemy not to accept *Capital* as it is written, the smallest departure from the text being taken as a sign of revisionist deviation. Such an inflexible attitude, however, diminishes the most valuable asset of Marxism. The objective knowledge of capitalist society, which Marx discovered in essence, and upon which the whole edifice of social science must be built, the knowledge that Marxists can truly pride themselves in, would be completely squandered if *Capital* were turned into a holy scripture permitting no legitimate questioning.

(c)   The Problem of Social Science

(α) So far I have used the expression 'objective knowledge' as synonymous with 'science', but in everyday language 'science' often means natural science, which, of course, is an older discipline than social science. Hence arises the popular misconception that natural science is bound to be, in some sense, more 'scientific' than social science, and that social science, in order to be 'scientific', must model itself after natural science. Such a superficial opinion, although openly espoused by one or more of the currently dominant schools of philosophy, is repugnant to reason. Any knowledge of the real world – whether it pertains to natural or to social phenomena – is scientific if and only if it is objectively defensible, instead of being subjective and arbitrary. From this point of view, it is natural science that is only half-scientific, since its objectivity is always open to question. One has to accept the fact that nature does not 'become grey', and that the validity of explanations in natural science must remain 'relative' to the current state of knowledge. Nature can never be totally or finally known. Only certain specific aspects of nature can be known with increasing precision. If this is the case, then the being (the ontic presence) of nature and its cognition are necessarily apart, and the distance that separates them – however much it may be shortened – can never be wholly eliminated. Hence, the cognitive method of natural science cannot circumvent the correspondence theory of truth. This point was perhaps most clearly established by Kant's philosophy, which insisted upon the unknowability of the *thing-in-itself.*

The issue is how theory and facts are related to each other in natural science. One of the simplest examples of 'theory' may be the Euclidean theorem, which states that the three inner angles of a triangle add up to a straight line. This theorem is an immediate consequence of the axiom of parallel lines, and is formally (tautologically) demonstrated to be true, but in order to apply this theorem to the study of nature and draw some substantive (that is, factually non-empty) conclusions, one must construct a physical triangle. Of course, any physical triangle is an imperfect representation of the mathematical triangle. Hence, in order to empirically observe the result predicted by the theorem, the construction of the physical triangle must be judged reasonably accurate. It is the lack of any universal standard, by which one physical triangle is judged admissible while another is not, that makes the correspondence of theory and fact purely *ad hoc* and pragmatic. An axiomatic (or tautological) statement such as the Euclidean theorem on triangles does not by itself constitute a natural-scientific theory. In order to make it relevant to the study of nature, such a statement must be translated into a factual statement by means of an *operational* directive, specifying how one may conduct its empirical testing (how one may construct a physical triangle). However, an operational directive is always more or less arbitrary and involves practical (that is, subjective) judgements.

This is not all. A scientific statement is usually phrased in the following *predictive* form: 'if conditions a, b, ..., n are satisfied, then the result x will follow'. If we suppose that all ambiguities concerning the factual significance of a, b, ..., n and x are already overcome, how many times must this observation be tested before we may conclusively accept the theoretical prediction $(a, b, ..., n) \rightarrow x$? This, of course, is the well-known problem of Hume. Even if the same result has always been observed, that does not warrant an *a priori* conclusion that the test may not fail in the next experiment, since no test is 'final'. This simply means that the truth of any natural-scientific proposition can never be absolutely established; it has only so far withstood 'falsification' (in the light of counter-evidence). Yet a *so-far-so-good hypothesis* can always be refuted tomorrow. In fact, it is this refutability that has been claimed as the mark of a sound scientific statement! This is just another way of affirming that nature does not become *grey,* and hence that the knowledge of nature is destined to remain tentative or 'relative' forever. Whether or not this state of affairs is satisfactory, there is no escaping this dilemma in natural science. Since nature cannot be wholly known, there remains in it Kant's thing-in-itself that is forever unknowable. Hence, the knowledge of nature necessarily remains partial and subjective.

The consequence of this fact is that natural science can only teach us how to 'conform to' nature. There is no question of abolishing existing nature and replacing it with something else. Whatever may be the natural order that God is alleged to have designed, man has to conform to it in order to derive the greatest benefit from it. This *conformism* is a practical wisdom of man in general, regardless of his individual or social values. There is consequently nothing ideological about it. It is perhaps for this reason that the lack of strict objectivity in natural science can be tolerated. For what is the point of knowing nature *in toto* and thus abolishing its unknowable thing-in-itself? Would this not be as impious as to arrogate the divine wisdom?

(β) If conformity to the forces of nature is thus free from ideology, conformity to the existing social order cannot be. An individual or a group of individuals can choose to either conform to the existing order or not. No social order is permanent and irrevocable; it only comes into being at a particular time in history and passes away at another. It is for this reason that no society is free from ideological divisions. Thus, a profound difference between the subject-matter of social science and that of natural science is already obvious. Nature is not created by man, and may, therefore, retain the unknowable thing-in-itself. But society, which is a human contrivance, cannot maintain the same degree of mystery within it. There is, therefore, no reason why the formation of human society, at least in its abstract generality, cannot be totally and objectively exposed. It goes without saying that man possesses the ability to know what he himself invents. There is no 'thing-in-itself' in mathematics or in any other man-made tautological (axiomatic) system. Even speculative philosophy (metaphysics), which is a much broader system of human thought, has been successfully synthesised by Hegel. It should not, therefore, be surprising to find that after the complete knowledge of thought, the second reliable kowledge of man turns out to be that of society rather than of nature.

A partial or one-sided view of society, however, necessarily involves an ethical judgement, a partisan bias, or an ideology. This fact may be most strikingly illustrated, in the history of political economy, by the split of the Ricardian School into the Harmonists and the Socialists. Classical political economy, built on the faith in the eternity of capitalism, reached its acme in Ricardo's doctrine in the early nineteenth-century. But Ricardo was unable to explain the relation between his labour theory of value and the formation of prices and a general profit-rate in the capitalist market. As the Ricardian School consequently disintegrated, the Harmonists chose to abandon the labour theory of value. They were impressed by the efficiency with which the price mechanism worked in a freely competitive market, apparently resolving all class conflicts. Their impression was not altogether false, for the capitalist market, with its anonymity, did tend to displace extra-economic coercion. However, the Harmonists unwarrantably generalised this aspect of capitalism and refused to see its other side. Indeed, by renouncing the labour theory of value, they deprived themselves of any conceivable insight into the class structure of capitalist society. The Socialists, on the other hand, who were outraged by evident injustices of the capitalist regime, took the distribution of wealth to be the central issue of political economy. With their eyes fixed on the distress of the working class, they could not be expected to see the sophisticated economic mechanism that capital unfolded from out of itself. The labour theory of value, in their hands, consequently degenerated into a naïve political dogma that the workers ought to be paid the whole product of their labour, a dogma devoid of sound economic analysis.

Both the Harmonists and the Socialists were one-sided and ideological in their subjective evaluation of capitalism. Instead of dispassionately pursuing an objective knowledge of capitalist society in its totality, they each persisted on a particular (one-sided), if empirically observable, aspect of capitalism that most readily supported their ideological claims. The Harmonists, who only paid attention to the positive qualities of capitalism, rendered it into a natural order, with regard to which they demanded nothing but conformism. No wonder they imported the analytical method of partial knowledge from natural science with great enthusiasm, and eventually ended up transforming political economy into the quantitative, positive and technical science of 'economics'.

The Socialists, to whom the evils of capitalism appeared as inevitable as natural cataclysms, were not even that consistent. Some desperately called for a revolution regardless of its consequences, as if to demand the abolition of nature in order to be freed from earthquakes and floods. Others only wanted to temper the severity of social conflicts with *ad hoc* policy measures, as if to mitigate the brute force of nature. Hence, the polarisation of the Socialists into the radical revolutionaries and parliamentary reformists. Marxists too, as soon as they lost sight of the dialectic of capital, could not escape the same fate.

In order to overcome the difficulty with which Socialists have involved themselves, an objective account of capitalism that transcended all ideologies, including socialist ones, was needed. Without a total comprehension of capitalist society as the dialectic of capital, it is not possible to save socialism from its deep-rooted confusion, nor is it possible to adequately criticise the intellectual legacy of the Harmonists. It is this that Marx foresaw when he undertook to 'criticise' political economy. The search for the dialectic of capital need not be terminated with Marx's death. This tradition can be, and must be, carried forward to its logical end, transcending even Marxism itself.

(γ) Although professional scientists think somewhat more systematically and rigorously than ordinary people, there is no qualitative difference between scientific logic and the logic of daily life. In fact, the former is only a more sophisticated version of the latter. Hence, in order to illustrate the contrast between the mode of natural scientific thinking and that of social scientific thinking, it is not necessary to look very far. It is sufficient to consider how one seeks to explain differently a typically natural phenomenon and a typically social (inter-human) phenomenon that occurs in one's own daily life.

Suppose that abnormal weather is experienced in a given 'spatio-temporal region', threatening a widespread famine. What has caused this unusual weather? This is a typical query concerning a natural phenomenon. In this case, a particular atmospheric condition affecting the region may be identified first. Various plausible hypotheses will then be offered to explain what might have caused that atmospheric condition. It may be agreed that the atmospheric condition (x) was caused by the simultaneous materialisation of prior conditions $(a, b, ..., n)$. But in that case, for each condition $a, b, c, ..., n$, the second-order explanations such as $(a^a, b^a, ..., m^a) \rightarrow a$ must be sought, and the same procedure will have to be repeated forever. Thus, it is evident that by continuing such operations one can never identify a single (ultimate) cause that lies behind all the proximate causes. In other words, prior to arriving at the ultimate explanation, one is forced to admit, at some stage, that the whole thing is an act of God or a matter of chance (that is to say, one is caught by Hegel's 'spurious infinite' without ever reaching the 'true infinite'!) It is quite obvious that a purely natural phenomenon – such as abnormal weather in a given spatio-temporal region – cannot be completely explained. One has to be satisfied with an explanation of its proximate causes, leaving the thing-in-itself unexplained, for by insisting on the ultimate cause, one is only led into the realm of religion, that is to say, beyond the capability of scientific explanation.

As a typical social (non-natural) phenomenon frequently encountered in daily life, consider an unsolved case of murder. The body of a victim has been discovered in a mysterious condition, and one wishes to know how the act of murder has been committed. Obviously, the criminal investigation cannot be closed until the mystery is *totally* exposed; at least, the court cannot convict anyone on uncertain evidence – such as on conjectural knowledge or on a falsifiable hypothesis. Solving the mystery of a murder case is obviously an altogether different business from accounting for the anomaly of weather conditions. The detective investigation requires one to reconstruct in one's own mind what must have necessarily taken place in the actual scene of the crime from whatever traces of it are left behind, while making sure not to be misled by deliberate attempts at concealing the truth. Of course, it may be said, quite correctly, that even a Sherlock Holmes cannot explain the psychological motivation of the crime, which may be hatred, greed, cruelty, jealousy, or whatever else. However, what happens in the inner psyche of the offender is not a purely social phenomenon, and does not belong to the investigation of the act of murder as such. Since no social event occurs in a vacuum, it is to be expected that social (inter-human) factors mingle with natural and environmental factors. So long as the murder is investigated strictly as a social phenomenon, it is enough to establish who perpetrated the offence, when, where, and how. However, within this scope, the explanation must be complete in order to be valid at all. To convict a suspect on anything less would make an 'open society' the crassest of all jokes.

What does 'the complete explanation' mean in the present context? It can only mean that the story told by the investigation (the theoretical reconstruction of the scene of the murder) is identical to the total confession by the accused (with regard to the actual occurrence of the murder), in case he subsequently becomes co-operative. In other words, the explanation of a social event is complete only when what must have happened is identical with what actually happened. That is, however, precisely the meaning of the identity of the subject and the object that the dialectic demands. The dialectic defines truth as the subject-object identity, or as the completeness of explanation, and thus avoids the correspondence theory of truth. Hegel's rejection of Kant's thing-in-itself has this simple meaning. The present example teaches the following important lesson. In solving the mystery of a social event occurring in one's daily life, one does not construct an axiomatic model, interpret it factually, and repeat experiments or observations, that is to say, one does not resort to the empirico-analytical method of natural science. Even if the model is rigorous and the factual interpretation plausible, a hypothetical theory of the unique case of murder cannot be 'repeatably' tested. In this way, the mystery of a social event can never be conclusively solved. It is the dialectical method, which defines truth as the subject-object identity, that must be applied to the solution of a social (inter-human) mystery. In what follows, therefore, I intend to show how the method of the dialectic can be effectively employed for the solution of the mystery of capitalism.

B   The Significance of the Dialectic

(a)   *Hegel's Dialectic*

(α) In a passage already quoted, Marx clearly recognises Hegel as being 'the first to present the general forms of working of the dialectic in a comprehensive and conscious manner'. Engels, who characterises the dialectic as 'the investigation of the forms of thought or of the thought determinations', also agrees that 'since Aristotle this has been systematically undertaken only by Hegel'. Indeed, the two founders of Marxism never stinted their praise of Hegel, to whom they had owed their intellectual formation. Yet the subsequent history of dialectical materialism has had the infamous record of politically persecuting 'Hegelianism' as a major threat to the revolutionary spirit of Marxism. There is little doubt that such wanton intellectual violence has seriously perverted Marxism and has contributed to its unlimited vulgarisation. Even the belated revival of Hegel studies after the discovery of the *Paris Manuscripts* has not sufficiently undone the profound damage wrought by the Stalinist inquisitors. It is my belief that the dialectic operates essentially in the same way, whether in idealism or in materialism, and that, therefore, Marx's thought can never be understood as it was intended to be, without a full comprehension of the significance of the Hegelian dialectic.

Hegel's *Encyclopaedia of the Philosophical Sciences* consists of the Logic, the Philosophy of Nature, and the Philosophy of the Finite Spirit. To Hegel, 'logic coincides with metaphysics',[10] and the metaphysical world is the world of pure thought. The word 'metaphysics' is nowadays frequently used in the pejorative

---

10   Hegel 1975, p. 36.

sense of a pseudo-science, but it must be recalled that the first systematic and self-contained knowledge of man was metaphysics. This is hardly surprising, since metaphysics does not study the external world, but rather the world of abstract concepts or thought-forms, that is, the internal operation of the human mind. The study of such subject matter can be purely idealist, and hence can circumvent much of the difficulty of the theory of knowledge. Hegel views the metaphysical world as being free and self-contained, unlike the material world that only imperfectly reflects the norms of the metaphysical world.

Hegel does not deny the existence of the material world, but believes that such a world does not hang together by itself as a coherent whole. Hence, the material world lacks true being or reality. Only the world of pure thought really exists, according to him, because it is self-consistent and rational. Such idealism is often scoffed at. Yet without appreciating the profound wisdom that this idealism implies, no-one can hope to understand the true nature of Hegel's dialectic. Let us begin with a simple, heuristic example. Anyone who has seen dogs can 'think' of them. Hence, there is a thought of dogs. But this thought is, of course, full of sensuous connotations. A dog-lover thinks of dogs fondly, while a dog-hater thinks of them with malice. Hence, there is no inter-subjectively unique thought of dogs. Such a thought is not 'pure' in the sense of being free from sensuousness, or material associations. The thought of dogs, however, can be generalised or universalised to the thought of all quadrupeds. In this case, the difference between the dog-lover and the dog-hater in their thinking is to some extent overcome, because the thought has become less specific and so more remote from day-to-day experience. Yet some may think of quadrupeds differently from others. Let the thought of all quadrupeds further universalise itself to the thought of all animals, of all living creatures, of life itself, of mortality as opposed to immortality, of the temporal in contrast to the permanent, and so on. In this process of self-universalisation, thought increasingly divests itself of all individually and subjectively particular sensuous associations, and becomes purer. Thought by itself becomes intersubjectively more general, and eventually enters the metaphysical world. This world, and that alone, is fully universal, intersubjective (=objective) and pure because its ingredients are free from 'sensuousness' or material associations, in the absence of which they cannot be interpreted differently by different individuals.

Not only are such pure thought-forms as infinity, essence, necessity, causality, subject versus object, and suchlike, perfectly universal, but they also cannot exist either disparately – unrelated piece-by-piece – without forming a logical unity. Being free of contingent factors that influence individual thinking, these concepts must automatically relate themselves and realise the unity of thought in the self-contained metaphysical system. It may be claimed that such formally-abstract concepts, as mathematical concepts too, are universal and pure. It is true that mathematics borrows from the metaphysical vocabulary when it employs words such as infinity and continuity. However, when adopted by mathematics these words are emptied of their real or substantive content, and are redefined to suit the requirement of a man-made language. These words are then meaningful only within the scope of a deliberate agreement. Metaphysics is not such an artificial language, constructed to serve a particular purpose. It is, figuratively speaking, the language of God, of reason, or of the whole universe. Man learns this spontaneous language by merely rising above his own individual subjectivity and arbitrariness. That is why the metaphysical world forms itself *without artificially prescribed axioms or a set of rules*, by the free action of thought itself. The metaphysical system, in other words, is self-contained; it hangs together of its own accord, not because it is artificially so constructed as to avoid formal inconsistencies, but because thought itself is self-contained. This is the crucial point. Pure thought synthesises itself by its own logic, not by virtue of any arbitrary form imposed on it from the outside. It is this self-synthesising process of thought that is called the dialectic. The dialectic, therefore, is a self-developing and self-explaining logic, that is to say, a spontaneous and living logic.

(β) Unlike formal logic, the dialectic is concrete. The word 'concrete' – as it is used in Hegel's 'concrete universals' or 'the concrete logical idea' – has a special meaning. It must not be confused with 'empirical', although such a confusion is very common. The general nature of the dialectic can be explained in terms of its three basic properties: (i) the view of a self-contained totality; (ii) the subject-object identity; (iii) the process of synthesising contradictions. The first two of these properties, to which I have already referred, amount to the same thing, and they define the scope of the dialectic. The last property has to do with the operational procedure of the dialectic.

The fundamental idea of the dialectic lies in its assertion that 'truth is the whole'. In simple language, this means that an incomplete story is a false story, because in the absence of vital connexions, the story is neither coherent nor credible. In the earlier example of a murder trial, this point is plain. The suspect cannot be convicted unless the whole story is told, but what is meant by the whole story or complete knowledge in this context? Surely, it does not mean accounting for all empirical details of the actual scene of the murder; it can only mean the logical completeness of the account, in the sense that it is a self-contained explanation that does not depend on any unverified hypothesis or conjecture. In other words, true knowledge must constitute a coherent and self-explanatory system, or what Hegel calls 'the concrete logical idea'.

If knowledge does not form a logically self-contained system, it represents only a part of the universe of discourse, the remainder being left unknown. The validity or truth of the knowledge is then wholly dependent on what this unknown remainder actually turns out to be. The dialectic refuses to accept an incomplete or hypothetical knowledge as true. But this is just another way of saying that the dialectic neither recognises the unknowable thing-in-itself, nor entertains any postulate or axiom as valid knowledge. The dialectic, which defines truth as 'the concrete logical idea', remains ineffective if the object of study does not by itself constitute a logical totality. It will do no good to simply 'view' something (for example, nature) as a totality or *Gestalt* if it cannot be logically synthesised as a self-contained system. In this sense, the dialectic is not an indiscriminate holism.

The second property of the dialectic – the identity of the subject and the object – further clarifies this point. If the observer (the subject) and the observed (the object) do not come together, then 'theory (or knowledge)' on the part of the subject and 'reality' on the part of the object are merely parallel and cannot be related except by arbitrary conventions or pragmatic rules. That is to say, cognition (epistemology) and being (ontology) are necessarily apart and unrelated, so that a 'correspondence theory of truth', with all its pitfalls, cannot be avoided. It has already been shown that the knowledge of nature is destined to suffer from this limitation and cannot be made dialectical. For the dialectic to be effective in establishing knowledge, it is necessary that the object of the study should reveal itself completely. For example, in the previous illustration of a murder, several witnesses who have observed disparate aspects of the crime scene might each have proffered different explanations. If the court could not overcome their one-sidedness in synthesising all the available information into a coherent story, and as a result had no alternative but to choose one or more of the explanations as the most plausible, by means of some 'empirical' test, then the truth about the crime would remain unknown. The suspect might have to be sent to the gallows on the basis of falsifiable hypotheses. Such a barbarous affront to reason can be avoided if the detective investigation is, in principle, capable of discovering the whole truth, which would consist of the identity of 'what actually happened' and 'what must theoretically have happened'.

A subject matter is thus totally (dialectically) comprehended only when its theoretical explanation is identical with the self-exposition by the subject matter. Hegel's logic that coincides with metaphysics is said to offer a philosophical account of the divine wisdom, but the philosopher cannot know God's design, unless He Himself intends to reveal it. Indeed, the construction of a dialectical system is possible only with respect to a totality that is willing, or is tending, to fully expose itself. In this case, the dialectic can accomplish total knowledge or the subject-object identity by merely 'copying' (or reflecting) the process of the self-revelation of the subject matter. There is no need to apply an external logic to it because the logic is inherent in the subject matter itself. The procedural property of the dialectic, the synthesis of contradictions, is determined by this fact.

In order to expose a subject matter totally, the dialectic proceeds step-by-step from the abstract to the concrete. The 'abstract' means the unspecified and empty, while the 'concrete' means the specified and synthetic. The dialectic always presupposes a totality of the subject matter, but does not exhibit all of its concrete features at once. It is as if an artist begins with rough contours before inserting the details, and finishes his picture by applying paint in layers. An initially empty whole is gradually enriched with specifications, until it becomes pregnant with all its logical ingredients. Every time a new specification is introduced, the level of abstraction is changed. At each level of abstraction, the dialectic recognises a 'contradiction', which, when synthesised, amounts to a new specification of the totality, thus enabling an advance to another level of abstraction. It is for this reason that the dialectic is often characterised as a logic of 'contradiction' or a negative logic. However, such a characterisation is often highly misleading and is particularly so when many popular exponents allude, undauntingly, to the meaningfulness of a 'contradictory logic'! Even more frequently the dialectic is characterised by the mystical triad of 'thesis-antithesis-synthesis', with a suggestion that the dialectic rationalises any apparent logical inconsistency. In both cases, 'contradiction' in the dialectical sense is confused with contradiction in the sense of formal logic.

Consider the famous Hegelian triad of being-naught-becoming. The following illustration may clarify the dialectical meaning of contradiction and its synthesis. Suppose that I ask a friend the question, 'Do you have a child?' If the answer is simultaneously 'Yes, I have' (being) and 'No, I have not' (non-being), the answer is *contradictory* in the formal-logical sense. Either my friend is a schizophrenic, or he does not want to answer my question. Obviously, such a contradiction can never be synthesised, for it is *not* a dialectical contradiction. Yet many self-appointed exponents of the dialectic come forward with the incredible claim that precisely this schizophrenia or elusiveness of my friend illustrates what Hegel calls 'becoming'. This is most decidedly *not* what *becoming* means. When my friend answers my query with 'Yes, I have' (being), he has not yet specified his child at all. Hence, the child may be a boy or a girl, a one-year old infant or an uncontrollable teenager, a whizz-kid or mentally challenged; in short, anything that a child can be. It is this *absence of any concrete information* that is called 'nothing' or 'naught'.

Indeed, without any further specification than merely that he exists, the child means pure 'nothing' to me. If I were to open his file it would remain totally blank, save perhaps for a hypothetical or tentative name or number that I may choose to give him for reference. Yet I cannot ignore the fact that there is a child in my friend's household. That is the dialectical *contradiction*.

'Becoming' means, in the present case, that I may ask more questions and proceed to complete a meaningful file of the child, or I may simply forget about it. I am formally free to let the child 'come to be' or 'pass away'. Since there is no compelling reason for me to opt for either of the two alternatives, the state of 'becoming' is said to be fluid and unstable. However, so long as my original question was not a frivolous one, and was genuinely motivated by curiosity, I must seek more information. If my friend responds to my further questioning, his child will not remain a *pure being*, but will become a *determinate (or specified) being*. At the same time, my thought of the child moves from one level of abstraction to another, that is, it progresses one step forward in its dialectical journey *from the abstract to the concrete*. Soon I will have obtained a very concrete image of the child so far as he can be externally described. Once his file is complete, I may wish to personally meet the child for an in-depth study of his character or inner motivation. That is, I will now seek his Essence, having already confirmed his Being.

In this way, the dialectic moves from abstract to concrete (more synthetic) knowledge, until the subject matter cannot be specified further. Dialectical concreteness, therefore, does not mean 'empirical' concreteness. It only means logical self-sufficiency or coherence. The dialectic ends with a fully synthesised totality called *the Absolute Idea*. (Sometimes it is also called the True Infinite or the Concrete Universal). In the present example, the Absolute Idea of the child is identical with what he actually is, apart from, of course, irrelevant (contingent) empirical details. The dialectic of Hegel's *Logic* proceeds in exactly the same way. Here, the Absolute (the philosophical term for God) is first externally described as *Being* (quality, quantity, measure), then inwardly analysed as *Essence* (intro-reflexion, appearance, actuality), until He is finally exposed as *the Notion* (the subjective notion, the object, the Idea). Roughly speaking, the Being, Essence and the Notion of God (the Absolute) may be understood to mean *how He is*, *what He is*, and *how He is because of what He is*, respectively.

(γ) Once the Logic that coincides with metaphysics was completed, Hegel applied it to Nature and the Finite Spirit, claiming that the material world reflected Reason (or Providence), albeit with some predictable disturbances and distortions. Although the material world is finite (unreal), external (crude) and contingent (incoherent), it is still essentially governed by Reason through its 'cunning', according to Hegel. This purely idealist philosophical system of Hegel may now appear somewhat quaint and outdated. Yet it is in essence not so different from the all too familiar Christian view of the world. It is, therefore, not surprising that the left-wing Hegelians, when they first sought to criticise their master's thought, almost exclusively preoccupied themselves with religion. Marxists too wished to abolish Hegel's *idealist* philosophy, that is, his philosophical system, the religious and political overtones of which they found particularly objectionable. But in their case, they rightly recognised the value of Hegel's dialectic, which they intended to preserve, even after abolishing the idealist philosophical system. Yet was this, after all, a feasible proposition?

If the proposed switch of the dialectic from idealism to materialism can in fact be accomplished, it will certainly be a striking revolution in philosophy. However, the question must be cautiously approached. Engels, for example, claimed that the dialectic and the concept of the Absolute were not mutually compatible, on the grounds that the Heraclitean view of the flux of matter could not possibly accommodate an absolute immutability. However, that was a superficial observation. To Hegel, it is the process of the self-revelation of the Absolute that is dialectical. Hence, it is impossible to preserve the dialectic after abolishing its subject, the Absolute, unless in His place another subject that is equally self-revealing is introduced. If one simply dethrones the Absolute without establishing what takes His place, the dialectic will also disappear. When Engels failed to show that nature exposes itself as completely as the Absolute, the dialectical materialists were left with nothing. Their critique of Hegel quite understandably degenerated into the mere accusation that Hegel was a reactionary collaborator with the Prussian autocracy. The rejection of Hegel on such frivolous grounds only contributed to the utter degradation of the dialectic itself.

It is generally believed that only the young Marx directly criticised Hegel's philosophy, while the mature Marx preoccupied himself with political economy, an empirical science. It is true that explicit references to Hegel are scarce in *Capital*, but what is all too often overlooked is the fact that a true critique of Hegel's 'logic which coincided with metaphysics' can be accomplished only with a 'logic which coincides with economic theory'.[11] The philosophical activity of the early Marx is really no more than a prelude, a guiding thread, to the implicit critique of Hegel's *Logic* accomplished later in Marx's *Capital*. This must be so because only in *Capital* can the materialistic substitute for Hegel's Absolute be found. Here, the dialectic of 'capital' replaces the dialectic of 'the Absolute'. For Marx, 'capital' plays the same role as 'the Absolute' for Hegel. In the introduction to *The Science of Logic*, Hegel states:

---

11   Hegel 1975, p. 36.

Accordingly, logic is to be understood as the system of pure reason, as the realm of pure thought. This realm is truth as it is without veil and in its own absolute nature. It can therefore be said that this content is the exposition of God as he is in his eternal essence before the creation of nature and a finite spirit.[12]

In exactly the same way, it is possible to characterise the content of the dialectic of capital as the exposition of 'capital' in its pure essence 'before the creation of capitalism in history'. However, in order to prove this claim, the first methodological point that must be established is how economic concepts can be as pure, objective and universal as Hegel's metaphysical categories.

Hegel constructed the objective and internally coherent system of metaphysics by releasing thought from sensuousness. Only when thought was freed from its material associations did it become pure, objective and metaphysical. Yet, as Hegel reckoned, thought possessed within itself the power to increasingly universalise itself, and, consequently, also to synthesise itself at its most universal level. Material objects, on the other hand, did not possess this power of self-universalisation and self-synthesis. Hegel, therefore, believed that philosophy must necessarily be idealist, and that the dialectic must coincide with metaphysics. Thus, Marx's proposition that the dialectic should be made to live with materialism would have been most vehemently objected to by Hegel himself. This crucial point has been very clearly realised by Lucio Colletti, according to whom the dialectic cannot be separated from idealism. Colletti claims that 'reality cannot contain dialectical contradictions but only real oppositions',[13] and yet 'capitalist oppositions are, for Marx, dialectical contradictions and not real oppositions'.[14] Colletti justifies this apparent incongruity with the proposition that 'for Marx, capitalism is contradictory not because it is a reality but because it is an upside-down, inverted reality (alienation, fetishism)'.[15]

These are certainly profound observations that strike at the heart of the question. Yet what is an 'inverted reality' such as capitalism if it is not also a special kind of reality? Surely capitalism cannot be an idea or a theoretical fiction just because it is not a 'natural' reality. It is true that nature contains only real oppositions, not dialectical oppositions. However, it does not follow that 'the fundamental principle of materialism and of science is the principle of non contradition', unless Colletti specifically means by 'materialism and science' natural materialism and natural science. Nor does it follow that 'science is the

12   Hegel 1969, p. 50.
13   Colletti 1975, p. 29.
14   Colletti 1974, p. 3.
15   Ibid.

only means of apprehending reality, the only means of gaining knowledge of the world', if, in this case, by 'science' he means only natural science. These equivocal statements come from Colletti's failure to admit that social reality is qualitatively different from natural reality, and that, as a result of being qualitatively distinct from natural science, social science has a place of its own. Why does Colletti hesitate to admit this? It is perhaps the horror of 'the spiritual idealism of Continental European philosophy in this century' that inhibits him from reaching the conclusion, to which his own argument naturally leads. To me, however, his insights are more admirable than his personal inhibitions. He has argued convincingly against dialectical materialism, and alluded to a possibility of the dialectic of capital. The right question to ask at this point is why – only in social history, and never in natural history – reality sometimes occurs 'inverted'. The answer to this question establishes the dialectic of capital, and with it the 'true foundation of the social sciences' that Colletti thinks has not yet been found. In what follows, I wish to demonstrate this point.

(b)   The Rational Kernel of the Dialectic

(α) Political economy studies the real economic life of man in society. Despite the fact that man has always led an economic life, it was not until the beginning of the Modern Age that political economy developed as a systematic knowledge, that is to say, as a science. Why? The reason is that economic life is ordinarily not easily separable from the political, socio-ethical and other ideological elements of human life. Economic relations do not appear transparently, unless they are liberated from the extra-economic contingencies of social life. Only the formation of an open, impersonal market, which relates humans indirectly through goods – through material objects called 'commodities' – enables economic relations to appear in their pure form, divested of all extra-economic contingencies. In the market, the social relations between humans appear 'objectified' as 'the social relation between things'. The market breaks down traditional master-servant relations and makes people free, equal and independent traders. It is, therefore, not by chance that political economy, which aims at an objective study of economic relations, became a possibility for the first time with the advent of capitalism, a global commodity-economy. The knowledge of economic life, which had previously been as sporadic and fragmentary as the commodity-economy itself, could then be formulated systematically. In other words, the 'inversion' of social reality, in the form of capitalism, is a necessary condition for a systematic study of economic life.

The first form of trade was a 'silent trade' between two independent and economically self-sufficient communities, not a direct face-to-face barter between the deer hunter and the beaver trapper, as Adam Smith would have us believe. Only silent trade, where 'silence' implied strict non-interference with the other party's internal affairs, developed into a more general trade characterised by the impersonal commodity-economic relations among participating traders. A mere barter of goods between known parties only ends with a ritualistic gift-giving practice, or a tributary relation, which is perhaps an early form of taxation and subsidisation, but it is certainly not an instance of commerce. Although commodity trade arises at first between independent communities at their border and as 'external relations', it does not for that reason leave those communities unaffected. As part of their economic life increasingly depends on external trade, members of each community begin to develop 'internal trade', in effect reducing themselves to individual trading units, and thereby also eroding communal economic life, which had hitherto formed an organic whole. It is the *internalisation* of the external trade relations that broadens the scope of a commodity-economy.

If, as in capitalism, even labour-power – the ultimate source of productivity – is 'commoditised' in this process, it is in principle possible for the whole of economic life to become completely saturated with the forms of the commodity-economy, leaving no trace of direct human relations. Capitalism is, thus, a social system in which all human relations tend to be external, anonymous and reified. It is this reification or impersonalisation of human relations that makes them objective. The dialectic of capital, therefore, envisages a purely capitalist society in which the reification of social relations is supposed to be complete. Such a society, which the dialectic of capital must presuppose, corresponds to the metaphysical world of Hegel in which thought is pure and objective. A *purely capitalist society* is, of course, not an empirical datum; it has to be mentally constructed, as is Hegel's metaphysical system. Yet the mental construction of such a society follows (or *copies*) the reifying force of the commodity-economy, which is a real rather than ideal process. What makes the dialectic of capital 'materialist' instead of 'idealist' is not the factual existence of a purely capitalist society, but the self-abstraction of capitalism itself, which reflects the 'real (not ideal)' commodity-economic force of reification. The self-purification of thought in Hegel is a strictly mental process, while the construction of a purely capitalist society is a *mental process that copies, and is aided by, the real process*. The purely capitalist society, in other words, is a theoretical (logical) system, in which the reifying force of the commodity-economy is hypothetically allowed to consummate itself. This reifying force is real and material (objective), not ideal or imaginary (subjective), even though its consummation may not be factual.

It should be quite clear that the purely capitalist society of the dialectic of capital is not a Weberian ideal type, as is, for example, the neoclassical economic model of perfect competition. The construction of an ideal type is an exclusively subjective operation. Since reality always presents itself as a welter of diverse forces and tendencies, the observer exercises his own discretion in 'accentuating' what appears to him to constitute its leading characteristics, while ignoring what he believes to be irrelevant details. He then proffers the one-sidedly (or subjectively) accentuated pattern of reality as its ideal type or image. His ideal type can be generally accepted to the extent that his subjective views (biases) are shared by others. Thus, for neoclassical economics the ideal image of capitalism is a perfectly competitive general equilibrium market, in which the unobstructed functioning of the price mechanism promises the blissful state of Pareto-optimality. I have, however, warned against the ideological elements that necessarily creep into any such ideal type of society. The purely capitalist society of the dialectic of capital – although it in fact shares many characteristics with the neoclassical perfect-competition model – is free from such ideological elements. This claim is made on the ground that the theoretical abstraction of a purely capitalist society is not subjective (one-sided) and arbitrary, but rather *copies or reflects* the self-abstraction of capitalism itself.

(β) This point is far from trivial, for it touches on the foundation of the materialistic dialectic, the only method of objective social science. Yet it appears to me that its full import has not been sufficiently appreciated by Marxists. Even Marx himself did not unambiguously explain why economic theory must presuppose a purely capitalist society. At the same time, Engels and later dialectical materialists went astray in their formulation of the materialist 'copy theory'. In the following pages, I intend to further elaborate on the implications of the present thesis.

As Marx writes:

> In theory it is assumed that the laws of capitalist production operate in their pure form. In reality there exists only approximation; but, this approximation is the greater, the more developed the capitalist mode of production and the less it is adulterated and amalgamated with survivals of former economic conditions.[16]

Although it is clear from this passage that Marx also presupposes a purely capitalist society in theory, he fails to clearly argue for the methodological necessity of such a presupposition. Elsewhere, he observes:

---

16   Marx 1967, *Capital*, Volume III, p. 175.

> Free competition is the adequate form of the productive process of capital. The further it [free competition] is developed, the purer the forms in which its [capital's] motion appears.[17]

Such an observation is almost as subjective as the neoclassical claim that 'perfect competition' is the ideal type of capitalism. Even more misleading is a passage such as the following:

> The actual movement of competition belongs beyond our scope, and we need present only the inner organization of the capitalist mode of production, in its ideal average, as it were.[18]

It is as though an ideal image of capitalism could be obtained by the mechanical device of 'averaging out' contingent irregularities and cyclical factors of the market. Writing in the middle of the nineteenth-century, Marx may have taken it for granted that capitalism had already approached perfection, at least in England, and may have thought it unnecessary to advise a specific procedure for the mental construction of a purely capitalist society.

After the liberal era, however, an ideal operation of capitalism becomes more remote from day-to-day experience. Statistical averages of empirical data cannot then hope to even faintly bring out the inner logic of the capitalist mode of production. This means that without a firmer methodological justification, the relevance of a purely capitalist society tends to escape notice. All the more vigorously, therefore, the dialectic of capital must claim the objectivity of a purely capitalist society on the ground that it is a *mental construct dictated by the motion of capital itself,* rather than one that is subjectively imposed on it from the outside. This, indeed, amounts to a reaffirmation of the 'copy theory' made much of by Engels and the dialectical materialists. However, the present version of the theory differs fundamentally from theirs, which I believe to be spineless. Let us first hear what Lenin has to say on the copy theory in his *Materialism and Empirio-Criticism*:

> The recognition of theory as a copy, as an approximate copy of objective reality, is materialism.[19]

---

17   Marx 1973, *Grundrisse*, p. 651.
18   Marx 1967, *Capital*, Volume III, p. 831.
19   Lenin 1964, p. 247.

> Engels ... constantly and without exception speaks ... of things and their mental pictures or images [Gedanken-Abbilder].[20]

> Engels speaks neither of symbols nor of hieroglyphs, but copies, photographs, images, mirror reflections of things.[21]

> It is beyond question that mechanics was a copy of real motions of moderate velocity, while the new physics is a copy of real motions of enormous velocity.[22]

These unilateral assertions hardly explain the materialist theory of knowledge. They do not even attempt to answer the question as to how thought reflects real things as concepts and relates them into an objective theory of reality.

In his 'Ludwig Feuerbach and the End of German Philosophy', Engels obtains his *Abbilder* theory from a sweeping criticism of Hegel's idealism, claiming that 'the self-movement of the concept' merely reflects real motions in 'nature and human history', and that 'the dialectic reduces itself to the science of the general laws of motion, both of the external world and of human thought', the two sets of laws being 'identical in substance'. Here, the criticism is not specifically directed at Hegel's 'logic that coincides with metaphysics', that is, to the gemstone of the idealistic dialectic, but instead aimed at Hegel's less dependable *Weltanschauung,* with all its crude idealistic perversions. From such a facile criticism that could only convince Engels's already committed allies, one can only expect the pronouncement of another *Weltanschauung,* not a strict vindication of the materialistic dialectic. As already remarked, thought copies the self-revelation of the Absolute in Hegel's *Logic.* In order to establish a materialistic version of the copy theory, therefore, Engels ought to have demonstrated that there is at least one form of self-revealing reality. By failing to do so, Engels handed down to his materialist followers a completely undependable and empty copy theory.

The difficulty with the Engelsian copy theory may be illustrated as follows. Suppose that one observes a pail containing no water. How is one supposed to copy it? To merely call it an empty pail would be no better than an exercise in name-giving – an association of the pail with the previously defined state of 'emptiness', wherever the latter concept came from. Is that pail empty because it never contained water, or because water once there has been drained? Since the pail does not by itself give any clues, one can only imagine its past history in the light of other similar instances. Clearly, there is no meaning in 'copying' the pail, which does not speak its own truth. It is quite otherwise if one observes a leaking pail and concludes that it will eventually be emptied of water. The fact that the pail is slowly being drained of water through a hole at its bottom dictates this conclusion, and does not permit the observer to indulge in arbitrary imagining. He *must* infer that if the present condition is not remedied in time, all water will eventually run out of the pail. This inference is true and objective even if – as luck would have it – someone presently rushes to the scene and plugs the hole so as to stop the emptying when it is only half consummated. In this case, the leaking pail tells its own story, which the observer's mind has no choice but to 'objectively copy'.

The moral of the above illustration is clear. It is futile to claim, as Lenin does, that mechanics is a copy of low-velocity motions in reality, for the physical world does not possess a teleological end. It does not reveal its own story; it does not grow to maturity and become 'grey'. Nor does it become purer either by divesting itself of contingent irregularities. Hence, mechanics cannot be a copy of the physical world, nor can it be a dialectical theory. It is merely an ideal type constructed by scientists to probe the mechanical aspect – and only that aspect – of the physical world. That is why mechanics is capable of axiomatic formulation, which implies the non-identity of the subject and the object, namely, of theory and reality. The correspondence of a theory of mechanics with real motion, therefore, must be tested by experiments and observations. It is a serious error to confuse this kind of theory with a dialectical theory.

Uno – who talked of *hôhô no mosha* (the copy of the object's own method of self-abstraction) – was the first to explicitly warn against an indiscriminate attribution of the dialectic to 'nature and history', and to establish the real meaning of a dialectical copy theory. By claiming that capitalism alone possesses a genuine materialistic dialectic, he did not in any way deprive the dialectic of its weight. On the contrary, he made the materialistic dialectic what it should be, namely, the method of objective social science and the theory of knowledge of materialism. Because it is a commodity-economy, capitalism unmistakably possesses a self-reifying force, and this fact justifies a purely capitalist society as the objective presupposition of economic theory. Since purely capitalist society is the outcome of *hôhô no mosha*, it is different from an arbitrarily constructed ideal type; it has an objective foundation. I know no methodological argument more decisive than this one. For how else can one hope to establish social science, or the knowledge of society, free from ideological one-sidedness and arbitrary subjectivity?

The copy theory that Uno has forcefully advanced is, however, not altogether absent in Marx. Glimpses of it appear in various parts of his writings. For example, in his celebrated introduction to the *Grundrisse*, Marx refers to the economic concept of labour in the following:

> Labour seems to be a very simple category. The notion of labour in this universal form, as labour in general, is also extremely old. Nevertheless, 'labour' in this simplicity is economically considered as modern a category as the relation which gives rise to this simple abstraction.[23]

Although in pre-capitalist societies a labour that produced all forms of wealth could only be conceived of as an ideal type, it becomes a reality in capitalist society. This is because the commodity-economy requires labour to be applied indifferently for the production of any use-value. Thus, according to Marx, 'labour, not only as a category but in reality, has become a means to create wealth in general'.[24] Here, the phrase 'not only as a category but also in reality' implies the dialectical copy theory, which justifies an abstraction in economic theory so long as it reflects the self-abstraction of the commodity-economy in reality.

This does not mean that simplifying assumptions for merely expository purposes are prohibited. It only means that such assumptions must be removed as theory undergoes further synthesis. For example, the organic composition of capital cannot be expected to become uniform in all industries, however much capitalist production develops. It is, nevertheless, warranted to assume its uniformity in early contexts of the theory, in which the production of diverse use-values can as yet be held implicit. Similarly, the development of capitalism does not tend to materialise a stationary state or 'simple reproduction', but for heuristic reasons, theory always explains simple reproduction before addressing itself to the more complicated process of expanded reproduction. This is because certain aspects of the inter-industry relation can be made perfectly clear even while the accumulation of capital is held implicit. On the other hand, the assumption that the rate of surplus value is the same in all industries can be maintained throughout the dialectic of capital, because if it is not so at present, due to contingent factors, the development of capitalist society is capable of removing such factors. Similarly, the simplification of the labour process is not merely an expository device; it is an abstraction dictated by the development of the capitalist method of production. The dialectic may,

---

23   Marx 1970, *Contribution*, p. 209.
24   Marx 1970, *Contribution*, p. 210.

therefore, retain assumptions of this kind to its end. Thus, the purely capitalist society, when fully synthesised, no longer depends on expository simplifications. Yet it remains as abstract as is warranted by the self-reifying force of the capitalist commodity-economy.

(γ) The purely capitalist society, thus synthesised, is a perfectly 'inverted' reality (in Colletti's sense). Here, all human relations appear 'upside down', as thing-to-thing relations. It is as if capitalist society were governed by natural laws. That an optical illusion of this sort arises from the very nature of capitalism has important methodological implications. What is genuinely natural is, of course, *real economic life* itself, which ordinarily cannot be clearly perceived because of the involvement of ideological factors in its social organisation. It appears transparently for the first time under capitalism, the global commodity-economy, since the latter tends to operate anonymously and, thus, also tends to cleanse itself of ideological factors. Yet this direct visibility of real economic life under capitalism (and not in other historical societies) has, in its turn, the perverse effect of attributing a 'natural appearance' to capitalism, which is a 'historical and social' institution. When 'the economic life common to all societies' and 'its specifically commodity-economic mode of operation' double and appear superposed, one upon the other, the relation between the two tends to appear inverted. The 'economic life common to all societies' becomes the apparent image of capitalism, and its 'specifically commodity-economic mode of operation' is the concealed reality. This is clearly an inversion of reality, since capitalism *is* the social and historical institution and not the natural order. (In other words, it appears as though 'hardware' dictates 'software', rather than vice versa).

This inversion of reality explains the true significance of *fetishism*. Only capitalist society makes its constituent human relations objective, and so enables the development of social science. Yet objectified social relations are never immediately observable, as they withdraw behind and underlie relations between material things. It is for this reason that social science is, from the beginning, saddled with a peculiar difficulty, and the failure to recognise this fact leads to the absurdity of a 'natural or physical science of society'. It is precisely this absurdity that has plagued economic theory in the Harmonist tradition. If one observes only the natural appearance of capitalism, without delving into its concealed reality, it seems as though this historical institution, just as nature, possesses an 'unknowable thing-in-itself'. Wherefrom arises fetishism, that is, the misconception of human relations that constitute society as 'social relations' that self-animated material objects unaccountably form among themselves. If one fails to break through such fetishism, one cannot even perceive capitalism as a social reality. A superficial study of capitalism at the level of its natural appearance cannot, therefore, constitute a genuine social science; it remains at most a spurious 'physics' of reified human relations.

An objective account of capitalism presupposes the unravelling of fetishism, that is to say, the exposition of the social reality hidden behind the natural appearance. Yet the relation between the social and the natural cannot be a relation of real opposition; it must be one of dialectical contradiction. For if real oppositions governed nature and relations between material things, to say that the natural and the social are related in terms of the same real oppositions would amount to denying the existence of the social as distinct from the natural. That would certainly make social science an outright impossibility. Social science has its justification in the recognition that the 'social' is distinct from the 'natural'. However, once this is admitted it is plain that political economy – a social science that studies the capitalist mode of production – cannot operate with the principle of non-contradiction (that is, exclusively with the principle of real opposition). The method of political economy, because of the peculiar nature of its subject matter, must necessarily be dialectical. In other words, the theory of political economy cannot be other than the dialectic of capital.

The dialectic of capital proceeds by solving the recurrent contradiction between value (the social) and use-value (the natural), and the synthesis must always occur by letting value prevail over use-values. This means that the analysis of capitalism consists of suppressing its natural appearance, and in bringing out its concealed social reality step-by-step. Purely capitalist society is fully synthesised only when the natural appearance is neutralised, and the concealed reality is totally exposed. In this respect too there is an exact correspondence between the dialectic of capital and Hegel's dialectic. In the case of Hegel, the construction of the *Logic* amounted to exposing the wisdom of the Absolute implicit in the sensuous materiality of finite things. Hence, when the concrete-synthetic totality of the Absolute is fully laid bare, materialism is suspended and pure idealism remains. One should not, however, conclude from this that material things simply vanish; they are merely sublated (*aufgehoben*), that is to say, preserved as an inactive substrate. (In the following section, however, I shall point out a difficulty that this drastic interpretation might raise for Hegel's idealism). That explains the transition from the Absolute Idea to Nature, in which material things refuse to remain inactive. In the same way, the use-values that the dialectic of capital subdues in order to fully divulge the logic of capitalism do not remain so tame in empirical history. Whence follows the necessity of the stages-theory of capitalist development. (More on this to follow).

Yet in a purely capitalist society, in which the reifying force of the commodity-economy is supposed to be consummated, use-values must be completely neutralised, so as to exhibit the social reality of capitalism crystal clearly, and free from the natural contingencies of economic life. Of course, capitalism in history never exists with such purity, but neither does the divine wisdom operate in an empty space uninhabited by corporeal things. The recognition of truth always requires the exercise of mental power to see beyond apparent contingencies. The dialectic is the method that enables the 'thinking intellect' to synthesise the inner truth, or hidden reality, of the object of study. There is, therefore, absolutely nothing illegitimate about the study of capitalism resorting to the dialectic. In fact, the very nature of capitalism compels such a method. Capitalism, of course, is not a mere idea or theoretical fiction; it is a social reality in a very real sense. The fact that it is not a natural reality, and as such cannot be comprehended with the application of the principle of non-contradiction, does not render the dialectic of capital 'a disguised religion' or 'spiritual philosophy', whatever Colletti may imply by such terms. On the contrary, it is the dialectic of capital that lays 'the true foundation of the social sciences'.

(c)   The Contradiction between Value and Use-values

(α) So far the similarity of the *materialistic dialectic of capital* to the *idealist dialectic of Hegel* has been emphasised, but an important difference between the two must not be overlooked. The difference is most readily apparent when the role of 'nothing' in Hegel's dialectic is compared with that of 'use-values' in the dialectic of capital. In the latter, value – the formative element of capitalism – stands opposed to use-values, which represent the material factors of economic life, devoid of commodity-economic specifications. Whereas *value* implies commodity-economic – and hence social – being, *use-values* connote its absence. Use-values, as elements of the economic life common to all societies, must be subdued by and subsumed under value in order for capitalism – a specifically commodity-economic and historical institution – to fully display its inner logic. In Hegel's Logic too, 'being' implies the presence of the Absolute, and 'naught' His absence. But what can the absence or non-being of the Absolute mean? It can only mean the material world prior to its absorption into the metaphysical world, or, more precisely, the thought of the material. The trouble, however, is that such a thing has no place in the 'logic that coincides with metaphysics'.

If the Absolute were present in only one of several material worlds, and if He were to reveal Himself in it by subsuming its materiality, then the non-being of the Absolute would mean that which is common to all these material worlds, and that which constrains the manifestation of the Absolute in any one of them. Such a premise, however, would be quite inconsistent with Hegel's idealism, for who then would have created the material worlds in which the Absolute is absent? Surely, the Absolute could not have created a material world without leaving within it traces of his own deed, that is, without inspiring it with his own wisdom. Idealism could not possibly admit the creation of a material world in which the Absolute has played no part. Therefore, it follows that, for Hegel, there can be only one material world created by the Absolute, and this world must be impregnated by his wisdom, which thought cannot do otherwise than copy. Yet as thought copies the action of the Absolute, the materiality of the external world is bound to be effaced, so that its shadow remains, in the purely logical context, only as 'nothing', that is to say, as the non-being of thought.

Much of the difficulty with Hegel's dialectic stems from the elusiveness of this concept of *naught*, which his idealism imposes. As is well known, Hegel begins his *Logic* with the contrast of being and naught, where being marks the awakening of thought, which is the first intimation of the presence of the Absolute. The naught that follows does not, and should not, mean simply the absence of the Absolute, but rather the impossibility of specifying Him in thought as anything further than pure being. A difficulty arises here because these opposing conceptions are not clearly demarcated. It is as though the non-specificity of the Absolute were no different from his simple absence in the sea of nirvana that effaces everything. Thus, one must constantly resist and overcome the somnolence of naught, as it were, in order not to lose sight of the just now recognised being of the Absolute. This ambiguity is responsible for the popular and false interpretation of Hegel's first triad – 'being-naught-becoming' – to which I have already referred. It must be conceded that idealism cannot overcome this ambiguity that threatens to cripple the dialectic, for, indeed, how can idealism claim that, were the Absolute abolished, there would remain materiality, just as use-values remain after the abolition of value, the formative element of capitalism? Idealism should assert that in the absence of the Absolute, there can be nothing left, 'nothing' in the sense of total blankness. This makes Hegel's dialectic lopsided, for its thesis (being) is *never really constrained by its antithesis (nothing)*, so that the triumph of the Absolute is predetermined before analysis.

Indeed, when Engels criticised the concept of the Absolute as being incompatible with the operation of a dialectic, he should have struck at this point, the Achilles heel of the Hegelian dialectic. He should have insisted that a dialectic is meaningful only when the overcoming of the antithesis by the thesis is not a foregone conclusion. He would then have initiated an immanent and therefore decisive critique of Hegel's idealist dialectic. The great advantage of the materialistic dialectic of capital lies in the fact that 'use-values' represent only the non-being of capitalism, a historical and transient social institution, the abolition of which does not reduce everything to ashes. If the commodity-economic integument of capitalism is discarded, real economic life common to all societies remains as virgin 'use-values'. Such use-values are, however, not by nature destined to be subsumed by the commodity-economic form of value. Only under a very particular set of circumstances does such an event occur historically. That is why the dialectical synthesis of a purely capitalist society becomes a meaningful exercise. The synthesis demonstrates the logical possibility of capitalism, a far from obvious credo with which to start.

In this book, I intend to show that theoretical arguments of the dialectic of capital often proceed in exactly the same manner as the metaphysical categories unfold in Hegel's Logic. At times the correspondence is so close that I am almost forced to believe what is unbelievable, namely, it is as if Hegel already had a complete knowledge of the dialectic of capital, but for some reason feigned ignorance and deliberately equivocated it with his metaphysical language! (What a cunning teacher!) Such an impression – false as it is – only testifies to Hegel's great philosophical acumen. Contrary to popular belief, his *Logic* consists not of Romantic poetry, but tightly-argued demonstrations. Yet there are several instances when his reasoning is rather forced and difficult to understand. In all these cases, I can show that the dialectic of capital performs better. The reason is that the concept of 'use-values' as opposed to value has a substance that is lacking in Hegel's concept of 'nothing'. The dialectic, which progresses by overcoming recurrent contradictions between value and use-values, is bound to be clearer than the dialectic that keeps harking back to the mystical inter-penetration of being and nothing.

(β) Let us consider a few examples. Hegel characterises 'becoming' as 'a double determination', that is, as containing two unities of being and nothing: coming-to-be and ceasing-to-be. He then says that 'both are the same, becoming, and although they differ in direction they interpenetrate and paralyse each other'.[25] 'The resultant equilibrium', according to Hegel, 'settles into a stable unity'.

> Becoming is a stable unrest which settles into a stable result ... This result is a vanishedness of becoming. It is the unity of being and nothing which has settled into a stable oneness. But this stable oneness is being, yet no longer as a determination on its own but as a determination as a whole.[26]

---

25   Hegel 1969, p. 106.
26   Ibid.

It is thus that Hegel deduces 'determinate being' from 'becoming'. Such reasoning is, of course, very difficult to follow, but it can be made quite plain if it is rephrased in the language of the dialectic of capital.

Translate the triad of 'being, naught and becoming' into the triad of 'value, use-value and exchange-value'. Then, one can easily deduce from 'exchange-value' the determinate being of value, or the 'forms of value expression'. Clearly, in an exchange of commodities, the seller wishes to realise the value of his commodity, which has a use-value that is of interest to the purchaser. Hence, in 'exchange-value', the seller foresees the realisation (or coming-to-be) of value, while the purchaser foresees the realisation of a use-value (the ceasing-to-be of value). Hegel would, therefore, be perfectly right in characterising exchange-value, or becoming, as 'a double determination'. However, what corresponds to determinate being, namely, the 'expression of value by the commodity-seller' does not follow from 'a stable unity or oneness' resulting from 'the interpenetration or mutual paralysis' of value and use-value. It comes from the fact that commodities, not being simply goods or plain use-values, must be priced (express their value by the use-value of another commodity) before any actual exchange can take place.

Hegel too intuitively realises that 'being' is the active factor and 'nothing' the passive factor of the dialectic, but in his reasoning he frequently treats both factors on equal terms and finds himself obliged to generate their synthesis by mechanically collapsing one into the other. Such an instance recurs in his theory of 'measure'. Hegel's measure, which unifies quality and quantity, corresponds to the capital-form, which combines the forms of both money and commodities. The three broad categories of 'specific quantum, the measureless and absolute indifference', respectively, bring out the fundamental characteristics of 'merchant capital, money-lending capital and industrial capital' quite well. However, with the belief that measure is realised everywhere in the sphere of nature, Hegel places himself under a strong Newtonian influence, which renders his reasoning at times thoroughly mechanical.

It is, of course, absolutely essential that measure should be understood as 'qualitative quantity' and not 'quantitative quality', for capital (measure) which takes on and off the forms of money (quantity) and the commodity (quality) begins and ends with money that externalises value, and not with the commodity that holds value immanently. Hegel fully realises this point when he characterises 'specific quantum' as the variability of quantum, which maintains the same determining quality. Indeed, in the form of merchant capital, M–C–M', the value of specific commodities (C) can be expressed by larger or smaller quantities of money (M and M') within limits, that is, to the extent that the price-differential can exist. Yet Hegel does not know where the limits come from, and is therefore forced to dwell on such ancient puzzles as 'whether a single grain makes a heap of wheat or whether it makes a bald-tail to tear out a single hair from the horse's tail'.[27] At such a level, the problem is reduced to mere mechanical relations between extensive and intensive quanta. All natural events occur in time and space. Sometimes time appears to be the intensive and space the extensive magnitude, but at other times the reverse may be true. It is not possible to determine *a priori* which constitutes the subject of the motion and which is its mere mediation. At this point, even the fundamental difference between 'qualitative quantity' and 'quantitative quality' is no longer clear.

Hegel's deduction of 'the measureless' and 'absolute indifference' is even more haphazard and abstruse, whereas the deduction of money-lending capital from merchant capital, and of industrial capital from money-lending capital, requires no such mental acrobatics. The reason why individual units of merchant capital constitute 'self-subsistent measures of material things'[28] is that they are involved with different use-values. Money-lending capital does not blend these differences by means of some mysterious 'affinity'. As the money-lender, it stands apart from merchant activity and removes itself from direct involvement with use-values. But precisely for that reason, money-lending capital tends to become 'measureless' (unprincipled). The side-stepping of trade in use-values makes money-lending capital an empty form of capital, a non-metamorphosis of value. The defect of this form must, therefore, be overcome by industrial capital, which, while involving itself with use-values, nevertheless achieves indifference to them. Industrial capital does not spring from the quantitative excess of money-lending capital, which oversteps its 'nodal points'.[29] Industrial capital realises an absolute indifference to use-values by purchasing labour-power as a commodity; labour-power that can render any form of productive labour.

As the third and last example, let us consider Hegel's doctrine of 'objectivity', which I believe is in close correspondence with the theory of rent in the dialectic of capital. The process whereby 'the Notion determines itself into objectivity' is, according to Hegel, 'identical in character with the ontological proof of the existence of God'.[30] 'God, as the living God, and still more as absolute spirit, is known only in his activity; man was early instructed to recognise

---

27   Hegel 1975, p. 159.
28   Hegel 1969, p. 348.
29   Hegel 1969, pp. 366ff.
30   Hegel 1969, p. 705.

God in his works'.[31] In the language of the dialectic of capital, this may be paraphrased as follows: if the distribution of surplus value in the capitalist market
is comprehended only from the point of view of capital (as in the theory of
profit), it remains the subjective Notion, which is neither 'realised' nor 'objectified'. It is necessary to understand the distribution principle in its activity or
working, as it involves a factor alien to capital, namely, landed property. In this
way the dialectical meaning of the theory of rent is very clearly defined. Hegel,
on the other hand, holds the material world in which 'the works of God' may
be observed nameless, although his dialectic of mechanism, chemism and teleology echoes the three broad divisions of his natural philosophy (mechanics,
physics and organics) very closely.

It is obvious that Hegel's objectivity, in fact, means nature or the material
world, which he cannot, however, make explicit in his metaphysical logic. Being unable to posit the entity external to the Notion of the Absolute, Hegel resorts at once to the 'twofold meaning' of objectivity, namely 'objectivity which
stands opposed to the self-subsistent Notion', and 'objectivity which is also the
being that is in and for itself' meaning 'that is free and above all contingency'.[32]
The latter may be interpreted as 'the realised or objectified distribution principle' that may emerge as the conclusion of the theory of rent. However, the
dialectic that leads up to that conclusion requires a clearer specification of
objectivity in the first sense. Thus, although with his 'mechanism, chemism
and teleology', Hegel in fact characterises the dialectical sequence of the three
forms of rent (differential rent of forms I and II, and absolute rent) with remarkable pertinence and accuracy, the detail of his speculative argument is
often too fanciful and erratic to be convincing. In this book, I will show how
the dialectical theory of rent can render Hegel's doctrine of objectivity easier
to grasp and more reasonable.

(γ) Thus, even from this cursory look at a few examples, it is clear that the
dialectic of capital can remove many ambiguities from Hegel's dialectic. This
is only to be expected, because the former is an immanent critique and a materialistic transposition of the latter. Just as 'the anatomy of man is a key to the
anatomy of the ape', so must the dialectic of capital be a key to the understanding of Hegel's *Logic*. Yet if, as is being contended here, the dialectic of capital is
a more developed form of Hegel's dialectic, they must be essentially identical
and homomorphic in structure, even though the one operates in the idealist
context of metaphysics and the other in the materialist context of economic

---

31   Hegel 1969, p. 706.
32   Hegel 1969, p. 709.

theory. This claim of the uniqueness of the dialectic might surprise some, because it appears at first sight to contradict the conventional view of materialism. An explanation is, therefore, in order.

As already stated, the dialectic defines truth as the subject-object identity. That is to say, it does not impose an external logic on the object of study, but allows the latter to reveal its own logic of synthesis. The dialectic merely spells out the logic inherent in the subject matter, and refuses to dictate to it a finite logic that the human mind invents for its explanation. This principle rigorously applies to Hegel's dialectic, which copies the self-revealing wisdom of the Absolute, in just the same way as it applies to the dialectic of capital, in which economic theory does nothing but follow the 'self-synthesising logic of capital'. If this is the case, the identity and homomorphism of the two dialectics can mean only one thing, namely, that the Absolute and capital possess the same logical structure, and, hence, that the object of study of metaphysics and that of economic theory are in fact the same thing with different names. Indeed, if they were different and unrelated, how would they possess the same logic of self-synthesis?

To say that the human mind comprehends only one logic, even though the objects of study are different, would certainly contradict the previous argument that the dialectic is the concrete logic inherent in the subject matter itself, and not an abstract logic subjectively or arbitrarily designed to assist human comprehension. There is clearly no escape from the conclusion that what Hegel believed to be the Absolute was in fact capital in disguise, and that he unknowingly described the economic theory of capitalism in the language of metaphysics. To some extent, this explains why I said above that this necessarily strikes one as 'unbelievable' at first glance, that is, the idea that it was as if Hegel, already in possession of a complete knowledge of the dialectic of capital, deliberately equivocated on this matter by using metaphysical jargon. Indeed, this contention may initially appear extravagant and too fanciful to be believed. But is it really so?

I believe that, in principle, there can be only one real totality capable of complete self-synthesis, and that totality is capitalism, which has an inner logic that the dialectic of capital copies. Hegel's Absolute is not a 'real' totality, but a mentally constructed one. From the point of view of materialism, the Absolute is clearly a product of human thought. The thought creates the Absolute first, and then pretends that it only passively copies His wisdom. This is like writing a novel, in which the author claims to have been asked by the principal character to tell the latter's story. Who then is the real story-teller – the fictional character or the author who invented him? Idealism asserts that the author invents nothing, but merely copies the story recounted to him by the fictional character. This voluntary disclaimer of originality may appear quaint in the present age in which the opposite practice flourishes. But the whole tradition of speculative philosophy is built on this principle of pious humility and self-effacement, and Hegel undoubtedly is the last great author of that school. The question is why his fictional character (the Absolute) so uncannily resembled real capitalism, that is to say, why Hegel's metaphysical system so closely adumbrated the system of economic theory.

One can answer this question only by invoking Hegel's genius. Hegel, who in 1807 enthusiastically applauded Napoleon's entry into Jena, was not an ivory-tower recluse engrossed in private thoughts. On the contrary, he was greatly perceptive of the spirit of the age (*Zeitgeist*), as capitalism was about to evolve into a new world order in the wake of bourgeois revolutions. As Feuerbach realised early on, the greatness of the German-idealist philosophy is that it is a system of 'reflective' thought. Hegel was not consciously aware of what his thought reflected; however, he certainly had premonitions of what was to come and knew how to express it in the allegorical, or metaphorical, language of speculative philosophy. Thought moves people only when it reflects an imminent reality. It was because the Absolute of Hegel was, in fact, capitalism that his philosophy appealed so decisively to the youth of his time.

This point is confirmed by the fact that the completion of Hegel's idealist philsophy almost instantly gave rise to its materialist critics. The young Hegelians, including Feuerbach, realised that the content of Hegelianism would remain intact even after the abolition of God, the Absolute. How was that possible, especially when Hegel had expressly stated that philosophy and religion were different only in form and not in content? Feuerbach thus taught his philosophy of *anthropomorphism*, which argued that God was an outward projection of man's inward nature, a thesis enthusiastically supported by young Marx and Engels. It was already clear that the Absolute of Hegel reflected something real, but the humanism of Feuerbach, because of its inability to preserve Hegel's dialectic, was not sufficient as a true materialist critique of idealism. What was required was to show not only that the Absolute was a reflection of something real, but also that the dialectic was the logic of the real.

Only when this is accomplished is God finally abolished, and the materialist critique of Hegel's philosophy complete. Conventional Marxism has not faced this issue, but has merely tried to graft onto Feuerbachian materialism a few questionable 'laws' or 'principles' of the dialectic. To me, that constitutes a pathetic anti-climax, a deplorable example of the 'poverty of philosophy'. Only the dialectic of capital, with its thesis of 'capital-morphism' (whereby the Absolute is regarded as capital), instead of the Feuerbachian anthropomorphism, can truly overcome Hegel's idealism and establish materialism unambiguously.

This, of course, does not definitively demonstrate that God exists nowhere. It only means that He does not exist in the Hegelian fashion. For only capitalism exists dialectically as the real.

C   Political Economy and Socialism

(a)   *The Scope of Political Economy*

(α) The superiority of the dialectic of capital (economic theory) over the Hegelian dialectic (metaphysics) stems, to a large extent, from the reinforcement of the antithetical term. That is to say, a solution of the contradiction between *value and use-value* generates a logical motion far clearer than an *ad hoc* recourse to the interpenetration of *being and nothing*. But precisely for this reason, political economy cannot take the role of 'use-values' lightly. Indeed, whenever society produces and consumes use-values, there is economic life. Yet the latter is not immediately comprehensible, *unless most of the use-values are produced and traded as commodities*. Only under capitalism do all use-values tend to be produced and traded as commodities, and it is this fact that enabled political economy to study economic life in general for the first time, after that mode of production (called 'capitalism') evolved historically. Even this fact, however, does not imply that the existence of capitalism in history requires a prior conversion of *all* use-values into commodities. Such a rigid condition would make it impossible for capitalism to evolve historically. Moreover, capitalism, once in existence, would not be transient if it ever actually satisfied such a condition. The operation of capitalism in history is, by its own nature, expected to be more or less imperfect, as some use-values refuse to submit themselves to the sway of the commodity-economy.

The dialectic of capital does not assert that use-values should always take the form of commodities, but rather that capitalism exists to the extent that they do. In general, use-values cannot be made to conform to the rules and principles of the commodity-economy. That is why the capitalist mode of production is a historically transient institution. Only when the use-values that society requires are manageable by the commodity-economy does capitalism approach its ideal image. Yet a purely capitalist society is never realised factually. If that were to occur, it would imply that society's economic life had been completely freed from the vagaries of use-values, an event just as unlikely as the miracle of levitation. In view of the perennial difficulty of commoditising use-values even under capitalism, political economy is compelled to study this institution at three distinct levels of abstraction. The pure theory of capitalism contemplates only use-values that are capable of being completely subsumed by the commodity-economic form, for otherwise it would not be possible to fully reveal the inner logic of capitalism. Such use-values may be described as *neutralised* or *idealised*. The stages-theory of capitalist development introduces use-values in a somewhat more concrete fashion as 'types'. Thus, the stages of mercantilism, liberalism, and imperialism, are characterised by wool, cotton, and steel, respectively, and by the technologies appropriate for the production of such use-values. Only in the economic history of capitalism are use-values permitted to remain in their raw form, that is, in their full variety and empirical detail.

Although economic life always involves use-values, they do not hang together by themselves, which is to say that they do not have a logic of their own. The kind of use-values a society most commonly produces and consumes is a historical, not a logical, question. A direct study of use-values produced and consumed under capitalism may reveal a capitalistic life-style, but it does not explain the laws of motion of capitalist society nor, through them, the norms of economic life common to all societies. Political economy must, therefore, *neutralise or inactivate* use-values in order to first discover the inner logic of capitalism. This procedure pays a high price in that it demands a significant departure from real capitalism as it is experienced in history. Yet to avoid such a cost is to ignore the logical nature of capitalism, and to fall into the fallacy of the logical-historical method (which I shall criticise in the next section). Capitalism never openly exhibits its inner logic. That is to say, capitalism in history, while it always contains a 'logical or pure capitalism' inside itself, never actually materialises it in a theoretically perfect form. That is why economic theory requires a 'mental abstraction' to reach the logical core of capitalism in history, and to find there a purely capitalist society.

This method is frequently opposed for two reasons. First, the theoretical presupposition of a purely capitalist society, which is not directly observable, appears to concede too much to idealism. Secondly, the concept of a purely capitalist society is hastily confused with the neoclassical model of a perfectly competitive market. These views stem from the total lack of comprehension of the dialectic. As already stated, the dialectic of capital is free from idealism not only because capital, unlike the Absolute, is not a fiction, but also because, for something to be real, it need not be apparent, that is, directly or empirically observable. Indeed, if the logic of capital were directly visible, abstract economic theory would be unnecessary. The abstract economic theory of the dialectic of capital is, however, quite different from the formal and mechanical economic theory of the neoclassical school, *which altogether ignores use-values as distinct from values (commodities)*. Neoclassical theory does not simply inactivate or idealise use-values, but also reduces them to 'scarcities', that is, to empty numbers with different labels. Since the formal mechanism of the market is, in that case, never really opposed or restricted by use-values, neoclassical theory develops the one-sided view that the economy is always market-based. The faith in the permanence of capitalism, once embraced by classical political economists, is here translated into what Karl Polanyi aptly describes as the 'market mentality', which hypostatises the market everywhere: the 'economistic postulate which argues the virtual presence of the market in every society, whether such a system is empirically present or not'.[33]

The dialectic of capital does not suffer from the market mentality, because it recognises the contradiction between value and use-values even in the pure theory, in which use-values are expressly said to be 'idealised'. Here, value must be understood, in the first instance, in its broad and primary sense of capitalist indifference to use-values. Although idealised in theory, use-values – representing the substantive aspect of economic life – continue to resist the uniformity of value, which seeks to integrate them. The purpose of the dialectic is to uncover the logic of capital, which eventually accomplishes this integration, to the extent that use-values are amenable to it. Since the present book is devoted to a detailed examination of that logic, I do not intend to summarise it here. However, the point must be made to the effect that even in pure economic theory, use-values cannot be dismissed as 'nothing'. Value, or the formative factor of capitalism, does not simply brush them aside, but instead subsumes them, and thus grounds itself on (and fills itself with) the substance of real economic life. The economic theory of the dialectic of capital, albeit abstract, does not study the formal mechanism of capitalist society in the absence of real economic life. Rather, it examines how capital seeks to embrace the real economic life of society within the commodity-economic integument.

Herein lies the truly revolutionary character of Marxian economic theory, for to demonstrate that capitalism is nothing but real economic life, temporarily wrapped in a commodity-economic skin, is to suggest the possibility of its removal. That is to say, as soon as use-values exceed the commodity-form, the self-regulation of the capitalist market is already foiled to that extent. This means that real economic life is not by nature market-based, but that its original and natural state is retrieved when 'the narrow bourgeois skin' is 'peeled away' from capitalism. The economic theory of the dialectic of capital, which exhibits the logical synthesis of capitalism as something so far-fetched and unnatural as to require the idealisation of use-values, may be called 'invertible' in a sense that neoclassical theory could never be. Indeed, remove the price

---

33   Polanyi 1968, p. 117.

mechanism of the self-regulating market from neoclassical theory, and there is nothing left of it. However, the peeling away of the commodity-economic skin from the purely capitalist society leaves behind, or reveals, the *general norms of economic life common to all societies* in a fully developed, if idealised, form.

(β) Once the inner logic of capital is comprehended in the context of a purely capitalist society, in which use-values are inactivated, and in which, therefore, history is held implicit, the next step is to reactivate use-values and to reinstate history, in an effort to return to actual (empirically observable) capitalism in history. Yet the return journey cannot be a direct one, for, indeed, how can once inactivated use-values of theory be suddenly revived and made to act like raw and naked use-values, as they are found in empirical history? The mediation between the abstract world of theory and that of concrete-empirical history must be found in the *stages-theory* of capitalist development, in which use-values reappear in the first place as *types*.

A stages-theory (*Stufentheorie*) of some sort is inevitable in any historical study, for without it the wealth of empirical details cannot be systematically explored. However, when economic historians mark off the three stages of capitalist development (mercantilism, liberalism, and imperialism), they can do more than build 'ideal types' because each stage can be characterised by the interplay of *a particular type of use-values* and the logic of capitalism. The latter operates differently depending, for example, on whether use-values are producible by light technology, characteristic of the English cotton industry of the mid-nineteenth-century, or are producible only by heavy technology, typical of the German steel mills at the turn of the century from the nineteenth to the twentieth. The stages-theory does not examine a particular episode of capitalist economic history. Rather, it portrays the *modus operandi* of logical capitalism as it subsumes an economic life involving specific *types* of use-values. Again, this task is very similar to that which is assigned to Hegel's *Natur-* and *Geistes-philosophie*. Hegel too believed that the logic that 'coincided with metaphysics' could not be directly linked to the empirical sciences, and that the philosophies of nature and finite spirits were required to mediate them.

These considerations reaffirm the nature of dialectical knowledge. Since it takes the problem of objectivity seriously, it does not permit a facile union or correspondence of 'super-sensible' theory with 'sensible' reality. Even when the latter is ultimately governed by the abstract laws of motion, which are in the true sense of the word 'objective', they are not expected to appear undistorted, or undeformed, in the real world, which is filled with empirical contingencies. Referring to 'the infinite wealth and variety of forms and, what is more irrational, the contingency which enters into the external arrangement of natural things', and to 'the impotence of Nature to adhere strictly to the Notion in its realisation', Hegel says: 'This impotence of Nature sets limits to philosophy and it is quite improper to expect the Notion to comprehend – or as it is said, construe or deduce – these contingent products of Nature'.[34] In exactly the same way, political economy must admit the impotence of history to strictly adhere to the logic of capitalism. It would be quite improper to expect the logic of capitalism to be able to explain all the empirical contingencies of capitalist history.

The adoption of a particular type of use-value specifies the technology appropriate for its production, and the type of capital that most effectively operates the existing technology constitutes the *dominant form of capital* in that stage. Each stage of capitalist development must, therefore, be studied with reference to the nature, the specific mode of accumulation and the economic policies adopted by the bourgeois state to assist the dominant form of capital.

The formative period of capitalism is characterised by the *mercantilist stage*. This stage is best represented by seventeenth- and eighteenth-century England, prior to the Industrial Revolution. The domestic handicraft production of woollen articles, chiefly for the international market, typifies the industrial activity of that stage. Throughout this stage, merchant capital, which operates the putting-out system, plays the dominant role. In order for merchant capital, which originally accumulates wealth in international trade, to successfully infiltrate a traditional society, not only should its agriculture be sufficiently productive, but the co-operation of the existing feudal powers is also essential. Only with the satisfaction of such pre-conditions can *merchant capital* gradually transform a traditional society into capitalism by promoting the disintegration of the guild system, expropriating small producers and separating manufacture from agriculture. The mercantilist stage represents the period of primitive accumulation, by means of which merchant capital reorganises national production in a way most conducive to foreign trade. The stage-theory of mercantilism is, however, different from the economic history of the period. Since chronological details are irrelevant, I believe that the following schema is sufficient to capture the fundamental characteristics of the mercantilist stage:

The Stage of Mercantilism

1. Merchant Capital as the Dominant Form
    a) *International trade and the accumulation of wealth*
    b) *Domestic industries and the putting-out system*
    c) *The separation of manufacture from agriculture*

---

34   Hegel 1970, pp. 23–4.

2.   The Mode of Accumulation of Merchant Capital
     a)   *The disintegration of the guild system*
     b)   *The expropriation of small producers*
     c)   *National industry subordinate to foreign trade*
3.   Mercantilist Economic Policies
     a)   *Chartered monopolies and navigation acts*
     b)   *Trade policies and corn laws*
     c)   *The primitive accumulation*

The liberal stage of development characterises the period in which capitalism securely establishes itself. This period is best represented by mid-nineteenth-century England in the wake of the Industrial Revolution. The bulk production of cotton articles in modern mechanised factories typifies the industrial activities of the stage. It is now *industrial capital*, subdivided into small independent and competing enterprises, that plays the dominant role. By this time, the *home (or national) market* is well established, and old restrictive practices having been removed. Since the direct producers are already 'free in the double sense', their labour-power being readily available as a commodity, industrial capital no longer needs the protective assistance of the state. Instead, the freely competitive market automatically and anonymously regulates the production of commodities, while an increasing mechanisation of industry deprives the working class of its traditional skills. This enables industrial capital to appropriate the fruit of surplus labour in the form of surplus value, that is, without having to resort to extra-economic coercion. Yet as the process of capital accumulation necessarily undergoes business cycles fraught with decennial crises, an intensification of class antagonism cannot be avoided. In view of the faith in the self-regulation of the market, liberal economic policies tend towards the elimination of restrictive trade practices (both domestically and internationally) and the retrenchment of public finances. The international free trade movement, however, is understandably resisted by the infant-industry argument for protection in less developed countries. The following may be suggested as a conspectus of the stage-characteristics of liberalism.

The Stage of Liberalism

1   Industrial Capital as the Dominant Form
    a)   *The establishment of the home market*
    b)   *Effects of the Industrial Revolution*
    c)   *The modern factory system*

2   The Mode of Accumulation of Industrial Capital
  a)   *Mechanisation and the deskilling of labour*
  b)   *Commodity production under free competition*
  c)   *The cyclical process of accumulation*
3   Liberal Economic Policies
  a)   *The free trade movement*
  b)   *Cheap government*
  c)   *International economic relations*

The free trade movement that reached its acme in the 1860s did not last forever. The long depression of the 1870s, in the aftermath of the Franco-Prussian War, profoundly changed the pattern of capitalist development, ushering in 'imperialism' as the third and last stage of capitalist dvelopment. During this stage, which is best represented by Imperial Germany, the economic activity of a capitalist nation revolves around the iron-and-steel industry. In view of the heavy hardware required for the production of such use-values as iron and steel, the form of the joint-stock enterprise, the scope of which had previously been limited to public utilities and commerce, now becomes prevalent in manufacturing industries. This means that the production of commodities tends to be 'remote-controlled' by finance-capital. The latter, as the dominant form of capital in the imperialist stage, develops various monopolist organisations so as to shelter the production of heavy use-values from the vicissitudes of the market. Free competition is, therefore, replaced by organised monopolies in heavy industry. As the market thus loses, to some extent, its self-regulating mechanism, industrially developed capitalist nations tend to suffer from a *chronic excess of capital*. The export of capital to colonies and satellites consequently becomes mandatory. To the extent that the market fails to effectively regulate economic activities, *finance-capital* demands the active policies of the imperialist state. Not only does the latter resort to fierce tariff wars, but it also addresses itself to colonial policies and *sozialpolitik*, thereby markedly inflating public expenditures. The following schema may roughly summarise the stage-characteristics of imperialism.

The Stage of Imperialism

1.   Finance-Capital as the Dominant Form
  a)   *The joint-stock company system*
  b)   *The importance of fixed capital in industry*
  c)   *The financial control of industry*

2.   The Mode of Accumulation of Finance-Capital
      a)   *The displacement of free competition by monopolies*
      b)   *Various methods of controlling the market*
      c)   *Chronic tendency to an excess of capital*
3.   Imperialist Economic Policies
      a)   *Custom duties and dumping*
      b)   *The export of capital to colonies and satellites*
      c)   *The division of the world into colonial empires*

(γ) In the above summary of the three stages, I have, to a great extent, sacrificed accuracy for brevity. Ideally, the exposition of the stage-characteristics should follow a certain logical order, since the purpose of the stages-theory is to demonstrate how motives (the logic of capitalism) are translated into stage-theoretic actions in an artificially contrived environment, determined by the specification of the type of use-values and the associated industrial technology. It is important to realise that the stages-theory is a 'mental experiment' in this sense, rather than a compressed description of historical facts, even though, in reality, the mental experiment is greatly assisted by the study of economic history. This is the reason for my statement earlier, namely, that economic historians can build more than ideal types, by marking off the three stages of capitalist development. In the preface to the First German Edition of *Capital*, Volume I, Marx himself wrote as follows:

> The physicist either observes physical phenomena where they occur in their most typical form and most free from disturbing influence, or whenever possible, he makes experiments under conditions that assure the occurrence of the phenomenon in its normality.[35]

This suggests that the economist should do likewise in his theoretical work. I believe that this experimental procedure is more appropriate for the stages-theory than for the pure theory of capitalism.

If the stages of capitalist development were mere ideal types, which economic historians subjectively constructed, the stages would not mediate between the pure theory and the history of capitalism, and would fail in the task specifically assigned to them. The mediation is possible only because the stages-theory stands exactly halfway between abstract-logical theory and concrete-empirical history, as a *mental experiment* in the above sense. It is the availability of such a mental experiment that gives the economic history

---

35   Marx 1967, *Capital*, Volume I, p. 8.

of capitalism an advantage that is not shared by other economic histories. Of course, history is always full of contingencies, but it is a natural impulse of the historian, regardless of his creed, to see the inevitable trend lurking behind contingent factors. Only in the history of capitalism can he separate the necessary from the contingent, without resorting to subjective ideal types. For empirical facts that agree with the predictions of the stages-theory may be viewed as logically necessary. This possibility, it seems to me, confirms the importance of the history of capitalism, in the study of economic history in general. Radical as it may seem, such a view is consistent with the fundamental proposition of historical materialism that capitalist society holds a mirror up to all pre-capitalist societies.

Needless to say, the present view does not imply that all historical facts under capitalism can or must be theoretically accounted for. An unrestrained 'application of theory' to history only does violence to facts. It is, as Hegel says, 'quite improper' to expect the inner logic of capitalism to explain all the 'contingent products' of history. (Only an empty theory purports to work such wonders. A real theory does not answer all our subjectively motivated queries. If it answers a question, it does so *on its own terms*, regardless of the subjective urgency with which the solution is sought. A dependable theory is not the one that is always forthcoming with ready-made answers). The pure theory of capitalism, in other words, applies to the study of capitalist history only heuristically, through the mediation of stages-theory, and never directly. Theory must be adapted to the study of history, not the other way around. It is this point that is ignored by the logical-historical method, which calls for an unmediated unity of logic and history. I intend to discuss the fallacy of this method in some detail below, for it essentially amounts to a mystification of the dialectic as a *universal logic of a self-unfolding reality*, as it seeks to sublate any arbitrary contradiction.

Since the logical-historical method regards history as process which unfolds itself, by resolving some sort of contradiction, it need only invent one in some broad sense, in order to arrive at a 'logical' explanation of *all* historical developments. This conveniently makes history deterministic and predictable. Whatever is historical then appears logical, and whatever is logical seems to hide history behind it. Indeed, according to this approach, a transition from one mode of production to another must be logically explained in the light of the principle of historical materialism that a contradiction or discrepancy between society's *productive powers* and its *relations of production* must entail some sort of transformation of quantity into quality. According to this method again, the dialectic of the commodity, money and capital is nothing but an abstract description of the historical fact that money arises from barter, and capital from monetary exchanges! In other words, this method makes no distinction between the commodity-economic logic of capital, which is peculiar to the modern age, and the development of general history, which may have nothing to do with the commodity-economy. Uno has quite rightly warned against such a conception of history, describing it as 'commodity-economic' rather than 'materialistic'. There is, indeed, a sense in which the 'commodity-economic conception of history' is a conventional-Marxist version of Polany's 'market mentality'. For just as the market mentality hypostatises the all-embracing market, where it does not exist, the commodity-economic conception of history generalises the logic of capital to a universal law of history.

Such a wanton generalisation, however, makes both the logic and history meaningless. It must be clearly understood that use-values do not possess their own logic; indeed, if they did, it would be quite different from the commodity-economic logic of capital. Thus, for example, it is not possible to logically explain why wool, cotton and steel appear in this order as the typical use-values in the three stages of capitalist development. Neither is it possible to logically account for the transition from one stage of deveolopment to another, for that would attribute a specifically commodity-economic logic to the autonomous development of history. This point is of particular importance at the present time, when the world economy has already left *capitalism proper* behind, and finds itself in a phase of transition away from capitalism to something else (socialism?). Both Uno and Polanyi are agreed in dating the end of *capitalism proper* (or the age of the self-regulating market) with the outbreak of the First World War. This means that an enquiry into the present as economic history demands a method quite different from that applicable to the economic history of capitalism. That is a difficult problem, a satisfactory treatment of which requires some more preliminary discussions.

(b)   The Fallacy of the Logical-historical Method

(α) Referring to the 'method which underlies Marx's critique of political economy', Engels states as follows:

> The logical method ... is indeed nothing but the historical method, only stripped of the historical form and diverting chance occurrences. The point where this history [of bourgeois society] begins must also be the starting point of the train of thought, and its further progress will be simply the reflection, in abstract and theoretically consistent form, of the historical course.[36]

---

36   Engels 1970b, p. 225.

As is rather typical with Engels, here he states a partially correct idea in a confused fashion. It is, of course, correct to say that bourgeois society, in the phase of its historical development, synthesises its own logic by divesting itself of contingencies, and that political economy assumes its logical form by merely copying this inner logic of capitalism. However, the same reasoning cannot be extended to apply to all societies. Ignoring this important restriction, Engels vigorously argues elsewhere that 'the course of any history is governed by inner general laws', claiming:

> Historical events thus appear on the whole to be governed by chance. But where on the surface accident holds sway, there actually it is always governed by inner, hidden laws and it is only a matter of discovering these laws.[37]

Such a generalisation is clearly untenable. The valid proposition contained in the earlier passage, namely, that the history of capitalism reflects its inner logic, in one way or another, is here transformed into the different proposition that every history, capitalist or not, must unfold according to a pre-established logical plan. In this manner, Engels might have thought he had successfully translated Hegel's *Philosophy of History* into its materialist counterpart, but such a historical determinism is 'materialist' only in name. It is, in fact, the most unconscionable form of spiritual idealism, the kind that understandably repelled Colleti (as we have already seen). Since history always proves to be right, so the argument seems to go, one merely has to stare at it hard enough until 'the hidden general laws' emerge from 'the leaps and bounds and zigzag line' of actual history!

Engels evidently substitutes for Hegel's world-spirit (*Weltgeist*) the operation of 'hidden general laws', which are presumed to have governed the history of humanity from its beginning. One must realise that this apparently innocent substitution, although it might greatly appeal to the popular mind, does irreparable damage to the dialectic. Since these 'general laws' cannot possibly be the specifically commodity-economic laws of capitalism, they allude to the general principles of historical materialism. It now appears that the specifically commodity-economic logic of capital is no more than a special variation of the more general 'logic' of historical materialism, rather than the latter being an insight gained only in the light of the former. However, if historical materialism is allowed to thus override political economy, the dialectic of capital becomes an impossible proposition. Capitalism can no longer be studied through a logic of its own, but only as an ideal type, which embodies the 'general laws' of history.

---

37   Engels 1970a, p. 366.

The extent to which such a procedure adulterates the dialectic is exemplified by the writings of Ronald Meek, who most faithfully abides by the Engelsian logical-historical method.

According to Meek, 'Marx developed a highly idiosyncratic method of enquiry – it might perhaps be called the "logical-historical" method – which was one of the more interesting and significant of the fruits of his early Hegelian studies'.[38] With this perception Meek arrives at the following monstrous interpretation of the law of value:

> Marx's theory of value can conveniently [!] be considered under the three headings of Pre-capitalist society [the abstract society of simple commodity production in which 'the labourers still owned the whole produce of their labour'], Early Capitalism [where 'capitalist relations of production suddenly impinged upon those of simple commodity production'], and Developed Capitalism [in which 'profit becomes proportional not to labour employed but to capital employed']. To each of these forms of society there may be conceived to correspond certain basic economic categories and certain basic logical problems. The task of the analysis of value as Marx understood it was to solve those basic problems in terms of the relations of production appropriate to the particular 'historical' stage which was under consideration.[39]

It is, of course, correct to say that the dialectic of capital, in its Doctrines of Circulation, Production, and Distribution, operates at three distinct logical stages of abstraction, so that certain specifications deliberately held implicit in earlier doctrines are made explicit in later ones. But this does not mean that one may 'in the development of economic categories' fail to 'remember that the subject, contemporary bourgeois society, is presupposed both in reality and in the mind'.[40] It is certainly incorrect to confuse the logical levels of abstraction with 'historical stages'. Strangely enough, Meek himself seems to be aware that such historical stages do not in fact exist, for in a footnote attached to the above passage, he says:

> A word of caution may be appropriate here, in order to forestall possible criticisms involving the fallacy of misplaced concreteness. The three forms of society mentioned here do not necessarily represent actual

---

38   Meek 1967, p. 99.
39   Ibid.
40   Marx 1970, *Contribution*, p. 212.

historically identifiable forms: They are merely the 'historical' counter-parts of the three main stages in Marx's logical analysis of the value problem. In Marx's view, it will be remembered, the course of logical analysis is a corrected mirror-image of the actual historical course.[41]

With this reservation, Meek in effect admits that the 'historical-logical' correspondence, whether it really exists or not, must always be imagined because its absence upsets him. In other words, logic must be tested by history for the sake of his peace of mind. This feeling seems to be widely shared by conventional Marxists, who have abandoned the dialectic for empiricism. What they fail to see is that not only is it impossible to empirically test a pure dialectical theory, but also, because of its subject-object identity, such a test is altogether unnecessary. Their insistence on the 'logical-historical' method – sometimes to the extent of fantasising non-existent histories – seems to stem from their lack of confidence in the objectivity of dialectical knowledge.

It is true that in the Doctrine of Circulation, in which the logic of transition prevails, the development of the theory appears to closely parallel the historical sequence of events. Thus, indeed 'money' originates from 'commodities' and 'capital' from 'money', both in theory and in history. But I emphatically disagree with Engels's claim that 'the logical exposition ... requires historical illustration and continuous contact with reality'.[42] For example, although the development of the value-forms, since it represents a generative logic, can be usefully illustrated with apposite historical instances, an excessive reliance on historico-anthropological facts[43] only does violence to theory.[44] Moreover, any parallel between the historical and the logical order of appearance of categories is limited to the Doctrine of Circulation. As Marx pointed out early on, 'it would be inexpedient and wrong to present the economic categories successively in the order in which they have played the dominant role in history',[45] so that, for example, agricultural rent cannot be introduced into theory until the capitalist market is fully developed. Indeed, contrary to popular belief, 'transition' is not the only dialectical method. In the Doctrines of Production and Distribution, where the methods of 'reflection' and 'unfolding' apply, the logical order frequently reverses the historical order.

It is this point that most conventional Marxists seem to overlook. With the fixed idea that the dialectic consists only of the logic of transition, and that

41   Meek 1967, p. 99.
42   Engels 1970b, p. 227.
43   For example, see Mandel 1970, pp. 49ff.
44   See Colletti 1973, pp. 131–2.
45   Marx 1970, *Contribution*, p. 213.

the latter reconfirms any historical sequence of events, they are led to a crude 'logical-historical' method. However, this historicism – an irrational combination of empiricism and historical determinism – profoundly distorts their conception of capitalism. Indeed, they see in the history of capitalism nothing but an unfolding of the devil's plan. Such a view, of course, has nothing to do with the dialectic. Capitalism, if it consisted only of negative properties, would not have formed a historical society. Political economy does not teach only the negative side of capitalism; rather, it teaches with what remarkable ingenuity, subtleness and cunning capital organises the economic life of society in a peculiarly commodity-economic fashion. Moreover, it was Marx's belief that no-one could truly criticise capitalism without first recognising its positive accomplishments. Thus, in reviewing capitalism in its historical perspective, one always has to bear in mind what it can and cannot do.

The tradition of the logical-historical method, which conveniently enables Marxists to ignore the dialectic of capital and to come forward with wishful interpretations of historical materialism, has long been established, so that those who approach Marxism through the secondary literature and textbooks are inevitably trapped by this mesmerising piece of 'epistemology'. 'Marx was the first economist of top rank', writes Schumpeter, 'to see and to teach systematically how economic theory may be turned into historical analysis and how the historical narrative may be turned into *histoire raisonnée*'.[46] Greatly impressed by the 'chemical mixture of theory and history' supposedly accomplished by Marx, Schumpeter reasons that the German historical school, whose record is less spectacular, ought in principle to have done equally well or better. His decisive effort to remedy that shortfall, therefore, results in the picturesque theory of 'creative destruction' and 'entrepreneurial innovation', but Schumpeter's artistry is magnificent only in its visionary subjectivity, the objective logic of capital having completely disappeared in his unrestrained eulogy of the 'entrepreneurial spirit'. In Schumpeter, one observes the logical-historical method both at its best (in its most subtle guise) and at its worst (in terms of its pernicious influence on economic theory). Understandably, Schumpeter continues to be idolised by the practitioners of bourgeois economics, who are increasingly wary of the ghostly emptiness of their non-invertible theory.

(β) In contrast to Schumpeter's, Karl Polanyi's economic thought is far more sensible and essentially in agreement with the presuppositions of the dialectic of capital. Although he eschews the use of the word 'capitalism', there is no doubt that what Polanyi calls 'the self-regulating (or price-making) market'

---

46   Schumpeter 1950, p. 44.

encapsulates the nature of capitalism. As an outstanding historian and anthropologist, Polanyi at once realises that the organisation of economic life exclusively by the principles of the market is both exceptional and devastating to humanity, and that such a thing is destined to be a brief historical interlude of no more than a century. Specifically, Polanyi considers the period between 1830 and 1914 to be the era of the self-regulating market. He also realises that for the market to be self-regulating, and hence the exclusive method of integrating economic life, three fictitious commodities are essential, namely, labour, land, and money. They are, in effect, the conversion of man, nature, and an institution, into commodities. While Polanyi does not explain the logic of this proposition, it clearly agrees with the claim of the dialectic of capital that the synthesis of a purely capitalist society requires the commoditisation of labour-power, land and idle funds.

Unfortunately, Polanyi does not present a theory of the self-regulating market, which is to say that he does not show how such a thing is logically possible. As I wish to show, this constitutes a major weakness in Polanyi's doctrine. However, that does not seem to impair the soundness of his historical intuition, as on the one hand, he admits the presence of the self-regulating market in history, and on the other, he interprets it as a 'liberal utopia', which cannot be completely achieved. Indeed, the acuteness of Polanyi's observation is striking, for what he sees is the essential fact that capitalism's perfection in pure theory can never be entirely materialised in reality. This insight shields him from the commodity-economic conception of history, which one might consider as a variation of the 'obsolete market mentality'. The market mentality consists of generalising the mechanism of the self-regulating market to where it cannot operate, because use-values spurn it. In other words, it ignores the fact that use-values resist the integration of economic life by the principle of value, expecting the substantive economy to always and willingly submit itself to the sway of the market. Polanyi quite rightly dismisses such an illusion, recognising the fact that substantive economic life not only can be, but also is, in most cases, independent of the market, that is, of commodity-economic regulation.

If it is unwarranted to expect that the economic life of all societies is, implicitly or explicitly, regulated by the market, neither is it reasonable to imagine that the dynamics of all societies, capitalist or not, should be governed by the same set of universal laws. Hence follows Polanyi's criticism of historical materialism. More specifically, Polanyi objects to 'the untenable stages theory of slavery, serfdom, and wage-labour that is traditional with Marxism' on the grounds that 'the character of the economy' is not exclusively 'set by the status of labour', since, for example, 'the integration of the soil into the economy is

hardly less vital'.[47] Clearly, what Polanyi criticises here is the textbook 'periodi-
sation' of historical materialism, which comes with the assertion that a mode
of production changes whenever a quantitative rise in its productive powers
requires a qualitative rearrangement of the relations of production. It is as
if historical progress could always be explained by a universal law of transition, which uncannily resembles the so-called dialectic of the transformation
of quantity into quality. Such a simplistic view of history understandably re-
pels Polanyi. However, as I have pointed out, the danger of the 'commodity-
economic conception of history' is not limited to the extended application of
the laws of capitalism to non-capitalist societies. It also dilutes, by reaction,
these capitalist laws themselves to axiomatic trivialities. Thus, the dialectic of
commodity, money and capital is understood no differently from the 'dialectic'
of slavery, serfdom and wage-labour. In the same vein, the economic theory
of capitalism is expected to demonstrate how monopoly 'springs' out of free
competition, how decennial crises necessarily 'lead to' the rising up of the
working class, and how capital accumulation 'foreshadows' the imminence of
socialism.

What makes Polanyi's economic thought both refreshing and valuable is its
resolute refusal to entertain the facile logical-historical method, even though
it unambiguously recognises the transience of capitalism in history. Following
Menger, Polanyi distinguishes the two senses of the word 'economic' – one being the formal sense of 'economising' (which has to do directly or indirectly
with the optimising behaviour of market-based individuals), and the other being the substantive sense of 'techno-economic' (which has to do with universal
human need for 'material want-satisfaction'). Broadly speaking, the same distinction has always been adopted by the dialectic of capital, which talks of the
'commodity-economic' organisation of society's 'real economic' life. Indeed,
in the Marxian tradition, the whole structure of economic theory is governed
by the single principle of the contradiction between value (the commodity-
economic) and use-values (the real-economic). The dialectic of capital by
itself signifies that capitalism, and only capitalism, is in principle capable of
synthesising the recurrent contradiction between the two opposing factors.
Polanyi does not appear to see the fact that the self-regulating market (pure
capiatlism) can be brought to completion by the synthesis of 'economising'
(value) and 'techno-economic' (use-value). As a historian, he rather seems to
stress the impossibility of such a 'liberal utopia'. This explains why Polanyi fails
to develop a theory of the self-regulating market. Yet for the same reason, he realises all the more clearly the absurdity and the precariousness of the regime,

---

47   Polanyi 1968, p. 156.

which leaves the techno-economic process of material want-satisfaction entirely to the economising behaviour of anonymous individuals.

This profound insight, however, compels Polanyi to face the difficult issue,
which has so far not been satisfactorily solved, namely, the old problem of
political economy in the wider sense or 'pre-capitalist theoretical economy',
which, as Engels wrote in 1894, was 'still to be brought into being' having been
undertaken 'only by Marx in general outline'.[48] Political economy, in the narrower sense of enquiry into the nature of capitalism, must seek its theoretical
foundation in the reifying force of the self-regulating market. Yet as Polanyi
discovers through his extensive investigations, markets play only a minor role
in integrating the economic life of non-capitalist societies. If so, the first task
of 'political economy in the wider sense' must be to establish a method for the
study of real economic life, without the assistance of commodity-economic
logic. Is this a feasible proposition? When Polanyi addresses himself to directly
categorising the substantive norms of economic life, circumventing the market, does he offer a defensible economic theory, that is to say, anything more
than the classificatory scheme of reciprocity, redistribution, and the market? It
is to this problem that we must now turn.

(γ) When Marx and Engels formulated the materialistic conception of history
(historical materialism) in *The German Ideology* of 1845–46, it was an ideological hypothesis, which led them to the study of political economy. However,
by 1859, when Marx summarised it in the introduction to *A Contribution to
the Critique of Political Economy*, it had acquired another meaning, for not
only had the study of political economy demonstrated the validity of historical materialism in the specific context of capitalist society, but in so doing
it also sharply redefined the terms of its original propositions. For example,
the meaning of the economic substructure, which was supposed to form the
base of the ideological superstructure, would have remained quite vague had
the dialectic of capital not demonstrated, by its self-conclusiveness, that there
are such things as the *general norms of economic life*, conceptually separable
from the state and other superstructural institutions. The class relations of society could also be shown rigorously in economic terms only in the capitalist
context. Neither would the idea of the correspondence between productive
forces and production-relations have become unambiguous, unless economic
theory established the dependence of the value-relation on the existing state
of technology. By being thus grounded on the economic theory of capitalism,
historical materialism not only acquired a greater credibility as a hypothesis,

---

48   Engels 1969 [1878], pp. 177ff.

but it also became a dependable method of enquiry into the economic life of pre-capitalist societies, relative to and in the light of capitalism, just as 'the anatomy of man is the key to the anatomy of the ape'.

Indeed, it was in this sense that Engels referred to political economy in the wider sense, by which he meant a comparative examination of pre-capitalist modes of production, *while employing capitalism as the referent.* When he credited Marx with having laid down the general outline of such studies, he presumably thought of various passing remarks in *Capital* and the *Grundrisse.* Engels himself subsequently made an important contribution to the field with his 1884 work on *The Origin of the Family, Private Property and the State,* based on the work of L.H. Morgan. As is well known, both Marx and Engels increasingly devoted their attention to the account of pre-capitalist economic formations in their later years, although they left nothing as systematic as *Capital* in that field of study. Evidently, they took empirical works in history and anthropology very seriously. There was little trace of the 'market mentality' in their approach, nor were they in this connection dogmatic 'periodisers' of past history. Their study was in no essential way different from Polanyi's 'comparative economy', except that the more recent empirical works that Polanyi falls back on were not available to Marx and Engels.

What is common to the founders of Marxism and Polanyi is the recognition that every society stands on the economy, that is, the production of use-values or 'the provision for material want-satisfaction', and that there are only different ways in which the economy is socially 'instituted'. The purpose of 'political economy in the wider sense' is to extract from the wealth of empirical studies in history and anthropology certain types of the 'economy as instituted process', and to contrast their differences with the capitalist economy. Since pre-capitalist economies, not being wholly regulated by the market, do not possess their own internal logic, the said 'types' are only approximations, and valid only by reference to capitalism. Of course, this does not mean that pre-capitalist economies should be observed as undeveloped forms of capitalism. On the contrary, their differences from capitalism must be emphatically stated, and the reasons examined. At this point Polanyi's classification of the three integrative methods of economic life – *reciprocity, redistribution,* and *markets* – becomes meaningful, even if different types of economy cannot be mechanically characterised by different combinations of these methods.

As Polanyi emphasises, *reciprocity,* which so struck Thurnwald and Malinowski, is a particularly pervasive institution in primitive communities before the advent of the state, and *redistribution* more distinctively belongs to the sphere of the state. Historical materialism attaches great importance to the evolution of the ancient state, which Polanyi appears to take too lightly. There is, of course, no single way in which the state evolves from primitive or 'tribal (or clannish)' communities. It may be that tribal wars or the harshness of natural conditions of production introduce so-called Asiatic despotism. This form of the state, often merely a tribal federation, most liberally preserves the clannish constitution, and remains stationary as long as it successfully withstands external influences of trade and warfare. The formation of the Greco-Roman state, on the other hand, cannot be explained without consideration of the devastating effects of trade and the monetary economy on prior tribal societies. This form of the ancient state, because of pervasive commerce and external conflicts motivated by it, cannot remain stationary. Thus, even though the two forms of the ancient state – Asiatic and Greco-Roman – both stand on slavery, the economic significance of slave-labour differs widely in the two cases. The Germanic form of the state, in which cities are conspicuously absent, may not even undergo a recognisable stage of slavery before it develops medieval serfdom directly from out of tribal societies.

This does not mean that the 'stages theory' of communal labour, slavery, serfdom and wage-labour is either untenable or irrelevant, as Polanyi might have construed it. It only means that empirical history is not meant to be axiomatically periodised according to this scheme. The stages (in the sense of the 'periods' of historical materialism) rather mark the extent to which man, the active agent of labour, is separated from nature, the objective conditions of man's labour. This separation, according to Marx, is most completely effected in the relation of wage-labour and capital.[49] In primitive societies, men live and work in a communal organisation, like animals in a herd, that is, as part of nature. When a master-servant relation establishes itself, the servant (a slave or a serf) becomes the active agent of labour vis-a-vis nature, but also belongs to the objective conditions of labour, from the point of view of the master. Only free labour under capitalism completely releases man from nature. If this is so, Polanyi's objection to historical materialism – that it lopsidedly emphasises labour and ignores the function of land and other natural conditions of the economy – cannot be defended. The stages of development of productive forces that provide the focus for historical materialism refers rather to the general conditions of use-value production (material want-satisfaction), including geographical, climatic, and other natural factors, and implies the degree to which human beings are liberated from their objective environment.

From this point of view, there is clearly no conflict between historical materialism and Polanyi's approach to the comparative economy. Indeed, a synthesis of the two is bound to prove fruitful, for in order to study the economy

---

49   Marx 1973, *Grundrisse*, p. 489.

of a past society, one must first establish its 'distance' from capitalism, which constitutes the referent, thus situating that society within a proper historical perspective. The lack of this consideration on Polanyi's part makes his classificatory scheme quite empty. It is true, for example, that reciprocity is primarily the communal method of economic integration. But communities themselves evolve from kinship to clannish and tribal groups, to geographical communes and medieval villages, and then further on to modern co-operatives. A *reciprocal* relation is always present, but its economic content cannot remain the same. Similarly, the state always acts as the redistributor of wealth, but ancient, feudal, bourgeois and socialist states obviously carry out different redistributive functions. The same thing can be said of the function of markets in different historical epochs. It would be rash to generalise without considering the degree to which man sets himself apart from nature, that is to say, the degree to which the production of use-values becomes a more genuinely human activity. Indeed, the study of a pre-capitalist economic institution can be made much more profound and concrete if the specific combination of reciprocity, redistribution and trade is appraised in historical context, rather than reduced to the relative preponderance of such abstract factors as 'symmetry', 'centricity' and 'exchange'.

As already stated, economic theory is *invertible* if it recognises the real economic life common to all societies within the capitalist integument of the universal market. It is the invertibility of economic theory that establishes historical materialism as the method of 'comparative economy' or 'political economy in the wider sense'. Although economic theory is not directly applicable to non-capitalist societies, the economic life of such societies can be studied comparatively in the light of capitalism, *as soon as historical materialism is grounded on the economic theory of capitalism.* A comparative method, employing capitalism as the referent, is unavoidable since a non-capitalist economy has no inner logic of its own. The relation between 'political economy in the narrower sense' and 'that in the wider sense' can be illustrated by Chart 0.2. At the top level is the concrete empirical study of economic history, and at the bottom level is the dialectic as a purely logical system. In the middle level is to be found the study of different types of instituted economies, of which the corresponding history is the concrete-empirical dynamics. Only under capitalism do instituted economies mediate 'capital's logic' and 'history' as 'stages of capitalist development'. In other societies, the institutions must be inferred from history, and the role of economic theory is limited to merely ensuring that these institutions satisfy the *general norms of economic life.* Recall that an economic institution that fails to satisfy these norms is bound to collapse and to give way to another.

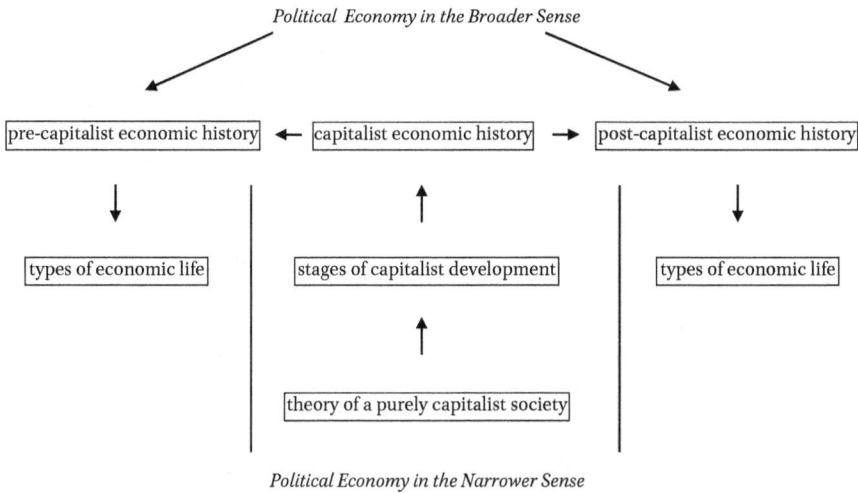

Political Economy in the Broader Sense

| pre-capitalist economic history | ← | capitalist economic history | → | post-capitalist economic history |

↓   ↑   ↓

| types of economic life | | stages of capitalist development | | types of economic life |

↑

| theory of a purely capitalist society |

Political Economy in the Narrower Sense

CHART 0.2

(c)   *From Capitalism to Socialism*[50]

(α) Now that the scope of political economy in its narrower and wider sense has been considered, it is necessary to discuss how, in that light, one may approach the economic problems of today, including the prospect of socialism (a new historical society to follow capitalism). The dialectic of capital is often criticised for its seemingly apolitical stance. Specifically, it is accused of ignoring class struggles and the question of the transition from capitalism to socialism. It is true that the purpose of the dialectic is to expose the inner logic of capitalism, and that such concrete problems as class struggles and socialism do not properly belong to that context. But that does not mean that the dialectic is irrelevant to them. For example, the fact that the logical exposition of capitalism deliberately holds the institution of the state implicit does not mean that the *theory of the bourgeois state* could or should be developed independently of the dialectic of capital. On the contrary, the dialectic specifies the level of abstraction (that of the stages-theory) at which such a problem can be correctly addressed. What characterises the approach of the dialectic

---

50   This section was written in the early years of the 1980s, and now, in retrospect, appears quite inadequate, especially from about the middle of (β) to the end. The author begs the readers interested in his more up-to-date view on the world economy in ex-capitalist transition to refer, for instance, to the article entitled 'Fiat money and how to combat debt deflation' in Yagi *et al.* 2013, pp. 208–25, or 'Towards a Critique of Bourgeois Economics', in Sekine 2013, pp. 238–75.

of capital is that it clearly distinguishes between what occurs logically to capitalism and what occurs to it for contingent and circumstantial reasons. The dialectic does not deny the importance of class struggles and socialism; it only claims that they are not exclusively logical problems, thus allowing them the maximum degree of freedom.

This proposition is frequently denounced as being counter-revolutionary by the adherents of the logical-historical method. But the refusal to accept their historical determinism is by itself neither revolutionary nor counter-revolutionary. The dialectic of capital merely proposes that it is both futile and foolhardy to discuss such questions as class struggle and socialism without a prior grasp of what capitalism is all about. Far too much has been said about these things by revolutionaries who appear to have no more than a popular and haphazard conception of capitalism. It is true that political economy shares much of its vocabulary with ordinary language, and this is often to its advantage. But an uncritical importation of day-to-day terms, with their inevitable ambiguity and imprecision, into political economy can also damage its scientific dependability. This danger is all too easily overlooked by those who ignore the dialectic of capital. Yet by circumventing it, nobody can hope to firmly grasp such a synthetic concept as capitalism.

To see this, let us first examine some popular conceptions of capitalism. According to dictionaries, 'capitalism' is supposed to mean the following. The Oxford dictionary says: 'The condition of possessing capital or using it for production; a system of society based on this; dominance of private capitalists'; Webster says: 'An economic system characterised by private or corporation ownership of capital goods, by investments that are determined by private decision rather than by state control, and by prices, production, and the distribution of goods that are determined mainly in a free market'; Funk and Wagnalls says: 'An economic system in which the means of production and distribution are, for the most part, privately owned and operated for private profit'; Random House says: 'An economic system in which investment in and ownership of the means of production, distribution, and exchange of wealth is made and maintained chiefly by private individuals or corporations, esp. as contrasted to cooperatively or state-owned means of wealth'; The American Heritage says: 'An economic system characterized by freedom of the market with increasing concentration of private and corporate ownership of production and distribution means, proportionate to increasing accumulation and reinvestment of profits; a political or social system regarded as being based on this'.

For the purposes of daily conversation and newspaper commentary, these conceptions of capitalism may be quite adequate. It is obvious, however, that they cannot pass for a scientific definition of capitalism in political economy.

What is immediately apparent from the above selections, however, is that the linguists could not have obtained material assistance from professional economists, for the latter, in most cases, have no more definite a conception of capitalism. Orthodox economists (particularly the neoclassical ones) simply refuse to define a 'socio-economic' concept such as capitalism, although they, nevertheless, do not hesitate to use the term to mean *the institution that realises the desirable 'supremacy of the market' and promotes the use of privately owned capital-goods*. Marxists, on the other hand, vacillate between two definitions of capitalism: one sees capitalism as *a system of universal commoditisation, in which even labour-power becomes a commodity;* the other sees capitalism as *a system in which the means of production are privately owned and are concentrated in the hands of a few*. These two definitions are often thought to be equivalent, although no convincing proof has ever been advanced to justify that presumption. The first definition is, of course, not incorrect, but its implication can be understood at quite different levels. That is to say, capitalism can be either firmly or haphazardly grasped by the same definition. The second definition is so broad that it may also apply to the slave society of ancient Greece or elsewhere, for if slaves could have exercised their right of private property robustly, they would not have been slaves.

The question arising at this point concerns how a concept as synthetic as capitalism can ever be comprehensively defined. Relatively simpler concepts – such as price, production, profits, and so on – may be defined and illustrated in the usual fashion, that is, as in law or mathematics, at appropriate levels of abstraction, but it is clearly impossible to sufficiently describe the whole of capitalism in a formal statement such as 'it is a social institution satisfying the following properties: A, B, C, and so forth'. If this were attempted, either the list of these properties would become endless, or each of the finite number of properties would have to be supplemented by a multitude of footnotes and cross-references between them. In other words, a definition calls for more definitions, until the subject to be defined evaporates in a process analogous to Hegel's 'spurious infinity'. Actually, this is precisely what a *synthetic concept* means, that is to say, a concept is synthetic if its formal descriptive definition degenerates into the bad infinity of Hegel. Clearly, capitalism is a synthetic concept in this sense. It is for this reason that many take refuge in vague "ideal types" of capitalism, rather than insisting upon *ineffective definitions*. But an ideal type of capitalism is bound to be subjective and one-sided, thus requiring a strong ideological determination to defend it, whenever it is confronted with another ideal type.

Does this mean that a concept as synthetic as capitalism can never be specified? Not so. For a synthetic concept to be objective, it must be a copy of the self-formation or self-synthesis of reality, and this is accomplished by the method of the dialectic. *Capitalism can be adequately defined only by the dialectic of capital, namely, as a self-contained logical system of the motion of capital itself.* Indeed, this is the method of Marx, who never proffered a Cartesian definition or a Weberian ideal type of capitalism, but only its definitional system as *a copy of capital as it synthesises itself.* In other words, Marx defined capitalism, if at all, as a *Begriff* (a linguistic grasp or rational comprehension) in the dialectical tradition of Hegel. Marx realised the vital point that only as a *Begriff* can a synthetic concept such as capitalism be defined objectively. The dialectic of capital merely refines what Marx has already done, by establishing a purely capitalist society as the concrete-synthetic definition of capitalism. If this is the case, it becomes perfectly clear that animated discussions on class struggles and socialism would be to no avail, unless they were firmly grounded on the dialectic of capital.

(β) Most Marxists appear to believe that the so-called free enterprise economy, which has evolved in the West after the Second World War, constitutes the most advanced stage of development of capitalism (often called 'state-monopoly capitalism'), and, consequently, that the present economic and political problems of the West can best be analysed in the light of the laws of capitalism. This also implies that the existing tension between the East and the West arises fundamentally from the confrontation of the two opposing regimes, the one socialist and the other capitalist. The same view seems to be shared, albeit with an opposing ideology, by anti-Marxists as well. Such an outlook, however, is at variance with the teachings of Uno and Polanyi, who have stated that *capitalism proper*, or the self-regulating market, ended its life with the First World War. According to Uno, the War of 1914 reflected the incapacity of finance-capital to settle the problems of its own making by commodity-economic means, and hence symbolised the end of the capitalist era in any meaningful sense. Indeed, the establishment of the Soviet state in Russia, in express opposition to capitalism, denied the latter once and for all any further claim to be a world-historic order. To Polanyi, the fall of the pure international gold-standard system marked the end of the same era, since it meant the abdication of commodity-money, one of the three 'fictitious' commodities essential to the integral functioning of the self-regulating market. Even the gold exchange standard, which briefly ruled in the late 1920s, intimated the arrival of a new monetary order: the managed currency system. On the heels of that system, moreover, followed the public control of effective demand, which was to undermine the other two fictitious commodities, labour and land, which were vital to the self-regulation of the market.

The classical doctrine regarded the class of landowners as unproductive, not only because they earned rental revenues (property income) through no effort of their own, but also because they consumed the whole of their income without adding to society's savings. The dialectic of capital accounts for this fact as stemming from the teleological coexistence of capital and landed property (Chapter 8), an essential condition of capitalism. If landed property collected more rent than it could consume through an aimless maximisation of rental revenues, society would save more than it could undertake to invest, making it possible for a Malthusian underconsumption to develop. Such a tendency, if not altogether absent, was quite limited during the liberal stage of capitalism, since the savings of the land-owning class generally financed social capital, to the securing of which the capitalist class made little contribution. During the stage of imperialism, the diffusion of joint-stock companies not only obscured the relation between capital and landed property, but also promoted the growth of intermediate classes, together with many rentiers. At the same time, investments in heavy fixed capital demanded not only the savings generated from within industry, but also massive long-term funds arising from elsewhere. The social mobilisation of such funds for industry was the task specifically entrusted to finance-capital, but the consequent growth of monopolies atrophied the home market and bred the chronic tendency of an excess of capital. This made foreign investments by finance-capital inevitable, which in turn led to the division of the world into colonies, and imperialist wars. The war of 1914, however, put an end to this mode of capital accumulation.

The policy of the state to boost the aggregate demand marks the demise of finance-capital. Indeed, if sufficient investment opportunities remained at home or abroad, finance-capital would have no difficulty in mobilising society's savings and converting them into profitable investments. Only when political considerations restrict naked imperialism does finance-capital (confined already to the atrophied home market) fail to maintain the savings-investment linkage at a full employment level. The creation of effective demand by the state for an adequate utilisation of society's resources, however, implies the *failure of capital as capital*. The monopoly firm, which once embodied finance-capital, now becomes an anemic 'satisficer', a curious hybrid of capital and landed property, parasitic on the economic activity of the state. This also means that the conversion of labour-power into a commodity loses its substance. The fact that this conversion is not accomplished by capital in its autonomous reproduction-process reveals itself in the low position of the aggregate demand curve for labour. This conjuncture, if left alone, would determine a market clearing wage-rate well below the value of labour-power, a condition which, under capitalism proper, would occur only cyclically in the trough of depression. Because of the absence of dynamism on the part of genuine private capital, capable of spontaneously pulling itself out of the depressionary economy, the state must artificially create effective demand so as to raise the position of the aggregate demand curve for labour, which in turn determines a market clearing wage-rate somewhat above the value of labour-power. The labour market is, thus, clearly not self-regulating, for even apart from collective bargaining, it determines a commodity-economically arbitrary price for labour-power.

Similar considerations apply to the pricing of land. At first sight, it might appear that land became more commodity-like after the liberal era because of the visible increase in real estate transactions in recent times, but a commodity-economically rational price of land must gravitate towards the capitalised value of rental revenues, in the light of the ruling rate of interest. Land prices today do not tend to settle to such a standard, because the fusion of capital and landed property makes the market regulation of rents impossible, and the 'managed currency system' consists of dictating any arbitrary rate of interest that circumstances warrant. Thus, the commoditisation of land also no longer retains its capitalist rationality. Indeed, in the absence of capital, the price of no commodity can be rationally explained. Universal commoditisation is, of course, an essential feature of capitalism, but this does not simply mean that use-values are extensively traded. Rather, it means that they tend to be traded for capitalistically rational prices, that is, prices that are consistent with the subsumption of the real economy by capital.

As Polanyi claims, the three fictitious commodities of money, labour, and land, are essential components of the self-regulating market. However, I have just shown that these are no longer commodities in any substantive (capitalist-rational) sense in the present-day 'free enterprise' system, even though they still retain the commodity-form superficially (formally, if not substantively). In this light, the dialectic of capital cannot recognise the present system as constituting a world-historic stage of capitalist development. Rather, it represents a phase of transition away from capitalism towards socialism. This means that the dynamics of this system cannot properly be studied as an episode of capitalist economic history, and that an application of the method of 'political economy in the wider sense' is required for its analysis. It also means that the present-day practice of class struggles can be neither dictated by nor accounted for strictly in terms of the laws of capitalism. It must instead be evaluated and developed in the light of the concrete working of the contemporary 'free enterprise' system. Although this is not an appropriate place for an in-depth examination of its basic features, the following brief remarks may nevertheless suffice.

If the effective demand policy of the state is not confined to mere pump-priming, which has, in any case, proven to be ineffective, but rather takes the form of regular government outlays of a magnitude approximating to 20 percent or more of GNP, a collusion of the bureaucracy and the large (oligopolistic) business enterprises becomes unavoidable, for, indeed, the purchase of goods and services from millions of scattered small firms is administratively cumbersome and inefficient. Government contracts tend to be awarded to large firms equipped with so-called 'technostructure', the development of which is in the interest of both the state and the firms. Indeed, as Galbraith has pointed out, the technostructure forms the core area in which the accumulation of wealth and the development of technology are concentrated in today's 'free enterprise' system. From this follows two significant trends. First, the market no longer functions as a rational allocator of resources, but turns into an expropiratory mechanism in favour of large firms at the expense of the small. Second, the development of mega-technology, namely, technology that is environmentally harmful and detracts from the enrichment of civilian economic life, tends to be encouraged. The reactionary character of the present system springs from these two related sources and has, indeed, become increasingly obvious through the 1960s and 1970s.

At first the postwar application of the aggregate demand policy by the state appeared to promise the realisation of an 'affluent society', free from the terror of periodic crises. Indeed, such a policy may have significantly raised the consumption level of the masses, but the vigorous pursuit of economic growth and the protracted Vietnam War during the 1960s profoundly distorted the structure of the American economy. Mega-technology, which devastates the living environment and squanders primary resources, was installed there as an arm of effective demand policy, while economically sounder and more traditional ways of life were, directly and indirectly, brought to ruin. The international competitiveness of the United States consequently deteriorated, until the suspension of the dollar's convertibility into gold became unavoidable. The weakening of the American economy, after the collapse of the IMF regime, was further aggravated by the international petroleum crisis in the early 1970s. Since that time the 'free enterprise' economy of the West has been unable to extricate itself from persistent and deepening *stagflation*, an ominous phenomenon, which implies a *divorce of money and credit from the real economy*.

Stagflation cannot be explained away as being merely due to technical errors in the application of macroeconomic policies. Nor can it be corrected by an appropriate mix of such policies. The demise of finance-capital has compelled the state to actively enforce effective demand policies. But the state cannot openly interfere with the supply side (in the literal sense) of the economy, so long as the principle of free enterprise continues to be upheld. Hence, in its lopsided economic planning, the state must depend on and promote the interest of the existing large oligopolistic firms. In other words, without arbitrarily reallocating resources to them, the state cannot fulfil its public responsibility of maintaining a high level of employment. At the same time, however, the productive capability and structure of society further depart from that which best serves the welfare of its population. If the state assists 'pyramid builders' by guaranteeing them high profits with tax money or printed money, a full employment may be achieved, but under such an artificially contrived full employment, the producers of other things that are more important to life find themselves deprived of resources and unable to run profitable businesses. Since the market is no longer 'self-regulating', it does not correct relative prices between 'pyramids' and other things. Instead, it accelerates inflation. If the state, therefore, restricts credit in order to control inflation, the pyramid builders cheerfully stop production, laying off their workers, for they can now earn usurious interest on their money, which they can no longer use for accumulation or real capital formation. (Recall that they are hybrids of capital and landed-property). Other producers, already weakened through years of neglect and exploitation, are powerless to reverse this trend. On the contrary, many go out of business, in view of the high cost of credit. Thus, money runs its course with little bite in the real economy.

(γ) Suprising as it may be to some, capitalism cannot be blamed for such an absurd situation. Indeed, stagflation could not occur if the market were truly self-regulating. Stagflation is undoubtedly an offspring of economic distortions created by the effective demand policy of the state, *the policy which arose only after the dissolution of finance-capital*, the last of the dominant forms of capital. Capitalism has many flaws, but not on account of its logic being self-contradictory, as is often erroneously believed. Capitalism can form a historical society because all its inner contradictions are logically (dialectically) synthesisable. The dialectic of capital, as opposed to conventional Marxism, proves that capitalism possesses a consistent system of logic, which enables it to satisfy the general norms of economic life common to all societies, and hence that it does not tend to permanently misallocate resources in the way the post-capitalist 'free enterprise' economy does. Contrary to the assertion of historical determinists, the operation of capitalism does not logically lead to its own self-destruction; rather, it ceases to exist *when external conditions on the use-value side become sufficiently unfavourable to the operation of its logic*, as they did after the War of 1914. The post-capitalist 'free enterprise' economy, in contrast, has no comparable logical integrity, and so its development can

produce an economically absurd result, that is, a situation that fails to satisfy the general norms of economic life. To ignore this important distinction
between capitalism proper and the post-capitalist 'free enterprise' economy,
by merely calling the latter 'state-monopoly capitalism', may satisfy the logical-
historical method, which argues that capitalism is now at last in its predictable
phase of logical disintegration. But such a view only serves to obscure a proper
image of socialism to come, and thus to misguide class struggles aimed at its
achievement.

Just as the 'free enterprise' system of the West cannot be regarded as capitalism, properly speaking, neither can the 'centrally planned command-economy'
of the East be regarded as socialism proper. Marxists generally take socialism
to be a transitional step towards communism. Although they refrain from
specifying the latter for fear of committing a utopian blunder, they nevertheless seem to vaguely conceptualise it as the ultimate dream of humanity, a land
of Cockaigne, where abundance prevails over scarcity. From this follows the
untenable idea that any mobilisation of resources, which is presumed to accelerate the advancement of productive powers, deserves to be named 'socialism'.
The speed with which the Soviet Union managed to build its industrial capability is, therefore, hailed as the finest example of socialist accomplishment.
However, socialism, properly speaking, must be an antithesis of capitalism and
cannot be meaningfully posited except as an inverse image of the dialectic of
capital. To simply conceive of socialism as an economic regime founded on
the public ownership of the means of production is just as unreasonable as to
define capitalism by the private ownership of the means of production. Socialists have always derived their inspiration from a critique of capitalism, and
this, of course, is as it should be. One must realise, however, that capitalism by
its very nature is an institution singularly open to criticisms. The fact that its
theoretical perfection can never be realised in history, or, as Polanyi would put
it, the fact that a completely self-regulating market is a liberal utopia, makes
criticisms of capitalism for its failures an easy matter. Such criticisms, however,
do not strike at the root of capitalism, nor do they clarify the essential properties of socialism as an alternative to it.

In order to arrive at the true sense of socialism, one must criticise capitalism
as a whole and at its best, rather than for its every contingent partial failings –
be it in terms of alienation, instability, inequity, misery or repression. The
dialectic of capital shows that capitalism, in its cyclical phase of 'average
activity', approximates an ideal state, a liberal utopia, in which the existing
resources tend to be optimally allocated for the production of all use-values.
These use-values are supposed to be produced with the most efficient
utilisation of available techniques, and in such quantities as exactly correspond

to the pattern of social demand, which, moreover, is freely and spontaneously formed without the intervention of extra-economic forces. The workers are paid adequate wages for the reproduction of their labour-power and enjoy a historically feasible standard of living in a state close to full employment. The majority of capitalists earn average profits in all industries. What is wrong with this near ideal situation, so appealing to the liberals, in which the partial failings of capitalism are minimised? Most Marxists would quickly point out that even in this case surplus value is appropriated, which is to say that a large number of workers, deprived of the means of production, are obliged to support the idle few belonging to the propertied class. If so, the simple way to placate their moral indignation would be to transfer the ownership of the means of production from the capitalist class to the state, so that part of surplus value which the capitalists used to consume privately would now be made available for public consumption. Indeed, it is on the basis of this understanding that the bureaucratic 'command economy' has been built.

I believe that this critique of the liberal utopia is fundamentally faulty, and the Marxist solution based on it quite inadequate. The true limitation of capitalism, even in its ideal state, lies in the fact that all use-values are produced as value, that is to say, they are produced with *indifferent labour*. Productive labour, an essential base of human activity, is under capitalism destined to be a necessary evil – unfulfilling drudgery and a source of disutility – which may be compensated by amenities to be enjoyed *later*. By making labour indifferent, capitalism logically prevents it from being 'life's prime want', as Marx described it. Even in a liberal utopia in which the standard of living may be considered 'affluent', this problem persists, for it is a systemic failure of capitalism as a human society, not a partial aberration resulting from contingent circumstances. From this follows the conclusion that socialism would be meaningless if it failed to promise a society so organised as to *overcome the disutility of labour*. Such a goal may not be immediately attainable, even with a widespread application of automation and robotics to industry. Yet the total lack of its consideration disqualifies the bureaucratic 'command economy' as genuine socialism. Indeed, such problems as material incentives for labour and the ideological education of the workers arise precisely because the command economy presupposes labour to be a form of punishment. On this basis, the central planning method of the East, which not only dictates the vector of social demand from above, but also directly interferes with the supply side of economic activity, tends to be even more repressive than the so-called 'free enterprise' system of the West. Indeed, in its most liberal form, the centrally planned economy, as conceived by economists today, is no better than a complete simulation of the market by the computer.

The above considerations suggest that conventional Marxism, with its facile logical-historical method, has thoroughly obfuscated the true problem of socialism versus capitalism. With the ambiguous notion of state-monopoly capitalism, it confuses that problem with the current East-West relation, and directs class struggles in the wrong direction, for class struggles aimed at the replacement of the contemporary 'free enterprise' system of the West with the centrally planned command-economy of the East will not accomplish a proper socialism at all. If a truly meaningful socialism is to be constructed, one must first grow out of conventional Marxism. In particular, one should resolutely break the spell of historical determinism, and examine the irrational and reactionary character of the existing regime without prejudice. The dialectic of capital is a basic conceptual framework that enables one to face this important task. Only through a rigorous study of the inner logic of capitalism, as presented by the dialectic of capital, can one see what the future course of human society might be like. At the end of this book, I intend to return to the problem of socialism again and outline its possibilities.

PART 1

The Doctrine of Circulation
(The Being of Capital)

∵

Introductory Remarks

In capitalist society, goods (or use-values) that are necessary and useful for its survival are in most cases *produced by capital as commodities*. It is true that there remain, in practice, a great many goods that are otherwise produced, but if they were to be allowed to divert one's attention, the basic character of capitalist society would not be made transparent. Hence, the dialectic of capital is obliged to envisage a *purely capitalist society*, in which *all* goods are produced by capital as commodities by means of commodities. It must, in other words, be understood that the economic life of capitalist society is entirely governed by the *form of the commodity*, or that capitalism is a global (or total) commodity-economy. The commodity is a *form* that goods or products assume when they are exchanged for one another. This form clearly does not issue from the process of production that constitutes the material foundation of economic life. Rather, the commodity-form originates in the exchange relation between one productive community and another. Yet capitalism consists in the fact that this *circulation-form* of the commodity, which originally arises outside the process of production, sinks deeply into it and radically reorganises it as the *production-process of capital*. Therefore, the dialectic of capital, which intends to logically comprehend the self-formation of capitalism (or Marx's so-called "the capitalist mode of production"), cannot begin with production in general. It must instead expose how the commodity-economy itself generates the instrument capable of subsuming the alien process of production. That instrument is the *form of capital*, which presupposes the form of money. The latter in turn arises from the form of the commodity.

It is true that the three basic circulation-forms of *the commodity*, *money*, and *capital*, existed long before the genesis of capitalism. But the scope of a pre-capitalist commodity-economy was always limited, as it was merely ancillary and subsidiary to the prevailing mode of production. Since, in pre-capitalist societies, economic life was largely not commodity-economic, these circulation-forms were themselves less than fully developed. It is quite otherwise in capitalist society, which organises its entire economic process according to the principles of the commodity-economy. Here, the full capabilities of the circulation-forms can be observed. For example, a product of capital is a genuine or intrinsic commodity, since it cannot be disposed of otherwise than as a commodity, whereas a good manufactured by a small producer is only accidentally a commodity, since it does not become a commodity through its own nature, but by mere chance or contingent circumstances. Only by studying the form of a *genuine commodity* can economic theory hope to clarify the logical necessity that the commodity contains *'moneyness'* as one of its essential properties. The fact that a commodity-economy as such, albeit not in a fully-fledged form, pre-existed capitalism merely confirms the present contention that a process of production need not be capitalistic in order to support a limited operation of the commodity-economy. Capitalism, however, is a peculiar economic system in which the process of production is operated by principles essentially alien to it. Thus, the doctrine of circulation studies the circulation-forms of the commodity, money and capital in a fully developed capitalist society, while deliberately holding its underlying process of production implicit, rather than focusing on commodities, money and capital as they existed historically in less developed forms in pre-capitalist societies.

Capitalistically produced commodities are materially heterogeneous as use-values, but socially homogeneous as value. It is this social homogeneity, as the expression of the value of a commodity, which reflects the self-relatedness of capitalist society in its most abstract (least specified) form. Value, which can never exist by itself but only correlatively with a specific use-value, is, however, only *immanent* in a commodity. Capitalist society would not be formed if the value aspect of a commodity were left where it first appears, and were not set free from the use-value that restricts its motion. In other words, the dialectic of capital cannot proceed without overcoming the so-called *contradiction between value and use-value*. This contradiction reflects the fact that the commodity-economic principles that bring capitalist society together are alien to the material aspect of its economic life, which is common to all societies. The contradiction, therefore, arises throughout the dialectic of capital, in one form or another, and must be overcome at every stage, until a purely capitalist society is logically synthesised as a self-explaining system. Indeed, the dialectic is completed only when the social uniformity of value finally prevails over the material incongruity of use-values, just as capitalist society establishes itself only when the commodity-economic mechanism irrevocably governs the material aspect of economic life. There are three distinct ways in which the contradiction between value and use-value arises and is resolved in the process of the formation of capitalist society. The dialectic of capital accordingly divides itself into the three doctrines of circulation, production, and distribution.

In the doctrine of circulation, the contradiction first arises in the simple fact that value must always coexist with a specific use-value in any commodity. In order to express its value, a commodity must suppress its own use-value. The commodity accomplishes this task by reflecting its value in the use-value of *another* commodity. Yet if this other commodity is chosen for its 'consumability' as a use-value by the owner of the original commodity, the latter's value expression still remains a private affair, which could hardly confirm the social worth of any commodity. Only when all commodities reflect their value in the use-value of a single commodity called money does the expression of value become the universal social act of *pricing*. The use-value of money, which consists of its immediate exchangeability for all other commodities, rather than of its direct consumability, becomes socially neutral, overcoming the constraints of private wants. Commodities other than money, therefore, adequately express their values in the special commodity called money, making the unrestricted exchange of all commodities among themselves possible. As money thus places all other commodities on a footing of equality, a commodity-owner transforms himself from a consumer into a merchant-trader, whose activity is perceptibly freed from the restrictions of use-values.

Money is the direct value-reflecting object, since the direct 'consumability' of its use-value is irrelevant. Hence, as the *means of purchase*, it can measure the value of all commodities. Yet the function of money as the *measure of value* occurs only as money intermediates commodity exchanges. As the *medium of exchange*, money is a mere instrument that facilitates the switching of one use-value for another, so the value that money explicitly represents need be present only formally. It is for this reason that token money can, to a large extent, replace full-bodied money as the medium of commodity circulation. Yet the integrity of the gold standard system, which automatically evolves from the commodity-economy, can be preserved if and only if money can freely move in and out of the sphere of commodity exchanges. This requires that part of society's stock of money must always be held in the form of *idle money* outside of the circulation-sphere. In this form, money functions as the *store of value*. Idle money that at first forms itself by dropping out of commodity exchanges, however, does not forever remain a passive residual of circulating money. Monetary funds are also positively accumulated with a view to future investment. Idle money in this form does not merely preserve value as the 'temporary abode of purchasing-power', but is already potentially *capital*. That is to say, it is ready to purchase a commodity, not for consumption, but for gainful resale.

Capital does not hold value immanently (as a commodity does), nor does it merely store a given value (as money does); instead, capital *augments* value within its motion, as it alternately assumes and discards the forms of money and the commodity. Three different types of capital are distinguished as merchant capital, money-lending capital and industrial capital, respectively. *Merchant capital* profits from buying a commodity at a cheap price and selling it at a more expensive price. But in this form the activity of capital is restricted to the sphere of circulation, where the merchant capitalist acts as a middleman between producers and consumers. Since the use-values that he trades are already produced and cannot be changed by him either quantitatively or qualitatively, his value augmentation is severely constrained by the availability and disposability of the use-values involved. *Money-lending capital,* which does not trade any use-values, and which, therefore, achieves a formal uniformity of value augmentation, is, however, an empty capitalist operation. It is a form of intercepting mercantile profit, on a contractual basis, from outside the sphere of circulation. The value augmentation of this parasitic form of capital cannot be self-dependent, nor is it necessarily congenial to the working of the commodity-economy. The only form of capital capable of overcoming the use-value restrictions is the one that can transform use-values within its own motion, which is to say, the form of *industrial capital.* Since industrial capital can choose any use-value that best serves it as the vehicle of value augmentation, it is as free from the specificity of use-values as any form of circulation can be.

The process of the dialectic that begins with the two elements of the commodity and ends with the notion of industrial capital is one that entails a search within the sphere of *simple circulation* for a more adequate and synthetic form capable of liberating value from the restrictions of specific use-values. Here, one form *passes over* to another in a step-by-step progression, until a more adequate and synthetic instrument of circulation cannot be found. The form of industrial capital cannot develop further within the sphere of circulation because its real activity involves the process of production. The *logic of transition* must, therefore, come to an end with the question: what real (as opposed to ideal or formal) condition must be fulfilled before industrial capital may commence its action? That condition must be found outside the sphere of circulation in the fact of the *conversion of labour-power into a commodity.* Labour-power is not a capitalistically producible commodity. It can become a commodity only under a historically particular social arrangement called 'capitalism'. The formation of the latter, through the process of primitive accumulation, cannot be logical. It can only be historical. It is with the *recollection* (internalisation) of this historical fact that the dialectic of capital closes its *doctrine of circulation* and opens its *doctrine of production.* When labour-power capable of producing any use-value is in fact available as a commodity, the form of industrial capital can subsume the whole of society's production-process.

The logic of simple circulation outlined above is identical in its structure to Hegel's *logic of being.* Hegel's Doctrine of Being examines the Absolute, not in His eternal essence, but in His transient immediacy. That is to say, the Absolute is here elaborated in terms of *how* He is rather than in terms of *what* He is. The Absolute first asserts His presence by pure being, which distinguishes itself from the sea of naught or nirvana. However, this *being,* too, insofar as it precedes all thought-determinations, is empty and 'being-less'. Thus, in Hegel's case, the dialectic consists of overcoming the emptiness (or nothingness) that originally overrules *being,* for if it failed to prevail over naught, being would perish and would not in the end reveal the fullness of the Absolute.[51] The process of the cognition of the Absolute is identical to the process of His self-revelation. Thus, in the Doctrine of Being, the increasing awareness of how and by what instrumentality the Absolute is present is traced step-by-step through the categories of *quality, quantity*, and *measure.* The dialectic that begins with pure being and ends with absolute indifference also forms the *logic of transition (or passing over) from one form to another,* and has an astonishingly close correspondence to the dialectic of the circulation-forms. The correspondence, however, will be of little interest to the reader who is not familiar with the logic of Hegel, although from the point of view of the method of the dialectic, it is of no negligible concern. In the following, I shall largely limit my comments on the correspondence to a few paragraphs at the close of the introductory remarks to each chapter. The reader weary of quasi-philosophical exegesis may skip these paragraphs in the first reading.

---

51 However, note what was said in the Introduction; see Section B, (c), (γ).

CHAPTER 1

The Form of the Commodity (*Quality*)

A fundamental feature of capitalist society is the transformation of social relations into relations between things. This tendency for the reification, or at least impersonalisation, of human relations follows from the fact that in capitalist society all goods tend to be produced as commodities. I say 'all goods', but not 'all goods and services', for services cannot be capitalistically produced as commodities, nor can they in fact be reified. It is necessary, therefore, to suppose that in a purely capitalist society, personal services are not directly rendered from one individual to another, but only via the consumption of traded commodities. For instance, it will have to be supposed that no barber exists in a purely capitalist society, but rather that various tools, instruments and cosmetic materials are produced as commodities, whose consumption (assumed costless) yields the haircutting service. Restrictive as it may appear, this simplification must be expressly adopted if the essential properties of capitalism are to be prominently exhibited, apart from irrelevant details. At least this much is implied by the celebrated passage with which Marx opens *Capital:*

> The wealth of those societies in which the capitalist mode of production prevails, presents itself as an immense accumulation of commodities, its unit being a single commodity. Our investigation must therefore begin with the analysis of a commodity.[52]

Commodities, in the dialectic of capital, are nothing but goods produced in capitalist society.

Commodities, however, existed long before the genesis of capitalism, and they can also exist, to a considerable extent, in socialist economies. In that light, therefore, an objection may be raised against the definition of commodities here as goods produced in capitalist society. It must be remembered, however, that in other societies the extent to which goods become commodities is always limited, since goods produced non-capitalistically are not *destined to* become commodities. The development of capitalism, on the other hand, tends to convert all products into commodities, so that a purely capitalist society cannot be envisioned without presupposing that all goods necessarily take the form of commodities. From the point of view of the dialectic of capital, commodities matter insofar as they contain the embryo of capitalism, and

---

52   Marx 1967, p. 35.

hence insofar as they provide the form in which fully developed capitalist society manifests itself externally. Commodities in other societies are meaningful to the dialectic of capital only to the extent that they share the same properties as capitalistically produced commodities. Indeed, viewed from the outside, capitalism presents itself immediately, that is, prior to any further specifications, as an immense collection of commodities. A commodity, therefore, is the simplest and the most abstract property of capitalism (or the capitalist mode of production).

It is, however, significant that the external form, or operating mode, of capitalism is already present, before the evolution in history of capitalist society. Indeed, capitalism never arises from the root of any production-process, but from the circulation-form of commodities, separable – conceptually as well as historically – from their productive source. Commodities as a circulation-form can, therefore, be investigated without explicit reference to the process of production from which they issue. That is why the dialectic of capital examines commodities, in the first instance, as a pure circulation-form. The word 'form', which frequently recurs in the dialectic of capital, means a 'contextual definition or specification'. For example, a good need not always be circulated before it is consumed, but if it is circulated, a good becomes or assumes the form of a commodity, and must as a consequence obey certain rules prescribed by the context of circulation. In other words, a commodity cannot always do what a mere good can do, such as be directly consumed by its owner. Thus, to say that the commodity is a circulation-form is to emphasise that it is not a mere good, but rather is a good insofar as it is an instrument of circulation.

Viewed as a pure circulation-form, a commodity has the two elements of value and use-value: *value* refers to its social quality, and *use-value* to its material or physical properties. A commodity distinguishes itself from a mere good in having value or a 'social dimension', in terms of which every item is qualitatively the same as any other. Thus, value cannot exist by itself. It can only exist correlatively with a use-value, in terms of which every commodity is qualitatively distinct from any other. Hence, in order to assert itself in an exchange, a commodity-value must 'negate' or suppress its correlative use-value, by expressing itself in the use-value of another commodity. By proposing an exchange, in other words, the owner of a commodity, as the seller, wants to part with its use-value in order to realise its value. Simultaneously, as the purchaser of another commodity, he is prepared to pay the value of that commodity in order to take possession of its use-value. The use-value of a commodity cannot become value to its owner, unless the value of another commodity becomes a use-value for him. If a direct exchange were to take place, the 'becoming' (realisation) of the value of one commodity, which would be concomitant with the surrender of its use-value, would be cancelled by the opposite relation: the 'becoming' (realisation) of the use-value of the other commodity, which would be concomitant with the vanishing of its value. In this way, the value of neither commodity could be held fast, its fleeting quality being destroyed as soon as it arises.

In order to fix value in a 'determinate form', therefore, the expression of value *must not be studied in an actual process of exchange*, but rather from the point of view of the seller, exclusive of the point of view of the purchaser. Indeed, when the seller of a commodity proposes an exchange, he places himself in a passive position, being unable to carry out the trade on his own initiative. The owner of the commodity-demanded, however, acquires an immediate purchasing-power of the commodity-offered, within the terms of the proposed exchange. When many exchange proposals are made by all commodity-owners, 'little monies' of this sort, each restricted by the terms of already proposed exchanges, multiply in the world of commodities. These 'monies' reflect the values of various commodities in a chaotic muddle. Such a muddle is inevitable so long as each commodity-owner expresses the value of his commodity in the use-values that he personally wants to consume. In a trading system, however, there are bound to be a few commodities called *general equivalents*, wanted by all commodity-owners, not because they are urgently needed for consumption, so much as their acquisition and use is associated with prestige and ostentation. Such commodities are natural candidates for money. Since all or many other commodities reflect their value in the use-value of general equivalents, the latter can always buy some quantity of many other commodities.

On the basis of their use-value, some general equivalents are superior to others, in acting as reflectors of values. Eventually, one unique general equivalent will supersede all others and monopolise the function of the reflector of values. The use-value of money does not lie in the sensuous quality of the commodity, thus excluded from the ranks of ordinary commodities as the general equivalent, but in the social quality of being the immediate purchasing-power of all other commodities. Hence, the expression of the value of an ordinary commodity in the use-value of money is set free from the desire of the commodity-owner for the consumption of other commodities. He can offer all of the supply of his commodity for whatever it is worth in terms of money. In the expression of the value of his commodity, in other words, the commodity-owner is no longer a mere consumer. He has grown into a merchant to whom the expression of value is the pricing of his commodity. Only at this point is the expression of commodity-values complete, the value of every commodity being uniformly reflected in the physical body of the monetary commodity. Value, as the homogeneous social quality of all commodities, is now fully established, not only as a negation of the specific use-value with which the value of a commodity must correlatively exist, but also of use-values in general as objects of consumption or use.

The Hegel Correspondence

The theory of the commodity just outlined will be studied in detail in the present chapter. Prior to that study, however, an amazingly close correspondence of this theory to Hegel's dialectic of quality (in the Doctrine of Being) must be emphasised. The celebrated triad of being, naught, and becoming, is here reproduced as the triad of value, use-value, and exchange-value. Value is the social being of a commodity, as use-value is its social non-being. The 'inseparability'[53] of these two mutually exclusive factors in a commodity sets it in motion, namely, as the exchange of one commodity for another. In the exchange, however, the arising of value from the use-value of one commodity is cancelled by the passage of the value of the other commodity into a use-value. 'Becoming contains being and nothing as two such unities, each of which is itself a unity of being and nothing; the one is being as immediate and as relation to nothing; and the other is nothing as immediate and as relation to being'.[54] Indeed, the exchange contains two commodities: one becomes value, even while the other ceases to be. 'Becoming, as this transition into the unity of being and nothing, a unity which is in the form of being [in which the value-side prevails] or which has the form of the one-sided immediate unity of these moments [as conceived by the seller of the commodity], is determinate being'.[55]

In Hegel's theory of determinate being, pure being is restated as quality, the negation of which is 'no longer an abstract nothing, but, as a determinate being and somewhat, is only a form of such being – it is as Otherness'.[56] Similarly, in the theory of value-form to be developed in this chapter, the social *quality* of the value of a commodity is not simply described as the opposite of its own use-value, but is of necessity expressed by its owner in terms of 'other use-values' of his choice. These use-values, selected because of his desire to consume them, serve as a form of the value of his commodity. The value-form of a commodity is, therefore, *limited* by the extent of its owner's desire for the consumption of other commodities. This limitation can only be overcome as the urgency of his desire for consumption is subdued, that is to say, as he reflects the value of his commodity in a use-value that he does not so urgently require.

---

53   Hegel 1969, p. 91.
54   Hegel 1969, p. 105.
55   Hegel 1969, p. 106. My interpretative remarks appear in square brackets.
56   Hegel 1975, p. 135.

If such a use-value is generally wanted by all commodity-owners, it is what Hegel calls *infinity*, because that use-value, being wanted by all commodity-owners, can automatically purchase some quantities of all commodities. Thus, the triad of 'quality, limit and infinity' has a close correspondence to the development of the value expression through 'the simple, the expanded and the general' form of value.

The ultimate of infinity, however, is the *true infinite* which can be restated as being-for-self. If the values of all commodities are expressed in the use-value of a single commodity, and of no other, that commodity is demanded no longer for its sensuous quality, but rather for its abstract social quality of having universal and unrestricted purchasing-power. That commodity is money or the value-reflector of all commodities, which, however, is no longer anything 'other' than value, for it is itself a mirror image or an alter ego of value. The physical attributes of money, in other words, reveal what value really is like. The three fundamental properties of value are: (1) it is qualitatively one and the same; (2) it can be split into parts and reside in the body of many different commodities; and (3) it brings together all commodities in a unified social interrelationship. Again, Hegel's dialectic of *being-for-self*, proceeding with the triad of 'one, many (repulsion) and attraction' appears to closely parallel the economic theory of the properties of value.

A   The Two Factors of a Commodity: Value and Use-value (The Pure Being of Value)

(a)   *The Value of a Commodity*

(α) A single commodity that constitutes 'a unit of the wealth of a capitalist society' is 'in the first place, an object outside us, a thing that by its properties satisfies human wants of some sort or another'.[57] This statement gives the impression that a commodity is first of all a use-value before it is a value. However, almost immediately afterwards, Marx also makes the following observation: 'The use-values of commodities furnish the material for a special study, that of the commercial knowledge of commodities. Use-values become a reality only by use or consumption: they also constitute the substance of all wealth, whatever may be the social form of that wealth'.[58] In other words, all wealth – capitalistic or otherwise – possesses a use-value, but the study

57   Marx 1967, *Capital,* Volume I, p. 35.
58   Marx 1967, *Capital,* Volume I, p. 36.

of use-values as such falls outside the scope of political economy. Here, the word 'use-value' refers to the physical properties of wealth, or, more specifically, of goods or products, which are in some sense useful to the consumer. All goods – whether commodities or not – possess a use-value, in this broad sense, almost by definition. Furthermore, it is true that goods are prior to commodities, because whatever is not a good cannot in any case be a commodity. However, goods do not automatically develop into commodities simply because they have use-values. Goods become commodities only under a definite social arrangement. That is to say, a commodity is a social and historic 'form' that goods may adopt when their owners are so related as to exchange them mutually.

It is for this reason that political economy must begin with the study of the commodity-form, rather than with a study of goods or wealth in general. The theory of political economy, or the dialectic of capital, aspiring to end with a total comprehension of capitalism in its abstract functioning, must begin with the simplest form, or contextual specification, that reflects the presence of capitalism as a historical society. That form is the commodity, which cannot exist independently of a social relation between a seller and a purchaser. Conversely, no social relation inheres in goods, which only imply consumers. Although a commodity is by itself a 'thing outside us', or a material object, the commodity-form has a social dimension that provides the dialectic of capital with its point of departure. It must be shown that the social and historic form of the commodity necessarily develops money, and that money automatically gives rise to the form of capital.

(β) Thus, a commodity contains the most abstract and, at this point, the least specified element of capitalism, in that it is value. The value of a commodity is not its physical property, but an expression of its social being. The fact that all commodities possess a value, and that as values they are of some homogeneous social quality, can scarcely be doubted; for otherwise it would be incomprehensible as to why they are all capable of being uniformly priced and made comparable *only quantitatively* with one another. If all commodities, however incongruous they may be with one another in their use-values, can nevertheless be made mutually comparable and measurable in some qualitatively homogeneous units, the reason must be sought in the social nature of the commodities, rather than in their physical or material properties. Therefore, value is, in the first instance, that which makes the reduction of all commodities to some socially homogeneous quality possible. For want of a better name, the value of a commodity may, at the present stage of abstraction, be described as the social worth or significance (or perhaps even the money-ness) of that commodity. By possessing value, a commodity represents a definite 'fraction' of the totality of all commodities existing in society.

Value, in this sense, is that which concerns the seller, not the purchaser, of the commodity. The seller is not its user or consumer, and so cannot take an interest in its use-value. Indeed, from the point of view of the seller, the commodity is a useless object, which can only be discarded if it fails to be purchased (exchanged for something else). The seller offers to trade his commodity, hoping that it is, in some way, socially significant or worthwhile, despite its being completely useless to himself. His sole concern is the extent to which his commodity is appreciated by others, that is, the extent to which it proves to be a value (a fraction of social worth). To consider a commodity from the point of view of its owner is mandatory for the dialectic of capital, because the owner is in fact the capitalist, as he appears at the present level of abstraction, simply as a seller of the commodity. Being an implicit capitalist, the seller has already specialised in owning a single kind of commodity, rather than a collection of different commodities. Of course, the seller cannot sell unless he finds a purchaser, but once a definite purchaser is found and the commodity is in the purchaser's hands, it immediately becomes a non-commodity, a mere good, or an object of use or consumption. A commodity always comes into the picture in the hands of a seller who has yet to find its purchaser. Hence, it makes sense to first examine a commodity from the point of view of its seller, that is, as a value.

Orthodox economics considers a commodity not from the viewpoint of the seller, but rather from the perspective of the purchaser who has already taken possession of it. In other words, the orthodox concern starts only from the point of view of the consumer. That is why a commodity is conceived as no more than a good, a use-value, or a source of individual satisfaction. The social and historic form of the commodity is, therefore, entirely overlooked. However, the consumer of a commodity cannot possibly develop into a capitalist, nor can the study of goods or the consumption plans of individual consumers reveal any significant aspect of capitalist society. To the dialectic of capital, therefore, subjective value theory and its modern extensions are altogether irrelevant.

(γ) The concept of value, at this stage, as some unspecified social substance (as a quality, which may be called social worth, social significance, or even moneyness), is admittedly abstract and difficult to grasp. Even Marx himself could not resist the temptation to identify that substance as abstract human labour at the very opening of *Capital*. But such a procedure contradicts the method of the dialectic, which requires that a self-synthesising totality should first be examined in its immediacy or external form, that is to say, by the categories of its 'being'. True to this method, Marx correctly began his dialectic of capital with the circulation-form of the commodity, not with production or labour. If one follows Marx in this respect, it is impossible to relate the concept of value, at this abstract stage of analysis, with such substantive economic activities as labour and production, which do not belong to the sphere of simple circulation. Moreover, to abruptly deduce from an exchange of two commodities – such as '1 quarter corn = x cwt. iron' – the claim that 'the common factor' in the two use-values is the same quantity of labour socially required for their production is clearly invalid, even in the absence of Böhm-Bawerk's well-known animadversion. All that the 'equation' says is that the two use-values have the same price. But what must be explained here is why all commodities have a (positive) price at all.

Orthodox economics purports to answer this question by claiming that 'all exchangeable goods' have 'the common property of being scarce in proportion to demand'.[59] Suppose then that there exist 100 million tons of coal in society. In what sense is this amount of coal 'scarce' relative to demand, other than that it is simply not freely available to all, and hence has a price? Unless the social demand for 100 million tons of coal implies 'a real economic quantity' independently of this price, the above claim amounts to the definitional tautology that they are scarce ≡ they have a positive price ≡ they are not free goods. It avails nothing to say that the demand is expressed by the quantity of other goods exchangeable for the 100 million tons of coal, because that merely says that the other goods also have the same price. The reason why they both have a (positive) price has still not been explained.

According to Walras, things are scarce if they are 'on the one hand, useful to us and, on the other hand, only available to us in limited quantity'.[60] If by 'useful to us' Walras means that scarce things give rise to social utility, and by 'available to us in limited quantity' he means that the marginal social utility of their existing quantity remains positive, his definition of scarcity[61] is free from the suspicion of *petitio principii,* for marginal social utility is independent of prices observable in the market. This is the reason why Wicksell defended Walras's rareté quite rightly against Cassel's 'refutation of the theory of value'.[62] However, orthodox economics has long since renounced its faith in 'social utility', the latter now being considered a 'metaphysical' concept unworthy of

---

59   Böhm-Bawerk 1975, p. 75.
60   Walras 1969, p. 65.
61   Walras 1969, p. 146.
62   Wicksell 1961, pp. 219ff.

positive science. When Robbins declares that scarcity involves the necessity to make a choice,[63] he takes the concept of prices much more broadly than market prices. But he certainly cannot say that society chooses a point on the transformation curve independently of market prices unless he, of all persons, resorts to the social utility function. By goods being scarce he, therefore, means that their marginal rate of transformation is a positive real number. Thus, if 'the economist is interested in the way different degrees of scarcity of different goods give rise to different ratios of valuation between them',[64] that economist is only interested in determining specific prices, which are already assumed to be positive in any case by the exclusion of all non-economic, that is, free or noxious goods.[65] Economic, that is to say, scarce goods have positive prices *by definition*. Thus, if 'the prices of different commodities and factors of production are expressions of relative scarcity or marginal valuations',[66] this can only mean that different commodities have particular positive prices, it being already presupposed that they must have some positive prices in any case. The nebulous notion of 'scarcity' gives the false impression that orthodox economics somehow explains why all commodities are positively priced, while in fact it does not.

By claiming that value is, in the first instance, social worth, or whatever makes the commodity socially significant, the dialectic of capital unambiguously explains that all commodities derive their positive price from their social dimension called 'value'. It is impossible to reduce the heterogeneous use-values of different commodities to a socially homogeneous quantity without rehabilitating the objectionable conception of social utility, which even orthodox economics has rejected as untenable. Value is a quality of the commodity quite independent of its use-value. A commodity derives this quality not from its material existence, but from its social being. It is the social dimension of a commodity that makes it a value, in terms of which it does not qualitatively differ from any other commodity. All commodities relate themselves with one another only quantitatively in prices, because they share the same property of being socially significant, not because they are, in some empty sense, scarce. The substantive content of the social significance, or what Marx calls the social substance, cannot, however, be revealed as yet. All that can be anticipated at this stage is that the unspecified social substance should be an objective quantity, instead of a merely imagined or metaphysical quantity such as social utility.

63   Robbins 1952, pp. 14ff.
64   Robbins 1952, p. 16.
65   Terms borrowed from Debreu 1959, p. 33.
66   Robbins 1952, p. 55.

(*b*)   The Use-value of a Commodity

(α) Although a commodity is a value from the point of view of its seller, it cannot have a value without being at the same time a use-value for the purchaser. Since a commodity presupposes its purchaser as well as its seller, it is at the same time a value and a use-value. The use-value property of a commodity reasserts the fact that a commodity is a material object 'outside us' and a 'thing', whereas a *service, which is rendered 'between us'*, and which is not a 'thing', cannot be a commodity. Only a material object, with a capacity to yield a useful service to us in its consumption-process, can assume the form of the commodity.

The social being of value and the non-social being of use-value are mutually exclusive. Indeed, they are sometimes said to 'contradict' each other. However, the contradiction between the two factors of a commodity is not such that their coexistence in a commodity is impossible. On the contrary, one cannot exist without the other. A commodity can be viewed as a value by its seller, just as it can be viewed as a use-value by its purchaser. If viewed as a value, a commodity differs from any other commodity only quantitatively, given that it is part of a homogeneous social mass of all commodities; if viewed as a use-value, each commodity is qualitatively distinct from every other commodity, given that it is a heterogeneous sample of the collection of all commodities. The two aspects of a commodity, although mutually exclusive, are also complementary because the value of a commodity cannot exist without its use-value; nor can the use-value of a commodity exist without its value.

(β) The use-value of a commodity is not simply the use-value of an object of consumption, but a use-value from the point of view of a potential purchaser of a commodity, while it is still in the possession of the seller. To reiterate, the use-value in question is not as yet in the hands of the purchaser, and is thus not yet ready to be consumed. In order to consume that use-value, the purchaser must first acquire the commodity which embodies it, by paying an appropriate price for it. But in so doing he also realises the value of the commodity to its seller. Neither the value nor the use-value of a commodity can be realised unless the commodity changes hands, that is, unless it is circulated. A commodity is a form that a good (product) assumes in the process of circulation. Once a commodity is circulated and falls into the hands of the purchaser, it at once becomes a non-commodity, which is ready to be consumed as a simple use-value. The use-value of a commodity (before its sale or purchase) is not of this kind, but a use-value, which must co-exist with value. It is a use-value, which can be realised only after the value of the commodity is also realised. The use-value, with which the dialectic of capital is concerned, is not a simple use-value, existing independently of value. Therefore, the use-value of a commodity is, so to speak, the negative correlative of its value.

(γ) Since the use-value of a commodity, as viewed by its purchaser, is not yet immediately consumable, he must first take possession of it from its seller in the process of circulation or exchange, in order to actually consume its use-value. The purchaser can take possession of someone else's commodity by paying its price, that is, by counter-offering his own commodity in an appropriate quantity. In other words, the purchaser of a commodity must also be the seller of another commodity. Thus, the circulation-process of a commodity is necessarily its exchange-process for another commodity. The purchaser and the seller are, thus, the two aspects or sides of the commodity-owner, just as value and use-value are the two factors of a commodity. As the seller, a commodity-owner is concerned with the value of his commodity; as the purchaser, he is interested in the use-value of a commodity, which he has not yet acquired.

If two commodities A and B are exchanged, the seller of A is simultaneously the purchaser of B, and the seller of B is at the same time the purchaser of A. This means that the realisation of the value of A requires the realisation of the use-value of B, and that the realisation of the value of B requires the realisation of the use-value of A. Here, the use-value of B, insofar as (and to the extent that) it expresses the value of A, is called the exchange-value of A, or the value in exchange of A; the use-value of A, insofar as (and to the extent that) it expresses the value of B, is said to be the exchange-value of B, or the value of B in exchange.

(c)   *Exchange-value or Value in Exchange*

(α) If a barter trade of A and B could be assumed, in which the quantity a of A is exchanged for the quantity b of B, then the exchange-value of A per unit would be the quantity b/a of B and the exchange-value of B per unit would be the quantity a/b of A. Value in exchange would, in that case, be reduced to a mere quantitative *exchange ratio* of one use-value to another. In fact, orthodox economics does make the 'heroic' assumption of universal barter, so as to reduce the exchange of commodities to the exchange of mere goods, and commodity values to mere ratios of use-values, comparable in terms of some arbitrary *numéraire*. This approach to commodity exchanges, however, is obviously faulty, because it cannot explain the use of money, without which commodity exchanges cannot occur on any significant scale. An economic theory which does not even show how the use of money necessarily evolves with the expansion of commodity exchanges is a far cry from any sensible analysis of the capitalist mode of production.

Although irregular barters that take place here and there, by chance, may be considered incipient forms of commodity exchange, the latter cannot develop at all without growing out of that form. Commodity exchanges of even a modest scope require that all commodities should be made exchangeable for all other commodities, and presuppose, for this reason, the *use of money,* which overcomes the stringent restrictions of barter (which is necessarily based on, and limited to, a double coincidence of wants). Money, in other words, makes the free and universal exchange of commodities possible. The concept of a general barter equilibrium is a mere figment of the imagination, which issues from a one-sided observation of commodity-exchanges *post festum.* When exchanges have already been concluded, the realisation of values is a *fait accompli* and can no longer be anyone's serious concern, given that there remain only simple use-values in some quantitative proportion ready to be consumed.

(β) The correct approach to the problem of exchange-value is not merely to calculate the ratio of use-values *already traded*, but to 'show that exchange-value is the only form in which the value of commodities can manifest itself or be expressed'.[67] The value of a commodity cannot reveal itself directly. It can reveal itself only in the form of value or value in exchange, that is to say, in a definite quantity of the use-value of another commodity. Even if the substance of value is later identified as labour, the actual quantity of labour spent for the production of a commodity is not always equal to its value. It is the quantity of labour that should have been spent for its production that constitutes the value-substance of the commodity. What quantity of labour should be spent for the production of a commodity depends on what quantity of labour should be spent for the production of all other commodities. At the present stage of abstraction, at which the substance of value cannot be specified, this proposition amounts to saying that the social significance of any one commodity cannot be evaluated independently of the social significance of all other commodities. This interdependence of all commodity-values, which springs from the unity of the trading society, makes the expression of value in the form of exchange-value both necessary and inevitable. Goods are not in themselves related; (capitalist) society operates in such a way that they *become interrelated*. It is this point that the so-called general equilibrium theory of the neoclassical school overlooks, despite its tedious protestation of the interdependence of all 'markets'. If that is the case, neoclassical economists should have questioned how a historical society could ever be formed based on such a crude hypothesis as universal (or generalised) barter.

---

67   Marx 1967, *Capital,* Volume I, p. 38.

(γ) Commodity exchanges in general do not permit any barter. Consider the exchange of **A** for **B** in quantities *a* and *b*, respectively. For this exchange to take place directly, that is, without the intervention of any other commodity, it is necessary that (1) the owner of **A** should be willing to part with the *a*-quantity of **A** in order to obtain the *b*-quantity of **B**, which he desires, and (2) the owner of **B** should be willing to part with the *b*-quantity of **B** in order to obtain the *a*-quantity of **A**, which he desires. Only by chance can these two conditions be simultaneously satisfied, that is to say, the fulfilment of these conditions does not follow from the nature of commodities, but is merely a matter of coincidence, or a 'double coincidence of wants', as it is often called.[68] The reality of commodity exchanges must be explained by the principle that issues from the nature of commodities themselves, namely, from the fact that every commodity has a value and a use-value.

In the rest of this chapter, it will be shown that the nature of commodities by itself generates money, and that the exchange of commodities is necessarily a monetary exchange of commodities. The exchange of **A** for **B** in quantities *a* and *b* is, thus, in fact, mediated by money. What appears to be the barter of **A** for **B** is no more than an *ex post* description of the fact that the owner of **A** sold the *a*-quantity of his commodity for, say, $5, and then purchased with that money the *b*-quantity of **B** in the open market. For this 'exchange' to take place, it is indeed necessary that there should be an owner of **B**, who sells the *b*-quantity of his commodity for $5. But it is not necessary that he should also be willing to buy the *a*-quantity of **A** for $5. Only when the exchange of commodities is released from the restrictions of barter, by the intervention of money, can the scope of a commodity-economy expand. Thus, in the following pages, it must be examined how money emerges from the social and historic form of the commodity. In the course of this examination, it will become clear that money is in fact nothing but the value or 'money-ness' of commodities released from the material contingencies of their correlative use-values.

B   **The Forms of Value or the Expressions of Value as Exchange-value (The Determinate Being of Value)**

(*a*)   *The Simple Form of Value*

(α) In capitalist society, all commodities express their value in a money price. Thus, Marx writes as follows:

---

68   Clower 1977, p. 207.

The busiest streets of London are crowded with shops whose showcases display all the riches of the world, Indian shawls, American revolvers, Chinese porcelain, Parisian corsets, furs from Russia and the spices from the tropics, but all these worldly things bear odious, white paper labels with Arabic numerals and their laconic symbols £.s.d. This is how commodities are presented in circulation.[69]

Indeed, even today all commodities in supermarkets, department stores or anywhere else are bound to have a price tag, asking to be purchased by someone with a definite amount of money. However, the money price is only a developed form of expression of the value of a commodity in the use-value of another commodity. If the purchasing-power of money becomes doubtful, for example, as in a state of hyperinflation, a more primitive expression of value – such as 'this bottle of wine is yours for three pounds of butter' – returns to the clearing-house of commodities.

The simplest and the most elementary expression of value takes that form, and may formally be stated by ordered pairs of two positive real numbers:

$$(a_b, b^a), \quad (b_c, c^b), \quad (c_d, d^c), \text{etc.,} \tag{I}$$

where (i_j, j^i) indicates a desired exchange proposition by the owner of commodity-I for commodity-J. For example, (a_b, b^a) will mean that the owner of commodity-A is willing to part with its a_b-quantity, if and only if the b^a-quantity of commodity-B is somehow made available to him. One may perhaps interpret such a statement as an announcement on the bulletin board of a clearing-house of commodities. Thus, if A is wine of some description, counted in numbers of bottles, and B is butter of a stated quality, measurable in pounds, then (wine, butter) = (1, 3) would announce the intention of the wine-owner who seeks to exchange a bottle of his wine for three pounds of butter. It is obvious that if the wine-owner does not want any butter (i.e., if $b^a = 0$), he will not take the trouble to make that announcement, since in that case he is prepared to offer no bottle of wine ($a_b = 0$) for butter. Formally, however, it makes no difference if he is obligated to exhibit a blank piece of paper on the bulletin board, which in that case would read $(a_b, b^a) = (0, 0)$. If such a practice is allowed, every commodity-owner must display at least one blank card for $(i_j, j^i) = (0, 0)$, because the owner of commodity-I clearly does not want to exchange any amount of it for the same commodity.

---

69   Marx 1970, *Contribution*, p. 87.

When the expression (a_b, b^a) has positive entries, commodity-**A** is said to be in the position of relative value-form, and commodity-**B** in the position of equivalent value-form. The value of **A** is projected onto the use-value of **B**, and is expressed by a definite quantity of **B**. The value of **A**, which cannot be seen in the physical body of **A** itself, and can in no way be expressed by its own use-value, now finds a determinate form of expression in a specified quantity of the use-value of **B**. The so-called 'contradiction' between the value and the use-value of **A** may be said to have externalised itself by means of **B**, now that the value of **A** can assume the form of b^a set against a_b.

In stating this relation, the owner of **A** desires a very specific quantity b^a of **B**, such as three pounds of butter, not two or four. Only against this pre-selected quantity of the use-value of **B** can he decide how much of his own commodity he will offer in exchange. Since the owner of **A** is interested in the use-value, not the value, of **B**, he must be quite specific about the quantity of **B** that he wants to acquire. On the other hand, since the owner of **A** is not interested in the use-value, but only in the value, of **A**, he cannot be as definite about the appropriate quantity of **A**. He only presumes that someone might accept his proposed trade. In other words, he cannot say 'Here is a bottle of wine. If you want it, bring three pounds of butter or more', because no-one may in fact respond to such a call. He must rather say 'I want three pounds of butter, for which I am willing to give away a bottle of wine, *perhaps more if necessary* (make an offer, try me), since I am not a drinker myself'. Clearly, in this expression, the wine-seller is not expressing the value of *one bottle of wine* in the use-value of butter, but the value, or the social worth, of wine as such, even though the butter-price of wine applies as yet only to one of the bottles that the wine-seller has to offer.

(β) The expression of value such as (a_b, b^a) does not imply an actual exchange of a_b of **A** for b^a of **B**. It is only a statement of the desired exchange proposition on the part of the owner of **A**, motivated by his need or want of b^a of **B**, and reflecting his subjective anticipation of the value, or social significance, of **A**. Although it is a search for an owner of **B**, who may be willing to accept the proposed trade, the presence of a **B**-owner does not follow from the expression (a_b, b^a). Even if there happens to be someone who wishes to dispose of **B**, he may either want no **A** at all, so that $(b_a, a^b) = (0, 0)$, or he may want, in his own expression (b_a, a^b) of the value of **B** in **A**, an a^b different from a_b for a b_a different from b^a. In fact, the owner of **A**, who proposes an exchange by the announcement (a_b, b^a), blindly faces an unknown market, and possesses no initiative in concluding the exchange. Having made the announcement, he must passively await telephone calls, or equivalent communications, from an owner of **B**, who alone has the power to actually carry out the trade, by accepting the proposal already made.

When all commodity-owners make an exchange proposition, all commodities assume the position of the relative value-form, in which their use-value does not matter to the owner. Their quantities are tentative and subject to revisions, depending on society's response to their exchange propositions. In this passivity, all commodities are values rather than use-values; they do not differ qualitatively but only quantitatively from one another, in the sense that one commodity may turn out to be socially more significant than another. Not so with the commodities standing in the position of equivalent value-form, for these commodities are already wanted as use-values. If someone offers a bottle of wine for three pounds of butter, whoever possesses three pounds of butter is free either to accept or to reject the offer. Three pounds of butter is already an immediate purchasing-power of a bottle of wine, by virtue of the fact that the owner of wine has proposed a trade in these terms. Thus, if the owner of **A** announces (a_b, b^a), the owner of **B** acquires the power to purchase a_b of **A** with b^a of **B**, at a moment's notice, whether he wants to exercise this power or not. In other words, the owner of **A**, who makes his exchange proposition known with (a_b, b^a), although himself incapable of actually consummating the proposed trade, converts b^a of **B** into a little 'money', so far as the purchase of the a_b-quantity of his **A** is concerned.

(γ) The simple expression of value, such as (a_b, b^a), must not be mistaken to represent a point on the so-called 'offer curve' of the owner of **A**. What orthodox economics calls the offer curve presupposes that both **A** and **B** are simple use-values (for the owner of **A**), and that both **A** and **B** are perfectly divisible for the purpose of his consumption. Even if the obviously questionable assumption of divisibility is abandoned, so that the curve reduces to a finite number of points, of which one is selected for some reason as the most relevant, that point has nothing to do with the present value expression (a_b, b^a), for the fundamental presupposition that **A** and **B** are both simple use-values, ready to be consumed, cannot be accepted by the dialectic of capital. The expression of value becomes necessary because **A** is not a use-value to its owner, and **B** is a use-value, which he does not possess. It is true that the simple expression of value contains an embryonic demand-and-supply relation, but the demand and supply are not those of a simple consumer. The owner of a commodity is not a simple consumer, but a merchant who eventually develops into a capitalist.

No doubt even a merchant engages in individual consumption, but his demand for commodities cannot be overwhelmingly determined by his personal consumption-plan. Thus, if the owner of **A** is said to demand **B** for consumption, the latter word must be understood to mean consumption in the broad sense of any use that can be made of **B**, including productive consumption and speculative holding, not in the narrow sense of direct consumption for individual enjoyment. From this point of view, it makes sense to say that the b^a-quantity of **B** that the owner of **A** pre-selects as requisite is a definite quantity. For example, the three pounds of butter that the wine merchant demands cannot as well be two pounds or four pounds, because two would be insufficient to, say, support his employees, and four would be wasteful in view of his general business plan. Indeed, when the merchant develops into a capitalist, it will be seen that he purchases productive elements in very definite quantities in such proportion as the given technique requires, and that his ability or desire to substitute one commodity for another is, in most cases, extremely limited. Moreover, so far as the substitution is concerned, there exists none between a commodity-**B** that the capitalist buys and the commodity-**A** that he sells, since the latter commodity is not even a use-value to him.

Thus, the demand-and-supply relation inherent in the simple value expression cannot be deduced from an offer curve (or a 'demand-and-supply curve', as Marshall called it) of orthodox economics. The demand and supply of a merchant-trader, or the owner of a commodity, cannot be as easily formalised as that of a consumer, as Friedman acutely remarks.[70] This, however, does not mean that the concepts of demand and supply are absent in the dialectic of capital. On the contrary, the governing principle of the activity of a merchant is to buy as cheaply as possible as a demander, and to sell as dearly as possible as a supplier. This principle is already implicit in the simple expression of value (a_b, b^a), in which the quantity b^a is definite and the quantity a_b is tentative. The owner of **A** is never certain that his exchange proposition will ever be accepted by an owner of **B**, but can make it more likely to be accepted by increasing the quantity a_b of **A**. At the same time, the owner of **A** is unwilling to part with a quantity of **A** any greater than is necessary to achieve his purpose, even though **A** is not a use-value to him. Here, he must follow the principle of raising the price if the commodity sells quickly, and reducing the price if it does not. This principle appears in the present context as the regulation of a_b given b^a, by the merchant-owner of **A**. Thus, the ratio of b^a to a_b is not a ratio of one use-value to another or an 'exchange ratio'; it is a ratio of a use-value to a non-use-value, that is, a tentatively 'proposed' terms of exchange.

---

70   Friedman 1962, pp. 14–15.

(*b*)   *The Expanded Form of Value*

(α) If the owner of commodity-A can express its value in the use-value of commodity-B, he should be able to do so with respect to any other commodity C, D, E, ... etc., in the use-value of which he takes an interest. Similarly, the owners of **B, C, D, E,** ... etc., must also be expected to reveal the value of their own commodity in terms of other commodities that they wish to obtain. Thus, the society-wide expression of commodity values takes an *expanded form of value*, which presents itself as in (II) below. Assuming that there are *n* commodities, the expanded form of value will be an *n* x *n* matrix of two-dimensional points(i_j, j^i), where i_j is the quantity of commodity-I, which its owner is willing to part with in order to acquire the j^i-quantity of commodity-J, owned by someone else. The diagonal entries of the matrix are bound to be a pair of two zeros; other entries are either a pair of zeros or of positive numbers.

$$
\begin{pmatrix}
(0,0) & (b_a, a^b) & (c_a, a^c) & \ldots & \ldots & \ldots & (n_a, a^n) \\
(a_b, b^a) & (0,0) & (c_b, b^c) & \ldots & \ldots & \ldots & (n_b, b^n) \\
(a_c, c^a) & (b_c, c^b) & (0,0) & \ldots & \ldots & \ldots & (n_c, c^n) \\
(a_d, d^a) & (b_d, d^b) & (c_d, d^c) & \ldots & \ldots & \ldots & (n_d, d^n) \\
\ldots & \ldots & \ldots & \ldots & \ldots & \ldots & \ldots \\
\ldots & \ldots & \ldots & \ldots & \ldots & \ldots & \ldots \\
(a_n, n^a) & (b_n, n^b) & (c_n, n^c) & \ldots & \ldots & \ldots & (0,0)
\end{pmatrix}
\tag{II}
$$

Let us take a particular column, say, the first, and examine it from the viewpoint of the owner of a commodity, which in this case is **A**. The owner of A need not be a single person. There may be several owners of A who may wish to acquire commodity-B in different quantities, by means of the different quantities of commodity-A, their subjective anticipation of the value of A in terms of B being different. For example, three owners of A may each propose an exchange of A for B by (1, 3), (1.2, 4), and (1.5, 6), respectively. In this case, 3.7 units of A are offered for 13 units of **B**, so that (a_b, b^a) should be equal to (3.7, 13), unless some or all of the owners of A revise their valuation, after seeing what others do. There is no question here as to which part of the joint trade proposition (3.7, 13) may in fact be successful, or as to how the result of actual exchanges will be shared among the owners of **A**. The point of the present discussion is to indicate how much social demand there is for **B** in terms of **A**; by means of the three trade propositions, 13 units of **B** have already become money, or immediate purchasing-power, with the proviso that the first three units of **B** can buy 1 unit of **A**, the second four units of **B** can buy 1.2 units of **A**, and the last six units of **B** can buy 1.5 units of **A**. How this restricted 'money' is in fact used by the owner of **B** is another question, which need not bother us now.

If there are only a very few owners of **A**, the variety of commodities, which could reflect the value of **A** as equivalents, would be limited because their desires or needs will not be extensive. However, when a large number of **A**-owners want to use **A** as the means of obtaining other commodities, a very large number of equivalent commodities, or value-reflectors, must arise. Thus, in each column of the matrix (11), the number of non-zero elements (in the matrix) should be expected to increase with the number of potential traders. Moreover, as potential traders increase, the variety of commodities offered for exchange also tends to increase, so that the number, *n*, of commodities existing today is not in any sense fixed forever. The expanded form of value contains the possibility of self-expansion, establishing and extending the social inter-connection of an increasing number of commodities.

(β) The expression of the value of a commodity, standing in the position of relative value-form, is now enriched and becomes more complex. For example, the value of wine is no longer merely expressed in the physical body of butter, but in that of many other equivalent commodities – such as tea, honey, linen, iron, and so on. The expression of the value of wine is thus released from the specific form of butter, which is only one of the modes of expression of the value of wine. If there are many ways of expressing one and the same thing, the latter's identity is more easily distinguished from its incidental forms of expression. (Indeed, since the falling of an apple is not the only way in which the force of gravitation manifests itself, it should be clear that gravitational force exists prior to the falling of an apple). However, if the value of a commodity is recognised as a quality that exists by itself, but is only observed in terms of the use-values of other commodities, it is clear that the value of the commodity possesses its own magnitude, which is not a consequence of particular exchanges. Only because wine has value of some magnitude can one bottle of it be offered for three pounds of butter, two bottles for ten ounces of honey, twelve bottles for twenty yards of linen, and so on, regardless of whether these proposed exchanges are in fact realisable. The value of wine thus pre-exists an exchange of it (or even its exchange proposal) for other commodities.

(γ) When all commodities express their value in the use-value of many other commodities, little 'monies' of all sorts proliferate in the commodity-exchange system, with each 'money' possessing the immediate power to purchase some other commodities under very complex qualitative and quantitative restrictions. Yet the restrictions imposed on these varied purchasing-powers are still too numerous and extensive to allow the exchange of all commodities for one another in any desired proportions. For example, one unit of commodity-B may be able to buy 2 units of commodity-A, and 2 units of commodity-B can buy 4 units of commodity-A, yet commodity-B may never be able to buy 3 units of commodity-A; or, if no owner of commodity-C expresses its value in terms of commodity-B, the latter cannot buy any amount of commodity-C. Even if, by miraculous chance, all proposed exchanges but two symmetric entries in (II) were capable of being realised, because of a suitable counter-proposition of trade, there would still remain two commodities un-exchanged after all other commodities are withdrawn for consumption. These commodities are not exchanged, even though society wants them, because their supply in each case does not agree with the demand, and hence their social worth or value cannot be realised. Since the value of a commodity presupposes the values of all other commodities, it means in this case that no commodity's value is yet correctly measured.

Thus, the present form of value expression is grossly deficient. It does not bring out the real value of any commodity, because it fails to permit the exchange of all commodities for other commodities. The world of commodities still lacks social unity, since there is no general way of expressing value, but only many arbitrary ways of doing so. In other words, the expression of value in this form is still a 'private business' of the many commodity-owners who hope to realise the social worth of their non-use-values, before society could properly accommodate their wishes by integrating the system of commodity-exchanges.

(c)   *The General Form of Value*

(α) However, the problem of the constantly expanding chaos of value expressions finds its own solution, in that any system of commodity exchanges is bound to generate a commodity, which is wanted by all the owners of other commodities. A commodity-world or commercial system, consisting of commodities A, B, C, ..., N, is said to be integrated if there exists among them a commodity-X, which stands in the position of the equivalent value-form in the value expression of all other commodities. Formally, this means that the matrix (II) contains a row such as:

$$[(a_x, x^a)\ (b_x, x^b)\ (c_x, x^c)\ \text{...}\ \text{...}\ \text{...}\ (n_x, x^n)] \tag{III}$$

No element of this – apart from (x_x, x^x) – is a pair of zeros. Such a commodity-X is called a general equivalent.

The existence of a commodity such as **X** must be logically demonstrated, rather than merely asserted with reference to empirical facts. The following procedure is, therefore, suggested. Take a row from (II) with the largest number of positive entries, and re-label commodities so that the $m \times m$ sub-matrix ($m < n$) at the upper-left corner contains the x-th row, which is all positive, apart from the diagonal entry. Then, we have the following:

$$[(a_x, x^a) \ (b_x, x^b) \ ... \ ... \ (x_x, x^x) \ ... \ (m_x, x^m)] \hspace{2cm} \text{(III-1)}$$
$$= [(+, +) \ (+, +) \ ... \ ... \ (0, 0) \ ... \ (+, +)].$$

Hence, commodities **A, B, ..., M**, under the new labelling, are already integrated by commodity-**X**, the latter being a general equivalent of the system [**A, B, ... M**]. This system excludes $n - m$ commodities, which for convenience have been labelled as **U, V, ..., W**. In that case, the owners of **U, V, ..., W** did not demand any quantity of **X** for their direct consumption originally. However, the fact that **X** can now purchase some quantities of **A, B, ..., M** at a moment's notice accords a new use-value to **X**, which the owners of **U, V, ..., W** did not realise earlier. Once this abstract-social use-value of **X** [see (β) below] is recognised, over and above its material use-value, it is inevitable that the owners of **U, V, ..., W** should also begin to contain in their value expression such terms as:

$$[(u_x, x^u) \ (v_x, x^v) \ ... \ ... \ (w_x, x^w)] \hspace{2cm} \text{(III-2)}$$

Consequently, it can be safely concluded that the matrix of the expanded value-form (II) always contains a row (III) in which entries are all positive, except for the diagonal entry.

On the other hand, a commodity-**X**, which integrates the system [**A, B, ..., N**] may not be unique to begin with. For example, both **X** and **Y** may be desired in exchange for other commodities. In that case, both are general equivalents, and as such they both become an immediate purchasing-power of all other commodities with different restrictions. It will be presently shown, however, that this non-uniqueness is the last hurdle to be overcome before an equivalent commodity becomes true money, or *the* general purchasing-power, with no restrictions. The solution to this problem, however, cannot be discussed under the present heading of the general form of value. Prior to that discussion, it will be necessary to examine the theoretical property of any general equivalent, which, by its own nature, tends to extricate itself from the various restrictions imposed on its purchasing-power.

(β) The general form of value (III) is characterised by the fact that all com-modities existing in the system, other than a general equivalent, X, project their value onto the use-value of X, which therefore becomes the common value-reflecting object of the system. Hence, in this form of value expression, all commodities are reduced to a homogeneous quality in the use-value of X, and become directly comparable with one another in quantitative terms. The social relation of all commodities as values is now concretely apparent, as the multifarious use-values of all other commodities are no longer relevant. The relative magnitude of values thus begins to be recognised more clearly.

If one commodity-X, which is universally wanted, emerges, the value ex-pression of other commodities tends to be released from the restrictions im-posed by the personal needs or wants of their owners. For example, if butter is a general equivalent, known to be desired by everyone, the owner of wine may not have to insist upon the exchange of a bottle of wine for 'three pounds' of butter, even though his personal requirement is restricted to only so many pounds. If, indeed, the counter-offer is five pounds of butter for two bottles of wine, why should he not accept that proposed trade and actually obtain five pounds of butter? For he may later be able to dispose of the two unneces-sary pounds of butter for some other commodities he desires. Since butter pos-sesses the immediate purchasing-power of all commodities, albeit with many restrictions yet to be overcome, the owner of wine may be able to buy with butter some use-values that he wants, even if the owners of these use-values do not want to buy any wine at all. If butter were not a general equivalent, the owner of wine would be unwise to obtain two extra pounds of butter unneces-sarily, the disposition of which would cause him significant troubles. However, the fact that butter is universally wanted makes the trading of two bottles of wine for five pounds of butter a possible advantage to the owner of wine.

If all commodity-owners realise that some use-values they cannot directly obtain in exchange for their own commodity may later be purchased with butter, and adopt the same strategy as the owner of wine, then the demand for butter will no longer be constrained by their strict personal wants or re-quirements. Not only will butter be demanded well beyond their immediate need, but they will also begin to cease expressing the value of their commod-ity directly in the use-value of the commodities that they eventually wish to consume. An increasing proportion of all commodities will begin to reflect their value exclusively in the use-value of butter, which has become a general equivalent. This means that X is no longer demanded for its own material use-value, but for its *social and abstract use-value,* in that all commodity-owners wish to have it, not for its direct use or consumption, but for its immediate purchasing-power of all other commodities. As much of X as can be obtained in exchange for each commodity will then be demanded by its owner.

(γ) Marx says that the 'general form of value results from the joint action of the whole world of commodities, and from that alone'.[71] Indeed, as commodity-owners demand **X**, not for its ordinary use-value, but for the abstract-social use-value of a general equivalent as well, they no longer demand it in specific quantities that have been pre-selected, according to their personal desire for consumption. The expression of values, consequently, will be formulated in a different manner. For example (a_x, x^a) will no longer mean 'Since the x^a-quantity of **X** is desired, this a_x-quantity of **A** is offered', but rather 'This a_x-quantity of **A** is offered for whatever it is worth in **X**'.

If the uniqueness of **X** could be taken for granted, the *general form of value* as currently interpreted would already be the *money form of value*, with **X** being the general equivalent. However, the uniqueness of **X** cannot be taken for granted at the present stage. If, therefore, another commodity **Y** is also a general equivalent, there must be another set of value expressions in **Y** in addition to (III), such as:

$$[(a_y, y^a) \quad (b_y, y^b) \quad \dots \quad \dots \quad (n_y, y^n)] \tag{III$'$}$$

Thus, the owners of **A**, **B**, ..., **N** express the value of their commodity partly by (III) and partly by (III$'$). The division of the total supply a of **A**, b of **B**, etc., into a_x and a_y, b_x and b_y, etc., will still be contingent and arbitrary, reflecting the individual judgment of the owners of **A**, **B**, ... , **N**. The only commodities, the whole supply of which will be found in the position of *relative value-form*, will be **X** and **Y**. But such value expressions as (x, y^x) by the owners of **X**, and (y, x^y) by the owners of **Y**, suggest that the exclusion of **X** and **Y**, as general equivalents, from the ranks of ordinary commodities is not yet complete. The first expression betrays that **X** is a commodity to be sold for **Y**, and the second that **Y** is a commodity that must be sold for **X**. In that case, neither **X** nor **Y** can be said to be *the* general equivalent, or true money, since true money must be such that its owners are exclusively the purchasers of other commodities, and no longer its sellers. As Tooke once stated, 'Money can always buy other commodities, whereas other commodities cannot always buy money'.[72]

By the same token, the exchange of all commodities for all commodities is impossible, so long as the value expressions of the form (x, y^x) and (y, x^y) coexist. Unless, by chance, these two expressions cancel each other out, so as to permit a direct exchange of **X** and **Y**, the owners of either commodity cannot directly purchase other commodities, **A**, **B**, and so on. Should one then exempt the owners of **X** and **Y** alone from expressing their value in a general

---

71 Marx 1967, *Capital,* Volume I, p. 66.
72 Quoted in Marx 1970, *Contribution,* p. 98n.

equivalent, and allow them to retain their previous value expressions in the expanded value-form (II)? In that case, however, the value expressions of the system as a whole would not be formally different from (II), except that (II') below contains more (0, 0) than the original (II). The form of value would not then have made decisive progress, the two 'monies' being still too restrictive to permit a system of universal commodity exchanges.

$$\begin{pmatrix} (0,0) & \dots & \dots & (x_a, a^x) & (y_a, a^y) & \dots & (n_a, a^n) \\ \dots & \dots & \dots & \dots & \dots & \dots & \dots \\ \dots & \dots & \dots & \dots & \dots & \dots & \dots \\ (a_x, x^a) & \dots & \dots & (0,0) & (y_x, x^y) & \dots & (n_x, x^n) \\ (a_y, y^a) & \dots & \dots & (x_y, x^y) & (0,0) & \dots & (n_y, y^n) \\ \dots & \dots & \dots & \dots & \dots & \dots & \dots \\ \dots & \dots & \dots & \dots & \dots & \dots & \dots \\ (a_n, n^a) & \dots & \dots & (x_n, n^x) & (y_n, n^y) & \dots & (0,0) \end{pmatrix} \quad (\mathrm{II}')$$

The present discussion, however, points to the solution of the problem thus posed. If an economically meaningful selection can be made between X and Y, or among any number of general equivalents, then the system of commodity exchanges will be completely freed from all restrictions. That selection must be made on the basis of whether X or Y is, *as a use-value*, more fit than the other to serve (or function) as the general equivalent of the system.

C   Money Prices or Values in the Form of Money (The Being-for-Self of Value)

(a)   *Money as the Value-reflector*

(α) The choice of a particular commodity as *the* general equivalent depends both on the physical property of the commodity, and on the nature of the world of commodities that it unifies. Thus, in primitive communities, such things as cattle, slaves, honey, oil, spits, shells, wampum and the like were often used as general equivalents, before various metals took their place. In most cases, the general equivalent is not a commodity, which has a use-value that is indispensable to the daily life of the community, or at any rate not a commodity that is to be immediately consumed. Often it is a foreign commodity or a commodity readily transferable to alien merchants. If the general equivalent arises from inside of the community, it is either a surplus commodity, which is habitually stored, or a material to be possessed for symbolic and ornamental purposes. An object of immediate consumption is least likely to become the general equivalent, because despite ubiquitous demand for it, the appreciation of its use-value tends to differ from one person to another, and at various times. A commodity that has a use-value that is remote from the urgency of day-to-day consumption is more likely to be chosen as the general reflector of values, since it is dispensable, that is, since its possession is more a matter of prestige and luxury than a matter of life and death.

The material property of primitive monies also depends on the lifestyle of the traders. Hunting tribes, sea-going fishermen, nomadic races, and so on, were obviously involved in the exchange of different types of commodities, from which different materials for money must have emerged. However, as trade developed, joining hitherto separate spheres of commodity exchanges, one general equivalent superseded another until metallic coins were eventually introduced to facilitate commercial activities, extending over a wide range of cultures and civilisations. The first known minting of metallic coins occurred both in China and in Asia Minor in the seventh-century B.C. So far as capitalism is concerned, money is, from the beginning, gold and silver. The pure theory of capitalism must, of course, presuppose gold money, which functions much as it did in 1860s England.

(β) Of all the precious metals gold is particularly well suited to serve as the universal reflector of values that are qualitatively homogeneous and differ only quantitatively. There are several reasons for this. Gold can be divided or fused in any desired amount without altering its quality; it has a high degree of social significance, even in its smallest portion, so that it is easy to carry and store; its material property may be preserved almost permanently, so that value can be retained in gold more adequately than in any other commodity. Furthermore, gold is not absolutely necessary for society's existence. This last property makes gold a dependable commodity in which to reflect values. Since its use-value is not indispensable to economic life, non-monetary gold is used mainly as material for luxury objects, which can readily be converted into money and *vice versa*. Such flexibility would be absent in the case of 'bricks' if they were to be used for both monetary and non-monetary purposes. Even if the demand for monetary bricks rises, building bricks are not automatically demanded less, so that a rise in their price must induce the production of more bricks at the expense of other commodities. If the production of other commodities cannot be swiftly curtailed, the brick price would have to rise sharply. Gold is protected from such instability because an increased demand for monetary gold is immediately met by the conversion of gold medals, candlesticks, watches, and such into money, before an expansion of gold production need be arranged.

Since gold is also a commodity, it has to have value and a (non-monetary) use-value. But the fact that its non-monetary use-value is relatively unimportant to economic life makes the value of gold relatively stable. The relative stability of value is an important qualification for the general equivalent.

Although gold is not originally money, money is almost naturally gold because its use-value best fits the requirements of the general equivalent. However, this theoretical explanation as to why gold, or in its absence, another rare metal, becomes money must not be confused with the historical fact that gold money actually emerged from the exchange of commodities. Money does not arise because it is convenient for the exchange of commodities, which in a limited scope can conceivably exist even without money. The exchange of all commodities for all commodities, the most universal and enduring exchange of commodities, must, however, presuppose the use of money from the beginning. For in any case some money must exist as the value-reflecting object of the commercial system. Of all the potential candidates for money, gold – on account of its specifically mercantile use-value properties – is theoretically best qualified to serve as money. If, indeed, gold became money with the development of commerce, the historical fact felicitously agrees with the theoretical expectation in this case. History, however, does not always realise what is a theoretical necessity, and so historical evidence must not be counted on to provide the ultimate verification of the theory.

(γ) The selection of gold as the general equivalent or money completes the value expression of all other commodities in the form of price. The values of all commodities can now be expressed exclusively in the use-value of gold, which is the single value-reflecting object or *the* general equivalent. When gold is confirmed in this position, all other commodities cease to act as an equivalent in the value expressions of their owners. By thus jointly abandoning value expressions in the use-value of any non-monetary commodity, the owners of other commodities definitively exclude gold as the general equivalent from the ranks of ordinary commodities. Gold, in consequence, can no longer stand in the position of the relative value-form, for, as Marx writes, 'if the linen, or any other commodity, serving as universal equivalent were to share in the relative form of value, it would have to serve as its own equivalent. We would then have 20 yards of linen = 20 yards of linen; this tautology expresses neither value, nor magnitude of value'.[73] Indeed, the value of gold cannot be expressed in the use-value of gold itself, nor is it necessary to express its value in the use-value of any other commodity. For gold is not a commodity to be sold, but a commodity that purchases all other commodities.

---

73   Marx 1967, *Capital,* Volume I, pp. 68–9.

The values of all commodities now become gold *in the minds of* their owners. At this point, commodity-values need no longer be differentiated qualitatively, as so much is residing in this or that commodity, for they are 'one' in
the Hegelian sense, in that they are all expressible by a definite quantity of
gold. This uniformity of value expression originates in the uniformity of values
themselves, which constitutes a homogeneous social quality, allowing difference only in magnitude. In this sense, the uniform expression of values in one
and the same quality of gold may be said to be the *being-for-self* of value, for the
question 'What kind of a thing (was für ein Ding) is value?' can be answered as
follows: 'It is gold-like in being perfectly homogeneous and divisible'. Although
values are thus qualitatively 'one', they are quantitatively 'many', namely, they
are expressible by many different prices. Hence, the dialectic of capital now
turns to *money prices* or the *money form of value*.

(b)   Money Prices or the Money Form of Value

(α) If **X** is gold or the general equivalent, the general form of value (III) is immediately converted into:

$$[(a, \overline{x}^a) \quad (b, \overline{x}^b) \quad ... \quad ... \quad (n, \overline{x}^n)] \tag{IV}$$

Here, a, b, ... , n are the total quantities supplied of commodities **A**, **B**, ... , **N**
in the system, and $\overline{x}^a$, $\overline{x}^b$, ... , $\overline{x}^n$ are the quantities of gold expected to be obtainable in exchange for them. This mode of expression of values is called the
money-form of value.

This form is not different from other value-forms, in that the value of every commodity is expressed in the use-value of another commodity. Since the
value of a commodity always coexists with its use-value, the latter must be
negated, or abstracted from, in order to observe the value independently of
its correlative use-value. However, the use-value of one commodity can only
be negated by the use-value of another commodity. Hence follows the need
for the expression of the value of one commodity in the use-value of *another*.
In the money-form of value, however, all values are expressed in gold, which
has a use-value that is abstract and as remote as possible from the urgency of
direct consumption. Gold, of course, is a use-value in (IV). Yet it is a use-value
that has been socially chosen as the most neutral and therefore the most appropriate material to reflect the values of all commodities. It is for this reason
that the quantities $\overline{x}^a$, $\overline{x}^b$, ... , $\overline{x}^n$, of **X** are not limited by the desire or want
of commodity-owners for the material use-value of **X**. Any socially realisable

quantity of gold is demanded in exchange for each commodity, rather than a definite quantity of gold pre-selected in view of its material usefulness to individuals. Consequently, if $(a, \bar{x}^a)$ means 'We want to sell 1,000 bottles of wine for 240 oz. of pure gold', it also means that 'The supply price of a bottle is 24/100 of an ounce of pure gold'. Since wine is not a use-value for its sellers, the marginal utility of wine, whether it falls or rises, is certainly irrelevant to them. Therefore, the money-form of value (IV) can be equivalently stated as:

$$[(1, p_a) \quad (1, p_b) \quad \cdots \quad \cdots \quad (1, p_n)] \tag{IV'}$$

Here, $p_i = \bar{x}^i / i$ ($i = a, b, \ldots, n$) are supply prices in terms of gold money. This mode of expressing the value of each commodity per unit by its money price may be called the *price-form of value.*

(β) When the form of value reaches the present stage of generality, the identity of the owners of X undergoes a very decisive alteration. The owners of money need no longer be the producers or the original owners of gold, hoping to realise its value by the sale of gold; all commodity-owners, who must have sold their commodities for gold in the past, are presently money-owners. Hence, the demand for other commodities by means of X can no longer be expressed by the xth column of (II) or (V), but by (VI). Whereas (V) is an expression of the value of X, which its original owners want to dispose of in return for other commodities that they personally desire to consume, (VI) is not even a form or expression of value by individual commodity-owners. In (VI), $\bar{x}^a, \bar{x}^b, \ldots, \bar{x}^n$ are society's demand for money by society's suppliers of A, B, ... , N. In other words, (VI) is society's *purchase-plan* and is no longer an expression of value by commodity-owners.

$$\begin{pmatrix} (x_a, a^x) \\ (x_b, b^x) \\ \cdots \\ \cdots \\ \cdots \\ (0, 0) \\ \cdots \\ \cdots \\ \cdots \\ (x_n, n^x) \end{pmatrix} \tag{v}$$

$$
\begin{pmatrix}
(\overline{x}_a, a) \\
(\overline{x}_b, b) \\
... \\
... \\
... \\
(0, 0) \\
... \\
... \\
... \\
(\overline{x}_n, n)
\end{pmatrix}
\tag{VI}
$$

Since (V) is still a value expression, it is expected that some entries other than $(x_x, x^x) = (0, 0)$ are a pair of zeros, but no entry of (VI) other than $(\overline{x}_x, x) = (0, 0)$ can possibly be a pair of zeros. For if society does not want to purchase any one of A, B, ... , N with money, there cannot be n commodities, which are assumed to exist in the system. Indeed, the existence of demand for all commodities must be taken for granted in the expression of values such as (IV) or (IV′). If it is not certain that some money-owners will purchase wine, why should wine be offered for a sum of money or with a money price in the market? In the absence of this certainty, the owners of wine would not express its value (which does not exist) in the use-value of gold. Thus, the mode of value expression (IV) or (IV′) presupposes that the owners of gold are now society at large, rather than a few individuals who may not want to buy some commodities with gold.

(γ) In the money-form (or price-form) of value, the expression of commodity-values is completed, that is to say, the expression of values is now translated into a matter of 'pricing commodities' in units of homogeneous gold, the use-value of which is its social function as money, rather than its material properties for direct use or consumption. When gold is used as the instrument of pricing, it is given special names such as pounds, dollars, euros, yens, etc., so as to socially assure the purity of gold to be used as money. The pricing, however, is the responsibility of the sellers, who want to realise the value of their commodities. If they overprice their commodities, they may fail to sell, and if they underprice them, they realise less value than they are capable of. Hence, they must constantly observe the reaction of the market, in the light of which they must revise their *supply prices*. By pricing commodities, however, the sellers only propose a trade without ever having the power to force

anyone to buy. Purchasers alone, as money-owners, have the initiative in concluding the proposed trade, for only money has direct purchasing-power over
all commodities.

When small 'monies' of restricted purchasing-power are eliminated, so as
to let a single commodity (gold) serve as universal money in the money-form
of value, society's purchase-plan (VI) has already formed itself. This purchase-
plan can also be expressed equivalently per unit of each commodity as:

$$[(p_a{}^*, 1) \quad (p_b{}^*, 1) \quad \cdots \quad \cdots \quad (p_n{}^*, 1)] \tag{VI$'$}$$

Here, $p^*_i = \bar{x}_i / i$ $(i = a, b, \ldots , n)$ are demand prices. Society's allocation of money to the purchase of all commodities, however determined, gives rise to these
demand prices. Commodity-sellers are not directly informed of the pleasure
of society, which they must probe by trial and error, but the formation of a
demand price in money for all commodities truly integrates a system of commodity exchanges, since the exchange of all commodities for all commodities
is now at last possible.

(c)   The Social Cohesion of all Values

(α) The value of a commodity originally implied that it was a non-use-value
to its owner, that is to say, a negation of its use-value. This negation, however,
is at first a private business; the owner of a commodity negates its use-value
by offering it in exchange for another use-value, which he wishes to consume,
rather than the use-value of his own commodity. This is a negation or dismissal
of one use-value, but not of another, so that the commodity is not yet free
from *all* use-values; it is dependent on the use-values that its owner wants to
consume. Hence, the expression of value is still constrained by the fact that
some commodities matter as use-values. This constraint is removed in the
money-form of value, in which commodities are no longer viewed as heterogeneous use-values that are of interest to individual commodity-owners, but
as qualitatively homogeneous units of gold, which possess the abstract-social
use-value of being the universal purchasing-power. The fact that commodities
are socially uniform as values, notwithstanding the heterogeneity of their use-
values, with which they have to coexist, is now concretely established not by
any arbitrary abstraction, but factually. All commodities are priced because
their values *become gold in the minds of their owners*.

However, if each commodity is priced, it at once becomes possible to aggregate all commodities offered for sale during any period of time and to talk
of the aggregate money value of all commodities, of which each commodity

is a fraction. The relation of the whole and its parts also becomes a reality when the system of commodity exchanges is truly integrated by money, which possesses immediate purchasing-power over all commodities. Hegel's idea of 'repulsion and attraction' at this stage of his dialectic might perhaps be interpreted to correspond to the perfect divisibility and additivity of value, as the social quality of commodities.

(β) What money prices express is not a relation between gold and other 'things'; it is a social relation of commodities among themselves as values. Money, which commodities themselves generate by excluding one of their own as the general equivalent, need not at this stage even physically exist (although it must exist in the minds of the commodity-owners) in establishing the social interconnection of all commodities. It is quite sufficient that commodities are merely priced in terms of gold money, since the actual purchase of commodities is not yet in question. The presence of money prices, for which commodities are offered in exchange, shows that their values cannot be adequately expressed by exchange ratios of one commodity for another, but only by the relation of universal exchangeability of all commodities among themselves. Money *in the minds of commodity-owners* establishes this relation.

Yet if commodities are thus interrelated by means of money, the relation of demand and supply, already implicit in the simplest form of value, is brought out more clearly. Ordinary commodities, which can no longer stand in the position of the equivalent value-form, but must always stand in the position of the relative value-form, are 'supplied' for money, and money, which never takes the position of the relative value-form, 'demands' commodities. That is why *money buys commodities and commodities do not buy money*, as was once pithily stated by Tooke. The potential sellers and the potential buyers of commodities come together to form a market, in which the sellers (or commodity-owners) represent the forces of supply, and the buyers (or money-owners) represent the forces of demand. The two forces of demand and supply are, thus, clearly separated with the evolution of money. The stage is now set for the actual exchanges of commodities. Commodities cannot be directly exchanged, or bartered, for other commodities. They can only be exchanged with the mediation of money. The generation of money from the value expression of commodities is, therefore, a prerequisite for a truly universal exchange of commodities.

(γ) The theory of commodities does not explicitly treat the actual process of exchange, but rather the forms of value expression by commodities (that is, by their owners or sellers). Although commodities are meant to be exchanged, they cannot be exchanged without the mediation of money. Commodities, as already stressed, cannot be directly bartered, even though goods may be. It is this fact that clearly distinguishes commodities from mere goods. Indeed, commodities do not presuppose definite consumers, whereas goods do; to 'barter commodities' is a contradictory expression because barter can take place only between two known consumers. A commodity-owner does not consume his own commodity and is unaware as to who its purchaser (consumer) will be. Since the purchase is potential rather than actual, commodities are required to express their values. Money, with which commodities must be purchased, is generated from the value expression of commodities, that is, from what commodities do because they are commodities. It is, indeed, common sense to think of money at the first mention of commodities, but it is more than common sense to theoretically identify money as an element lying hidden in the very concept of a commodity – an object possessed by an individual, willing to dispose of it socially.

Although a commodity is a non-use-value to its owner, it is too valuable to be simply discarded. A commodity is valuable because it has a social significance, which will be proved in exchange. Nevertheless, the value of a commodity must be asserted by its owner in anticipation of society's acknowledgement, whence follows the need for the expression of value. In expressing the value of a commodity, its owner in effect says: 'This commodity is useless to me, but must be useful to someone in society'. However, in order for the expression of value to perfect itself, the identity of this 'someone' must increasingly become abstract and impersonal. For if this 'someone' is a clearly identifiable person, with whom the commodity-owner can conclude a barter agreement, the two parties possess not commodities, but mere goods, which have no value to express. Thus, even in the simplest expression of value, the 'someone' must be impersonal enough to be described as 'whoever is willing to take my commodity for so much of such and such a use-value'. The 'someone' becomes less specific in the expanded form of value, in which he may be the possessor of any of the use-values that the commodity-owner may want for his consumption. In the general form of value, the 'someone' is even more general, being no longer strictly dependent on the commodity-owner's interest in this or that use-value. In the money-form of value, the 'someone' is completely general, because he is in no way restricted by the commodity-owner's desire for any material use-value.

The value of a commodity must be expressed in terms of the use-value of another commodity, it is true. However, the expression of value is imperfect to the extent that the commodity-owner views the use-value of the value-reflecting commodity as substantive and material. The imperfection of the expression of value, in other words, is proportional to the extent to which the commodity-owner is a consumer. The nature of the commodity demands, however, that its owner should not remain a consumer, but must grow into a genuine merchant. Only then will he become a full member of capitalist society. Thus, what the theory of the commodity accomplishes in the dialectic of capital is nothing other than to bring out the true nature of the commodity. A commodity is not a mere good, exchangeable for its use-value, but a social and historic form, by means of which a good is transformed into an instrument of trade. As an instrument of trade, the commodity matters as value, not as a use-value, even though it never ceases to be a use-value. By the same token, a commodity-owner becomes primarily a merchant, not a consumer, even though he cannot survive without consuming commodities. The so-called contradiction between the value and the use-value of a commodity lies in the fact that its social significance (or money-ness) is brought into the open only by subordinating its material properties, even though the latter can never be altogether expunged. Thus, even money, the value-reflecting object *par excellence,* is not free from the physical body of gold.

CHAPTER 2

The Form of Money (*Quantity*)

The study of the commodity-form in the previous chapter brought out what the commodity is by exposing what it (or its owner) does. A commodity, not being a mere good or product, cannot exist by itself in isolation from other commodities; it must express its value in the body of another commodity, so as to assert its belonging to the world of commodities and, thus, to establish its social identity therein. Unless the value-reflecting object becomes common to all commodities as money, however, the social relation of all commodities among themselves cannot be fully expressed. Only in the money-form of value, in which the value of every commodity becomes a definite quantity of gold (the material for money) in the mind of its owner, do all commodities enter the market as peers, such that any one of them can be exchanged for any other. The qualitative homogeneity of all commodities as values is, thus, established by the fact that they all possess a money price.

By simply expressing the value of his commodity in money, however, a commodity-seller acquires not a particle of gold. The amount of gold that the price of his commodity represents exists as yet only in the seller's imagination as a 'desideratum'. This imaginary gold must be converted into real gold for the value of a commodity to be realised (and *measured*), rather than merely expressed, and for that commodity to be actually traded rather than merely offered for sale. A commodity must be purchased with *physical gold,* payable to the seller, in order to be recognised as socially significant. Money, which as the general equivalent possesses the immediate purchasing-power of any commodity, now goes into action as the *means of purchase*. The definition of money as the means of purchase marks, however, only the point of departure for the dialectical exposition of the nature of money. The latter must be exposed again by the examination of what money (or its owner) does. Having no proper price of its own (other than unity by definition), money does not express its value, which is to say, money is never offered for sale. Money instead *purchases* commodities and, as the means of purchase, develops its three distinct functions.

The first function of money is to *measure the value* of a commodity. This function immediately follows from money's act of purchase. If, for example, a commodity is offered for sale for $5 a unit, only three units may be purchased at that price. The seller may therefore reduce the price to $3 and sell the rest of his current supply immediately. In the next round of trade, the seller offers the same commodity for $4.5, selling perhaps five units. But after reducing the price to \$3.5, he sells the remaining units of his supply easily. In the third round of trade, he offers the commodity for \$4 apiece and, with a reasonable delay, sells all units that he offers for sale. In view of this experience, he thus always offers his commodity for \$4 apiece and sells as many units as he can supply. In this case, it is obvious that \$4 apiece is the *normal price* of the commodity, that is, the price at which society wants to trade it normally. By actually purchasing a commodity, money forces its sellers to revise their money-form of value (or supply price), until they offer the commodity at a normal price. Money's function as the measure of value, therefore, consists in regulating the monetary expression of the value of every commodity that is actually traded (or its supply price). Thus, no commodity can be traded at an arbitrary price for long, but rather must settle at a *normal price*, which correctly reflects its social significance (or value).

How much money is needed to reveal the normal price of a particular commodity depends on many fortuitous circumstances and cannot be generally determined. However, apart from the gold producers who must presently be left out of consideration, all money-owners who purchase a commodity obtain money by selling their own commodity. Money to purchase a commodity in M – C′ is obtained by the sale of a commodity in C – M. The sequence of a sale and a purchase, C – M – C′, thus defines the function of money as *the medium of circulation*, that is, as the instrument of commodity exchanges. Since commodity-prices tend to their normal level, the quantity of money that society needs in order to carry out the requisite exchanges, in any period of time, can be determined as a *definite quantity*. It is not without cost to society to keep that much money in full-bodied gold in the sphere of circulation at all times, but the gold standard system permits only a limited substitution of *fiat* money for gold coins. The maintenance of the gold standard system requires the free entry and exit of money into and out of the circulation-sphere.

Money that stays outside the sphere of commodity circulation is generally called *idle money* or *funds*. The third function of money, then, is to store and preserve value in this form. Idle money first arises as a direct consequence of commodity exchanges, that is, from the separation of the sale, C – M, and the purchase, M – C′. Money earned but not spent immediately, for whatever reason, drops out of the circulation-sphere for a longer or shorter period of time. During that period, therefore, a trader in possession of idle money can extend a *credit* to another trader. The latter, who purchases a commodity, M – C′, before he has sold his own, C – M, however, contracts a debt, which must be settled within a specified period of time. Money, as the *means of payment*, or what comes to the same thing, a 'cash reserve' to back up the trader's credit money (his non-cash means of purchase), must be set aside, quite apart from the means of circulation required for the current exchange of commodities. No doubt, the terms of credit must be extended or shortened, depending on the availability of a cash reserve or money, as the means of payment. The quantity of idle money in this form influences the state of commodity exchanges, rather than the other way around. At this point, the production of new gold, so far neglected, can be viewed in a new light. Those who directly or indirectly obtain newly produced gold hold it for some time as accumulation-funds, for the purpose of expanding the scale of their trade. Idle money of this kind, charged with a *latent* energy for commodity-economic growth, is bound to be converted sooner or later into capital.

The Hegel Correspondence

The correspondence between the theory of money and Hegel's logic of 'quantity' is not as close as that between the theory of the commodity and the logic of 'quality'. Yet the exposition of the theory of money, which must follow its own inner necessity, nevertheless, appears to shed new light on the interpretation of the dialectic of quantity, although this has not been seriously studied hitherto. The reader may, in fact, realise that money offers a better illustration of 'quantity' than early nineteenth-century mathematics, to which Hegel made frequent and sometimes misleading reference. The triad of quantity, quantum, and the quantitative relation (ratio), in this chapter, appear to correspond to the three functions of money as: the measure of value, the circulating medium, and idle money (or funds).

In defining pure quantity, Hegel says: 'Quantity is pure being, where the mode or character is no longer taken as one with the being itself, but explicitly put as superseded or indifferent'.[74] This may be translated into the following: 'Money is value, which is no longer tied to a specific use-value; the use-value of money as the general equivalent has already been shown to be non-specific and neutral'. Money then becomes the *means of purchase*, with no qualitative limit. For the aggregate quantity of money as the means of purchase that measures the value of commodities cannot be determined. It is like space and time, both continuous and discrete. Money measures the value of a commodity by purchasing it *repetitively*. In revealing the normal price of a commodity, an unspecifiable quantity of money purchases it continuously – because no specific part of that totality of money does the work, and also discretely – because in each individual act of purchase, a particular fraction of that totality of money

---

74   Hegel 1975, p. 145.

must be used. The fact that in each individual purchase money, as the means of purchase, must have a discrete magnitude introduces 'the limitation of quantity'; yet a money owner obtains the necessary quantity of the means of purchase by selling his own commodity. He is not qualitatively restricted in his purchase, but he is quantitatively restricted, inasmuch as he has no more money than that which he has earned by his previous sale.

Money acting as the means of purchase, immediately after it has been earned by the sale of a commodity, is called the circulating medium, and corresponds to 'quantum which is quantity with a determinateness or limit'.[75] A quantum, or a limited quantity, has the property of a (real) number, the magnitude of which is described as both extensive and intensive. Although the interpretation of these two aspects of a magnitude is far from straightforward, the following reasoning may be suggested. As an extensive magnitude, the quantity of the circulating medium has its determination outside of itself, as a mere plurality of gold units. Here, a particular amount of gold serves as the medium of circulation; no more and no less. As an intensive magnitude, however, the quantity of the circulating medium has its limitation within itself as an embodiment of value. Whether gold contains more value or less determines the amount of gold necessary for the circulation of commodities. Despite this duplication, however, the aggregate quantity of the circulating medium cannot autonomously determine itself. It is always determined by the money value of the commodities being circulated, which is external to the circulating medium. From this follows the possibility of substituting monetary tokens for full-bodied gold money, which if unrestrained results in what Hegel calls 'quantitative spurious infinite', or the spiral of fiscal inflation. The true infinite of the circulating medium, however, lies in its ability to preserve value outside the sphere of commodity circulation.

Hegel's logic of the quantitative relation (or ratio) is even more difficult to interpret from the point of view of the theory of money. Yet the following interpretation may be suggested. Outside of the circulation-sphere, money is at rest or is idle. The theory of money requires that idle money should be increasingly specified in relation to active money (or the circulating medium), which mediates commodity exchanges. First, the magnitude of idle money, as mercantile wealth, that may exist in society is directly determined by the magnitude of the circulating medium as a residual. Secondly, the magnitude of idle money, as society's cash reserve or the means of payment, inversely determines the quantity of credit money that may be used to replace the medium of circulation. Thirdly, to the extent that the magnitude of idle money can be increased

---

75   Hegel 1969, p. 203.

by the production of new gold, idle money is pregnant with capital, which can raise commodity exchanges to their powers and enables the scope of commodity exchanges to grow. Thus, Hegel's 'direct relation', 'inverse relation', and 'the relation of powers', have some bearing on the dialectic of idle money or funds.

A   Money's Function as the Measure of Value (Money as Pure Quantity)

(a)   *Money as the Means of Purchase*

(α) All commodities present themselves in the market (or the sphere of circulation) with a price in gold due to the fact that the value of a commodity has already become 'gold in the mind of its owner'. The supply price of a commodity, however, is no more than a subjective expression of value by the owner of the commodity, who possesses no initiative in actualising the proposed trade. Hence, the supply price cannot be realised unless the commodity is purchased, that is, unless its demand price agrees with its supply price. The realisation of the supply price, whether it accurately reflects the value of the commodity or not, thus requires the conversion of *imaginary gold* in the mind of the seller into *physical gold* payable by the purchaser in exchange for the commodity. This conversion is accomplished by the act of purchase, which involves money as the means of purchase. It is in this capacity that the presence of physical gold, whether directly in the form of coins or indirectly in the form of a reserve (which backs up other monetary instruments), becomes for the first time a necessity.

(β) Nothing short of a commodity possessed of its own value can act as money, that is to say, as the means of purchase, for otherwise it would not have been demanded as an equivalent or a value-reflecting object. Nor would it ever have acquired the immediate purchasing-power of any commodity. A commodity-money must, of course, possess a use-value, the quantity of which is countable in some physical or natural units. Gold, for instance, is a metal, the quantity of which is usually reckoned in units of weight, after its purity is determined. If the weight-unit for ordinary gold and the weight-unit for monetary gold are different, the ratio is called a *mint-price*. For example, gold money of sterling purity is counted in pounds sterling, but gold of the same purity may also be counted in pounds troy, if it is not used as money. The mint-price, however, does not fix an invariable measure of value. For instance, suppose that linen were a monetary commodity and that the mint-price was defined as 'three ordinary yards of linen ≡ one monetary yard of linen'. This would in no sense fix the value of linen. On the contrary, it could change as freely as may be imagined. What would remain unchanged is the mint-price of 3 : 1, even if the linen value today were ten times more than yesterday's. The mint-price only stipulates a social agreement that all commodity prices shall be made comparable in monetary yards of linen, and that the latter shall bear a fixed ratio to ordinary yards of linen. That merely amounts to the adoption of the standard of price, but not to the fixation of the measure of value in Marx's well-chosen terminology.[76]

(γ) How, then, is it possible for a monetary commodity such as gold, the value of which is never fixed, to measure the value of other commodities? Clearly, the operation of measuring the value of a commodity cannot be understood in the same way as applying a ruler externally to a physical object so as to find its length. As the standard of length, the ruler must be made of such a material as would vary least in length under the effects of temperature, humidity, and other surrounding conditions. Yet the absolute invariability in the length of the ruler itself may be difficult to obtain. Even in that case, a close enough approximation to the length of a physical object can be determined.

Let us suppose, then, that both the length of the object to be measured and the ruler, which measures the length of the object, are variable in length. Then, after a number of experiments, the statistics of measurement can be recorded as being between, say, 3cm and 5cm. If the statistics do not converge to some average, such as 4.3cm, as the frequency of experiments increases, it can be concluded that the object has no definite length. If the statistics do converge to a definite average, such as 4.3cm, this number can be taken to be an adequate measure of the object's length. In other words, the length of the object can be determined, subject to the statistical 'law of large numbers'.

The validity of this measurement is dependent on the (assumed) invariance of the frequency distribution that the statistics of the measurement give rise to. It is precisely the absence of such invariance that characterises the measurement of commodity values. Suppose that two persons wish to sell similar apples, one offering 100 apples for 30¢ apiece, while the other offers 100 apples for 50¢ apiece. The statistical average is, of course, 40¢ apiece, but in fact the price of an apple may never tend to this level, since both parties can change their supply prices in the light of market conditions. Suppose that, in the first instance, ten apples are sold for 30¢ apiece, and five apples for 50¢ apiece. Then,

76   Marx 1967, *Capital,* Volume I, pp. 97–8.

in the light of that market response, the first seller may now revise his price to 38¢, and the second seller to 44¢. This time, let us suppose that eight apples are sold for 38¢ apiece, and seven apples for 42¢ apiece. Again, further revisions of the supply price will occur. If, in this fashion, the apple price eventually tends to center around 43¢ apiece, this tendency has not been generated by the law of large numbers, but by the *principle of demand and supply*. Here, the ruler (the demand) wants to measure (accept) shorter (cheaper) samples of the object (or the commodity) more willingly, and the object (or the commodity) wants to provide (supply) as many longer (dearer) samples as possible. The measurement of the value of a commodity implies the effort, on the part of its sellers, to make it as dear as possible, and the counter-effort, on the part of its purchasers, to make it as cheap as possible. It is as if the object (the commodity) were animated by supranatural powers!

(b)   The Formation of Normal Prices

(α) The principle of demand and supply does not, however, reveal the value of any commodity in a once-for-all isolated trade. If, for example, a small painting by Picasso is sold by auction for half a million dollars, this price does not reflect the value of that unique sample of Picasso's paintings. Its value is economically nil because the painting cannot be capitalistically reproduced. It is only a 'good', which accidentally took the form of a commodity on this occasion. An auction may be a convenient method for the seller, but it does not necessarily follow from the economic nature of the painting. The seller may perhaps achieve a better deal by visiting a few rich collectors to negotiate the price. In that case, the price will be agreed upon between the two persons known to each other, as in barter. However, the negotiation of the price does not, in general, apply to a capitalistically produced commodity, which is the matter in question here.

A capitalistically produced commodity is reproducible, and hence can, in principle, be supplied in any quantity (that is, in any number of interchangeable samples). It is widely and frequently traded in an impersonal (or reified) market, in which a large number of unidentified sellers face a large number of unidentified buyers. Since they cannot come into direct contact with one another and agree upon the price by way of negotiation, they can only respond to the market price already made observable by the previous trade. If the market price is too high, the purchasers take a small quantity, forcing the sellers to reduce the price. If the price is too low, the purchasers begin to queue up outside the store, enabling the sellers to raise the price. The sellers, therefore, constantly revise their supply price, as they 'grope' for the right price, in which the pleasure of the market is correctly reflected. The social dimension of a commodity asserts itself only in frequent repetitions of such an impersonal trade.

(β) From the point of view of the seller, the intensity of the demand for his commodity is perceived by the rapidity with which it is sold. A merchant seller of a commodity cannot wait indefinitely, because time can spoil its use-value or otherwise cause him expenses. Nor can he expect to sell immediately after he obtains the commodity, for the selling of a commodity is a time-consuming business. Each seller, therefore, allows for a given length of time, T^0, to be the normal period within which he should dispose of his commodity. Yet the actual length of the selling time is dependent on the price of his commodity, $T(p)$. If the price, p, is set too high, the market responds slowly, so that $T(p) > T^0$. If the price is set too low, the reverse is the case, so that $T(p) < T^0$. It is reasonable to suppose that the real-valued function $T(p)$, defined on real $p > 0$, is continuous with a continuous derivative, $T'(p) > 0$. It is also reasonable to suppose that the seller reduces the price if the commodity is slow to sell, and raises the price if it sells promptly. Thus, the revision of the price by the commodity seller can be formally expressed by the relation $dp/dt = R(p) = f[T^0 - T(p)]$, with a continuous positive transformation f, indicating the speed of the adjustment. Since $R(p)$ is continuous, and for some p it is positive and for some other p negative, there is a p^* such that $R(p^*) = 0$. Moreover, this p^* is locally stable since $R'(p) < 0$. (See Figure 2.1).

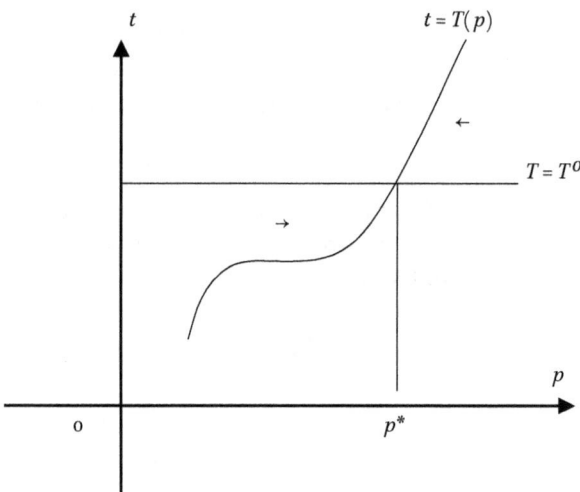

FIGURE 2.1

It may be thought that the allowance for the reasonable length, T^0, of the selling time differs from one seller to another, even when the same commodity is involved. Of course, some dispersion of T^0 around a mean may not be avoided, so that, if the sellers operate in the market, in which the same $T(p)$ prevails, those with a relatively greater T^0 tend to sell at a p^* greater than those with a relatively lower T^0. The difference, however, cannot be too great because those with the lowest T^0 will be the first ones to sell and those with the highest T^0 the last. Experience teaches merchants the wisdom of quick sales at small profits. They declare themselves 'not to be knowingly undersold', and vie with each other in reducing T^0 and p^*. Thus, even though a small dispersion may remain around an average, reflecting the competence or incompetence of individual sellers, T^0 tends to settle to a socially given length, and hence p^* as well to a definite level. This price, p^*, may be called the *normal price* of the commodity.

By establishing the normal price, money, as the means of purchase, is said to measure the value of the commodity. A normal price must, however, be distinguished from an equilibrium price, and the measurement of value from the determination of value. An equilibrium price of the commodity in the capitalist market cannot be specified until the underlying condition of its demand and supply is made more explicit. For example, the price of 43¢ for a capitalistically produced apple may be said to be an equilibrium price of the apple only when it is known how many apples are wanted in society, under what technical conditions these apples are produced with socially necessary labour, and what level of the general rate of profit then prevails in the market. These details are deliberately left implicit in the doctrine of *simple* circulation, which deals only with the commodity-economic *modus operandi* of capitalist society, when the latter is yet to be grounded on real economic life. A normal price, in other words, is a more abstract (that is, less specified and emptier) concept than an equilibrium price. Thus, if the normal price of apples is said to be 43¢ per piece, at a given time and place, no substantive explanation for it is yet given apart from the purely formal market-behaviour of the participating traders.

For the same reason, the normal price *measures* the value of a commodity, but does not *determine* it. In order to determine the magnitude of the substance of value ('socially necessary labour', as it will later turn out to be), one must know the substantive manner in which the socially necessary quantity of the commodity is produced. The normal price of 43¢ an apple does not tell us how much socially necessary labour must have been spent to produce the apple. It only shows that the apple possesses a social worth, which expresses itself in the price of 43¢. Even in this case, however, it must be stressed that value cannot be measured without a normal price. That is to say, the formation of a normal price implies, and is implied by, a definite magnitude (to be specified later) of value, so that the normal price, p^*, must be known first, before discovering the corresponding value of the commodity in question. Hence, a commodity, which cannot be repeatedly traded and cannot form a normal price, does not possess a value. Such a 'commodity' is not a *genuine* commodity; rather, it is only an *accidental* commodity.

(γ) Money cannot measure the value (or social significance) of a commodity with a single (once-and-for-all) act of purchase. Many units of the same commodity must be purchased *a great number of times* for its normal price to be established. It is quite impossible, however, to say what quantity of money as the means of purchase is required in measuring the value of a commodity. Money that measures the value of a commodity is, therefore, an *indefinite or pure quantity*, as Hegel puts it. This quantity of money in its indefinite totality is said to be 'continuous', in the sense that it is self-same and undifferentiating. 'Continuity is simple, self-same self-relation, which is not interrupted by any limit or exclusion'.[77] Yet in measuring the value of a commodity, money must be used in *many repeated acts of purchase,* and in each individual act of purchase, a fraction of the entire means of purchase is involved. The means of purchase, as it consists of such individual fractions, may be said to be a 'discrete' quantity, again according to Hegel's usage. A quantity, which is both continuous and discrete (that is, both infinitesimally and discretely divisible) is simply a 'magnitude', although how large or small it is cannot as yet be specified. The quantity of money that establishes the normal price of a commodity is an unspecifiable magnitude, consisting of the self-same units of gold, some of which must be used together in each individual act of purchase.

(c)   The Source of the Means of Purchase

(α) If the normal prices of all commodities, $p^* = (p_1^*, p_2^*, \ldots, p_n^*)$, are established in a given market, the aggregate money value, p^*x, of all the commodities that are traded during a specified period of time, $x = (x_1, x_2, \ldots, x_n)$, can be known. This aggregate is the monetary expression of the total value of the traded commodities. For example, if 1,000 apples and 500 pears are traded at the normal prices of 43¢ and 50¢ each, respectively, then the aggregate money value is $680. It is not known how much money has to be spent before the normal prices will be established, but once they have been established, no more means of purchase than $680 will be needed to realise the value of all these

---

77   Hegel 1969, p. 185.

commodities. In fact, considerably less than this sum of money will be needed for the purpose, since each dollar can be used several times during a given market period. Thus, as prices converge to the normal, and as the values of the commodities are being measured, the quantity of the means of purchase required, in a given market period, acquires an upper limit.

(β) When normal prices are established, the quantity, M, of money that society needs to purchase all commodities in a given market does not exceed the aggregate money value, p^*x, of these commodities, but it is not as yet possible to know the difference of M from p^*x. In the meantime, every individual purchaser must own a definite quantity of money, in order to be able to buy the desired commodities in specific amounts. For instance, if he wants to buy ten apples for 43¢ apiece, and five pears for 50¢ apiece, the purchaser must have $6.80 ready to effect the purchase. Every individual act of purchase, in other words, must presuppose an appropriate quantity of money in the possession of the individual purchaser of commodities. The question, therefore, immediately follows as to how and where he has obtained the necessary means of purchase.

Gold too is a capitalistically produced commodity. It is true that the producers of gold can immediately purchase other commodities without having sold any commodity for gold, but this is a very special case (the discussion of which can be postponed until later in the chapter). In that case, every money-owner, who alone can freely purchase commodities, must have obtained gold as the means of purchase by selling his own commodity. A money-owner, in other words, is (or has been) a commodity-seller, who converts the proceeds of his sales into means of purchase. Thus, in the market or the circulation-sphere of commodities, there is no pure consumer who acquires the means of purchase for some unknown reason. Both the sellers and the purchasers are merchant traders. The forces of demand and supply in the market, therefore, do not represent consumers on one side, and producers on the other, but rather merchant traders on both sides. The commodity-economy is thus fundamentally a mercantile system.

(γ) That the act of purchase, M – C', can only take place in consequence of the act of sale, C – M, specifies the quantity, M, of the means of purchase more concretely. In the act of sale, C – M, money is not acquired as an article of consumption, and therefore can only be used as the means of purchase of other commodities. Having been acquired by the sale of a commodity, the means of purchase is *qualitatively free*, in the sense that it possesses the immediate purchasing-power of any other commodity. But it is not *quantitatively free*, because its quantity is constrained by the value of the commodity previously sold. For example, if someone has sold ten apples for 43¢ apiece, and now possesses $4.30, he can purchase only 8.6 pears. As to his ability to buy some pears, no qualitative restriction applies because the $4.30 that he possesses has the immediate purchasing-power of any commodity. However, the quantitative restriction cannot be overcome because he can never buy more than 8.6 units of that commodity (the pear).

If, in this way, the means of purchase is qualitatively free, but quantitatively restricted, it follows that the function of *money as the measure of value* is also subject to that restriction. Money measures the value of a commodity by purchasing it repetitively, but in each case the money used as the means of purchase has been acquired by prior sales of other commodities, and so is limited in quantity. The totality of the means of purchase, functioning as the measure of value is, therefore, also a limited quantity. It is money in C – M – C′ that in fact measures the values of all commodities. That is to say, money measures value, while acting as the means (or medium) of circulation.

B   Money's Function as the Medium of Circulation (Money as Quantum)

(a)   The Chain of Commodity Transactions

(α) Except for the direct producers of gold, every trader acquires money needed for the purchase, M – C′, of commodities belonging to others by the sale, C – M, of his own commodity. If the purchase follows the sale almost immediately, that is, in the same market period, he keeps money in his pocket only for a very short while, and never carries it over to the following market period. Money, which does not stay long in the pocket of the seller, intermediates the exchange of a commodity, C, for another commodity (or other commodities), C′. It is not a mere means of purchase, but the medium (or means) of circulation, that is, the medium of commodity exchanges. In the sale, C – M, of a commodity, however, its owner has no initiative, and cannot for his part enforce the trade. For someone to be able to sell, C – M, someone else must purchase, M – C. Thus, if an individual trader has accomplished the exchange of a commodity, C, for another, C′, in the process described by C – M – C′, this already implies the presence of a buyer of C and the seller of C′. If the first of these persons has sold C″ and the second purchases C‴, the complete exchange of a C for C′ 'implies four extremes, and three dramatis personae',[78] namely, C,

---

78   Marx 1967, *Capital,* Volume I, p. 111.

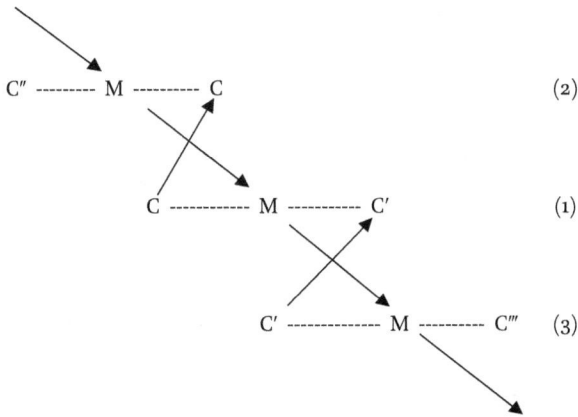

CHART 2.1

C', C", C''' and (1), (2), (3), at the least – as in Chart 2.1 above. However, for the second person (2) to be able to sell, C" – M, there must be another person behind this chain, who buys, M – C". And if the third person (3) has purchased, M – C''', someone behind the scene must have sold, C''' – M, and so on. Hence, the above network of commodity transactions is self-extensive upwards and downwards.

It is supposed here that all commodities are traded at normal prices and, also, for the sake of simplicity, that each person buys and sells commodities of the same money value. In reality, however, prices may diverge from the normal, and a person either may not spend all the money that he earns, or may spend more than he earns during the same market period. Hence, the network of commodity transactions is in fact more complex and involved than is schematically represented here. However, even apart from such complexities, the following two facts have already become obvious: (1) the exchange of commodities cannot be accomplished simply by an individual person; rather, it can be accomplished only as a joint action of all individuals who make up the commodity-economic society; and (2) the network of commodity exchanges is self-extensive, tending to involve more and more traders and an increasing variety of commodities.

(β) It is through this system of commodity exchanges that real economic relations between men can be integrated more extensively than otherwise. Since commodities are products, commodity exchanges imply both interpersonal transfers of products, and, consequently, social interrelations between producers and consumers. A working community of persons, in which products are to be transferred directly (by expropriation, collective consumption, and/ or non-market exchanges) cannot develop as generally and as extensively as a commodity-economic system, because only the latter possesses the market or the circulation-sphere of commodities, in which products can be *impersonally* traded. In the latter case, questions are not raised as to how and by whom the commodities C, C', C'', C''', and so forth, were produced, or how and by whom they will be consumed. The market, in other words, ignores the past and the future of commodities. Thus, Marx writes:

> The circulation becomes the great social retort into which everything is thrown, to come out again as a gold-crystal. Not even are the bones of saints, and still less are more delicate *res sacrosanctae, extra commercium hominum* able to withstand this alchemy. Just as every qualitative difference between commodities is extinguished in money, so money, on its side, like the radical leveller that it is, does away with all distinctions.[79]

For this reason the social interrelations of producers (and consumers), which constitute a working community of people, are no longer directly visible and appear reified as physical relations of commodities. In this system of universal commodity exchanges, a people's economic relations can break all traditional, cultural and geographical barriers and form a truly extensive and integrated whole.

(γ) Although the chain of commodity exchanges is inherently self-extensive, it cannot extend indefinitely because the market in a given time and place contains only a finite number of traders and commodities, however many that may be. It is, of course, true that the sale, C – M, and the purchase, M – C', of an individual trader can always be interrupted (that is to say, it need not be connected together in the same market). But it is surely incorrect to over-emphasise that possibility at this juncture, as Marx seems to do, with the gratuitous suggestion of capitalist crises.[80] A chain of commodity transactions can always be closed by equating the first commodity to enter the market with the last commodity to exit from it, that is, by letting C'' = C''', in the case of the simplest chain involving three persons (see Chart 2.2).

In this simplest case, there are only three traders (1), (2), (3) and three commodities C, C', C''. All traders sell and buy, and all commodities are sold and bought. Hence, society's exchange system may be represented by: $(C + C' + C'') - M - (C + C' + C'')$, or more generally by: $p^*x - M - p^*x$. This representation

---

79   Marx 1967, *Capital,* Volume I, p. 132.
80   Marx 1967, *Capital,* Volume I, pp. 113–4.

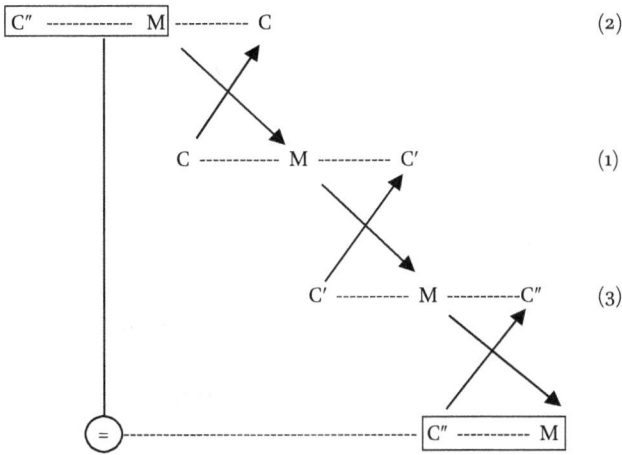

CHART 2.2

has the advantage of showing that society exchanges all commodities for all commodities with the mediation of money, although individual traders always exchange their commodities for different commodities.

It is important to note that money that mediates an individual exchange of commodities in C – M – C', and money that accomplishes the social exchange of all commodities for all commodities, $p^*x - M - p^*x$, are one and the same thing. In this connection, a passing reference to Hegel's triad of 'unit-sum (or amount)-number' may not be completely out of place. According to Hegel, 'quantum reaches its highest development and perfect mode in number', which involves sum (= amount) as the factor of discreteness and unity (= unit) as the factor of continuity.[81] Adopting this terminology, I might state that a definite (real) number can be assigned to money as the medium of circulation, M, a quantum, since the latter mediates individual transactions, which can be viewed both as consisting of separate units and as forming a combined sum of all transactions. The chain of commodity transactions consists of individual links. Money, as the medium of circulation, must be understood as the factor that brings these links together into a whole chain. Since money, in this capacity, is never held for long in the pockets of traders, it may be viewed as staying permanently in the circulation market as a definite quantity, M. This quantity of money divides itself into units of various magnitudes as it assists the circulation or temporary passage through the market of commodities, which originate in the sphere of production and retire into the sphere of consumption.

---

81   Hegel 1969, p. 202; Hegel 1975, p. 203.

Money as the medium of circulation socially unites all commodities as they pass through the market.

(b)   The Circulation of Money

(α) A given sum of gold, M_c, that permanently stays in the market, mediating the exchange of commodities, is said to be in circulation, since it always moves back and forth from the hands of one trader to the hands of another. The quantity of money in circulation may be one million dollars in one market and two million in another. The first question, then, concerns what determines the different quantities of money in circulation in different markets. The answer is given by Marx as follows: 'The quantity of money functioning as the circulating medium [M_c] is equal to the sum of the prices of the commodities [px] divided by the number of moves made by coins of the same denomination [v]'.[82] This is quite correct, if the phrase 'the commodities' in this sentence means the *commodities that are actually being circulated,* rather than the *commodities merely offered for circulation* (but not yet actually traded), although Marx does not make that distinction clear. If a commodity is not actually purchased, its price involves no physical money, but only imagined money.

The formula, $M_c = px/v$, must not be confused with the apparently similar identity advanced by the so-called 'quantity theory of money'. The present formula is not an identity, but a function, $M_c = f(p, x, v)$, which determines the quantity of money to be in circulation, M_c, once prices, p, commodities actually circulated in physical units, x, and the 'velocity of circulation', v, are given. The quantity of money, M_c, is here strictly a dependent variable. No suggestion is made to the effect that the price level is dependent on the money supply, when other variables are given. 'The commodities are equated beforehand in imagination, by their prices, to definite quantities of money. And since, in the form of circulation now under consideration, money and commodities always come bodily face to face, one at the positive pole of purchase, the other at the negative pole of sale, it is clear that the amount of the means of circulation required is determined beforehand by the sum of the prices of all these commodities'.[83] Indeed, no commodity presents itself in the market without a price or value expression, even if the price is provisional and subject to revisions. The price, moreover, *tends to settle to its normal level* as it is revised in the course of actual trade.

---

82   Marx 1967, *Capital,* Volume I, p. 120.
83   Marx 1967, *Capital,* Volume I, p. 117.

The average velocity of the circulation of money (*v*), which is 'measured by the number of moves made by a given piece of money in a given time',[84] reflects the rapidity with which commodities are exchanged in the market by a given amount of money. The briskness, or stagnation, of commodity exchanges is not caused by the quantity of the circulating medium. For example, a merchant who has sold 20 yards of linen for $200 today may either immediately spend it to buy four gallons of brandy today, or may wait to do so until tomorrow. His choice depends on the urgency of his need for brandy and not on his having, or not having, $200 to pay for it. The urgency with which traders wish to acquire commodities with the means of purchase already in their possession determines the velocity of circulation of money. It can be said in general that if business conditions are promising, traders spend money more quickly; if not, *vice versa*. However, in a period of average business conditions, the rapidity with which traders part with the circulating medium will be 'normal', so that one can talk of a *normal velocity of circulation of money* (*v**) in a given market.

(β) Thus, if the size of the market is given by the volume of transactions, *x*, and if the set of normal prices, p*, and the normal velocity of circulation, v*, are known, the normal quantity of the circulating medium, M_c*, is fully determined. Under normal circumstances, the sphere of circulation cannot absorb more than this quantity of gold.[85] This quantity of gold is an 'extensive' magnitude in the sense of Hegel. It is a number of units of the use-value of gold. However, gold is a commodity, and as such it also embodies value. The same quantity of gold, as the embodiment of value, can be considered as an 'intensive' magnitude in Hegel's sense. It is now necessary to study the quantity, M_c, of the circulating medium from both points of view. The following argument can be considerably simplified by the harmless assumption that the velocity of circulation of money is equal to one ($v = 1$), for in that case, the monetary expression, *px*, of the value of all ordinary (non-monetary) commodities in circulation, *x*, is the same as M_c.

The value of no commodity can be expressed in its own use-value. Therefore, the monetary commodity has no meaningful *money-form of value* or money-price, except for the trivial fact that it is always equal to one. However, this does not mean that money has no value, nor that it has a fixed and invariable value. It only means that money's physical body is sufficient to guarantee its homogeneity with other commodities. Even when the values of all

---

84   Marx 1967, *Capital,* Volume I, p. 120.
85   Ibid.

commodities are correctly measured, so that, say, $100 = M_c^* = p^*x$ $(v^* = 1)$, this need not mean that M_c^* and p^*x contain the same magnitude of value, no assertion having so far been made to the effect that normal prices should be proportional to values. Since the definition of the magnitude of value is not yet given, it may be supposed, for example, that M^* contains 20 units of value and p^*x contains 25 units of value. This causes no difficulty in confirming Marx's following proposition, provided that the ratio 20 : 25 of the value contained in money and that contained in all the other circulated commodities taken together is maintained. The proposition is the same as the following: 'The values of commodities remaining constant, their prices vary with the value of gold (the material of money), rising in proportion as it falls, and falling in proportion as it rises'.[86] Since it is supposed that 100 units of gold contain 20 value units, the unit-value of gold is 1/5 at present. Suppose that it rises to 1/4. Then 100 units of gold now contain 25 value units. But since the value contained in other commodities taken as a whole is unchanged at 25 units, only as many units of gold as would embody 20 value units – namely, 80 units of gold – are needed for the circulation of commodities. Consequently, 20 units of gold embodying 5 value units are dismissed, as prices fall by 20 percent. Indeed, given $x = (x_1, \dots , x_n)$, the comparison of $100 = px$ and $80 = p'x$ shows only that p_i : $p_i' = 5 : 4$ (for all $i = 1, \dots , n$).

'The change in the quantity of the circulating medium is, in this case, it is true, caused by money itself, yet not in virtue of its function as a medium of circulation, but of its function as a measure of value. First, the price of the commodities varies inversely as the value of money, and then the quantity of the medium of circulation varies directly as the price of the commodities'.[87] In other words, the measure of value function of money requires that the commodities express their value of 25 in the quantity of gold that contains 20 units of value. If, indeed, the value of money has risen from 1/5 to 1/4, the money-form of value of the circulated commodities should have fallen to $p'x = 80$. As a consequence, that requires only $M_c = 80$, instead of $M_c = 100$. After further elaborating on this point, Marx writes:

> A one-sided observation of the results that followed upon the discovery of fresh supplies of gold and silver, led some economists in the 17th, and particularly in the 18th, century to the false conclusion that the prices of commodities had gone up in consequence of the increased quantity of gold and silver serving as means of circulation.[88]

---

86   Marx 1967, *Capital*, Volume I, p. 117.
87   Ibid.
88   Marx 1967, *Capital*, Volume I, p. 118.

One can clearly grasp the reasoning behind Marx's refutation of the quantity theory of money, only if one examines the quantity, M_c, of the circulating medium as an embodiment of value, that is to say, as an 'intensive' rather than 'extensive' magnitude.

(γ) Since the value of money is never fixed, the quantity required to circulate the same aggregate of commodity values can rise and fall. This fact may be interpreted as Hegel's 'alteration of quantum'.[89] However, there is a more important economic problem, which immediately follows from the fact that the circulating medium (gold) is itself an embodiment of value. Suppose that a quantity of gold that possesses the value of 20 is needed to circulate commodities, which have an aggregate value of 25. Since gold, as the circulating medium, is not withdrawn from the market for consumption, it is not necessary to currently produce all the required quantity of gold of, say, 80 units. However, as they circulate, gold coins are abraded, lost or stolen. Thus, a small fraction, say, one-tenth, of gold, serving as the circulating medium, must be replenished in each market period. In the present case, 8 units of gold containing 2 value units must be capitalistically produced in each period, in addition to all other commodities containing 25 value units. This means that society must produce commodities embodying 27 value units, but can only consume commodities embodying 25 value units, the difference being a *cost* to a society which organises itself on the basis of circulation economy.

This cost is incurred even when the volume of commodity transactions, x, is unchanged. If society grows over periods of time, and if x consequently increases, a greater *cost of circulation* must be borne. Capitalist society must endeavour to reduce such a cost as far as possible because if that kind of cost is too heavy, it can outweigh the advantages of the commodity-economic management of the economy. Fortunately, the solution to this problem lies in the nature of the circulating medium. Experience shows that gold coins, already somewhat abraded, may circulate at their face value, provided that they can be converted into the stated quantity of gold when they are withdrawn from circulation. That implies that a dependable representation of gold can function as the medium of circulation just as well as genuine gold, or that full-bodied gold can circulate commodities *by proxy*.

This property of the circulating medium stems from the fact that it is not a store of value. For a trader, whose purchase immediately follows his sale, the receipt and the payment of money are mere formalities, or a sort of commodity-economic ritual. All he wants to ascertain by the use of 'transactions money' is that the money value of the commodity he has sold is equal to

---

89   Hegel 1969, pp. 224–5.

the money value of the commodities he purchases. To the extent that nominal gold can satisfy the trader in this regard, real gold may withdraw from the sphere of commodity exchanges.

(c)   *Currency or the Institutional Medium of Circulation*

(α) The medium of circulation in actual use will be called *currency* here.[90] The currency of capitalist society generally consists of full-bodied gold coins and tokens (or gold symbols) made of silver, copper, nickel, etc., and paper. 'As wealth increases, the less precious metal is thrust out by the more precious from its place as a measure of value, copper by silver, silver by gold'.[91]

> The practical difficulties in the way of coining extremely minute quantities of gold or silver, and the circumstance that at first the less precious metal is used as a measure of value instead of the more precious ... and that the less precious circulates as money until dethroned by the more precious – all these facts explain the parts historically played by silver and copper tokens as substitute for gold coins.[92]

Thus, even when gold has established itself as the standard money, copper and silver may continue to circulate as subsidiary money in small or localised transactions, without undermining the supremacy of gold.

Just as the circulation of gold is spontaneous, so that of the less precious metals must also have originated spontaneously from commodity exchanges. Once the circulation of different metals becomes customary, however, there arises the need for minting coins. 'Coining, like the establishment of a standard of prices, is the business of the State'.[93] It may at first sight appear awkward to have to invoke the State in the theory of a purely capitalist society, but in the present context, the State does not mean much more than an 'institutionalised agreement of traders'. Since the development of commodity exchanges requires 'law and order', it is reasonable to implicitly assume the presence of institutions that maintain them. Economic theory, of course, cannot tell exactly how such institutions are formed, but it may imply that suitable commercial

---

90   This usage differs from Marx's. In the translation of *Capital,* volume I, the word 'currency' is frequently used to mean 'circulation' [Umlauf], as in 'the currency of money = cours de la monnaie'; Marx 1967, pp. 114–5. See also the Fowkes translation in Marx 1977 [1867], p. 210.

91   Marx 1967, *Capital,* Volume I, p. 99.

92   Marx 1967, *Capital,* Volume I, p. 126.

93   Marx 1967, *Capital,* Volume I, pp. 124–5.

habits and customs, based on agreements among individuals, are institutionalised and stabilised in order to guarantee the sound development of commerce. The State is, therefore, understood here as a typical institution, which
oversees the working of a commodity-economy from the outside. The functions of the State include the minting of coins and the issuing of inconvertible
paper money.

'We allude here only to inconvertible paper money issued by the State and
having compulsory circulation'[94] because *fiat paper money* is the most extreme
form of token money. It can be surmised that even fiat money originally arose
from the commercial practice of issuing vouchers, stamps or tickets for specific
commodity transactions. These money-substitutes may be a useful device to
a group of traders collectively, if their mutual trade is sufficiently regular and
predictable. However, the money substitutes introduced for the purpose of saving circulation-costs to society at large must be distinguished from those designed to save individual circulation-costs. Traders themselves cannot develop
the former into a general medium of circulation; only public authorities can
enforce the general circulation of fiat money as the legal tender. It is important
to realise that the production of monetary gold is a *cost of circulation* to society at large, if not directly to individuals. Therefore, the commodity-economy
cannot by itself save such a cost through its own internal mechanism. It has to
depend on an institution external to it.

For this reason, fiat money must be distinguished from credit money.

> Money based upon credit implies ... conditions, which, from our stand-
> point of the simple circulation of commodities, are as yet totally unknown
> to us. But we may affirm this much, that just as true paper money takes
> its rise in the function of money as the circulating medium, so money
> based upon credit takes root spontaneously in the function of money as
> the means of payment.[95]

As will be seen later, credit is an instrument that allows traders to minimise
their individual circulation-costs. Traders do not have to depend on any institution external to the commodity-economy in order to develop a complex
credit system, which perceptively reduces the individual burden of circulation-
costs. The banking system automatically evolves from within the commodity-
economy, while *credit money*, which the system issues, generally circulates
widely enough that it is not necessary to seek extra-economic assistance.

---

94   Marx 1967, *Capital*, Volume I, p. 127.
95   Ibid.

Fiat money, which unlike credit money saves circulation-costs to society at large, cannot automatically develop in the hands of traders themselves, and hence must be issued and administered by public authorities alien to the commodity-economy, so as to ascertain the general circulation. It is precisely for this reason that the issue of fiat money possesses no commodity-economic rationality, while the quantity of its issue has no inherent limit.

(β) If the State issues *fiat money* under the gold standard regime – which we must in any case suppose is integral to the monetary system of a purely capitalist society – it can remain gold-equivalent only for so long as its total issue does not exceed the quantity of gold that would otherwise be required as the medium of circulation. That is to say, only for so long as the nominal sum of fiat money in circulation does not exceed $M_c = px/v$. If the issue of fiat money falls short of M_c, then some gold coins must still circulate in order to take up the slack. Thus, the production of gold for use as the medium of circulation cannot be completely eliminated. Yet to always issue fiat money in the correct maximum amount is virtually impossible given that the money value of the commodities being circulated (px) changes all the time. Hence, the issue of fiat money – which costs virtually nothing to the issuer but enables him to purchase commodities in the same way as gold producers – easily tends to exceed the proper limit. In that case, the nominal value of, say, one pound of fiat money, no longer represents one pound of gold money, since fiat money once issued cannot be easily withdrawn from circulation.

Unlike gold coins, which can be readily melted into bullion and preserves its gold value outside of the circulation market, fiat money consists of worthless pieces of paper once it leaves the sphere of circulation. Thus, no trader can retire fiat money from circulation and hold it for long as a store of value. Only the issuer can retire fiat money from circulation if he has commodities to sell. However, the issuer is not a commodity seller; he only purchases commodities. Thus, for example, if 250 fiat pounds are issued while the current commodity trade warrants only 200 gold pounds, the purchasing-power of one fiat pound will equal to that of only 0.8 gold pound. A commodity, which has a gold price of 2 pounds, will then cost 2.5 pounds in depreciated fiat money. Since the issuer of fiat money is if anything a pure purchaser, the declining purchasing-power of fiat money only tempts him to issue even more of it. If the velocity of circulation of fiat money may be supposed unchanged, an unrestrained issue of fiat money will lead to the proportional depreciation of its purchasing-power, as well as the proportional rise of commodity prices in terms of it.

This relation between the quantity of fiat money and commodity prices is reminiscent of Hegel's 'spurious quantitative infinite', in which 'the two terms flee from each other',[96] and that is pontificated by the so-called Quantity Theory of Money, which claims that the money prices of commodities will be proportional to the quantity of money supplied. In fact, the latter theory applies only to fiat money, or inconvertible paper money, endowed with the power of compulsory circulation, and follows directly from the true relation, $M_c = px/v$. Let fiat money, F, be issued $\alpha > 1$ times the quantity of gold, M_c, needed for the circulation of commodities, which has a money value in gold of px. Then, $F = \alpha M_c = \alpha px/v \equiv qx/v$, where $q_i \equiv \alpha p_i$ is the price of the i-th commodity in terms of the depreciated paper money. The equation of exchange, $F = qx/v$, deliberately skips the true economic relation, $M_c = px/v$, when it proclaims that it offers an empirically more general law of money and prices. In fact, the equation of exchange is an application of the true economic relation that determines the necessary quantity of the circulating medium to a very special case. Over-issued fiat money is really pseudo-money, which cannot be withdrawn from the market as a store of value, but which asserts its presence regardless of the value expression of the circulated commodities. The quantity theory of pseudo-money, therefore, merely shows the economic meaninglessness of the absolute level of fiat money prices.

(γ) The truth of the quantity theory, therefore, does not lie in the relation, $F \to q$, but rather in the reverse relation, $F/\alpha \leftarrow q/\alpha$. In other words, the commodity-economy permits the institutionalisation of the medium of circulation as currency, only insofar as the relation, $M_c = px/v$, is preserved. The commodity-economy defeats any attempt by external institutions to impose an arbitrary currency that violates that relation. Thus, in capitalist society, if the State indulges in a spiral of fiscal inflation, the currency of that State will continue to depreciate, relative to gold and other currencies, until that currency fails even to function as a medium of circulation. So long as gold remains the general equivalent, capitalist society insists upon an unadulterated gold standard, and permits the use of monetary tokens (including fiat money) only to the extent that they conform to that standard. It is only within this limit that the use of monetary tokens is beneficial to commodity trade, as it saves society some of the burden of circulation-costs. Under the system of the gold standard, however, the circulation of gold coins cannot be completely eliminated, for otherwise gold symbols would lose their legitimacy. Hence, the production of monetary gold as the circulating medium cannot be altogether avoided either.

The gold standard implies free minting, that is to say, the automatic conversion of gold coins into bullion and of bullion into coins. It is this automatic

---

96   Hegel 1969, p. 228.

conversion that guarantees the entry and exit of money into and out of the sphere of circulation, as the money value of circulated commodities varies from time to time. Thus, even though gold symbols always constitute a significant portion of the circulating medium, the latter can remain genuine money only to the extent that its quantity is flexibly adjustable. The money-ness of the circulating medium, in other words, depends on the existence of money outside of the sphere of circulation. Money, which does not circulate, remains idle (or inactive) money. Money in capitalist society is, therefore, classifiable into two large categories: the circulating medium or active money, M_c, and idle money (or money at rest), M_r. Under the gold standard, only part of M_c may be non-gold tokens. In the following section, the function of money as the *store of value* or idle money (M_r) will be investigated.

C   Money's Function as the Store of Value

(a)   The Formation of Idle Money

(α) Idle or inactive money arises most simply and automatically as reserve money, which is accumulated with the expectation of future purchases of commodities. Since the exchange of commodities, C – M – C', is mediated by money, the sale, C – M, and the purchase, M – C', can always be separated. Thus, the merchant who has sold 20 yards of linen for $200 today need not immediately spend them on 4 gallons of brandy; he may hold them for a day, two days, three days, or more, separating the sale of linen for $200 and the purchase of brandy for the same amount of money for a longer or shorter interval of time. However, *if the market period is a whole week*, and if the merchant will return the $200 that he earns today back to circulation before the end of the week, the longer or shorter lapse of time during which he holds the money within the week only affects the velocity of the circulation of transactions money for that period. Reserve money arises when he holds the money that he receives today *beyond the week to a future market period*.

There is no necessity for the trader to spend all the money that he earns in one market period before the expiry of the same. On the contrary, such a practice may not even be possible because of the nature of the use-values involved in his transactions. For example, a trader may have to sell a commodity of small value for several weeks before he obtains sufficient money to buy a more valuable commodity. Conversely, he may have sold an expensive commodity, the proceeds of which he may spend over several weeks on less expensive commodities. Alternatively, perhaps a farmer who sells his crop in autumn may not find agricultural implements in the market that he wants to buy until the following spring. The possibility of separating the sale and the purchase meets the requirements of traders, who want maximum freedom from the use-value restrictions of their transactions. In their effort to sell dear and to buy cheap in the best of all possible markets, traders automatically build *reserve money* while waiting for an opportunity.

If, however, money is withheld for only a few market periods, as the 'temporary abode of purchasing-power' (to borrow Milton Friedman's apposite expression), then that money temporarily kept idle is not very different from active transactions money qualitatively. Money of that kind, held in reserve with a fairly clear prospect of being spent on the purchase of commodities, is in any case the first form of idle money. For this type of idle money to be formed, only the natural separation of the sale, C – M, and the purchase, M – C', that permits traders to overcome the use-value restrictions of their transactions is sufficient. The building of reserve money also increases the bargaining-power of the trader and enables him to operate in the market more advantageously.

(β) A trader can accumulate reserve money by selling more and buying less. Since he is not a consumer, he does not sell a large volume of his commodity merely to buy goods for his own consumption. Only an insignificant part of his sales proceeds will have to be spent to satisfy his daily needs. His merchant skill is exercised when he buys shrewdly in a favourable market, without wasting precious money on unnecessary or less than desirable commodities. The trader is a discriminating buyer. Thus, he would prefer to hold on to gold rather than convert it into burdensome commodities. This preference can no longer be explained by the convenience of trade in ordinary use-values, but rather by the fact that gold preserves value more effectively than other use-values.

Gold is a better store of value than other commodities for two reasons. Firstly, it need not be consumed. And secondly, it is the direct purchasing-power. An ordinary commodity, once purchased, must typically be used or consumed almost immediately before its use-value is lost. Even a durable commodity, unless it is irreproducible, which is ruled out here, loses its use-value by simply becoming old. Even if it preserves its use-value almost intact, it must first be resold for money in order to be exchanged for other commodities. Often the resale price of an old commodity is less than the price of a comparable new commodity. Gold, on the other hand, preserves its use-value almost perfectly and permanently, even if it is, in the meantime, used as a luxury article – such as a candlestick, medal, or ring. Nor is it necessary to sell gold for money in order to purchase commodities, since gold itself is already money. (The small seigniorage fee that may be charged to convert gold bullion into coins can be neglected in the present context).

This does not mean that the value of gold is invariable over time, although, as already explained, the fluctuation of gold value is expected to be less pronounced than the fluctuation in the value of other commodities.[97] If gold loses its value, it is certainly not because the use-value of gold diminishes or deteriorates over time. Technical progress, or the discovery of new gold mines, can of course reduce the value of gold, but such contingencies must be expected with regard to all commodities. That merely puts gold on the same footing as any other commodity. Gold is the best store of value because it almost perfectly preserves its use-value over time, and because its use-value is general rather than particular, in the sense of being immediately convertible into any desired use-value. In other words, gold is mercantile (or commodity-economic) wealth *par excellence*; its use-value being both self-preserving and universal.

Since the use-value of gold is general, the marginal utility of money cannot decline. The trader's desire to accumulate gold money is consequently unbounded. Money is no longer held simply as a reserve with a view to eventually purchasing certain commodities. Money is saved as mercantile wealth, which must be spent wisely and sparingly. The trader accumulates money, wanting to keep it away from circulation as much and for as long as possible. This propensity of the trader may perhaps be represented more adequately by the concept of 'monetary saving' than by Marx's concept of 'hoarding'. For example, Marx writes as follows:

> An outward expression of the desire to withdraw money from the stream of circulation and to save it from the social metabolism is the burying of it, so that social wealth is turned into an imperishable subterranean hoard with an entire furtive private relationship to the commodity-owner.[98]

The *auri sacra fames*, à la Midas, that manifested itself in exaggerated forms in pre-capitalist societies may be a useful reminder of the non-diminishing marginal utility of gold, but this must not overshadow the commodity-economic rationality of monetary saving. Indeed, the trader does not blindly worship money, which to him is an instrument of his operation rather than the ultimate end itself.

(γ) Monetary saving and monetary spending are two sides of the same coin. Money withdrawn from the market is saved, such that: $\Delta M_c + \Delta M_r = 0$. Thus, even though individual traders want to accumulate money indefinitely, the

---

97   See Chapter 1, Section C, (a), (β); see also Marx 1970, *Contribution,* p. 155.
98   Marx 1970, *Contribution,* p. 130.

quantity of money that society may withhold from circulation cannot exceed the quantity of the circulating medium that has become redundant, because commodity exchanges require a definite quantity, M_c, of the circulating medium. There would be no reason for traders to save money at the expense of commodity exchanges, which mediate the metabolic process of society's economic life. Those who unilaterally hoard money, never to spend it again, cannot be merchant traders, who mediate the social exchange of commodities. Thus, if some traders withdraw money in any period from the market, others disgorge money into it from their past saving, so that the existence of the necessary means of circulation, M_c, in the sphere of commodity exchanges is secured.

This conclusion is inevitable, inasmuch as the production of new gold, other than that which replaces the abrasion of circulating gold coins, is as yet left out of consideration. A trader can save only from the money that he obtains by the sale, C – M, of his own commodity. If the stock of gold existing in society, M, is unchanged, and if the quantity of gold required as the circulating medium, M_c, is also given by the money value of commodities being circulated, then idle money that can be saved in society, M_r, must be determined residually as $(M_r = M - M_c)$. Part of society's stock of gold is active as the medium of circulation, while the other part remains idle as accumulated monetary savings. The two parts bear to each other a relation such that the quantity of M_c directly determines the quantity of $M_r (= M - M_c)$ as the residual. Hegel's 'direct ratio' (das direkte Verhältniss) may perhaps be interpreted in this sense.

(b)   Money as the Means of Payment

(α) A market in which certain commodities are regularly traded suggests that a social system of reproduction underlies it. But the production of use-values is in many ways conditioned by technical, geographical and seasonal factors, so that, for example, when farmers market their crop (C), they do not necessarily find the fertiliser (C') ready to be purchased in the market. The separability of their sale, C – M, and their purchase, M – C', is therefore convenient to their desired exchange of commodities. The opposite situation can also arise when farmers need the fertiliser, which is already marketed, but are unable to buy it until some time later when the crop becomes saleable. It would be much more convenient for farmers if they could buy fertiliser now, without money, N – C' (where N is a non-cash trade instrument), and pay off the debt later when they have sold their crop for money, C – M. This is, in fact, frequently possible because the manufacturers of fertiliser have often saved up sufficient money to permit this. They can use this money for their present purchases and wait until the farmers have sold their crop. At the same time, the manufacturers are freed from the responsibility of storing the fertiliser and preventing its use-value from being spoiled. It is to their advantage to sell the fertiliser *on credit*, letting the farmers use it immediately. The farmers, who purchase the fertiliser today, however, will be obligated to pay its price when the credit period expires, whether they have actually sold their crop or not. The money that the indebted farmers pay back on the day of settlement can no longer be viewed as the medium of circulation; instead, it is the means of payment.

The non-cash trade instrument, N, that the farmers use in the purchase of the fertiliser, represents their I.O.U. or promissory note to pay the price with a specified period of delay. This is another case in which gold money purchases a commodity by proxy. It has already been explained that within a certain limit, gold symbols (including fiat money) can circulate as the means of purchase without detracting from the integrity of the gold standard system. If gold symbols are exchanged for a commodity, gold standing behind them purchases it and measures its value, provided that these symbols are convertible into gold, whenever the money value that they represent is ready to leave the sphere of circulation. The same applies to promissory notes. The only difference is that their day of conversion into gold is pre-determined. As long as physical gold is present when the credit period expires, the promissory note stands for a genuine representative of gold and can purchase a commodity and measure its value in the name of gold. It is, therefore, quite wrong to claim that the value of a commodity purchased with a promissory note is measured only when the note is cashed. Value is measured by the act of purchase, not by the subsequent cancellation of the debt. The act of purchase takes place when the purchaser acquires the right to consume the commodity in return for the promissory note, not when he honours it.

This explanation does not contradict the earlier proposition that the value of a commodity is measured only when it becomes physical gold payable to the seller, rather than remaining imaginary gold in his unilateral value expression. Thus, if a seller of the fertiliser merely puts it on the shelf with the price tag of $5 per kilogram, the value of the fertiliser has not yet been measured, but so long as the farmer purchases 10kg of it for $50 – either with cash or with a promise to pay $50 plus some interest – the value of the fertiliser must have been measured. Even if the farmer defaults later, and the seller of the fertiliser fails to receive the promised money, that does not change the fact that the 10kg of fertiliser have been socially acknowledged as worth $5 per kilogram, revealing to that extent the value of the fertiliser. The farmer purchases it not with imaginary money, but with physical money that is payable later. As a matter of fact, it may be supposed that when he purchases the fertiliser on credit, he also purchases $50 worth of agricultural implements in cash. In that case, he can, in the first instance, pay the $50 cash to the seller of the fertiliser and immediately receive from him the credit of $50, with which to buy the agricultural implements. All commodities are then paid for in cash and only a debtor-creditor relation remains between the two traders after the acts of purchase have been concluded. This is a plausible explanation because no trader can conceivably purchase all commodities on credit during any given market period. It is, however, simpler to say that the promise to pay money is not as unreal as 'imagined' money in the mind of the seller. A promissory note represents a social recognition, in principle, of the money value of the commodity.

(β) If a trader purchases a commodity on credit, that is to say, with a promissory note, he places himself under the absolute obligation to have the means of payment ready by a specific previously agreed upon date. If he fails to liquidate his debt by that time, he will be declared insolvent. Consequently, the saving of money as the means of payment becomes a categorical imperative to the indebted trader; his is a 'forced saving' rather than a freely chosen decision not to spend. The amount of money that society withdraws from circulation as the means of payment, however, is far less than the money value of the commodities that promissory notes have circulated. If N_{ab} is the promise by trader-(a) to pay a given sum of money, with a given delay, to trader-(b), then for all N of the same money sum and the same delay period, the operations, $N_{ab} \rightarrow N_{bc} = N_{ac}$ and $N_{ii} = 0$ $(i = a, b, ...)$ are possible. Hence, a complete circuit of debts and credits, such as $N_{ab} \rightarrow N_{bc} \rightarrow N_{ca} = N_{aa} = 0$, would leave no balance to be settled in the physical means of payment. If that were the case, money would function purely as abstract money of accounts among traders (a), (b), and (c), with the exchange of commodities requiring no more than joint bookkeeping, in which receipts and payments mutually cancel. A system of trade credits among independent traders, however, can never be organised so perfectly as to leave no balance to be settled in hard cash. (The details of this will be studied in Chapter 9). It is in the nature of a commodity-economy to always require some means of payment.

If the issuer-(a) of the promissory note, N_{ab}, has a good credit standing, N_{ab} becomes credit money in the form *of* a 'bill of exchange', and can circulate by 'endorsement' among many traders, prior to the date of its expiry, as Marx explains:

> Credit-money springs directly out of the function of money as a means of payment. Certificates of the debts owing for purchased commodities circulate for the purpose of transferring those debts to others. On the other hand, to the same extent as the system of credit is extended, so is the function of money as a means of payment. In that character it takes

various forms peculiar to itself under which it makes itself at home in the sphere of great commercial transactions. Gold and silver coin, on the other hand, are mostly relegated to the sphere of retail trade.[99]

The wholesale trade and other inter-business transactions make an extensive use of commercial bills. But they are hardly used in retail trade, where purchasers are final consumers. Since a trade bill implies a credit given by the seller of a specific commodity to its purchaser, it is in general impossible for the bill to eventually return to its issuer and to liquidate itself without involving cash money as the means of payment.

If banks discount a trade bill, however, they may issue banknotes instead of paying in gold. Banknotes, or, equivalently, demand deposits at the bank (convertible into gold on demand), are a more developed form of credit money than trade bills. In an advanced capitalist economy, an overwhelming part of the medium of circulation takes the form of central banknotes, acting as the legal tender, drastically economising the circulation of gold. The central bank must, however, always stand ready to maintain the convertibility of its notes into gold. In this case, the gold reserve in the vault of the central bank circulates commodities, measures their values, and acts as the means of payment, all by proxy. All functions of money, in other words, presuppose the existence of the physical gold reserve in the vault of the central bank. Although, within a country, the means of payment may take the form of central banknotes, the transfer of these notes from the debtor to the creditor, as means of payment, implies the transfer of the claim to that gold. If the debtor and the creditor live in different nations, however, the settlement can be accomplished only by an actual shipment of gold. Since the partition of a purely capitalist society into different central banking jurisdictions is, however, purely arbitrary, the settlement of debts in gold must be considered to be the general rule, which, in some exceptional cases, may be accomplished without physically moving gold from one place to another.

(γ) So far it has been supposed that the need for the means of payment arises only from commercial debts, incurred by past purchases of commodities. However, any other contractual obligation to pay money – be it wages, rents, or taxes – also gives rise to the demand for the means of payment.

In every country, certain days of the year become by habit recognised settling days for various large and recurrent payments. These dates depend, apart from other revolutions in the wheel of reproduction, on conditions closely connected with the seasons. They also regulate the dates for payments that have no direct connexion with the circulation of commodities such as taxes, rents, and so on. The quantity of money requisite to make the payments falling due on those dates all over the country causes periodical, though merely superficial perturbations in the economy of the medium of payment.[100]

The 'quantity of money requisite to make payments' of all sorts, during any market period, may, therefore, be quite independent of the quantity of the circulating medium required to carry out commodity exchanges during that period. Even if one restricts the source of demand for the means of payment to commercial debts that were incurred in the past, the necessary quantity of M_r, which must be ready today as the means of payment, is determined independently of the necessary quantity of M_c, which mediates today's commodity transactions. Thus, for example, if $M_r = 50$, this is not because M_c is a particular number rather than any other; $M_r = 50$ is determined independently of whether $M_c = 100$, or $= 50$, or anything else.

This independence from the money value of the currently circulated commodities transforms the means of payment into funds. The source of funds can no longer be found in the circulation-sphere, since their quantity cannot be determined residually as $M_r = M - M_c$. If, for example, $M_c = 50$ and $M_r = 50$, then society's stock of money must be $M = 100$. However, if $M = 90$, a difficulty obviously arises, so long as the production of new gold (or at least the conversion of non-monetary gold into monetary gold) is still neglected. The difficulty can be overcome only if M_c becomes dependent on M_r, rather than the other way around. This 'inverse relation', as Hegel would call it, can best be seen in the *modus operandi* of the banking system. It is well known that the banking system issues notes and creates demand deposits only up to a certain multiple of its cash reserve in gold. It cannot create these immediately convertible (on-demand) liabilities without limit, in response to the demand for the circulating medium, M_c, of which they constitute a major component. If the cash reserve is redundant, the banking system may provide more means of circulation, and, in the contrary case, the reverse. The system accomplishes this adjustment by easing and tightening bank credit, which, in the present abstract context, may be taken to mean the lengthening and shortening of the periods of deferred payment.

---

100   Marx 1967, *Capital*, Volume I, p. 141.

Thus, if traders possess plentiful funds, they give liberal credits to each other and stimulate active commodity exchanges; if they are short of funds, they can afford to extend only limited credits to each other, thus restricting the scope of commodity exchanges correspondingly. It is, therefore, not the volume of commodity transactions that determines the gold stock of society, but the other way around. The stock of gold viewed in this active role is *funds*, or Marx's *universal money*. Here, M_r does not arise solely as a consequence of the non-purchase of commodities or the liquidation of liabilities. Rather, *money as funds acts as the regulator of commodity exchanges*. Money, which possesses an initiative in actualising a proposed trade, now returns to itself in the present context, as money that sets the pace of commodity exchanges in general.

(c)   *Funds or Universal Money*

(α) The concept of funds can be widely interpreted to include all forms of idle money when its concrete function is specified. In that way, *reserve money* and the *means of payment,* which have already been treated, may be viewed as special forms of funds. Such common expressions as consumption-funds, loanable funds, depreciation funds, wage-funds, and so on, suggest that the word 'funds', in the sense of 'money in hand or pecuniary resources', can be used to describe various applications of idle money, of which reserve money and the means of payments are two special cases. But they do not unveil the full potential of money as funds. Funds must now be studied in their own right, rather than as something different from the medium of circulation, that is to say, as 'inactive' money, the quantity of which does not depend on the state of commodity exchanges. Funds, in this narrower sense, must be viewed as gold flowing into the sphere of circulation, rather than as gold withdrawn from it; they must be viewed as money with a *latent* influence on trade rather than as money simply dropping out of it.

This change of emphasis entails the reinstatement of gold producers, who have so far been neglected. Newly produced gold enters the sphere of circulation by the 'purchase without sale' of the gold producers and accrues to those who have sold them commodities. Those who sell commodities to gold producers, directly or indirectly, may hold the received gold in hand as funds, returning it to circulation as and when they see fit. The traders, who thus hold newly produced gold for some time, activate it only when they are ready to *expand the scale of their business*. In other words, funds, properly speaking, are funds for accumulation or new investment. They constitute money at rest. They are not simply dormant, having been withdrawn from the market, but are actively awaiting the opportunity to pour into the circulation-sphere, with a view to expanding the existing scale of commodity exchanges. No trader can expand his business, or begin a new business, without first accumulating enough money to be able to do so. If, however, the accumulation of money by one trader is at the expense of another, the scale of society's commodity exchanges will remain unchanged. The commodity-economy, as a whole, must accumulate money prior to its physical growth. Money as funds is now viewed as the potential source of commodity-economic growth.

In a particular capitalist country, funds may be accumulated in the form of central banknotes, if these are legal tender. However, when the whole country envisions an expanded scale of its commodity exchanges, additional banknotes and/or demand deposits must be created in advance. This, of course, cannot be done unless the gold reserve of the central bank is correspondingly increased. The country's economic expansion, in this case, requires a prior accumulation of gold in the vault of the central bank. The gold reserve of the central bank can, however, increase only by the production of new gold (or the conversion of non-monetary gold into monetary gold), if the inflow of gold from a foreign country is excluded. In the theory of a purely capitalist society, foreign trade must be left out of consideration, so that the only way in which society's stock of gold is increased in preparation for economic expansion is by the production of new gold.

(β) The above characterisation of money as funds might, at first sight, appear unrelated to Marx's concept of 'universal money', or 'money of the world'. He seems to define 'world money' simply as gold and silver used in the settlement of international trade. Thus, Marx writes:

> Just as every country needs a reserve of money for its home circulation, so, too, it requires one for external circulation in the markets of the world. The functions of hoards, therefore, arise in part out of the function of money as the medium of the home circulation and home payments, and in part out of its function of money of the world. For this latter function, the genuine money-commodity, actual gold and silver, is necessary. On that account, Sir James Steuart, in order to distinguish them from their purely local substitutes, calls gold and silver 'money of the world'.[101]

Indeed, the gold stock of a particular nation rises and falls in response to changes in its trade balance. But for capitalist society as a whole, the flow of gold from one country to another merely changes the world distribution of the

---

101   Marx 1967, *Capital*, Volume I, p. 144.

precious metal and does not affect the aggregate quantity of monetary gold. Thus, from the point of view of an entire capitalist society, the inflow of gold must be 'internalised' as the production of (or the conversion of non-monetary into monetary) gold. Marx himself recommends the following procedure:

> The involvement of foreign commerce in analysing the annually repro- duced value of products can therefore only confuse without contributing any new element of the problem, or of its solution. For this reason it must be entirely disregarded. And consequently gold too is to be treated here as a direct element of annual reproduction and not as a commodity ele- ment imported from abroad by means of exchange.[102]

This procedure must be adopted throughout the theory of a purely capitalist society.

If gold flows into a country in response to its trade surplus, the latter oc- curs because it has produced more than it has consumed. Society can produce more commodities (excluding durable commodities other than gold) than it can directly or productively consume, only by producing the unconsumable commodity, namely, monetary gold. Alternatively, if society consumes all of its production of ordinary commodities, it can at least reduce the 'consumption' of gold by converting more non-monetary gold into monetary gold. Similarly, if gold flows out of a country in response to its trade deficit, it must have con- sumed more than it has produced. For society to consume more commodities than it produces (excluding, once again, durable commodities other than gold, produced in the past and stored up until the present), it can only 'consume' gold by shifting it from its unconsumable monetary form to its consumable non-monetary form, or by abrading monetary gold in circulation. Hence, in the analysis of a purely capitalist society, the inflow and the outflow of gold money must be a consequence of one of the following: either as the conversion of non-monetary gold into monetary gold and its reverse, or the production of new gold, which is either more or less than the abrasion of monetary gold.

Since gold too is a capitalistically producible commodity, it will be pro- duced only in such quantities as society desires relative to other commodi- ties. Even when society's scale of reproduction remains unchanged, monetary gold, abraded in circulation, must be automatically replaced. A shortage of gold reveals itself in a uniform depression of the market prices of other com- modities below their normal prices, enabling a unit of gold to buy more of all commodities. This cannot fail to stimulate gold producers to increase their output, until their 'purchase without sale' of commodities restores normal

102   Marx 1967, *Capital,* Volume II, p. 470.

prices in the market. It is, however, premature at this abstract stage of discussion to fully explain the mechanism of adjustment in the production of gold. Ideally, the 'production' of gold should be altogether left implicit, when *money as funds*, required for the expansion of commodity trade, is studied in the doctrine of simple circulation. Marx's reference to 'money of the world' or 'universal money', rather than 'accumulation funds', indicates the subtle judgment with which he treated this difficult problem of dialectical exposition.

(γ) It is, however, important to realise that the formation of funds here alludes to the holding of idle money as a necessary step in the conversion of surplus value into capital, which will be discussed more explicitly later. The relation of accumulation-funds to commodity exchanges is such that the former provide the latter with a potency or energy to grow, suggesting the aptness of Hegel's 'the relation of powers' (das Potenzen-verhältniss). Funds are meant to be 'capitalised', not to be dissipated by consumption. Thus, when they go into circulation via the act of purchase, M – C, it is for the purpose of gainful resale, C – M'. Money as funds is the motor of the chrematistic process, M – C – M', which we may legitimately refer to as *capital*, not the mere instrument of commodity exchanges, C – M – C'. Traders do not merely exchange commodities; they profit from commodity exchanges by buying cheap in M – C and selling dear in C – M'. It is the chrematistic activity of traders, called arbitrage, that brings unity and order to the commodity-exchange market.

Without active *arbitrage* that closes price-differentials over an extended territory, society would not be integrated wholly under a single market. Commodity-economic society would be partitioned into several localised markets, which if not totally isolated would be only loosely connected with one another. Simply as the medium of circulating commodities, however, money would not be able to remedy the disarray of separate markets. It is the function of money as funds, or as 'money of the world', that enables traders to profit from price-differentials, thereby eliminating local disparities and universalising the market. The theory of a purely capitalist society does not merely assert the principle of a unique price for the same commodity, taking the operation of a perfect arbitrage for granted. Unlike vulgar economic theory, which always assumes what it cannot explain, the dialectic of capital shows why money as funds necessarily universalises a commodity-economy. This unifying power of money also accomplishes the growth of commodity trading.

In the trader's act of arbitrage is already implied the general form of capital, M – C – M', which consists of making a sum of money M into a greater sum of money M' with the intermediation of a commodity C. The dialectic of capital must now proceed to the examination of this particular circulation-form as a metamorphosis of value, or value in motion.

CHAPTER 3

The Form of Capital (*Measure*)

Already implicit in the notion of *money as funds* is the capitalist activity of buying a commodity not for direct consumption or use, but instead for gainful resale. If a sum of money, M, is thrown into the sphere of circulation with a view to acquiring a greater sum of money, M', this chrematistic operation is called *capital*. Capital is not a thing; it must be understood strictly as an *operation* or activity. The *commodity*, it will be recalled, expresses its value in the use-value of another commodity, but it cannot take the initiative of actualising the proposed trade. The commodity, in other words, must passively wait to be purchased because its value remains immanent in it. The commodity can be active only in its value expression, that is, in making a trade proposal. *Money*, in contrast, is the universal equivalent, and as such externalises the value of all other commodities. As the general embodiment of commodity values, money purchases commodities, realising and perhaps even storing their value instead of merely expressing it. Thus, money functions as an explicit value-object, standing apart from ordinary commodities. *Capital* is a *chrematistic operation*, which combines the externality and the immanence of value in its *metamorphosis*, that is to say, value grows in capital, while it takes on and off alternately the forms of the commodity and of money.

The most general form of capital is that of merchant capital, M – C – M'. A merchant buys a commodity (or an assortment of commodities) in order to sell it dearer. The greater the price-differential, the greater is his profit, which is the monetary expression of the *surplus value* that he earns. If the merchant profits from a price-differential over space, his operation is an *arbitrage*. If, on the other hand, he profits from a price-differential over time, his operation is a *speculation*. In both cases, the merchant activity tends to close price-differentials, and to join hitherto separate markets into a single whole. While profitable opportunities increasingly disappear with the unification of the market, the latter fact also undermines and erodes the traditional mode of production from without, preparing the ground for the formation of capitalism. Yet the form of merchant capital has an important limitation in that it has to trade use-values, which are not its own products. The success of the merchant's chrematistic, therefore, depends on the trader's skill, contacts, luck and other contingent factors, directly tied to the specificity of the use-values that he handles. There is consequently no likelihood for the profit-rate to become uniform in all mercantile operations.

The form of money-lending capital, M ...... M', circumvents this difficulty by sidestepping mercantile activities. A money-lender makes money available to traders, who employ it in their chrematistics, and later intercepts part of their profits as interest. In this way, the money-lender need not be directly concerned with the specific use-values that the merchants choose to trade. What matters to him is merely the general profitability of the trading sector to which he lends money. The trading sector must always involve specific use-values, some of which are more conducive to profitable business than others. But the money-lender has the advantage of not being tied down to any specific use-value, his success depending on the overall performance of the trading sector. The money-lender's remoteness from use-value constraints makes the operation of money-lending capital both free and unprincipled. A sum of money advanced as capital by money-lending capital collects a previously agreed upon interest in due course, and so grows of its own accord, without being troubled by the vicissitudes of individual commerce. On the other hand, there is no general principle that stipulates how far the money-lender may partake of the mercantile profit earned in the trading sector. Consequently, it is easy for him to let his predatory nature loose, which instead of merely imposing order and discipline on mercantile activities, may actually lead to their exhaustion and ruin.

The form of industrial capital, M – C ... P ... C' – M', which includes within itself the production of a commodity by means of commodities, C ... P ... C', is the most developed form of capital. It does not circumvent use-value restrictions, but produces *any* use-value as C' as the occasion demands. In other words, the chrematistic of industrial capital is not restricted by particular use-values, but only by use-values in general. This is the adequate form of capital, in which value can grow indifferently to particular use-values. Since it can produce value in the form of a freely chosen use-value, industrial capital can displace the traditional mode of production and establish capitalism. This formal possibility, however, becomes reality only when *labour-power* is converted into a commodity, for it is labour-power that produces any desired use-value, and also produces more value than it consumes. However, the conversion of labour-power into a commodity does not automatically follow from the development of commodity exchanges. The so-called 'primitive accumulation', which released the direct producers from land and transformed them into mere owners of labour-power, is a historical fact implying the use of extra-economic forces.

The Hegel Correspondence

The theory of capital as a circulation-form, to be developed in the present chapter, corresponds to the dialectic of 'measure' in Hegel's *Logic*. Just as measure is the unity of quality and quantity, so capital is a unity of the forms of the commodity and of money. However, the concept of the metamorphosis of value, M – C – M', prohibits from the beginning a parallel treatment of the commodity value (C = determinateness or quality) and money (M = magnitude or quantity), for money always represents value 'externally and immediately', while a commodity holds it only 'immanently'. Although Hegel defines *measure* in the beginning as 'qualitative quantity'[103] or 'a quantum with a qualitative significance',[104] and never as 'quantitative quality', his exposition soon obscures the priority of quantity over quality and appears to take them as two equally significant factors of measure. It is perhaps here that the difference between the idealist and materialist dialectics becomes most strikingly apparent, as already mentioned in the Introduction. Indeed, providential measure is permanent and predetermined. It is observed everywhere and always. Capital, on the other hand, is merely a historic agent, which organises society's economic life, provided that the value-relation can successfully subordinate use-values. All the more reason, then, why capital cannot remain a mere state of balance or proportion of the two elements – quality (value object) and quantity (money). It must be a value-augmenting motion, which seeks a quantitative growth of quality (the value that inheres in the commodity).

In the category of 'specific quantum', Hegel quite rightly sets out to show that quantum can to some extent alter, without thereby also changing its 'defining quality as, for instance, a heap does not cease to be a heap if only a grain is removed'.[105] If the change of an external magnitude, $s(x + 1) = as(x)$, merely reflects a growth of the corresponding immanent quality, $t(x) = t_o e^{bx}$ (where $a = 1 + b > 0$), the measure relation between s and t is maintained. Yet Hegel claims that 'the different forms in which measure is realised belong also to different spheres of natural reality',[106] where 'space and time are the purest forms of externality'.[107] Thus, if s and t stand for space and time, it is impossible to say, in their measure relation, which of the two variables constitutes the external side and which the immanent side. Hegel is, therefore, obliged to deduce the

---

103   Hegel 1969, p. 333.
104   Hegel 1969, p. 330.
105   Hegel 1969, p. 335.
106   Hegel 1969, p. 331.
107   Ibid.

'self-subsistent measure' of a material thing as the twofold measure relation, consisting of the measure relation between internal t and external t', and the measure relation between external s and internal s'.[108] There are, however, as many measures as there are material things, some of which, being qualitatively indifferent, coalesce together by 'affinity' to share the same kind of measure, or 'real measure'. The series of measures accordingly form a nodal line, such that between any two nodes quality is invariant to quantitative alterations. Only by overstepping a node or quantitative limit does the thing become 'measureless'.[109] In other words, the nodal points are where a quantitative change suddenly entails a qualitative change. If, however, quality is indifferent to a quantitative change that does not exceed the node, that quality constitutes the substrate of the corresponding real measure. In that case, it is natural for Hegel to further deduce the final category of 'the absolute indifference'[110] as the perennial substrate of all things. What lies behind material things and their qualitative classifications is the essence, or self-identity, which differentiates itself into external 'states' determined by the quantum.

The laborious treatment of measure in the larger Logic, however, is too readily influenced by Hegel's preoccupation with the unity of 'the quantitative and the qualitative aspects of natural object'.[111] The dialectic of capital cannot accept this naturalistic outlook and the reasoning that follows from it. On the other hand, the main outline of the dialectic of measure, proceeding from 'specific quantum' through 'the measureless' to 'the simple relation-to-self' – portrayed with far less outlandish frills in the smaller Logic – remains absolutely valid. Hegel wants to discover the permanent substratum, or essence, underneath the fleeting world of 'being' or 'immediacy'. He, therefore, constructs 'measure' as the most synthetic mode or form of being which despite its variability and transfiguration, remains self-identical and capable of containing within itself the permanent. In political economy, the circulation-form of capital plays exactly the same part. The commodity, in which value is immanent, and money, which externalises value, are both simpler forms of circulation. Value figures as a passing moment in the exchange of commodities. Even value that is stored in money does not forever rest in that state. Only in capital, which endlessly repeats its metamorphosis, does value find its permanent abode where it can grow self-identically, that is, as 'the simple relation-to-self'. Capital is the mode

---

108   Hegel 1969, p. 347.
109   Hegel 1969, p. 366–74.
110   Hegel 1969, p. 375.
111   Hegel 1969, p. 331.

of circulation rich enough to subsume value completely. It is in the motion of capital, and in this alone, that value reveals its supra-historical substance.

The form of merchant capital closely resembles the category of *specific quantum* because the chrematistic of a merchant is never free from the specific use-values that he handles. The determinateness of *quality* restricts the alteration of quantum. The form of money-lending capital corresponds to Hegel's 'real measure' in that a money-lender deals with several self-subsistent merchants, his operation being only indirectly restricted by the use-values that the indebted merchants trade with one another. However, the money-lender can easily exceed his proper limit and become 'measureless', since his activity only *circumvents* use-values, instead of really *overcoming* them. The form of industrial capital alone is truly free from the restrictions posed by specific use-values on the motion of value, because industrial capital can produce any use-value that best fits the occasion. The Hegelian state of the *absolute indifference* to quality or determinateness is accomplished by *the true infinite of measure*. The parallel state is achieved in the dialectic of capital with the form of industrial capital, which can freely produce any use-value it chooses. The present chapter follows this broad interpretation of Hegel's *measure*, while ignoring the details of its naturalistic illustration.

A   The Form of Merchant Capital (Capital as Specific Quantum)

(a)   *The General Formula for Capital*

(α) When idle money becomes funds, or universal money, it is already pregnant with capital. Universal money, however, does not merely remain idle by simply renouncing the purchase of a commodity for consumption; universal money is employed for the purchase of commodities *for resale* with a pecuniary gain. As soon as funds are thus spent, the operation of capital, as the chrematistic operation of advancing a sum of money, M, for the purpose of acquiring a greater sum of money, M', has already begun. Since capital is nothing but a chrematistic use of funds, only the owner of funds can become a capitalist by using them as capital.

The general formula for capital, M – C – M', states the fact that value, in the form of money, quantitatively grows from M(> o) to M'(> M) by undergoing the form of a commodity, C. Capital, therefore, unifies the two simpler forms of circulation – money and the commodity – in a definite sequence, which must be taken as a whole. Neither money nor the commodity by themselves apart from this sequence constitutes capital. Nor can the order of the sequence be reversed, since capital must always begin and end with the form of money, while undergoing the form of the commodity in the course of its motion. Universal money simply held, or a commodity (whether as a real asset or means of production) merely possessed, is not capital. For example, if someone owns a house, the market price of which appreciates over time, that does not by itself make him a capitalist. A capitalist who speculates on the house should have purchased it with money, which would otherwise have lain idle, and should be willing to sell the house for money as soon as sufficient profit is earned. In other words, a gain in value of a commodity (sometimes called its 'capital gain') that is not realised in money does not by itself constitute capital; the operation of capital requires an increase of value in the socially acknowledged form of money.

Since capital begins and ends with money, the explicit form of value, its circuit can be readily recognised by the turnover of capital. The difference in the value of its end-point, M', over the value of its starting point, M, is called *surplus value*, the monetary expression of which, M' − M = m, is *profit*. The efficiency of the value augmentation of capital can, therefore, be measured purely quantitatively by the rate of profit, and the shorter the turnover-time the more efficient is the motion of capital.

(β) Ideally, capital should entail the highest possible rate of the self-growth of value over time in the form of money. However, the motion of capital must go through the form of the commodity, in which value is immanent. This means that the value augmentation of capital directly or indirectly involves and is constrained by a use-value. From this point of view, capital is described as a *metamorphosis*, that is to say, capital, in its motion, must alternately assume the forms of money and the commodity.

Although Marx applies the expression 'metamorphosis' not only to the motion of capital, M − C − M', but also to the process of a commodity-exchange, C − M − C', the latter application is not quite as felicitous as the former. It will be recalled that money can buy a commodity, but a commodity cannot buy money. A commodity, which prices itself, must await its purchase without any initiative on its part in actually conducting the trade. Hence, the owner of a commodity cannot set the process, C − M − C', into motion by himself, transforming his commodity, C, into another commodity, C'. Capital, by contrast, arises from universal money with the spontaneous impulse to purchase a commodity. Although in the latter half of the motion of capital, the act of resale, C − M', which involves a 'deadly leap (*salto mortale*)', must indeed take place, a commodity, which was not likely to be resold with some profit, would not have been purchased in the first place. At least the owner of money can take a risk on his own initiative and responsibility. This is what the owner of a mere commodity cannot do. It seems, therefore, appropriate to reserve the expression 'metamorphosis' for the self-propelled change of forms that the motion of capital undergoes, rather than apply it indiscriminately to any change of forms.

The concept of a metamorphosis brings out the restrictions on the motion of capital imposed by the use-value of the commodity with which it is involved. Indeed, the value of capital cannot grow from M to M' unless the use-value of C permits this growth. In this respect, the Hegelian category of 'specific quantum', which is 'the simple relation of the quantum to itself, its own determinateness within itself',[112] describes well this essential property of capital. The development of the forms of capital does not eliminate such use-value restrictions altogether, but only neutralises them until they become unspecific and indifferent to the motion of capital. The order of exposition of the theory of capital-forms thus follows the progress of capital as it increasingly overcomes these restrictions. The chrematistic of merchant capital is most directly constrained by the 'specific' use-values of the commodities that it handles, while money-lending capital circumvents direct involvement in use-values altogether by removing itself from merchandise trade. Only the form of industrial capital truly overcomes the restrictions of *specific* use-values by presupposing the capacity to produce any of them.

(γ) The fact that the metamorphosis of capital begins and ends with the same form of money, which is free from the specific quality of a use-value, signifies that the motion of capital, M – C – M', unlike the process of a commodity-exchange, C – M – C', is inherently self-perpetuating. The exchange of a commodity, C, for another commodity, C', is a once-and-for-all affair, since both commodities are absorbed by consumption once the exchange is over. But this is not the case with capital. If, in the beginning, M was idle money convertible into capital, this must also be true of the M recovered in M', together with a profit, m, when capital has turned over once. Hence, at least the M in M' will have to be reinvested as capital to repeat the same operation, unless external conditions so change as to make that repetition impossible. Accordingly, the circulation-form, M – C – M', must be only one of the circuits in the successive process:

M – C – M' · M – C – M' · M – C – M' · M – , ... , etc.

This process is expected to continue *ad inifinitum*.

---

112   Hegel 1969, p. 332.

Moreover, a profit, m = M' – M, is also earned in the form of money, namely, in the form of immediate purchasing-power. Thus, surplus value too can be invested as additional capital, if there is a suitable use-value, which may be resold (either as is, or transformed) profitably. As much of surplus value as circumstances permit will, therefore, be converted into capital, or will be accumulated, so as to expand the scale of the chrematistic operation. Thus, the circulation of capital is never a once-and-for-all affair, but a self-repeating and naturally expanding process. Capital endlessly pursues profit, but is not disposed to merely 'hoard' the result of its chrematistic. As Marx says:

> This boundless greed after riches, this passionate chase after exchange-value, is common to the capitalist and the miser; but while the miser is merely a capitalist gone mad, the capitalist is a rational miser. The never-ending augmentation of exchange-value, which the miser strives after, by seeking to save his money from circulation, is attained by the more acute capitalist, by constantly throwing it afresh into circulation.[113]

The rationality of capital lies in its constant return to circulation, for only in the continuing motion of capital can value grow without limit.

(b)   The Activity of Merchant Capital

(α) The general formula for capital, M – C – M', applies in an unmodified fashion to the form of merchant capital, which buys a commodity cheap and sells it dearer, either as a consequence of arbitrage or speculation. Concretely, one may conceive of a merchant trader who profits from a price-differential, either in time or over space, but who subjectively rationalises his profit as a reward for his risk bearing. In discussing the activity of this form of capital, it is desirable to make careful distinctions between the theoretical merchant and the historical merchant, for strictly speaking the latter does not belong to the theory of a purely capitalist society. However, there are reasons why the study of merchant capital cannot avoid frequent references to its historical form.

In the dialectic of capital, a theoretically rudimentary concept does not always play a dominant part in the working of a fully developed capitalist society. Thus, for example, the simple value-form, which is theoretically prior to the money-form of value, can no longer be directly observed whether in a capitalist society, or indeed in any historical commercial practice. The development of a commodity-economy, it is true, does not eradicate the simple expression of value, which invariably returns to the clearing-house of commodity-exchanges,

---

113   Marx 1967, *Capital*, Volume I, p. 153.

whenever money loses its credibility, for instance, in a state of hyperinflation. Yet the normal functioning of a commodity-economy, instead of exhibiting the simple value-form as it is, contains it in the more developed money-form of value as a theoretical or conceptual ingredient. Similarly, the form of merchant capital, which historically played the dominant role in the early phase of capitalist development, as well as in pre-capitalist commodity-economies, is no longer conspicuously observable in a developed capitalist society. This does not mean that the form of merchant capital disappears with the development of capitalism. Even in a fully developed capitalist society, capitalists are inveterate merchants, willing to profit from arbitrage and speculation, whenever an opportunity presents itself to them. However, because price-differentials tend to disappear as capitalism develops, capital must seek profits from sources other than strictly mercantile activity. In a well-developed capitalist society, the form of merchant capital, although always present as an atavistic feature of capital, does not appear with the concreteness characteristic of historical merchant capital. Similar considerations apply to money-lending capital.

The historical prominence of these two forms of capital in pre-capitalist (or early capitalist) societies does not justify Marx's proposal to 'entirely leave out of consideration the antediluvian forms of merchants' capital and money-lenders' capital, in analysing the standard form of capital, the form under which it determines the economic organisation of modern society'.[114] Although the forms of merchant capital and money-lending capital cannot by themselves organise a capitalist society, they both survive as essential ingredients of industrial capital. That is why industrial capital, when it organises a capitalist society, can delegate part of its operation to commercial capital and loan-capital (see Chapter 9), which are the reinstatements of merchant capital, and money-lending capital, respectively, in the context of capitalist society. If these two forms of capital played their historical part more prominently before the full evolution of capitalism, this fact only confirms that capitalism needs more than these forms of capital to be historically present, namely, the conversion of labour-power into a commodity. It does not follow that 'merchant's capital is an impossibility', or that 'to account for the conversion of money into capital by circulation alone is impossible'.[115] The form of industrial capital too originates in circulation as a synthesis of merchant and money-lending capital.

(β) The activity of merchant capital presupposes the existence of price-differentials, which imply a segmentation of society's market. Even in a purely

114   Marx 1967, *Capital,* Volume I, p. 163.
115   Marx 1967, *Capital,* Volume I, p. 164.

capitalist society, the market is not always or by definition unified. On the contrary, the smallest changes in the conditions of demand and supply constantly disturb and disrupt the integrity of the market. However, the more developed is the capitalist economy, the stronger are the forces that automatically correct these disturbances and disruptions. It is for this reason that the persistence of chronic price-differentials is a more common feature of the commodity-economy prior to the full development of capitalism. Merchant capital is, therefore, the dominant form of capital in that environment. Yet the activity of merchant capital goes a long way towards uniting hitherto separate markets, as it closes existing price-differentials and extends the scope of the commodity-economy.

This fact explains why the development of commerce contributed often to the erosion of the traditional mode of production from without, and consequently to its decay. Just as commodities originated in inter-community trade, rather than in communal economic life itself, so the origin of capital was external. As soon as the use of money established itself as a more or less general commercial custom, merchant traders travelled far and wide, bringing exotic commodities to isolated places. The contact with alien merchants, in turn, often stimulated the formation of local trading activities, which gradually undermined the foundation of the existing economic order. Capital, being an operation, rather than just a function (for example, of money) or a mode of value expression (for example, of the commodity), has the power to affect real economic life, although by itself it remains an insubstantial form of circulation. In the case of merchant capital, its effect on real economic life was limited to the erosion of the self-sufficiency and independence of isolated economic communities, and to the establishment of a more extensive commodity-economic network. The operation of merchant capital did not lead to a complete subversion of the traditional economic order, since the scope of merchant activity was confined to the sphere of circulation, where it did not strike at the productive root of any economy. Even then, the growth of commerce in Europe from the fourteenth-century spelled the doom of feudal society, the soundness and integrity of which were increasingly hard to maintain. Neither was Japanese feudalism, which attained near perfection under the Tokugawa rule, exempt from frequent reforms to curb the development of commerce.

So long as commerce remains an economic activity external to the prevailing mode of production, however, the unification of a society-wide market is never complete. Hence, merchant capital always finds lucrative opportunities in the sphere of circulation. Only when society's production-process itself becomes radically commodity-economic, with the genesis of capitalism, does the formation of a 'home market' or 'national market' swiftly ensue, wherein price-differentials are progressively eliminated. The once dominant merchant capital, therefore, finds the scope of its activity increasingly restricted, until its hegemony passes finally to industrial capital.

(γ) In capitalist society, merchant capital cannot for long remain the dominant form of chrematistic operation because surplus value cannot be created in circulation. In its motion capital takes, alternately, the form of money, and the form of the commodity. But whether as a money-owner or as a commodity-owner, the capitalist must buy and sell in the market, exactly as any other trader, with no particular advantage or disadvantage. Since no trader earns a surplus value by merely buying and selling commodities at normal prices, there is no reason why the capitalist alone should do so. Within a unified market, the opportunity of trading commodities at prices above or below the normal is, in principle, absent. This does not mean that a trader cannot regularly buy a commodity from another trader, or sell a commodity to another trader, at a price diverging from the normal. But in that case, one trader's gain is the other's loss, so that society as a whole has made no net profit. The mercantilist conception of 'profit upon alienation' thus fails to explain why surplus value accrues to society as a whole.

Since the development of capitalism, accompanied by the increasing perfection and unification of the market, deprives merchant capital of its traditional sphere of action, it cannot continue to play the leading part in the commodity-economy. But its energy is sublimated and makes its presence known in the behaviour of industrial capital. Even an industrial capitalist cannot realise his surplus value except through the sale of his commodity. Thus, if he advances $100 and recovers, after his capital operation, $110 with the profit of $10, he neither knows nor cares whether that $10 has sprung from production as distinct from circulation. He may, in fact, have produced the surplus value worth $9, but in addition, he may luckily have made $1 in the sale of his commodity. Alternatively, he may have produced the surplus value of $11, but for some reason lost $1 in the purchase of his elements of production. Whatever the case, he reckons that he has earned the profit of 10 percent through his judicious capitalist operation. His characteristic unconcern with the real source of profit exposes his genealogy, which may be traced back to his merchant ancestors.

(c)   The Limitation of Merchant Capital

(α) The purpose of the operation, M – C – M′, of merchant capital is to achieve the highest rate of profit in the shortest period of time. Merchant capital does not buy a commodity for its own consumption, but rather for gainful re-sale. Hence, the material use-value of the commodity is relevant only as an instrument of chrematistic. Therefore, if commodity **A** is less efficient as an instrument of the chrematistic than commodity **B**, merchant capital must at once abandon **A** and switch to **B**. Without this freedom of choice, merchant capital cannot be a purely chrematistic operation. Yet precisely this freedom is restricted in the case of merchant capital, which by its very nature is unable to fully overcome the specificity of the use-values that it handles.

Since merchant capital does not produce commodities of its own liking, it can only choose from use-values that are already produced. The merchant always acts as a middleman interposing himself between producers and con-sumers. The scope of his freedom is, consequently, limited to the sphere of circulation, outside of which both producers and consumers remain beyond his control. Thus, for example, even if the merchant wants to sell five gallons of whisky of a particular quality, he may find only four gallons of such whisky produced, or perhaps the merchant can acquire wool fabrics at a bargain price, but consumers may be interested only in cotton fabrics. The merchant, there-fore, has to cajole and threaten – sometimes even cheat and swindle – his cus-tomers in order to promote his own interest. But as the market becomes more established and competitive, even this traditional method of merchant capital begins to find its limit.

The merchant is, of course, not altogether removed from production, inas-much as such para-productive activities as the transportation and storage of goods are often an integral part of mercantile business. But the degree to which such activities can transform already produced use-values is limited. The mer-chant, therefore, endeavours to subordinate producers as much as he can, dic-tating the particular quality and quantity of the use-values that he purchases. If producers are disorganised and unable to bargain fairly with the merchant, they become easy prey to his crude expropriatory practice. But even in the case of the commission-system (or putting-out system), in which the merchant maintained unchallenged pre-eminence, he could not exploit the producers to their ruin without hurting himself. When the producers organised themselves in a capitalist industry, it was the merchant who eventually yielded.

(β) Just as 'the exchange of commodities first begins on the boundaries of [in-dependent] communities, at this point of contact with other similar commu-nities, or with members of the latter',[116] so capital originates in inter-communal trade, namely, in the activity of the merchant who brings products of one com-munity to another for profitable sale. Although the scope of the merchant's activity generally presupposes the separation of producers and consumers, his individual success or failure depends, more immediately, on his personal

---

116   Marx 1967, *Capital,* Volume I, p. 87.

skill, experience and luck. How cheaply the merchant buys a commodity from producers and how dearly he sells it to consumers cannot be determined by any objective standard, as they are dependent on contingent and idiosyncratic factors. Thus, for example, a merchant who is highly successful in the fur trade may be practically incompetent in the selling of spices and perfumes, simply because he does not have the easy way with tropical farmers that he has with northland trappers.

The merchant's inability to easily shift his operation from one class of use-values to another severely limits competition, and contributes to the reactionary and parasitic character of merchant capital. A large firm established in a particular line of trade may develop into a powerful institution with privileges and protection granted by the state. Such an institution is normally difficult to compete with, but may suddenly decline when fortune turns against it. The history of mercantilism illustrates the collusion of established merchant capital with the powers of the absolute monarchy. Since merchant capital fails to overcome the use-value restrictions to its chrematistic operation, it has the tendency to lean on extra-economic powers.

(γ) If competition among merchants is inherently limited, so is the tendency towards the equalisation of profit-rates. Thus, whether the investment of $100 yields the profit of $20 or $5 depends on who makes the investment, the efficiency of the value augmentation of capital being determined by such contingent factors as the individual merchant's speculative skill, luck, personal connections, or exclusive privileges. In that case, A's $100 and B's $100 are qualitatively different as capital. To that extent, merchant capital is not yet an accomplished form of capitalist chrematistic; it is not yet a self-augmenting motion of value, regardless of who operates it, and regardless of which use-value it involves. Until the motion of capital is freed from the specific properties of use-values and becomes fully impersonal, the commodity-economy must fall short of its ideal, which would doubtless entail the complete reification of human relations. It is for this reason that another type of capital, free from these limitations, must now be sought.

B   The Form of Money-Lending Capital (Capital as the Measureless)

(a)   *The Nature of Money-lending Capital*

(α) Merchant capital, to which the general formula for capital, $M - C - M'$, directly applies, has been found incapable of subordinating use-values sufficiently so as to let value augment itself freely. Money-lending capital, by contrast, with its formula, M ...... M', where the dots indicate the total exclusion of commodity exchanges from its operation, represents the chrematistic of capital in its ideal purity, inasmuch as no use-value interferes with the self-growth of value.

The apparent simplicity of money-lending capital poses the question as to why this form of capital has not been treated as the first, that is, as the most rudimentary form of capital. The answer is that money-lending capital is not by itself a viable proposition, in that it must rely on a self-subsistent merchant capital that is already present and in operation. The chrematistic of money-lending capital presupposes commodity exchanges outside of itself; it consists of intercepting part of the merchants' profits, which are being earned in the sphere of commodity exchanges. Money-lending capital can circumvent direct involvement in use-values simply because merchant capital already handles them. Hence, money-lending capital stands apart from merchant capital, and is thus one step away from the frontline of capitalist activities.

The owner of funds, who is not particularly enamoured with the excitement of commerce, may become a moneylender. He may be a retired merchant, or he may have a comparative aptitude for money-lending, rather than for trading merchandise. Perhaps he may be in the practice simply because he is following his family tradition. For whatever reason, there were professional money-lenders in pre-capitalist societies who were not simultaneously merchants. This fact, however, must not obscure the fact that funds, which were temporarily inconvertible into capital, frequently arose in the hands of the merchant himself. In that case, he could practice money lending as a subsidiary capitalist operation. As capitalism develops, however, the class of professional money-lenders (those who always lend their money for an interest and never invest it in the circulation or production of commodities for a profit) tends to disappear, and the lending of funds, temporarily inconvertible into capital, becomes a subsidiary capitalist operation known as finance (later called *loan-capital*), which is practiced by all capitalists, whether industrial or commercial.

(β) Money-lending capital can avoid direct involvement in use-values by standing above or aside from self-subsistent merchant capitals. If, for example, the money-lender makes his funds available to fur traders, his relation to the use-value of fur has already become indirect. The money-lender may, however, make loans to a number of merchants whose trade involves a variety of use-values. In such cases, he is no longer even indirectly related to any specific use-value, but to a class of use-values, no element of which is of particular significance. What matters to the money-lender is not the profitability of trade in a particular use-value, but more generally the profitability of trade as a whole, involving many and varied use-values. Thus, if the fur trade is currently depressed, the silk trade may be prosperous. The money-lender, in that event, simply makes his funds more readily available to silk traders than to fur traders. Since the money-lender is perfectly free to make loans to whoever are the most credit-worthy, he is indifferent to the specific branch of use-value trade that he happens to encourage.

This desirable indifference, however, is obtained at the cost of abandoning the *metamorphosis*, which is an essential property of capital. The money-lender does not part with his capital when he makes a loan. Rather, he relinquishes his funds to the borrower, retaining only the contractual right to a given sum of money on a specified date. The legal document stating his right has, of course, no value, either implicitly or explicitly. Thus, the value of capital does not remain all the while with the money-lender, albeit under different guises. Hence, money-lending capital cannot be said to undergo a metamorphosis of value in its motion; it is the emptiness of its capitalist activity that characterises money-lending capital and which the dots in the formula M ..... M' are meant to represent. The indifference to use-values on the part of money-lending capital also implies its indifference to the way in which the merchant uses the loaned funds. The money-lender may take collateral or charge a risk premium on top of the interest. But once the loan is made, it is up to the borrower to use the loaned funds in whatever manner he sees fit.

Because of the emptiness of this type of capitalist activity, the value augmentation of money-lending capital is purely formal. A given sum of money, M, is converted into the contractual right to a greater sum of money, M', after a specified period of time, by the force of a pre-agreed interest $(1 + r)$. Once the contract is signed, there remains no capitalist activity but the enforcement of the law, by virtue of which M becomes M' or 'money begets more money'. From the point of view of capital, it is as if the augmentation of value were automatic and self-enforcing. This is an ideal form of chrematistics, since capital never needs to question where it in fact pumps the surplus-value from.

(γ) The monetary expression, m = M' − M, of the surplus value that money-lending capital earns is called 'interest' instead of profit. An interest is the price of funds payable at the end of the lending period if funds are regarded as a special commodity. This interest forms a certain percentage of the loaned principal. The price is agreed upon and fixed at the time that funds are transferred from the lender to the borrower, and in principle it cannot be changed later. The merchant receives a loan with the expectation of profiting from his trade in due course. But his contractual obligation to repay the loan with an interest does not disappear, even if he fails to realise the expected profit. The borrower, therefore, is never certain whether he will be, in the end, in a position to pay the interest; the lender, by contrast, sustains no economic uncertainty, since the contractual rate always remains binding.

This does not mean that money-lending is a risk-free operation. It is quite possible that the debtor will turn out to be insolvent, in which case, even with the foreclosing of the defaulter's assets, the lender may lose not only the interest but part of the principal as well. Yet a risk of this kind is 'insurable', that is to say, statistically convertible into the cost of lending, which the lender can charge on top of the interest. The so-called risk premium is normally distributed in such a way that less credit-worthy borrowers pay the greater share of it, and fully qualified borrowers pay hardly any. Quite apart from such conventional details, the risk premium may be theoretically understood to offset the cost of lending arising from bad loans. This kind of insurable risk must be distinguished from the 'uninsurable risk' that the merchant bears in his operation. The merchant gambles on an expected profit, which cannot be statistically estimated in advance, since his success or failure depends on chance, just as much as on his shrewdness or skill.

The merchant's profit is, therefore, properly due to his genuine risk taking, from which the money-lender is exempt. For this reason, the money-lender does not earn a profit, but only interest. In order to earn interest, one need not have capitalist acumen; one only need possess loanable money. Money-lending capital is, therefore, a formally ideal method of chrematistic, in which 'money bears fruit' of its own accord, compounding itself with an interest. Money-lending capital is not concerned with the ups and downs of trade in any specific use-value, nor with the individual skills or luck of a particular trader.

(b)   The Activity of Money-lending Capital

(α) Money-lending capital, as already mentioned, stands apart from commodity exchanges, and reigns over self-subsistent merchant capitals. It can, therefore, regulate the activity of the merchants from without, imposing upon them some order and discipline. A merchant who borrows money has to return it with interest, and so cannot as freely gamble on borrowed money as he would on his own. Unless his business was already sound, he could not have obtained a loan for a reasonable rate of interest in the first place. If he obtains a loan, his expected profit must be large enough, relative to the contractual payment of the interest, in order to justify an investment. Even if the contemplated investment is promising enough, the high degree of risk involved may subdue his

166   CHAPTER 3

'animal spirit'. The activity of merchant capital, consequently, becomes more disciplined and less prone to reckless gambling.

At the same time, the presence of money-lending capital can contribute, to some extent, to the rational allocation of funds to various branches of trade. Since money-lending capital is not tied to any specific use-value, it can make more funds available on easier terms to the branch of trade, which is relatively more profitable. Thus, if the silk trade is more profitable than the fur trade, merchants themselves may be slow to shift their capital from fur to silk. But money-lenders do not hesitate to quickly patronise silk traders at the expense of fur traders. In this way, more funds are automatically channelled into the growing sector of the commodity-economy. To the extent that it is not directly restricted by a specific use-value, in other words, money-lending capital can be more capitalistically rational than merchant capital.

(β) This rationality comes from the fact that money-lending capital makes loans to anyone who is credit-worthy, regardless of what he does. However, the credit-worthiness of the borrower does not depend so much on his 'expected' ability to make a large profit in the present venture, as on his past record and his possession of valuable assets. Since the money-lender is indifferent to how the loaned funds are actually used, he is quite prepared to lend to the pure consumer as well, especially if the latter is a landlord, king or church in possession of considerable wealth. In pre-capitalist society, the chief customer of money-lending capital was, indeed, such a pure consumer, whose rental or tax revenue depended fundamentally on agricultural productivity. In such a case, money-lending capital, even more so than merchant capital, could exert a destructive effect on traditional society and its mode of production.

For instance, a lord may have to borrow money in view of a famine, or a king to supplement the expenses of a war. Unless the famine is followed within a few years by a bumper crop, or the war by a resounding victory, there is little assurance that the borrower will find easy means to repay the loan, let alone the accumulated interest. Money-lending capital – or usurer capital, as it may better be called in this context – then turns into a relentless dispossessor of the debtor in plight. In order to avoid the threat to his property, the lord will be obliged to raise the rent, and the king to impose heavier taxes, which cannot but strain an already impoverished agriculture even more. The stability of the feudal mode of production can thus be easily shaken when money-lending capital begins to suck its blood. No wonder the medieval church condemned usury as the worst form of injustice.

(γ) With the development of capitalism, however, the classical form of money-lending capital tends to disappear, because merchant capital loses its profitable sphere of action, as price-differentials close with the unification of the market. The once dreaded usurers disappear, or become mere pawnbrokers, who vegetate in the restricted sphere of popular finance beyond the reach of ordinary banks. Yet money-lending as such does not disappear even in capitalist society. If merchant capitalists lose their profits upon alienation, industrial and commercial capitalists now earn average profits from which an interest can be paid. The need for capitalist finance merely converts the traditional form of money-lending capital into the modern form of *loan-capital*. Only professional money-lenders will decline, that is to say, the species of half-capitalists who always lend their money for an interest, but who never invest it for an average profit.

In a purely capitalist society, Marx's so-called 'money-capitalists',[117] who are presumably 'modernised' money-lending capitalists, cannot survive except in the restricted sphere of popular finance, which in any case is irrelevant to theory. The reason for this fact is that idle money, inconvertible into capital, cannot arise except temporarily in a purely capitalist society. Only the capitalists – whose profession is to convert as much idle money as possible into capital in order to earn an average profit – can possess idle money, which may be temporarily incapable of conversion into capital. For example, depreciation funds must be accumulated for some time in the form of money before they can be reinvested in fixed capital. Funds of all sorts, which must wait for a longer or shorter period of time before they can be converted into capital, arise as normal attendants of the circulation-process of capital (see Chapter 5). It is such funds, temporarily forced to remain idle, that are loaned through the money market to other capitalists, who are capable of using them as additional capital. Thus, money-lending is conducted by industrial or commercial capitalists whose main purpose is to earn an average profit. Since no capitalist is content to earn only an interest when he can also earn an average profit, a professional money-capitalist cannot exist in a purely capitalist society (see Chapter 9 for more detail).

The form of money-lending capital is thus absorbed by the subsidiary operation of loan-capital by industrial and commercial capitalists. The disappearance of the professional money-lender, however, does not in the least abate the desire of capital to aim for the formal ideal of money-lending capital, namely, to achieve the self-growth of value by transcending any involvement with use-values. As will be discussed later in full detail, capital eventually accomplishes this ideal in the form of *interest-bearing capital*, the highest and the most fetishistic form of capital.

---

117   Marx 1967, *Capital,* Volume III, pp. 370ff.

(c)   *The Limitation of Money-lending Capital*

(α) Money-lending capital realises the ideal form of the self-growth of value by standing apart from not only the production but also the circulation of commodities, that is, by presupposing the real cause of its chrematistic outside of its motion. Yet in doing so, it fails to constitute the metamorphosis of value, which the general formula for capital requires. Therefore, it does not qualify as a genuine form of capital. It is a capitalistically empty operation of self-enrichment, external and parasitic to the commodity-economy. For this reason, the monetary form of surplus value accruing to money-lending capital is not profit, but interest alone. The latter, instead of resulting from the uncertainty of capitalist activity, consists of a contractually fixed claim to money, ensured by the rigour and certitude of the law.

The rate of interest may be regarded as the 'price' of funds made available for a definite period of time, but even if the money market is well developed, this particular price has no normal level, as it is determined, quite arbitrarily, by the temporary forces of demand and supply. Any capitalistically produced commodity has a normal price, since its supply can be adjusted to the demand for it, as the trade in it recurs a great number of times. Funds, on the other hand, are not capitalistically producible commodities, and their supply cannot be increased or decreased to conform to the demand for them. Nor is the demand for funds stable over time. Consequently, the market rate of interest reflects nothing more than shifting equality of the demand for and the supply of funds, having no tendency necessarily to settle to any *normal* level, as more and more funds are bought and sold over many market periods. Having no physical use-value or commodity value, funds are a 'pseudo-commodity' unable to form a normal price. For this reason, if funds are absolutely short relative to the demand for them at any moment, the rate of interest can rise without restraint, readily surpassing the rate of profit. However, if the rate of interest is higher than the rate of profit, no further investment of capital is possible; if value can no longer augment itself in the form of capital, the commodity-economy reaches its absolute limit.

Thus, even in a fully developed money market, loan-capital can charge a rate of interest that may arrest and prohibit further capitalist activity. If the money market is not developed, as in pre-capitalist societies, the determination of the rate of interest is still more arbitrary. Here, the extent to which the money-lender intercepts the merchant's profit depends on the balance of the one's greed and the other's ability to circumvent it.

(β) If it were capable of self-restraint, money-lending capital could make a positive contribution to the commodity-economy, by imposing order and

discipline on the activity of merchant capital, and by promoting a more rational allocation of funds. However, precisely because of the emptiness of its
form of chrematistic, which is due to its circumvention of use-values, money-
lending capital possesses no internal check on its predatory and expropriatory
nature. It can exceed its measure and become 'measureless', to use the Hegelian locution, or to put it more colloquially, money-lending capital is by nature
a 'loan shark'. Thus, not only did it tend to thwart the healthy development
of pre-capitalist societies, as pointed out earlier, but it could also become a
dangerous parasite, which would even feed on the commodity-economy itself. Money-lending capital is 'irrational' to the extent that it paralyses rather
than assists the normal functioning of commodity exchanges, for by forcing
a standstill of the commodity-economy, and by rendering merchandise trade
unprofitable, money-lending capital can deprive itself of the basis of its own
existence.

This irrationality of money-lending capital is preserved even in capitalist
society by loan-capital (to be discussed later in Chapter 9), since even there the
rate of interest rises in most cases when the rate of profit falls. As will be seen
later (Chapter 7), it is the technological constraint on the accumulation of capital that is increasingly reflected by the 'falling rate of profit'. Yet being a subsidiary capitalist operation essentially independent of use-values, loan-capital, in
such a circumstance, cannot offer any fundamental solution to the problem,
nor even forewarn of the impending crisis. Instead, it precipitates the excess of
capital by accelerating the so-called widening-process, namely, the extensive
accumulation of capital at a constant organic composition, without involving
technical progress (Chapter 9).

(γ) The only economic activity reserved to money-lending capital is the selling of funds for interest. But the interest, $M' - M = m$, does not as yet exist at
the moment of sale. Hence, the legal process of collecting the interest does
not always parallel the economic process of generating what is to be paid as
the interest. If a divergence between the two processes arises, it is the extra-
economic force of the law that must prevail over the self-functioning of the
commodity-economy. The exchange of commodities already presupposes
some *law and order*, in general terms, including the prevention of fraud and violence, the minting of coins, and so on, it is true. But these measures are there
merely to ensure that the commodity-economy should work smoothly, according to its own internal rules. For example, it may be a punishable offence to
sell a commodity at gunpoint, or to purchase a commodity with counterfeit
money, simply because such activities would obstruct the smooth unfolding
of commodity-economic principles. However, to declare a large number of
borrowers insolvent and to foreclose their property, in the name of the law,

because the commodity-economy did not work as had been foreseen would be quite a different story. In that case, the commodity-economy has already developed in a particular way when the law insists that it should have developed in another way. The enforcement of the law then interferes with the working of the commodity-economy, rather than assisting it.

To the extent that money-lending capital requires an enforcement of the law against the internal working of the commodity-economy, this form of capital introduces an *extra-economic coercion*, alien to the logic of the commodity-economy. By sidestepping all use-values, and by thus realising an ideal form for the self-augmentation of value, the operation of money-lending capital ironically reverts to an extra-economic compulsion that is entirely alien to the concept of value, which objectifies social relations as impersonal commodity relations. The failure of money-lending capital, however, suggests how the form of capital must in fact develop in order to truly subordinate the restrictions of use-values. The form of capital must stay in the sphere of circulation where it originates. It must not merely exclude or circumvent use-values, but must internalise and absorb them. Only when the motion of capital can settle the contradiction between value and use-value within itself does it become truly free. Industrial capital is the form that is expected to accomplish this feat.

C   The Form of Industrial Capital (Capital as Absolute Indifference)

(a)   The Nature of Industrial Capital

(α) Use-values must not be merely circumvented, but rather must be contained and neutralised within the form of capital, which arises in the sphere of circulation and abides by the principle of metamorphosis. From this requirement follows *industrial capital*, with the formula $M - C \ldots P \ldots C' - M'$ (where $C \ldots P \ldots C'$ indicates an interruption of circulation by the production-process of capital). The production-process does interrupt the circulation of capital but does not lie outside of capital; the production-process is subsumed under the circulatory motion of capital, as an integral part of its value augmentation. It is in the form of industrial capital that the process of value augmentation finally sets itself free from the restrictions of specific use-values. In this case, the commodity, C', is not a use-value already produced by non-capitalist means and subsequently found by capital in the market as incapable of further transformation. It is a use-value that capital itself transforms, as it likes, provided that the socially available technology permits that transformation. If capital can produce *any* use-value that best fits its chrematistic, it is no longer constrained by a particular use-value, but only by use-values in general. Capital, therefore, achieves *absolute indifference* to the specificity of the use-value that it sells; it can sell any commodity, C', that will yield to it the greatest surplus value. Its *elements of production* represented by C in the above formula, in contrast, are as restrictive as the commodities that merchant capital trades. Many of these elements of production are, in fact, produced as commodities by capital when industrial capital takes over society's process of production. But there is one commodity that must belong to C, although it is not a product of capital. That is, labour-power. Moreover, industrial capital cannot in any case purchase an element of production as a commodity, unless it is already made available so in the market. It must, therefore, be understood that labour-power is already made available as a commodity in the market.

Both C and C' are commodities in which value is immanent. If they both tend to be bought and sold at normal prices, they must not be different only as use-values, but in terms of the magnitude of value as well. In other words, C' must contain more value than C for industrial capital to augment value. Surplus value must be produced in the production-process of capital, C ... P ... C'. This fact requires that C should contain a commodity, which forms and augments value rather than merely preserving it within the production-process of capital. Labour-power is such a commodity.

Thus, so far as industrial capital is concerned, it must demonstrate its skill not simply in buying and selling ready-made commodities at the most advantageous terms; rather, it must do so by selecting the commodity that promises to yield the maximum return, and producing it from the necessary elements of production, including labour-power, which it has purchased at normal prices. It still abides by the basic principle of 'buying cheap and selling dear'. But it involves a little extra effort in buying suitable productive elements with which to produce a commodity, which in light of its resources it can sell most advantageously in the market.

(β) In order for C ... P ... C' to represent the production-process of capital, that is to say, in order for C' to be a capitalistically produced commodity, it is mandatory that labour-power, L_p, be purchased as a commodity in C. Hence, the production-process of capital may be more explicitly shown by:

$$C \begin{cases} L_p \\ \\ P_m \end{cases} \text{...} \quad P \quad \text{...} \quad C'$$

Here, P_m stands for the means of production, that is, commodities other than labour-power, L_p, purchased by industrial capital. If, for example, a small commodity producer purchases only the means of production, P_m, as commodities in order to produce his commodity, C′, with his own labour-power, or with the labour-power of others appropriated by a method other than commodity-economic, his production-process is in no sense that of industrial capital, even if C′ is sold for a higher price than that for which C is bought. That sort of production-process depends on a factor exogenous to the commodity-economy, namely, non-commoditised labour-power, which restricts the production of a commodity from the outside.

Such a restriction is far more serious than any use-value restriction so far encountered. The latter kind of restriction hinders the activity of capital, but not the conversion of funds into capital. For example, if A's advance of $100 for a year earns him the profit of $10, while B's identical advance earns him the profit of only $5, then this difference remains only for so long as B is unable to trade the same use-value under the same condition as A does. In contrast, if A and B produce the same use-value with the same technique, but if A – who can count on his son's labour-power in addition to his own – invests $100 in the means of production, while B – whose son is sick – can only invest $50 in the same, B's production is handicapped by a factor altogether alien to the commodity-economy. If the production-process of capital depended on such a contingency, industrial capital could not be said to be a more adequate form of value augmentation than the forms of merchant capital or of money-lending capital. The popular confusion that even a small commodity producer invests his means of production as 'capital' and capitalistically produces his commodity must be laid aside, once and for all, for otherwise the significance of the form of industrial capital would never be truly understood.

Labour-power, which industrial capital must purchase as a component of C, is expected to liberate the chrematistic of capital from entanglement with a particular use-value. This requires that within the scope of the socially available technology, labour-power must be able to produce any use-value that capital wishes. For example, if the capitalist wants to produce brandy, but the labour-power he has purchased in the market can only produce whisky, the chrematistic of industrial capital would be as constrained by the use-value of whisky as that of merchant capital. In that case, the development of the forms of industrial capital, as a more advanced step beyond the form of merchant capital, would be meaningless. Of course, no labour-power can produce that which is technically impossible to produce (for example, an aeroplane before such a product is invented). But society's demand in that case may be safely neglected, because a normal price for it could not be established in any case, which, of course, would disqualify it as a *genuine* commodity.

(γ) The form of industrial capital contains as an intermediate phase the production-process, C ... P ... C′, within the circulation of capital, M – C · C′ – M′.
The production-process of capital does not lie outside the sphere of circulation, but is enveloped in it. In this manner, industrial capital can subsume the
entire production-process of a society, converting the latter into a *capitalist*
society in which all use-values are capitalistically produced as commodities by
means of commodities alone. Capitalism can form a historically viable society
because the form of industrial capital, unlike the other forms of capital so far
mentioned, can directly govern the social production-process. For the same
reason, the activity of industrial capital need not and cannot be studied in its
historical form in pre-capitalist societies because the activity of industrial capital *ipso facto* forms capitalist society.

It is true that the activities of both merchant and money-lending capital
worked against the traditional mode of production. Indeed, they powerfully
contributed towards the disintegration and decay of feudal societies over centuries, prior to the birth of capitalism. However, in the end, these two forms of
capital did not by themselves radically alter the existing mode of production,
nor did they by themselves usher in capitalism. Operating exclusively outside
the sphere of production, these two forms of capital never struck at the root of
traditional societies. However, when industrial capital commenced its action,
an altogether different situation had to evolve because this form of capital did
not spare the productive base of society. Industrial capital was, of course, not
the dominant form of capital from the beginning. But as it penetrated deeper
into society's production-process, reorganising it into the value-formation-
and-augmentation process of capital, industrial capital established itself as the
governing mode of capitalist society.

While, in the rest of the dialectic of capital, the activity of industrial capital
will be studied in all its theoretical detail, here, the nature of its *form* prior
to its action must be investigated. Quite apart from what it does, industrial
capital, which subsumes the process of production as an intermediate phase
of its circulation, so as to overcome the restrictions of specific use-values,
formally accomplishes the perfect mode of capital, or what corresponds to
Hegel's 'true infinite of measure'. From the point of view of simple circulation
or commodity-exchanges, the social quality of value immanent in a commodity cannot be more liberated than in the form of industrial capital. For in this
form alone, value can grow freely in its never-ending, self-propelled motion,
without being derailed by any *particular* use-value. The operating principle
of capitalism is already fully exposed by the form of industrial capital, which
within the sphere of simple circulation cannot pass over to a more synthetic
form. However, the conversion of labour-power into a commodity, which constitutes the necessary and sufficient condition for the form of industrial capital

to launch its real action, cannot be logically deduced from the development of a commodity-economy.

(b)   Labour-power as a Commodity

(α) Without the conversion of labour-power into a commodity, industrial capital cannot in practice begin its operation. Yet labour-power is not inherently a commodity because it is not a product of capital. No capitalist can sell labour-power, which never belongs to C′, whereas all industrial capitalists must purchase labour-power as a commodity, since it always forms a part of C. Even as a commodity, labour-power is inseparable from the person of the worker, and cannot be reproduced except in his individual consumption-process. In the production-process of capital, labour-power does not retain its value because the capitalist cannot resell it as a commodity; it can only be consumed as productive labour, which is its use-value as it is realised in the production-process. The conversion of labour-power into a commodity is, indeed, a historical institution peculiar to the capitalist mode of production. It is, therefore, necessary here to specify this special commodity labour-power a little more explicitly.

Marx gives the following definition:

> By labour-power or capacity for labour is to be understood the aggregate of those mental and physical capabilities existing in a human being which he exercises whenever he produces a use-value of any description.[118]

'The aggregate of those mental and physical capabilities' in the possession of a human being, and expendable as productive labour for the production of a use-value, however, need not always be so expended. It can also be exercised as unproductive labour, or can even be dissipated in recreation or loafing. In order for labour-power to be converted into a commodity, the aggregate of those productive capabilities, both mental and physical, must be alienated from the human being who possesses it. A very special social condition is required to accomplish this formal separation of the work-capacity from its *natural owner*. That social condition is met with the emergence in the market of the free worker, that is to say, the one 'free in the double sense, that as a free man he can dispose of his labour-power as his own commodity, and that on the other

---

118   Marx 1967, *Capital,* Volume I, p. 167.

hand he has no other commodity for sale, is short of everything necessary for the realisation of his labour-power'.[119]

In order for the worker to be *free* in the disposition of his labour-power as a commodity, he must, of course, be a free person, untrammelled by the feudal or any other master-servant relation. Otherwise his appearance in the market as the seller of his labour-power may be legally forbidden or restricted. When he sells his labour-power as a commodity, moreover, the worker must not sell it 'rump and stump, once for all', but only 'for a definite period of time',[120] for otherwise he would be converting himself from a free man into a slave. In order for the worker to be *free* from the possession of any other commodity but labour-power, he should be deprived of the means of production with which to produce a commodity for sale, and the means of subsistence to sustain his life until he finishes his production. Indeed, if he has these means sufficient for the production of a commodity, from the sale of which he may earn his livelihood, he has the choice of not selling his labour-power as a commodity.

By 'subsistence' is here meant the minimum of the means of livelihood, which when consumed enables the worker to adequately reproduce his labour-power. This subsistence cannot be biologically ascertained or medically prescribed. Indeed, as Marx writes:

> If the owner of labour-power works today, tomorrow he must again be able to repeat the same process in the same conditions as regards health and strength. His means of subsistence must therefore be sufficient to maintain him in his normal state as a labouring individual. His natural wants, such as food, clothing, fuel, and housing, vary according to the climatic and other physical conditions of his country. On the other hand, the number and extent of his so-called necessary wants, as also the modes of satisfying them, are themselves the product of historical development, and depend therefore to a great extent on the degree of civilisation of a country, more particularly on the conditions under which, and consequently on the habits and degree of comfort in which the class of free labourers has been formed.[121]

The determination of the subsistence of the worker, therefore, is not free from 'a historical and moral element'.[122] However, in any given social context, it is

119 Marx 1967, *Capital,* Volume I, p. 169.
120 Marx 1967, *Capital,* Volume I, p. 168.
121 Marx 1967, *Capital,* Volume I, p. 171.
122 Ibid.

always 'practically known' as a datum.[123] Since, however, labour-power does not survive its mortal owner, his subsistence must include enough means of livelihood for the worker to raise and educate his children, who will take his place when he retires from active working life. In other words, the subsistence standard of living of the worker must be such as to perpetuate the normal family life of the working class, for it is in family life that labour-power is reproduced, not only from day to day, but also from one generation to another. The maintenance of such a family life does not exclude a natural growth of the working population.

It is the value of the means of subsistence, so defined, that is equal to the value of labour-power. Indeed, when the free worker prices his labour-power by way of its value expression, the normal price of his labour-power tends to settle to the *normal price of his means of subsistence*. For if the normal price of labour-power exceeds that of his means of subsistence today, the worker can buy more means of livelihood than is sufficient to reproduce his labour-power, and so may fail to market his labour-power tomorrow. If its normal price falls short of the normal price for his means of subsistence, the worker will be unable to supply his labour-power tomorrow *in the same health and strength*. Hence, society's existing labour-power can at least be maintained if and only if the normal price of labour-power is equal to that of the worker's means of subsistence.[124] Since labour-power is not a capitalistically produced commodity, it does not possess a value other than that which is imputed by the value of the worker's means of subsistence.

(β) As already emphatically mentioned, the advent of the working class, 'free in the double sense', does not follow logically in the doctrine of simple circulation. Nor does history demonstrate that capitalist society automatically evolved as soon as the commodity-economy reached a state of considerable sophistication. It was surely not the development of simple commodity production that gradually introduced capitalism. Nor was it simply the contradiction between the rising productive powers and the constrictions of feudal production-relations (which disintegrated under the deleterious influence of commerce) that provided the material conditions for the emergence of capitalist production-relations.[125] The historical fact that only in sixteenth-century England did the so-called enclosure movement occur, for the first time, setting off the 'primitive accumulation' that eventually led to *the conversion of*

---

123   Ibid.; Marx 1977, p. 275.
124   See Chapter 4, Section B, for more detail.
125   Marx 1970, *Contribution*, p. 21.

labour-power into a commodity, cannot be simply explained by commodity-economic logic, let alone by an axiom of historical materialism.

The dialectic of capital cannot and does not explain the historical cause of the primitive accumulation, which was necessary for the formation of capitalist society. Primitive accumulation can only be presupposed as the 'mute recollection of the past' on the part of a purely capitalist society, which as a theoretical construct has no beginning or end. Marx, who wrote eight vivid chapters on primitive accumulation, treated them as an appendix to the first volume of *Capital*, rather than integrating them into the logical structure of his theory of capitalism. That was the case, even though he stressed the fact that 'Nature does not produce on the one side owners of money or commodities, and on the other men possessing nothing but their own labour-power'.[126] This procedure confirms the dependability of Marx's method. From the point of view of history, the importance of primitive accumulation can hardly be doubted, but the dialectic of capital does not explain capitalism in its historical context, that is, 'in its birth, development, and decline'. The dialectic of capital, which exposes the inner logic of capitalism, cannot show how primitive accumulation came to pass.

(γ) If the cause of the primitive accumulation cannot be explained by theory, its effect and significance, which the theory of a purely capitalist society always presupposes, must be thoroughly grasped. It is vitally important, in other words, to know what this primitive accumulation accomplished, regardless of why and how it in fact occurred. Primitive accumulation essentially means the release of the direct producers from the land. In traditional societies, the direct producers were tied to land as peasants and were subject, in one form or another, to the master-servant relation based on pre-capitalist landownership. When peasants were evicted from the land, whether by the enclosure movement or otherwise, and were denied access to the natural means of production represented by land, they found themselves not only free from feudal bondage, but also free from the means of production and livelihood, and were left with nothing else to sell but their own labour-power. Since primitive accumulation did not occur overnight, and was not locally restricted either, a variety of different methods must have been employed to turn the peasants into propertyless wage-workers. Nevertheless, the formation of the worker 'free in the double sense' could not have been accomplished without his expulsion from the land upon which his previous life depended.

---

126   Marx 1967, *Capital,* Volume I, p. 169.

Only when the worker is detached from land can capital purchase his labour-power as a commodity and appropriate the productivity of his labour. At the same time, the traditional landowner, whose land is now practically empty of peasants, cannot by himself exploit the natural means of production that he possesses (particularly after the halcyon days of sheep grazing). He is, therefore, obliged to rent his land to capital for productive exploitation. In this way, capital obtains ready access to both labour-power and land, the two original sources of productivity. Since capital can, by itself, produce all intermediate products once the original elements of production are at its disposal, there remains nothing that limits the productive activity of capital. The mercantile wealth that has been accumulated in the sphere of circulation can now be poured into the sphere of production, establishing the unchallenged supremacy of industrial capital.

So far as the relation between capital and landed property is concerned, the above schema needs some modifications, since capital's access to land by a rental contract, rather than by the purchase of a commodity, is never free. Up to this point, however, the dialectic of capital has not developed its peculiarly capitalist method of dealing with the renting of land.[127] Hence, the relation between capital and landed property must be left implicit in the following analysis. That is to say, it must be presupposed that capital somehow obtains free access to land of uniform quality, pending the exposure of the specifications governing the relationship between capital and landed property at the appropriate juncture. With this pre-supposition (*voraus-setzung*), capital is now seen to be the omnipotent producer of all use-values as commodities by means of commodities. Society's production-process is, therefore, placed under the unrestricted governance of capital.

(c)   *The Transition to the Doctrine of Production*

(α) The form of industrial capital, which contains the phase of production, C ... P ... C', between the circulation phases M – C and C' – M' is no longer strictly a form of circulation, because the production-process interrupts the circulation of capital, as the dots in the formula indicate. This interruption is necessary because of the nature of labour-power as a commodity, for if capital purchased a horse, this interruption would not occur. The horse, as a capitalistically produced commodity, has a value of its own, even though the 'horse-power' (which cannot be traded separately from the horse itself) does not. As the horse is consumed productively in the production-process of capital, a new product will emerge. The value of the horse, however, is preserved

---

127   This will be treated fully in Chapter 8.

in this production-process, partly in the form of the 'depreciated' horse, and partly in the form of the new product, which emerges in consequence of the consumption of the horse. Since the capitalist is free to sell either the depreciated horse or the new product as a commodity (as an embodiment of value), or both as commodities, whenever he chooses to do so, it is impossible for the original value of the horse to disappear at any moment, unless either the horse dies or the new product turns out to be socially useless. When the horse is completely depreciated, its value is entirely transferred to the new product.

It is, however, impossible for any production (that is, the conversion of a use-value into another) to take place without the intervention of human productive labour. Let us, therefore, substitute a slave for the horse in the same example. In that case, however, the slave is not a product of capital and, hence, has no value. It is, therefore, purely a fiction to suppose, for the sake of argument, that the value of the slave is somehow considered equal to the value of his labour-power. In this case, the transformation of C into C' in possession of a higher price may be thought possible, without interrupting the circulation of capital, as M – C – C' – M, since throughout the production-process the slave (or slave-power) would remain just as saleable as any other means of production and the new product. A slave-owning capitalist would, however, be a contradiction in terms, since a slave-owner can appropriate surplus labour only by means of extra-economic coercion, while a capitalist produces surplus value without having to resort to it.

The labour-power of a free worker is a commodity, which the purchaser-capitalist may consume only during a given period of time. If the capitalist fails to use it during this time, labour-power vanishes without producing a use-value; yet the capitalist who has bought more labour-power than he can use within a contractual period, cannot sell the redundant labour-power as a commodity, since its natural owner, the worker, who alone can do so, has already sold it to the capitalist. This means that, in the production-process of capital, the capitalist does not retain the value of labour-power, which he pays to the worker in return for the use-value of the latter's labour-power, in much the same way as the money-lender hands over funds to his borrower. Instead of an IOU, however, the industrial capitalist retains the use-value of, or more specifically the right to use, the labour-power he has purchased for a specified period. During this period, the capitalist must consume the labour-power 'productively', that is to say, for the production of a use-value, so that the value of the new product, finished at the end of the period, C', should possess more than the value of the labour-power and the means of production advanced as capital, and consumed productively during the same period, C. In other words, labour-power must form a value greater than its own in the production-process of capital in which it is consumed.

(β) For industrial capital, the use-value of labour-power is productive labour that transforms the means of production, P_m, into a new commodity, C'. This commodity, C', must, however, be *any* use-value that the capitalist may choose to designate, and the worker for his part must be *indifferent* to the way in which his labour-power is used. Although the worker himself exerts labour, *he is not the consumer of his labour-power*, which has already been sold to the capitalist. The worker is, therefore, incapable of exercising his labour-power without obeying the capitalist's specific *instructions*. If the capitalist fails to give necessary instructions, the worker is quite free to waste his time on recreation, loafing or on irrelevant labour. On the other hand, the worker is in no position to refuse the capitalist's instructions pertaining to the use of his labour-power, provided, of course, that they are free from extra-economic coercion.

In the production-process of capital, labour-power must be able to produce *any* commodity in just the same way as money can buy *any* commodity in the sphere of circulation. Money externally represents value in the circulation-sphere because its use-value no longer lies in the sensuous quality of gold, or any other money-materials, but in the general purchasing-power of all commodities. Similarly, labour-power forms value in the production-process of capital because its use is not restricted to the production of a given use-value as a commodity, but is adaptable to the production of all commodities. Labour-power is, therefore, a unique commodity capable of forming the social quality of value that inheres in any commodity. The statement that *labour-power does not preserve its value in the production-process of capital* reflects the fact that *it may produce no value at all, if the capitalist fails to give its natural owner proper instructions as to how to use it*. Yet if his instructions are appropriate, labour-power must be able to produce more value than it itself possesses, or else capital, which is solely interested in the augmentation of value, would not have purchased this labour-power.

When labour-power satisfies this requirement, industrial capital can buy and sell all commodities at normal prices, and still earn the surplus value that is created in the production-process of capital. Like merchant capital, industrial capital too does not hesitate to buy cheap and sell dear, if there is a chance to do so. However, even when the market approaches perfection, and allows little room for profits upon alienation, industrial capital can still draw surplus value *from within* its production-process. It is for this reason that the activity of industrial capital, once set into motion, sinks more and more deeply into the production-process of society, until the whole of it is reorganised capitalistically.

(γ) When capital produces a use-value, it is intrinsically a commodity, that is to say, it is destined to be sold as a commodity. Since the production-process of capital is essentially a value-formation-and-augmentation process, and is only secondarily the process of producing a use-value, no use-value can be produced by capital without at the same time forming the social quality of value in that commodity. The inseparability of the production of both value and a specific use-value makes the capitalistically produced commodity an intrinsic one. A use-value produced by a non-capitalist, say, by a simple commodity producer, is not an intrinsic commodity. It is a commodity *by chance* depending on the free choice of the producer. A small producer may, or may not, intend to produce a commodity because his production-process is essentially that of a use-value, not of value. Whether or not his production-process is also a value-formation process depends on contingent factors outside of the production-process, such as the decision or intention of the small producer to sell his output in the market, rather than disposing of it otherwise. For example, a small producer, who originally meant to produce a commodity for the market, can change his mind later and convert his product into a gift. The production-process of capital is not similarly free. Indeed, no use-value can be produced by capital, except as a by-product of its value-formation-and-augmentation process, because capitalist production consumes labour-power, which is indifferent to all use-values. Labour-power, consumed in simple commodity production, is never so general; it is restricted in the scope of its useful application.

The production-process of capital, which is primarily a value-formation-and-augmentation process, is radically commodity-economic. It automatically ousts all exogenous factors that interfere with the economic nature of production. Thus, unlike the traditional mode of production, in which the material substructure of society appears more or less blended with its ideological superstructure, capitalist production exhibits the productive organisation of society in its pure form, that is, as a set of production-relations unencumbered with extra-economic interventions.

It is precisely for this reason that the labour-and-production process common to all societies that forms the material base of their existence is most clearly identifiable as the social substance, or as the *unchanging substratum*, of the production-process of capital. Although no society can ever exist without the labour-and-production process, the latter cannot be visualised as a systematic whole by merely comparing different types of society, and by arbitrarily piecing together those aspects that appear to be common to all of them. Not only in theory, but also in reality, the labour-and-production process must evolve, divested of irrelevant contortions and deformities, as the underlying substance of the production-process of capital. Just as *absolute indifference* finally reveals 'the permanent' in Hegel's *Logic,* so the *operation of industrial capital* reveals the labour-and-production process in the dialectic of capital.

PART 2

The Doctrine of Production (The Essence of Capital)

∴

Introductory Remarks

The doctrine of circulation, it will be recalled, opened with the proposition that the value of a commodity is always tied to a specific use-value. It was shown that in order to release the socially uniform quality of value from the materially heterogeneous use-value, the form of the commodity must 'pass over' to the form of money, and that the latter must further pass over to the form of capital. Only industrial capital, which in principle can produce any desired use-value, was then shown to be capable of attaining the required freedom for the motion of value, a form of value augmentation absolutely indifferent to the specificity of use-values. In the doctrine of circulation, therefore, one form of circulation passed over to another, as each one in turn attempted to suppress the restriction of particular use-values. By contrast, industrial capital, as a circulation-form, is free to deal with *any* use-value of its choice, because of its presumed capacity to produce all use-values *with indifference*; its value augmentation, therefore, is dependent only on 'use-value production in general', and not on the production of specific use-values. The circulation of commodities that is recurrent and ongoing, rather than intermittent and sporadic, must indeed presuppose a continuing production of all use-values as commodities. This fact, however, can only be sensed in the sphere of circulation, in which commodities are exchanged for one another, without questioning their origin. Only with the emergence of industrial capital – the form of *absolute indifference* to the circulation of specific use-values – does the *process of production in general* become a real issue. For it is this fundamental fact that unleashes the action of industrial capital. The doctrine of production, accordingly, begins with the production of use-values in general, or what is to be called the *labour-and-production process*, which forms the underlying substance of the production-process of capital.

From the viewpoint of the commodity-economy, the labour-and-production process *common to all societies* is an 'other' (to use the Hegelian expression) to begin with. Yet it is not an 'other' to which the commodity-economy can simply 'pass over', sublating itself. The sphere of circulation cannot generate a form more synthetic than industrial capital, which if it 'became' or 'passed over to' the supra-historic labour-and-production process would summarily destroy itself, without preserving its historically peculiar commodity-economic principle of operation. The contradiction between value (capital as the form of value augmentation) and use-value (the production of use-values in general) can no longer be circumvented by the *dialectic of transition or becoming*. For the contradiction that now arises is not between socially uniform value and materially specific use-values, but rather between the *historic form of value augmentation* and the *supra-historic process of use-value production* as such. In this case, the contradiction cannot be overcome by suppressing particular use-values in order to release value, but by letting the form of value wholly *absorb and internalise* the production of use-values itself. It is the dialectic of *reflection or grounding* (rather than of transition or becoming) that one must now count upon.

Reflection consists of specifying a concept not by an 'other' that lies outside of it, but by an 'other' that is posited inside of itself. In other words, a reflected concept is dual, consisting of a positive and a negative side, such that the concept explains itself only when the mutual relation between the two sides is adequately specified. For example, productive labour is said to be at one and the same time 'concrete-useful' and 'abstract-human', just as the commodity is at once a use-value and value. In the case of the commodity, the coexistence of value with a use-value immediately led to the suppression of the original use-value in the synthetic concept of exchange-value, in which value expresses itself in the use-value of *another* commodity. In the case of productive labour, however, its abstract-human aspect does not attempt to suppress its concrete-useful aspect by any means. Abstract-human labour cannot be released, or become free, from concrete-useful labour by becoming something else; productive labour is abstract-human only because it is also concrete-useful in one way or another. The concept of productive labour is enriched by its duality, by virtue of which its real significance to the labour-and-production process is properly apprehended. Hence, in this case, the dialectic does not take the form of 'being, naught and becoming', but rather takes the form of 'identity, difference and the ground'. This means approximately the following: every concept in the doctrine of production that at first appears self-same or identical (such as productive labour) contains differences within it. These differences must be so posited as to form two contrasting aspects of the whole (such as the concrete-useful and the abstract-human aspect of productive labour). Only when the relation between these two aspects is established specifically does the original concept become 'non-empty or well grounded', namely, explain itself as something real. The contradiction between value and use-value is not absent, since one of the dual aspects has to do (at least implicitly or indirectly) with value, and the other with use-value. The use-value aspect, however, pertains not to a specific use-value that is to be circulated, but rather to *any* use-value that is to be produced. Hence, the value aspect cannot discard the use-value aspect, which it must instead contain and absorb as its own material or substance. Only when use-value production in general is fully contained by and is submitted to the sway of the value augmenting motion of capital can capitalist society constitute itself as a self-dependent system.

The doctrine of production consists of three parts: the production-process, the circulation-process, and the reproduction-process of capital. In the *production-process of capital*, the motion of industrial capital in the sphere of circulation is temporarily laid aside, in order to concentrate on the conversion of use-value production in general into the production of value by capital. If **a** represents use-value production as such, and **a′** the production-process of capital, the main proposition here may be expressed as: **a → a′** (or **a′** is built on **a**).

Although the supra-historic process of use-value production, **a**, or what is to be called the *labour-and-production process*, is unencumbered by commodity-economic specifications, it consists of a purely natural side, **n**, and a techno-organisational side, **s**. The latter side later adopts the specifically capitalistic *modus operandi*. When capital takes over its management, the labour-and-production process, **a = n ⇆ s**, becomes the instrument of value augmentation, **v′**. Capital cannot afford to produce a use-value that is not socially demanded, through its consumption of the labour-power that it has purchased as a commodity, because capital is unable to appropriate the fruit of surplus labour, except in the form of surplus value embodied in a commodity. This compels capital to follow the motion of prices in identifying the right use-value to produce. The productive labour of society is, in consequence, efficiently allocated so that only so much of each use-value (as much as society wants) tends to be produced. Since capital produces any use-value without inhibition as the occasion demands, all use-values are produced by capital *indifferently* as value, **a ⇆ v′ = a′**. This converts the production of use-values, **a**, into that of value, **a′**. It now remains to show how **a′** can liberate the productive powers of labour in **a** to their fullest potential. The capitalist production of absolute and relative surplus value, however, leaves no productive powers of labour unexploited. Capital furthers its aim of surplus-value production by simplifying the labour-process through *co-operation, manufacture* and *mechanisation*; labour-power consequently becomes a standardised commodity, perfectly indifferent to the concrete-useful form of labour. Capital, which thus completes the commoditisation of labour-power, L_p, no longer distinguishes it from the means of production, P_m, which are also bought as commodities in C. In other words, both constant and variable capital are regarded by capital indiscriminately as production-costs.

The capitalist conception of production-costs raises the problem of the circulation-process of capital because capital consumes time and resources not only in production, but in circulation as well. If the production of value, **a′**, is contrasted to the unproductive metamorphosis of value, **u′**, which capital must undergo in its entire circulation-process, **b′ = a′ ⇆ u′**, the leading proposition of this part of the dialectic may be expressed as: **a′ → b′** (or **a′** is embedded in **b′**). Indeed, if the production of use-values, **a**, has to be carried out as the production of value by capital, **a'**, then the same fact also requires that **a'** be further contained in **b'**; for capital, after all, is a circulation-form. The productive activity, **a'**, and the unproductive activity, **u'**, of capital now constitute the two contrasting elements of the circulation-process of capital, **b'**.

In its circulation over time, industrial capital takes on and off the three forms of money-capital, productive capital, and commodity-capital. Capital, in each form, has its own cycle or circuit, which always goes through a production-period and a circulation-period. Total capital advanced at any moment of time must, accordingly, be divided into productive capital and circulation capital (that is, money-capital or commodity-capital). The longer the period of circulation, the more value must be held in the unproductive form of circulation capital, and the greater must also be the pure circulation costs that must be defrayed from out of already-earned surplus value. The unavoidability of the circulation-period, therefore, detracts much from the production and disposition of surplus value. Capital, in its effort to raise the efficiency of value augmentation, does not distinguish, however, between the circulation- and the production-period. Both periods add up to the turnover-time of capital. Variable capital, which does not preserve its value in the production-process, does not turn over in the same sense as constant capital. But during the turnover-time of circulating constant capital, variable capital renews itself. Therefore, the shorter the turnover-time of circulating constant capital, the greater is the *annual rate of surplus value*, which contributes positively to the *efficiency of value augmentation*. So far as is technically feasible, capital seeks, not without reason, to turnover as promptly as possible, minimising the waste of time and resources. Yet the circulation of capital presupposes and entails the circulation of the capitalist's income, i.e., of surplus value. The study of this problem brings out the fact that each capital, in order to successfully circulate, must exchange its output with the output of other capitals as commodities. The interaction of all capitals in the exchange of commodities, however, goes beyond the scope of the circulation-process of capital.

The reproduction-process of capital unifies the production- and circulation- processes of capital from the point of view of the aggregate-social capital. If **A'** is the production-process and **B'** the circulation-process of the aggregate-social capital, the dialectic, in this section, aims to establish the proposition '**A'** → **B'** = **R** (the unity of **A'** and **B'** constitutes the social totality, **R**, which shall be called the capitalist mode of production)'. All societies must operate their production-process continually as a *reproduction-process*. But the method of ascertaining an uninterrupted flow of production differs from one society to another. In a socialist society, it may be conscious socialist planning, **P**, that must mediate its social production of use-values, **A**, as **A** ⇆ **P**.

In capitalist society, the production of use-values is carried out as the production of value by the aggregate-social capital, **A'**, and its continuity is ensured by the circulation of the aggregate-social capital, **B'**, which here in particular means the exchange of the products of capital as commodities.

The reproduction-process of capitalist society must take the form of the accumulation of capital. If the production of value by capital, **a'**, is studied from the viewpoint of the aggregate social capital, as **A'**, rather than of an individual capital, the workers-versus-capitalist relation in a capitalist enterprise will become the global value relation between the class of workers and the class of capitalists. The reproduction of these two classes is mediated by the reproduction of the aggregate-social capital. The case of a *simple reproduction* poses no problem. But an *expanded reproduction*, in which part of surplus value must be converted into new capital, is constrained by the natural growth of the working population, insofar as technical progress in the method of production is, for the moment, left out of consideration. On the other hand, the reproduction of the value relation, **A'**, implies the reproduction and circulation of commodities, **B'**. Capitalist society must reproduce *basic goods*, for the replacement of the means of production currently consumed, and *non-basic goods*, for consumption by the two classes of capitalists and workers. Both types of goods are produced by capital as commodities and exchanged by the medium of money. Again, no problem arises in the case of a simple reproduction, but in an expanded reproduction, the replacement of fixed capital raises a peculiar complication, even if the supply of additional labour-power that the accumulation requires is taken for granted. Depreciation funds would tend to grow faster than is necessary for the replacement of worn out capital, if accumulation were to continue without technical progress. In the actual process of capital accumulation, however, worn out fixed capital of the old generation is always replaced with a new type of fixed capital, which is technically superior and of greater value. Hence, the excess of depreciation funds over the replacement cost merely lightens the burden of technological innovations. Fixed capital constrains the actual process of capital accumulation, such that the periodic alternation of the widening phase, which introduces no significant technical progress, and the deepening phase, which involves a cluster of innovations, cannot be avoided. It is in the deepening phase that capital creates a relative surplus population, which can be gradually absorbed in the subsequent phase of widening. The law of surplus population peculiar to capitalism ensures the availability of labour-power as a commodity that the accumulation of capital requires. In view of this law, the accumulation of capital is no longer restricted by any factor internal to itself. The capitalist mode of production, **R**, consequently establishes itself as a self-sufficient totality.

The doctrine of production, the content of which has just been outlined, seems to closely parallel Hegel's Doctrine of Essence, in which the eternal essence of the Absolute is described through the stages of intro-reflection, appearance and actuality. When the Absolute reveals Himself as totally indifferent to His specific mode of being (or combination of quality and quantity), it becomes clear that behind His 'immediacy' lies 'something else' and 'that this background constitutes the truth of being'.[128] Intro-reflection consists of discovering this background and showing how the real existence of the Absolute is mediated by (and dependent upon) it. In other words, intro-reflection establishes what the Absolute essentially is. Yet the knowledge of what He is (essence) would be incomplete without the knowledge of why He appears as He does (appearance), for the outer appearance of the Absolute is conditioned by His inner self, just as much as His inner self is conditioned by His outer appearance. Hence, appearance and essence are not distinct; the same light shines both inward and outward. If this is the case, the truth or actuality of the Absolute cannot lie only in His inner self, nor only in His outer appearance, but in their unity. In actuality, the inner and the outer collapse to form one totality, which absorbs its own condition, for the inner that conditions the outer and the outer that conditions the inner blend together and manifest themselves as Actuality. In turn, this means that actuality is a totality that depends upon nothing other than itself, thus, establishing the Absolute as a self-dependent totality. Although, in broad outlines, Hegel's dialectic of essence appears to parallel the doctrine of production in economic theory reasonably closely, there are also many conspicuous divergences in detail. Moreover, the exposition of essence by Hegel himself is not the same in the larger as in the smaller *Logic*. My interpretation in the following pages, by and large, depends upon the smaller *Logic*, although occasionally I make use of the text of the larger *Logic*. The reader who is not interested in the Hegel correspondence may skip the introductory remarks related to it at the beginning of each chapter.

---

128   Hegel 1969, p. 389.

CHAPTER 4

The Production-process of Capital
(*Intro-Reflection*)

Introduction

No society would survive, even for a few years, if it ceased to *produce*, that is to say, if it ceased to work on nature by transforming part of it into goods (use-values) that are directly or indirectly useful to human existence. The stock of consumption-goods would soon be exhausted, and that of industrial materials wasted. Tools, machinery and plants, if left idle, would gradually decay and fall into ruins. The material foundation of any society's existence is undoubtedly the production of use-values, which always involves the expenditure of human labour. The labour-and-production process in which people organise their labour to produce use-values (or material goods) is the unchanging *substratum* of economic life, regardless of its historical form. Capitalism, which is a particular form of economic life, must also stand on this *supra-historical and material ground*. From the point of view of production, therefore, the circulation-form of capital becomes *inessential*; it is viewed as a mere seeming, shadow or illusory being. The process of capitalist production will be studied, first, under the title of the labour-and-production process, which, however, would not clearly stand out unless its performance were unobstructed by non-economic factors. Not until the whole of society's production is conducted under the chrematistic form of capital will the process of labour and production reveal itself transparently, that is, undisturbed by extra-economic factors. Thus, even this supra-historical process common to all societies cannot be fully comprehended until capitalism evolves and lets it manifest itself in broad daylight, as the abstract essence of the production-process *of capital*.

The labour-and-production process, or the production-process of use-values that is common to all societies, is a simple substance, untouched by commodity-economic specifications. Yet it contains a contrast between the purely natural or biological aspect on the one hand, and the socio-technical or organisational aspect on the other. Since the latter aspect becomes specifically capitalist later, the distinction must be clearly posited. Thus, the labour-and-production process is strictly a nature-imposed condition of human survival, if viewed simply as the *labour-process*, namely, as man's purposive action on nature for obtaining use-values. But it implies, at the same time, an integrated productive organisation of one sort or another, if viewed as the *production-process*. Neither should one consider productive labour, the leading constituent of the labour-and-production process, only in its *concrete-useful* aspect as performed by isolated individual workers, for in its *abstract-human* aspect it alludes to a working community of people, systematically producing a given set of use-values. Similarly, the *necessary labour* of the direct producer, although it would have to be performed, even if he lived in isolation, and the specific manner in which his *surplus labour* is allocated and disposed of, distinguishes different types of society.

The labour-and-production process, operated capitalistically, namely, under the chrematistic form of capital, is the process of value formation and augmentation, in which a capitalist and a group of wage-earners confront each other as the purchaser and the sellers of labour-power as a commodity. Labour-power loses its value as soon as it is purchased, that is, at the outset of the production-process; labour-power, however, cannot recreate its own value without at the same time creating a new surplus value, while it is consumed during the production-process. A capitalist who invests $100 in the means of production and another $100 in labour-power must, therefore, produce a commodity worth more than $200 by the end of the production-process in order to earn any surplus value at all. If the social demand for that commodity is such that its price can only be $200 or less, no amount of 'exploitation' enables the capitalist to realise a surplus value. Since the sole purpose of capitalist production is the augmentation of value, all capitalists must strive to produce nothing but the best-selling commodity, at any time and place. All use-values consequently tend to be produced in *socially necessary quantities*, which imply an optimum allocation of society's productive labour relative to the existing techniques. However, this means, whether one likes it or not, that each capitalistically produced use-value embodies the expenditure of no more or less than *socially necessary labour* for its production. Moreover, since this is the only homogeneous social substance (or social real cost) that a commodity can embody, it follows that the value of the commodity is determined by the expenditure of socially necessary productive labour, thus confirming the *labour theory of value*.

The demonstration of the labour theory of value depends on the *conversion of labour-power into a commodity*, the existential condition of capitalist society. Now, in reverse, it can also be shown that the validity of the labour theory of value makes capitalist society historically viable. Capitalist society, as any other society, guarantees that if productive labour is optimally allocated, the direct producers can always acquire the entire product of their necessary labour, even though the product of their surplus labour may fall into the hands of members of society other than the direct producers themselves. This proposition confirms the historical viability of capitalism. Thus, the validity of the labour theory of value and the historical existence of capitalist society imply each other; they are indeed identical. This fact is referred to as the necessity of the law of value, 'necessity' in this case signifying that one cannot be established without presuming the other. However, the labour theory of value, as stated here, does not imply that values are necessarily proportional to equilibrium (or normal) prices, that is, the prices that will prevail when society's productive labour is optimally allocated. Any set of prices that accomplishes the desired allocation of labour will suffice. Since, however, the formation of prices in the capitalist market cannot be discussed until the *actuality of capitalism* is already established, the dialectic of capital assumes, for the sake of simplicity and heuristics, that prices are proportional to values throughout the doctrine of production. This assumption, as it turns out, implies an absence of differentiation within capital, according to the different use-values that its individual units in different sectors happen to produce.

By converting the production of use-values into the production of value, capital also accelerates the development of the productive powers of labour. Being a form of value augmentation, industrial capital automatically seeks to raise the rate of surplus value to its maximum, whereas in a non-capitalist society the degree of the 'exploitation' of surplus labour is always circumscribed by the material need of the ruling class. The direct producers under capitalism are, therefore, compelled to work to the limit of their physical strength, whatever the technology of production that currently prevails may be. At the same time, the pursuit of *extra surplus value* by capital entails technical changes that further promote the rate of surplus value. Yet the production of surplus value would be restricted if the labour-process were not simplified, and if, consequently, labour-power were not 'standardised'. Handicraft production would not develop into capitalist production if skilled workmen were of overwhelming importance to the provision of all use-values. The *capitalist method of production,* based on co-operation, manufacture and mechanisation, however, tends to reduce craftsman skills, which are largely irrelevant in the factory production of most use-values, so that at least their marginal output may be produced with unskilled *simple labour.* Consequently, the mobility of labour from one industry to another becomes sufficiently free so as to ensure the swift adjustment of varying goods supplied, in response to the changing pattern of social demand for these goods. The working of the law of value (including, specifically, the production of surplus value) depends on the formation of labour-power that is totally indifferent to any specific form of concrete-useful labour.

The simplification of the labour-process by the capitalist method of production perfects *labour-power as a commodity*, the use-value of which becomes dependably uniform, regardless of where and from whom it is bought. The normal money wage that forms itself in the labour market then expresses nothing but the value (or reproduction-cost) of standardised labour-power. Yet, because of the misleading complexities peculiar to the form of wages, both the workers and the capitalists confuse the value of labour-power with the value that labour-power produces. In consequence of this confusion, the money wage now appears as the compensation for the use-value of labour-power, or labour itself, which can be bought in the market in just the same way as means of production. Hence, both variable and constant capital are reduced to mere production-costs, which, together with circulation-costs and a 'mark up', are seen as forming the price of a commodity. The source of surplus value is, thus, expunged and mystified. But the concept of individual cost (as distinct from social real cost) now establishes itself, and proceeds to govern the circulation-process of capital.

The Hegel Correspondence

The production-process of capital corresponds to Hegel's intro-reflection, or 'essence as reflection within itself', which proceeds with the triad of 'the ground, existence, and the thing' (according to the *Smaller Logic*). Essence is characterised by Hegel, in the first instance, as an unchanging substratum of being or 'a permanent in things',[129] from which viewpoint the categories of being are inessential. The ground is thus bare essence, divested of the immediacy of being, and must therefore be explained by the 'pure categories of reflection', which consist of the triad of 'identity, difference, and the ground'. Hegel, however, explains how the second term of this triad – 'difference', which at first refers to mere dissimilarity or variety – intensifies itself into contrast and then further into polar opposition or contradiction. The sub-triad of 'distinction, duality, and opposition' may represent these successive specifications of 'difference'. In the exposition of the labour-and-production process, the main triad of 'identity, difference and the ground' is repeated three times, and each time the second term ('difference') progresses through the stages of 'distinction, duality and opposition'. First, the production of use-values in general is taken to be an identity, in which, however, the labour-process and the production-process can be distinguished as the two different elements.

---

129   Hegel 1975, p. 163.

The unity of these two constitutes the labour-and-production process. The latter is totally dependent upon productive labour, which at first may be viewed as an identity. This identity turns out to be a dual one consisting of a concrete-useful and an abstract-human aspect. From the concept of dual productive labour issues the notion of the expenditure of labour, or *labour-time*, which is again considered, first, as an identity. This identity, however, is *bipartite*, being composed of necessary labour and surplus labour. The concept of bipartite productive labour implies an opposition such that one part of it cannot be increased without decreasing the other. The labour-and-production process, with productive labour as its central core, is thus 'grounded' three times as the solid 'negativity' of essence.

The labour-and-production process common to all societies is, however, a socio-technical organisation without a self-motivating force. A historically particular principle of management must always operate this otherwise inactive organisation. 'The ground is not yet determined by objective principles of its own, nor is it an end or final cause: hence it is not active'.[130] It is like an orchestra without a conductor. 'It becomes a motive and effects something through its reception into a will'.[131] This is done by reinstating being, which was once considered inessential, as something to be grounded. The unity of the ground and the grounded is existence. Yet the existence of capitalism means, in exactly the same manner, that the labour-and-production process common to all societies is activated by the specifically commodity-economic principle of capital. Thus activated, the labour-and-production process becomes the process of value-formation-and-augmentation. However, the former is not discarded or abandoned when the latter arises. 'Having issued from the ground, existence contains the ground in it; the ground does not remain, as it were, behind existence, but by its very nature supersedes itself and translates itself into existence'.[132] If the supra-historical labour-and-production process is thus translated into the capitalist mode of production, however, each use-value is produced as value by an independent capitalist operation. Hence, 'existence is the indefinite multitude of existents',[133] interacting among themselves. That is to say, capitalism is a network of independent capitalist operations, each producing a particular use-value. The law of value ensures the unity of this network.

---

130   Hegel 1975, p. 179.
131   Ibid.
132   Hegel 1975, p. 180.
133   Hegel 1975, p. 179.

The working of the law of value, or the production of value and surplus value, however, crucially depends on the conversion of labour-power into a commodity. This translates the ground into existence, and as such it can suitably be called 'the thing'. 'The thing is the totality – the development in explicit unity – of the categories of the ground and of existence'.[134] From the point of view of existence, labour-power as a commodity produces different surplus products in different capitalist operations. Labour-power therefore possesses concrete skills or 'the thing has properties'. That means, from the point of view of the ground, that labour-power has abstract working capacities, which Hegel calls 'matters or abstract characters'.[135] The development of the capitalist method of production, however, simplifies the labour-process and renders the mobility of labour virtually costless. Labour-power is 'standardised' and is reduced to the single 'matter' of unskilled working capacity, 'indifferent towards [the] specific character'[136] of labour. 'The numerous diverse matters coalesce into the one matter'.[137] To this matter, however, attaches the 'form' of cost, because the capitalist – whose production no longer depends on specific but only standardised labour-power, readily purchasable in the market – does not recognise the difference of this particular 'thing' from the other elements of production. Thus, the matter is submerged in the form, which attaches to other things as well. 'The form embraces in it the matter or subsistence as one of its characteristics'.[138] Indeed, this is exactly what the dialectic of capital asserts when the value of standardised labour-power is converted into the money wage. The form of wages enables the capitalist to view the value of labour-power, once it has been duly standardised, as the labour cost in just the same way as he views the value of the other productive elements as the non-labour cost of production.

A   The Labour-and-Production Process (The Foundation of Capitalist Production)

(a)   The Labour-process and the Production-process

(α) All historical societies, that is, societies that exist in history rather than merely in the imagination, must produce use-values systematically. The

---

134   Hegel 1975, p. 181.
135   Hegel 1975, p. 183.
136   Hegel 1975, p. 184.
137   Ibid.
138   Hegel 1975, p. 188.

totality of this supra-historical economic activity, the production of use-values for society's existence, is called the *labour-and-production process*. Although this process is expressly said to be common to all societies, regardless of their historical form, it cannot be conceptualised by the general study of all (or many) historically existent societies, abstracting in some subjective manner from their transient peculiarities. The labour-and-production process is not an ideal type, thus obtained; rather, it is nothing other than the production-process of capitalist society, once its integument (commodity-economic mode of operation) has been deliberately set aside as illusory or inessential. The reason why even such a universal reality as the *production of use-values* must be abstracted through the medium of the historically particular capitalist society is that only capitalism tends to eliminate, through its commodity-economic *modus operandi*, extra-economic human relations that interfere with the process of production. For example, in a feudal society, the production of wheat under identical natural and technical conditions may, in different cases, result in varying quantities of output because the master-servant relation differs from one case to another. In capitalist society, this sort of thing cannot in principle occur because the production of the same commodity under identical natural and technical conditions always gives the same result (that is to say, the most efficient or optimal outcome), regardless of which capitalist operates it.

Not only is the production of use-values largely free from the idiosyncrasies of the operator, his good fortune and other contingent factors, but real economic life in capitalist society also tends to substitute material use-values for personal services, whenever this is technically feasible. This tendency for the 'materialisation' of real economic life makes the production of use-values more important for the continued existence of a society. For example, in a traditional society, there is little reason to produce an alarm clock, because an early-rising servant can always wake up the master. If this service is not readily available, extra-economic force may be applied to generate it. Capital, however, cannot directly generate, by its chrematistic operation, more human service than is available already. But it can produce alarm clocks as commodities, if they are demanded, in order to partially substitute for the servants' duties. Thus, if it were technically feasible, barbers would be eliminated from capitalist society, while haircutting instruments and lotions would be abundantly produced as commodities. This tendency for the materialisation of real economic life might appear to be contradicted by the empirical fact that even when capitalism approximated its ideal image in the 1860s in England, not only did a sizeable class of domestic servants remain, but also collectively demanded services – such as entertainment, private education, and so on – were, in some cases, more widely supplied by profit-seeking (albeit, strictly speaking, non-capitalist) enterprises than before. The explanation of these empirical facts, however, belongs not to the pure theory of capitalism, but rather to economic history, which, through the mediation of the stages-theory, must demonstrate that they do not significantly undermine the operation of the fundamental laws of capitalism. In order to establish these fundamental laws, the pure theory must recognise the real force of the materialisation of economic life, which, if not always obvious in empirical terms, follows directly from the nature of capitalist production.

Indeed, capitalism, which tends to *reify* all human relations and to make them appear only as relations between commodities (material objects), automatically implies the materialisation of economic life. Personal services, other than the ones directly attendant to the trading activity of capital, cannot be regulated by commodity-economic principles, and hence cannot dispense with the involvement of extra-economic forces. If such contingent factors could not be overcome, a logical synthesis of capitalism as a global commodity-economy would be impossible. (If so, however, the historical capitalism that constitutes the presupposition of the dialectic could not have existed). Indeed, the purpose of the dialectic of capital is to demonstrate the logical possibility of capitalism, once its historical existence is presupposed (*vorausgesetzt*). It is, therefore, both necessary and justified to proceed here with the understanding that an economic life free from all extra-economic contingencies is, in principle, possible, to the extent that the existing productive technology permits it. (This procedure will, in any case, be vindicated later by the closure of the dialectic). The dialectic of capital, accordingly, considers the labour-and-production process, or the process of producing use-values, to be the sufficient representation of real economic life in capitalist society, thus openly excluding the category of interpersonal services meant for individual consumption, such as the haircutting service of the barber, the services of domestic servants, and suchlike. The other two categories of services that are indispensable to the organisation of society will be discussed later.

In the dialectic of capital, the word 'production' always refers to the creation of a use-value, which is, by definition, a material object capable of yielding a useful service in its consumption-process: 'production' here never means the provision of an interpersonal service of whatever category. Labour that involves the production of a use-value is termed 'productive', and labour that does not is referred to as 'unproductive'. Labour that is directly involved in the rendering of a useful service is, therefore, unproductive. This does not mean that the dialectic considers all unproductive service-labour to be unimportant or dispensable. Indeed, no society can be organised through productive labour alone. Since unproductive workers, without themselves producing a use-value, must nevertheless consume a collection of use-values in order to live, productive workers in all societies must perform *surplus labour*. It is necessary that the definition of productive labour should be clearly stated in the context of the labour-and-production process common to all societies, or else the specific manner in which productive labour appears in capitalist society would not be correctly understood.

(β) The production of use-values common to all societies is first of all a labour-process of man, that is, a process in which humans work with the definite purpose of transforming natural objects into more readily (directly or productively) consumable use-values. The productive activity of man considered as a labour-process is only a direct extension of his biological life, even though, unlike animals, man is not motivated by instinct. In expending labour so as to create a use-value, a human being always acts consciously with a definite design in mind. Yet the ultimate purpose of labour is the survival of man as a natural being, in harmony with the rest of the ecological system. Labour, as an activity for the self-preservation of man, is said to mediate the *metabolic* process that takes place between nature and man, for by the consumption of the products of labour, man reproduces his labour-power, with which he further adapts natural objects to his own needs.

In the labour-process, man works directly or indirectly on nature, which may be represented by *land*. Indeed, land is the original source of supply of all the objects of labour, namely, the objects to which human (productive) labour may be applied. These objects can be the raw produce of land, upon which scarcely any labour has yet been expended. But in most cases, objects are already, to varying degrees, transformed by labour, as is the case, for example, with processed industrial materials. These objects of labour are distinguished from the means of labour – such as tools, machines and plants, which are designed to make the application of labour more effective. The distinction is meant to emphasise the indirect method with which man works on nature with a view to acquiring the wherewithal to live. So-called supplementary or auxiliary materials – such as engine fuels, lubricating oils, dyestuffs, and so forth – are used, perhaps even more *indirectly*, to make the objects and the means of labour easier to handle.

In the labour-process, the subject of the action is man himself, who works consciously and purposively on nature. It is his desire to live in security and comfort that impels him to work, so as to adapt the natural environment to his needs. In a more complex technological society, this fundamental economic reality may not be immediately apparent. But if, for example, an airliner is stranded in a no-man's land, and if the means of livelihood brought from the civilised world are exhausted before the rescuers arrive, the passengers and the aircraft crew are forced to realise the bare truth of the labour-process. Opera singers may have to plant, teachers may have to cut trees, salesmen may have to build, and doctors may have to hunt. Indeed, without productive labour, which involves a direct or indirect transformation of nature, no human community can hope to survive.

By consuming his labour-power, that is, by applying productive labour to an object of labour, assisted by various means of labour, man transforms part of nature into readily consumable use-values. These use-values are the *products*, which now leave the labour-process of man and confront him as independent objects. Just as nature is external to man, produced objects too can become external to him. From the viewpoint of the products, the human labour-process may therefore be regarded as a production-process of things by things, that is to say, a technical process, in which both the objects and the means of labour may be grouped together as the means of production, and in which even labour-power – the single source of productive labour – may be counted as a factor (or element) of production, along with the non-human means of production. This, indeed, is the only way in which orthodox economics understands the labour-and-production process, namely, in terms of the so-called 'production function'. The latter represents a purely technical process of transforming certain use-values into other use-values. This viewpoint is not incorrect, but it is one-sided, because no economic process is strictly a thing-to-thing relation. The dialectic of capital insists that what appears to be a technical process of production is but one special aspect of the whole labour-and-production process; that is to say, it can never be independent of, or separable from, the labour-process. The truth of this Marxian view is conceded, if reluctantly, by orthodox economics as well, which states that 'even in our presently advanced state of automation, every act of production requires the input of human resources'.[139]

It must be repeated that 'production' in the dialectic of capital strictly means the 'fabrication of material goods', excluding such services as 'rendering legal advice, writing a book, showing a motion picture, and servicing a bank account'. This is not for the mere reason that 'the concept of producing is', in some subjective sense, 'much clearer, when we speak only of goods',[140] rather than of services. The *production-process* is another way of viewing the *labour-process*, in which man acts on nature so as to transform natural objects into directly or indirectly (productively) consumable use-values. The expenditure of unproductive labour, which does not involve direct or indirect action on nature, does not constitute a labour-process; nor can it be viewed as a production-process 'from the point of view of the product', which in that case would not even exist.

---

139   Ferguson and Gould 1975, p. 123.
140   Ibid.

As already stated, the exclusion of services from the concept of production does not imply that they are unimportant. On the contrary, some services are absolutely indispensable to any human society. Yet to confuse the concept of production, which involves a physical adaptation of the natural environment to human need, with the strictly person-to-person transfer of services, which does not do so, would expunge the distinction between the natural and the social, and would eventually lead to an empty social science. It is the expenditure of productive not unproductive labour that forms the material foundation for the existence of all societies.

(γ) Marx discusses 'the labour-process as the production of use-values' in contrast to the 'production of value and surplus value', at the beginning of his theory of production,[141] defining the labour-process as follows:

> The labour-process, resolved as above into its simple elementary factors, is human action with a view to the production of use-values, appropriation of natural substances to human requirements; it is the necessary condition for effecting exchange of matter between man and Nature; it is the everlasting Nature-imposed condition of human existence, and therefore is independent of every social phase of that existence, or rather, is common to every such phase. It was, therefore, not necessary to represent our labourer in connexion with other labourers; man and his labour on one side, Nature and its materials on the other sufficed.[142]

That the labour-process is 'the everlasting Nature-imposed condition of human existence' is incontrovertible, but the supra-historical character of the labour-process does not really make it unnecessary 'to represent our labourer in connexion with other labourers', and particularly so if the labour-process, examined 'from the point of view of its result, the product',[143] is also a production-process.

> Though a use-value, in the form of a product, issues from the labour-process, yet other use-values, products of previous labour, enter into it as means of production. The same use-value is both the product of a

141   See *Capital*, Volume I, Part III, Chapter VII, Section 1.
142   Marx 1967, *Capital*, Volume I, pp. 183–4.
143   Marx 1967, *Capital*, Volume I, p. 181.

previous process, and a means of production in a later process. Products are therefore not only results but also essential conditions of labour.[144]

Thus, the production of a use-value is not an isolated process, but an organic part of the interrelated production of all use-values. Indeed, society's production of use-values, even in its supra-historical generality, must presuppose a socio-technical organisation of production, namely, the allocation of productive labour in various fields of use-value production. Therefore, the labour-and-production process cannot be reduced to a purely technical input-output relation at the disposal of isolated individuals. The interconnection of all productive workers engaged in different parts of an integrated system of production cannot be altogether ignored.

Underlying the production-process of capital, as its unchanging (supra-historical) substratum, the labour-and-production process constitutes not only a human-nature intercourse, but also a socio-technical organisation, the abstract generality of which is common to all forms of society. Only as such can the labour-and-production process be grasped as the 'social substance' capable of being subsumed by the specifically capitalistic mode of operation. This point of view, which was first advanced by Uno, differs fundamentally from Marx's, according to which the capitalist production of commodities is a mere synthesis of the labour-process and the value (formation and) augmentation process, in just the same way as the commodity is a unity of use-value and value. From Marx's method follows the common fallacy that the duality of productive labour is specific to commodity production, since the labour-process appears to involve only the type of labour that produces specific use-values, namely, so-called 'concrete-useful labour'. It is, however, impossible to neglect the other aspect of productive labour, that of 'abstract-human labour', even in the supra-historical labour-and-production process.

The production-process unites many labour-processes, in which diverse use-values are produced, within an integrated system that produces all socially demanded use-values. That is the reason why the labour-and-production process may be regarded as the material foundation of any society, regardless of its particular historical form. If some use-values that a society needs could not be produced in its labour-and-production process, that society would not be historically viable. The production of all socially necessary use-values, however, implies an appropriate allocation of society's productive labour, regardless of how this allocation is in fact accomplished. Various forms of 'concrete-useful' labour, therefore, hang together and constitute a whole, which may be divided

---

144   Ibid.

into homogeneous parts as 'abstract human' labour. Thus, the distinction between the two aspects of the labour-and-production process is closely related
to the duality of productive labour.

(b)   The Dual Nature of Productive Labour

(α) Although the production-process of useful things is a technical process,
labour-power and the means of production do not function in the same way,
even in that context. Labour-power is the active factor, and the means of production the passive elements, in the process of production. This is due to the
fact that the means of production are specific to the particular process of use-
value production, whereas labour-power, which is needed in all processes, is
indifferent to their particular form. For example, a spinning machine cannot be
used to mill flour, leather cannot be made into a wineglass, and a screwdriver is
not needed, at least not directly, to pasteurise milk. Labour-power, by contrast,
is consumed in every field of production. It may be true that labour-power
cannot be easily shifted from one field of production to another, because different productive activities require different skills and training, or because the
labour-power of different persons is of varying degrees of efficiency. However,
this in no sense contradicts the basic fact that labour-power can, in principle,
produce whatever it is technically feasible to produce.

If this were not the case, a community of people could be permanently short
of food, shelter, or any other essential articles of consumption, and could easily
perish because of the inflexibility of the productive structure. Even the story of
Robinson Crusoe reminds one of the extent to which a single man can diversify
his productive activities sufficiently to maintain his own life. A community of
a large number of people can do so, all the more flexibly, by reallocating its
labour-power, as occasion demands, to the various fields of production. If a
passenger plane is stranded on an uninhabited island, and if the natural conditions of that island are not too harsh for human existence, the crew and the
passengers can survive without necessarily possessing professional skills, directly or indirectly, in the provision of the means of livelihood.

Thus, in all economic communities, regardless of the particular form of their
organisation, labour is always performed in two distinct senses: on the one
hand, as *concrete-useful* labour, and on the other, as *abstract-human* labour.
When a worker spins cotton yarn, he renders the concretely useful labour of
spinning. But the same worker under different circumstances could have made
a spinning machine. In that case, his concrete-useful labour would have been
the machine-making. The manner in which society assigns him specific labour
to perform may not be the same in all cases, but it makes no difference in that

his work is part of the total social labour, whether in the form of spinning or machine-making. In this sense, he always performs abstract-human labour. Labour-power is a general input in all production-processes for this reason. The basic use-value of labour-power, therefore, lies in that it can be adapted to produce any desired good, not in that it can only produce specific goods.

Abstract-human labour must first of all be distinguished from the instinctive animal labour. On this point Marx writes as follows:

> We are not now dealing with those primitive instinctive forms of labour that remind us of the mere animal. An immeasurable interval of time separates the state of things in which a man brings his labour-power to market for sale as a commodity, from that state in which human labour was still in its first instinctive stage. We pre-suppose labour in a form that stamps it as exclusively human. A spider conducts operations that resemble those of a weaver, and a bee puts to shame many an architect in the construction of her cells. But what distinguishes the worst architect from the best bees is this, that the architect raises his structures in imagination before he erects it in reality. At the end of every labour-process, we get a result that already existed in the imagination of the labourer at its commencement.[145]

Indeed, a spider's labour is restricted to the concrete-useful form of webbing, and a bee's labour to the form of collecting honey and making a hive in which to store it. Man's labour is not restricted in this way, for 'by acting on the external world and changing it, he at the same time changes his own nature. He develops his slumbering powers and compels them to act in obedience to his sway'.[146] Thus, it is exclusively human labour that is, by its very nature, adaptable to all purposes preconceived in the imagination. It is, therefore, appropriate to call it 'abstract' human labour.

This fundamental nature of abstract-human labour may perhaps be most readily understood in reference to Robinson Crusoe, who is supposed to have individually performed many forms of concrete-useful labour with careful premedition. Because of his faculty of planning in advance and in abstract terms, he could appropriately allocate his productive labour, as abstract-human labour, to the production of all use-values necessary for his survival. Society does the same thing as Robinson Crusoe; it must, in one way or another, plan

---

145   Marx 1967, *Capital,* Volume I, pp. 177–8.
146   Marx 1967, *Capital,* Volume I, p. 177.

what to produce, and how, before actually undertaking to produce. The actual expenditure of productive labour in all societies is, therefore, preceded by an exercise of unproductive mental labour, which does not itself produce anything, but which formulates the strategy of production. Thus, even though it is productive labour that forms the material foundation of society, productive labour is not operative by itself. Even to put it into operation, the unproductive labour of planning and decision-making is absolutely indispensable to any society. Who performs this kind of unproductive labour, and in what specific manner, however, differs a great deal from one society to another. In capitalist society, it is, of course, individual capitalists who perform this sort of unproductive labour, by the method of trial and error. In socialist society, it may be planning agencies at all levels of the government that are entrusted to perform this duty.

(β) Because human labour is always abstract, in addition to being concrete, it makes sense to say that a given use-value requires so many hours of labour overall to produce. Suppose, for example, that 8kg of raw cotton are converted into 6kg of cotton yarn by 6 hours of spinning labour, with the assistance of a spinning machine. Clearly, the total labour required to produce the 6kg of cotton yarn cannot be just the 6 hours of spinning labour. If the 8kg of raw cotton themselves require 20 hours of labour to produce, and if part of the machine, representing 4 hours of labour, wears out in the process, 24 hours of labour must have already been spent on the means of production alone. Therefore, the 6kg of cotton yarn required 30 hours of labour in all to produce. Such a calculation depends upon the reducibility of all kinds of concretely useful labour to some homogeneous units of abstract-human labour.

This reduction does not require that everyone's labour is equally productive. For example, children may take twice as long as adults to produce the same quantity and quality of product in every field. If this is the case, there are two categories of labour-power, children's labour-power being equivalent to half of adults' labour-power. Even if there are many more categories, of which the relative efficiency is sometimes difficult to assess, society can always work out through experience a reasonably accurate weighting system, so far as the main core of material production is concerned. For example, in planting a field an experienced peasant can, in a given time, cover more area than an inexperienced one. This, then, may be taken to be a rough measure of relative productivity in agricultural labour. In hunting, the average number of rabbits per day, if they are the commonest catch, may be used to grade the relative skill of hunters. Even though manufacturing production is often more complex, there are job categories in which the relative productivity of workers can be readily measured in quantitative terms, and all the more so if the labour-process is simplified.

As will be explained later, capitalist society possesses an inherent tendency to simplify and standardise all forms of productive labour, so that the abstract aspect of human labour is made apparent *not only theoretically but also historically*. In other societies, this may not be expected. In feudal societies, for example, relatively simple labour is largely confined to agricultural production, which is not only subject to a wide range of natural irregularities, but is also conducted under extra-economic master-servant relations. Hence, the simplicity of agricultural labour is not strikingly obvious. Even then, a medieval peasant can raise grains almost as easily as he grows green crops; he can irrigate a rice field and pasture cattle, shifting from one form of farm labour to another with little trouble or hesitation. It must be emphasised that the material foundation of all societies is, by and large, secured by *simple* (or simplified) productive labour. If this were not the case, a large number of direct producers would be unable to shift from one form of essential labour to another, as occasion demands, and the survival of society would rest on a precarious ground.

Labour can be described as simple if direct producers can switch from one form of concrete-useful labour to another without serious difficulty. In medieval societies, agricultural labour was largely simple, but not manufacturing labour to any considerable extent; skilled craftsmen were rare and could not easily be trained. At the same time, however, the material foundation of feudal societies rested not on skilled manufacture, but rather on predominantly simple labour in agriculture. Capitalist society extended the scope of simple labour to non-agricultural production as well, rendering professional and individual skills in all fields of material production largely irrelevant. This does not mean that skilled labour is ever entirely absent in capitalist society; it only means that, apart from luxury items – such as artistic objects – unskilled labour tends to be able to produce more or less the same things as does skilled labour. The only sphere in which highly sophisticated training cannot be avoided is that of professional services. But such services can effectively function only after the material foundation of capitalist society is secured by productive labour. The sophistication of professional services in capitalist society rests on the condition that simple labour becomes universal in all forms of use-value production.

(γ) Thus, productive labour, which the labour-and-production process involves, must simultaneously be 'concrete-useful' and 'abstract-human'. The supra-historical character of the labour-and-production process does not render productive labour exclusively concrete-useful. The abstract-human aspect of productive labour, which is present in all societies, becomes specifically value-forming labour when capitalist commodity production embraces the supra-historical labour-and-production process, transforming it into the value-formation-and-augmentation process. This point is essential to the correct understanding of the labour theory of value.

Marx's method of demonstrating the labour theory of value by the so-called 'process of distillation'[147] in the exchange of two commodities fails to bring out the real significance of the concept of value. If two commodities are exchanged in a certain quantitative ratio – say, two apples for one peach – and this ratio is then recurrently observed in a given market, that does not prove that the same quantity of 'socially necessary' labour constitutes the value of two apples and the value of one peach. It only shows that two apples and one peach have the same price, as already mentioned. In the context of commodity exchanges, the substance or the real content of value cannot be specified. Value can only be identified there as *some homogeneous social quality* present in all commodities. In order to establish that the substance of commodity value is the socially necessary expenditure of abstract-human labour, it must first be shown that the historically particular form of capital is capable of subsuming the process of labour and production, which forms the material foundation of any society, and that productive labour in any society possesses the aspect of abstract-human labour.

It is not incorrect to say that the labour-process is a process of producing use-values. But the uncoordinated production of use-values, carried out at random by isolated labourers, does not secure the material condition for any society's survival. In all viable societies, it is necessary that the production of use-values should be organised as an integrated whole. It is the particular principle of this organisation that differs historically. In capitalist society, the principle that governs the anarchic production of commodities is the *law of value*. The law of value necessarily implies the labour theory of value, because the co-ordinated production of use-values in all societies involves the expenditure of productive labour as abstract-human labour. To say that the substance of commodity values is abstract labour merely amounts to stating that the material foundation of capitalist society, as of any other society, lies in the labour-and-production process. From this point of view, it is obvious that the labour theory of value cannot be established by 'distilling' labour as the common factor of two commodities that are exchanged in the market. The labour-and-production process must first be seen as a co-ordinated social complex of use-value production.

It must be admitted, however, that all aspects of the labour-and-production process and their significance cannot readily be exposed and grasped except

---

147 Böhm-Bawerk 1975, p. 69.

insofar as that process forms the material foundation of capitalist society. This is because the simplification of productive labour does not become universal before the evolution of capitalism, as Marx himself tells us:

> The example of labour strikingly demonstrates how even the most abstract categories, despite their validity in all epochs – precisely because they are abstractions – are equally a product of historical conditions even in the specific form of abstractions, and they retain their full validity only for and within the framework of these conditions.[148]

In other words, the concept of labour that produces all forms of wealth, which dates from Adam Smith, 'despite its validity in all epochs', is a product of the capitalist era, because 'labour, not only as a category but in reality, has become a means to create wealth in general'[149] only with the evolution of capitalism. Hence, the labour theory of value not only clarifies the specifically capitalist principle of co-ordinating commodity production, it also throws light on the general necessity of co-ordinating the production of use-values in all forms of society.

(c)   *Surplus Labour and Necessary Labour*

(α) Productive labour that forms the material foundation of all societies must therefore be abstract-human in addition to being concrete-useful. However, this duality is not the only property of productive labour. It is also *bipartite*, in that it consists of 'necessary' and 'surplus' labour. *Necessary labour* is productive labour performed for the purpose of reproducing the labour-power currently being consumed in the process of production; *surplus labour* refers to productive labour otherwise expended. This division of productive labour into a necessary and a surplus part presupposes the concept of abstract-human labour. For example, society as a whole may spend 6 million hours of productive labour during a week consisting of, say, 5 working days. If the weekly production of wage-goods for the consumption of productive workers requires, directly or indirectly, 3 million hours, and if the wage-goods are both necessary and sufficient to reproduce society's labour-power, which is productively consumed during the week, then the total labour-time of 6 million hours is partitioned into the necessary labour-time of 3 million hours and the surplus labour-time of 3 million hours. On a daily basis, the total labour-time will be

---

148   Marx 1970, *Contribution*, p. 210.
149   Ibid.

1.2 million hours, and both the necessary and the surplus labour-time will be 0.6 million hours. If there are 100,000 workers, each individual worker must be working 12 hours a day, performing 6 hours of necessary labour and 6 hours of surplus labour. One can also say that every productive hour of labour in this society consists of half an hour of necessary labour and half an hour of surplus labour. Thus, with the concept of abstract-human labour, any unit-expenditure of productive labour may be partitioned into a necessary part and a surplus part.

The formal definition that the necessary labour-time of a productive worker per day is 6 hours means that he can produce in 6 hours, if he is assigned to do so, the assortment of use-values that are just sufficient for the daily reproduction of his labour-power. Suppose that x, y, z are the quantities of goods, X, Y, Z, that are just sufficient for this purpose. Suppose also that $\lambda_x, \lambda_y, \lambda_z$ are the number of hours of simple labour socially required for the production per unit of X, Y, Z. Then, '$\lambda_x x + \lambda_y y + \lambda_z z = 6$' is equivalent to saying that the necessary labour-time is six hours. The productivities of labour ($\lambda_x, \lambda_y, \lambda_z$) depend on the technology available to society, as well as the manner in which that society organises its labour-and-production process. Given these parameters, however, any productive worker, who spends $\lambda_x x$ hours wherever X is generally produced, $\lambda_y y$ hours where Y is generally produced, and $\lambda_z z$ hours where Z is generally produced, should be able to complete the basket (x, y, z) in six hours.

The assortment (x, y, z) of use-values just sufficient for the reproduction of labour-power, or what was previously called the *subsistence*, cannot be determined *a priori*. It is certainly above the so-called biological minimum, but how far above it depends on historical circumstances.[150] Nor is the assortment identical with respect to every productive worker.[151] In all cases, however, the subsistence must reflect the 'permanent' consumption of wage-goods by the workers rather than their 'temporary' or immediate consumption. Even an isolated individual (such as Robinson Crusoe) normally works more than is necessary to live for that day, in order to provide for a rainy day. Society must do the same, for otherwise the slightest anomaly of weather conditions or other natural calamity, which frequently deprives human society of its ordinary working environment, would at once cause its downfall due to a shortage of wage-goods. Necessary labour must, therefore, always produce enough to stockpile some wage-goods against all contingencies, which may also include epidemics, conflagrations, ravages caused by war, and so forth, in addition to natural catastrophes. The stockpiling of some surplus wage-goods, however,

---

150 See Chapter 6.
151 See Chapter 7.

does not mean that surplus labour is performed. This becomes particularly obvious in the Robinsonian fable. Indeed, if an isolated individual who can produce his daily means of livelihood in 6 hours works for 12 hours every other day, surely he does not perform any surplus labour.

A historical society must not only provide for a rainy day, but must also maintain its stock of labour-power (which may increase over time with the natural growth of the population) when one generation of productive workers is superseded by another. In other words, the currently active generation of workers must produce enough wage-goods to raise their children. The children must, of course, be adequately fed, clothed, and otherwise looked after, as they are the next generation of productive workers. Use-values that are consumed in the children's education, healthcare, and so forth, are included as wage-goods to the extent that they are indispensable to the formation of a full-fledged productive worker. Although the product of necessary labour must include such use-values as are needed for the raising and training of the workers' children, it does not include use-values needed for the caring of the old and the terminally sick, who are not capable of performing productive labour either now or in the future. Indeed, anthropological studies have revealed that in some primitive communities the old and the sick, who could no longer work, were left to die in order that others might live. If a human community must survive in a very harsh natural environment with a primitive technology of production, the room for surplus labour may be so limited that even such cruelty has to be accepted, if not condoned, as a way of life. It may be remarked, however, that an economic community, in which productivity is so low and surplus labour so scarce, cannot reliably satisfy the material condition for its lasting existence, as a slight worsening of the environment can easily destroy it. Political economy must, in any case, envisage a society productive enough, relative to the niggardliness of nature, to be able to form a firm material base for its existence. This would mean that all societies studied by political economy must be in possession of labour-power sufficiently productive to render considerable surplus labour.

(β) In order to understand the nature of surplus labour, let us begin by considering how much, if any, surplus labour Robinson Crusoe might perform. Suppose that if he works for 5 hours he can produce just barely enough to survive for the day, but that in order to enjoy some luxury, and also to provide for unpredictable contingencies, he in fact works for 6 hours a day. Since he has no family to look after, and since a sufficient stock of provisions has already been built, he clearly has no reason to further produce use-values that he himself cannot consume, even in future. If, therefore, he is already satisfied with the present standard of living and comfort, and if he has no ambition to explore a new technology, the rest of his time can be devoted to the unproductive labour of management and personal recreation. *Robinson Crusoe then performs no surplus labour,* his productive labour being wholly spent for the acquisition of use-values that are 'necessary' directly or indirectly for the reproduction of his own labour-power. Of course, luxury and comfort do not always involve surplus labour. Robinson Crusoe may choose to work for 7 hours, rather than 6 hours, in order to improve his standard of living, that is, in order to obtain either more use-values or use-values of higher quality. Even in that case, he does not perform an hour of surplus labour in addition to 6 hours of necessary labour, but just 7 hours of necessary labour for the more costly reproduction of his own labour-power. An isolated individual like Robinson Crusoe cannot perform surplus labour.

It is, therefore, quite clear that surplus labour arises only in a social context. Productive workers perform surplus labour in addition to necessary labour, because there are members of society who consume use-values without producing them at all. Specifically, the aged and the sick, who cannot work, and the mental workers, who specialise in unproductive labour, are members of society who must be supported by the surplus labour of the productive workers or *direct producers*. The aged and the sick may be described as *natural or welfare dependants*; civilised society supports these dependants for humanitarian reasons. Often, however, their wisdom and experience contribute to the better management of society, in which case they should be considered as mental workers. Mental workers – including administrators, ritualists, soldiers and intellectuals – may be considered to form a class of *social dependants*. Society supports these dependants on the understanding that they enrich social life by indirectly contributing to the production of use-values. Sometimes it is incorrectly and irresponsibly asserted that all social dependants are purely parasitic 'exploiters' whose status must be summarily terminated. It is hardly necessary to point out the senselessness of such a view, for even crude revolutionaries are aware that some technicians, intelligentsia, and so on, are needed in any society. In fact, no society can be constituted by productive labour alone. Although productive labour is absolutely indispensable to the formation of every society's material base, productive labour as abstract-human labour is never expended blindly. The application of productive labour, as already remarked, always presupposes a prior process of planning and decision-making. Moreover, a society that lacks law and order, and that is frequently harassed by hostile aliens, or plagued by epidemic diseases, cannot make the most of its available productivity. Therefore, some if not all of the social dependants must be present in all societies to protect and oversee the functioning of the labour-and-production process from the outside. This justifies the need for surplus labour in any society.

Suppose that every productive worker of a society can reproduce his labour-power in 6 hours a day, but he can technically work for 12 hours without exhausting his daily labour-power. This does not immediately mean that they all work for 12 hours a day, while performing 6 hours of surplus labour. It is possible that 3 hours of surplus labour per worker per day is quite sufficient to satisfy all social needs – such as caring for the sick and the old, and relieving the mental workers from the burden of productive labour. If the population is stationary or increasing only slightly, if it is not exposed to aggressive alien forces, and if little incentive exists to improve the present living conditions, there is no reason to believe that the surplus labour-time per worker should be more than 3 hours a day, since if labour-power is not exhausted it can always be consumed by recreation.

History shows, however, that human communities seldom led such a peaceful and complacent life, and that if they *had* done, then the development and differentiation of civilisation would have been much slower. A growth in population may force a tribe to relocate itself in search of a better natural environment; a hunting tribe, which is constantly on the move, may sometimes come into violent conflict with another. The necessity of developing more adequate defences and other urgent considerations may impose a more regimented and disciplined social organisation on sedentary communities. Thus, from time immemorial, the members of a human community divided themselves into productive workers and their dependants. The more the dependants, social and natural, the more surplus labour had to be performed by productive workers.

Natural dependants, however, do not tend to increase relative to the productive workers beyond a certain limit, at least under normal circumstances. Not so with social dependants. The latter can theoretically increase up to the limit dictated only by the technical availability of surplus labour. Since social dependants, once relieved from productive labour, acquire ready access to extra-economic forces, which may be applied to impose further discipline on the productive organisation of society, it is to be expected that they would develop themselves into a class of unproductive superiors, in a position to appropriate surplus products from the working members of society. At this point, it is not only possible but also likely that the class of social dependants will increase beyond the proper proportion, that is, more than is necessary for the efficient management of the labour-and-production process. Some social dependants do not even perform unproductive labour for the good of society, but merely squander their time and energy on recreation, while being supported by the productive members of society. Such social dependants are indeed purely parasitic, and their status may be abolished without doing harm to society. Given that the class structure of a society is dependent upon the particular method of management of the labour-and-production process, it is generally impossible to abolish the undesirable portion of the existing class of social dependants, unless this method itself is altered.

(γ) At a certain stage of the development of human history, class societies emerge, which are of different types according to the particular mode of appropriation of the surplus products that are produced through surplus labour. In class societies, the extent to which surplus labour is actually carried out in the labour-and-production process depends on the relation between productive workers (or direct producers) and their social dependants, or, in other words, on the class relation, which characterises the particular social organisation of the labour-and-production process. This relation may in short be called the 'production-relation', which differs historically from one class society to another. One generic form of production-relation is represented by slavery, in which the labour-power and the persons of productive workers (or direct producers) are wholly owned, either by the state or by individual slave-masters. Another form is represented by serfdom, in which productive workers, tied to the land, are under a contractual obligation to perform surplus labour for their feudal lord. The capitalist production-relation differs from either of these in that the capitalists' access to the labour-power of the direct producers involves, in principle, no exercise of extra-economic forces, but merely the trade in 'commoditised' labour-power, as distinct from the persons of productive workers.

In view of the specific character of the capitalist production-relation, the unproductive mental labour that capitalist society needs for its constitution can be divided into two broad categories: the *labour of economic management*, performed directly by the capitalists themselves, or their hired assistants, and the *non-economic institutional labour*, the organisation of which is the direct responsibility of the capitalist state. The former category will be examined in concrete terms in the following chapter; in the present chapter, it is held implicit in the *chrematistic form* of the value augmentation of capital. The latter category, however, is entirely neglected in the dialectic of capital, because a purely capitalist society only presupposes the function of the state as a background condition, without bringing it out into the open. It is in the context of the stages-theory that the nature of the capitalist state, with all its paraphernalia, must be explicitly treated.

Capitalism is a fully developed commodity-economy in the sense that commodity-economic rules and principles pervade even its labour-and-production process. A commodity-economy arises when self-dependent economic communities, in possession of some disposable surplus products, come into peaceful contact with one another. As exchanges of such disposable products, in the form of commodities, develop to the advantage of these communities, a significant part of their ordinary economic activity is transformed into the production of commodities. The consequent evolution of commerce – inter-communal as well as intra-communal – does not, however, radically alter the traditional mode of production, unless it is accompanied by the conversion of labour-power into a commodity. History abounds with instances of flourishing trade in ancient and medieval societies, the material foundation of which continued to depend upon slavery or serfdom. Even the revival of active international commerce, at the beginning of the modern age, when feudalism gradually decayed, did not immediately give birth to capitalism. The genesis of capitalist society required, together with the accumulation of commercial wealth, the formation in large numbers of propertyless workers who had to trade their labour-power as a commodity through the so-called process of 'primitive accumulation'.

When labour-power, the single source of productive labour, is converted into a commodity, a global commodity-economy, known as capitalism, evolves. Since labour-power can be purchased as a commodity, an overwhelming part of society's labour-and-production process is now operated under the form of capital. The motion of capital is a never-ending process of value augmentation, in which the capitalist appropriates the surplus labour of productive workers in the form of the surplus *value* embodied in a commodity. The appropriation of surplus labour, being motivated by the chrematistic incentive of capital, is bound to be pushed to its physical limit. The accelerated accumulation of capital and the spectacular rise of the productive powers of labour, thus, characterise the labour-and-production process under capitalism.

The labour-and-production process, which forms the material base of all societies, is the 'social substance' (or the 'unchanging substratum', to use Hegel's locution), from the point of view of which the commodity-economic forms of circulation are mere integuments (or Hegel's 'Schein'). Capitalism, however, exists in a unity of form and substance, that is, in the subsumption under the chrematistic motion of capital (form) of the labour-and-production process (substance). The 'existence' (in Hegel's sense) of capitalism must, therefore, be demonstrated by the compatibility of the commodity-economic form of value and the supra-historical substance of the labour-and-production process, as the material foundation (or what Hegel calls the 'ground') of all societies. The process of value-formation and augmentation by capital exhibits this compatibility by way of the *law of value*, which is a historically particular (the peculiarly capitalistic) mode of socially organising the labour-and-production process.

The law of value, in other words, is the ultimate proof of the existence of the capitalist mode of production.

The method of exposition of the doctrine of production (of the 'essence' of capitalism) demands that the labour-and-production process, which forms the material base of all societies, be explained prior to its peculiar operation, as integral to the value-formation-and-augmentation process of capital. It must not be forgotten, however, that the method of enquiry, which proceeds from the concrete-empirical to the abstract-theoretical, begins with the image of a fully developed capitalist economy. The concept of simple labour, which produces all forms of wealth, develops 'not only theoretically but also in reality', together with the evolution of capitalism. This fact makes the material foundation of all societies transparent. This transparency can be attained because the commodity-economic forms with which capitalism organises its labour-and-production process tend to replace interventions by extra-economic forces. The labour-and-production process, divested of extra-economic coercion, together with any super-structural ideology that might motivate it, forms the economic base of society. It is for this reason that the exact sense of the materialistic conception of history, which claims the substructure (or the base) of all societies to be economic, can be confirmed to be true for capitalism by Marxian political economy, which studies it as a historically specific form of society.

B   The Value-Formation-and-Augmentation Process (The Existence of Capitalist Production)

(*a*)   *The Labour Theory of Value*

(α) In the production-process of capital, not only the means of production but also labour-power itself is purchased as a commodity. That is to say, labour-power can enter the production-process of capital only after being purchased by capital as a commodity. Yet as soon as it is purchased, labour-power loses its value and is not re-saleable as a commodity. Thus, the only way in which the capitalist, who has purchased labour-power, may recover its money value is to consume it in the production-process of capital, thereby creating a new commodity for sale. For example, if a capitalist advances $100 in the means of production and purchases labour-power with another $100, his output must be sold for more than $200, otherwise his chrematistic operation will have been a failure. The capitalist will, of course, endeavour to purchase the elements of production as cheaply as possible, and to sell his product as dearly as possible, so as to realise a maximum profit. If all commodities tend to be bought and sold for normal prices, however, the capitalist cannot in general make a relative profit at the expense of other commodity-sellers. He can make a genuine profit if and only if the labour-power that he purchased is consumed, in the manner described, during the production-process of capital, so that it yields a commodity containing a greater new value than the value of the labour-power itself. In other words, the labour-power, which cost the capitalist $100, must produce a commodity worth more than $200, considering that the $100, which represents the value of the means of production, is preserved throughout the production-process and is simply transferred to the new product.

When an industrial capitalist purchases the means of production (P_m) and labour-power (L_p) in the process, M – C, the value of the former is called *constant capital* (denoted by c), and that of the latter is called *variable capital* (denoted by v). The purpose of the production-process (....P....) is to render the value of the new commodity to be sold, C', in the process C' – M', greater than the value of the original advance, C, purchased in M – C. If the difference is called *surplus value* (denoted by s), it follows that M = C = c + v and C' = M' = c + v + s. In other words, the capitalist, who invests the value c + v > o in the elements of production, must realise at least as much value as he advanced, namely, c + v + s > c + v (so that s > o), by selling his commodity. It goes without saying that if surplus value were zero or negative (s ≤ o), the chrematistic of capital would have been meaningless. Hence, the production-process of capital can exist only when surplus value is distinctly positive (s > o).

Although the same symbol, v, applies to variable capital in the original investment (c + v) and the variable-capital component of the product value (c + v + s), and although by definition they are quantitatively equal, they do not qualitatively represent the same value. Variable capital represents the value of the labour-power purchased at the beginning of the production-process and consumed in it. This value disappears as soon as it is purchased, and indeed even prior to its entering the production-process of capital. The variable-capital component of the product value has been *newly created* during the production-process, together with surplus value. Thus the v in c + v pre-exists the production-process, and is as 'old' as constant capital, whereas v in c + v + s arises in consequence of the production-process and is as 'new' as surplus value, s. The expression 'variable capital' implies not only that the newly formed value, v + s, may be greater than the original value, v, by the amount of the positive surplus value, s, but also that the new value, v + s, can easily turn out to be less than the old consumed value, v, if, for example, an inappropriate (that is, unwanted) use-value is produced, realising a negative surplus value. Moreover, if labour-power were kept idle in the production-process of capital, it would produce nothing – not even the equivalent of what is required to renew itself – although the means of production, left unused, can always be disposed of as commodities. Constant capital, therefore, preserves its value in the production-process, which merely transfers the old value of the means of production consumed to the newly created product; variable capital, by contrast, loses its value in the first instance, but preserves its use-value that reproduces itself along with surplus value in the production-process of capital.

Being a form of value augmentation, capital seeks to earn a maximum profit by producing a commodity that is most urgently wanted by society. If the commodity is socially wanted, then its price will be high enough to yield a positive profit, which is the monetary expression of surplus value. However, if the commodity is not socially wanted, its price will fall short of its cost of production, inflicting a loss on the producer. During any period of time, society needs many use-values, if not all. It is patently impossible for a society to need or want no use-value at all during a year, month, week or day. Consequently, the production of some use-values is bound to be profitable in any period, which means that some surplus value can always be earned. It is up to capital to find out, through trial and error, which use-values may be the most profitable ones to produce.

If a capital is not alert and fails to identify a good use-value, no amount of 'exploitation' can maximise the profit. Labour-power must, in any case, be consumed exhaustively in the production-process of capital, rather than being left idle so to waste its productive capacity. Yet even if labour-power is overworked, that alone does not guarantee that the commodity will sell for a price that permits a significant profit. The capitalist, in other words, cannot produce surplus value by simply 'exploiting' his workers, that is, by simply forcing them to work hard and long hours. If the wrong use-value is produced, the price that it fetches in the market may be so low that a negative profit may accrue. In such a case, both surplus labour and necessary labour will have been wastefully performed. A capital must, therefore, always strive to find a use-value that is most intensely demanded in society.

(β) Suppose that a capitalist, who invests $200 in the means of production and labour-power, sells his product for $250. His profit-rate then is 25%. If he could do better by producing another use-value, he would have done so. All capitalists, after a search by trial and error, find a use-value that when produced will be no less profitable than the production of any other commodity. So long as circumstances permit, capital always endeavours to produce more of the better selling commodities and less of those that sell poorly. This is what makes capital a genuine form of value augmentation. Thus, even though the search for the most profitable use-value may never end, and even though the shift from one branch of production to another may not be immediate or instantaneous, there is always a tendency in capitalist society for just as much of all socially desired use-values to be produced in the end. Indeed, if capital produced a use-value in a quantity that did not meet demand, its price would inevitably rise so as to make its production relatively more profitable than the production of other commodities. Conversely, if capital produced a use-value in excess of the socially desired quantity, its price would necessarily fall so as to render its production less lucrative than that of other commodities. Being a commodity-seller a capitalist cannot dictate the choice of the use-values that must be sold. He may, however, attempt to fathom the pleasure of society by observing the movement of prices, before producing such commodities as are likely to yield the highest rate of profit.

If all use-values, thus, tend to be produced in the socially desired quantities, and if society's productive labour tends to be allocated by capital accordingly, then this allocation of productive labour must eventually be optimal, because under the existing technology, each use-value will be produced with no more labour than that which is socially necessary, directly or indirectly, for its production. Since society wants as much of all use-values as can be technically produced with a given order of priorities, if a particular use-value were to absorb more labour than was socially necessary, then commodities of a lesser priority could not be produced in the socially desired quantities. If a particular use-value were to consume less labour than was socially necessary, that use-value would, of course, fail to be produced in the socially desired quantity. However, once the capitalist allocation of resources eventually achieves conformity with the pattern of social demand for use-values, no fraction of the available productive labour is wasted, that is, every hour of surplus labour is realised as surplus value accruing to capital. This ideal situation may in fact only be approached, but it nevertheless constitutes the centre of gravity, or the limit to which production in capitalist society is always attracted.

Thus, every capitalistically produced commodity tends to embody or represent a definite fraction of the totality of society's productive labour, viewed as abstract-human labour. Indeed, that is equivalent to saying that every such commodity embodies the social substance, real cost, or 'socially necessary labour for its production'. It was said earlier that every capitalistically produced commodity possesses the 'socially uniform quality of value'. The substance of the value of a commodity, however, could not be identified in that context, because no real economic quantity which was socially uniform, objective (rather than imagined), and not tautologically identical to price, existed as yet. 'Socially necessary labour' is, however, a real economic quantity that satisfies all these requirements. Hence, if it is also established that socially necessary labour is the only such quantity, the *labour theory of value* follows inevitably.

Since a socially homogeneous 'real economic quantity' could not be found in the Doctrine of Circulation, it must necessarily be sought in the production-process of a commodity. The production of a use-value involves the consumption of productive elements, which, as stated earlier, may be broadly classified into labour-power (L_p) and man-made means of production (P_m). Through the consumption of these *elements (or factors) of production* a socially homogeneous 'real economic quantity' arises. The *natural means of production* represented by land, being 'indestructible', cannot be consumed in the production of a commodity, nor can they give rise to such a quantity. They do not even possess value themselves, since they are not capitalistically producible commodities. The rich variety of their free services, though essential to the production of use-values, cannot consequently be reduced to any socially uniform substance. Even man-made or reproducible means of production, which are indeed consumed in the production of a use-value, cannot be directly reduced to such a substance either. As use-values, they are of heterogeneous qualities and are quite specific to the production of the use-value to which they are applied. They are, indeed, no more reducible to a socially homogeneous substance than the natural means of production. As opposed to the natural means of production, however, man-made instruments of production are themselves capitalistically produced commodities in possession of value, in terms of which they are measurable in homogeneous units. Hence, if the substance of value is discovered elsewhere, it is possible to evaluate, in real terms, the consumption of the man-made means of production. There is only one more element of production left, namely, labour-power. It is clearly in the productive consumption of labour-power that the 'real economic quantity' must be identified. Moreover, the consumption of labour-power generates productive labour, which is homogeneous in its abstract-human aspect. If, by virtue of this property, productive labour is capitalistically allocated to various branches of use-value production, it becomes *socially necessary labour*. The latter, therefore, is the only 'real economic quantity' that can be considered to form the substance of value.

The labour theory of value, which is thus inevitably established, has, however, been subjected to various uninformed criticisms. When orthodox economists, under the influence of Knight, Schumpeter, Samuelson *et al,* claim that land and capital (in the sense of man-made instruments of production) are as productive of value as labour, they do not seem to have the faintest idea of what the term *value* actually refers to in the dialectic of capital. Since value is that which brings all capitalistically produced commodities together in real terms, its substance must be a socially uniform 'real economic quantity', independent of prices. Having rejected the artifice of social utility, however, bourgeois economics no longer possesses anything that even remotely resembles such a quantity. From the viewpoint of an economic doctrine, which refuses to concern itself with the material and social foundation of the capitalist market, and which merely takes its existence as an axiom, or a matter of faith in that empirical fact, the concept of value is manifestly irrelevant. Such a pragmatic approach uncritically takes the commodity-economic relations that appear in a reified form on the surface of the market to be mechanical interrelations of 'things' among themselves, rather than the reflection of the socio-historical human relations that constitute capitalism. The market-economy, it is proclaimed, consists of 'things' called 'goods and services' and supra-historic individuals who are, for some reason, animated by the mysterious power of self-optimisation. Capitalism, to bourgeois economics, means no more than such a fantasy world, a toy-land, far away from the reality of human history.

(γ) The labour theory of value is the proposition that every capitalistically produced commodity tends to embody as value the socially necessary labour for its production. (This proposition does not imply that prices should be proportional to values, although it implies that a commodity without value has no normal or equilibrium price either. More on this later). The validity of the labour theory of value, therefore, presupposes the existence of capitalist society, or more specifically the conversion of labour-power into a commodity. If labour-power is not fully commoditised, industrial capital cannot produce all use-values indifferently as value. Hence, the tendency for commodities to be produced with socially necessary labour may be too weak to make itself felt, even in the long run. The labour theory of value cannot be demonstrated in such a context. This is particularly the case with the so-called system of simple commodity production, in which independent producers are supposed to own their means of production, and in which labour-power cannot consequently be a commodity. Simple commodity production may exist in capitalist or non-capitalist society as a subsidiary or peripheral economic activity, but it can never by itself constitute a mode of production. Since no society's labour-and-production process can conceivably be organised by the activities of independent small producers, a society-wide system of simple commodity production is a pure figment of the imagination, having no real economic meaning.

Even if such a system existed initially, it would not survive a minor change in the pattern of social demand. Suppose that after a conflagration society needs a great amount of building materials and is willing to sacrifice the production of other commodities to a considerable extent in order to meet the pressing need for them. Small producers of other objects, however, cannot just stop or reduce their conventional supplies and increase the supply of building materials, in the production of which they possess no skills, experience or tools. Nor can the producers of building materials work for twenty-four hours a day until the social demand is satisfied. Consequently, no matter how high the price of building materials soars in the market, and no matter how low the relative prices of other commodities sink in the market, the society of small producers cannot adjust its supplies to its demands beyond a certain limit. This is not all. It is quite possible that a counter-adjustment might take place. For if the high price of building materials is expected to be more than temporary, the producers of such materials may even reduce their output, hoping to enjoy an easier life with less labour, rather than overworking themselves in order to serve the cause of public welfare. The producers of other commodities (the prices of which have been depressed), instead of curtailing their supply and sustaining a further loss of income, may increase their production in a desperate attempt to fight against the worsened terms of trade. Since these small producers are nothing other than master-craftsmen, in possession of particular skills, experience and instruments, they cannot be expected to be indifferent to the concrete-useful form of their labour.

The labour-power of an independent small producer is not a commodity, and hence has no value. That is to say, the reproduction cost of his labour-power cannot be objectively determined in the market. The cost of living (or the real wage paid to himself) of an independent craftsman is, therefore, quite subjective and arbitrary, as is his concept of profit. That is why he can continue to produce a commodity in which he has a stake for as long as he lives, if he so chooses, just as he may stop producing his commodity the moment his life becomes sufficiently comfortable. The labour-power of a small producer, therefore, is either incapable of moving from one branch of production to another, or is at least extraordinarily slow to do so. In that case, however, it cannot reasonably be expected that any use-value produced by a small producer would ever be made available in the socially desired quantity, even in the long run. A society depending solely on simple commodity production would almost permanently waste productive labour in producing some useless articles, while at the same time suffering from a chronic shortage of use-values that are more urgently needed. The labour-and-production process so inefficiently organised and managed could not possibly assure any society of the material conditions for its survival.

The reason why capital, unlike simple commodity producers, can successfully organise and manage the labour-and-production process, according to the principles of the commodity-economy, is that the production-process of capital consumes labour-power that has been purchased as a commodity. Labour-power, bought and sold in the open market, is already dispossessed of any means of production or of livelihood; skills and experience are also irrelevant to such labour-power. It can for that reason be the source of the labour that produces any use-value, quite indifferently to its concrete-useful forms. Only because such labour-power is available in the market can capital expand or contract its production of a use-value at will, migrating from one branch of industry to another in response to the dictates of social demand. Since commoditised labour-power has value, together with a corresponding normal price, objectively determined in the market, profitability is an unambiguous concept to capital. Being sensitive to the profit-rate, capital swiftly and flexibly adapts to the pattern of social demand. The fact that the prices of all capitalistically produced commodities tend to settle to normal (or equilibrium) levels, reflecting their values, which are in their turn determined by the socially necessary labour, makes the capitalist production of use-values the production of value. This point is essential to *the labour theory of value*.

The labour theory of value, however, has not always been understood in this sense. More often its (pre-Marxian) classical version, which claims the proportionality of prices to values, has been uncritically taken to be the exclusive meaning of the labour theory of value. Yet that is an egregious error. Apart from very special cases, most capitalistically produced commodities do not tend to be bought and sold for normal (or equilibrium) prices that are proportional to values. This fact in no sense conflicts with the proposition of the labour theory of value that the substance of value is socially necessary labour. It is the obsession with proportionality that caused many authors, and even Marx himself to some extent, to overlook the significance of value as the property of capitalistically produced commodities. In a futile attempt to confirm an 'undiluted' labour theory of value, some Marxist authors – particularly Engels,[152] Hilferding,[153] and Stalin[154] – argue as if capitalism were preceded by a more 'genuine' (!) commodity-economic society, founded upon simple commodity production. This is much worse than Adam Smith's fairy tale of beaver-and-deer hunters, 'in that early and rude state of society'. Since the Marxists, being materialists, cannot tell a fairy tale (instead of a real story of hard experience in history), these authors openly insist that historical capitalism arose amid the disintegration of simple commodity production, even though that is most

---

152   See the 'Law of Value and Rate of Profit' section in Engels 1967.
153   See Hilferding 1975.
154   See Stalin 1971.

decidedly untrue. Far from contributing to genuine understanding, such a fabrication diverts attention from the true significance of the labour theory of value.

I do not claim that a commodity produced by a handicraftsman does not have a value, but only that the value of such commodity cannot be known unless the same commodity is simultaneously produced by capital. Indeed, only by chance may a commodity be simply (that is, non-capitalistically) produced in the socially desired quantity, and thus have a price that is equivalent to a normal price in a capitalist economy. This is but a reflection of the fact that only a capitalistically produced commodity is a genuine commodity, whereas a commodity produced otherwise is a commodity *by chance*. Capital does not produce a use-value for its own sake; capital produces value in whatever use-value that happens to be the most convenient for that purpose. That is why the product of capital is necessarily a commodity. A simple commodity producer produces a use-value, an artefact, which does not typically have a normal price; he cannot be said to produce value except by chance. The labour theory of value is, thus, a necessary consequence of the capitalist mode of production, and not of simple commodity production.

(b)   The Viability of Capitalist Society

(α) The existence of capitalist society has been shown to imply the validity of the labour theory of value, in the sense that all use-values tend to be produced as commodities, with socially necessary labour. The reverse is also true. If the labour theory of value holds so that all use-values are produced as commodities with socially necessary labour, then capitalist society can exist as a historical society. In order for any society to be historically viable, the following condition must be satisfied: *the direct producers must have guaranteed access to the product of their necessary labour*. This condition is fulfilled by capitalist society, if all use-values are produced as commodities in the socially desired quantities, that is to say, with socially necessary labour. In that case, all capitalistically produced commodities may be exchanged at their normal prices, with the result that the wage-earners will be able to buy back the entire product of their necessary labour, while the capitalists will not only recover the value of their capital, but will also wholly appropriate the product of surplus labour. In turn, this means that the wage-earners will not receive any more than what is necessary and sufficient to reproduce their labour-power, so that they will have to sell it again as a commodity. This fact, as already stated, is equivalent to establishing the existence of capitalist society. Thus, the *condition of viability of capitalist society* amounts to the proposition that every wage-worker buys back the value of his labour-power as wage-goods, and that, as a corollary, the surplus value that he produces falls entirely into the hands of the capitalist.

In order to demonstrate this position, I will deliberately begin by envisaging a capitalist society in which no surplus labour is performed. Needless to say, no such society in fact exists, be it capitalist or otherwise. Yet this drastic abstraction is warranted in the theory of value, in just the same way as the abstract system of simple reproduction is warranted in the theory of accumulation. It is inconceivable that capitalist society would fail to accumulate, that is, fail to convert part of surplus value into capital. Nevertheless, the reproduction-process of capital must first be studied in the context of a simple reproduction, in which the capitalist class individually consumes the whole of the produced surplus value. The reason is that simple reproduction already contains the minimum conditions of reproduction, which must be preserved even under expanded reproduction. In other words, a simple reproduction is always embedded in all cases of expanded reproduction. The same thing can be said of the present abstraction of a capitalist society that contains only necessary labour. Even if, in reality, surplus labour is always performed, the fact that wage-workers must perform necessary labour, so as to produce the collection of wage-goods necessary and sufficient for the reproduction of their labour-power, does not disappear. It is, therefore, warranted to study this fundamental fact in isolation from other more complicated relations that characterise capitalist society.

In order to avoid any misunderstanding, however, it must be stressed that this abstraction is not the same thing as reducing capitalist society to a society of simple commodity production. Simple commodity production, as already stated, does not commoditise labour-power. In the present context, on the contrary, labour-power is supposed to be a fully-fledged commodity in possession of value. Yet its purchaser, the capitalist, is not present in flesh and blood. This abstraction, in other words, merely focuses on a particular aspect of capitalist society for the purpose of exposition; it is an expository (and heuristic) simplification at the present level of abstraction that prepares the way for a more concrete development of the theory, which will follow. Hence, although his physical existence is held implicit, the capitalist is nevertheless present behind the scenes, if only as a ghost-like operator of capitalist chrematistics. This simplification in no way alludes to the actual historical existence of what remains a strictly imaginary regime of simple commodity production.

Let the basket of wage-goods, which is just enough to reproduce the labour-power of a simple worker per day, be one unit of Y, and let one unit of Y be producible in 6 hours of necessary labour. Suppose that a capitalist employs one worker for a day for 6 hours, and produces 3 units of Y, in which 18 hours of labour are embodied. If this output sells for 9 dollars, then, with the assumption of no surplus labour, the capitalist's capital (or output) composition will be as follows:

	(c)		(v)		(s)		
(in hours of labour)	12	+	6	+	0	=	18,
(in dollars)	6	+	3	+	0	=	9,
(in units of Y)	2	+	1	+	0	=	3;

The value and the price of Y per unit are $\lambda_y = 6$, $p_y = 3$. Since the worker must be able to buy back one unit of Y, after having performed the six hours of necessary labour, $p_y = 3$ requires that he should be paid the money wage of three dollars. The capitalist invests 6 dollars in the means of production and 3 dollars in labour-power, but sells his output for 9 dollars realising no profit (which is shown in the second line of the above tabulation). The same thing is stated both in value (the first line) and quantities (the third line).

Suppose that another capitalist produces X, which may be a component of Y, or an item of the means of production to be consumed in the production of Y. If he too hires one worker for a day and produces 6 units of X, which embody 30 hours of labour, and which sells for 15 dollars, then this capitalist's capital (or output) composition must be the following:

	(c)		(v)		(s)		
(in value terms)	24	+	6	+	0	=	30
(in price terms)	12	+	3	+	0	=	15
(in quantity terms)	4.8	+	1.2	+	0	=	6,

and $\lambda_x = 5$, $p_x = 2.5$. In this case again, the worker must be paid the wage of 3 dollars, so as to be able to buy back one unit of Y, with which to reproduce his labour-power. The capitalist invests 12 dollars in constant capital, which he recovers by selling 4.8 units of X, and 3 dollars in variable capital, which he recovers by selling 1.2 units of X. He makes no profit.

Here, the exchange of the two commodities, X and Y, may be written as '1.2 units of X = 1 unit of Y', since they are both equal to 3 dollars. This 'equation' of exchange not only reflects the common price of 3 dollars, but also the real common factor, namely, 6 hours of socially necessary labour. This equation of exchange is not like Marx's '1 quarter corn = x cwt. iron', which merely states that both sides have the same price, without explaining why, in terms of socially necessary labour, they are also equal. In this case, the above equation of exchange directly reveals the substance of value because values and prices are proportional:

$$p_x 1.2 \; = \; p_y 1 \; = \; 3 \text{ dollars,}$$
$$\lambda_x 1.2 \; = \; \lambda_y 1 \; = \; 6 \text{ hours.}$$

This proportionality holds only in the absence of surplus labour. Suppose that the capitalist, who produces X, sold 6 units of his output for 12 dollars, instead of 15 dollars. In that case, his capital (= output) composition would be:

	(c)		(v)		(s)		
(in value terms)	24	+	6	+	0	=	30,
(in price terms)	9	+	3	+	0	=	12,
(in quantity terms)	4.5	+	1.5	+	0	=	6,

so that $\lambda_x = 5$ and $p_x = 2$ would follow. However, that would be an impossible situation, since $\lambda_x = 5$ would mean that 1.5 units of X should embody 7.5 hours of labour, whereas the above table shows that 1.5 units of X are the product of 6 necessary hours of labour. The same contradiction occurs if the output quantity is divided into the constant-capital component and the variable-capital component in terms of any price other than $p_x = 2.5$.[155] This suggests that, in the absence of surplus labour, values and prices must necessarily be proportional.

The proportionality, in this case, reflects the fact that if society produces wage-goods alone, directly and indirectly, that society is like a union of Robinson Crusoes who perform no surplus labour. Suppose that a, b, c, d, e and f are the use-values produced in society, and that they are either directly items of wage-goods or indirectly items of the means of producing wage-goods. If, for example, society allocates one-sixth of its labour to the production of each of these items, the same result can be obtained in one of two ways: either one-sixth of the working population devotes all of its necessary labour-time of 6 hours a day to the production of one item, or each individual worker produces all these items, devoting to each one hour of their necessary labour-time.

---

155   This price is calculated as follows: Divide the necessary labour-time (6) by the known value of X ($\lambda_x = 5$) to obtain 1.2 units of X; then $1.2p_x = 3$, since one basket of wage-goods is 3 dollars. It follows that $p_x = 2.5$.

The former case of the *social division of labour* can be reduced to the latter case of *non-specialisation with the exchange of one use-value for another, produced in an equal number of labour-hours*. If the consumption pattern differs from one worker to another, then each of the non-specialised workers of the second case can obtain the desired basket for consumption in one of two ways: either he exchanges with other workers wage-goods that he wants less of for wage-goods that he wants more of, or he reduces the production of wage-goods that he wants less of and increases the production of wage-goods that he wants more of. The former case of exchange achieves the same result as the latter case of production adjustment if use-values of an equal labour cost are exchanged. The moral of the story is now quite obvious: in the union of Robinson Crusoes, exchange is just another way of accomplishing what the individual adjustment of production would have achieved in any case, even if, in the case of the production adjustment, one hour of labour sacrificed in one branch of industry is one hour of labour gained in another branch of industry. In each case, what occurs is the exchange of the product of one labour-hour for the product of one labour-hour. This primitive fact compels the proportionality of values and prices for all the products of the abstract capitalist society, which performs no surplus labour.

(β) If a pirate ship appears on the scene and requires the community of Robinson Crusoes to produce not only wage-goods for themselves, but also tributary goods for the pirates, the situation undergoes a drastic change. The pirates are not productive workers; they merely apply extra-economic coercion, perhaps with intimidating gunshots, to the Robinson Crusoes in order to make them produce tributary goods e, f, g and h. How many hours of surplus labour must now be performed will depend on how greedy the pirates are. The expropriators do not have any conception of cost in terms of productive labour; they are only aware of the cost of appropriating the fruits of surplus labour. Thus, if the pirates were rational and capable of calculating, in money terms, the average cost, m_j, of appropriating one unit of tributary good, j, where j = e, f, g, h,[156] then they would exchange the tributary goods among themselves at prices proportional to the money cost of appropriation: $q_j = km_j, j$ = e, f, g, h, where k is a positive constant. In this case, however, e and f are also wage-goods, and their valuation among the direct producers and that among the expropriators will, in general, be different:

$$m_e:m_f = q_e:q_f \neq p_e:p_f = \lambda_e:\lambda_f$$

---

156 The definition of m_j's will become clearer in the next paragraph.

In a non-commodity-economic society, such an inconsistency between the two sets of valuation of use-values causes no serious problem. Nor is the constant, k, rationally determined, as it is largely dependent on contingent factors. In capitalist society, by contrast, neither any inconsistency in the valuation of use-values, nor any indeterminacy of the factor-k, can be tolerated. Both problems will, in fact, be solved by capital's peculiarly commodity-economic method of appropriating surplus value. That is to say, instead of applying extra-economic force to the productive community from the outside, so as to expropriate surplus products, capital turns the whole system of use-value production into an instrument of value augmentation. Capital, as a consequence, manages to allocate the productive labour of society in just the same way as the community of Robinson Crusoes did before the arrival of the pirates, such that every socially wanted use-value is produced with socially necessary labour. For this reason, the prices of commodities in capitalist society cannot be wholly independent of their values.

Let us now suppose that the daily labour-time of each productive worker is 12 hours, of which 6 are necessary and the other 6 are surplus labour-time ($6v + 6s$). Suppose that the capitalist who employs one such worker produces during each day 5 units of Y, in which 30 hours of labour are embodied, and sells this output for 15 dollars. Then the compositions of his output in terms of value, price and quantity are, respectively, as follows:

	(c)		(v)		(s)			
(in value terms)	18	+	6	+	0	=	30,	$\lambda_y = 6$,
(in price terms)	9.5	+	3	+	2.5	=	15,	$p_y = 3$,
(in quantity terms)	3.17	+	1	+	0.83	=	5,	$r = 0.2$.

Since the price of Y per unit is $p_y = 3$, the worker must receive 3 dollars in order to buy back one basket of wage-goods. It is assumed that the capitalist invests 9.5 dollars in the means of production, so that the rate of profit is 20% [since $(9.5 + 3)(1 + r) = 15, r = 0.2$]. Clearly, in this case, the worker can buy back the product of his necessary labour with 3 dollars that are paid to him as his wage. The product of surplus labour, that is, 0.83 unit of Y, belongs wholly to the capitalist, because its money value, p_y 0.83 = 2.5, is 20% of the money value of capital invested, 9.5 + 3 = 12.5. In order to appropriate one unit of Y as surplus product, it would be necessary to invest 15.06 dollars, instead of 12.5 dollars, and produce 6.024 units of Y instead of 5 units of Y, as the daily output. In that case, 15.06/6.024 = 2.5 dollars would have to be invested per unit of Y. (The same sum of money can be directly obtained from the above tabulation, by dividing 12.5 = 9.5 + 3 dollars by 5, that is, by dividing the cost of production of Y by the number of units of Y produced). This amount may be regarded as the 'average cost of appropriating one unit of Y as a tributary good', that is to say, as m_y. Then, from $km_y = p_y$, it follows that $k = 1 + r = 1.2$.

Since the labour theory of value is assumed to hold, that is to say, since all use-values are assumed to be produced in the socially desired quantities, if another commodity X is to be produced, its production must be equally profitable. Let us suppose, therefore, that the capitalist who employs one worker and invests 22 dollars in the means of production produces 15 units of X, in which 45 hours of labour are embodied. In that case, his production data in value, price and quantity terms will be the following:

	(c)		(v)		(s)			
(in value terms)	33	+	6	+	6	= 45	$\lambda_x = 3$,
(in price terms)	22	+	3	+	5	= 30	$p_x = 2$,
(in quantity terms)	11	+	1.5	+	2.5	= 15	$r = 0.2$.

The price of X per unit must be $p_x = 2$ [since $(22 + 3)(1 + 0.2) = 30$ and $30/15 = 2$]. Again, the worker, whose necessary labour of 6 hours produces 1.5 units of X, is paid $p_x1.5 = 3$ dollars, as the wage with which he can buy one basket of wage-goods. As for the capitalist, he appropriates 2.5 units of X as the surplus product, since $p_x2.5 = 5$ is 20% of the money value of capital invested, 22 + 3 = 25. In order to appropriate one unit of X as surplus product, he should have invested 10 dollars instead of 25 dollars, and produced 6 units of X rather than 15 units of X. The average cost of appropriating one unit of X will then be 10/6 = 1.67. (The same number is directly obtained by dividing 25 dollars invested by 15 units of X). If this number is multiplied by $k = 1 + r = 1.2$, one obtains the price of 2 dollars per unit of X. Since X represents any commodity other than Y that is being produced in the present capitalist economy, the above explains how the prices of all commodities are determined once p_y and r are given.

Clearly, in the presence of surplus labour, the capitalist pricing by the method of the pirates violates the proportionality of values and prices. In particular, the following fact must be observed. If a worker produces 1.5 units of X in 6 hours of necessary labour, it does not necessarily follow that 60 hours of labour are, on the whole, needed for the production of 15 units. It is more rational for the capitalist to reason that if 1.5 units of X cost 3 dollars, 15 units should cost 30 dollars. In the production of X, which is not a wage-good, the latter reasoning of the capitalist overrules the former reasoning of the productive worker. However, in the production of Y, which is the basket of wage-goods, both methods of reasoning are equally valid. One would say that since one basket is produced in 6 hours, 5 baskets must be produced in 30 hours. The other would say that since one basket costs 3 dollars, 5 baskets should cost 15 dollars. This fact shows *the fundamental importance of the production of Y in a capitalist economy*. The conversion of labour-power presupposes the conversion of wage-goods into commodities. In all societies, a certain number of baskets of wage-goods must be produced in order to maintain the productive core of the working population. In capitalist society, there is a corresponding money value of capital that must be invested therein. Hence, depending on the price of wage-goods (p_y), the rate of profit (r) is determined. Since all other commodities are produced in the socially desired quantities with some money value of capital investment, this profit-rate further determines the prices of those commodities relative to p_y. The exchange of commodities according to these prices ensures: (1) that every wage-worker receives the product of his necessary labour; and (2) that the product of his surplus labour belongs to the capitalist. It is, therefore, demonstrated that if all commodities are produced with socially necessary labour, capitalist society can exist just as any other historical society.

(γ) The above discussion must not be confused with the theory of the formation of equilibrium prices and the general rate of profit (to be developed in the doctrine of distribution). Here, prices and the rate of profit cannot be simultaneously determined, because the technology available for the production of all use-values is not as yet made explicit. In fact, the choice of a combination (p_y, r) amounts to naming the particular point through which a 'factor-price frontier' is passing. The frontier implies a particular set of techniques. For that reason, the price of the basket of wage-goods and the money value of capital invested in all fields of production must be 'assumed' in order to arrive at the prices of other commodities. The purpose of the present analysis is merely to establish a proposition of the following kind: 'The validity of the labour theory of value, i.e., the production of all use-values with socially necessary labour, implies a set of normal prices such that the exchange of commodities at those prices guarantees the historical viability of capitalist society'. The labour theory of value does not imply, nor does it depend upon, a set of prices that are proportional to values, but rather it depends upon any set of prices that are consistent with the optimum allocation of productive labour. The doctrine of production, however, often assumes that normal prices and values are proportional, even when surplus value is produced. This assumption is made only for the sake of expository simplicity. It is, however, important to know what this assumption actually implies, and why that implication does not contradict the purpose of the doctrine of production.

Let us first demonstrate the fact that in a capitalist economy in which surplus value is produced, *prices and values are proportional, if and only if the value composition of capital is the same in all branches of industry*. Assume, as before, that the value of 5 units of Y, produced by one worker in one day, has the composition $18c + 6v + 6s = 30$, and that the money value of this output is 15 dollars. If the proportionality of values and prices is assumed, the production data in value, price and quantity terms will be:

	(c)		(v)		(s)			
(in value terms)	18	+	6	+	6	=	30,	$\lambda_y = 6,$
(in price terms)	9	+	3	+	3	=	15,	$p_y = 3,$
(in quantity terms)	3	+	1	+	1	=	5,	$r = 0.25,$

because the price-to-value ratio of the output must be the same as that of the means of production, $15/30 = 9/18$. It is then true that $r = s/(c + v) = 0.25$. Yet if the newly formed value is always $6v + 6s$, this profit-rate requires that the value of constant capital used up by one worker per day is always 18. Hence, the value composition of capital $c/v = 3$ must be the same in all branches of industry.

Conversely, let us assume that the value composition of capital is the same in the production of X and of Y. It is already known that:

	in Y							in X					
18	+	6	+	6	=	30,	18	+	6	+	6	=	30,
?	+	3	+	?	=	15,	?	+	3	+	?	=	?,
?	+	1	+	?	=	5,	?	+	?	+	?	=	15.

If the common rate of profit is $r = 0.25$, the table for Y will be as before, and already satisfies the proportionality, $9/18 = 15/30 = 0.5$. Suppose then that the table for X is as follows:

18	+	6	+	6	=	30,	$\lambda_x = 2,$
13.8	+	3	+	4.2	=	21,	$p_x = 1.4,$
9.86	+	2.14	+	3	=	15,	$r = 0.25.$

At first sight, it appears that nothing is wrong here. Yet the price-to-value ratio of the product is $21/30 = 0.7$, and that of the means of production is $13.8/18 = 0.77$. Suppose that the means of production of 18 value units are also produced with the same value composition of capital, $c/v = 3$, and the same rate of surplus value, $s/v = 1$. Then, the price-to-value ratio of the 'means of production of the means of production of X' is 9.24/ 10.8 = 0.86. If the experiment is repeated, it will be found that the ratio keeps increasing as one moves back the 'stages' of production. Now, let us suppose that the table for X is as follows:

$$18 \; + \; 6 \; + \; 6 \; = \; 30, \quad \lambda_x \; = \; 2,$$
$$7 \; + \; 3 \; + \; 2.5 \; = \; 12.5, \quad p_x \; = \; 0.83,$$
$$8.4 \; + \; 3.6 \; + \; 3 \; = \; 15, \quad r \; = \; 0.25.$$

In this case, the price-to-value ratio of the product is 12.5/30 = 0.42, and that of the means of production 7/18 = 0.39. If one moves back one 'stage', assuming the same value composition, then the price-to-value ratio of the 'means of production of the means of production of X' is 3.8/10.8 = 0.35. If the same experiment is repeated, it will be found that the ratio keeps decreasing as one moves back the 'stages' of production. It is, however, not possible to infinitely regress in this way because basic goods (means of production) form a system such that, for example, coal is needed to produce iron and iron is needed to produce coal. Thus, if the price-to-value ratio of iron is greater than that of coal in the first instance, the reverse must be the case in the second instance. It then follows that if the value composition of capital is the same in all branches of industry, the price-to-value ratio of the product and that of the means of production must be the same. By virtue of this fact, the second line of the table for X must satisfy the condition $(18\alpha + 3)(1 + 0.25) = 30\alpha$, from where $\alpha = 0.5$ is obtained. In that light, the table becomes:

$$18 \; + \; 6 \; + \; 6 \; = \; 30, \quad \lambda_x \; = \; 2$$
$$9 \; + \; 3 \; + \; 3 \; = \; 15, \quad p_x \; = \; 1$$
$$9 \; + \; 3 \; + \; 3 \; = \; 15, \quad r \; = \; 0.25,$$

so that $\lambda_x/p_x = 2 = \lambda_y/p_y$. This establishes the proportionality of values and prices.

In an actual capitalist economy, the value composition of capital differs, of course, from one industry to another, reflecting differences in the production of use-values, and such differences do not tend to disappear with the development of capitalism. The dialectic of capital must, therefore, take that fact into full consideration when the time comes, that is to say, when the theory of prices and profit is developed in the Doctrine of Distribution. At the present stage, however, the theory is not yet sufficiently concrete to explicitly treat that problem, just as the theory of money in the doctrine of circulation, while discussing the function of money as the means of payment, had to eschew a detailed account of credit and banking. Since the dialectic proceeds on a spiral path, the same ground is often revisited with increasing light in order to bring out the details of what was earlier left in rough contours. If, at one stage of abstraction, some aspects of the problem are deliberately left implicit, there is a good reason for that. In the present case, the validity of the labour theory of value presupposes a set of normal prices, and these 'normal prices' will themselves be more concrete-synthetically specified later as 'equilibrium prices or production-prices'. At this point in the development of the theory, any set of prices that is consistent with the optimum allocation of productive labour will serve our purpose. What is important in the present discussion is not so much the existence of a particular set of equilibrium prices as the stability of such prices. That is to say, we need only take cognisance of the fact that an excess demand (supply) for any commodity raises (lowers) its price, inducing capital to produce more (less) of it. Hence, if there is a set of prices that are proportional to values, and if that set does not restrict the scope of the doctrine of production, there is no reason why it should not, for simplicity's sake, be adopted for the purpose of the present discussion. The same consideration applies to the rate of profit. The theory cannot, at the present stage, determine exactly what rate of profit should prevail, when productive labour is optimally allocated. Any positive rate of profit will do, provided that it is consistent with the assumed set of prices. What is important now is that the same rate of profit must apply to all branches of production. Since the rate of profit, $r = s/(c + v)$, is consistent with the set of prices that are proportional to values, there is no reason why that rate of profit should not be adopted in the present discussion.

To explicitly take into account differences in the value composition of capital in different industries implies a technical differentiation of capitalists, according to the use-values that they specialise in producing. Some capitalists produce fabrics and others make steel; the value composition of capital is usually higher in a heavy industry than in a light industry. Yet it is precisely this kind of differentiation between capitalists, or operating units of capital, that is irrelevant to (or held deliberately implicit in) the doctrine of production, since the production-relation between the capitalist and his workers does not differ depending on whether the firm makes a fabric or steel. The production-relation, or value-relation in the present case, is invariant to the specific use-value that the capitalist currently chances to produce. The value-relation is formed because the workers are indifferent to the concrete-useful form of labour, and because the capitalist is free to produce any use-value that may be in demand in society. This essential argument of the doctrine of production would only be obscured rather than emphasised if the question of the specialisation of capital in various branches of use-value production were prematurely introduced. It is, therefore, perfectly consistent with the method of the dialectic to keep the concept of capitalist specialisation (and hence inter-industrial differences in the value composition of capital, c/v) implicit at this stage, pending the formation of the capitalist market. Only when the capitalist mode of production is demonstrated to be a self-sustaining motion can capital proceed to form its own market. In the meantime, therefore, it must be understood that all use-values can be produced with such techniques as give rise to a common value composition of capital throughout the economy. This restrictive assumption may be removed only when it is necessary to do so, namely, only in the Doctrine of Distribution.

(c)   *The Necessity of the Law of Value*

(α) If the existence of capitalist society is presupposed, the labour theory of value must necessarily hold. Conversely, if the validity of the labour theory of value is presupposed, then capitalist society must be viable. It is impossible for one to be true without the other also being true. The historical existence of capitalism and the functioning of the labour theory of value are, therefore, identical. This fact is referred to as the *necessity of the law of value*. The law of value, in other words, is the labour theory of value, as it implies the existence of capitalism, or the existential law of capitalism with specific reference to the labour theory of value. If the labour-and-production process is capitalistically operated as the value-formation-and-augmentation process, the 'law of value' necessarily enforces itself. It is, therefore, the most fundamental law upon which capitalism revolves. Why, then, is there such a close relation between capitalism and the determination of value by socially necessary labour? It is because the existence of all historical societies depends, in the final analysis, on human exertion of productive labour on nature. No human society can survive without establishing a metabolic relation with the surrounding nature, that is, without working on nature and transforming part of it into use-values that are directly or indirectly useful to human life, with the mediation of productive labour. It is the particular manner in which this process is carried out, or the particular 'mode of production' for short, that historically characterises different types of society. Capitalist society certainly is not exempt from the primitive fact that man obtains his wherewithal to live from nature, in exchange for the expenditure of productive labour. Thus, according to Adam Smith, 'Labour was the first price, the original purchase-money that was paid for all things. It was not by gold or by silver, but by labour that all the wealth of the world was originally purchased'.[157] Although Smith fails to distinguish what is specific to capitalist society from what is common to all societies, it is true that all use-values are originally acquired by productive labour, and that the 'real price' or value of a commodity is ultimately dependent upon 'the toil and trouble of acquiring it'[158] from nature.

In capitalist society, however, this primitive fact does not appear in its simplest form, but rather in a form adapted to the operation of capital. The Charts 4.1 and 4.2 below illustrate the difference. In the first Chart (4.1), the direct producers (L) expend productive labour on nature (N) to obtain use-values. In a class society, some of the use-values thus obtained are in the form of surplus products, due to the ruling class (X), which appropriates them from the direct producers by means of extra-economic forces. In this case, the extra-economic mechanism of the appropriation of surplus products remains outside of the metabolic exchange of matter between man and nature. In capitalist society, by contrast, capital (K) directly intervenes in this man-nature exchange of matter, as in the second Chart 4.2.

The Simpler Form

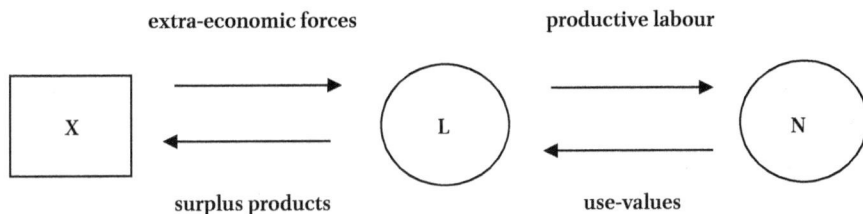

CHART 4.1

The Capitalistic Form

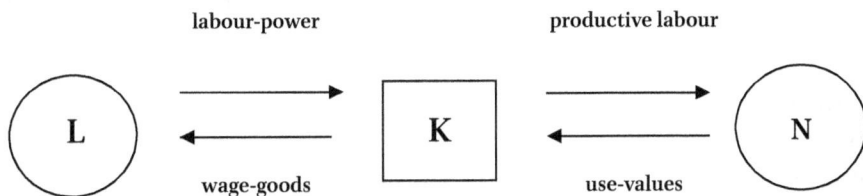

CHART 4.2

---

157   Smith 1937, p. 30.
158   Ibid.

The application of productive labour to nature is possible there *only through capital*, which in its production-process consumes the labour-power of the direct producers, purchased as a commodity. Consequently, all the products of labour (use-values) belong to capital in the first instance, and only wage-goods are returned to the direct producers in exchange for labour-power. Only in form, and not in substance, is the exchange of labour-power for wage-goods identical to the exchange of ordinary commodities. When, for instance, the owner of linen and the owner of wine exchange these use-values through the mediation of money, both traders already possess what is to be exchanged. Yet when labour-power is purchased, the capitalist does not own wage-goods; wage-goods or their equivalent must be produced by the productive consumption of labour-power itself, after it is purchased. It is true that the workers are paid only at the end of the contractual period, so that capital already possesses wage-goods by the time wages are paid. Yet at the beginning of the contractual period, when labour-power is purchased, and when capital consequently obtains the right to consume it, no output at all of the contractual period, whether wage-goods or otherwise, is present. Hence, the exchange of labour-power for wage-goods is not an exchange of already existing commodities, but an exchange of commodities through the process of production (that is, through the capital-operated man-nature exchange of matter), which is yet to take place.

It is on the basis of this fundamental exchange of labour-power for wage-goods that capitalism hangs together. Here, the law of value appears in its purest form, for if the value of labour-power is, say, six hours of labour, the wage-goods must also be the product of six hours of labour. Value must be exchanged for value regardless of what money wages turn out to be, because the consumption of labour-power by capital for six hours forms the six hours' worth of value in the wage-goods. In this fundamental value relation, standing upon the primitive exchange of matter between man and nature, productive labour unmistakably forms value. Yet if the expenditure of labour for six hours forms value, there is no reason why labour expended beyond six hours does not form value. Such labour forms surplus value or 'augments' value. In this way, it is clear that the division of newly produced value into what corresponds to the value of variable capital and surplus value is not a matter of the 'distribution of the product'. Distribution usually implies the division of a pre-existing whole into shares. Hence, if the value product, v + s, is already present, without any pre-judgement as to how it must be divided, then and only then does the question of its distribution meaningfully arise. However, in the present case, the distribution is a foregone conclusion. Before any production begins, labour-power must be purchased, for production *ipso facto* means the consumption of labour-power. Whether any new value is, in consequence, formed or not, capital must pay the full value of the labour-power that it has purchased as a commodity, under pain of self-destruction or bankruptcy. The owner of the labour-power, once it is sold, must receive its value, even if it, by any chance, ends by producing no new value. Surely he cannot 'share' or receive the dividend of a value product, which may never even exist.

(β) In capitalist society, productive labour is not expended merely to create use-values, but to produce commodities. Hence, the duality of productive labour, consisting of concrete-useful and abstract-human labour, now becomes the duality of productive labour, consisting of use-value creating labour and value-forming labour. Therefore, if 8kg of raw cotton are converted into 6kg of cotton yarn in 6 hours of spinning labour, with the assistance of a spinning machine, and if the 8kg of raw cotton contain 20 hours of labour, and the wear and tear of the machine represent 4 hours of labour, then the 6kg of cotton yarn are not merely the product of 30 hours of labour; they are a commodity embodying 30 hours of labour as value. Thus, if society spends 3 million hours of labour in all to produce the total output of its commodities, then the 6kg of cotton yarn, as a commodity, represent one hundred-thousandth of the homogeneous mass of all commodities. All capitalistically produced commodities are interrelated, because as value they are nothing but a fraction of the total expenditure of society's productive labour.

The productivity of labour in spinning may, however, rise in such a way that 12kg of raw cotton are converted into 9kg of cotton yarn, in the same 6 hours of spinning labour. If 12kg of raw cotton then contain 30 hours of labour, and the wear and tear of the spinning machine are in this case 6 hours, the 9kg of cotton yarn is the product of 42 hours of labour. The value of cotton yarn per kg, which was 5 hours earlier, has now fallen to 4.67 hours. The fall in the unit value of about 7% results from the fact that the 50% increase in the quantity of yarn (from 6kg to 9kg) requires only a 40% increase in the value of the output (from 30 hours to 42 hours), because despite the 50% increase in the value of the means of production (from 24 hours to 36 hours), the new value of 6 hours, formed by spinning, remains unchanged. If, however, no change takes place in the productivity of spinning labour, while the value of the means of production alone rises by 50%, then the value of the 6kg of cotton yarn merely rises by 40%, so that the value per kg is now 7 hours instead of 5 hours.

Exercises of this kind confirm the fact that the pre-existing value of the means of production (such as raw cotton and the spinning machine), while it may increase or decrease with the quantity of the output (cotton yarn), remains absolutely unaffected by productivity changes that occur in the process of production in question (spinning), in which they are used. Raw cotton and the spinning machine are the products of cotton-growing labour and machine-building labour, but do not perform any spinning labour, or abstract-human labour concomitant with it, in the production of cotton yarn. Hence, they cannot add any new value in the spinning process. It is the property of the concrete-useful labour (of spinning) that transfers a greater or lesser value of the means of production (raw cotton and wear and tear of the spinning machine) depending on how productive it is. Similarly, the natural means of production, which have no value, make no contribution to the formation of value, however useful or indispensable they may be for the production of a use-value. By the same token, means of labour, such as tools and machines, transfer their value to the product only to the extent of their wear and tear, although contributing to the creation of the product as a functioning whole. By the same token again, the waste of raw cotton that cannot be technically avoided does transfer its value to the newly produced cotton yarn, in the same way as supplementary or auxiliary materials, if there exist any. Thus, concrete-useful labour, now regarded as labour that creates the use-value of a commodity, not only converts a collection of the means of production into a new product, but also transfers their pre-existing value to the new product.

The duality of productive labour thus acquires new specifications in the production-process of capital. This is not all. Since individual capitalists produce commodities through the method of trial and error, without the requisite knowledge of what other capitalists may be doing, it is not possible to calculate the value of a commodity in advance. Thus, when a commodity is produced, neither the capitalist nor the workers can know whether the labour actually being performed is in fact socially necessary. Only when the commodity is sold for an expected price, namely, the price that yields a profit-rate as good as anywhere else, can it be surmised that the commodity has realised its value. Even this, however, is a theoretical proposition because the general rate of profit is never empirically observable, nor are all commodities necessarily bought and sold at normal prices. Hence, if a particular commodity, cotton yarn, is sold with the profit rate of, say, 15%, which is generally considered to be a good rate, there is no assurance that it has not resulted from contingent factors, such as the purchase of raw cotton at a price well below the normal. In some factories, it may be possible to actually measure an average duration of labour-time needed to convert a set of means of production into a unit of the finished commodity. Yet this so-called 'time study' is never a general practice, nor is it expected to be either accurate or complete enough to be of any economic significance, although it may serve some managerial or technical purpose.

This means that 'socially necessary labour' that is supposed to form the value of a commodity is not an observable substance, even though privately planned and executed labour for the production of a use-value is obviously perceptible to the senses. The duality of abstract-human labour and concrete-useful labour, therefore, becomes the duality of hardly apprehensible social labour that forms value and immediately palpable private labour that creates a use-value. The secret of the so-called *fetishism of commodities* is to be found here. A commodity is plain as a use-value, but is 'enigmatic' as the embodiment of value, given that everyone can see or feel concrete-useful labour, while no one has ever seen or felt 'socially necessary labour'. This substance is elusive to the untrained eye, and cannot be seen by the empiricist observer, and so it has often been ignored as unscientific or 'metaphysical'. Indeed, when the labour theory of value declares that the value of a commodity is commensurate with socially necessary labour, empiricists and positivists are stricken by terror. 'Beware of the labour theory of value', admonish the teachers of bourgeois economics, as if to echo Newton's warning to beware of metaphysics. Yet if they shirk the law of value, how can they possibly 'know' for sure that capitalism is more than an illusion?

(γ) The law of value *enforces itself through the motion of prices*. If particular use-values are overproduced, that is to say, produced more than is enough to satisfy the social demand, their prices will fall and that discourages further expansion of their production by capital. If other use-values are under-produced, namely, produced less than is enough to satisfy the social demand, their prices will rise and this encourages a more rapid expansion of their production by capital. In this way, all use-values will eventually tend to be produced *in the socially desired quantities*, and their prices will tend to settle to normal prices that reflect the values of the commodities. These prices, which will later be called 'production-prices or equilibrium prices', therefore can be said to be governed or regulated by values. For otherwise, for example, if the production of a commodity by capital did not respond to the motion of prices as described above, so that a commodity could not be supplied in the socially desired quantity (if that commodity could not be produced with socially necessary labour, and thus fails to possess a definite value), then it would not have a production-price, a full-equilibrium price or even a normal price. In other words, its price would remain arbitrary, temporary and theoretically indeterminate. To say that the capitalistically produced commodity has an equilibrium (or normal) price means *ipso facto* that the latter reflects its value. This proposition, however, does not mean that equilibrium prices must be derived, or calculated, from some previously known values by some quantitative 'transformation'. Values are in fact not empirically measureable quantities. Even theoretically, insofar as the priority in time is concerned, values do not exist prior to equilibrium prices, for they can only be determined simultaneously.[159] That which must be emphasised here is that values are not merely supply-determined or technologically determined without reference to social demand. On the contrary, capital could not continue to operate for long if it ignored the existing pattern of social demand, as reflected in the motion of prices.

To say that value cannot be determined without taking into consideration both the demand side condition (the pattern of the social demand) and the supply side condition (the technology) does not, of course, mean that the interaction of demand and supply in the abstract is sufficient to determine values. If that were the case, a commodity that is not even capitalistically produced, such as an antique or an artistic object, would also have a value. Such a thing can have an arbitrary 'monopoly price', at which the forces of demand and those of supply come to a settlement of some kind, so that the excess demand for and the excess supply of that commodity are eliminated. It may therefore be *formally* claimed that a market price reached equilibrium in the monopoly market. Yet such a price depends on so many contingent (not logically explainable) factors that it cannot be regarded as a normal (or equilibrium) price of the capitalist market. Since neither a value nor a true equilibrium price can be deduced from supply conditions alone, the interplay of demand and supply is, of course, absolutely essential to the 'measurement' of the value of a commodity, namely, to the establishment of its normal price. Further discussion of the subject belongs to the Doctrine of Distribution.[160] Suffice it to say here that a capitalistically produced commodity is a *genuine commodity* in possession of a normal price that reflects its value, the determination of which must take into consideration both the supply side and the demand side conditions.

The importance of the price mechanism arises from the so-called *anarchy* of capitalist production. In general, an individual capitalist does not produce by contract; *he produces for an open market,* just as a commodity-owner sells in an impersonal market rather than to known purchasers. Therefore, the capitalist does not know in advance the real marketability of his commodity, nor the intensity of competition that he will actually face. Only after the commodity is produced and marketed is he made aware of whether or not his expectation, on the basis of past experience, was warranted. The fact that the law of value thus regulates the anarchy of production *ex post facto,* so as to adapt it to the social demand, appears to the capitalist as if he and others were subject to an external force, such as a law of nature, which exercises an enforcement or compulsion, which is beyond human control. The law of value is not, of

---

159   More on this to come in Chapter 7.
160   See Chapter 7.

course, a statutory law, but neither is it a natural law that cannot be humanly rescinded. It is a historical law that governs the capitalistic operation of the labour-and-production process. In the final analysis, therefore, it is a man-made law that was historically adopted and that can be historically revoked. Only the choice of human society to operate the labour-and-production process by the anarchic method of capitalism compels the enforcement of the law of value. However, the law of value reifies human relations and imposes a thoroughly impersonal regulation on capitalist producers, who therefore find themselves spellbound by the consequences of their own actions, just as the primitives felt overpowered by the animistic spell of the totem pole, which they themselves carved and painted. The fetishism of commodities, or 'the thing-in-itself [of capitalism], shows itself here in its genesis'.[161]

C   The Development of the Capitalist Method of Production: Labour-Power as a Commodity (The Thing-in-Itself of Capitalist Production)

(a)   *The Rate of Surplus Value*

(α) As soon as the value-formation-and-augmentation process establishes itself as the capitalistic mode of operating the labour-and-production process, a new problem poses itself. How does capital exploit and develop the potential productivity of labour? Not in all societies is the productive power of labour either exhaustively utilised or vigorously advanced. Indeed, in some societies direct producers need not work to the limit of their physical capacity, nor is there any strong incentive to improve upon the existing technology of production. It is, however, well known that the opposite is the case in capitalist society. This fact must be explained by the peculiarity of the capitalist mode of production, that is to say, the capitalist method of operating the labour-and-production process. In the production-process of capital, the pre-existing value of the means of production, or of constant capital, is simply 'transferred' to the new product. It is true that productive labour, which forms and augments value, cannot take place without means of production, so that capitalists are obliged to invest money in constant capital. Yet the latter is only an instrument that enables variable capital to produce surplus value. Suppose that a capitalist invests $410 in constant capital, $90 in variable capital, and obtains a surplus value of $90, during a given time period. Then the value of the product

---

161   Hegel 1975, p. 180.

(410c + 90v + 90s) is $590, and the capitalist augments the value of $500 to $590. However, if instead he invested $600 in constant capital, the value of the product (600c + 90v + 90s) would be $780; the augmentation of value would then be from $690 to $780. Although the rate of profit, $s/(c + v)$, which is the sole concern of the capitalist, is 18% in the first case, and a little over 13% in the second, there is no difference in the two cases in the fact that the newly produced value is $180 (=90v + 90s), or that the self-reproducing variable capital of $90 currently adds the surplus value of $90. The relation between the capitalist and his workers, which is invariant to the rate of profit, is measured by the rate of surplus value (s/v) and it is 100% in both cases.

If the rate of surplus value is 100%, this means that half of the working day is devoted to the reproduction of labour-power, and the remaining half to the production of surplus value for the capitalist class. It is this rate that defines the fundamental production-relation between productive workers, who sell their labour-power, and the capitalist, who purchases it. 'At first sight it appears a strange proceeding to equate the constant capital to zero' in the rate of profit, $r = s / (c + v)$, so as to define the *rate of surplus value* as $e = s/v$. However, Marx explains as follows:

> Of course the ratio of surplus value not only to that portion of the capital from which it immediately springs, and whose change of value it represents, but also to the sum total of capital advanced is economically of very great importance. We shall, therefore, in the third book, treat of this ratio exhaustively. In order to enable one portion of a capital to expand its value by being converted into labour-power, it is necessary that another portion be converted into means of production. In order that variable capital may perform its function, constant capital must be advanced in proper proportion, a proportion given by the special technical conditions of each labour-process. The circumstance, however, that retorts and other vessels are necessary to a chemical process does not compel the chemist to notice them in the result of his analysis.[162]

In other words, the pre-existing value of constant capital must be deliberately suppressed in order to fix one's attention on that aspect of the formation and augmentation of value that determines the workers-versus-capitalist relation. Through this relation, as expressed by the rate of surplus value, capital exploits and develops the productive powers of labour, even though this relation is never directly visible either to the capitalist or to the workers. The development of

---

162   Marx 1967, *Capital*, Volume I, p. 215.

the capitalist method of production is in fact nothing but the development of the method of promoting the rate of surplus value.

The rate of surplus value can be said to be determined by the length of the working day, given the length of the necessary labour-time. Alternatively, it can be said to be determined by the length of the necessary labour-time, given the length of the working day. If the production of surplus value is investigated on the assumption that the length of the necessary labour-time is given, the production of absolute surplus value is said to occur. If the production of surplus value is investigated on the assumption that the length of the working day is fixed, the production of relative surplus value is said to occur. Suppose, for example, that a worker who reproduces his labour-power in 6 hours works for 12 hours a day. Then he produces absolute surplus value at the rate of 100%. Yet if instead he works for 18 hours a day, his production of absolute surplus value will be at the rate of 200%. Suppose, on the other hand, that a worker who works for 12 hours a day reproduces his labour-power in 6 hours. Then, he produces relative surplus value at the rate of 100%. However, if instead he reproduces his labour-power in 4 hours, his production of relative surplus value will be at the rate of 200%. This definition might be construed as differing from Marx's, which is as follows:

> The surplus value produced by prolongation of the working day, I call absolute surplus value. On the other hand, the surplus value arising from the curtailment of the necessary labour-time, and from the corresponding alteration in the respective lengths of the two components of the working day, I call relative surplus value.[163]

Marx's definition gives the false impression that there are some initial lengths of the working day and of the necessary labour-time, in reference to which neither absolute nor relative surplus value is produced, and that only when there is a change from such initial lengths is there a production of either absolute or relative surplus value. Thus, for example, Sweezy writes:

> The rate of surplus value may be raised either by an extension of the working day, or by a lowering of the real wage, or by an increase in the productiveness of labor, or finally, by some combination of the three movements. In case of an increase in the length of the working day, Marx speaks of the production of absolute surplus value, while either a lowering of the real

163 Marx 1967, *Capital,* Volume I, p. 315.

wage or an increase in productivity, leading to a reduction of necessary labor, results in the production of relative surplus value.[164]

However, if this were the case, neither absolute nor relative surplus value could be produced unless there were a 'change' in the working day and/or the quantity of necessary labour. I find such a definition of surplus value, applicable only when it varies, difficult to accept. Any production of surplus value is both absolute and relative, depending upon how one looks at it. If it is viewed simply as an excess of newly produced value over the reproduced value of labour-power, surplus value is absolute. If it is viewed relative to the technical condition that determines the value of labour-power, then surplus value is relative.

The rate of surplus value, which thus defines the worker-versus-capitalist relation, must first be investigated from the point of view of the production of absolute surplus value rather than of relative surplus value. This is for the following reason. If the basket of wage-goods contains some given quantities x, y, z of commodities X, Y, Z, and if the number of hours of labour required for the production per unit of these commodities are $\lambda_x, \lambda_y, \lambda_z$ then the length of the necessary labour-time is equal to $\lambda_x x + \lambda_y y + \lambda_z z$. Since x, y, z are given quantities, this magnitude depends on the values $\lambda_x, \lambda_y, \lambda_z$ (at x, y, z), which further depend on the productivity of labour affecting industries X, Y, Z directly or indirectly. Hence, to say that $\lambda_x x + \lambda_y y + \lambda_z z$ is a constant means fixing society's productive technology and organisation apart from irrelevant changes in the productivity of labour in luxury-good industries, which do not influence the value of wage-goods. The point of view of absolute surplus value, in other words, enables one to study the production of surplus value in simpler terms, that is, broadly under a given state of arts in society's production of commodities. Indeed, once (x, y, z) and the technology of producing the wage-goods are given, the quantity of necessary labour can be uniquely determined. In reference to this quantity, capital wants as extensive and intensive a working day as possible. Only after this fundamental principle of capital is established can the possibility of curtailing the quantity of necessary labour be investigated.

(β) Having purchased labour-power as a commodity, capital, of course, intends to use it as thoroughly as possible. The same principle applies to any other element of production. It is impossible for capital to waste a portion of already purchased raw materials, for example, without fully exploiting its use-value; that would be inconsistent with its principle of chrematistics. However, labour-power is a special commodity, which cannot be separated from the person of

---

its natural owner, who daily reproduces it through his individual consumption. If labour-power is consumed too unscrupulously in the production-process, the owner of labour-power may not be able to reproduce it adequately by his subsequent consumption and rest. Exactly to what extent labour-power may be used during the day, without jeopardising its reproducibility, cannot be theoretically determined, since that sort of thing depends upon physical and historical conditions that are contingent to the commodity-economy. Theory, therefore, merely states that given the quantity of necessary labour, the production of absolute surplus value is possible up to a certain physical limit, and that capital, as a form of value augmentation, always strives to attain that limit. In concrete terms, the production of absolute surplus value is pursued by (1) the extension of the working day, (2) the intensification of labour, and (3) the reduction of real wages. Of these, by far the most typical is the method of extending the length of the working day.

In the early period of capitalism, many industries were still largely dependent upon traditional handicraft production, and even after primitive accumulation, the degree of commoditisation of labour-power was limited. Craftsmen and erstwhile peasants could not be easily subjected to the demands of capital, so that even the extension of the working day had to be enforced by legislation. Marx writes about the history of such legislation, from the middle of the fourteenth-century to the end of the seventeenth-century.[165] With the development of capitalism, however, a class of industrial workers evolved whose living habits were no longer even partially or indirectly tied to peasant life, while the mechanisation of industry, particularly after the Industrial Revolution, released the capitalist method of production from dependence on skilled craftsmanship. Not only did public legislation become unnecessary at this stage in order for capital to prolong the working day, but the advantage of running its machinery with the least interruptions goaded capital into resorting to this practice, and indeed without restraint or scruples. Its effect was alarming to capitalist society, if not to individual capitalists, as the normal reproduction of labour-power could no longer be assured. A moral outcry then led to several successive legislative changes towards the middle of the nineteenth-century that compulsorily and increasingly limited the length of the working day. Again, Marx has a detailed account of working class conditions and labour legislation in that period.[166] All this is a familiar episode of the history of modern labour and can to some extent be taken to illustrate an aspect of the production of absolute surplus value. It is, however, important not to confuse

---

165   Marx 1967, *Capital,* Volume I, pp. 264ff.
166   Ibid.

history with theory. Economic theory can indeed show that there is a limit beyond which the working day may not be prolonged. But it cannot explain what that limit is empirically, nor how historically such a limit was concretely established, since neither the dynamics of legislation nor the working class movement depend solely on commodity-economic factors.

The intensification of labour is another method of increasing the production of absolute surplus value. The measurement of productive labour by the hour presupposes, of course, a certain standard intensity of labour. If T is the number of hours of labour of standard intensity, and b is the factor of intensity, $t \equiv bT$ may be used to calculate the rate of surplus value as $e = (t - v)/v$, where v is the value of labour-power or the length of necessary labour-time measured at $b = 1$. Then, the rate of surplus value,

$$e = (t - v)/v, \quad t \equiv bT,$$

can clearly be raised, even if T and v are both given, by raising $b > 1$. For example, even if the law requires that the working day must not exceed 12 hours ($T = 12$), a 5% increase in the intensity of labour ($b = 1.05$) will raise the rate of surplus value by 10%, since $t = bT = 12.6$, which makes $s = 6.6$ and $e = 1.1$. The reason why capital readily yielded to the English Factory Acts, which gradually restricted the permissible length of the working day, during the period 1833–64, is perfectly understandable. By this time, capitalist factories were equipped with machinery, the operating speed of which had to be raised only slightly in order to compensate for the foregone extension of the working day. The length of the working day and the intensity of labour together determine what is broadly known as the condition of labour. Economic theory cannot determine this condition in concrete terms; it is, however, expected to be generally bad in the period of stagnation and relatively good in the period of high prosperity, so that whatever prevails in the phase of average activity during the present business cycle must be taken to represent the normal condition of labour, relative to the productive technology currently employed by capital.

The third method of promoting the production of absolute surplus value is the reduction of real wages. Since the reduction of (x, y, z), under a given technology, reduces the quantity of necessary labour-time, v, it might, at first sight, appear that one should treat this case as an increased production of relative surplus value, as Sweezy does in the above-quoted passage. Yet this reduction of necessary labour-time does not involve any technical change, so that only in form but not in substance does this case agree with the definition of a gain in relative surplus value. This kind of ambivalence arises because the so-called basket of wage-goods, presumed to be necessary for the reproduction of labour-power, is a flexible concept. It is certain that it cannot be medically, nutritionally or otherwise prescribed. Therefore, as will be seen later, real wages do vary in the phase of accumulation, which does not involve a significant technical change. If (x, y, z) represents a real wage in the period of average activity, much less is earned in the period of stagnation and recovery, and considerably more in the period of high prosperity. Thus, the condition of the labour market sometimes enables capital to buy labour-power at less than its normal price, and consequently to produce more than 'normal' absolute surplus value, although the reverse is the case when the labour market is tight. It must also be recalled that when capital employs women and children in place of men, real wages are generally reduced and the production of absolute surplus value is enhanced. Historically, this was one of the important consequences of mechanisation. If a working class family supplies two workers instead of one, it usually need not receive a double wage in order to reproduce itself. Moreover, the competition with women and children forces adult male workers to accept a lower real wage. Regardless of the concrete circumstances that lead to the depression of real wages, capital invariably takes advantage of it, so as to realise an increased production of absolute surplus value.

The last-mentioned case of women's and children's participation in the labour force has another effect beneficial to capital. The total surplus value (S) that capital can produce is the product of three factors: the number of workers (n), the value of their individual labour-power (v), and the rate of surplus value (e), i.e., $S = n \cdot v \cdot e$. Thus, if v is given, S can be doubled, either by doubling n or by doubling e. It is obvious that the doubling of the rate of surplus value is virtually impossible, unless v is very small to begin with. Yet if capital has resources and if the labour-force is extensive, doubling the number of workers is not difficult. It is for this reason that a small unit of capital cannot, even with a harsher condition of labour, produce as much surplus value as a large unit of capital. If, for example, the length of the working day is restricted by legislation, capital must resort to the shift-work system, so as to minimise the time during which productive equipment lies idle. A large unit of capital can relatively easily employ shift-workers and produce more surplus value, while raising the efficiency of transferring the old value of the means of production to the new product; the same thing would be difficult for a small unit of capital. This also implies that the minimum quantity of accumulated money, capable of being converted into capital, becomes greater as capitalism develops.

(γ) Even if the length of the working day is fixed and the intensity of labour unchanged, it is still possible to extend the duration of the surplus labour-time, by shortening the time devoted to necessary labour. Necessary labour-time is shortened, if it takes less time to produce the basket of wage-goods required for the reproduction of labour-power. Hence, any rise in the productivity of labour that directly or indirectly facilitates the production of wage-goods leads to an increase in the rate of surplus value. The method of raising the rate of surplus value in this way can be studied only from the point of view of the production of relative surplus value. It is this method that conforms best to the need of capital, because there is no limit to the advancement of productive powers. It is also this method that justifies capitalism as a historical mode of production, since technical progress becomes an automatic consequence of the chrematistic of capital.

Not all improvements in industrial technology entail a higher productivity in wage-goods production. For instance, a technical innovation in the luxury-goods industry does not immediately affect the production of wage-goods, unless the new technique is somehow adapted for use in wage-goods industries. However, an innovation in the steel manufacturing technique may reduce the cost of a textile machine, which is directly employed to produce workingmen's trousers, in which case a higher productivity in steel (a non-wage good) has an indirect effect on the production of the trousers (a wage-good). In general, all manner of technical progress, with the exception of those restricted to non-wage consumer goods, will have some positive effect on the productivity of wage-goods production, and hence will lead to a rise in the rate of surplus value.

No individual capital is, however, directly concerned with the raising of social productive powers. Even if a general improvement in the technical method of production promotes the rate of surplus value by reducing the reproduction cost of labour-power, it does not motivate an individual capital to adopt a new productive technique. A special incentive to introduce a new technique must, therefore, be explained by the theory of *extra surplus value*.

The following example illustrates this theory. Suppose that all cotton yarn manufacturers, except one, invest 270 dollars a day, to convert 160kg of raw cotton into 120kg of cotton yarn, by depreciating 80 hours' worth of spinning machines. They all employ 10 workers for 12 hours a day, paying the money wage of 3 dollars to each. If the daily output of each of these capitalists sells for 300 dollars, the surplus value of 30 dollars will be realised, which comes to 100% of variable capital. The one exceptional capitalist may, however, be supposed to have introduced a new technique, which enables him to transform 200kg of raw cotton into 160kg of cotton yarn in one day, depreciating 80 hours' worth of improved machines and employing 10 workers for 12 hours a day, at the same wage rate of 3 dollars each. If 160kg of raw cotton cost 200 dollars, 200kg of it will cost 250 dollars. Hence, the daily investment of this capitalist will be 320 dollars, instead of 270 dollars. However, if 120kg of cotton yarn are generally sold for 300 dollars, 160kg of it can be sold for 400 dollars. Consequently, this innovating capitalist will earn the surplus value of 80 dollars, which is about 266.7% of variable capital.

If 160kg of raw cotton are the product of 400 hours of labour, the other capitalists are selling the product of 600 hours of labour (480c + 60v + 60s) for 300 dollars. Yet this innovating capitalist is selling the product of 700 hours of labour (580c + 60v + 60s) for 400 dollars, which in fact should represent the product of 800 hours of labour. The difference of 100 hours of labour represents the excess of social value over the 'individual' value of the output of the innovating capitalist; this difference is defined as his *extra surplus value* in terms of labour. Yet the currently prevailing money value of the product of 100 hours of labour is 50 dollars, which is exactly equal to the difference between the 80 dollars that the innovating capitalist earns over his investment of 320 dollars, and the 30 dollars that the other capitalists earn over their investment of 270 dollars.

The possibility of gaining an extra surplus value is a strong incentive for any individual capital to adopt a new method of production. However, this advantage cannot be enjoyed permanently by the innovating capital, for sooner or later other capitals begin to introduce the same method. As the new method is more and more widely adopted, it becomes difficult, and eventually impossible, to sell the product of 700 hours of labour for what represents 800 hours of labour. By the time all capitals employ the new method of production, the money value of 160kg of cotton yarn, in which only 700 hours of labour are embodied, will be sold for 350 dollars rather than 400 dollars. The extra surplus value of 50 dollars will be eliminated. Since all the cotton yarn manufacturers now invest 320 dollars and sell their product for 350 dollars, the surplus value that they earn will again be only 30 dollars, or just 100% of their variable capital.

What remains, however, is the fall in the value of cotton yarn. Before the innovation, 120kg of cotton yarn, embodying 600 hours of labour, were sold at 300 dollars; after the innovation, 160kg of cotton yarn, embodying 700 hours of labour, are sold for 350 dollars. Hence, 1kg of cotton yarn, which was produced with 5 hours of labour, and which cost 2.5 dollars, is now producible with approximately 4.4 hours of labour, and can be purchased at about 2.19 dollars. If any wage-goods are made of cotton fabric, the basket of wage-goods required for the reproduction of labour-power can be produced with less than 6 hours of labour, and be purchased for less than 3 dollars. For example, the basket may now be produced with 5.5 hours of labour and may cost 2.75 dollars, in which case, the rate of surplus value is raised to about 118% from the original 100%. This additional 18% reflects an increased production of relative surplus value, which remains, and this benefit is not restricted to the cotton yarn manufacturers, but will be shared by the whole class of capitalists.

Although the concept of extra surplus value, or what is commonly known as quasi-rent, is indispensable here in order to explain why capital can increase the production of relative surplus value, the full implication of that concept cannot be exposed in the present context. The reason is that extra surplus value involves relations among capitalists themselves, rather than just relations between capitalists and workers. Later, in the chapter on profit (Chapter 7), the concept of extra surplus value will be treated again, as underlying a special case of *surplus profit*; only then will the full economic significance of extra surplus value be made clear. In the meantime, however, Marx's well-known claim that extra surplus value contains the value substance because 'the exceptionally productive labour operates as intensified labour'[167] must be questioned. Extra surplus value is not earned simply because labour becomes more productive or 'intensified' with the innovative technique, but rather because the social value of the commodity in question is not yet determined by that technique. When, with the diffusion of the innovative technique, the social value of the commodity is determined by that technique, labour is still 'intensified' or more productive, but no extra surplus value can be produced. What is produced by 'intensified' or more productive labour is the increment of relative surplus value, which is, of course, not the same thing as extra surplus value.

Two more points must be stressed before this section is concluded. First, the effect of an innovation usually increases the total outlay of capital, as well as the total output of the industry in which the innovation occurs. In the above example, each of the cotton-yarn producing capitalists invested 270 dollars before the innovation and augmented that value to 300 dollars. However, the outlay of capital per capitalist became 320 dollars and the value of output became 350 dollars after the innovation was generally adopted. This shows that a greater concentration of capital and production tends to occur in the course of acquiring more relative surplus value.

The second point is that most types of innovation are embodied in fixed capital equipment, such as the spinning machine in the above example. That explains why there is ordinarily a long enough period, during which extra surplus value may be enjoyed by a few progressive capitalists. If a new productive method, adopted by innovating capitalists, was instantly copied by all the others in an industry, extra surplus value could not reward the innovators sufficiently; the incentive to introduce a costly innovation might not be great. In actual practice, industrial secrets or patent rights may protect the interests of innovators, but the pure theory of capitalism cannot allow for such contingent factors. The reason why the gap between social and 'individual' value can

---

167   Marx 1967, *Capital*, Volume I, p. 318.

subsist for a considerable period of time must be attributed to the fact that the innovative technique is, in most cases, embodied in fixed capital equipment. In that case, the introduction of a new technique will become a reasonable business proposition for the majority of the capitalists in an industry only after their old equipment is sufficiently depreciated. No one introduces a new machine, however productive it may be, when the old machine is not even half depreciated, unless there are other compelling reasons to do so.

(b)   The Modern Factory System

(α) Even when a mass of propertyless workers is created in the process of primitive accumulation, that does not immediately enable the capitalist to employ these workers with advantage, unless he has a factory well adapted to make use of their labour-power. The production of absolute and relative surplus value presupposes an industrial process in which capital can consume the labour-power of wage-earning workers without vocational or occupational restrictions. Such a condition is satisfied only with the establishment of the modern factory, from which craftsmanship and specialised skills are by and large eliminated. The evolution of the modern factory system shows that there are three features essential to any capitalist enterprise; these features are called *co-operation, manufacture,* and *mechanisation.* Here, however, they are studied not as the actual historical steps in the development of the modern factory system, but rather as the underlying concepts of the concrete environment in which the production-process of capital takes place.

   In order to invest capital in an industrial enterprise, some definite quantity of money must have been accumulated in advance. This prior possession of investible money is that which distinguishes a capitalist from a worker. But as the quantity of money required for an industrial operation increases, the separation of those capable of developing as capitalists and those destined to remain permanent members of the working class becomes more and more definite and irreversible. The pre-eminence of a capitalist over workers first appears in his ability to employ a significant number of workers under his supervision. Indeed, if he employed only one worker, his living standard would not be much better than that of the worker, even with a rate of surplus value of 100%. The so-called method of *co-operation* consists of the gathering of a certain number of workmen in one place, in order to exploit the productive powers of collective labour. Whereas other societies too occasionally resorted to the same method in carrying out heavier works, it was not until the formation of capitalism that co-operation became a more or less universal feature of all productive enterprises.

Co-operation socialises the labour-and-production process. The craftsmen-like skills of independent workers are no longer the most desirable qualities of those working together side by side. Rather, punctuality, regular performance, and the ability to endure the discipline of collective work, tend to be more highly valued. By cultivating an average standard of efficiency, the method of co-operation makes labour-power more uniform and exploits the productivity of collective labour, rather than the excellence of individual workers. It is in this process that the capitalist emerges as the authority in the workplace, rather than as the patient and compliant patron of whimsical craftsmen. Moreover, some means of production are bound to be used co-operatively under the capitalist's supervision, which not only saves his initial cost of investment, but also enables him to guard against its wasteful and improper use. As the capitalist thus imposes his authority, the collective productivity of the enterprise is enhanced.

In capitalist society, the productiveness of collective labour can be exploited only under the leadership of the capitalist, whose factory is organised according to the method of *co-operation*. Since workers are unable by themselves to socially organise their own labour, and since the productive powers of concentrated labour grow more or less in proportion to the scale of capitalist enterprise, which is determined by the magnitude of invested capital, the productive powers of labour necessarily appear as the productive powers of capital. The true source of productivity is, thus, already enshrouded within the phenomenal form of the capitalist enterprise.

It is important to clearly understand that the theoretical concept of co-operation does not imply the existence of a historical period in which capitalist production depended only or primarily on co-operation. There was, in fact, no such epoch in history. On the contrary, the early phase of capitalist production was characterised by the putting-out system or the system of domestic handicraft industry, whereby co-operation was not at all a salient feature of production. This fact of history does not, however, contradict the theoretical treatment of co-operation as the most general and abstract feature of the modern factory system, established after the Industrial Revolution. For without co-operation the development of the manufacture division of labour, to be discussed in the following subsection, would be inherently limited. Even though, in history, an early tendency for the manufacture division of labour to develop may already be observed in the domestic system (and there is nothing strange about it), that does not justify the contention that co-operation is logically dispensable to a full development of the organised division of labour among working people, labouring side by side.

(β) The assembling of a number of traditional handicraft workers in a capitalist factory in the form of co-operation almost immediately gives rise to an organised division of labour within that factory. The co-operation that involves such a division of labour is called *manufacture*. This division of labour within a capitalist enterprise must be distinguished from the specialisation of industrial activities, or the *social division of labour*, which occurs among capitalists themselves. When the capitalist is already specialised in the production of, say, woollen yarn, his workers may be assigned to a number of different jobs, ranging from the preparatory work of blending, carding, and suchlike, to the various subsequent operations of spinning, twisting, winding and packaging. No single worker goes through the whole process of production, but only a narrowly subdivided part of it. This has the decisive effect of reducing each worker to a partial operative of the organised process of production. As the workers thus lose touch with the integrated whole of productive activity, and as they are no longer capable of functioning as independent craftsmen, the speed and the intensity of organised labour are more readily enforced, so as to raise the productivity of the capitalist enterprise.

Manufacture, however, is a preparatory step towards the fully mechanised capitalist factory. The organised division of labour promotes the skill and efficiency of the workers in each specialised section of the capitalist factory, and differentiates tools and machines so as to suit sectional requirements. Although the simplification of labour accomplished by manufacture is such that even completely unskilled workers can be employed to some extent, they are as yet subordinate to their more trained colleagues, whose technical skills cannot be dispensed with. It is for this reason that the capitalist command of the working class cannot be complete under the method of manufacture. Indeed, in the early period of capitalism, prior to the Industrial Revolution, manufacture production by industrial capital was never in a position to challenge the predominance of merchant capital, which operated within the commission (or putting-out) system.

Marx actually talks of 'the manufacturing period properly so-called', referring to 'that period, roughly speaking, [that] extends from the middle of the 16th to the last third of the 18th century'.[168] From this reference, however, one should not draw the conclusion that during that period manufacture was in fact the predominant method of capitalist production. Economic history suggests otherwise. Although large manufactories were present already in the fifteenth and the sixteenth centuries, they did not appear to have

---

168   Marx 1967, *Capital,* Volume I, p. 336.

overpowered domestic handicraft industry, even in the seventeenth and eighteenth centuries. Yet the fact that manufacture was in reality a rather exceptional method of production, prior to the Industrial Revolution, does not in the least bit contradict the theoretical proposition that a modern factory, deprived of machinery, would be virtually identical to a *manufactory*, which differs from simple co-operation in having a well developed division of labour. Here again, logical development is not reproduced in step with the historical process of capitalist development, which just reconfirms the need for a stages-theory to mediate between the pure logic and empirical history. In the doctrine of simple circulation, the logic of transition could often find a historical parallel, although even then the correspondence was by no means accurate, and must not be relied upon to demonstrate the dialectical necessity of the theory. The logic of reflection that governs the doctrine of production is never corroborated by a parallel development in history; in fact, the logical order often reverses the historical sequence. For instance, only after the existential proof of capitalism is given, on the assumption that labour is already simplified, can it be shown that labour in fact tends to be simplified with the development of the capitalist method of production. One should not be misled by the facile 'logical-historical method' into believing that the dialectic must rely on a historical or empirical parallel to prove its validity. That would make the dialectic a perfectly futile exercise.

It is true that the manufacture division of labour within the factory presupposes the social division of labour, which is a natural outcome of the commodity-economy. It is also true that the two forms of the division of labour stimulate each other. But the manufacture division of labour does not consist of the independent operation of handicraft workers. On the contrary, they are integrated in an organic whole of interdependent workers, whose collective productivity is to be exploited by the capitalist. To the extent that this method of production makes room for the employment of totally unskilled wage-earners, and to the extent that it differentiates and specialises the tools of production, the manufacture division of labour constitutes an important precondition of the Industrial Revolution.

(γ) The last hurdle to be overcome in order to complete the modern factory is the *mechanisation* of industry. Industrial machines are generally classifiable into (i) power machines, (ii) transmission machines, and (iii) working machines. The first two magnify the productivity of the last, which are the traditional hand-tools, snatched away from the hands of the workers and fitted into a mechanical system. Working machines are no longer the docile instrument of production, which handicraft workers operate on their own initiative, but are instead a mechanism operated by the capitalist, demanding the workers' submission. The mechanised labour-and-production process is an engineering process into which labour-power is fed like raw materials. The co-operation and the division of labour, combined with mechanisation, no longer permit the survival of handicraft skills. The entire working-process can be simplified and requires no more than totally unskilled labour with the exception perhaps of a few skilled workers in supervisory positions, working in part as the capitalist's assistants.

The productivity of the mechanised factory is spectacular, relative to anything known before, as the Industrial Revolution demonstrated. Machines are, however, not adopted by the capitalist because they lessen the quantity of labour required for the production of use-values, but because they raise the rate of surplus value. In other words, a more productive machine is introduced because an extra surplus value accrues to the innovating capitalist. It is, therefore, quite consistent that the mechanisation of industry does not imply any relief with regard to the expenditure of productive labour. On the contrary, the immediate effect of the Industrial Revolution was the intensification of labour and the extension of the working day.

More important to the social position of the working class, however, is the fact that the simplification of labour, accomplished by mechanisation, confirms the conversion of labour-power into a commodity. When machines render the skills and the extra physical strength of workers useless, women and children could be employed quite as effectively as grown-up men. The extended scope of the labour force makes it possible for the capitalist to pay less wages per worker than before, because the maintenance of a working class family does not depend on the wages of an adult male 'bread winner' alone, but on those of all of its working members. The simplification of labour also standardises labour-power, which can be purchased in the open market as easily as it can be dismissed. A mass of unskilled wage earners cannot now survive except by selling their labour-power to a capitalist at a wage-rate determined in the labour market. In the consumption of labour-power, purchased as a commodity, the capitalist is therefore assured of maximum freedom.

The dialectic of co-operation-manufacture-mechanisation can be looked at from two sides. On one side, it exhibits the logical composition of the modern factory system: mechanisation presupposes manufacture and manufacture presupposes co-operation. Hence, a modern factory consists of (1) assembling workers, (2) dividing their labour, and (3) subjecting them to the operation of the machinery. These are necessary and sufficient steps to form a modern factory. On the other side, the dialectic also implicitly recognises what it is that secures the conversion of labour-power into a commodity: the simplification of labour presupposes the division of labour, which presupposes collective labour. Hence, a modern worker is characterised by (1) lack of individuality, (2) loss of craftsman skill, and (3) mechanical indifference to labour. It is possible that the worker in a feudal system might also satisfy these conditions, due to some contingent factors, such as mental retardation. However, it is quite another thing to have virtually all workers satisfy these conditions, thereby reducing society's labour-power to a standardised object, susceptible of conversion into a commodity. The discussion of this section does not immediately answer – nor is it meant to answer – economic historians' perennial question, namely, how did an industrial capitalist emerge? They must find out for themselves why, at a particular time and place in history, the commission (or putting-out) system no longer effectively competed with modern factory production. Pure theory can say only that merchant capital is not an adequate form of capital, and that with the conversion of labour-power into a commodity, industrial capital commences its action (Chapter 3). We are discussing here the logical ingredients (or presuppositions) of the action of industrial capital, not the historical process in which they actually emerged.

The mechanisation of the production-process does not occur in all industries equally. Some industries are bound to be more difficult than others to mechanise, enabling handicraft production to survive longer, just as the division of labour in some industries could be relatively easily accomplished, while in others it was harder to come by. Yet in any one industry the mechanised method of production, once introduced, generally tends to displace the traditional method swiftly because of its incomparably greater productivity. If one industry is well mechanised, related industries often follow suit. Thus, the powerful force of mechanisation, once set in motion, has a revolutionary effect on the whole economy, leading to the greater concentration of capital, as well as the formation *en masse* of commoditised labour-power. The groundwork of capitalist production is thereby laid.

(c)   The Form of Wages

(α) Labour-power is not a product; it does not become a commodity in the same way as products, namely, by being capitalistically produced. Moreover, labour-power cannot be exchanged for products that are already in existence. Labour-power can only be exchanged for what it itself produces. A particular type of production-relation must, therefore, be implied by the conversion of labour-power into a commodity; capitalism is just another name given to this particular type of production-relation. Indeed, the whole existence of capitalism hinges so crucially on the fact of labour-power being a commodity that without a full appreciation of this fact, nothing meaningful can ever be said about capitalist society. Yet it is in the nature of capitalist society to hide this fundamental relationship under the 'phenomenal' form of wages. Neither capitalists nor wage-earners are consciously made aware that they are trading labour-power as a commodity.

Even though the capitalist pays money corresponding to his variable capital in order to buy labour-power, the latter is a commodity only at the moment of purchase, because as soon as it is purchased, it can no longer be resold, and hence it ceases to be a commodity altogether. For this reason the capitalist does not see that he has bought labour-power as a commodity. What he sees is merely that labour services make products, and so he believes that he has purchased labour services rather than labour-power as a commodity. However, a service is not a 'thing outside us', nor can it ever be a commodity. Labour flows only in the consumption of the use-value of labour-power. Since the capitalist has purchased this labour-power for a definite period, he has the right to consume it as he pleases during the same period. Yet this point is bound to be obscured because labour-power is a special commodity *inseparable from the person of its natural owner*. It is, therefore, necessary for the worker himself to work in order to generate labour. Hence, it appears as if the worker were consuming his own labour-power rather than the capitalist, who is the purchaser of the labour-power as a commodity. When labour-power is simplified and standardised, however, the purchaser must tell its natural owner (the worker) how to use it; the worker does not himself know how to consume his own labour-power without detailed instructions from its purchaser.

It will be a different story if someone hires a mechanic to repair a car. The mechanic knows exactly what must be done with it and employs his labour-power as he sees fit. Even if the customer dictates all the details of the work to be done, the mechanic is at least free to say when the car will be ready; he may even say that certain jobs are beyond his competence and cannot be done. He will be paid for the useful work he does on the car, *not for the value of his labour-power*, which he consumes at his will. The practice of paying daily or weekly wages for a regularly performed useful work by a carpenter, a gardener, a cook, or a seamstress, originated long before the advent of capitalism. This practice never by itself created the class of propertyless wage-earners as in a capitalist society. If someone is paid a daily or weekly wage or salary, this does not automatically mean that he is selling his labour-power. The prime minister of a socialist state can also be paid a money wage or a salary, but his labour-power can hardly be described as a 'commodity'. In capitalist society, labour-power is a commodity despite rather than because of the phenomenal form of wage-payment, which misleads the capitalist into believing that he pays money in the same way as a non-capitalist employer pays for the useful labour services performed for him.

Even workers themselves, and their socialist spokesmen too, often fail to penetrate, through this apparent form of wages, to the capitalist reality that underlies it. The value of labour-power is always paid after the expenditure of productive labour, of which the abstract and the concrete aspect are performed simultaneously. Therefore, it is often overlooked that productive labour produces value at the same time as it produces a use-value. Moreover, a day's labour can never be clearly divided in the minds of workers into a necessary and a surplus part; no bell rings, no siren sounds to tell the workers that from this or that moment their labour becomes surplus labour to be appropriated by the capitalist. If they are paid 3 dollars each, after having worked for 12 hours a day, it will appear that the wage is paid for the 12 hours of work, and particularly so because less than 3 dollars will be paid to those on a reduced workload, and because an extra wage is usually granted to those who have done overtime work.

The reason why the value of labour-power is paid after labour is performed rather than before, however, is that this commodity cannot be separated from the person of the worker. If the worker becomes sick or otherwise unable to work, the capitalist will fail to consume his labour-power. Any purchaser of a commodity would indignantly demand a refund if it later turns out to be defective. Foreseeing this outcome, any decent seller would market his commodity with a 'complete satisfaction or your money back' guarantee. Labour-power is also sold with a similar concession that 'no payment is accepted, until its use-value is duly delivered'. Such a concession was already customary with pre-capitalist service workers for an obvious reason: they never sold their labour-power, but the result of their labour. Only those who were either known or expected to be competent in producing a desired effect were asked to perform specific labour in return for money. In that case, a wage was necessarily post-paid as a reward for the work done. Yet pre-capitalist service workers obtained a contract by announcing 'I can do this or that for you'. Capitalist wage workers cannot offer their labour-power in the same way. In selling their standardised labour-power, they can only ask 'try it as you see fit'.

Despite the fundamental difference in substance, the wage form is the same whether paid to a traditional service worker or to a capitalist productive worker. Hence, there arises the confusion between the value of labour-power (v) and the value-product (v + s) that it produces. This confusion, moreover, is perfectly congenial to the merchant soul of capital, which rationalises its operation as buying v + s cheap and selling it dear. No wonder the classical school of political economy – the spokesman of the nineteenth-century bourgeoisie – never surmounted this confusion.

(β) If capitalists and workers alike, bewildered by the traditional form of wage payment, fail to see that they trade labour-power as a commodity, economic analysis must show that this is in fact the case. Economic theory shows this truth by demonstrating the law of value. The law of value which makes the existence of capitalism identical with the validity of labour theory of value does not permit the classical confusion of v and v + s, for if wage-earners received more than the product of their necessary labour, labour-power would not be reproduced as a commodity, and hence capitalism would not exist as a historical society. The failure of the classical labour theory of value stems not only from its inability to clearly distinguish between concrete-useful and abstract-human labour, but also from its confusion of the value of labour-power with the value-product of labour. Even Ricardo, who regarded 'the natural price of labour' (labour-power) to 'depend on the price of the food, necessaries, and conveniences required for the support of the labourer and his family',[169] left the determination of this natural price to mere demand and supply.[170] His labour theory, therefore, remains inconclusive and useless on the most vital issue, namely, the existential proof of capitalism. For what is the use of the labour theory, or of any real cost theory, if it cannot uncover the production-relation of capitalism, or the value-relation, that lies behind the mere interplay of demand and supply?

The existence of surplus value, as a condition of capitalist production, manifestly militates against the view that money wages correspond to the value-product, v + s, of productive labour. Yet if this point was already established with the law of value in the preceding section, why is it necessary to emphasise once again the *conversion of the value of labour-power into wages*, after the discussion of the modern factory system? The reason is that the Marxian method is not content with an abstract proposition that labour-power is a commodity. It was not so originally, nor will it always be. Labour-power becomes a commodity *under a given social formation*, which is capitalism. It must, therefore, be shown not only that capitalism requires 'commoditised' labour-power for its existence, but also that the concrete working of the production-process of capital itself repeatedly confirms that conversion of labour-power into a commodity.

However, the production-process of capital does not simply complete the commoditisation of labour-power; it mystifies and conceals what it has accomplished by adopting the traditional form of wages. The payment of wages to industrial workers gives the impression that labour itself, instead

---

169   Sraffa 1961, p. 93.
170   Marx 1971, *Theories of Surplus Value*, p. 400.

of labour-power, is traded between the capitalists and the workers, and this impression is strengthened by the so-called form of *time wages*. The workers believe that they are paid, say, 3 dollars for 12 hours' work, because they can sometimes be hired for 0.25 dollar per hour. The hourly wage is merely the daily wage divided by the number of hours normally worked by the majority of workers. This form of wage is convenient for the capitalist who wants to hire additional workers for half a day or at odd hours. Some workers may survive by working irregular hours at different places, without being employed full time at any given factory. The insecurity, as well as the easy mobility, of these irregular workers only reinforce and confirm the commoditisation of labour-power.

So-called *piece-wages* are an even stronger form of concealing the conversion of the value of labour-power into wages. Here, the daily output of a normal worker is divided by the number of pieces of the product. For instance, if a normal worker is paid 3 dollars for producing 12kg of cotton yarn a day, the piece-wage, payable to a spinning worker, is 0.25 dollar per kilogram of cotton yarn produced. In this case, the semblance of wages being a *payment for useful work done* is even more firmly entrenched. It was, in fact, with this form of wages that merchant capitalists exploited rural handicraft workers in the early period of capitalist development. Yet as the factory production of the same commodity developed in the cities, the piece-wages of rural handicraftsmen only preserved the appearance of compensation for the useful services rendered by them, and became a disguised form of payment for the value of their labour-power. They too were reduced to the ordinary ranks of the proletariat.

Thus, these forms of wage-payment are certainly not inconsistent with the proposition that in capitalism the substance or the real content of money wages is nothing but the value, or the reproduction cost, of labour-power. Any change in the quantity of labour, required for the production of a standard worker's basket of wage-goods, must be reflected in the variation of wages.

It must be emphasised, however, that the labour market cannot determine an equilibrium wage-rate, but only a feasible wage-rate. This is because labour-power is not a capitalistically produced commodity. The supply of any other commodity is regulated by the price mechanism, so that if a commodity is overproduced, a fall in its price restrains over-expansion, and if it is underproduced, a rise in its price encourages further expansion. Only in the state of balanced growth are the market prices normal and revelatory, in one way or another, of the values of the commodities. The same thing, however, cannot be expected in the case of labour-power because the rise and fall of its price does not call forth a swift adjustment of its supply. The value of labour-power cannot be determined in the same way as the value of other commodities; it will be explained later that the value of labour-power, relative to the existing complex of productive technology, can only be identified as the labour cost of reproducing labour-power *in the period of average activity* during the current business cycle (Chapter 6).

All this, however, does not mean that labour-power cannot become a commodity, although it means that labour-power does not become one as a matter of course. The first condition for the conversion of labour-power into a commodity is met when a mass of free propertyless workers is created in the course of primitive accumulation, but this condition must be increasingly perfected with the development of modern mechanised factories. Industrial capital becomes a true form of chrematistics only when it can produce any use-value at will, within the range of technical feasibility. Labour-power, or the capacity of man to perform productive labour, becomes a genuine commodity when it is freed from vocational and occupational restrictions, and becomes indifferent to the specific kind of labour that may be assigned to it. If, in order to run his business, the capitalist must depend on a few irreplaceable and highly experienced craftsmen, who have, say, served his family since his grandfather's generation, he cannot be a true personification of industrial capital. The skill and craftsmanship of these workmen determine the quality of his product, and his business thrives only insofar as the public continues to appreciate such a product. Hence, the true nature of industrial capital cannot be represented by such a special case, for capital must typically be able to produce anything that promises the maximum gain. In a purely capitalist society, all capitalists must be able to operate in an environment in which any worker is as good as any other. That is the environment in which labour-power is truly reduced to a commodity, a commodity that is capable of producing any use-value that fits the capitalist need during the entire period of its employment. It is, therefore, both natural and inevitable that the capitalists regard the money wages that they pay as their labour cost of production.

(γ) Clearly, however, what costs the capitalist is different from what costs society. If a direct producer works for 12 hours a day and reproduces his labour-power in the first 6 hours, the real cost to society is 12 hours of productive labour, but the capitalist employer only pays the equivalent of the first 6 hours. By regarding money wages as the price of labour rather than of labour-power, the capitalist fails to see how he acquires the surplus value, representing 6 hours of surplus labour, in the production-process of capital. Since the money value of his investment, $c + v$, represents the cost of production to the capitalist, his output C' of $C \dots P \dots C'$ cannot contain any more than the money value of $c + v$. Thus, from the viewpoint of the capitalist, the production of surplus value is *ipso facto* the realisation of surplus value in the process, $C' - M'$. The capitalist's conception of cost, therefore, makes it impossible to isolate from the sphere of circulation, the production-process of capital, $C \dots P \dots C'$.

Industrial capital, like merchant capital, but unlike money-lending capital, constitutes a metamorphosis of value. That is to say, the value of capital assumes and discards, alternately, the forms of money, productive elements and a saleable commodity, while always remaining in the hands of the operator. The elements of production, however, consist of the means of production, which retain their value in the production-process, and labour-power, which does not. To this latter productive element, therefore, the concept of metamorphosis does not strictly apply, and so a special consideration of the topic is needed. Since labour-power is not a capitalistically produced commodity, it is not inherently an embodiment of value; labour-power acquires value, like a simply produced commodity, only in the act of sale, which is conditioned by factors outside of labour-power itself. A wage earner reproduces his labour-power as a use-value in his individual consumption-process. He has not chosen this particular use-value from many other use-values because it is the best way to form and augment value, but because he cannot do anything else. In reproducing his labour-power, therefore, the wage earner does not produce a value, but a use-value, which acquires value indirectly through the working of capitalist society. It is the social relation peculiar to capitalism that converts labour-power into a commodity. A commodity, which is not inherently an embodiment of value, but to which value attaches because of conditions external to itself, is called a 'simple commodity'. Labour-power is *the only simple commodity within the capitalist mode of production*. A simple commodity is not capitalistically produced as value. The loss of value by labour-power in the production-process of capital is but a reflection of this fact.

Why, then, does capital, the metamorphosis of value in principle, purchase such a risky commodity as labour-power, which loses its value as soon as it is purchased? It is because labour-power, which forms new value greater than its own value, in the production-process of capital, may be paid *after the work is performed*. The newly produced commodity contains the reproduced value of labour-power and surplus value, as well as the value of constant capital used up. Since wages are paid after the labour is performed, capital need not conceive of wages as the direct expression of the value of labour-power, but as the expression of the reproduced value of labour-power, present in the newly produced commodity. In other words, with the adoption of the form of wages, capital need no longer view its production-process as interrupting its circulation-process as in:

$$M - C \begin{cases} P_m \\ \quad\quad\ldots\ldots\ldots P\ldots\ldots\ldots \quad\quad C' - M' \\ L_p \end{cases}$$

Instead, capital may subjectively dissolve its production-process into an uninterrupted flow of its circulation-process as follows:

$$M - P_m \underset{[K, L]}{\text{------}} C' - M' \begin{cases} P_m \\ \\ W + R \end{cases}$$

where [K, L] is the co-operation of managerial and productive labour, R and W
are, respectively, the capitalist's and the wage earners' revenue. The interruption of circulation by the production-process is accurately indicated by means
of the dots in the scientifically correct first formula, but industrial capital is
no longer even present inside the second formula, in which only the means
of production are considered 'capital'. Indeed, if wages can be paid out of
the product, variable capital need not even be 'advanced', the wage bill being
reduced to a distributive share in the new product.

This capitalist rationalisation irrevocably mystifies the true source of surplus value, but at the same time reasserts the original concept of capital as
the circulation-form, where nothing but the metamorphosis of value can
take place. In other words, it is in the nature of capital itself to dissolve its
production-process into its circulation-process, suppressing the distinction
between the production of value and its formal transformation. With this new
conception of things, which is admittedly facilitated by capitalism's own misleading appearance, capital is now ready to return to the sphere of circulation.
The dialectic cannot move from one sphere of investigation to another unless
the subject matter itself compels that passage. In order to bring into focus the
circulation of industrial capital which has so far been left out of sight, it is
necessary for industrial capital to rediscover itself as a circulation-form. This
rediscovery is made possible only when, in the view of industrial capital itself,
the distinction between variable and constant capital is obliterated, that is,
only when the value of labour-power is converted into wages.

CHAPTER 5

The Circulation-process of Capital (*Appearance*)

Capital does not merely transform productive elements into use-values. In so doing, it also simultaneously forms and augments value. Unlike use-value, *value that is not realised is not produced either*. Only by the sale of the commodity for money is the production of value by capital confirmed. Capital, as a form of circulation, is fully aware of this fact and *considers the sale of a commodity just as important as its production*. Indeed, with the adoption of the form of wages, capital goes so far as to dissolve its production-process into its total circulation-process, thus mystifying the productive source of surplus value. Although such a mystification is not by itself defensible, it nevertheless reflects the fundamental fact that the productive phase of industrial capital cannot be fully comprehended in isolation from its circulatory phases of the buying and selling of commodities. The production-process of capital (C ... P ... C′) is necessarily hemmed in by the circulatory phases (M – C and C′ – M′), such that the whole motion of capital (M – C ... P ... C′ – M′) constitutes the circulation-process of capital.

The word 'circulation-process' is sometimes used in two distinct senses: in one sense, it means the simple circulation processes of capital in buying and selling commodities (that is what I have just called the 'circulatory phases' in reference to industrial capital); in the other sense, it means the whole circulatory motion of industrial capital, including the process of production which is embedded in it. The title of the present chapter refers to the latter sense. This particular usage might be confusing at first. But this difficulty stems from the nature of the subject itself. While the processes of simple circulation (the buying and selling of commodities) are pure empty forms that capital, as a particular type of commodity-seller, must also undergo, the whole motion of capital itself constitutes a circulation-form, in which capital is grounded on its production-process. It is the form that is inseparable from the matter (just as the *outer* is inseparable from the *inner*) that must now be studied. Just as the simple processes of circulation by capital are the antecedents of the production-process of capital, the whole circulation-process of capital is its consequence. To put it more directly, the capitalist is now viewed as a merchant-producer rather than merely a merchant or producer. The capitalist, being a merchant-producer, cannot just produce a commodity; he must also trade commodities.

In view of this fact, the motion of industrial capital must now be seen in its three distinct aspects, none of which, taken separately from the others, adequately represents the whole nature of capital. The motion of capital is the unity of the *three circuits of capital*, namely the circuit of money-capital (M – C ... P ... C' – M), the circuit of productive capital (P ... C' – M'. M – C ... P) and the circuit of commodity-capital (C' – M'.M – C ... P ... C'). The *circuit of money-capital* represents the 'mercantilist view' that capital is a chrematistic operation motivated by the individual desire for self-enrichment. The *circuit of productive capital* represents the 'classical view' that the continuing motion of capital has as its base the nature-imposed necessity of reproducing use-values. The *circuit of commodity-capital* differs from the other two, in beginning and ending, not with the advance of capital, be it in monetary or in real form, but rather with the result of capitalist production. This circuit views the motion of capital as the unceasing supplier of use-values in the form of commodities, as did the Physiocrats in their *Tableaux économiques*. Each of these circuits stresses one important aspect of the motion of capital, which, however, can be fully comprehended only as a unity of all the three circuits.

This fact becomes obvious when any individual capitalist operation is examined. A capitalist enterprise must continually produce its commodity, even while selling and buying commodities, because an interruption of the production-process becomes prohibitively costly with the development of the capitalist method of production. Consequently, when part of capital is already in the form of finished goods as commodity-capital, or in the form of money, ready to purchase productive elements as money-capital, the other part of capital is still in the form, either of productive elements or of half-finished goods (goods in pipeline), as productive capital. Capital, thus, divides itself into *circulation-capital* (money-capital and/or commodity-capital) and *productive capital*, in proportion to the time periods that capital spends for (simple) circulation and for production, that is, in proportion to the lengths of the circulation-period and of the production-period.

Since the circulation-process of capital is a time-consuming process, both in its productive phase and its circulatory phases, the passage of time is itself a cost to capital. During the circulatory phases, in which a merely formal metamorphosis occurs, value is not augmented. Yet circulation-capital must be held in proportion to the length of the circulation-period in order to avoid a costly interruption of production. *The sterile holding of circulation-capital over time is thus a cost to capital.* Even if the purchase cost of productive elements is given, a long or short production-period makes a difference to capital. In general, however, the length of the production-period is technically determined,

while the length of the circulation-period depends largely on contingent factors. This is the reason why circulation-costs become a particularly important
consideration for capital. In addition to the cost of merely holding circulation-
capital, which does not directly contribute to the augmentation of value, there
are also *pure costs of circulation*, which capital must deduct from its surplus
value. These are the human and non-human costs of buying and selling commodities. The nature of these costs becomes clearer if one maintains a sharp
distinction between productive and unproductive labour. In all societies, both
types of labour are absolutely indispensable; in a purely capitalist society, however, unproductive labour is performed essentially as the capitalists' own labour, or its extensions. The theoretically flawless definition of productive and
unproductive labour does not, however, mean that every empirically concrete
labour can be easily classified into either one of these two categories. Labour,
expended in such activities as *transportation and storage*, which is closely allied to the circulation of commodities, can be either productive or unproductive depending on the circumstances.

   Given the nature of the circulation-process of capital, it becomes a categorical imperative for capital to minimise the cost, and maximise the efficiency, of value augmentation, because if capital took too much time in circulating commodities, the unproductive waste of resources could outweigh
the advantage of capitalist production, which raises the productive powers
of labour through mechanisation. Moreover, the force of competition automatically requires that each individual capital should strive for a maximum
efficiency of value augmentation. If production-costs, namely, the purchase-
costs of productive elements, are technically given, a maximum efficiency of
value augmentation can be achieved only by the shortening of the *turnover-
time of capital*, which consists of the total duration of the production and the
circulation-period. From the point of view of capital, the turnover-time is simply the length of time required for the money advanced as capital to be recovered in the form of money, through the sale of its commodity. Theoretically,
however, the turnover-time must be defined as the time intervening between
the purchase of a productive element and the next purchase of the same productive element.

   This means that the concept of the turnover-time must be studied in the
light of both the circuit of money-capital and that of productive capital. For
instance, the value of *fixed capital* is transferred to the new product piecemeal
as it wears out, so that every sale of the product recovers part of the advanced
value in the form of money. Yet depreciation-funds cannot be re-advanced as
money-capital until the renewal time arrives. Hence, the turnover-time of fixed
capital is determined by its durability. Since constant capital always includes

some fixed components, it has many turnover-times, the shortest of which is the turnover-time of circulating (*constant*) capital, which transfers its value wholly to the product in one production-process. It can, however, be shown that the efficiency of value augmentation depends only on the initial value of fixed capital, but not on its varied turnover-times. The reason is that the turnover-time of circulating constant capital agrees with the *turnover-time of variable capital*, which forms and augments value rather than merely transferring pre-existing value to the commodity-product.

What determines the efficiency of value augmentation is essentially *the turnover-time of variable capital*. Yet for variable capital one cannot talk of the turnover-time in the same sense as for constant capital because *the value of labour-power*, once purchased as a productive element, is handed over to the workers and is (productively) consumed by them, never returning to the hands of the capitalist. What accrues to the latter, when he sells his commodity, is not the old value of the variable capital that he originally advanced, but instead a newly produced value corresponding to it, together with surplus value. The turnover-time of variable capital is, therefore, not the duration of time required for the reappearance in monetary form of the old value advanced, but rather the duration of time required for the reproduction (reappearance or renewal) in the newly produced commodity of the old value of labour-power already consumed in the production-process. Thus, apart from technical constraints, the annual *efficiency of value augmentation* is fundamentally determined by the *annual rate of surplus value*, which is the product of the rate of surplus value and the number of times that variable capital turns over during a year. The pursuit by capital of a maximum efficiency of value augmentation, therefore, consists of its efforts to raise the rate of surplus value, on the one hand, and to accelerate the speed of turnover, on the other. From the point of view of the circulation-process of capital, it is immaterial whether the efficiency of value augmentation is in fact raised by an increased rate of surplus value, or by an accelerated speed of the turnover of capital.

Every turnover of capital realises surplus value, but the value corresponding to it was not advanced earlier. In the case of a simple reproduction, the consumption-fund of the capitalist, spent earlier as his income, will be integrated in the circulation-process of capital in order to realise surplus value. Yet as soon as surplus value is realised in money, it falls away from the circulation-process of capital, and forms a *freely disposable income* for the capitalist. The circulation of capitalists' income (surplus value) and the circulation of capital, therefore, complement each other. This fact is particularly apparent if the motion of capital is examined in the light of the circuit of commodity-capital, which begins and ends with a capitalistically produced commodity. By the working of the law of value, capital can and indeed tends to produce all commodities in the socially desired and necessary quantities. Hence, if in order to circulate the aggregate of capitalistically produced commodities ($\Sigma C'$), society needs more means of circulation than exist already, $\Sigma C'$ must be supposed to already include enough new monetary gold to meet the deficit.

Since gold too is a capitalistically produced commodity, it cannot fail to be supplied in such a quantity as society demands, whether for monetary or non-monetary use. Thus, there cannot be any permanent shortage of money that might obstruct the circulation-process of capital, whether the latter implies a simple reproduction or an expanded reproduction. It is not the quantity of money that influences the circulation-process of capital, but rather the function of money in the disposition of surplus value. If surplus value is spent entirely for consumption, money functions as means of circulation over the turnover-time of capital. However, if part of surplus value is saved, and is held as accumulation-funds, over several turnover-times of capital, pending their growth into an appropriate magnitude for real investment, money remains *idle*. The formation of accumulation-funds is a necessary prerequisite for the real accumulation of capital. This special requirement of capitalist society that *the accumulation of the monetary metal should precede the accumulation of real wealth* must be fully appreciated, before the reproduction-process of capital is investigated in the following chapter.

The Hegel Correspondence

This part of the dialectic of capital corresponds to Hegel's doctrine of appearance. 'The essence must appear or shine forth', says Hegel. 'Its shining or reflection in it is the suspension and translation of it to immediacy, which, while as reflection-on-self it is matter or subsistence, is also form, reflection-on-something-else, a subsistence which sets itself aside'.[171] This admittedly difficult passage may perhaps be paraphrased as follows: the production of value by capital cannot stand by itself, because value must be realised in order to be actually produced. The production of a commodity and its circulation presuppose each other. If the same thing (the operation of capital) is looked at from the side of production, 'it is matter or subsistence'; if it is looked at from the side of circulation, it 'is also form'. Yet it is always capital that both produces and circulates. If it only produced or circulated, it would not be capital at all. Thus, the 'appearance [or circulation-process of capital] holds in combination the two

---

171   Hegel 1975, p. 186.

elements of reflection into self and reflection into another'.[172] 'Reflection into
self' may be interpreted to mean what capital does inside its own factory, and
'reflection into another' what capital does in the open market.

The first part of the doctrine of appearance Hegel called the world of appearance, or the phenomenal world. 'The apparent or phenomenal exists in such a
way, that its subsistence is ipso facto thrown into abeyance, or suspended, and
is only one stage in the form itself'.[173] In the circulation-process of capital, production is only one of its phases; hence, capital must take not only the form of
the elements of production, but also the forms of money and the commodity.
'The form embraces in it the matter or substance as one of its characteristics.
In this way the phenomenal has its ground in this (form) as its essence ... but,
in so doing, has it only in another aspect of the form'.[174] In other words, capital
now appears under the form of assets in the balance sheet of an enterprise,
where some assets do represent productive elements, but other assets are
unproductive money and commodities. 'This ground of it [the phenomenal]
is no less phenomenal than itself, and the phenomenon accordingly goes on
to an endless mediation of subsistence by means of form, and thus equally
by non-subsistence'.[175] This could mean that from the point of view of the
circulation-process of capital, the productive activity, upon which it is grounded, is completely submerged in the phenomenal form of assets and costs. 'This
endless intermediation is at the same time a unity of self-relation'[176] because
the motion of capital is in fact a unity of the circuit of money-capital, the circuit of commodity-capital and the circuit of productive capital. 'Existence is
developed into a totality, into a world of phenomena – of reflected finitude'.[177]
The existence of capital thus appears as a *balance sheet*, an asset portfolio, no
item of which is more essential than another.

When the process of value formation and augmentation is thus enveloped
in the phenomenal world of 'assets and costs', matter is lost in the form, but
the form does not lack content. Now 'content and matter are distinguished
by this circumstance, that matter, though implicitly not without form, still in
its existence manifests a disregard of form, whereas the content, as such, is
what it is, only because the matured form is included in it'.[178] In another statement, Hegel asserts that 'the form is content: and in its mature phase is the

172   Hegel 1975, p. 187.
173   Hegel 1975, p. 188.
174   Ibid.
175   Ibid.
176   Ibid.
177   Ibid.
178   Hegel 1975, p. 189.

law of phenomenon'.[179] The efficiency of value augmentation is the matured form, having as its content the annual rate of surplus value. If the rate of surplus value was 'matter', which 'manifested a disregard of the form', the annual rate of surplus value is the 'content', which apart from technical parameters is identical with the form of the efficiency of value augmentation. Capital does not 'exploit' direct producers for the sake of exploitation; it raises the rate of surplus value, in its general effort to raise the efficiency of value augmentation. This is 'the law of phenomenon'. In other words, the production of value and surplus value is, in the final analysis, governed by the mercantile principle of capital.

Hegel then proceeds to the theory of 'correlation (*Verhältnis*)', stating that 'the phenomenon is relativity or correlation: where one and the same thing, viz. the content or the developed form, is seen as the externality and antithesis of independent existences'.[180] In the first place, the content lies in the whole or togetherness, as opposed to the parts that make up the whole; then, the content is understood as 'force' as opposed to its expressions; finally, the content becomes the inner as opposed to the outer. Through these steps, Hegel apparently reasons that the content and its independent existences are fused into an identity, which is called actuality. Unfortunately, the dialectic of capital cannot follow the same reasoning here, because there is the economic problem of the circulation of surplus value, which complements the circulation-process of capital. The actuality of the reproduction-process of capital cannot be directly deduced from the 'content' of the circulation-process of capital, but only from the 'separability of income from capital' which makes the circulation of surplus value both the condition and the consequence of the circulation-process of capital.

A   The Circular Motion of Capital (The Phenomenal World of Capital)

(a)   *The Three Circuits of Capital*

(α) The capitalist's motivation notwithstanding, the return of capital to the sphere of circulation does not obliterate the production-process, which involves the real transformation of use-values, a process that is quite apart from the formal metamorphosis of value. The circulation-process of industrial capital must now be studied as being dependent on this real transformation. From

---

179   Ibid.
180   Hegel 1975, p. 191.

this point of view, the circulation-process of industrial capital becomes more complex than its original circulation-formula connoted. The circular motion of capital cannot be adequately represented, except by the triplex of the circuits of money-capital, productive capital, and commodity-capital. When capital is in the form of money, it is called *money-capital*; when it is in the form of productive elements or goods in the pipeline, it is called *productive capital*; and when it is in the form of a saleable commodity, it is called *commodity-capital*. The circulation-process of industrial capital is made up of three phases, viz.: (1) M – C; (2) ... P ...; (3) C′ – M′. The circuit of money-capital is in the form (1)(2) (3); the circuit of productive capital is in the form (2)(3)(1)(2); and the circuit of commodity-capital is in the form (3)(1)(2)(3). These circuits are explained in what follows.

The circuit of money-capital (M – C ... P ... C′ – M′) is formally identical to the already familiar circulation formula for industrial capital, first introduced in the doctrine of circulation. In simple circulation, however, the production-process of capital could only be anticipated. By now, its reality has been fully exposed. Hence, the sequence of the three phases (1)(2)(3) can be studied again with the knowledge that (1) is preparatory to (2), as (3) is consequent upon (2). Yet this circuit is still fundamentally 'mercantilist', since production here is no more than an instrument of the capitalist chrematistic, which originates and concludes itself in the form of money. While presupposing the capitalist mode of production, the circuit of money-capital is still motivated by the individual desire for self-enrichment. This subjective aspect does not disappear from the motion of capital, even when it integrates the production-process of society; on the contrary, it is this pervasive momentum that sustains and regulates capitalist production. Let us therefore examine the three phases of this circuit, one after another.

In the first phase, M – C, money functions simply as the means of purchase, but the same function simultaneously constitutes part of the operation of capital, inasmuch as the commodities purchased (C) are the elements of production, including labour-power. The conversion of labour-power into a commodity does not originate in the purchasing-power of money. Money can buy labour-power because the latter is already available in the market as a commodity. A money-owner becomes an industrial capitalist by virtue of the fact that he purchases labour-power as a commodity. This fact now compels that the second phase, C ... P ... C′, is not just any production-process, but quite specifically the production-process of capital. The elements of production, purchased as commodities by capital, must function in its production-process as productive capital. Since labour-power, once purchased, cannot be resold as a commodity, capital cannot immediately conclude the process of circulation that it has begun, by letting the third phase, C′ – M′, follow the first phase, M – C. The circulation-process must necessarily be interrupted by the production-process, in which labour-power purchased as variable capital forms and augments value. Hence, the result of the second phase, C ... P ... C', is an embodiment of value, which cannot be disposed of otherwise than as a commodity. Since the capitalistically produced commodity cannot be consumed before it is sold, the third phase, C' – M', must necessarily follow. Capital, therefore, reappears in the circulation-sphere, this time as the seller of a commodity. The produced commodity (C') does not further increase its value in the sphere of circulation, but must remain there for some time before it can be sold, incurring some extra expenses to capital in the meantime. However, surplus value contained in the commodity is realised, and the chrematistic purpose of capital accomplished, only by the sale of the commodity.

With the conversion of the produced commodity, C', into money, M', the original advance of capital, M, and surplus value, m, can be separated in M'. The circuit of money-capital accordingly completes itself, with the M in M', although the circulation of surplus value, c', contained in C' has only finished its first phase, c' – m, and must be followed by the second phase, m – c, to conclude itself. For the circuit of money-capital, however, the completion of the circulation of surplus value is immaterial, because the recovery of the capital-value advanced, M, together with the realisation of surplus value in money, m, accomplishes its goal. Although M', or any part thereof, can be reinvested as capital, M' is not by itself money-capital, but simply money. Its conversion into money-capital, or the operation, M'.M, requires a reassertion of the chrematistic motive, on the part of the capitalist. In fact, money acts quite differently in M – C from C' – M'. In the first phase, money actively sets capital into motion as money-capital; in the last phase, money is a mere result of the sale of the commodity. Even the fact that the commodity was produced in the course of value augmentation is only vaguely recollected in M', in which form, the motion of capital is almost extinct. The circuit of money-capital, thus, describes the motion of industrial capital in its purely capitalist aspect, that is to say, as an individual operation of chrematistic. Use-values are, therefore, totally irrelevant to this circuit, which ignores the consumption either of the capitalist or of the workers. This circuit is even indifferent to whether any part of the monetised surplus value, m, is consumed as revenue or converted into additional capital. Only the self-enrichment of the individual capitalist matters, for which the original possession of money-capital, M, is no doubt the absolute condition. Yet the individual capitalist is not in fact unconditionally in possession of money-capital; capitalist society must have enough money-capital, whoever may be in a position to advance it. For an individual circuit of money-capital to complete itself, the market must be so organised as to absorb its product in exchange for its elements of production. In other words, the circuit of money-capital by one capitalist presupposes the continuing circuits of money-capital by others. But if the circuit of money-capital is repeated twice as

$$M - C \quad .... \quad P \quad .... \quad C' - M'.M - C \quad .... \quad P \quad .... \quad C' \quad - \quad M',$$

the other two aspects of the motion of capital immediately exhibit themselves, namely, the circuit of productive capital, P → P, and the circuit of commodity-capital, C' → C'. The circuit of money-capital, M → M' cannot repeat itself without being accompanied by the other two circuits.

(β) The circuit of productive capital is written as P ... C' – M'.M – C ... P, rather than C ... P ... C' – M'.M – C. It is, therefore, not with the value of the productive elements that this circuit begins and ends, but rather with the collection of productive elements as use-values. Here, P must represent all the productive elements at the outset of the production-process, because, as soon as the latter begins its operation, part of the productive elements must already be transformed into either a finished (or at least a partially finished) product. As the production-process nears its end, more and more productive capital will be absorbed into commodity-capital. In order to clearly separate the circuit of productive capital from that of commodity-capital, it is therefore necessary that the collection of the productive elements needed for the capitalist operation should be observed before any commodity is, or begins to be, sent to the warehouse in a finished form. In this way, P can be properly understood as an index of the scale of capitalist production *in real terms*. The expression, P ... C'– M'.M – C ... P, stresses, moreover, the view that the circuit of productive capital is interrupted by the circulation of commodities, which is a view diametrically opposed to that of the circuit of money-capital.

Thus, the circuit of productive capital represents the 'classical' view of capital; indeed, the classical school was primarily concerned with the accumulation of wealth, and insisted on the definition of capital in real terms. This circuit therefore emphasises the periodic renewal of real capital, which is necessary for the reproduction of wealth. In order to begin a new production-process with P, however, the disposition of the surplus value arising from the prior production-process must already be settled. If the P at the end of the circuit is quantitatively the same as the P at the beginning, the surplus value must be wholly consumed by the capitalist; thus, a 'simple reproduction' must be taking place. If the P at the end is greater than the P at the beginning, part of the surplus value must have been accumulated, and the scale of reproduction must be 'expanding'. The circuit of productive capital, however, considers the problem of the scale of reproduction from the viewpoint of an individual capitalist operation.

In the latter half of the circulation-process, C′ – M′. M – C, the spending of revenue, m – c, is disjoined from the advance of capital, M – C, whereas, in the first half, C′ – M′, the formation of the capitalist's revenue, c′ – m′, is contained within the circulation of capital, from which it cannot actually be separated. However, the circulation of surplus value, c′ – m – c, is a simple exchange of commodities. Even the phase C′ – M′. M – C in the circuit of productive capital takes the simple form of an exchange of commodities, C′ – M – C, rather than the form of metamorphosis, M – C – M′, characteristic of capital. Since the circuit of productive capital insists on the repetition of the production-process, the separation of C′ – M′ from M – C cannot be tolerated. This means that from the point of view of this circuit, money functions only as the medium of circulation. Of course, the exchange of the variable-capital component of C′ for the labour-power component of C cannot be treated in the same way as the exchange of ordinary commodities. However, from the point of view of capital, the fact that the workers buy back the product of their necessary labour is conceived as the exchange of the workers' share of the product for labour-power. Since, in this circuit, money does not represent the original advance of the capital-value, but the mere instrument of exchanging C′ for C, money appears to be a veil over the real activity of capital. The criticism of mercantilism by the classical school was based on this view of capital, which emphasises the natural basis of the production of commodities. Unlike the circuit of money-capital, which considered money, as the prime mover of capitalist operation, and which, consequently, remained indifferent to the use-value aspect of production, this circuit regards the continuity of production to be the vital issue, and hence takes use-values seriously. For unless the specific product, C′, is exchanged for the specific collection of productive elements, C, the real activity of capital cannot be expected to continue.

Since the present circuit still represents the viewpoint of an individual capitalist, however, it is not as yet questioned here whether or not capitalists as a whole may be able to socially accomplish the exchange of C′ for C. Hence, if C′ is sold by the producer, it need not be actually consumed before he purchases the requisite elements of production, C, from the market and continues production. In fact, a large stock of C′ produced by many capitalists may well remain in the circulation sphere, being speculatively held by the commercial sector. Although such a situation frequently foreshadows an impending crisis, individual producers will hardly notice it. With their faith in Say's law and the quantity theory of money, they are bound to overlook the functions of money other than as the means of circulation, always producing as much and as quickly as they can while overstocking the market, until one day it collapses in a crisis as if yielding to the brute force of nature.

The classical view of the pre-determined harmony is, of course, perfectly consistent with the accumulation of wealth. If any part of the monetised surplus value, m, is accumulated, or, in other words, converted into additional capital, an *expanded reproduction* takes place, increasing the scale of production from P to P'. However, the expansion, P → P', of the circuit of productive capital is quite different from the self-enrichment, M → M', of the circuit of money-capital. The form, M → M', merely shows that capital augments value, and does not imply that surplus value has been accumulated, whereas the form P → P', rather than P → P, is a clear indication that the scale of reproduction has expanded, in view of a conversion of surplus value into additional capital. If any surplus value is produced, it does not *ipso facto* make the accumulation of capital possible, since an expansion of the scale of reproduction often requires that certain technical conditions should also be met. Hence, in most cases, surplus value, produced over a span of time, must be kept in the form of *accumulation-funds*, before reaching a sufficient magnitude capable of being converted into additional capital. In this case, money does not simply function as the medium of circulation in C' – M – C. Part of the money obtained by C' – M', but neither advanced as capital in M – C nor spent as revenue in m – c, must now function as the store of value. Money held as accumulation-funds is *potential* capital, and must be distinguished from mere reserve funds, which are often held to satisfy the precautionary motive, in addition to the usual transactions money. (Reserve funds do not originate in the circulation-process of capital. Rather, they are held outside the circulation-process of capital in order that they may be ready to supplement it in case it is stalled or disrupted, whether in simple or in expanded reproduction).

When accumulation-funds reach a magnitude that is technically sufficient to be converted into additional capital, the capitalist, whose turn for accumulation has arrived, must find in the market additional elements of production. Unless other capitalists simultaneously contract their scale of reproduction, so as to release enough resources for the accumulating capitalist to employ, society as a whole now requires more productive elements than before. Whether such a thing is possible or not cannot, however, be understood from the point of view of the individual circuit of productive capital. The individual accumulator must merely 'assume' that external conditions are somehow met for him to be able to expand his operation. In this way, the limitation of the present circuit becomes quite obvious; clearly, this circuit by itself cannot explain the whole complexity of the motion of capital. Indeed, let this circuit be repeated only twice as

$$\overbrace{P \, ... \, C' - M' \, . \, M - C}^{} \, ... \, \overbrace{P \, ... \, C' - M' \, . \, M}^{} \, ... \, P.$$

Then, not only the circuit of money-capital M → M', but also the circuit of commodity-capital C' → C', reassert their presence. The latter circuit must now be examined.

(γ) The circuit of commodity capital begins with C', which already contains surplus value. A value augmentation therefore is a *fait accompli* at the point of departure of this circuit. Unlike the other two circuits, which only anticipated the production-relation in their departing point, M or P, this circuit 'recollects' the capital-labour relation from the beginning. The fundamental difference of C' from C is also obvious. Although C too is in the commodity-form, it cannot enter the circulation-sphere immediately, because it includes labour-power. Both labour-power and the means of production are, so to speak, commodities purchased from others and meant to be consumed as use-values in the production-process of capital. In contrast, C' is the commodity that capital has just produced as value, and thus cannot be consumed until it is circulated. It is the product of capital destined to enter the sphere of circulation. Since C' is a capitalistically produced commodity, its sale must recover the value of capital advanced, while at the same time realising a surplus value. In form, C' – M' is a simple act of sale, which any commodity must undergo, but the fact that C' is a capitalistically produced commodity asserts itself in the inseparability of C' – M' from the subsequent M – C, which perforce must immediately follow.

In the circuit of money-capital, M' marked its end point, whether or not any part of M' was then reconverted into a new money-capital. M depended on the capitalist's (subjective) will, and not on the circuit itself. In the circuit of productive capital, the unbroken sequence of C' – M' and M – C followed from the natural necessity of reproduction. In the present circuit of commodity-capital, the need for M – C as the immediate sequel of C' – M' is due to the fact that C' has been capitalistically produced and is a commodity-capital. Here, part of M' must, as M, purchase productive elements, C, immediately, not for the purpose of reopening the production-process, in which the use-value must be created again, but rather for the purpose of ensuring a further supply of C', which is the capitalistically produced commodity. Production is here a mere instrumentality, whereby C' is repeatedly supplied to the market. The circuit of commodity-capital, in other words, renders the commodity exchange, C' – M – C, an ongoing rather than once-and-for-all process. Even the spending of revenue, m – c, must immediately follow C' – M' so as to render the circulation of surplus value, c' – m – c, regularly recurrent. This implies that capitalistically produced commodities must be productively and individually consumed in due course, in order to assure the flow of new capitalistically produced commodities. From this point of view, the circulation of surplus value no longer occupies a subordinate role to the circulation of capital. The two circulations depend on each other.

Unlike other circuits, the circuit of commodity-capital does not begin with the advance of capital, either in value or in real terms. Hence, this circuit is not concerned with the recovery or retrieval of capital advanced. Specifically, C' – M' is not a step taken for the purpose of regaining the value of capital previously advanced in money form; C' – M' must occur simply because C' is an intrinsic (capitalistically produced) commodity. Yet for one capitalist to effect C' – M', it is necessary that other capitalists should simultaneously undergo M – C, and for one capitalist to successfully undergo M – C, it is necessary that other capitalists should simultaneously effect C' – M'. Since the exchange of commodities is a socially interrelated act, even M – C cannot, in the present context, be taken exclusively as the advance of capital by an individual capitalist. Socially, M – C presupposes C' – M', just as C' – M' presupposes M – C. Therefore, the sale, C' – M', already implies the subsequent purchase, M – C, in the circuit of commodity-capital, in which the viewpoint cannot remain exclusively individual. This is the reason why the present circuit is capable of containing the motion of the *aggregate-social* capital as a self-dependent whole, and also why the study of the so-called *reproduction-schemes*, or *the circular flow of a capitalist economy*, is crucially dependent on this circuit.

This point becomes even more apparent if it is realised that the end point, C', of the present circuit is the result of production, not circulation. The conclusion of this circuit therefore does not depend on the external presence of money or commodities. Once the circulation of commodity-capital, C' – M – C, is successfully accomplished, the new commodity, C', arises from the production-process automatically. However, every C' – M – C takes it for granted that the preceding C' – M – C was successfully completed, so that C' can never be a historical point of departure of the motion of capital. Nor can this circuit stop the motion of capital at C, because in that case why would the preceding C′ – M – C ever have taken place? Thus, there is no beginning or end in the circuit of commodity-capital, and this is so not because reproduction is a natural imperative, but *because capital is capital*. Although the circuit of money-capital is purely commodity-economic, the other two circuits are based on a general norm of real economic life. Thus, if the circuit of productive capital is the capitalist expression of the seeding-to-seeding cycle of a real economy, the circuit of commodity-capital represents the crop-to-crop cycle capitalistically. It is significant that the former circuit suggests an individual operation, while the latter circuit implies a social interaction. In capitalist society, individual units initiate production anarchically, but the output must be sold as a commodity in the market. It is the social exchange of commodities that organises capitalist society, and that imposes a commodity-economic regulation on individual initiatives. The anarchy of the seeding-to-seeding cycle must, so to speak, be corrected *ex post facto* by the social consistency of the crop-to-crop cycle. Thus, the latter cycle contains the three fundamental characteristics of the circuit of commodity-capital already explained. They are: (1) The current crop must be productively and individually consumed, in an appropriate fashion, in order to ensure the production of next year's crop. Thus, the direct consumption of the surplus crop is as important as the use of the crop as productive elements; (2) A farmer must exchange his product for the products of other farmers, in order to ensure his next year's crop, so that he necessarily enters a social relation with others; (3) The crop arises from his own farm and not from his shopping basket. Thus, the harvesting of his crop immediately sends the farmer to the market, unless he is in a state of self-sufficient autarky. Indeed, this is how François Quesnay visualised the circular flow of an agricultural economy, in his celebrated *Tableau économique,* starting with an annual gross product worth, say, five thousand million livres.

The circuit of commodity-capital, which begins and ends with C′, thus represents the motion of capital as part of the socially interacting whole, consisting of commodity exchanges. The circuit of productive capital, which begins and ends with P, represents the motion of capital as an individually planned and executed continuum of the production and accumulation of wealth. The circuit of money-capital, which begins and ends with money, represents the motion of capital as the self-inspired chrematistic of an individual money-owner. None of these circuits, taken separately from the others, can exhaustively characterise the whole circular motion of industrial capital, which must always be understood as the triplex of these circuits. The motion of industrial capital, unlike that of merchant capital and of money-lending capital, cannot be grasped from the point of view only of the circuit of money-capital.

(*b*)   Productive Capital and Circulation-capital

(α) With the development of mechanised industry, it becomes not only possible but also necessary for capital to operate its production-process continuously without interruption. Thus, part of capital must remain in the production-process as means of labour and other elements of production, even while another part, already in the form of a finished commodity, leaves for the sphere of circulation. As the commodity is absorbed into its market, moreover, the corresponding part of capital becomes money, which is once again advanced as money-capital to feed the production-process with new productive elements. Thus, every enterprise holds part of its capital as productive elements or half-finished products, another part as commodities, and the rest as money, at every moment. This only means that the capitalist does not operate exclusively as a producer at one time, then as the seller of his commodity at another, and as a purchaser of productive elements at yet another time. He never shuts down his factory when a certain bulk of his commodity is produced in order to go to the market to sell it. Nor does he wait until he has sold all of it before buying productive elements. If an industrial factory is closed, even for a short while, it will easily become a shambles, with rusted machines and spoiled materials, which to be put into operation again will cost a considerable sum of money in refurbishment. Productive labour must ceaselessly flow simply to preserve the value of the means of production to be transferred to the new product. Precisely for this reason, capital loathes the shutdown of its factory even at night and on Sundays. Capital must continue to produce, even while it trades, so as to avoid a costly interruption of its production-process.

Let us now extend the concept of productive capital so as to include all elements of production and 'goods-in-the-pipeline' that remain in the production-process of capital. The rest of capital, either in the form of money or of the commodity, will henceforth be *referred to as circulation-capital*. A capitalist firm, in order not to interrupt its production-process, must always hold its capital partly in the form of productive capital and partly in that of circulation-capital, that is, of money-capital and commodity-capital. This division of capital closely corresponds with the observed fact that every industrial firm consists of a factory, a sales office, and a purchasing department. To the factory supervisor, capital appears to consist primarily of productive elements, particularly of the means of production. To the sales manager, the stock of the saleable commodity in the warehouse most readily represents capital, and to the clerk of the requisition office, capital above all means money. It is obvious, however, that these conceptions of capital are all one-sided. Capital must be all of these, and in practice these are represented, albeit in a 'phenomenal' form, in the balance sheet of the firm as its different assets.

A balance sheet represents, indeed, the practical wisdom of the capitalist, who intuitively realises the triplex character of the motion of industrial capital. That is why orthodox economists have always wanted to relate economic theory to the 'balance-sheet concept of capital', despite showing a striking lack of success in doing so. Milton Friedman frequently alludes to a portfolio theory of capital, but fails to ever make it explicit,[181] because he realises, quite correctly, that the 'ultimate wealth-owning unit' holds money only as one of its assets. Unfortunately, it is in terms of the subjective theory of consumption and of the market theory of returns that he wishes to explain the portfolio of an 'ultimate wealth-owning unit'.[182] Economic theory, however, becomes empty if it is made so general as to apply equally well to a capitalist industrial firm and to a supra-historical individual. Instead of inventing a historically meaningless entity such as the 'ultimate wealth-owning unit' or the 'consumer', and artificially (ideologically) inspiring it with the market-oriented 'economic rationality' as a matter of 'ought', the dialectic of capital derives its theory from the historical reality of industrial capital. If industrial capital cannot afford to interrupt its production, it has to divide its capital into productive capital and circulation-capital, and further divide the latter into money-capital and commodity-capital. The proportion in which capital must be held in those various forms is determined by the proportional lengths of time taken by the production-process and by the circulation-process, that is, by the proportional lengths of the *production-period* and of the *circulation-period*, with the latter being further divided into the *selling-period* and the *purchasing-period.*[183]

In order to illustrate this point, an example will be presented in the following subsection, showing how a balance sheet may be deduced from the motion of industrial capital. Since the balance sheet is a 'phenomenal' (to use Hegel's term) expression of capital, however, many arbitrary, that is to say, practical conventions must be adopted in order to represent the true motion of capital in this form. Moreover, simplicity also requires a few harmless assumptions.

---

181 For example, see Friedman 1969, p. 73.

182 A far more promising approach proposed by Kenneth E. Boulding in *A Reconstruction of Economics* has found few followers; see Boulding 1950 and 1962.

183 It must be noted that the production-period here means the span of time during which productive elements, purchased as commodities, are converted into the commodity-product, and that this concept has nothing in common with the 'production-period' of the Austrian capital theory; see Chapter 7.

In particular, it will be understood that as soon as capital is recovered in the form of money, M', its M-component is considered to form money-capital. In fact, M' contains not only M but also surplus value, m; the first is to be re-converted into money-capital by the operation, M'.M, and the second forms either the consumption-fund of the capitalist or his accumulation-fund. In the present context, however, these funds (as well as surplus value, c', already contained in the commodity-capital, C') will be integrated into the capital structure of the firm.

(β) Let us suppose that the capitalist invests a sum of money, M, at the beginning of the first week, to buy the elements of production, C_1, which are (productively) consumed, during the second and the third week, as C_2 and C_3, still in the production-process, until they reemerge as the finished product, C'_4, at the beginning of the fourth week. Suppose also that this product, C'_4, remains in the form of an inventory or stock at the beginning of the fifth week, as C'_5, and is sold only at the beginning of the sixth week for money, M'_6. Suppose further that this money, M'_6, cannot be immediately reinvested, but can purchase the elements of production only at the beginning of the seventh week, as M = C_1, to repeat the same process. If the capitalist endeavours to avoid any interruption of production, he should divide his capital into six equal portions, and should keep investing each portion at the beginning of every week, as in Table 5.1 below.

TABLE 5.1

Week	1	2	3	4	5	6	7	8	9	10	11	12
1st portion	C_1	C_2	C_3	C'_4	C'_5	M'_6						
2nd		C_1	C_2	C_3	C'_4	C'_5	M'_6					
3rd			C_1	C_2	C_3	C'_4	C'_5	M'_6				
4th				C_1	C_2	C_3	C'_4	C'_5	M'_6			
5th					C_1	C_2	C_3	C'_4	C'_5	M'_6		
6th						C_1	C_2	C_3	C'_4	C'_5	M'_6	
1st (again)							C_1	C_2	C_3	C'_4	C'_5	M'_6

It is, of course, assumed that technical and other conditions permit such a regular flow of weekly investments. If no expansion of business is envisaged, the structure of capital (M'_6, C'_5, C'_4, C_3, C_2, C_1) will remain constant after the

sixth week, and may be shown in the form of a balance sheet, as in Table 5.2
below. Here all values are shown in money terms at the beginning of each week
after the sixth.

TABLE 5.2

money-capital and funds	M'_6	capital advanced	$6C_1$
commodity-capital	C'_5, C'_4		
productive capital	C_3, C_2, C_1	net worth	$3m$

There are, of course, many complications. The capitalist knows only the
money value of total capital advanced ($6C_1$) and the money value of cash
on hand (M'_6) exactly. The money value of inventories (C'_5, C'_4) must, however, be estimated as expected values. The money value of productive capital
(C_3, C_2, C_1) also requires some conventional technique to be evaluated, even
when fixed capital and its depreciation are left out of consideration. Indeed,
no balance sheet is entirely free from some arbitrary calculations, because it
is merely a phenomenal expression of the true existence of capital. Even the
fact that labour-power, purchased as part of C, immediately loses its value is
ignored, since the labour-cost, or wage-fund, is considered here as part of productive capital. It is therefore not unreasonable to make further assumptions
with a view to simplifying the following exposition: (1) $C'_4 + C'_5 = 2C' = 2M'$,
which means that the market price of the commodity is expected to be unchanged, and that the commodity does not lose any part of its use-value during the storage period; (2) $C_1 + C_2 + C_3 = 3C = 3M$, which means that the money
value of productive elements (assuming the absence of fixed capital) remains
unchanged, while production is in progress; (3) $m = M' - M = C' - C$, which
means that some surplus value is gained when goods emerge as finished products, and that productive capital suddenly switches into commodity-capital at
the end of the third week. Thus, if, for example, $M = 120$ and $M' = 140$ in some
monetary units, the balance sheet may be numerically stated as in Table 5.3
below.

TABLE 5.3

$M' = 140$	$6M = 720$
$2C' = 280$	
$3C = 360$	$3m = 60$
780	780

Capital takes time both in production and in circulation. That is why it has to maintain a balance sheet structure, such as is illustrated above, ensuring at all times the continuity of the productive operation. Since two weeks are needed to sell the product, and one more week to purchase productive elements in the present illustration, the circulation-capital (money-capital and commodity-capital) of 420 (= M' + 2C') is needed, in contrast to the productive capital of 360 (= 3C), which corresponds to the three weeks required for production. Total capital advanced is 720 (= 6M) because the entire turnover-time of capital, including the periods for production and for circulation, is six weeks. Thus, apart from the net worth of 60 (= 3m), which is here included in circulation-capital, total capital advanced is divided into circulation-capital and productive capital, in proportion to the length of time required by the circulation- and production-phases, respectively, of the entire turnover-time of capital.

Let us now examine the structure of productive capital somewhat more closely. If capital takes three weeks for its production-phase, it may be assumed that regardless of how a portion M of capital is invested in the elements of production in the course of the three weeks, the entire output, the price of which contains the whole of M, emerges at the end of the third week (or at the beginning of the fourth week). This, of course, means that no fixed capital exists. It also means that no part of C, even if it is almost finished as a commodity, is ready for sale before the beginning of the fourth week. However, the process of investing M in the elements of production cannot be treated so simply. The elements of production consist of non-fixed constant capital such as raw materials, and variable capital or labour-power. Even if all the raw materials are purchased at the beginning of the first week, the workers can only be employed at the beginning of the week and paid at the end of it.

In order to illustrate the changing structure of capital, let us visualise an artificial and stylised process of producing orange juice from fresh oranges. For simplicity, any semi-product such as concentrate, which is neither juice nor fresh fruit, will be ignored, so that at the end of each week in the production-period, the use-value of productive capital, apart from labour, takes the form of either fresh oranges or orange juice. (The depreciation of the plant, and so on, will be neglected). Let the capitalist, at the beginning of each week, n, purchase three kilograms of oranges, $R = r(1) + r(2) + r(3)$, and the labour-power of three workers, to whom he pays the wages of $W = w(1) + w(2) + w(3)$, at the end of the week. By the beginning of the next week, one gallon of orange juice, $t(1) + v(1)$, is already made, and fills one-third of the jug, but two kilograms of fresh oranges, $r(2) + r(3)$, still remain intact in the squashing barrel. Two workers, therefore, continue to work in the second week and are paid $w(2) + w(3)$ at its end. By the beginning of the third week, another gallon of orange juice, $t(2) + v(2)$, is ready, and the jug is two-thirds full. Since one more kilogram of fresh oranges, r(3), remains, one worker must continue to work through the third week, and is paid w(3) at its end. Only at this point, that is to say, at the beginning of the fourth week, is the jug of orange juice completely full, requiring no further production. The law, it is assumed, prescribes that the capitalist should possess, at the beginning of every week, enough wage-funds out of which to pay the workers engaged during that week, at its end. We will assume that the technology is such that production cannot begin unless the squashing barrel is first filled with three kilograms of fresh oranges.

Under this supposition it is possible to decompose C_1, C_2, C_3 and C'_4 as follows:

$$C_1 = r(1) + r(2) + r(3) + w(1) + w(2) + w(3) = R + W,$$
$$C_2 = \underline{t(1)} + r(2) + r(3) + \underline{v(1)} + w(2) + w(3) = \tfrac{1}{3}(T + V) + \tfrac{2}{3}(R + W),$$
$$C_3 = \underline{t(1) + t(2)} + r(3) + \underline{v(1) + v(2)} + w(3) = \tfrac{2}{3}(T + V) + \tfrac{2}{3}(R + W),$$
$$C'_4 = \underline{t(1) + t(2) + t(3)} + \underline{v(1) + v(2) + v(3)} = T + V.$$

The value of the raw material, R, transferred to the product, is denoted by T, and the value of labour-power, W, reproduced in the product, is denoted by V. Thus, when the capital structure becomes stationary, its productive components, $3C = (C_1, C_2, C_3)$, in the above balance sheet can be stated in greater details as follows:

raw materials $2R = r(1) + 2r(2) + 3r(3),$

wage funds $2W = w(1) + 2w(2) + 3w(3),$

unfinished goods $T + V = 2t(1) + t(2) + 2v(1) + v(2).$

For example, if M = 120 is divided into R = 60 and W = 60 initially, the numerical balance-sheet will be as in Table 5.4 below:

TABLE 5.4

commodity in stock (2C') = 280	capital advanced (6M) = 720
raw materials in stock (2R) = 120	
unfinished product (T + V) = 120	
wage-fund on hand (2W) = 120	net worth (3m) = 60
cash available (M') = 140	
780	780

In this example, it is assumed that at the end of every week (after the sixth) the money wage of $W = w(1) + w(2) + w(3) = 60$ is paid for the value of labour-power consumed during that week. Although simultaneously the net worth of 60 accrues to the capitalist, only one-third of it, namely, 20, is actually realised in money, and represents the surplus value earned during that week. The remaining 40 of net worth, being in the form of the commodity, constitutes 'appropriable' surplus labour not yet realised as surplus value. Hence, the rate of surplus value per week is approximately 33.3%. If the *weekly efficiency of value augmentation* is defined as the ratio of realised surplus value to total capital advanced, it is 20/720 or approximately 2.8%. The question of the efficiency of value augmentation will have to be studied in greater detail later. Here, the primary issue is that even if the rate of surplus value is 33.3%, capital, of the magnitude of 720, must be tied up every week in order to earn the weekly surplus value of 20, and this total capital must be divided into various items appropriate to both the production and the circulation of the commodity.

(γ) Whereas capital in the process of production is actively engaged in the formation and augmentation of value, capital that remains outside of this process, whether in the form of money or the commodity, creates no value, undergoing merely a formal metamorphosis. It is, however, not possible to regard only productive capital, or only circulation-capital, as an adequate representation of the whole of capital. Capital is never merely money, a commodity, means of production or a wage-fund. It is all of them simultaneously, as synthesised in an organic unity. So long as the market is active, it is, of course, to the advantage of the capitalist to maximise the magnitude of productive capital, which has a direct bearing on value augmentation. His desire to do so, however, is constrained 'capitalist-socially' by the unavoidability of time, which is required for the circulation of his commodity. To ignore this constraint would have the disastrous consequence of forcing a production stoppage, if not outright insolvency. Hence, the capitalist must always keep part of his capital in the *unproductive* forms of money and commodities. Indeed, the asset structure of his capital is sometimes interpreted to reflect the wisdom of his 'risk aversion' or 'liquidity preference'. It has already been remarked that the lack of this conception led classical political economy to emphasise productive capital exclusively. This view, together with the inadequate understanding of the form of wages, has led to the uncritical identification of capital with the means of production. In consequence, the historic and commodity-economic significance of capital was altogether missed. Indeed, if capitalism simply meant the use of capital in the sense of the means of production, every production would *ipso facto* become capitalist production, and the capitalist mode of production would become a pure pleonasm.

Although the length of the production-period is mainly determined by technical factors, the circulation-period can be long or short, depending on the changing conditions of the market. Thus, even if production always takes three weeks, as in the above example, and as a consequence tying up the capital-value of 360, the selling and buying may take less or more than three weeks, due to largely unpredictable factors. If the circulation-period is long, more capital must be tied up in the operation; if it is short, some idle funds may be released. Moreover, to the extent that the factors affecting the length of the circulation-period are uncertain, or to the extent that the prices of the productive elements or those of the product may fluctuate in the market, no capitalist enterprise is safe if it does not hold additional money as reserve funds. As previously mentioned, reserve funds are not part of capital (although capitalists often believe them to be so), but constitute precautionary money held beside capital, so as to shelter its motion from unpredictable contingencies in the short run. If more permanent changes occur, either in productive technology or in the pattern of social demand, such as to alter the values of commodities, industrial capital may be forced to move from the production of one use-value to another, requiring some considerable expense in the process. The concrete manner by which such an adjustment is carried out cannot and need not be studied in the present context. It may be supposed that the representative unit of industrial capital always has enough resources, apart from the value of its advance, to withstand such contingencies. Even in that case, the lengthening and shortening of either the production-period or the circulation-period affect the magnitude of capital that must be advanced for the production of a given amount of surplus value.

It therefore follows that the period of time required, whether for production or for circulation, becomes an overriding consideration in the determination of the cost of value augmentation. In the above example, if the weekly sale of the commodity is 140 value units, of which 20 are the surplus value, and if total capital of 720 must be tied up every week, then at least the interest payable on the unrecovered value of capital (600 = 720 − 120) might appear to cause a deduction from the surplus-value of 20. That is to say, if, for example, the weekly rate of interest is 1%, disposable surplus value might appear to be reduced to 14 = 20 − 600 × 0.01. At the present stage, however, a cost calculation such as this is premature because no theory for the determination of the rate of interest has yet been formulated. Moreover, as will be seen later, interest turns out to be merely a transfer of surplus value from one capitalist to another, and as such cannot be said to form a cost to the capitalist class as a whole. Here, the real issue is how much of the existing capital-value must be held in an unproductive form, and how much that detracts from the production of surplus value in capitalist society. That raises the problem of *time*, as the cost of value augmentation.

Suppose that the productive method illustrated previously is the only technique known to the capitalist. Suppose, however, that the circulation-period is now reduced from three to two weeks, because commodity-capital, C'_4, need be stocked for only one week before it is sold for M'_5 at the beginning of the fifth week. If the capital value of 720 is divided into five equal instalments of 144, and one instalment is invested each week, the structure of capital (M'_5, C'_4, C_3, C_2, C_1) will become stationary after the fifth week, barring, of course, any expansion in the scale of business. This means that the wage-bill or variable capital per week is $W = 72$ (or half of 144), which produces the surplus value of 24 per week at the rate of 33.3%. The balance sheet, in that case, is as in Table 5.5 below, which yields the efficiency of value augmentation of 24/720 or roughly 3.3%.

TABLE 5.5

M' = 168	5M = 720
C' = 168	
3C = 432	2m = 48
768	768

TABLE 5.6

M' = 168	5M = 720
2C' = 336	
2C = 288	3m = 72
792	792

In contrast to the previous example, this case shows that capital of the magnitude of 720 can now produce surplus value of 24, because the circulation-period is two weeks, whereas capital of the same magnitude produced the surplus value of only 20 when the circulation-period was three weeks. Consequently, it may be concluded that the extension of the circulation-time from two to three weeks would, in this case, 'cost' 4 = 24 − 20 in surplus value. Unlike interest, this cost is not a mere transfer of surplus value from one capitalist to another, but rather the cost that the capitalist class as a whole must bear, because of the extension of the circulation-period, that is, because of the need to allocate a greater proportion of capital to the unproductive sphere of circulation. This type of cost will henceforth be called the *ordinary cost of circulation*. Since the circulation-period is never zero, every industrial capital must ordinarily bear this cost, in proportion to the length of the circulation-period.

If that is the case, however, the shortening of the production-period must also be treated in the same way. Let the circulation-period be three weeks, as in the example of the previous sub-section, but let the production-period be two, instead of three, weeks. In that case, after the fifth week the structure of capital will become stationary as $(M'_5, C'_4, C'_3, C_2, C_1)$, with the weekly investment of 144. In this case too $W = 72$ will produce the surplus value of 24 per week, at the rate of 33.3%. Although the balance sheet is somewhat different (see Table 5.6 above), the efficiency of value augmentation of 3.3% = 24/720 turns out to be the same as in the earlier case. Hence, the cost of extending the production-period from two to three weeks would also 'cost' the capitalist 4 value units in surplus value. This kind of cost may be called the *time-cost of production,* which is in addition to the labour and non-labour cost of the weekly output that was, in the case of the production-period of three weeks, 60W + 60R + (24 – 4)m = 140. The time-cost of production is of the same nature as the ordinary cost of circulation, in that it is surplus value foregone rather than an actual deduction from surplus value. How these costs are borne by capitalist society as a whole and by individual capitalists will be made clearer in the doctrine of distribution. What must be emphasised in the present context is that, in the circulation-process of capital, which contains the production-process, *time* itself becomes an important cost of value augmentation to the capitalist, whether that time is specifically for the production of a use-value or for a purely formal metamorphosis. This concept of cost is quite new and distinct from that of the production-costs referred to earlier. Between the production-costs, or the costs of purchasing productive elements, and the costs of surplus value foregone due to simply holding capital in one form or another over time, there are pure circulation-costs, which must be actually deducted from surplus value already produced.

(c)   *The Costs of Circulation*

(α) Quite apart from the ordinary circulation-cost, which is the difference between the surplus value that could have been earned in the absence of the circulation-period, and the surplus value actually realised in the presence of the circulation-period, there are more obvious costs that capital must bear during its phase of circulation. Even the purely circulatory operation of buying and selling commodities costs capital labour-power and material resources. For example, a sales shop must be maintained, commercial correspondence must be exchanged, and books must be kept. All these activities give rise to so-called pure circulation-costs, which are sometimes also called the capitalists' unproductive costs or 'faux frais' (or '*Unkosten*'). Pure circulation-costs must be defrayed from surplus value actually realised, and must cause a deduction from it. Thus, even if the circulation-period is only two weeks, enabling the capitalist to earn the surplus value of 24 per week, the weekly compensation for office workers and salesmen, the depreciation of office equipment, the consumption of paper and ink, and so on, may add up to 4 value units, reducing the surplus value at the disposal of the capitalist to 20. Pure circulation-costs generally tend to increase with the length of the circulation-period, though not necessarily in the same proportion. If it takes a long time to sell a commodity, a more active and determined sales campaign is called for, requiring more resources. Hence, if the circulation-period is three weeks instead of two, more than 4 value units may have to be deducted from the already diminished surplus value of 20. It is thus all the more necessary for capital to strive for a shorter circulation-period.

Purely commercial labour does not form or augment any value, nor does it even transfer to the new product the value of the material resources that it (productively) consumes. Such labour is unproductive and must be distinguished from productive labour, which directly creates a use-value as a material object. Since unproductive labour does not produce surplus value, it cannot be divided into necessary labour and surplus labour; thus, it is not a question of the appropriation of surplus labour. This, however, does not mean that unproductive workers are free from 'exploitation' in the ordinary sense. Indeed, by paying commercial labourers as little as possible and by letting them work as much as possible, the capitalist benefits greatly because his deduction of pure circulation-costs from surplus value is that much less. This 'exploitation', however unconscionable it may be, does not increase surplus value in any way, nor does it affect the production-relation between the capitalist and his productive workers, which was already established in the production-process of capital.

The pure circulation-costs being discussed here are those that are borne by the capitalist individually, and paid out of his surplus value. They must be clearly distinguished from the social cost of circulation, such as monetary gold, which is borne collectively by society at large. It is true that monetary gold, which cannot be consumed either individually or productively, constitutes *faux frais* to society and may therefore also be called 'unproductive'. However, monetary gold has a use-value, if more social rather than sensuous, that is, as a material object. The labour that produces it cannot, for this reason, be unproductive. Gold serves as money, because it is a capitalistically producible commodity. Of course, it goes without saying that unless surplus value were produced in gold (monetary or otherwise), no capitalist would undertake to produce it. Hence, it is quite wrong to treat monetary gold as one of the items of pure circulation-costs presently under discussion, although Marx's exposition gives the contrary impression. As previously mentioned (in Chapter 2), capital cannot by itself save the social cost of circulation, which is not sustained by individual capitalists in isolation. Specifically, capital cannot issue *fiat money* and enforce its circulation so as to economise the circulation of full-bodied gold money, although it can issue *credit money* or banknotes. Traders always know how to minimise their own costs, but they do not know how to save costs to society in general, unless the latter saving is an immediate consequence of their individual action. They are only willing to make use of the convenience of monetary gold provided at public expense (and thus a public good), if they are themselves not (directly) responsible for supplying it.

Somewhat similar to monetary gold are armaments, which can be neither productively nor individually consumed, and extreme luxury goods or morally repugnant goods, the absence of which does not deprive capitalist society of any essential use-value. These goods may be 'unproductive' or 'counterproductive' in themselves; however, the labour that produces them need not be unproductive of value, unless more are produced than is socially demanded. For example, a pornographic object or a narcotic drug is perfectly objectionable and counter-productive in the general sense. Yet so long as there is demand for it, capital has no scruples about producing it, thus squandering society's productive labour, which could be used for the production of worthier use-values. Capital does not itself avoid such a waste of productive labour, so long as there is some market demand, fuelled by a number of consumers who are ready to pay for such a noxious use-value. Extra-economic force must therefore intervene either to stop or to restrict the production of an inappropriate use-value. On the other hand, if the production of a counter-productive use-value is prohibited or restricted by law, that does not, in any essential respect, deter the motion of capital, just as the issue of fiat money by a public body does not inconvenience capitalism if its issue is kept within a proper limit. On the contrary, capitalist society becomes more 'productive' if productive labour need not be wasted in the fabrication of objectionable use-values.

(β) A sharp distinction between productive and unproductive labour in the dialectic of capital has often been criticised by those who are unashamedly ignorant of the meaning of the labour theory of value. Yet Marx himself is, to some extent, to blame for causing unnecessary confusion. Often he is torn between his own logic and the excess baggage of his knowledge of classical writings, unable to quite make up his mind. The first definition of productive labour given by Marx is as follows: 'If we examine the whole [labour] process from the point of view of its result, the product, it is plain ... that the labour itself is productive labour'.[184] Here, productive labour is clearly the human labour that acquires a product, a material object, or a use-value, directly or indirectly from nature herself. However, instead of elaborating on that point further, Marx attaches a footnote to this passage, which states:

> This method of determining, from the standpoint of the labour-process alone, what is productive labour is by no means directly applicable to the case of the capitalist process of production.[185]

When, later in volume I of *Capital*, he returns to the same subject, Marx writes:

> The first definition given above of productive labour, a definition deduced from the very nature of the production of material objects, still remains correct for the collective labourer, considered as a whole. But it no longer holds good for each member taken individually.[186]

Marx goes on to explain that 'in order to labour productively it is no longer necessary for you to do manual work yourself; enough, if you are an organ of the collective labourer, and perform one of its subordinate functions'.[187] From this point of view, the significance of the above quoted footnote is now expanded as follows:

> Capitalist production is not merely the production of commodities; it is essentially the production of surplus value. The labourer produces, not for himself, but for capital. It no longer suffices, therefore, that he should simply produce. He must produce surplus value. That labourer alone is productive, who produces surplus value for the capitalist, and thus works for the self-expansion of capital.[188]

---

184   Marx 1967, *Capital*, Volume I, p. 181.
185   Ibid.
186   Marx 1967, *Capital*, Volume I, p. 509.
187   Ibid.
188   Ibid.

Yet immediately after this passage, we find such an erroneous illustration as the following:

> If we may take an example from outside the sphere of production of material objects, a school master is a productive labourer, when, in addition to belabouring the heads of his scholars, he works like a horse to enrich the school proprietor.[189]

A salesman may also 'work like a horse' to enrich the business proprietor, but is he, for that reason, productive?

In the *Theories of Surplus Value,* the same error is repeated. Here, Marx refers to two explanations of Adam Smith of the distinction between productive and unproductive labour: (1) 'the view of productive labour as labour exchanged for capital'; and (2) 'the view of productive labour as labour which is realised in a commodity'. Marx has the following to say in response to these two views:

> Adam Smith's opponents have disregarded his first pertinent definition, and instead have concentrated on the second, pointing out the unavoidable contradiction and inconsistencies to which it gives rise. And their attacks were made all the easier for them by their insistence on the material content of the labour and particularly the specific requirement that the labour must fix itself in a more or less permanent product.[190]

To the extent that the second definition of Adam Smith involves, in its illustration, such an empirical question as how 'material' a commodity should be, Marx may be right in guarding against 'the unavoidable contradiction and inconsistencies'. But even the first definition of Smith is not free from misleading empiricism, when Marx claims that:

> Included among the productive workers, of course, are all those who contribute in one way or another to the production of the commodity, from the actual operative to the manager or engineer (as distinct from the capitalist). And so even the latest English official report on the factories 'explicitly' includes in the category of employed wage-labourers all

189   Ibid.
190   Marx 1971, *Theories of Surplus Value,* Part 1, p. 168.

persons employed in the factories and in the offices attached to them, with the exception of the manufacturers themselves.[191]

If a sales office were attached to the factory, then, would not the English official report classify all commercial workers, accountants and salesmen, as productive workers? What Marx does not seem to realise is that without the distinction of productive and unproductive labour (by his own first definition), even capital, as distinguished from revenue (surplus value), cannot be unambiguously defined. Thus, when circulation-costs are later converted into commercial capital, the same commercial worker, who was unproductive in volume II of *Capital,* suddenly becomes productive in volume III, only because he is presumed to be more systematically exploitable in the new context. If this were the case, one could also argue that a servant who is unproductive when gently employed need only be pushed around 'like a horse' in order to become productive. 'Exploitation' would then be a purely empirical and subjective conception, even harder to measure than the materiality of a commodity.

Marx was obviously misled by the writings of classical authors whose labour theory of value was thoroughly confused because of the absence of a general definition of productive labour, such as Marx's first definition, and because of their related failure to distinguish the labour theory of value from the explanation of equilibrium or natural prices. Marx's dialectical method enabled him to begin with the commodity, which is 'a thing outside us', rather than 'a personal service rendered between us', and to establish the first fundamental definition of productive labour as the labour that acquires a use-value, directly or indirectly, from nature. Once this was accomplished, what Marx should have done was to establish that under capitalism his original definition becomes equivalent to the second definition ('productive labour is the labour that forms value'), as well as the third definition ('productive labour is the labour that produces surplus value'). The proof is very simple. Since, in a purely capitalist society, no use-value can be produced except as a commodity, which must possess a value, productive labour that produces a use-value necessarily forms value. Since, moreover, no use-value can be produced there except as an instrument of capitalist chrematistics, labour that produces a use-value necessarily produces surplus value as well. Thus, under (pure) capitalism, all the three definitions of productive labour are theoretically equivalent. From this point of view, not only commercial labour, but all forms of mental or service labour as

---

191   Marx 1971, *Theories of Surplus Value,* Part 1, p. 152.

well, which does not produce a use-value (that is, which does not directly or indirectly involve transformation of nature) are without question unproductive.

I have already stated that the dialectic of capital need not be concerned with direct personal services, which cannot be reified by virtue of the commodity-economic tendency to materialise real economic life. This is in keeping with Marx's fundamental view that 'the commodity is the most elementary form of bourgeois wealth',[192] the reason being that the commodity, as 'a thing outside us', reifies the human relations of bourgeois society. Direct personal relations, which can never be completely reified, are not only irrelevant to the study of a purely capitalist society, but are also incapable of commodity-economic and thus objective explanation, and so fall outside the realm of political economy. They must be treated as empirical issues in light of the theoretical distinction (already established in their absence) between productive and unproductive labour. The distinction without a firm theory, but merely in reference to a multitude of empirical instances, is bound to degenerate into 'the hobby-horse of the second-rate fellows and especially of the school-masterish compilers and writers of compendia as well as dilettanti with facile pens and vulgarisers'[193] in the field of political economy. Marx should not have become embroiled in that level of discussion.

Apart from direct personal services, there are two other kinds of unproductive labour. One is the capitalist's own labour and its extensions; it is this kind that must be studied in the present context. The other kind, which may be broadly called socio-organisational labour, is essential to the formation of any society, but is largely non-economic (particularly in capitalist society); the study of this kind of labour belongs to the theory of the state, not to political economy. In capitalist society this second kind of unproductive labour becomes residual, together with the state itself, which manages such labour. For the constitution of capitalist society, only the first kind is of any theoretical significance. This is consistent with the presupposition of the dialectic of capital that capital does not depend on any principle other than its own to form a capitalist society. The dialectic of capital therefore deliberately holds the state implicit, while not denying its historical existence, and shows how the law of value integrates the anarchic production of use-values into a self-contained commodity-economic system. For the working of the law of value only *the unproductive labour of the capitalists and its extensions* are necessary accompaniments to the productive labour of the direct producers.

---

192   Marx 1971, *Theories of Surplus Value*, Part 1, p. 168.
193   Marx 1971, *Theories of Surplus Value*, Part 1, p. 170.

If commercial labour is thus viewed as the extension of the capitalist's own labour, it must include all forms of labour involved in the broad category of so-called 'business administration'. Those who sell and purchase commodities may not be the same as those who design the product, who do the market and technical research, and who make decisions as to how the business should in general be developed. Indeed, they are in the final analysis doing what the capitalist himself would do in the absence of diversification, that is, if business were not as complex as it is today. Even the top engineers and personnel managers are merely advisors to the capitalist because he himself cannot oversee all aspects of the administration of business. They are therefore commercial workers in the extended sense. It might be objected that factory supervisors, whose work is not at all connected with the circulation of a commodity, but only its production, cannot possibly be classified as commercial workers. One must not forget, however, that a factory supervisor is not a slave-driver, who must constantly exercise extra-economic coercion. His duty, theoretically, is limited to communicating to the workers how the capitalist wants their labour-power to be (productively) consumed. If the supervisor had to police them or regiment them like a military officer, it would mean that their labour-power was not a commodity. The development of the capitalist method of production, in perfecting labour-power as a commodity, is expected to eliminate all such policing eventually. Moreover, when labour-power was still a very imperfect commodity, as in the commission system, it was the job of the merchant capitalist and his representatives to guard against the pilfering of materials, the laziness of the workers and the excessive damage to which the instruments entrusted to the workers might be exposed. Hence, even the supervisory labour cannot be as vastly different from ordinary commercial labour as it might appear at first sight.

As long as the capitalist appropriates the surplus labour of productive workers, therefore, he can always pay his unproductive workers, by transferring to them part of his surplus value. He will do so willingly if the labour of these unproductive workers contributes indirectly towards the acquisition of more surplus value, by raising the efficiency of the operation of his business (by shortening the unproductive period of circulation, for example). The extent to which the capitalist 'exploits' his salesmen and other unproductive workers determines only how much of the surplus value that he has already appropriated will have to be shared with the productive workers. But it does not determine the rate of surplus value that applies to productive workers. The existential base of capitalist society is not affected by the distribution of surplus value; it only depends on the production of surplus value. It is worth pointing out here that the capitalist's unproductive labour, unlike the productive labour of wage earners, does not tend to be simplified with the development of the capitalist method of production. On the contrary, not only does it become diversified, requiring more and more specialised personnel, but it also becomes more complex in each of the specialised fields. For instance, as the market for his commodity expands, the capitalist may have to employ a salesperson capable of speaking several languages, who is aware of different cultures, and who is at the same time sufficiently knowledgeable with respect to the technical properties of the merchandise. The salesperson, in that case, does not sell his labour-power as a commodity to his employer. Recall that labour-power is 'the aggregate of those mental and physical capabilities existing in a human being, which he exercises whenever he produces a use-value of any description'.[194] The salesperson sells his professional expertise, rather than simply his labour-power. Yet the dependence of capital on professionally trained salespersons does not pose as serious a problem to the integrity of a purely capitalist society as the dependence of capital on professionally trained productive workers would, because salesmen do not produce surplus value; they merely partake of surplus value already produced by productive workers.

(γ) In all societies, some unproductive labour is not only useful, but also necessary, to make productive labour more productive. Yet to say that unproductive labour too is in fact 'productive' because it contributes indirectly, if not directly, to production would be as thoughtless as to say that a waiter is in fact a cook, just because the cook could not concentrate on culinary work if he also had to wait at the table. The concept of production was originally defined as a man-to-nature relation, not as a man-to-man relation; the dialectic can further specify or specialise the concept which was at first defined abstractly in broad outlines, but it cannot 'generalise it formally' in such a way as to make it emptier and less meaningful. On the other hand, how much unproductive labour is really conducive to higher productivity is not always apparent except in a competitive capitalist society, in which the capitalist himself weighs the desirability of such labour against the deduction of its cost from his surplus value. Since the capitalist considers even circulation-costs as part of his capital, he does not engage any unproductive service unless it is profitable for him to do so. In other societies, in which the idea of profitability is either absent or only vaguely realised, even the type of unproductive labour, which has direct bearing on productivity, is often governed by extra-economic contingencies. In other words, business administration and public administration are in most cases inseparable.

---

194   Marx 1967, *Capital,* Volume I, p. 167.

If therefore the type of unproductive activity that could belong to public administration, rather than to the administration of a business enterprise, that is, of a productive unit, is laid aside, there remains the purely circulatory activity of buying and selling products as commodities. It is quite clear that this kind of activity, which is peculiar to a commodity-economy, and which does not belong to the real economic life common to all societies, cannot be productive. There are, however, two categories of para-productive activities that are closely related to strictly circulatory activity. These are *storage* and *transportation*. The activities of storing productive materials and products, and of transporting them, though closely allied to the operation of buying and selling, also materially affect the consumability of use-values. This is apparent from the fact that these activities are indispensable to non-capitalist societies as well. Not only does the production-process include these activities within itself, but they are also often carried out as direct extensions of the production-process.

The extent to which products and productive materials must be stored often depends on the technology of production, and no society can function without any kind of storage activity. The storage of goods can roughly be classified into (i) the producer's stock of materials, (ii) the middleman's stock of commodities, and (iii) the household stock of immediately consumable goods. In capitalist society, (i) and (iii) can be drastically reduced because (ii) becomes overwhelming. Unless market conditions are uncertain, no producer or consumer would store up unnecessarily large quantities of materials or products, because they are readily available at predictable prices. However, when market conditions are volatile, abnormally large stocks are sought by many, and particularly by the merchants who intend to realise speculative profits. If commodities are stored for a period longer than is technically required, because of the various conditions of the circulation-sphere, it must be concluded that storage acquires a peculiarly commodity-economic character. Storage of this nature is definitely unproductive. Labour and material resources consumed by this type of storage activity add to the pure cost of circulation.

Similar considerations apply to the case of transportation. If goods or productive materials are produced at a place distant from the place of direct or productive consumption, it is necessary to transport them. To the extent that the transportation is technically unavoidable, it belongs to the productive activity of supplying use-values where they are needed. The transportation of goods or productive materials for this purpose is not peculiar to the capitalist commodity-economy, and so must be judged productive. However, sometimes goods and productive materials are transported not for technical reasons, but for purely capitalistic purposes, such as to make speculative profits. In that case, the transportation cannot be qualified as productive, just as it cannot be productive if goods and productive materials must be needlessly shipped back and forth in a poorly organised socialist economy; labour-power and material resources, consumed in the process, must be counted as adding to the *pure cost of circulation*, deductible from surplus value. It may be remarked that, in the present context, no specific reference need be made to passenger transportation. The industry of passenger transportation has no direct bearing on the production of use-values, and hence may be omitted from the theory of pure capitalism. Theoretically, productive workers need not be transported because they must be supposed to be available at any place where capitalist production occurs. The transportation of capitalists and their assistants, if necessary for the purpose of selling and buying commodities, should be included in the pure cost of circulation. No other form of passenger transportation is economically relevant.

The cases of storage and transportation illustrate an important aspect of the labour theory of value, namely, that the substance of value is supra-historical, although its form is strictly commodity-economic. Without a commodity, there is no value; hence, productive labour does not form value in all societies. Yet in capitalist society, which organises its economic life by the form of the commodity, value is not formed by labour that is specifically commodity-economic. Value is simply the commodity-economic expression of what is supra-historically universal, that is, of the fact that in all societies a use-value costs productive labour. An objective analysis of the capitalist mode of production would be impossible if this concept of *social real cost* could not be distinguished from the capitalist concept of private individual costs.

B   The Turnover of Capital (The Law of Phenomenon of Capital)

(a)   *The Efficiency of Value Augmentation*

(α) Capital produces a use-value as a commodity, that is, as a value (embodying) object, but *if value is not realised, it is not produced either*; the production of value must be confirmed as actual by its realisation. Since the realisation of value by itself takes time and costs money, the capitalist production of a use-value is constrained by the capitalist production of value. That is to say, it is not enough for the capitalist to merely produce a use-value; that use-value must be sold as a commodity in order to prove that the production of the use-value was also the production of value. The relation between value and use-value is now reversed. Earlier, in the production-process of capital, it was the production of value that was technically constrained by the production of a use-value.

Capital, which wanted to form and augment value, could not do so *in vacuo;* it had to produce a use-value that embodied value. Now, contrariwise, in the circulation-process of capital, a use-value is already produced as a potential value-object, yet the potential value must next be converted into actual value by the sale of the commodity. The production of a use-value as a commodity requires the realisation of value in the circulation-process of capital as a necessary sequel. Thus, capital cannot waste time and money in its circulation any more than it can in its production. Indeed, if the cost of circulating the product were excessive, the advantage of surplus value production in raising the productive powers of labour would be largely offset. Individual capitalists too would find the augmentation of value to be an unchallenging operation if only a small amount of surplus value were earned for a large advance of capital, or if a great deal of surplus value had to be earmarked as circulation-costs. Capital therefore seeks to minimise the cost of value augmentation as far as it can, which is effectively accomplished by the shortening of the turnover-time of capital overall.

It has already been shown that the shortening of the period of circulation raises the efficiency of value augmentation by saving all costs of circulation. If it is possible to reduce the length of the production-period, that too will save the time-cost of production, while raising the efficiency of value augmentation. Hence, capital does not distinguish the circulation-period from the production-period in its effort to minimise cost. It is by accelerating the speed of the turnover of capital that capital achieves the most efficient method of value augmentation. Whereas, in Part A of this chapter, the general properties of the motion of capital were simply laid out, here, in Part B, the cost-minimising behaviour of capital, in the light of those properties, must be examined. The concept of the *turnover-time of capital* is essential from this point of view. Although this concept is not easy to define in precise terms, it should be understood as the sum of the circulation-period and the production-period, while setting aside for the moment any consideration of the role played by the fixed component of constant capital. The turnover-time of capital is 'the period from the moment of the advance of capital-value in a definite form to the return of the functioning capital-value in the same form'.[195] Since capital can only be advanced either in money-form, M, or in the real form of productive elements, P, the turnover of capital can be studied *only from the point of view of the circuits of money-capital and of productive capital.* The circuit of commodity-capital, which does not begin with the advance of capital, cannot explain the turnover of capital. In practice, the turnover-time may be understood to be the period of time intervening between the moment, C, of

---

the conversion of money-capital, M, into productive elements, P, *and* the next similar conversion, C. Since productive elements, P, consist of various items, the turnover of capital must be studied with respect to each of these representative items. Prior to the differentiation of the productive elements, however, the relation between the turnover and the advance of capital may be specified by the concept of the *efficiency of value augmentation*.

In the previous part, A, it was assumed that the capitalist could always advance a capital of the value of, say, 720, whether for five or six weeks, investing either 144 or 120 every week, in each of these cases. Such a flexible adjustment may, however, not be possible because of the existing size of the plant. If therefore the weekly investment of capital is technically determined as 120, regardless of the length of the turnover-time, its extension from six to seven weeks increases the magnitude of capital advanced from 720 to 840 while the contraction from six to five weeks decreases it from 720 to 600. In other words, a variation by one week of the length of the turnover-time either ties up or releases the funds of 120. Assuming M = 120, W = 60, m = 20, m/W = 33.3% in all cases, let us compare the balance sheets in Table 5.7 below. Here, balance sheet I shows the original situation, in which the circulation-period and the production-period are both three weeks. (This was previously shown as Table 5.3). The efficiency of value augmentation there was m/6M = 2.8%, as already stated in part A, section (*b*), (β). The balance sheets IIa and IIb show the cases in which the turnover-time is reduced to five weeks, because either the circulation-period (*IIa*), or the production-period (*IIb*), is shortened from three to two weeks. The efficiency of value augmentation, m/5M, has thus risen equally to 3.3% in both cases. The balance sheets IIIa and IIIb show the reverse case, in which the turnover-time of capital is extended to seven weeks, because either the circulation-period (IIIa), or the production-period (IIIb), is lengthened from three to four weeks. The efficiency of value augmentation, m/7M, has fallen equally to 2.4% in both cases.

In the light of these examples, it can be generally concluded that any shortening of the turnover-time of capital reduces the magnitude of total capital advanced and increases the efficiency of value augmentation, and *vice versa*. In order to find out the implicit cost of the extension of the turnover-time, suppose that 7M = 720 were invested alike in IIIa and IIIb. Then surplus value of 17 (= 720 ÷ 7 ÷ 2 × 0.33) would be produced, so that a subtraction by 120 of capital advanced would have cost about 3 units in surplus value. Conversely, if 5M = 720 were advanced alike, as in IIa and IIb, the surplus value of 24 (= 720 ÷ 5 ÷ 2 × 0.33) would be produced, so that an addition of 120 to the capital advanced would have produced 4 additional units of surplus value.

It can also be easily confirmed that if the turnover-time of capital is unchanged, the proportion of the circulation-period to the production-period

TABLE 5.7

I. The original balance sheet (same as Table 5.3)

M′ = 140	6M = 720
2C′ = 280	
3C = 360	3m = 60
‾780‾	‾780‾

IIa. Contraction by one week of the circulation-period	*IIb. Contraction by one week of the production-period*

M′ = 140	5M = 600
2C′ = 140	
3C = 360	2m = 40
640	640

M′ = 140	5M = 600
2C′ = 280	
3C = 240	3m = 60
660	660

IIIa. Extension by one week of the circulation-period	*IIIb. Extension by one week of the production-period*

M′ = 140	7M = 840
3C′ = 420	
3C = 360	4m = 80
920	920

M′ = 140	5M = 840
2C′ = 280	
4C = 480	3m = 60
900	900

affects neither the magnitude of total capital advanced, nor the efficiency of value augmentation. For instance, the balance-sheets in Table 5.8 overleaf show the case in which the turnover-time of capital is six weeks, as in *I*, but in one case (*IVa*) the circulation-period is two weeks and the production-period four weeks, whereas in the other (*IVb*) the circulation-period is four weeks and the production-period two weeks. In both cases, the value of capital advanced is 6M = 720 and the efficiency of value augmentation is m/6M = 2.8%.

(β) Even if the turnover-time of capital is unchanged, however, there is one case in which both the value of capital advanced and the efficiency of value

TABLE 5.8

$IVa.$			$IVb.$	
$M' = 140$	$6M = 720$		$M' = 140$	$6M = 720$
$C' = 140$			$3C' = 420$	
$4C = 480$	$2m = \ \ 40$		$2C = 240$	$4m = \ \ 80$
760	760		800	800

augmentation are affected. This is the case when the productive technique is such that the labour-process is interrupted during the production-period. The so-called 'non-working period' within the production-period arises for various reasons. For example, raw materials may have to be dried before labour is applied to them, or high-quality wine may require a lengthy period of aging, without involving any labour between the initial stage of fermentation and the final stage of bottling and shipping. In agriculture and forestry, the interruption of the labour-process is a common occurrence, but even in manufacturing industries there are cases in which the labour-process must be suspended for some time for technical or other reasons. The non-working period within the production-period is indispensable to the production of the use-value, but sterile as far as the formation and augmentation of value is concerned.

It is perfectly obvious that an interruption of the production-period by a *non-working period*, that is, by the time-period in which no labour-process occurs, is a burden on the efficiency of the value augmentation of capital, just as an extension of the circulation-period is a burden. The non-working period, which is essential to the production of some use-values, must of course be clearly distinguished from the circulation-period. Yet from the point of view of the efficiency of value augmentation, the distinction becomes academic. It is for this reason that the flow of capital to agriculture and forestry, which involves a regular or lengthy non-working period, is often discouraged. This explains, to some extent, why in these industries capitalism often fails to develop as vigorously as elsewhere.

Consider, for example, the case in which the productive technology of I is changed, so as to make $v(2) = w(2) = 0$. This means that the production-period is still three weeks, but the second week involves no application of labour. If the other properties of the technology are unchanged, then every week $M = 100$ must be invested in $R = 60 = r(1) + r(2) + r(3)$, and $W = 40 = w(1) + 0 + w(3)$, in order not to interrupt production. If the rate of surplus value is 33.3%, the balance sheet may be stated as in Table 5.9 below. Surplus value realised per week is approximately 13.3, and that divided by total capital advanced of

TABLE 5.9

Commodity in stock (2C′)	= 227	capital advanced (6M) = 600
Raw materials in stock (2R)	= 120	
Unfinished product (T + 2V/3)	= 127	net worth (3m) = 40
Wage-fund on hand (4/3)/W	= 53	
Cash available (M′)	= 113	
	640	640

600 reduces the efficiency of value augmentation to about 2.2%. This implies that if a capital of the value of 720, instead of 600, were invested in the same technology, the surplus value realisable per week would be about 16. In comparison to I of Table 5.7 above, in which the surplus value realisable per week was 20, the implicit cost of interrupting the labour-process by one week would amount to 4 of the 20 units of surplus value. This cost is quite similar to what has been called the ordinary cost of circulation.

In the present example, it is assumed that even in the second week of the production-period, in which the labour-process is suspended, the value of raw materials, $r(2)$, will be transferred to the new product as $t(2)$. Hence, it may be questioned how, in the absence of productive labour, such a thing is possible. It is quite correct to say that the transfer of old value to a new product is due to the concretely useful property of productive labour, and that no concretely useful labour can be performed without a simultaneous expenditure of abstract human labour. Actually if, in the above example, R = 60 were divided into $r(1) = r(3) = 30 = t(1) = t(3)$ while $r(2) = 0 = t(2)$, that would make no difference to the conclusion. Yet to regard the 'automated' process of the second week as not consuming any means of production is at least as unnatural as to assume otherwise. It is therefore not unreasonable to adopt the convention which allows for the transfer of old value to the new product, even during the case of a temporary suspension of the labour-process.

(γ) No capitalist, however, is conscious of the fact that the process of value formation and augmentation takes place *only* during the working-period during which a labour-process actually occurs. It appears to the capitalist that the non-working portion of the production-period, in which a labour-process does not occur, just as the circulation-period, is as 'productive' as the period of production. This is only to be expected, inasmuch as he regards even the pure circulation-costs, which must be deducted from surplus value, as forming part of his capital (see Chapter 9). Hence, from the point of view of the capitalist, the efficiency of capital seems enhanced by simply shortening the turnover-time of capital, without regard to the component periods of the turnover-time. The capitalist rationality of the 'quick turnover', therefore, compels not only the shortening of the circulation-period as much as possible, but also the shortening of the production-period by the intensification of labour, shift-work, and other methods consistent with the increased and accelerated production of surplus value.

What concerns the capitalist, then, is how to acquire the maximum surplus value within the shortest period of time, given the magnitude of capital, or how to do the same with the smallest quantity of capital, given the turnover-time of capital. By making sure that no time is wasted in mobilising a given magnitude of capital, and by making sure that no capital-value stands idle within a given turnover-time, the capitalist ensures the greatest efficiency of value formation and augmentation that is technically possible currently. The so-called principle of 'cost minimisation' is a capitalist expression of this reality.

At this stage, it might be instructive to formulate the analytical structure of the balance sheet with the help of abstract symbols. The turnover-time of capital, t, consists of the production-period, t_p, and the circulation-period, t_c, so that $t = t_p + t_c$. The production-period is further divided into the working-period, t_w, and the non-working period, t_n, so that $t_p = t_w + t_n$. The circulation-period is made up of the selling-period, t_s, and the buying-period, t_b, so that $t_c = t_s + t_b$. Let M be the money value of weekly investment, m, a weekly surplus value realised; and let R be the money value of raw materials, of which the physical embodiment in unfinished goods is T; and let W be the weekly wage-fund, the corresponding value of which, in the form of unfinished goods, will be denoted

TABLE 5.10

money	$T_b(M + m)$	capital advanced	tM
commodity	$t_s(M + m)$		
productive capital	$t_p M$		
– raw materials	$\dfrac{(t_p + 1)R}{2}$	net worth	$t_c m$
– wage fund	$\dfrac{(t_p + 1)W}{2} - \left(\dfrac{W}{t_p}\right)\sum_x \theta_x$		
– unfinished goods	$\dfrac{(t_p - 1)(T + V)}{2}$		
	$- \left(\dfrac{V}{t_p}\right)\sum_x (t_p - \theta_x)$		
	$t_p M + t_c(M + m)$		$tM + t_c m,$

by V. Of course, $M = T + V = R + W$. Then, the balance sheet can be stated simply as in Table 5.10 below, where θ_x is the x-th week of the production-period during which time the labour-process is suspended. [See the end of this section for an explanation of the terms involving θ_x.] Thus, for example, if the second of the three weeks constituting the production-period is the non-working week, the wage-fund will be $2W - \frac{2}{3}W = (4/3)W$, and unfinished goods will be equal to $(T + V) - \frac{1}{3}V = T + \frac{2}{3}V$, as in the example of ($\beta$) above. If, however, there is no non-working week, the money values of the 'wage-fund' and of 'unfinished goods' are respectively $(t_p + 1)W/2$ and $(t_p - 1)(T + V)/2$. The rate of surplus value is m/W, and the efficiency of value augmentation is m/tM. If the magnitude of m is fixed, it is in the interest of capital to minimise either t given M, or M given t.

Since t is the number of weeks required for the turnover of capital, if we let T^* stand for the number of weeks in a year, it follows that $n = T^*/t$ will be equal to the annual frequency of the turnover of capital. To minimise t is then to maximise n, hence capital pursues the greatest annual frequency (n) of its turnover. If, for example, $1,000 are invested every week, the investment of capital per annum, assuming $T = 50$, is always $50,000. However, if $t = 5$ for one capital and $t = 10$ for another, the first capital turns over ten times while the second capital does so only five times. Whereas the first capital advances $tM = $5,000 throughout the year, the second capital must advance $tM = $10,000 at all times. If, each week, both capitals earn the surplus value of $200, the efficiency of value augmentation of the first capital will be 4%, and that for the second capital will be only 2%. Hence, unless a compensatory distribution of surplus value occurs, as will be explained in the doctrine of distribution, no capitalist will actually invest in an industry with a longer t and a smaller n (see Chapter 7).

Note: For the purpose of the present note, let us write $t_p = n$ and $\theta_x = x$, at first, for simplicity. (Here, n does not mean the turnover frequency capital, but an arbitrary integer). Then, the structure of productive capital can be expressed more generally as follows:

$C_1 =$ $[r(1), r(2), ..., r(n-1), r(n); w(1), w(2), ..., w(x), ..., w(n-1), w(n)]$,
$C_2 =$ $[t(1), r(2), ..., r(n-1), r(n); v(1), w(2), ..., w(x), ..., w(n-1), w(n)]$,

....

$C_x =$ $[t(1), t(2), ..., r(n-1), r(n); v(1), v(2), ..., w(x), ..., w(n-1), w(n)]$,
$C_{x+1} =$ $[t(1), t(2), ..., r(n-1), r(n); v(1), v(2), ..., v(x), ..., w(n-1), w(n)]$,

....

$C_n =$ $[t(1), t(2), ..., t(n-1), r(n); v(1), v(2), ..., v(x), ..., v(n-1), w(n)]$,

Where $r(i) = R/n$, $w(i) = W/n$, $t(i) = T/n$, $v(i) = V/n$ for all $i = 1, ..., n$. Hence

$$\sum r(i) = \frac{R}{n}[n + (n-1) + \ldots +1] = \frac{R}{n}\left[\frac{n}{2}(n+1)\right] \tag{1}$$
$$= \frac{R(n+1)}{2} = \frac{(t_p+1)R}{2}.$$

Similarly,

$$\sum w(i) = \frac{(t_p+1)W}{2}. \tag{2}$$

On the other hand,

$$\sum t(i) = \frac{T}{n}[(n-1) + (n-2) + \ldots + \{n - (n-1)\}]$$
$$= \frac{T}{n}\left[n(n-1) - \frac{(n-1)n}{2}\right]$$
$$= \frac{T(n-1)}{2} = \frac{(t_p-1)T}{2}. \tag{3}$$

Similarly,

$$\sum v(i) = \frac{(t_p-1)V}{2}. \tag{4}$$

However, if $x = \theta_x$ is the non-working week, the above $\sum w(i)$ will include such terms as

$$\frac{xW}{n} = \frac{\theta_x W}{t_p}, \qquad \text{all } x. \tag{5}$$

And the above $\sum v(i)$ will also include such terms as

$$\frac{(n-x)V}{n} = \frac{(t_p - \theta_x)V}{t_p}, \text{all } x. \tag{6}$$

Since, in the presence of non-working weeks, all such terms as (5) and (6) must be deducted from (2) and (3) & (4) respectively, the entry for 'wage funds' is $(t_p+1)W/2 - (W/t_p)\Sigma_x\theta_x$, and the entry for 'unfinished goods' is $(t_p-1)(T+V)/2 - (V/t_p)\Sigma_x(t_p-\theta_x)$, as shown in the above balance-sheet (Table 5.10).

(b)   The Turnover of Constant Capital

(α) Productive capital first takes the form of productive elements, that is, the means of production (P_m) and labour-power (L_p). Capital-value invested in the means of production is called constant capital; this value, which pre-exists the inception of the production-process, is simply transferred to the new product during the process. The turnover of constant capital therefore completes itself when the money invested in the means of production is recovered by the sale of the commodity (in the formation of which the means of production are productively consumed), and is ready to be reinvested. However, the manner in which constant capital is consumed in the production-process differs according to whether it belongs to the category of fixed capital or to the category of circulating capital. Means of labour such as tools and machines are not entirely consumed in one production-process, whereas objects of labour, such as raw materials, are entirely consumed. From the point of view of the transfer of value, this means that such things as tools and machines transfer only that part of their value, which corresponds to wear and tear, to the new product in a single production-period, whereas such things as raw materials transfer all of their value to the new product in each production-period.

The distinction between fixed and circulating capital is strictly due to the difference in the mode of transferring value in the production process, so that, theoretically, it makes no sense to apply the same distinction to material resources either held or consumed in the circulation-process. For example, so-called *circulation-capital* (that is, capital that takes the forms of money and commodities) is neither fixed nor circulating, although in popular literature they are often confused with *circulating constant capital.* The material resources consumed in the circulation-process do not transfer their value to the new product; they are unproductive costs of circulation to be defrayed by a deduction from the surplus-value component of the value product. The capitalist, however, distinguishes between current circulation costs, deductible from the current production of surplus value (such as bookkeeping and correspondence costs), and heavier circulation-costs, deductible from surplus value, produced over a lengthy span of time (such as the cost of an office building or equipment needed only for circulatory purposes). The extended use of the terms fixed and circulating capital to refer to these different types of circulation-costs reflects the limitation of the capitalist's conception, according to which 'capital' embraces all but labour costs.

The distinction between fixed and circulating capital depends neither on the length of time required to produce the thing, nor on its durability. For example, an aircraft engine might require a long time to build and it may last for a lengthy period of time, but it is a circulating capital in the production-process of an aircraft. Thus, what is popularly known as 'hardware' or 'heavy' equipment does not necessarily become fixed capital. The same physical object can be classified either as fixed or as circulating capital, depending on how it is used in the production-process. For example, cattle used in capitalist farming or milking are fixed capital, but the same cattle raised for the capitalist production of meat are circulating capital. Moreover, when the cattle are sold as commodities, they are not even productive capital but commodity-capital, and hence neither fixed nor circulating.

In addition to the means and the objects of labour, means of production include supplementary or auxiliary materials, such as coal for steam engines or electricity for the lighting of a factory, and so on. These materials are conducive to the production of use-values only indirectly. Since they are indispensable to the current production of the use-value, however, they may be considered to be circulating capital, the value of which is transferred to the new product in each production-period. The use of fixed capital sometimes involves the consumption of material resources for repair and maintenance. To the extent that the consumption of these resources is regular and indispensable to the production-process, their average consumption must be considered as circulating capital. However, if a machine breaks down by accident and material resources and manpower are needed to repair it, the cost cannot be included in the value of circulating capital. If expenses are incurred to guard against such an accident in the form of an insurance policy, those unproductive expenses must be deducted from surplus value.

(β) The turnover of constant capital, accordingly, consists of the turnover of circulating capital and the turnover of fixed capital. In the case of circulating capital, its turnover-time is determined by the sum of the production-period and the circulation-period, because together they form the length of time between the moment when circulating capital is purchased as the means of production, and the moment when its value, already recovered in the form of money, is capable of re-purchasing the same items. If it takes ten weeks for circulating capital to turn over ($t = 10$), it turns over five times a year, assuming that one year consists of fifty weeks. If $R = \$1,000$ are invested in circulating capital every week, the sum of $tR = \$10,000$ must be advanced as circulating capital at all times. Should the turnover-period be reduced to nine weeks, for whatever reason, no more than $tR = \$9,000$ would be needed. The magnitude of circulating capital that must be advanced is thus directly proportional to the length of its turnover-time, and affects its efficiency of value augmentation, m/tR, once the magnitude of variable capital and the rate of surplus value are known.

The turnover of fixed capital cannot be settled so simply, because it takes a number of production-processes over a lengthy period of time to complete itself. Suppose that the durability of a productive machine is five years and that the turnover-time of circulating capital is 10 weeks. Then, assuming again that a year consists of 50 weeks, there are five production-processes in each of the five years, during which the machine is active. Hence, it takes 25 production-processes for the machine to be completely consumed. The turnover-time of the fixed capital, therefore, is 250 weeks. It is true that the first twenty-fifth of its value is already recovered in the form of money in 10 weeks, the second twenty-fifth in 20 weeks, and so on, if the straight-line method of depreciation is adopted. However, the money so recovered must be accumulated as depreciation funds and cannot be used to re-purchase the depreciated part of fixed capital until the renewal time arrives. Hence, the capital-value invested in the machine of durability of five years cannot 'turnover' in less than five years. This example clearly shows that the concept of the turnover of capital must be studied from the viewpoint of the circuit of productive capital, as well as from the viewpoint of the circuit of money-capital. The problem of turnover must not be simply reduced to that of the recovery of capital value in the form of money. As a matter of fact, even from the point of view of the circuit of money-capital, it would be a mistake to confuse depreciation funds with money-capital. Although they are sometimes described as 'idle' money-capital, it is important to make a clear distinction between idle funds (money convertible into capital) and money-capital (which no longer remains 'idle'). The former is only potentially capital, whereas the latter already represents the value of capital in the functioning form of money.

Fixed capital, however, consists of many items with differing levels of durability. Even if the machine as a whole has an average life of five years, some of its parts may have to be replaced every year or two, while other parts may last for three or four years. If hand-tools and small instruments are used together with the machine, the durability of each will differ. Therefore, for each item of fixed capital, there is in principle a different turnover-time. It is not possible to accurately calculate an average turnover-time of all fixed items. Nor is such an average a significant economic concept. Marx's effort (in Chapter IX of Volume II of *Capital*) to define the aggregate turnover and cycles of turnover was related to his explanation of the periodicity of crises. It is true that the durability of fixed capital has an important bearing on the decennial cycles of the capitalist economy. However, in that case, it is an average durability of machines and plants in leading industries that determines the length of business cycles, not the average durability of all fixed items operating in a firm (see the following subsection). It is noteworthy that regardless of its variety, the turnover-time of fixed capital does not affect the efficiency of value augmentation.

This can be seen from the balance-sheet in Table 5.11 below, where F stands for the initial value of fixed capital, f for the weekly transfer of its value to the product, H for the unconsumed value of fixed capital, and D for the depreciation fund. The value of fixed capital, F, is clearly equal to $H + tf + D$. Here it

TABLE 5.11

money	$T_b(M + m)$	capital advanced	$\underline{tM + F}$
commodity	$t_s(M + f + m)$		
productive capital	$t_pM + H$		
– raw materials	$\dfrac{(t_p + 1)R}{2}$	net worth	t_cm
– wage fund	$\dfrac{(t_p + 1)W}{2}$		
– unfinished goods	$\dfrac{(t_p - 1)(T + V)}{2}$		
– undepreciated value of fixed capital	H		
– depreciation fund	D		
$t_pM + t_c(M + m)+(t_sf + H + D)$		$tM + t_cm + F$	

is assumed that there is no non-working production-period. The rate of surplus value, m/W, is, of course, not affected by the presence of fixed capital. The efficiency of value augmentation, $m/(tM + F)$, depends on the initial value of fixed capital, F, and the turnover-time of circulating capital, t, together with the weekly investment of money-capital, M, when surplus value, m, is given. But it does not depend specifically on the turnover-time (= durability) of fixed capital. Hence, from the point of view of the capitalist, it is the magnitude of fixed capital, not its various turnover-times, that is relevant to the efficiency of value augmentation. This can be seen from the balanced sheet in Table 5.11 above.

(γ) The balance-sheet, however, now implies that the structure of assets is no longer stationary, even when no accumulation takes place, because the depreciation fund, D, increases and the unconsumed value of fixed capital, H, decreases steadily, as the renewal time of fixed capital approaches. For items of short durability, small cycles occur, which are superposed on larger cycles generated by items of longer durability. Some of these cycles are cancelled out when the balance-sheets of many firms are consolidated over diverse branches of industry. However, if investments in heavy machinery and plant by all firms occur more or less at the same time, the turnover-cycle of these items cannot fail to be reflected in the economy as a whole. 'One may assume that in the essential branches of modern industry this life-cycle now averages ten years', wrote Marx. 'The cycle of interconnected turnovers embracing a number of years, in which capital is held fast by its fixed constituent part, furnishes a material basis for the periodic crises'.[196] This important point, however, can be elaborated only later in connection with the accumulation-process of capital (see Chapter 6). In the meantime, the formation of the depreciation-fund, side by side with actually functioning machinery and the plant, has another important consequence. Since the depreciation fund can neither be immediately converted into money-capital, nor spent for the capitalist's consumption, it must be held by the capitalist *in the form of idle money or funds* (convertible into capital, but not yet converted into capital). Thus, in the course of its turnover, fixed capital regularly generates idle money in the form of depreciation funds, which does not circulate until the time for the renewal arrives. The capitalist must therefore find a way to make the best use of such idle funds, together with idle funds released by the contraction of the circulation-period and reserve funds not currently needed. The development of the 'money market' is a consequence of this fact. If idle money, which is not immediately needed, can be loaned for a specified time-interval, the borrowers may be able to save some of their money-capital required for the circulation of commodities. In that case, capitalist society as a whole can reduce the ordinary cost of circulation, being able to allocate a greater proportion of total capital to productive purposes. The whole theory of finance and the interest rate will be developed later on this basis (in Chapter 9).

Another important problem arising from the use of fixed capital is that its value is not generally proportional to the physical quantity of its use-value. It is not always the case that a new machine is more productive than an equivalent machine that has been used for several years. If the initial cost of a machine with a durability of five years is $100,000, and its depreciated value in the second year is $80,000, this does not mean that the one-year old machine is 20% or so less productive. As a use-value, the machine may be supposed to maintain a constant efficiency during its lifetime, before it suddenly breaks down or evaporates at the end of the fifth year. This is very different from the case of raw materials, the value of which is transferred to the new product almost exactly as the use-value is consumed. In the present case of a machine, only its life-expectancy (future use-value), not its productive capacity (present use-value), is diminished as its value is transferred to the product. This means that the portion of the present use-value of the machine that corresponds to the depreciated value works more or less in the same way as a free gift of nature. Since the old machine, estimated to have the current value of $80,000, works just as well as the new machine of value $100,000, it is as though the capitalist is given

196   Marx 1967, *Capital*, Volume II, pp. 185–6.

20,000 dollars' worth of free machine-capacity. As will be seen later, this causes a certain technical problem for the labour theory of value, while the capitalist solution to this problem involves an adjustment, which is nothing other than the occurrence of periodic crises (Chapter 6).

Finally, it must be pointed out that the dependence of capitalist production on fixed capital becomes decisive with the mechanisation of the production-process, which completes the conversion of labour-power into a commodity. At least, in leading industries a considerable use of fixed capital cannot be avoided. The presence of fixed capital adds to the magnitude of total capital, which must be advanced for an industrial operation and causes the concentration of capital and production. A small saving of money no longer suffices to purchase an expensive machine, and hence cannot automatically be converted into industrial capital. This is not all. As heavy industries develop, investment in fixed capital requires such an enormous amount of capital that the very regime of free competition among many small capitalists cannot be maintained in some important sectors of the economy. At that stage, the impact of fixed capital is not limited to the quantitative increase of the organic composition of capital, but goes well beyond the scope of the pure theory of capitalism, requiring a more concretely historical study of the stage of imperialism, in which *finance-capital* evolves as the dominant form of capital.

(c)   The Turnover of Variable Capital

(α) Although each item of fixed capital has a turnover-time, which differs from that of circulating capital, it is only the latter turnover-time (t) that is relevant to the determination of the efficiency of value augmentation. As shown by its formula,

$$\varepsilon = \frac{m}{tM + F},$$

the turnover-time of no item of fixed capital influences this efficiency, although it depends on the initial value, F, of fixed capital. The reason why the turnover-time of circulating capital alone is a determinant of the efficiency of value augmentation is not apparent from the theory of the turnover of constant capital. In fact, circulating capital always turns over with variable capital, and it is the turnover-time of variable capital that determines the efficiency. The efficiency has so far been defined in weekly terms, that is, as the ratio of surplus value realised per week to total value of capital advanced. Hence, the *annual* efficiency of value augmentation is εT^*, where T^* is the number of weeks in one year. From the above formula, the *annual* efficiency is accordingly derived as follows:

$$\varepsilon T^* = \frac{mT^*/tW}{1 + \dfrac{tR + F}{tW}} = \frac{en}{1 + k}$$

Here, e $(= m/W)$ is the rate of surplus value, n $(= T^*/t)$ is the annual frequency of turnover, and k is the value composition of capital, or the ratio of constant capital advanced to variable capital advanced. If k is taken to be a technical parameter, the annual efficiency of value augmentation is uniquely determined by the product $e \cdot n$, which Marx calls the *annual rate of surplus value*.

Suppose that someone invests \$1,000 every week in variable capital, and its turnover-time is ten weeks. Then, if the rate of surplus value is 50%, the surplus value of \$500 is realised every week. In this case, however, the variable capital of \$10,000 must always be advanced, which assumes $T^* = 50$ and turns over five times a year. If constant capital is neglected $(R = F = 0)$, the annual rate of surplus value, which is equal to the annual efficiency of value augmentation, is 250%. Suppose another capitalist also invests \$1,000 every week in variable capital that has a turnover-time of 20 weeks. If the rate of surplus value is again 50%, the surplus value of \$500 is realised every week, as in the other case. Now, however, the variable capital of \$20,000 must always be advanced, which turns over only two and a half times a year. The annual rate of surplus value is 125%, which, if constant capital is neglected, is the same as the annual efficiency of value augmentation. The comparison of these two cases shows at once that the first capital is twice as efficient as the second capital in appropriating surplus value, despite the fact that they both employ and 'exploit' the same number of workers for the same length of time with the same intensity of labour. The difference arises from the different ratios of 'employed (or invested) variable capital' to 'advanced (or tied up) variable capital' in the two cases. Employed, or invested, variable capital is \$1,000 per week, and \$50,000 per year, in both cases; however, advanced, or tied up, variable capital is \$10,000 in the first case, and \$20,000 in the second.

The *annual rate of surplus value*, which is defined by:

$$\frac{e \times (\text{annually employed variable capital})}{\text{advanced variable capital}}$$

will come to 250% and 125% in the first and the second cases, respectively. The *weekly rate of surplus value,* which is defined by:

$$\frac{e \times (\text{weekly employed variable capital})}{\text{advanced variable capital}}$$

will be calculated to be 5% and 2.5%, respectively, in the first and the second case.

Even though the two capitals are both supplying the new value product of $1,500 per week, paying the wage-bill of $1,000, and realising the surplus value of $500, throughout the year, the first capital must advance (tie down) $10,000, and the second capital, $20,000, for their respective operations, because the turnover-time of capital is 10 weeks in the first case, and 20 weeks in the second case. This difference can as well be explained by saying that the first capital has a shorter, and the second capital a longer, 'incubation (or gestation) period' for their respective productions. In order for the first capital to sell its product of $1,500 this week, it must have started its preparation 10 weeks ago. For the second capital to do the same, the preparation had to start 20 weeks ago. In other words, the first capital has so far advanced only 10 weekly payments of wages, whereas the second capital has had to advance as much as 20 weekly payments. In the current sale of $1,500, the first capital recovers the wage-bill of $1,000 that it paid 10 weeks ago, and the second capital that of 20 weeks ago. In the next week's sale, the first capital recovers the wage-bill of 9 weeks ago, and the second capital that of 19 weeks ago, and so forth. The appropriation of surplus value is the leading principle of capitalist production; however, the magnitude of total capital needed to annually maintain a given rate of appropriation is determined by the turnover-time of variable capital. Thus, the annual rate of surplus value, which determines the efficiency of value augmentation, is crucially dependent on the turnover-time of variable capital.

The rate of surplus value is the fundamental measure of the workers-*versus*-capitalist production-relation. It was shown in the previous chapter that capital, in its production of absolute and relative surplus value, seeks to raise this rate to a maximum under the given circumstances. Since capital is a value-augmenting form, its tendency to strive for the maximum rate of surplus value cannot be doubted. But this sort of explanation is still very abstract and general. Here, in the context of the turnover-time of capital, one can and must explain this tendency a little more concretely, namely, by saying that each individual capitalist seeks to obtain the greatest annual rate of surplus value (*en*), as part of his general effort to minimise cost and to raise the efficiency of value augmentation. For instance, the lengthening of the working day and the intensification of labour not only raise the rate of surplus value, but also accelerate the turnover of capital. Hence, unless counteracting forces are at work, the efficiency of value augmentation is increased. It does not matter to the capitalist how he has earned his weekly or annual income, although producing surplus value with a lesser advance of capital would be one of his preferred ways. Yet if the value composition (k) is already at its technical minimum, and the frequency of turnover of capital (n) at its technical maximum, the gain in the efficiency of value augmentation must be due to an increase in the rate of surplus value. In other words, no capitalist need be aware of such a theoretical measure as the rate of surplus value, in order to strive for its maximum, since its maximisation is an automatic consequence of the capitalist pursuit of efficiency.

(β) The turnover-time of capital is thus fundamentally determined by the turnover-time of *variable* capital, which produces surplus value. Yet variable capital does not turn over in the same sense as constant capital, nor is it even appropriate to apply the term 'turnover' to variable capital without reservation. Constant capital literally turns over because the same value is preserved throughout the periods of production and circulation, undergoing only a formal metamorphosis. First, constant capital, in the form of money, purchases productive elements. These productive elements transfer their value to the product, and the product is then sold for money. The pre-existing value comes back again in the same form, and is ready to begin another cycle. However, the same thing cannot be said of variable capital, which loses its value as soon as it purchases labour-power. The value of the original variable capital is paid out as wages; the wages are then spent by the workers, not as capital but as revenue, and are entirely consumed. Hence, the original value of variable capital is destroyed, once and for all, in the individual consumption of the waged workers. These workers, however, reproduce the value of their labour-power, and embody it in the commodity-product; the reproduced value of labour-power appears, for the first time, in the newly produced commodity, together with surplus value. It is this newly reproduced value of labour-power, not the original value advanced as variable capital, that flows back to the capitalist in the form of money, when the commodity is sold, and that can be invested once again as his variable capital. To the capitalist, it may come to the same thing if he either recovers the money that he advanced, as the same old value of constant capital that has simply returned to him, or a newly produced value, equivalent to the old value of variable capital, which was destroyed, that now accrues to him for the first time. However, theory must not overlook the fundamental difference.

What appears to the capitalist as the return of his son is in fact the first visit of his grandson. The turnover of variable capital involves a change of generation, so to speak, such that the grandson, who comes to the house for the first time, is the living image of the son, who once left home never to return. In the case of human beings, the change of generation may take about twenty to thirty years. However, in the case of a simpler life, it is considerably shorter. For example, red radish in summertime reproduces itself in three to four weeks. Just as the lifecycles of species differ from one case to another, so the turnover-time of variable capital differs from one enterprise to another. Only variable capital possesses a lifecycle of its own, and this determines the turnover-time of constant capital as well. So if, for example, a capitalist enterprise invests $2,000 every week, putting $1,000 in circulating constant capital and $1,000 in variable capital, and if variable capital has the lifecycle of ten weeks, then the whole capital of $2,000 turns over in the same ten-week period. That is to say, the constant capital of $1,000, advanced ten weeks ago, returns to the capitalist in the same form as it was once advanced, since the same value has undergone a cycle of formal metamorphosis, without a quantitative increase or decrease, while the variable capital of $1,000 paid out as wages in the meantime and consumed by the workers, has been reproduced and accrues to the capitalist in the same form as it was once advanced, except that he realises greater new value than has been consumed in the production-process of capital. If, however, the lifecycle of variable capital is twenty weeks, instead of ten weeks, the $2,000 advanced ten weeks ago does not return in the same form, nor does surplus value accrue to the capitalist until ten more weeks have passed.

Capital with a shorter turnover-time has a faster self-reproducing, or self-renewing, force. Thus, capital that turns over in ten weeks invests $2,000 every week only for the first ten weeks. After advancing $20,000 in this way, it needs no further money to continue its operation. The capital that turns over in twenty weeks does the same thing as the first capital, in that in the first ten weeks it too advances $20,000. By this time, however, it has not sold its commodity; thus, in order to continue its production, this capital must keep investing $2,000 every week for ten more weeks. Only after advancing the total of $40,000 can this capital reinvest the proceeds of its own sale, since it needs no further money. The difference between the two cases therefore lies in how fast each capital becomes self-supporting, through the sale of its own commodity. The first capital becomes self-dependent in ten weeks, after advancing $20,000; the second capital does so in twenty weeks, after advancing $40,000. The length of time that must intervene between the original advance of $2,000 and the first reinvestment of $2,000, from out of the sales proceeds of the enterprise, constitutes its 'life-cycle' or the turnover-time of its capital.

(γ) If the turnover-time of capital is long, this capital purchases both labour-power and the means of production for an extended duration, without itself supplying any commodity. The wages paid for labour-power are almost immediately spent by the workers on wage-goods, so the capitalist must live in the meantime by spending the money set aside for his own consumption. Thus, the operation of this capital unilaterally absorbs from the market not only the means of production, but also wage-goods and the capitalist's consumption-goods for some duration, without offering its own goods in exchange. This is what happens whenever a long-term project, such as the building of a railway system, is launched on a large scale. Of course, even the introduction of a short-range project requires a series of initial investments so that, if the turn-over-time is six weeks – as supposed above in section A, (*b*), (α) above – capital unilaterally purchases commodities in the first five weeks without selling its own commodity. Yet there are firms going out of business that sell commodities without continuing to purchase commodities. Alternatively, even in the absence of such firms, a shortening of the circulation-period releases enough commodities that have already been produced and stocked in warehouses. However, a heavy project, requiring initial investments over an extended period of time, is likely to strain the market far more seriously.

Indeed, Marx wrote as follows:

> If we conceive society as being not capitalist but communistic, there will be no money-capital at all in the first place, nor the disguises cloaking the transactions arising on account of it. The question then comes down to the need of society to calculate beforehand how much labour, means of production, and means of subsistence it can invest, without detriment, in such lines of business as, for instance, the building of railways, which do not furnish any means of production or subsistence, nor produce any useful effect for perhaps a year, or even much longer, while they extract labour, means of production and means of subsistence from the total annual production. In capitalist society, however, where social reason always asserts itself only post festum, great disturbances may and must constantly occur.[197]

The first effect is felt in the money market. A great project with a long incubation period absorbs an enormous amount of funds from the money market, and converts them into money-capital. The money market lends temporarily idle funds of all sorts, including accumulation-funds, pending their own

---

197   Marx 1967, *Capital,* Volume II, p. 315.

transformation into money-capital. A sudden demand for these funds, how-ever, strains the money market, exerting an upward pressure on rates of inter-est. Higher rates of interest do not necessarily generate a greater supply of idle funds, at least not in sufficient quantities to ease the money market. Hence, other spheres of production, in which the turnover-time of capital is short-er, may be deprived of money-capital, which would otherwise have flowed to them easily. Unless the expected profit-rate is high enough to compensate for the rising rates of interest, small businesses may be caught in a 'financial squeeze' and may cease to produce altogether. The second effect is felt in the market for productive elements. Since a great project unilaterally purchases goods and labour-power, if not enough of them are already present in the mar-ket, a sharp rise in prices and wages cannot be avoided. In such a case, specu-lative activities tend to be incited, raising commodity prices well above the level that the increase of real demand justifies. Consequently, the rising real wage, which depresses the general rate of profit, can be concealed for some time; in the meantime, the appearance of continued prosperity abets reckless gambles and adventures even further. A considerable disturbance to the mar-kets for goods, labour-power and 'loanable funds' can occur in consequence of heavy projects, carried out at random by private promoters and speculators. Often this kind of investment occurs well past the prosperity phase of business cycles, when the market for labour-power is already tight enough, and only precipitates the outbreak of an excess of capital (see Chapter 6).

A project with a long turnover-time of capital need not involve a long pro-duction-period. Marx quotes the example of long-distance trade between Eng-land and India in the middle of the nineteenth-century. Because of primitive transportation facilities, the selling of English goods in India took a long time. Although exporters paid cash to English manufacturers before the shipment of goods to India, the money thus advanced by the exporters did not represent the money-form of the value of these goods (M'). It was money-capital (M), which unilaterally absorbed English goods, without a counter-supply of Indian goods having yet been supplied to the English market. Not only was the British money market strained because of the need to finance the large-scale Indian trade, but also to the extent that English manufacturers purchased elements of production with the money advanced by exporters, before the arrival of Indian goods, the English market for commodities and labour-power also necessarily experienced an inflationary pressure. The situation was thus quite similar to the building of railways.

These examples illustrate the economic effects of a long turnover-time of capital. These effects are, of course, frequently combined with other fac-tors, which are not completely accounted for by the theory of the turnover of variable capital. Nevertheless, situations arise in capitalist societies such that part of society's productive labour has to be engaged in activities whose outputs are not immediately available either for direct or productive consumption. The greater is the proportion of social capital that is advanced over a long turnover-time, the more labour must be devoted to the production of future use-values. Capitalist society must be mature enough to permit undertakings with a long life-cycle without significant disruptions of the market.

C   The Circulation of Surplus Value (No Correspondence with Hegel's 'correlation')

(*a*)   *The Realisation of Surplus Value*

(α) The value augmentation of capital requires that some surplus value is realised when the commodity is sold for money. Yet only when commodity-capital, C′, which already embodies a potential surplus value, is actually converted into its money-form, M′, is the presence of the surplus value unambiguously confirmed. Consequently, the conversion of C′ into M′ is, to the capitalist, a matter of vital concern, or a 'deadly leap (*salto mortale*)', to use Marx's more graphic expression. In the process of this conversion, the capitalist is no more than a commodity-seller, having no initiative in the actualisation of the value of his commodity. He may, indeed, realise more or less than the expected magnitude of surplus value, depending on how favourable the market turns out to be. To each individual capitalist, in other words, there always remains the danger of not realising enough surplus value to be able to maintain even the present scale of his chrematistic operation. If all capitalists were permanently obliged to contract their operation, however, capitalist society would be impossible; thus, it is normally the case that when some fail, others must succeed. The representative capitalist may therefore be regarded as maintaining an average performance, realising more or less the expected magnitude of surplus value in the conversion of his C′ into M′.

In that case, however, the question arises as to how it is possible at all for the capitalist to successfully transform his C′ into M′. In order to produce the commodity, C′, the capitalist has already purchased various elements of production of value, C; hence, the means of circulation, M, adequate for the purchase of C should have been put in the market and must exist there. Consequently, if the capitalist produces his commodity in conformity with the existing social demand, there is little doubt that he can recover at least the same quantity, M, of the means of circulation, which he himself has released to the commodity market. However, in order to realise the surplus value embodied in the commodity, it appears at first sight as though an additional quantity of money is needed. If, on average, all capitalists spend a sum, M, of the means of circulation, and absorb a greater sum, M', of money from the circulation-sphere, the source of the additional money, M' – M = m, must be explained. *This problem must be explained even in the absence of capital accumulation.*

It is impossible to explain this problem by an increased velocity of the circulation of money. Although the velocity of monetary circulation varies from time to time, it cannot regularly and permanently increase with every turnover of capital. Indeed, if that were the case, capitalist society would eventually approach the state of an infinite velocity of monetary circulation, which is clearly inconceivable. Neither is it possible to explain the problem by an increase in the production of gold, the monetary commodity. For in that case, the gold-producing sector alone would have to expand even when all other sectors in the economy maintain a simple reproduction. Although such a thing may occasionally happen, it is impossible to expect that it should be the case systematically and permanently.

Some classical economists posed the problem of locating the source of the additional means of circulation and found no solution, because, according to Marx, they considered the circulation-process of capital exclusively from the point of view of the circuit of money-capital. If, indeed, the motion of capital is represented by M – C ... P ... C' – M', and if, furthermore, the operation M'.M is conceived merely as a process of hoarding monetised surplus value, m = M' – M, by the capitalist, the problem becomes quite incomprehensible. Such a view one-sidedly reduces the capitalist to no more than a pathological gold-eater. If he were such an irrational being, capitalist society would not be an economically viable proposition. In order to avoid such a crude misapprehension, the motion of capital must now be examined primarily from the point of view of the *circuit of commodity-capital.*

(β) In the circuit of commodity-capital, C' – M'.M – C ... P ... C', the circulatory metamorphosis of C' into C is the major consideration; however, this metamorphosis cannot occur independently of the circulation of surplus value, c' – m – c. In order for the capitalist to be able to exchange his commodity, C', for the necessary elements of production, C, the capitalist class as a whole must produce, in the form of commodities, all the use-values needed for the reproduction of capitalist society. This means that the aggregate-social supply of commodities ($\Sigma C'$) must include not only the means of production (P_m), but also *wage-goods* necessary for the reproduction of labour-power (W_g). This is not all. Capitalists and their associates must also live if capitalist society is to function. Thus, the aggregate-social supply of commodities must also include their consumption-goods, which I call *luxury goods* (L_x). Of this aggregate supply of commodities, the means of production are directly purchased by each individual capitalist in the process, C' – M'.M – C, while wage-goods are purchased by the workers, who receive wages in return for the labour-power made available to the capitalist. Both categories of goods are therefore purchased with the money, which is originally advanced as capital. However, the third category of goods, namely, those produced for consumption by capitalists and their associates, or luxury goods, can only be purchased with *money, which is not advanced as capital*, that is to say, with the consumption-fund of the capitalists.

Because he can 'wait', the capitalist can advance, as capital, a sum of money, M, which will be recovered in M', only after a certain lapse of time. Yet 'waiting' in this instance does not mean total abstinence or lack of consumption; he can wait only *because he purchases goods from his personal consumption-fund* in the meantime. The possession of such money is a prerequisite of his acting as a capitalist. If his capital turns over once a year, he must at least possess a consumption-fund adequate to live through the year. If his capital turns over five times a year, he only needs such a fund to last for ten weeks or so. Yet in any case the advance of money, M, as capital is always accompanied by the simultaneous expenditure, m, of money by the capitalist out of his personal consumption-fund. The quantity of money required for the circulation of all capitalistically produced commodities is therefore greater than the quantity of money advanced as capital by the amount of the aggregate consumption-fund of capitalists. The circuit of commodity-capital, of which the first and emphatic part may be elaborated as follows,

$$C' - M'. \begin{cases} M - C \dots P \\ m - c. \end{cases}$$

exhibits this point without any ambiguity.

It does not matter how the capitalist originally acquired his consumption-fund, m, because once the circulation-process of capital is well established and repeated, this money regularly comes back to him in the realisation of surplus value. In every turnover of capital, the capitalist spends his consumption-fund, which he regains when the surplus-value component of his commodity is sold for money. It is obvious that capitalist production cannot continue unless the capitalist earns enough surplus value in every turnover of capital to at least enable him to maintain an adequate standard of living during the following turnover. To say that the whole surplus value that he earns in each turnover of capital is used as a consumption-fund is simply to define a so-called simple reproduction. A simple reproduction, in other words, sets the minimal condition of the circulation-process of capital.

The circuit of commodity-capital shows that the capitalist must exchange his commodity, C′, not only for the elements of further production, C, but also for his consumption-goods, c, and hence divide his sales proceeds, M′, into money-capital, M, and a consumption-fund, m. Whereas the elements of production, acquired in this process, are at once integrated in the production-process, C ... P ... C′, and re-emerge in the circulation-market as a new commodity, consumption-goods that are purchased by the capitalist with m, simply vanish from that market, leaving the corresponding sum of money or means of circulation behind. That is why the amount of money, corresponding to M + m = M′, is available by the time C′ emerges in the market to be circulated. In recapturing m, which he has spent on luxury goods, the capitalist does not 'recover' the money that he has advanced as capital; he earns the money afresh by the current production of surplus value.

A simple reproduction is, of course, a drastic abstraction. It means that the extent of value augmentation is limited by the scope of the capitalist's consumption. Suppose that the permanent consumption of the capitalist and his associates is about $10,000 a year, and that his capital turns over once a year. If he earns less, he cannot maintain his present scale of operation for long; if he earns more, he must eventually accumulate. The assumption of a simple reproduction permits neither possibility, so long as all goods are being produced in the socially desired quantities. This condition must, of course, be presupposed in the present context. Hence, if the commodity that the present capitalist produces is neither overproduced nor underproduced in society, the surplus value that he earns annually must be exactly $10,000. Such a thing, however, is manifestly impossible, because being a capitalist he must not hesitate to earn more surplus value if it is at all feasible. He must try to turn over his capital faster; he must intensify labour and stretch the working day; or alternatively, he must look for a technical innovation. In short, he must always strive for a surplus value greater than $10,000. Therefore, sooner or later, the capitalist must overstep the limitation of simple reproduction, earning a surplus value more than is sufficient to provide for his and his associates' consumption.

(γ) If the surplus value is greater than the consumption-fund of the capitalist, the realisation of this excess clearly requires more means of circulation than was originally spent by the capitalist for his consumption. The supply of the additional means of circulation in such a case will be studied in detail in the following section. Here, attention is called to the fact that surplus value, once realised in the form of money, drops out of the circulation-process of capital as the capitalist's 'income or revenue'. Money that is so released from the circulation-process of capital becomes *freely disposable*, so that it can be disposed of as the consumption-fund of the capitalist. However, the free disposability of income also implies that it need not be wholly spent; it can also be *saved* with a view to future investment. The purpose of the circulation of capital is not an endless hoarding of monetised surplus value, nor is it a pursuit of luxury by the capitalist. So long as an adequate standard of living, proportional to the prestige of the business, is achieved, the capitalist does not consume more lavishly, but instead will endeavour to save his income for further accumulation. By the conversion of the freely disposable income into an *accumulation-fund*, and then further into *additional capital*, the scale of reproduction can be expanded. An expanded reproduction means a greater scope for the value augmentation of capital. The acquisition of surplus value is the purpose of the capitalist operation, precisely because surplus value may be converted into additional capital. It is the accumulation of capital, rather than the hoarding of money or the enjoyment of sybaritic life, that is the capitalist rationale for the pursuit of surplus value. Individual consumption, just as the payment of rewards to his associates, is from the point of view of the capitalist a deduction from surplus value, and thus a necessary evil that must be minimised if possible. Surplus value that constitutes the capitalist's freely disposable income is either consumed or saved, that is, divided into the consumption-fund and the accumulation-fund. Money that realises surplus value therefore cannot be considered merely as the means of circulation in this context. If the turnover-time of capital is long, even the consumption-fund cannot be spent immediately as the means of purchase; part of it may have to be held idle for a year or more. In the case of the accumulation-fund, it must certainly be held idle for a lengthy period of time and through many turnovers of capital, until it grows into a size adequate for conversion into additional capital. How the capitalist disposes of surplus value over time, once it has been converted into money, cannot therefore be a matter of total indifference to the circulation-process of capital, even though the latter ostensibly disconnects itself from the circulation of surplus value as soon as the new commodity is sold for money.

(*b*) The Supply of the Monetary Commodity

(α) At the abstract level of the doctrine of simple circulation, the existing stock of money was divided into *active* means of circulation and *idle* money, or funds, 'hoarded' away from the circulation market. In a purely capitalist society, composed of capitalists and workers, 'hoarding' does not mean an irrational accumulation of precious metals, but the temporary holding of idle money or funds, which occurs naturally in the circulation-process of capital. The circulation of capital generates funds in a variety of ways. On the asset side of the balance-sheet, $t_b m$ is a freely disposable fund of the capitalist, while part of the wage-fund, $(t_p + 1)W/2$, which need not be spent for some time, must also be considered idle money. The depreciation fund, D, is most certainly lying idle until the renewal time of fixed capital arrives. In addition to these funds, a shortening of the circulation-period releases idle money, while the reserve fund, which is always held against unpredictable price fluctuations, tends to increase whenever uncertainty prevails in the market. Hence, the existing stock of money is not always ready to be spent, either in conjunction with the advance of capital or personally in consumption, as active means of circulation.

The quantity of money needed as active means of circulation depends primarily on the volume of trade, that is, the value of the aggregate-social supply of commodities ($\Sigma C'$). Hence, given the existing stock of money, an increased volume of trade tends to drain the pool of idle funds. In the short run, however, the velocity of the circulation of active money, to some extent, counteracts this tendency so as to relieve the market for funds of excessive strain. There are, of course, other well-known mechanisms contributing to the overall monetary flexibility of capitalist society, such as the ready inflow of specie and the conversion of non-monetary gold into monetary gold. None of these short run flexibilities, however, can be relied upon permanently; thus, in what follows, it must be assumed that the additional supply of the monetary commodity, such as gold, is procured only by its increased production.

(β) In the case of a simple reproduction, if no part of the existing stock of the monetary metal is abraded or lost, it is not necessary to produce gold in order to supply more money. The gold-producing industry, however, must maintain a scale of operation just large enough to meet the non-monetary demand for gold. That scale is stationary in the context of a society-wide simple reproduction. Even when simple reproduction prevails, however, some *abrasion and loss* of circulating monetary gold are, in most cases, unavoidable. The production of gold should therefore normally include the supply of new monetary gold, corresponding to the physical depletion of the existing stock of money. In that case, the production of gold, either for a monetary or non-monetary purpose, is a part of social reproduction, even when society maintains the scale of simple reproduction.

It will be supposed, in the present context, that society's productive labour is so allocated that all use-values, including gold, are capitalistically produced in socially desired quantities. If this were not the case, an adjustment of production would no doubt take place, thus eliminating any unnecessary waste of productive labour. When such an adjustment has already been accomplished through the working of the law of value, no use-value can either be overproduced or underproduced, relative to the social need.

What distinguishes the gold-producing industry from the other industries is the fact that its product, C', is already in the form of money, M', and requires no selling operation. Hence, the producers of the monetary metal, who advance money-capital, M, and spend a consumption-fund, m, throw the sum, M + m, of money into the circulation-market. However, when new gold, C' = M', is produced, they absorb no money from the market. The gold-producing sector therefore unilaterally injects money into the circulation-sphere, that is to say, purchases commodities without selling any. If the provision of non-monetary gold is for the moment ignored, the newly produced gold must be just sufficient to compensate for the abrasion and loss of circulating gold coins, for otherwise gold would be either overproduced or underproduced. The production of gold too is a capitalistic operation. Therefore, if more is produced than is necessary to satisfy society's demand for gold, monetary or non-monetary, its value must fall below the quantity of labour actually spent for its production. This fact will be reflected in a general rise in the market prices of all commodities *above normal*, which will affect the profitability of the gold-producing sector adversely. Hence, the production of gold will be contracted, and the production of other commodities expanded, until normal prices for all commodities are restored. Once that state of equilibrium is attained, the quantity of newly produced gold, apart from that meant for non-monetary purposes, must exactly correspond to the current abrasion and loss of gold coins. The reverse adjustment will take place if less gold is produced than is socially needed.

(γ) There is no alteration to this principle, even when accumulation or expanded reproduction requires more production of the monetary metal. An accumulation means the conversion of a part of surplus value into additional capital, which in consequence generally leads to a greater mass and value of commodities (ΣC') in need of circulation. Other things being equal, more means of circulation must be injected into the circulation-market by the gold-producing sector of the economy. An expanding scale of the circulation-process of capital demands more of both active and idle money so that, even if the velocity of circulation, the inflow of gold from abroad, the conversion of non-monetary into monetary gold, the lengthening of the terms of lending, and so on, can render the short run adjustment flexible enough, the shortage of the monetary metal will sooner or later entail a rise in the value of money, justifying the allocation of more social labour, current and stored-up, to the gold-producing industry.

The adjustment of production that automatically ensues is exactly the same as in a simple reproduction. The rising value of the monetary metal is reflected by a general fall in the market prices of other commodities below their normal levels. These commodities, of course, include productive elements that the gold-producing sector purchases in the open market. Hence, in order to produce the same amount of gold as before, this sector needs to pay less than before for the necessary elements of production. The production of gold inevitably becomes more profitable than the production of any other use-value, and the expansion of the gold-producing sector continues until the socially necessary output of gold flows into the market. Thus, there cannot be a permanent shortage of the monetary metal in capitalist society, any more than its permanent excess. The circulation-process of capital, whether in a simple reproduction or in an expanded reproduction, is therefore in no way restricted by the production of gold, which can be trusted to automatically supply whatever quantity of gold society may require at any moment of time.

(c)   The Conversion of Surplus Value into Capital

(α) As already stated, capital primarily aims at expanding the scope of value augmentation through accumulation, rather than facilitating the pursuit of a sybaritic life or the mere hoarding of monetised surplus value by capitalists. The constant exhortation of frugality and saving, which characterised the moral code of the nineteenth-century bourgeoisie, accurately reflected this self-denying virtue of capital. If, therefore, the magnitude of surplus value rises beyond the immediate need for consumption, the capitalist begins to form accumulation-funds. Normally, the funds must grow over a number of turnovers of capital to reach a sufficient magnitude, capable of being advanced as additional capital; in the meantime, this money is kept aside from the circulation-market. The amount of accumulation-funds that an individual capitalist sets aside from the market may have a limited effect on the overall quantity of the means of circulation existing in society. Yet when practically all of the capitalists plan to expand the scale of their reproduction, the effect cannot be negligible. More and more money is held as accumulation-funds and fails to be spent on goods, resulting in a shortage of the monetary metal as active money. The consequent rise in its value calls forth an increased production of the monetary metal by raising the profitability (or the efficiency of value augmentation) of that industry.

The accumulation of precious metals, the form of commercial wealth *par excellence,* was no doubt a historical precondition of the capitalist mode of production. However, the development of capitalism changes the character of the accumulation of money. In well-developed capitalism, it is not an autonomous hoarding of money that eventually breaks into capital accumulation. Rather, it is an intended accumulation of capital that induces a prior pooling of the monetary commodity. In other words, the holding of money in the form of accumulation-funds is an instrument rather than the object of the capitalist accumulation of wealth. Money, in this form, is from the beginning held as potential capital or as universal money, ready to purchase productive elements as soon as the first chance arises. If surplus value were already in the form of additional productive elements – as is the case to some extent in traditional agriculture – it would not be necessary to first convert it into money, before purchasing the desired elements of production. Capital must, however, produce a commodity that is most intensely demanded by society, and that commodity need not take the form of productive elements suitable for accumulation. Surplus value must therefore be converted into money, in the first instance, and only in this form of immediate purchasing-power can it be exchanged for desired elements of production. It is in the nature of capitalist production that the conversion of surplus value into capital must always occur through the intermediation of money. Nor does money function merely as the medium of circulation here, for this conversion requires time, pending the growth of accumulation-funds to an adequate magnitude.

(β) In order to convert surplus value into capital, therefore, the preparatory process of accumulating investible funds must first take place. Yet this process alone is sufficient to stimulate the production of more gold, or the monetary metal. This is a phenomenon peculiar to capitalist society. When an expanded reproduction occurs in other societies, it is not necessary that the production of gold should be the first to expand; the material condition of accumulation is directly satisfied by the presence of additional means of production and labour-power. However, in capitalist society, the formation of the material condition for accumulation must follow a prior expansion of the production of money, an object not directly useful to either direct or productive consumption.

The cost of producing money is certainly not an unproductive cost to its capitalist producers; however, from the social point of view, it cannot be other than unproductive *faux frais.* Only capitalist society has to allocate productive resources to produce a monetary metal, such as gold, more than is necessary for its direct consumption, or for the production of other use-values, simply because commodities must be circulated. Capitalist society cannot survive without money, and so long as money is a commodity it has to be produced according to the same principle that governs the production of any other commodity. Moreover, only such a commodity, which is capable of being produced in any desired amount, can function as money in a purely capitalist society.

Capitalism is, however, a rational economic system, which loathes a wasteful use of resources. Thus, even money, the commodity-economic *sine qua non*, must be economised in capitalist society, as long as its basic operation is preserved. That is why the modern credit system develops, the purpose of which is to activate the idle money generated by the circulation-process of capital. All kinds of funds currently held by the capitalist – whether for accumulation, consumption, depreciation, or wage-payments, but not immediately needed as the means of circulation – are deposited with the banking system, which loans them out to other capitalists in need of active money for specified periods of time. The credit system accomplishes the most efficient use of the existing stock of money, and goes a long way towards minimising the need for the additional production of the monetary metal. Yet even in that case, the accumulation of capital cannot occur without some additional production of the monetary metal, which claims the first right to the use of additional productive resources.

(γ) If a large number of capitalists decide to hold money as accumulation-funds, rather than to use that gold immediately as the medium of circulation, the market soon begins to feel the shortage of the circulating medium, as it becomes increasingly harder to sell other commodities for their normal prices. The gold-producing sector can, however, expand even without additional money-capital, since it can now purchase more productive elements for the same outlay of money as before. The consequent increase in the production of gold enables this sector to expand further. Since the gold-producing sector now purchases commodities by spending more gold, which it has produced rather than acquired by the sale of a commodity, an additional supply of gold necessarily flows out of this sector into the open market. If the gold-producing sector expands sufficiently, together with directly allied fields, the shortage of the circulating medium will be removed, even when capitalists at large hold as much money as they wish as accumulation-funds. Sooner or later, however, these accumulation-funds reach a magnitude sufficient for conversion into real capital; real accumulation can therefore take place in all fields of production. Thus, if A stands for the gold-producing sector, and B for the rest of the economy, an expansion of output must always occur in A first, so as to entail the expansion of B. Whenever a capitalist economy prepares itself for an accumulation, the purchasing-power of the monetary metal rises. In consequence, A expands to A + a, where a is additional gold production, sufficient to accommodate the present building of accumulation-funds, without causing a shortage of the circulating medium. Only when these accumulation-funds reach an adequate magnitude for real investment can B increase to B + b. However, this accumulation produces more commodities to be circulated, which requires more of the circulating medium. At the same time, the circulation-process of capital, involving an expanded reproduction, gives rise to the holding of more idle funds, even when further accumulation is not envisaged. The ensuing shortage of gold leads to another expansion of A + a to A + a + a'. If this a' now includes enough new gold to provide for more accumulation-funds, the expansion of B + b to B + b + b' follows in due course.

Thus, the growth of a capitalist economy involves the peculiar procedure, in which A automatically expands before B follows. Yet the problem of real accumulation is not yet solved. Instead, it is just introduced, for when accumulation-funds reach a magnitude sufficient for conversion into real capital, the material condition for B to actually expand the scope of its production must be present. That is to say, the actual conversion of surplus value into capital requires a prior presence of additional labour-power and means of production that are capable of being purchased by these accumulation-funds. When the problem is so posed, however, it cannot be answered within the scope of the circulation-process of capital alone, because the circulation of capital-value can no longer be discussed independently from the circulation of product-values. The more synthetic viewpoint of the *reproduction-process of capital* must be introduced to tackle this problem. In the meantime, it can only be assumed that the accumulation-fund converts itself into additional capital by somehow finding the necessary elements of production including labour-power in the market. Even the original metamorphosis of money-capital, M, into productive elements, C, tacitly assumed the same thing.

CHAPTER 6

The Reproduction-process of Capital (*Actuality*)

Whatever the form of the process of production in a society, it must be a continuous process, must continue to go periodically through the same phases. A society can no more cease to produce than it can cease to consume. When viewed, therefore, as a connected whole, and as flowing on with incessant renewal, every social process of production is, at the same time, a process of reproduction.[198]

Thus, regardless of the form of economic organisation, a social process of production by its very nature repeats itself as a reproduction-process. The reproduction of goods on a social scale, however, implies a reproduction of the production-relation, that is, the social organisation of people in the activity of use-value production. Indeed, every society reproduces its production-relation as it reproduces goods or use-values for its survival and comfort. In feudal society, for example, where goods are produced under a master-servant relation, the reproduction of goods reconfirms and perpetuates that relation. In capitalist society, where goods are produced as commodities, the reproduction of goods secures the endurance of the commodity-economic production-relation, that is, of the workers-versus-capitalist relation.

If the production-process of capital, which produces commodities, is viewed as the inner ground of capitalist society, the circulation-process of capital, which circulates produced commodities, may be considered as the outer appearance of capitalist society. Yet the inner and the outer cannot exist independently of one another; actual capitalist society is founded on an inseparable unity of the two, which is accomplished in the *reproduction-process of capital*. In the examination of the production-process, it was sufficient to consider the operation of the 'representative' individual capital, with the assumption that it can always purchase the required elements of production, including labour-power, in the market. The examination of the circulation-process too envisaged, by and large, the operation of the representative capital on the assumption that it could always buy and sell in the market whatever use-values it chose. The study of the reproduction-process of capital, however, requires the point of view of the aggregate-social capital, because only from that point of view can the totality of capitalist society – in which alone the production- and the circulation-process of capital are unified – be

---

apprehended at all. Capitalism forms a historical society because the entire process of its production and circulation can be carried out by the principle of capital. Here, the ability of capital to organise the whole of society's reproduction must be investigated.

The reproduction-process of capital is first of all the process of reproducing the capitalists and the workers. Unless the capitalists continue to appropriate enough surplus value in the form of freely disposable income, detachable from the circulation-process of capital, their existence cannot be ensured. However, surplus value is produced only in the production-process of capital, the continuity of which is now taken for granted from the point of view of the reproduction-process. Hence, the conversion of the output, C', of the aggregate-social capital into the necessary elements of production, C, of the aggregate-social capital and the consumption-goods, c, of the capitalist class may in the first instance be left implicit. This procedure enables one to concentrate on the continuum of the production-process, P, of the aggregate-social capital in which productive capital, variable and constant, is reproduced, together with surplus value. Variable capital is at first a sum of money in the hands of capitalists, who purchase labour-power from the working class. Variable capital, in its functioning form of labour-power, however, converts itself into the output of wage-goods in the production-process of capital. Wages are paid, as labour-power is consumed and as wage-goods emerge in the market. Hence, capital pays money wages for the consumption of labour-power, with its right hand as it were, while receiving the money value of the wage-goods, with its left hand. When it hands over these wage-goods to the working class, the money wages just paid out invariably return to capital. Since the sum of money paid and received by the aggregate-social capital is equal to the value, or the reproduction cost, of the labour-power it has consumed, its variable component reproduces itself, both in money and in real terms. The reproduction of capital by capital itself depends on this fundamental mechanism. The working class and the capitalist class, as well as the social relation that ties them together, are reproduced by virtue of this ingeniously contrived commodity-economic mechanism.

The reproduction of the capitalists and the workers is, however, contingent upon the appropriate conversion of the aggregate product, C', into the necessary elements of production, C, together with the consumption-goods for the capitalist class, c. The circulation of the aggregate supply of commodities, C', must now be studied as the problem of the *circular flow of products in the economy*, that is, as the problem of the *Tableau économique*. The reproduction-schemes, constructed by Marx, divide the economy into two sectors, producing, respectively, the means of production and the articles of consumption.

The schemes show how the annual flow of goods and the counterflow of money in the complex network of classes and sectors do accomplish the required conversion of C′ into C *plus* c, on a society-wide basis. However, the theoretical significance of the *reproduction-schemes* has been widely misunderstood. The first misunderstanding consists of overlooking the fact that the reproduction-schemes do not exhibit the total picture of capital accumulation. The theory of the schemes throws light on one important aspect of the reproduction-process of capital, but by no means on all of them. The schemes offer a framework within which the reproducibility of capitalist society may be studied from the point of view of produced commodities, *deliberately holding the presence of labour-power as a commodity implicit.* It is not the *actual process of capital accumulation* that the schemes are supposed to explain, but the more abstract fact that capitalist society, as any other society, can adequately reproduce all goods, so long as the supply of labour-power is guaranteed. The second misunderstanding, which is closely connected to the first, lies in the confusion of the circular-flow theory of the schemes with a theory of market equilibrium. The theory of the reproduction-schemes, as part of the doctrine of production, does not provide an explicit theory of the capitalist market; instead it takes a general equilibrium of the market for granted, without analysis. Hence, the celebrated inter-sectoral condition of reproduction cannot be interpreted as an 'equilibrium' condition between the two sectors; it is a technical constraint, to which all self-reproducing economic systems must be subject. A breach of the constraint therefore means that the underlying technology is inadequate, even for the simple reproduction of economic life; it does not specifically mean that a capitalist crisis is about to break out, or that capitalism is destined to collapse. In this chapter, I develop a general theory of the reproduction-schemes, free from these traditional misconceptions.

The reproduction of the capitalist production-relation *and* the reproduction of goods (products) as commodities are the two aspects of the reproduction of capitalist society, which expands its scope in the actual process of capital accumulation. Capital is a form of value augmentation. Just as an individual capital cannot really be itself without constantly growing, so the aggregate-social capital must grow by always expanding the scale of social reproduction that it embraces. The reproduction-process of capital is therefore necessarily the process of capital accumulation. Now, if the desired growth rate of capital value were less than the natural growth rate of the working population, capitalism would not be a self-sufficient mode of production. It is, of course, only by chance that the two growth rates will coincide, and the existence of capitalism cannot depend on chance. However, if the desired growth rate of capital value exceeds the natural growth rate of the working population, the shortage of labour-power – the crucial element of production, which capital cannot itself directly produce – will sooner or later impede the accumulation of capital. The aggregate-social capital is therefore left with only one choice, namely, to introduce technical innovations such as to raise the organic composition of capital, thereby creating a 'relative surplus population'. The capitalist law of surplus population must, however, not be misunderstood to be the assertion of a tendency for widespread and chronic unemployment under capitalism. Capitalism, as a historical mode of production, cannot permanently under-employ its productive workers. Yet the accumulation of capital requires that readily employable labour-power should always be present in the form of the commodity; this compels capital to periodically form a social reservoir of labour-power, or an *industrial reserve army*, which it drains in the course of subsequent accumulation. When the reservoir is almost empty, and when capital accumulation reaches a stalemate known as the *excess of capital*, the necessity of innovating the technological base of society is forced upon capital. The law of population peculiar to capitalism explains the ability of capital to successfully cope with the crisis, and thus to ensure the self-containedness and self-sufficiency of the capitalist mode of production.

The Hegel Correspondence

In his doctrine of 'actuality', Hegel describes the self-manifestation or mode of the Absolute. In the present context, the Absolute may be taken to mean the aggregate-social capital. If so, the actuality of the aggregate-social capital is undoubtedly the reproduction-process of capital, or the capitalist mode of production as it reproduces itself. For capitalism to be *actual* it must, of course, be *possible*. If capitalism is actual, because it is one of the many possibilities, its presence may be said to be 'formally necessary' or 'contingent'. If capitalism is actual, because it satisfies all conditions that make it in itself or in principle a possibility, capitalism is said to be a 'real possibility', or 'relative necessity'. If, however, the presence of capitalism is self-determined in such a way that its actuality and possibility are no longer separable, so that capitalism not only depends on its conditions, but also produces these conditions of existence for itself, then capitalism is said to be an 'absolute necessity' or 'unconditioned actuality'. Thus, the triplex of actuality-possibility-necessity proceeds from the formal stage (the stage of contingency) through the real stage (the stage of conditionality) to the absolute stage (the stage of self-sufficiency). In the last stage, actuality, possibility, and necessity, are identical, and there remains nothing but the self-relation or *activity* of the Absolute, which now transforms 'necessity' into 'freedom', through the sub-triad of substantiality, causality, and reciprocity.

Broadly speaking, if Hegel's doctrine of actuality may be understood in this way, a close correspondence between that doctrine and the present part of the dialectic of capital can scarcely be doubted. The reproduction-process of capital has already been described as the unity of the production-process and the circulation-process of capital, that is, as 'the unity, become immediate, of essence with existence, or of inward with outward'.[199] The study of the reproduction-process also requires the point of view of the aggregate-social capital, the mode of which is 'a determining which would make it not another, but only that which it already is, the transparent externality which is the manifestation of itself, a movement out of itself'.[200] Indeed, the self-reproducing capitalist mode of production is the manifestation of the aggregate-social capital in its chrematistic activity. The capitalist mode of production does not 'pass over' to another form, nor does it have to 'appear' as something different from what it is; it simply manifests itself as actuality, that is, as possibility become necessity.

The formal stage of actuality may be interpreted to mean the reproduction of capital by capital itself, contingent upon the conversion of labour-power into a commodity. For so long as and to the extent that labour-power is available as a commodity, the reproduction of variable capital is ensured. Through this fundamental reproduction, constant capital and surplus value can also be reproduced, and consequently the capitalist production-relation as well. The way capital secures the working population is, however, not yet questioned at this formal stage. Primitive accumulation, in other words, is a mere formal possibility, which may or may not have happened. 'The contingent is only one side of the actual – the side, namely, of reflection on somewhat else'.[201] In the real stage of actuality, it is shown that the reproduction of goods by capital in the form of commodities satisfies all conditions for capitalism to actualise itself. In other words, capitalist society can, as can any other society, produce all goods that are required or useful for its existence. The *reproduction-schemes* ascertain the possibility of the capitalist mode of production. 'If one brings into account the determinations, circumstances and conditions of something in order to ascertain its possibility, one is no longer at the stage of formal possibility, but is considering its real possibility'.[202] Yet the reproduction-scheme as 'real necessity is in itself also contingency', since although it is 'necessary as regards form,

199　Hegel 1975, p. 200.
200　Hegel 1969, p. 536.
201　Hegel 1975, p. 205.
202　Hegel 1969, p. 547.

as regards content it is limited, and through this has its contingency'.[203] In fact, the analysis of the reproduction-schemes accomplishes its formal consistency by deliberately holding the contingency (labour-power as a commodity) implicit. Hence, the reproduction of capital is, only in principle, 'really' possible.

However, 'that which is simply necessary only is because it is; it has neither condition nor ground'.[204] When the necessary becomes self-dependent or self-conditioned, it 'simply and positively is, as unconditioned actuality'.[205] The actual process of capital accumulation is unconditioned in this sense. It no longer depends on a contingency, for with the law of relative surplus population, capital can by itself make labour-power available as a commodity. The law of value is thus no longer subject to any external restriction. The activity of the aggregate-social capital has become 'absolute necessity', as a self-dependent totality capable of unfolding itself. A self-determined necessity, however, is 'freedom', since it is free from an alien principle. The capitalist mode of production, having established itself as absolute necessity, is now ready to develop its own ideal environment in which it proposes to function freely without internal restrictions. At this point, the doctrine of production comes to an end, and the doctrine of distribution must begin, just as, in Hegel's Logic, the Doctrine of Essence gives way to that of the Notion.

A   **The Reproduction of the Capitalist Production-Relation**
        (The Formal Necessity of Capitalism)

(*a*)   *The Production of Capital by Capital*

(α) The continuity of the capitalist process of production presupposes the circulation of capital. Unless a definite part of total capital advanced takes the unproductive form of circulation-capital, the production-process of capital cannot avoid interruptions. The significance of this truth cannot be understood by merely 'assum[ing] that capital circulates in its normal way'.[206] The theory of the reproduction-process of capital, in other words, cannot be adequately developed until after detailed discussions of the production- and the circulation-process of capital have already been concluded. To regard the reproduction-process as the total process that synthesises these two processes of

---

203   Hegel 1969, p. 550.
204   Hegel 1969, p. 552.
205   Hegel 1975, p. 212.
206   Marx 1967, *Capital*, Volume I, p. 564.

capital amounts to viewing capitalist society as a self-reproducing whole. The activity of capital is no longer studied simply from the viewpoint of production that constitutes the inner base of capitalism, or simply from the viewpoint of circulation that constitutes its outer appearance. Rather, it is recognised that the unity of the inner (the production-process) and the outer (the circulation-process) constitutes the reproduction of capital by capital itself. Only by demonstrating the necessity of capital to reproduce itself of its own accord can one hope to establish the self-dependence of capitalist society.

The reproduction of capital by capital is, however, accomplished through the reproduction of goods or use-values, which are material objects. Indeed, all societies reproduce themselves by reproducing 'things'. If goods are reproduced under a specific social relation, that relation is also cemented by the recurrent production of use-values or goods. Thus, in a feudal society, since goods are reproduced under a *master-servant relation*, the reproduction of goods by itself entails the reproduction of the master-servant relation as well. In capitalist society, goods are reproduced by capital as commodities; this fact also implies the simultaneous reproduction of the capitalist (commodity-economic) production-relation. If we refer to the specific manner in which goods are reproduced as the *mode of production*, the latter should be seen not only as reaffirming the corresponding production-relation, but also as presupposing it. Indeed, the reproduction of goods by humankind is never exclusively a natural activity; it is a natural activity constrained by the social organisation of production under which it occurs. To put it otherwise, the labour-and-production process, taken by itself, does not contain the moment of continuity. That moment must be sought in the reproducibility of the production-relation.

That is the reason why the reproduction of the capitalist production-relation must first be established (here in Part A), before the investigation (in the following Part B) into what the capitalist reproduction of goods (or use-values) *specifically as commodities* entails in more concrete terms. The first problem is clarified by studying the production-process of the aggregate-social capital, and the second problem by studying the circulation-process of the aggregate-social capital. In Part C, which concludes this chapter, the two aspects will be synthesised as the *actual process* of capital accumulation.

(β) It might appear strange that the reproduction-process of capital, which is already posed as a synthesis of the production- and the circulation-process of capital, must again be studied, first, from the point of view of the production-process, and, secondly, from the point of view of the circulation-process, as if to repeat what has already been accomplished. However, it should not be unexpected that the spiral motion of the dialectic should tread over the same ground, each time to arrive at increasingly enlightened knowledge. So far, both the production-process and the circulation-process of capital have been studied with reference to the activity of the representative sample of individual capital-units. Given its environment, an individual capital produces and circulates in such a way as to form and augment value most efficiently. Yet if the environment is simply given or posed, the self-reproduction of capital cannot be wholly grasped. It is necessary now to focus on the behaviour of the *aggregate-social capital*, rather than that of the representative individual capital. The necessity of *shifting the focus of attention from the individual to the social* has arisen in the treatment of the circulation of surplus value. The analysis of the circulation of surplus value requires the point of view of the *circuit of commodity-capital*, which is the only circuit capable of explicitly accounting for the social interaction of the motion of capital. The circuit of commodity-capital demands that the capitalistically produced commodity (C′) should be exchanged, via money, for the elements of production (C), together with whatever is to be purchased by surplus value (c). In order for an individual capital to successfully complete C′ – M – (C, c), however, the aggregate-social output, ΣC′, should have an appropriate composition of use-values. If this point is now taken into consideration, the production-process of capital can no longer be adequately represented by P in C... P... C′, but only by P in ΣC ... P ... ΣC′; that is to say, P must be viewed as the production-process of the aggregate-social capital. On the basis of that P, the circulation-process of capital too becomes ΣC′ – M – (ΣC ... P ...)ΣC′, or the exchange of the aggregate commodity-capital (ΣC′) for itself.

Thus, the first aspect of the problem of the reproduction-process of capital is the production-process of the aggregate-social capital, while taking the exchange of ΣC′ for ΣC′ for granted. The second aspect of the problem then turns out to be the exchange of the aggregate-social commodity-capital, ΣC′, for itself, through the mediation of money, while making the production of commodities implicit. It is obvious – even from the title of the third part of *Capital*, Volume II ('The Reproduction and Circulation of the Aggregate Social Capital') – that the second aspect of the problem must be treated as the *circulation of the aggregate-social capital*, not as that of an individual capital. I wish to emphasise here that the first aspect of the problem also requires the same treatment, since Marx does not specifically mention it at the outset of his accumulation theory (*Capital* I, Part 7). Precisely because of this omission, however, Marx is obliged to later insert, at several places throughout the relevant chapters, such remarks as: 'The matter takes quite another aspect, when we contemplate, not the single capitalist, and the single labourer, but the capitalist class and the labouring class, not an isolated process of production, but capitalist production in full swing, and on its actual social scale'.[207] No aspect of the reproduction-process of capital can be understood solely from the point of view of the representative individual capital; it is the operation of the aggregate-social capital that constitutes the reproduction-process of capital.

(γ) Regardless of the assignment of its individual component units, the aggregate of social capital must continually supply the market with the means of production and articles of consumption, while it 'also produces and reproduces the capitalist relation; on the one side the capitalist, on the other the wage-labourer'.[208] In order to disclose the reproduction of the capitalists and the workers, it is not necessary to explicitly consider the exchange process of commodities; it is enough to consider one gigantic capital, which produces all the socially needed use-values, and thus makes the division of the economy into sectors irrelevant. The total output of the aggregate-social capital may therefore be supposed to have the value composition, $C^* + V^* + S^*$. If the constant-capital component, C^*, of the total output is physically in the form of the means of production, and if the value-added component, $V^* + S^*$, is entirely in the form of the articles of consumption, a *simple reproduction* is said to occur. If part of the surplus-value component, S^*, of the total output contains some means of production, an *expanded reproduction* is said to take place. It cannot be said of a single capital that the constant-capital component (c) of its output always represents means of production, or its value-added component (v + s) the articles of consumption, even in the case of a simple reproduction. To the total output of the aggregate-social capital, however, the above definition applies.

Consider, for example, a simple capitalist economy with two independent capitals. The first produces 15 units of steel (the means of production) with 10 units of steel and 10 hours of labour. The second produces 10 units of corn (the article of consumption) with 5 units of steel and 10 hours of labour. If the value of steel and corn are both equal to 2, the following table shows the value composition of the output of the two independent capitals, and of the aggregate-social capital as indicated in Table 6.1.

TABLE 6.1

	c		v + s			
Capital I	20	+	10	=	30	the value of steel produced
Capital II	10	+	10	=	20	the value of corn produced
	30	+	20	=	50	

207   Marx 1967, *Capital,* Volume I, p. 572.
208   Marx 1967, *Capital,* Volume I, p. 578.

Clearly, for the first capital, $c = 20$ and $v + s = 10$ both represent the value of steel; for the second capital, $c = 10$ and $v + s = 10$ both represent the value of corn. Yet for the aggregate-social capital, $C^* = 30$ represents the value of steel, and $V^* + S^* = 20$ represents the value of corn. This fact provides the foundation upon which the following analysis (in Part A) is based. Notice that the present example implies a simple reproduction, since the value of steel produced is equal to the value of steel used up. Hence, there is no new investment, and 'national income' (= social value added) consists entirely of the consumption of corn. Of course, this does not mean that steel is not currently reproduced. On the contrary, its production is of fundamental importance from the point of view of society's reproduction-process, even under a simple reproduction. It is for this reason that Marx severely criticised 'Adam Smith's dogma that the price of any commodity resolves itself into wages, profit, and rent'.[209] Indeed, the product-value, $c + v + s$, of any commodity does not exclusively consist of the value-added (or new value) component $v + s$. Nor does aggregation eliminate C^* from society's product-value $C^* + V^* + S^*$. The product-value must always include the 'old value'-component consumed (productively), i.e., transferred to the new product.

Throughout the following, the working of the law of value – the ultimate regulator of the capitalist production of commodities – is presupposed, so that no use-value is either over-produced or under-produced, relative to the existing pattern of social demand. Of course, this does not mean that the over-production or under-production of a use-value can never occur. On the contrary, the anarchic mode of production always tends to either over-produce or under-produce any use-value. Yet for the purpose of the present enquiry, it is best to conceive of a state in which the law of value has already worked its way through the economy, and all outputs are consequently in the socially necessary (and desired) quantities. It will also be assumed that the turnover-time of capital is a unit conventional period (such as a year) in the production of all use-values.

(b)   The Simple Reproduction of the Production-relation

(α) The case of a simple reproduction must be considered first, because the fundamental mechanism of the reproduction of the capitalist production-relation is already apparent in this context. In order to maintain the existing capitalist class, it is necessary that surplus labour should be appropriated

---

209   Marx 1967, *Capital*, Volume I, p. 370.

as surplus value, and that this surplus value should be sufficient to form the consumption-fund of the capitalist class. However, in order to yield a regular income to the capitalist year after year, a given magnitude of capital must be invested in the continual production-process both as constant and variable capital. Labour-power, which variable capital purchases, functions as productive labour in the production-process of capital, transferring the old value used up to the new product, while at the same time forming and augmenting new value. Consequently, the continuity of the production-process requires that an appropriate quantity of labour-power should always be reproduced and be made available as variable capital.

Capital, of course, cannot directly reproduce labour-power; its reproduction must occur in the individual consumption of wage-goods by the workers. Moreover, since wage-goods are produced as commodities, capital, as a commodity-seller, always owns the entire supply of wage-goods; the workers must *buy back* these goods from the capitalists with the wage that is paid in return for the value of their labour-power. It is necessary then that the value of wage-goods required for the reproduction of labour-power should be equal to the value of labour-power itself. For if the real wage that the workers receive were more than is necessary for the reproduction of their labour-power, part of the presently employed labour-power would not return to the market as a commodity purchasable by the capitalist class. Alternatively, if the real wage were less than is necessary for the reproduction of labour-power, it would clearly be impossible to maintain the presently employed labour-power. It does not matter here what assortment of use-values forms the real wage, provided that it is just enough to reproduce labour-power as a commodity. That is to say, provided that the total wage-bill paid to the working class purchases such use-values as are just adequate to maintain the present working population in the same condition. There is no unique mechanism that determines the value of labour-power, since it depends on economic as well as non-economic factors. But for the purpose of the present discussion, some feasible wage-rate may be assumed initially (see Section (c) of Part C below). The maintenance of the variable part of the aggregate-social capital then reduces to the payment of wages, corresponding to the currently prevailing value of labour-power.

Although, by the payment of wages, the aggregate-social capital parts with the value that it initially possessed in the form of money as variable capital, it now possesses the same value of variable capital in the form of commodities – in particular, in the form of wage-goods. In a sense, the working class therefore sells its labour-power on credit, and is paid wages in money as the means of payment. From the point of view of an individual capitalist, who has advanced wages, it is true that the value of variable capital paid out may not immediately return as the value of the finished commodity. Yet from the point of view of the aggregate-social capital, the payment of wages must be simultaneous with the completion of wage-goods as commodities. For otherwise, the workers' wages could not be immediately spent to purchase wage-goods, which would have a serious consequence for the stability of capitalist society, since in that case labour-power could not be adequately reproduced. Therefore, if wages are paid at the same time as wage-goods are supplied to the market, it is obvious that the money that the aggregate-social capital pays out as wages immediately returns to it in exchange for the wage-goods. Thus, if labour-power is reproduced, the variable part of the aggregate-social capital is 'reproduced', that is, restored in the form of money as new variable capital.

This foolproof mechanism is ensured by the production of wage-goods as commodities. If the direct producers' articles of consumption are not produced as commodities – as in the case of peasants under the obligation of corvée services[210] – no such mechanism applies. Corvée peasants produce, during their necessary labour-time, their own means of livelihood, which they do not have to buy back with wages. Since the lord cannot then control the reproduction of their labour-power, over which they maintain responsibility, there is no reason why the peasants should willingly come forward with another offer of surplus labour tomorrow. Extra-economic compulsion must therefore be applied. Capitalist wage earners, by contrast, do not own the fruit of their own necessary labour; they can reproduce their labour-power only by purchasing wage-goods that they themselves have produced, returning to the aggregate-social capital the whole amount of wages they receive from it. Hence, the reproduction of labour-power under capitalism cannot occur without simultaneously restoring the instrument of its 'exploitation', namely, variable capital in the hands of capital.

This outcome necessarily follows from the fact that the entire product of labour, including wage-goods, belongs to capital, because it (with the advance of variable capital) purchases labour-power as a commodity. It is true that labour-power does not become productive capital as an embodiment of value, but only as a use-value. However, labour-power purchased as a commodity cannot, through the consumption of its use-value, materialise labour in a commodity belonging to the worker. The consumption of labour-power in the production-process of capital forms value in a commodity that belongs to capital. Hence, wage-goods – being part of the total output of labour expended in

---

210   Marx 1967, *Capital,* Volume I, p. 568.

the production-process of capital – are also commodities possessed by capital, which the working class must *buy back* with wages. The aggregate-social capital produces just as much value of wage-goods as can be purchased by the wages, and the wage-goods that the working class buys back from capital as commodities are no more than is necessary for the reproduction of the working class.

(β) If the reproduction of labour-power thus automatically restores variable capital in the hands of the capitalists, they cannot fail to maintain full control of society's productive labour. Moreover, productive labour has the property of *preserving old value* by transferring it from the means of production to the new product. Therefore, the work of maintenance of constant capital is automatically performed by productive labour, which capital consumes in its process of value formation and augmentation. Means of production, if left outside of the labour-process, decay naturally and lose their value, together with their use-value; constant capital, in other words, has no power to reproduce itself. It must depend on the concrete-useful aspect of productive labour that labour-power continuously furnishes. Moreover, since the social aggregate of constant capital, C^*, always consists of means of production, the reproduction of constant capital signifies the transformation of old means of production into new means of production. This transformation can only be undertaken by the continued application of productive labour. Thus, capital's ceaseless access to labour-power, the only source of productive labour, is both necessary and sufficient to maintain the existing value of constant capital.

When this process is viewed from the outside, without an adequate knowledge of the inner structure of the capitalist process of production, it appears as though capital itself maintains its own value through time. The preservation of the value of constant capital, the transfer of the pre-existing value to a new product and the transformation of one type of constant capital into another, all appear to depend on some mystical force in possession of capital, unrelated to the expenditure of productive labour. Such a view stems from observations of the commodity-economic operation of an individual capital, which always recovers the value of constant capital in the form of money, and converts that money into necessary means of production in the market. However, the possibility of selling a commodity for a price that recovers the value of the consumed means of production, and the availability of suitable means of production in the market for the continuing motion of an individual capital, cannot be taken for granted by the aggregate-social capital. When the reproduction of constant capital is studied from this point of view, it is no longer possible to maintain the mystery of 'self-maintaining capital' to survive. The reproduction of constant capital manifestly depends on the reproduction of variable capital.

Therefore, it follows that as long as the presently employed labour-power can be reproduced as a commodity, both the variable *and* the constant component of the aggregate-social capital can be maintained and 'reproduced' in the desired form. The maintenance of capital value, $C^* + V^*$, however, also ensures the regular formation of capitalists' income.

(γ) Under the assumption of simple reproduction, the surplus value, S^*, that the aggregate-social capital appropriates consists of articles of consumption for capitalists. The class of capitalists maintains itself by consuming these articles, while keeping the value of the aggregate-social capital intact. Hence, the capitalist class too is permanently 'reproduced'. It may be true that the original capitalists did not live on the surplus labour of their employees, but once the reproduction-process of capital is well established, the capitalists cannot continue to live on their own labour. For instance, suppose that a simple reproduction repeats itself annually as $20C + 20V + 20S = 60$. Then, even if the original capitalists acquired the capital value, $40 = 20C + 20V$, and their consumption-fund, $20 = 20S$, through their own labour, the total value of 60, with which they started the reproduction-process, is equal to only $60 = 20S \times 3$, which means that in the first three years they have completely consumed the fruit of their own labour, and that after the fourth year neither the capital value $40 = 20C + 20V^*$ nor the capitalist's income $20S$ represent the result of their own labour.

Since the capitalists and their associates do not perform productive labour, they can only live on the output of the surplus labour of productive workers, which capital appropriates in the form of surplus value. Productive workers cannot reproduce themselves without donating the fruit of their surplus labour to their employers; capitalists cannot maintain themselves without appropriating the surplus labour of their productive employees. Thus, the classes of workers and capitalists are formed and maintained. The owners of labour-power and the owners of capital are permanently segregated so long as labour-power has no direct access to the means of production.

The reproduction of capital therefore implies, and is implied by, the separation of the direct producers from the means of production. It is this separation that appropriately divides the new value-product, $V^* + S^*$, into a variable-capital component and a surplus-value component. The value-product, $V^* + S^*$, may be entirely consumed while keeping the existing capital intact because it is being newly produced during the same period in which it is consumed. Neither the surplus-value component nor the variable-capital component of the sold commodity recovers an old value; both are newly produced value, emerging for the first time in the capitalist market. The surplus value of the preceding year is already consumed as articles of consumption for the capitalist class, while the variable capital of the preceding year is likewise consumed as wage-goods by the working class. The old value of luxury goods (capitalists' consumption-goods) and wage-goods has disappeared, and is replaced with the newly produced value embodied in the output of consumption-goods of the present year. Moreover, the division of the annual product of consumer goods into wage-goods and non-wage-goods is also essential for the preservation of the existing capital. If this division does not accomplish the separation of the direct producers from the means of production, capital cannot be reproduced.

Thus, capital reproduces itself on one condition only, namely, by paying wages with which the direct producers may purchase wage-goods that are necessary and sufficient for the reproduction of their labour-power. In purely abstract terms, it may be argued that the reproduction of capital, and therefore the continued existence of capitalist society, depend on a contingency. However, the dialectic does not predict what will happen in an empty future; it is not an exercise in fortune-telling. A dialectical theory, which is 'grey', only shows the logical necessity of the accepted or pre-supposed fact (*Voraus-setzung*) that capitalist society has existed. In order to show that capitalism, which has undoubtedly existed historically, can also exist logically, it is sufficient to establish that labour-power continues to be traded as a commodity, if and only if its value equals the value of the wage-goods necessary for its reproduction. This has now been shown.

(c)   *The Possibility of an Expanded Reproduction*

(α) It is true that a capitalist production-relation first arises in consequence of primitive accumulation. If, however, this relation simply reproduced itself and merely maintained its original scale, capitalism would not become a predominant mode of production in society. In order for capitalism to form a historical society, the scale of reproduction cannot be rigidly fixed. It must therefore be shown that a simple reproduction of the capitalist production-relation always contains the germ of its own expansion. The fact that surplus value forms a freely disposable income for capitalists, however, also implies that it can be saved and added to the existing value of capital. The capitalist production-relation always generates surplus value, which capital can dispose of freely without detracting from the existing capital-value. Yet the free disposal of surplus value means that it may be consumed or otherwise employed as capital sees fit. A formal possibility of converting surplus value into capital is already present in the free disposability of surplus value as income.

Surplus value, however, cannot be wholly set aside as accumulation-funds; part of surplus value must, in any case, be devoted to the capitalist's consumption, ensuring him a certain standard of living. This standard of living, which must, of course, be higher than that of the working class, is dependent on historical conditions and cannot be completely determined in theory. The capitalist, as a personification of capital, however, does not endlessly pursue comfort and luxury. The consumption of the capitalist is always bounded or kept within limits. The capitalist thus begins to save his income as soon as the latter becomes more than is adequate to support his predetermined standard of living, forming funds for accumulation. It has already been noted that from the point of view of capital, the individual consumption of the capitalist is a necessary evil, which constrains the conversion of surplus value into capital. Capital is the form of value augmentation, which automatically seeks to expand its scope. The fact that the operation of capital has to be mediated by the person of the capitalist does not alter this fundamental principle. The so-called abstinence theory of saving merely takes what is apparent for what is real. It is not the capitalist virtue of abstinence and frugality that entails the accumulation of capital; it is the nature of capital itself that enforces the ceaseless expansion of the scope of value augmentation, and that asserts itself in the 'Protestant ethic' of the capitalist. In other societies, in which the production-process is not governed by capital, surplus products are often dissipated through ostentatious consumption, not because the ruling class is less virtuous, but because it does not personify the motion of capital.

When accumulation-funds reach a magnitude suitable for investment, that is, for the purchase of additional productive elements, surplus value is convertible into capital. The ratio of accumulation funds to surplus value, from which they are generated, will be called *the rate of accumulation*; it is sometimes also known as the capitalists' *propensity to save*. For an individual capitalist, it takes a while before his accumulation-funds reach a magnitude suitable for additional capital formation. But for the aggregate-social capital, even the smallest saving of the capitalist class may be considered adequate for some investment, in view of the mechanism here as yet held implicit of collecting capitalist-social savings and channelling them to the appropriate spheres of investment (see Chapter 9). At the present level of abstraction, in other words, the propensity to save of the capitalist class may be identified with its propensity to invest. Thus, whenever S^* is more than adequate to maintain an exogenously given level of consumption of the capitalist class, an accumulation of capital becomes possible.

(β) Even if its possibility exists, the accumulation of capital cannot become real unless additional capital, variable and constant, in the form of money finds necessary elements of production in the market. There is, however, no inherent difficulty in the investment of additional constant capital in the means of production, which the aggregate-social capital can directly produce and supply to the market. The fact that the capitalist class has saved accumulation-funds implies that it does not demand consumption goods to the full extent of its income, but demands some additional means of production for accumulation as well. The price mechanism, implicitly assumed here, will see to it that these means of production will be produced, since there is no fundamental impediment to capital in the production of one use-value instead of another within its capacity. The conversion of surplus value into constant capital, in other words, means only a change in the use-value structure of S^*, which the existing capital produces in any case.

This flexibility is absent in the conversion of surplus value into variable capital because capital cannot directly produce labour-power, even though it can always produce wage-goods in place of capitalists' consumption-goods. The accumulation of capital cannot become real unless additional labour-power is somehow made available to capital. It is important to bear in mind this fundamental restriction as a matter of principle, although there are special circumstances that permit the accumulation of capital in reality. For example, an extension of the working day or an intensification of labour may, in some cases, be sufficient to set additional means of production to work.

Apart from these special circumstances, which cannot always be depended upon, there is an important factor that causes an actual accumulation of capital, even under a full employment of the existing stock of labour-power. That is the *natural growth of the labouring population*. If the wage-rate is adequate to reproduce the labour-power of a productive worker, it must also be adequate to reproduce the normal conditions of his family life. Indeed, if capital paid wages that were sufficient only to support single workers, the working population could not be maintained beyond one generation, and capitalism would not survive when the present workers ended their active life. It is therefore necessary that the wage-rate paid to a productive worker should be enough to support his family life, in which not only his individual labour-power is reproduced, but also his children are raised and educated. Only in that case can the supply of new labour-power be made available, when part of the existing labour-power regularly disappears with the retirement of aged productive workers. Although that is the case, the wage-bill that maintains the existing stock of labour-power also allows for some natural growth of the working population because some population increase is part of normal family life.

If capitalist reproduction rigidly maintained a stationary scale, and were unable to absorb the incremental growth of the working population, capitalism would fail to organise a whole society under its own principle. The aggregate-social capital, however, is always ready to accumulate as long as additional labour-power can be found. Even empirically, it has been observed that rapid population growth under a genuine capitalism often leads to accelerated economic growth. The theoretical view, in the present context, is that the conversion of surplus value into capital becomes a necessity to the extent that the natural growth of the working population permits it.

(γ) Given the level of productivity, such that not all of S* need be consumed by the capitalists, the formal possibility of accumulation on the part of capital necessarily develops into an actual accumulation, in correspondence with the natural growth of the working population. Thus, *out of surplus value springs capital*. This is due to the fact that the money that realises surplus value forms a *freely disposable fund*. In order to set capital into motion, it is necessary, first, to accumulate freely disposable universal money of a certain magnitude. Part of this money may be converted into capital if the remainder guarantees the capitalist's consumption over the turnover-time of that capital. For the moment, it does not matter how and where such freely disposable funds originally arose; once the capitalist mode of production is in progress, however, the only source of such funds convertible into capital is none other than monetised surplus value. Hence, additional capital must always arise from surplus value. An overwhelming proportion, if not all, of the existing capital was accumulated at some time in the past, and so could only have arisen from surplus value.

Suppose that originally the capital of $12,000 is advanced. If the value composition of capital is c/v = 3/1, the rate of surplus value is 100% and 4/5 of surplus value is always consumed, then, ignoring all other complicating factors such as the presence of fixed capital, changes in the turnover-time of capital and so on, the accumulation of capital will proceed as in Table 6.2 overleaf, provided that the necessary labour-power is available.

Thus, within 15 years, more than half of the existing capital will have arisen from surplus value. In 30 years, only less than one-fourth of the existing capital accounts for the original advance. Since its growth rate is 5%, the existing capital after 50 years is over 11 times, after 100 years over 131 times, and after 150 years more than 1,507 times the original advance. It is this fact that Marx described as 'the transition of the laws of property that characterise production of commodities into laws of capitalist appropriation'.[211] Marx further wrote as follows:

> At first the rights of property seemed to us to be based on a man's own labour. At least, some such assumption was necessary since only commodity-owners with equal rights confronted each other, and the sole

---

211   Marx 1967, *Capital,* Volume I, p. 579.

means by which a man could become possessed of the commodities of others, was by alienating his own commodities; and these could be replaced by labour alone. Now, however, property turns out to be the right on the part of the capitalist, to appropriate the unpaid labour of others or its product, and to be the impossibility, on the part of the labourer, of appropriating his own product. The separation of property from labour has become the necessary consequence of a law that apparently originated in their identity.[212]

TABLE 6.2

Year	Capital Value advanced	The value composition of the output	Surplus value	
			Accumulated	Consumed
1	12,000	$9,000c + 3,000v + 3,000s = 15,000$	600	2,400
2	12,600	$9,450c + 3,150v + 3,150s = 15,750$	630	2,520
3	13,230	$9,923c + 3,308v + 3,308s = 16,538$	662	2,646
4	13,892	$10,419c + 3,473v + 3,473s = 17,364$	695	2,778
5	14,586	$10,940c + 3,647v + 3,647s = 18,233$	729	2,917
6	15,315	$11,487c + 3,829v + 3,829s = 19,144$	766	3,063
7	16,081	$12,061c + 4,020v + 4,020s = 20,102$	804	3,216
8	16,885	$12,664c + 4,221v + 4,221s = 21,107$	844	3,377
9	17,730	$13,297c + 4,432v + 4,432s = 22,162$	877	3,546
10	18,616			

Indeed, the original possession of $12,000 turns into the instrument of appropriating not only $3,000 in the first year, but $3,000 $(1 + 0.05)^n$ over $n(\rightarrow \infty)$ years. The growth rate of 5%, however, applies to the value figures here, not to the quantity of use-values. Hence, if in the meantime there is technical progress (not reflected in a change in the value composition of capital), the accumulation of real wealth can be more than 5% per year. By the same token, the capitalist's consumption may also improve faster than this rate, permitting considerable luxury as years pass by, without sacrificing a steady accumulation of wealth. If technical progress enables the same value of capital to purchase more means of production, a more-than-5% increase in the working

---

212   Marx 1967, *Capital*, Volume I, p. 583–4.

population does not necessarily worsen the worker's standard of living, contrary to the assertion of the so-called wage-fund theory. The accumulation of real wealth is thus in no sense limited by the growth rate of the value of capital originally advanced.

At this stage, however, the accumulation of capital is still dependent upon a factor alien to the principle of capital, namely, the natural growth of the wage-earning population. There is no reason to expect then that the natural growth rate of the labouring population should always be equal to the *desired rate of accumulation* on the part of capital. If the two rates do not generally coincide, the actual process of capital accumulation must develop an adequate mechanism so as to adjust the availability of the labouring population to its own requirement. Prior to dealing with this important problem, however, the transformation, so far implicitly assumed, of the aggregate-social product, $\Sigma C'$, into the productive elements, ΣC, of the aggregate-social capital must be analysed in detail.

B   The Reproduction of Goods as Commodities by Capital – The Reproduction-Schemes (The Real Possibility of Capitalism)

(a)   The Material Aspect of Reproduction

(α) So far the reproduction-process of capital has been considered as a continual process of production by the aggregate-social capital that contains within itself the circulation of commodities. Now the same thing must be studied as the recurrent process of circulation of all commodities, produced by the aggregate-social capital, presupposing the continuity of society-wide production, that is to say, as the *circular flow* of the whole economy, or as its *Tableau économique*. Marx treats this aspect of the reproduction-process of capital with his celebrated *reproduction-schemes*. This ingenious device has been widely praised as one of the most remarkable contributions to economic theory and continues to attract the attention of both Marxists and non-Marxists alike. Precisely for that reason, however, the interpretation of the schemes has been varied and controversial, and often totally divorced from its proper context in the dialectic of capital. It is therefore all the more necessary here to give the theory of the reproduction-schemes its proper place in the system.

The first point to emphasise in this connection is that the schemes belong to the theory of the reproduction-process of capital within the doctrine of production. The second point to emphasise is that the theory of the reproduction-process of capital does not exclusively consist of the study of the schemes. Since the reproduction-schemes belong to the doctrine of production, prior to the development of the capitalist market, it is obvious that the schemes do not and cannot furnish an explicit theory of prices, or any theory of equilibrium or disequilibrium in the capitalist market. The schemes, in other words, must be studied in terms of values rather than prices. Moreover, the schemes examine the reproducibility of capitalist society from the point of view of the commodities, after the same problem has been examined from the point of view of the social relation. In other words, the reproduction of capitalist society is treated, first, in its social aspect, and, second, in its material aspect. Neither aspect, however, constitutes by itself the whole process of the reproduction of capitalist society, which will be treated as the *actual process of capital accumulation* in the concluding part of this chapter. The theory of the schemes thus aims at clarifying one important aspect, but not the entirety of the reproduction-process of capitalist society.

Three specific problems are dealt with within the scope of the theory of the schemes. They are as follows: (1) What properties does capitalist society have in common with any other society in the reproduction of goods? (2) How does capitalist society adequately transfer all of its goods from their producers to their direct or productive consumers with the mediation of money? (3) In what technical respect does the reproduction of goods fail to fully conform to the commodity-economic principles of capitalist society? I will investigate in this section the first of these problems.

Quesnay's *Tableau économique*, which originally inspired the reproduction-schemes, divides society into the classes of farmers, landowners and manufacturers, and establishes how land-services, agricultural products and manufactured goods annually flow from one class to another. Each class sells as much money value as it purchases. However, the *Tableau* involves only *accounting identities* and no *behaviour equations* capable of determining a specific equilibrium, either in prices or in outputs. The system of national accounts, which the Keynesian theory of income determination presupposes, is also a circular flow model of the same kind. Here the national economy is divided into the household, business, government and foreign sectors. Accounting identities represent the transfers of goods and services among these four sectors. Still, the national accounts system as such does not contain behaviour equations, which under the constraints of the accounting identities, determine an equilibrium level of income. A circular flow model, which divides the whole economy into several sectors, and which may also classify the circulating money-value into several categories, consists of accounting identities solely, exclusive of behaviour equations, which together with the identities may determine a general equilibrium. In this respect, Marx's reproduction-scheme is not an exception. It always involves the two classes of capitalists and productive workers; it classifies the commodities into the means of production and the articles of consumption. It contains two accounting identities and one inter-sectoral constraint. There is no behaviour equation capable of determining a point of equilibrium.

On the other hand, a circular flow model can always presuppose a state of equilibrium, without making explicit the exact manner in which it is attained. If, indeed, a circular flow model is employed to exhibit the reproduction of an economy, it cannot do otherwise, because to say that a disequilibrium state is annually reproduced forever implies the absence of a tendency for the economy to restore equilibrium. A circular flow model, while it does not specify the nature of such a tendency, does not expressly deny its presence either. In the reproduction-schemes of Marx, the presupposition of equilibrium is obvious from the fact that all variables are represented there in terms of values. The value of the commodity is not in general commensurate with the number of hours of labour actually performed, but to the number of hours of *socially necessary labour*. The socially necessary labour for the production of a commodity is that quantity of labour technically required to produce it in the socially necessary or desired quantity. In other words, socially necessary labour is labour that produces an equilibrium quantity of the commodity. Thus, even if society actually spends 3 hours of labour to produce one unit of a commodity, its value may be 2 hours of socially necessary labour if the commodity is overproduced, or 4 hours if it is under-produced. Since a reproduction-scheme represents commodities in value terms, it shows a hypothetical state in which they are produced in socially desired quantities. Hence, it is impossible for a reproduction-scheme to exhibit a 'disproportion', 'under-consumption', or any other state of disequilibrium.

The rationale for envisaging capitalist society as consisting of the capitalist class and the working class, exclusive of the class of landowners, is in keeping with the context of the doctrine of production, which establishes that the existential base of capitalist society depends not on the specification of landed property, but only on the purchase and sale of labour-power as a commodity. Landed property, which will be made explicit in the doctrine of distribution, may at the present stage be treated as part of capital. Since landowners – just as other unproductive associates of the capitalists – merely share in surplus value, the reproduction of the aggregate-social capital is no more constrained by their consumption than by the consumption of the capitalists themselves. Hence, for the demonstration of the reproducibility of capitalist society, the subdivision of the capitalist class into its specialised or derivative branches is not relevant.

The classification of commodities into means of production and articles of consumption is also fundamental from the point of view of the production-process. Here, *basic goods*, which are outputs as well as inputs of the production-process, must be functionally distinguished from *non-basic goods*, which are outputs but never inputs, of the production-process. (Wage-goods, or the articles of consumption of productive workers, are here treated as 'non-basic' because they are not direct inputs of the production-process of capital). A similar distinction was emphasised by Piero Sraffa.[213] It is hardly necessary to reiterate that this classification is fundamentally different from the industrial classification of commodities due to capitalist specialisation. Means of production (basic goods) and articles of consumption (non-basic goods) are here functionally distinguished in relation to the production-process. Hence, the same use-value (for example, coal) may serve both as a means of production and as an article of consumption. It is therefore quite incorrect to view the two-sectoral division of the reproduction-schemes as a first step towards the more elaborate disaggregation of industry, which becomes necessary only in the doctrine of distribution. Even when the economy is fully disaggregated, the distinction between basic and non-basic goods remains in the fact that the prices and values of basic goods do not depend on those of non-basic goods, while the prices and values of non-basic goods do depend on those of basic goods.

Marx's reproduction-scheme may now be formally introduced as follows:

$$
\left.
\begin{aligned}
U_x &\equiv C_x + V_x + S_x, \\
U_y &\equiv C_y + V_y + S_y, \\
C_y &\leq V_x + S_x,
\end{aligned}
\right\}
\tag{1}
$$

Here C, V and S are, respectively, the constant-capital component, the variable-capital component, and the surplus-value component, of the product-value, U. The subscripts, x and y, refer, respectively, to the means of production (X-goods) and the articles of consumption (Y-goods). All the magnitudes are expressed in value terms, either directly in the number of hours of labour or in some monetary units, proportional to the amount of embodied labour. The first two lines of the above system (1) are definitional (or accounting) identities, and the last line is the inter-sectoral constraint. Since $V_x + S_x \equiv U_x - C_x$, the inter-sectoral

---

213   See Sraffa 1961.

constraint may also be stated as $C_x + C_y \leq U_x$. That is to say, the value of the means of production annually consumed must not exceed the value of those annually produced. When this equality holds, the economy is said to be undergoing *simple reproduction*; otherwise it is undergoing *expanded reproduction*. Since, in general, surplus value is partly consumed and partly accumulated, one may write:

$$
\left.
\begin{aligned}
S_x &\equiv C_x' + V_x' + S_x', \\
S_y &\equiv C_y' + V_y' + S_y',
\end{aligned}
\right\}
\tag{2}
$$

Here the primes on C_x, C_y and V_x, V_y indicate the additional constant and variable capital, and the primes on S_x, S_y indicate the consumption of surplus value. In a simple reproduction, $S = S'$, and $C' = V' = 0$ for both x and y. If the notation $C'' = C + C'$, $V'' = V + V'$ is adopted for both x and y, the first two identities of (1) may be rearranged to:

$$
\left.
\begin{aligned}
U_x &\equiv C_x'' + C_y'', \\
U_y &\equiv V_x'' + V_y'' + S_x' + S_y',
\end{aligned}
\right\}
\tag{3}
$$

with the understanding that, in the case of a simple reproduction, all primes must be omitted.

If, for the moment, it is supposed that there is only one means of production (X) and only one article of consumption (Y) – as, for example, iron and corn – the first two lines of (1) may be restated as:

$$
\left.
\begin{aligned}
\lambda_x X_x + L_x &\equiv \lambda_x X, \\
\lambda_y X_y + L_y &\equiv \lambda_y Y,
\end{aligned}
\right\}
\tag{4}
$$

where λ_x and λ_y are the number of hours of labour embodied per unit of X and Y; X_x and X_y are the number of units of X productively consumed in the two sectors; L_x and L_y are the number of hours of labour currently employed in the two sectors. Since, however, X and Y are assumed to be in the socially desired quantities in the present context, λ_x and λ_y can be taken to be the values of X and Y, and may be restated as:

$$
\lambda_x \equiv L_x / (X - X_x), \quad \lambda_y \equiv (\lambda_x X_y + L_y) / Y
\tag{5}
$$

It is certainly not justified to conclude from this that the values are determined by technical conditions alone, regardless of social demand. If X and Y were not assumed to be in socially demanded quantities, λ_x and λ_y would not be values, but merely the labour actually spent per unit of X and Y for their production. The inter-sectoral constraint can now be written as:

$$\lambda_x X_y \leq L_x = \lambda_x (X - X_x), \quad \text{or} \quad X_x + X_y \leq X. \tag{6}$$

This weak inequality in (6) means that the quantity of iron productively consumed during the current year must not exceed the quantity of iron produced during the same year. This condition is stronger than what Sraffa calls the 'assumption of self-replacing state' with respect to basic goods only, which in the present notation must be written as $X - X_x > 0$. Sraffa's condition must, in any case, be satisfied for values to be positive. Yet (6) says more than that. It says that there must be a positive surplus of iron produced over iron used up not only in the basic-good sector, but also in the economy as a whole, for any accumulation of capital to be possible.

Since it makes good economic sense to say that some basic goods should be produced in greater quantities than are used up in the economy as a whole, in order for the scale of reproduction to be expanded, I propose to generalise the condition of reproduction to the case in which there are many (say, $m > 1$) means of production as follows:

$$
\begin{aligned}
x_1 &\geq x_{11} + x_{21} + \ldots + x_{nl}, \\
x_2 &\geq x_{12} + x_{22} + \ldots + x_{n2}, \\
&\vdots \\
x_m &\leq x_{1m} + x_{2m} + \ldots + x_{nm},
\end{aligned}
\tag{7}
$$

where x_j ($j = 1, \ldots, m$) is the quantity produced of the j-th means of production, and x_{ij} ($i = 1, \ldots\ldots, n; j = 1, \ldots\ldots, m; n > m$) is the quantity of the j-th means of production consumed in the i-th branch of production. It is, of course, assumed that there are n commodities, of which m are basic goods and $n - m$ are non-basic goods. When the equality holds for all lines of (7), a simple reproduction is said to occur; the possibility of an expanded reproduction requires that (7) contains at least one strong inequality. It is easy to see that (7) implies Marx's inter-sectoral constraint, $C_y \leq V_x + S_x$, when X is disaggregated into m means of production, $x_1, \ldots\ldots, x_m$.

(β) With the above characterisation, the reproduction-schemes are freed from their common misuses and attendant fallacies, which abound in the traditional Marxist writings. As Rosdolsky reports, the reproduction-schemes were used as a theoretical weapon in at least two major Marxist controversies.[214] The first controversy took place in Russia towards the end of the nineteenth-century between the Narodniks and their Marxist opponents. The issue was whether or not the nascent capitalism in Russia could successfully develop a home-market, without heavily depending on the external market. The second controversy followed Hilferding's criticism[215] of Tugan Baranowski's earlier work, which contained an analysis of the schemes in the Marxist tradition of the first controversy. This time the schemes were used either to bolster or dismiss the 'breakdown theory' of capitalism by the radical and the revisionist factions of the Austro-German Social Democratic Party. Rosa Luxemburg's 1913 work *The Accumulation of Capital* is probably the best known and most representative writing of the polemic, which tapered off only after Henryk Grossman's massive work of 1929, *Law of the Accumulation and Breakdown*. As if that were not enough, Moritarô Yamada established a new tradition in Japan in 1931 with his influential book on the reproduction-schemes, which propelled a direct application of the schematic technique to the analysis of the development of Japanese capitalism. This tradition is still alive in Japan, although it is not as triumphant as it once was. As Rosdolsky correctly mentions, many Marxist writers, particularly the Austro-Marxists, in refuting Rosa Luxemburg, erred by confusing the abstract theoretical context in which the reproduction-schemes are laid out, and the more immediate context in which the trend of a concrete-historical capitalist economy must be diagnosed. Between the two contexts one must indeed find many 'intermediary links'.[216]

It is, however, not this confusion alone that is responsible for the many incorrect applications of the reproduction-schemes. Rosdolsky himself does not appear to be firmly on the right track in the purely theoretical comprehension of the schemes, which constitute circular-flow models instead of equilibrium models. It is this confusion between the theory of circular flows and the theory of equilibrium that seems to me to constitute the real source of errors. By expressing all terms in value, and not in actual labour expended, the reproduction-schemes exclude the possibility of disequilibrium of any sort, as already mentioned. Hence, it is impossible to logically construct a theory of 'realisation crises' on the basis of the schemes. Since this point is important, the following illustration may be in order at the risk of some repetition.

Consider the following table, in which all numbers represent actual labour performed:

---

214   See Rosdolsky 1977, esp. Chapter 30.
215   See Hilferding 1955.
216   Rosdolsky 1977, p. 453.

$$I \quad 1680 = 840c + 420v + 420s,$$
$$II \quad 1800 = 900c + 450v + 450s. \qquad (8)$$
$$IIc = 900 > 840 = I(v + s)$$

This table is *not* a reproduction-scheme, because it does not satisfy the inter-sectoral constraint, $C_y \leq V_x + S_x$, or the condition of reproduction more commonly written as $IIc \leq I(v + s)$. Indeed, $IIc = 900 > 840 = I(v + s)$ in the present case, with the consequences that $I(v + s) + II (v + s) = 1740 < 1800 = U_y$, and $Ic + IIc = 1740 > 1680 = U_x$. It is, however, absolutely incorrect to infer from these consequences that in a capitalist economy the demand for articles of consumption is inevitably limited, and that the demand for the means of production is necessarily excessive. It is still worse to envisage an accumulation under these circumstances in order to demonstrate a quantitative magnification of the 'contradiction'. In fact, no contradiction of any sort exists in this table, which simply says that this year more means of production are used up than are produced $(X < X_x + X_y)$. Such a thing may be possible temporarily, if the economy possesses a large surplus of unused means of production stockpiled from previous years. However, unless the surplus stock is extraordinarily large, it is impossible for society's demand to continue unchanged. In a socialist economy, a decree would soon be issued so as to expand the first sector and to contract the second sector; in a capitalist economy, the prices of the means of production would rise and those of the articles of consumption would fall. In that case, one hour of labour actually spent to produce a means of production will be realised as more than one hour of socially necessary labour, and one hour of labour actually spent to produce an article of consumption will be realised as less than one hour of socially necessary labour.

A reproduction-scheme must always be stated in values, that is, in terms of socially necessary labour, and not in terms of actually spent labour. If the difference between the two kinds of labour is about 7% up in the first sector, and 7% down in the second sector, the scheme for this year turns out to be:

$$I \quad 1800 = 900c + 450v + 450s,$$
$$II \quad 1680 = 840c + 420v + 420s, \qquad (9)$$
$$IIc = 840 < 900 = I(v + s),$$

instead of (8). [Whenever a reproduction-scheme (1) is concretely illustrated with numbers, I shall, henceforth, write it in the same fashion as (9) above]. If, even in terms of value, the condition of reproduction is not fulfilled, it merely shows an abnormal and temporary state, in which the current stock of surplus means of production is still abundant. Yet such an abnormal state cannot last for long, even if a simple reproduction is repeated; an accumulation will restore the inter-sectoral condition sooner or later. The point of this illustration is to drive home the impossibility of inferring from the schemes either 'under-consumption' or a 'disproportion', which cannot be corrected by the equilibrating forces operating implicitly behind the schemes. If there is a fundamental disequilibrium, which cannot be corrected even with the working of the law of value, such a disequilibrium, which might cause periodic crises, must be identified outside the schemes. Indeed, in Part C of this chapter, a fundamental disequilibrium of that sort will be studied. That disequilibrium, however, does not arise between one capitalistically produced commodity and another, but rather arises between the capitalistically produced commodities and *labour-power which capital cannot directly produce*. The schemes, however, do not treat labour-power as a commodity explicitly; the schemes treat only wage-goods, and their relation with other capitalistically producible goods. Hence, the schemes cannot openly exhibit a fundamental disequilibrium, even when it exists.

This proposition in no way implies surrender to the Harmonist view of the capitalist mode of production, and to Say's law in particular, as Rosdolsky seems to fear. Say's law has to do with the capitalist market, which can be disrupted by the fundamental disequilibrium between labour-power and the capitalistically produced commodities, not with the reproduction-schemes, which deliberately hold labour-power implicit. Once again, it must be stressed that the theory of the reproduction-schemes does not shed light on the whole of the reproduction-process of capital; rather, the theory illuminates only one aspect of it. This aspect, which does not explicitly involve labour-power as a commodity, must of course be free from the *fundamental contradiction* of the capitalist mode of production. If, in this particular aspect, the reproduction-process of capital is free from the contradiction, it does not follow that the whole process – namely, the actual process of capital accumulation – is also free of it. Rosa Luxemburg and her Austro-Marxist critics were not only wrong in confusing the abstract and the concrete, as pointed out by Rosdolsky; they were also wrong in confusing the expressly one-sided theory of the reproduction-schemes, with its limited ambitions, and the more overarching theory of capital accumulation.

The real significance of the schemes, within the theory of the reproduction-process of capital as a whole, lies in the confirmation that capitalist society can in principle do what any other historical society does, insofar as the reproduction of goods (of use-values) is concerned. In order to exist as a historical society, capitalism too must reproduce basic goods and non-basic goods in an appropriate proportion. This *general economic norm* is common to all societies, and cannot be ignored even when all goods are produced as commodities. The division of the economy into the two major sectors – one producing basic goods, and the other non-basic goods – is therefore absolutely fundamental from the point of view of reproduction. Any other multi-sectoral division is meaningless for this purpose. Thus, even in the incredible 'corn-economy', which is supposed to produce only one good called 'corn', seed-corn (X) must be functionally distinguished from food-corn (Y) in order to study its reproducibility. If the productivity of growing corn is such that $1kg$ of seed-corn annually yields b kg of corn for all purposes, the 'inter-sectoral' condition of reproduction amounts to $(b-1)X \geq Y$. In other words, the corn-economy can never afford to eat more than the net output of seed-corn.

If an economy produces three goods, of which the first two are basic goods, the reproduction system such as:

$$\left.\begin{array}{l} \lambda_1 X_{11} + \lambda_2 X_{12} + L_1 \equiv \lambda_1 X_{1'} \\ \lambda_1 X_{21} + \lambda_2 X_{22} + L_2 \equiv \lambda_2 X_{2'} \\ \lambda_1 X_{31} + \lambda_2 X_{32} + L_3 \equiv \lambda_3 X_{3'} \end{array}\right\} \tag{10}$$

must still be dichotomised into the basic sector,

$$\begin{pmatrix} X_1 - X_{11} & -X_{12} \\ -X_{21} & X_2 - X_{22} \end{pmatrix} \begin{pmatrix} \lambda_1 \\ \lambda_2 \end{pmatrix} \equiv \begin{pmatrix} L_1 \\ L_2 \end{pmatrix} \tag{10-a}$$

and the non-basic sector, consisting of the last identity of (10). If the condition (7) applies to (10), that is to say, if:

$$X_1 \geq X_{11} + X_{21} + X_{31}, \quad X_2 \geq X_{12} + X_{22} + X_{32}, \tag{11}$$

then:

$$\lambda_1 X_{31} + \lambda_2 X_{32} \leq [\lambda_1(X_1 - X_{11}) - \lambda_2 X_{22}] + [\lambda_2(X_2 - X_{22}) - \lambda_1 X_{21}]$$
$$= L_1 + L_2, \tag{12}$$

which is the same as Marx's condition of reproduction IIc $\leq$ I($v + s$), or alternatively, the inter-sectoral constraint, $C_y \leq V_x + S_x$. Hence, regardless of the number of use-values that are produced in the economy, basic goods form a self-consistent system among themselves, and the relation between that system and the rest of the economy must satisfy Marx's condition of reproduction, or the inter-sectoral constraint, if the economy is to reproduce itself.

The purpose of a reproduction system, such as (10), is not to determine values, although (10-a) consistently solves for the values of basic goods and, on that basis, the values of non-basic goods too can be determined in (10) if all outputs are already in equilibrium quantities. A reproduction system must always confirm its reproducibility, that is, whether or not the implied technology is productive enough to satisfy the condition (7). If it is satisfied, Marx's inter-sectoral constraint is bound to be met as well. The theory of the reproduction-schemes therefore does not demonstrate whether a capitalist economy can or cannot maintain its equilibrium; the theory shows whether or not the capitalist economy would be technically viable if it always maintained its equilibrium. Since the demonstration of equilibrium is not the issue in the reproduction-schemes, neither is the behaviour of individual capitals. The two sectors of the economy must therefore not be supposed to compete with each other in the same way as two individual capitalists, or two groups of individual capitalists. The economy is not divided into the two sectors on account of capitalists' specialisation. In other words, it is quite wrong to take for granted at this level of abstraction that each of the two sectors is managed by a single capitalist or by a union of individual capitalists. The aggregate-social capital produces both basic goods and non-basic goods in its two different factories, as it were. Since capitalistically produced goods are always commodities, they are circulated or exchanged one for another within and between sectors. Yet that does not necessarily mean that the two sectors confront one another as two independent and competitive capitalists. It is impossible for capitalist society to have only two capitalists, or to have two competitive unions of capitalists. Many individual capitalists in atomistic competition produce all goods. It would involve an egregious fallacy of composition to regard each suprahistorically functional sector of production as if it were an independently competing capitalist. This point must be clearly borne in mind before the question of accumulation is introduced into the schemes.

(γ) In order for a reproduction-scheme to permit accumulation, the inter-sectoral constraint, IIc $\leq$ I(v + s), must satisfy the strong inequality. If surplus value (s) is divided into additional constant capital (c'), additional variable capital (v'), and consumption by capitalists (s'), so that s $\equiv$ c' + v' + s', and if c" $\equiv$ c + c' and v" $\equiv$ v + v', then the scheme must satisfy the equality, IIc" = I(v" + s'), in order to commence an accumulation. Consider the following scheme:

$$
\begin{array}{ll}
\text{I} & 6000 = 4000c + 1000v + 1000s, \\
\text{II} & 3000 = 1500c + 750v + 750s, \\
& \text{IIc} = 1500 < 2000 = \text{I}(v + s).
\end{array} \right\} \qquad (13)
$$

If, in each sector, half of surplus value is devoted to accumulation and divided according to the sectoral value composition of capital, then:

$$\text{I} \quad 1000s = 400c' + 100v' + 500s',$$
$$\text{II} \quad 750s = 250c' + 125v' + 375s',$$

so that the scheme will be rearranged to:

$$\text{I} \quad 6000 = 4400c'' + 1100v'' + 500s',$$
$$\text{II} \quad 3000 = 1750c'' + 875v'' + 375s',$$
$$\text{IIc}'' = 1750 \ne 1600 = \text{I}(v'' + s'). \tag{13'}$$

This statement shows that the accumulation is impossible. Indeed, (13′) is a contradictory rearrangement of (13), because according to (13), the socially desired quantity of the means of production has been produced with 6000 hours of labour, but according to (13′), society wants a quantity of the means of production that can only be produced with $6150 = 4400c'' + 1750c''$ hours of labour. Similarly, according to (13), society wants to allocate 3000 hours of labour to produce the articles of consumption, while according to (13′), only $2850 (= 1100v'' + 875v'' + 500s' + 375s')$ hours of labour need be allocated for the purpose.

It might therefore appear that the rate of accumulation, or the capitalists' propensity to save, cannot be as high as 50% of surplus value. In order to determine a feasible accumulation-rate, α, such as to satisfy the equality, $6000 = \text{Ic}'' + \text{IIc}''$, one may solve the simple equation $\alpha\,1000(4/5) + 4000 + \alpha\,750\,(2/3) + 1500 = 6000$, to find $\alpha = 0.3846$. If this rate is applied, (13′) can be changed to:

$$\text{I} \quad 6000 = 4307.69c'' + 1076.91v'' + 615.40s',$$
$$\text{II} \quad 3000 = 1692.31c'' + 846.15v'' + 461.54s',$$
$$\text{IIc}'' = 1692.31 = \text{I}(v'' + s'), \tag{13''}$$

which permits the intended accumulation. In the second year, assuming that the rate of surplus value ($e = 1$) is unchanged, the scheme becomes the following:

$$\text{I} \quad (+7.7\%)\ 6461.63 = 4307.69c + 1076.97v + 1076.97s,$$
$$\text{II} \quad (+12.8\%)\ 3384.61 = 1692.31c + 846.15v + 846.15s,$$
$$\alpha = 0.3238.$$

Proceeding in the same way, in the third year the scheme will be:

I   (+6.5%) 6880.07 = 4586.65c + 1146.71v + 1146.71s.
II (+10.8%) 3749.92 = 1874.96c + 937.48v + 937.48s,
    α = 0.2713,

and in the fourth year:

I   (+5.4%) 7253.40 = 4835.54c + 1208.93v + 1208.93s,
II (+9.0%) 4089.04 = 2044.52c + 1022.26v + 1022.26s,
    α = 0.2265.

However, it is quite obvious that the accumulation of capital does not actually proceed in this manner, that is, with a steadily decreasing α. Yet this is the only possible path of accumulation, so long as a common rate of accumulation in both sectors must be insisted upon.

Morishima, who believes that this condition is absolutely indispensable, offers what he calls 'the fundamental equations of the theory of reproduction', assuming a constant α.[217] Thus, the equations applied to the present example with α = 0.3846 will be:

$$U_x (t) = 6011.89 (1.0928)^t - 11.89 (9.29)^t,$$
$$U_y (t) = 2986.71 (1.0928)^t + 13.29 (9.29)^t,$$

approximately, where $U_x(t)$, $U_y(t)$ are the outputs in value, at time, t, of the means of production and of the articles of consumption. From these follow $U_x(1) = 6459$, $U_y(1) = 3387$, which are close enough to the value outputs of the second year as stated above. However, already in the third year, further accumulation will become impossible, for the system such as the following emerges and violates the inter-sectoral constraints, viz:

$$U_x (2) = 6163.72 = 4109.15c + 1027.29v + 1027.29s,$$
$$U_y (2) = 4707.27 = 2353.64c + 1176.82v + 1176.82,$$
$$IIc = 2353.64 > 2054.58 = I(v + s).$$

The process of expanded reproduction, as Marx explains from the initial state, (13), is quite different. He first assumes the rate of accumulation of the first sector as α_x = 0.5, and determines α_y from 0.5 × 1000(4/5) + 4000 + α_y750(2/3) + 1500 = 6000, as α_y = 0.2. This relation can also be written as $C'_x + C'_y = \alpha_x S_x [k_x/$

$(1 + k_x)] + \alpha_y S_y[k_y/(1 + k_y)]$, if k_x, k_y are the value compositions of capital and α_x, α_y are the rates of accumulation in the two sectors. Surplus value is accordingly divided as:

I $1000s = 400c' + 100v' + 500s'$,
II $750s = 100c' + 50v' + 600s'$,

so that the rearrangement of (13) is:

I $6000 = 4400c'' + 1100v'' + 500s'$,
II $3000 = 1600c'' + 800v'' + 600s'$,   (13''')
    $IIc'' = 1600 = I(v'' + s')$.

From the second year onward, assuming always that $\alpha_x = 0.5$, the scheme will expand as follows:

Second year

I $(+10\%) 6600 = 4400c + 1100v + 1100s$
II $(+6.7\%) 3200 = 1600c + 800v + 800s$,
    $\alpha_y = 0.3$.

Third year

I $(+10\%) 7260 = 4840c + 1210v + 1210s$,
II $(+10\%) 3520 = 1760c + 880v + 880s$,
    $\alpha_y = 0.3$.

Fourth year

I $(+10\%) 7986 = 5324c + 1331v + 1331s$,
II $(+10\%) 3872 = 1936c + 968v + 968s$,
    $\alpha_y = 0.3$,

and so on. Thus, the economy grows at the uniform rate of 10% after the second year, and the rates of accumulation are $\alpha_x = 0.5$ and $\alpha_y = 0.3$ in the two sectors.

At this point, let us confirm that if the value composition of capital in the two sectors, k_i ($i = x, y$), and the rate of surplus value, e, are assumed to be constant, there is then a unique relation between the rates of accumulation, α_i, and the growth rates of capital, g_i, for ($i = x, y$). Since $\alpha_i S_i = C'_x + C'_y$ ($i = x, y$)

divide both sides by C_i and write $C'_i / C_i = g_i$, $V_i = C'_i / k_i$ on the right-hand side, and $C_i = k_i V_i$ on the left-hand side. Then it will be clear that:

$$\alpha_i e = g_i(1 + k_i) \quad \text{or} \quad \alpha_i = g_i(1 + k_i)/e, \quad \text{for} \quad i = x, y.$$

Thus, given that $k_x = 4$, $k_y = 2$, $e = 1$ in the present example, $\alpha_x = 0.5$ and $\alpha_y = 0.3$ imply $g_x = g_y = 0.1$, while $\alpha_y = 0.2$ implies that $g_y = 0.067$. Thus, *it is only in the first year that the growth rate of the second sector differs from 10%*. This exception for the first year, however, does not depend on the specific numerical example of (13), as Morishima has demonstrated.[218] Indeed, IIc" = I(v" + s') requires that:

$$U_x(0) - C_x(0) - C_y(0) = C'_x(0) + C'_y(0)$$
$$\text{or} \quad U_x(0) = C_x(0)(1 + g_x) + C_y(0)(1 + g_y).$$

At this point, g_y is in general different from g_x. But in the second year the relation is:

$$U_x(1) = U_x(0)(1 + g_x) = C_x(1)(1 + g_x) + C_y(1)(1 + g_y).$$

Thus, it necessarily follows that $g_x = g_y$, since $C_i(1) = C_i(0) + C'_i(0)$ for $i = x, y$.

If the value composition of capital is the same in the two sectors, a permanent difference between α_x and α_y does not occur. For example, the following scheme:

$$
\left.
\begin{array}{ll}
\text{I} & 6000 = 4000c + 1000v + 1000s \\
\text{II} & 2250 = 1500 \quad + 375v + 375s \\
& \text{IIc} = 1500 < 2000 = \text{I}(v + s)
\end{array}
\right\}
\tag{14}
$$

may grow at the uniform rate of 10% after the second year, with $\alpha_x = \alpha_y = 0.5$, although in the first year alone, $\alpha_x = 0.5$, $\alpha_y = 0.33$, and the rate of growth of the second sector is 6.7%. However, it may be difficult to always assume a common value composition of capital for both sectors. Therefore, the question arises as to whether or not Marx's allegedly 'strange investment function' is 'unnatural' or 'conflicts with his reasoning on the formation of the equilibrium rate of profit'.[219] The answer to this question is that (a) the process of accumulation exhibited by the reproduction-schemes does not represent an investment function, and (b) this process does not conflict with the law of average profit. The second point can be demonstrated immediately. Let us begin with

218   Morishima 1973, pp. 120–2.
219   Morishima 1973, p. 122.

the scheme (13) and assume that $(\lambda_x, \lambda_y, e) = (1.2, 1, 1)$. The scheme can then be alternatively written as:

$$\lambda_x\, 3333.3 + 1000(1 + e) = \lambda_x\, 5000,$$
$$\lambda_x\, 1250 \quad + \quad 750(1 + e) = \lambda_y\, 3000.$$

However, in Chapter 7, it will be shown that the assumed values and the rate of surplus value correspond to equilibrium prices and the general rate of profit $(p_x, p_y, r) = (1.089, 0.9693, 0.22)$, given that the wage rate, w, is $= 1$. Hence, in terms of prices, the same scheme can be written as:

$$(p_x\, 3333.3 + 1000)(1 + r) = p_x\, 5000,$$
$$(p_x\, 1250 \quad + \quad 750)(1 + r) = p_y\, 3000,$$

or

I $6534 = 4356\hat{c} + 1000\hat{v} + 1178\hat{s},$

II $2908 = 1634\hat{c} + 75\hat{v} \quad + 524\hat{s},$

II$\hat{c} = 1634 < 2178 = I(\hat{v} + \hat{s}),$

where the 'circumflex' on the top refers to magnitudes evaluated in prices. If the first sector accumulates its capital by 10%, as Marx supposed, surplus value in prices must be divided up as:

$$1178\hat{s} = 436\hat{c}' + 100\hat{v}' + 642\hat{s}',$$
$$524\hat{s} = 109\hat{c}' + 50\hat{v}' + 365\hat{s}',$$

so that $\hat{a}_x = 0.455$, $\hat{a}_y = 0.304$ (approximately). The difference in the rates of accumulation is not as pronounced in price terms as in value terms, $(\alpha_x = 0.5, \alpha_y = 0.2)$.

The remaining difference in the capitalists' propensity to consume is neither 'unnatural' nor irrational. Suppose that there are 642 capitalists in the first sector and 365 capitalists in the second sector. Then, on average, a capitalist in the first sector invests, say, 8.35 million dollars and earns the income of 1.83 million dollars (the general rate of profit being 22%), of which he consumes 1 million dollars and accumulates 0.83 million dollars. A capitalist in the second sector, on average, invests 6.53 million dollars and earns a profit of 1.44 million dollars (at the same rate of profit of 22%); he also spends 1 million dollars on consumption and accumulates 0.44 million dollars. There is nothing strange in the fact that a larger capitalist can save more than a smaller capitalist. This is only a special case of the common sense knowledge that a poor family usually has a greater Engel coefficient. The social propensity to save is only an average of different propensities to save of individual persons, even in orthodox 'macroeconomics'; there is no single propensity to save that applies to every person, rich or poor, as soon as he is better off than a 'worker'. An average depends on the statistical population. Therefore, if in the sector of the economy producing articles of consumption, there are a greater number of smaller capitalists than in the sector producing means of production, the average propensity to save of the non-basic sector should be expected to be smaller than that of the basic sector. The fact that the value composition of capital is higher in the basic sector than in the non-basic sector suggests that an average firm in the basic sector has a greater concentration of capital than in the other sector.

Although the permanent difference between α_x and α_y is thus not inconsistent with the behaviour of the capitalists composing each of the two sectors, it is not correct to view the process of accumulation exhibited in the scheme as an 'investment function'. The scheme does not explain why the basic sector chooses the rate of accumulation of $\alpha_x = 0.5$. There are many other alternatives that satisfy the condition, $IIc'' = I(v'' + s')$; some such alternatives are listed in Table 6.3 below. Any of these, and many others, will enable a capitalist economy, characterised by the initial state (13), to expand at a uniform growth-rate after the second year. An investment function worthy of the name

TABLE 6.3

C'_x	V'_x	S'_x	C'_y	V'_y	S'_y	α_x	α_y	g
500	125	375	0	0	750	0.625	0.375 (0)[a]	0.125 (0)[b]
480	120	400	20	10	720	0.6	0.36 (0.04)	0.12 (0.013)
440	110	450	60	30	660	0.55	0.33 (0.12)	0.11 (0.04)
400	100	500	100	50	600	0.5	0.3 (0.2)	0.10 (0.067)
320	80	600	180	90	480	0.4	0.24 (0.36)	0.08 (0.12)
240	60	700	260	130	360	0.3	0.18 (0.52)	0.06 (0.173)
100	25	875	400	200	150	0.125	0.075 (0.8)	0.025 (0.267)

a   The permanent rate of accumulation of the second sector observed after the second year is shown outside the parentheses. Inside them, the exceptional accumulation-rate in the first year is shown.

b   Outside the parentheses, the uniform rate of growth is shown, and inside them, the growth-rate of the second sector during the first year is shown.

must indicate which particular growth path is actually followed by the capitalist economy starting from (13). Yet that is precisely the information that the
reproduction-scheme does not offer. Marx merely used the path underlined
in the table as a possible illustration, presumably because of arithmetic convenience; he could have used any alternative example to demonstrate the fact
that every reproduction-scheme satisfying the inter-sectoral constraint can
reach a balanced growth path within one year, or that the balanced growth-
rate of the economy is set by the growth-rate of the basic sector, consistent
with the rate of accumulation of that sector. This is already a powerful enough
conclusion, which orthodox economics – with its flourish of growth theories –
has not yet grasped. However, even more is implied.

The above table also shows that the maximal rate of growth of the capitalist economy can be achieved if, and only if, all the available surplus of the
means of production is reinvested in the first year in the first sector. The reason is readily understandable. Consider again that iron (X) is the only basic
good. Then, the available surplus of iron, $X - X_x - X_y = \Delta X_0$, may be used, either
in the basic or in the non-basic sector. However, if all of ΔX_0 is reinvested in
the basic sector, the next year's ΔX, can be made the largest. On the other
hand, if only a small fraction of surplus iron is reinvested in the basic sector,
the next year's ΔX, may be much less than this year's ΔX_0. In the second year
and onward, ΔX_{t+1} is always the balanced growth rate times ΔX_t (t = 1, 2, …), if
the same α_x is maintained. Hence, only in the first year is the choice of a balanced growth rate possible. The decision to expand the non-basic sector very
modestly in the first year will have a satisfactory payoff from the second year
onward.

However, this does not endorse the doctrine that calls for a permanent priority of the basic sector, because in some cases the scheme itself does not permit the reinvestment of the entire ΔX_0 in the basic sector. For example, let the
first sector of (13) grow at its maximum rate of 12.5% with α_x = 0.625 and α_y = 0.
Then in the following year, the scheme will be:

I   (+12.5 %) 6750 = 4500c + 1125v + 1125s,
II   (0%) 3000   = 1500c + 750v + 750s.

If, instead of maintaining α_x = 0.625, all the surplus means of production are
again reinvested in the first sector, the latter will grow at the rate of 16.7%, with
α_x = 0.883 and α_y = 0 to:

I   (+16.7%) 7875 = 5250c + 1312.5v + 1312.5s,
II   (0 %) 3000   = 1500c + 750v   + 750s.

The present scheme, however, can no longer be expanded in the first sector only. For let $\alpha_y = 0$ in:

$$\alpha_x \, 1312.5 \, (4/5) + 5250 + \alpha_y \, 750 \, (2/3) + 1500 = 7875.$$

Then, it follows that $\alpha_x = 1.07$, but that is obviously impossible. The maximum priority that can be given to the first sector implies $\alpha_x = 1$ and $\alpha_y = 0.15$. The scheme in the following year will accordingly be:

I   (+20%) 9450 = 6300c + 1575 + 1575s,
II (+5%) 3150   = 1575c + 787.5v + 787.5s.

If, again, $\alpha_x = 1$ is assumed, $\alpha_y = 0.6$ follows. Consequently, the scheme expands over the year to the following:

I   (+20%) 11340 = 7560c + 1890v + 1890s,
II (+20%) 3780 = 1890c + 945v + 945s.

In a socialist country, in which labour-power is abundant, it may not be impossible to opt for a growth rate consistent with $\alpha_x = 1$. Yet once $\alpha_x = 1$ is adopted, it becomes necessary to expand the scale of the non-basic sector as well, with α_y that is consistent with the balanced rate of growth. Failure to observe this rule can only lead to inefficiency in socialist planning. Perhaps this point was sometimes overlooked in early experiments with socialism. Since the reproduction of goods has been studied in its general aspect, which is common to all societies, it is time now to examine the same thing in its specifically capitalist aspect. Capitalist society reproduces goods as commodities; commodities cannot be consumed either directly or productively before they are exchanged. The exchange of commodities for other commodities requires the mediation of money. That is to say, the circular flow of goods in a capitalist economy implies a counter flow of money as the means of circulation. Hence, the reproduction of goods in capitalist society must presuppose the existence and the provision of an adequate quantity of the medium of circulation. This problem will be considered in the following section.

(b)   The Circulation of Money in the Reproduction-schemes

(α) The circulation of commodities in the context of the reproduction-scheme is customarily divided into three processes: (i) the internal circulation of the means of production within their own sector, that is, the circulation of C_x;

(ii) the internal circulation of the articles of consumption within their own sector, that is, the circulation of $V_y + S_y$; and (iii) the inter-sectoral circulation of commodities, involving an exchange of $V_x + S_x$ and C_y. Let us first consider the case of a simple reproduction. For definiteness it will be assumed that all goods are produced and circulated within one year, and in particular it will be assumed that all goods emerge as finished goods on the last day of September from the production-process, which begins on the first day of January, and are completely circulated by the year-end. It is also assumed that wages are wholly paid at the end of September, and that both the workers and the capitalists live on the articles of consumption, purchased during the last quarter of the year, until the end of September in the following year.

These drastic assumptions involve a great deal of artificiality. For example, the aggregate-social capital is supposed to turn over exactly once a year, of which the first three quarters constitute the production-period, and the last quarter alone constitutes the circulation-period. Not only is the presence of any fixed capital assumed away, but inevitable differences in the turnover-time and structure of the individual components of the aggregate-social capital are also ignored. The production-process is supposed to be interrupted during the last quarter, in which the aggregate-social capital does nothing but circulate commodities, although such a thing can never in fact happen. The payment of wages, which normally occurs a great number of times throughout the year, is also represented by a once-a-year instalment. Regrettable as they are, these unrealistic assumptions must be tolerated in order to focus attention on the special nature of the problem at hand.

In the case of a simple reproduction, every act of selling commodities is followed by the act of purchasing an equal amount of money value, during the circulation-period. Hence, the means of circulation, paid out from any part of the system, always *return to the point of origin* in the same period. By means of this principle of monetary restitution, the distribution of the means of circulation, before and after the quarter-long circulation-period, is unchanged. In the following discussion, no special monetary units are introduced, with the understanding that the words 'value' and 'money value' are interchangeably used. For definiteness, the following scheme will be referred to for illustration:

$$\text{I} \quad 4500 = 3000c + 750v + 750s,$$
$$\text{II} \quad 3000 = 1500c + 750v + 750s,$$
$$\text{IIc} = 1500 = \text{I}(v + s).$$

(*i*) The circulation of C_x
The quantity of the means of circulation required for the realisation of this part of the output of capital-goods is $M_1 = k_1 C_x$, where k_1 is the reciprocal of the

velocity of circulation of M_r. [Note that in this and the following Sections (b) and (c), k does not stand for the value composition of capital, k]. Since C_x = 3000, it follows that M_I = 600, if k_I = 0.2. It does not matter which capitalists of this sector first pay out this amount of money; the latter always returns to whoever pays it by the end of the circulation-period. Marx divides the capitalists of this sector into those belonging to group-A, who first spend M_I = 600, and those belonging to group-B, who need not do so. The capitalists of group-A must then purchase some new means of production before selling their own products. If credit institutions are left out of consideration, the question naturally arises as to which capitalists initially possess M_I = 600, which they can 'advance' for the circulation of C_x = 3000.

In order to understand this problem, it should be recalled that all capitalists must hold the total value of their capital, advanced in the three forms of money-capital, commodity-capital and productive capital, at every moment of time, and hence that no capitalist is ever without some money-capital. Since it is assumed, in the present illustration, that the production-period (from January to September) is artificially separated from the circulation-period (from October to December), one must pretend that no commodity-capital exists in the first three quarters of the year, and no productive capital functions in the last quarter of the year. One must also pretend that money-capital lies idle during the entire production-period, but is activated in the subsequent circulation-period. This means that it is all the more necessary that every capitalist must hold his entire money-capital at the opening of the market in October. Therefore, the capitalists of group-A are not particular capitalists, whose behaviour differs from those of group-B, but are instead personifications of that part of total capital held in the form of money in this sector.

Money-capital, however, is destined to be spent on productive elements, as soon as possible, in order to shorten the turnover-time of capital (and in the present case, by the year-end at any rate). Capital, being a value-augmenting motion, cannot hold idle money unless technically obliged to do so. Moreover, C_x is assumed to possess just the kind of use-value that is most desirable for the value augmentation of whoever possesses a portion of M_I as money-capital. Consequently, the presence of M_{II} as part of the aggregate money-capital of this sector, is sufficient for the circulation of C_x. This M_{II}, of course, returns to where it originally started once the circulation of C_x is accomplished, restoring this part of the aggregate of money-capital. [In the present case, because of the artificial suspension of circulation during the production-period, this money-capital must lie idle until the market reopens again in the following year].

(ii) The circulation of $V_y + S_y$

The quantity of the means of circulation necessary to realise this part of the output of consumption-goods is $M_2 = M_2{}^v + M_2{}^s = k_2{}^v V_y + k_2{}^s S_y$, where $k_2{}^v$ and $k_2{}^s$ are the reciprocals of the velocity of circulation of the $M_2{}^v$-component, and the $M_2{}^s$-component, respectively, of M_2. Wage-goods worth $V_y = 750$ are produced and consumed in the second sector, and the money needed for their transaction is $M_2{}^s = k_2{}^v 750$. Yet all workers who have produced V_y, must be paid on the last day of September, their labour-power having already been consumed. The payment of $V_y = 750$ cannot occur on any other date, since no capitalist can wait until his share of the output, V_y, is sold for wages paid out earlier by other capitalists of the same sector. Hence, because $k_2{}^v = 1$ is necessary, the consequence is that $M_2 = 750$. This is due to the present assumption of the simultaneous, once-a-year payment of the entire wages-bill. Normally, wages are paid many times throughout the year and not necessarily on the same date by all firms, so that $k_2{}^v = 1$ may appear to contradict reality. Yet in any case, $M_2{}^v$ must already be in the hands of the capitalists on the day of wage-payment as 'variable capital in the form of money', or as a wage-fund. This amount of money, paid out as wages, circulates the V_y-portion of the output of consumption-goods during the last quarter of the year, and returns to where it originated by the year-end, restoring the wage-fund of this sector.

The quantity, $M_2{}^s$, of money, necessary to circulate capitalists' consumption-goods, $S = 750$, springs not from money-capital, but from the consumption-fund of the capitalists of this sector. Since the turnover-time of capital is one year, all capitalists must possess enough money to purchase their annual basket of consumption-goods, quite apart from the capital value in the form of money. The capitalists of this sector, however, need not possess the whole value of $S = 750$ in the form of money, but only a fraction of that value spendable immediately on the first day of October. If $M_2{}^s = 225$ is spent initially, it may circulate $1/k_2{}^s = 1/0.3$ times during the last quarter of the year to realise the whole of $S = 750$. It is again possible to adopt the explanatory device of Marx, and divide the capitalists of this sector into those belonging to group-A and those belonging to group-B, claiming that only the A-group capitalists originally spend $M_2{}^s$. This theoretical device, however, must not be taken to mean that some capitalists may circulate their capital without prior possession of an adequate consumption-fund. The capitalists of group-A merely represent the property of every capitalist as the possessor of a consumption-fund.

(iii) The exchange of C_y for $V_x + S_x$

The quantity of money necessary to circulate $C_y = 1500$, $V_x = 750$, and $S_x = 750$ will be denoted by $M_3{}^c + M_3{}^v + M_3{}^s = M_3$. First, $M_3{}^v = 750$ must be entirely spent by the capitalists of the first sector, on 30 September, out of their wage-funds. However, this money will be spent by the workers on wage-goods (to buy half of C_y in this case), enabling the capitalists of the second sector to purchase the means of production corresponding to V_x. Hence, $M_3{}^v = 750$ returns to the capitalists of the first sector after purchasing commodities worth $(1/2)C_y - V_x = 2V_x$. This means that $M_3 = k_3{}^v(2\,V_x) = 750$ circulates commodities worth $2V_x = 1500$, so that $k_3{}^v = 0.5$.

There remains the exchange of $S_x = 750$ for $C_y - V_x = 750$. For this transaction, there are two sources of money: $M_3{}^c$ and $M_3{}^s$, and they are spent in some appropriate combination. For example, it may be supposed that the capitalists of the second sector spend $M_3{}^c = 100$ and use the same money twice to buy means of production worth $0.267(C_y - V_x) = 200$. This implies that the capitalists of the first sector return the same $M_3{}^c = 100$ twice to buy consumption-goods worth $0.267S_x = 200$. Hence, $M_3{}^c = 100$, spent by the capitalists of the second sector, returns to the point of origin, after having mediated the sale of commodities worth $0.267(C_y - V_x + S_x) = 400$, meaning that $k_3{}^c = 0.25$. There remains the exchange of $0.733(C_y - V_x) = 550$ for $0.733S_x = 550$. For this transaction, let us suppose that the capitalists of the first sector spend $M_3{}^s = 137.5$ out of their consumption funds, and use the same four times to buy consumption goods worth $0.733S_x = 550$. Then, this also means that the capitalists of the second sector return the same $M_3{}^s = 137.5$ four times to buy means of production worth $0.733(C_y - V_x) = 550$. Hence, $M_3{}^s = 137.5$ mediates the sale of commodities worth the total of $0.733(C_y - V_x + S_x) = 1100$, and $k_3{}^s = 0.125$. Chart 6.1 below illustrates the flow of money just explained. Here it is assumed that the proportion $0.733 = \theta_I$ of the transaction, $C_y - V_x + S_x = 1500$, is effected by money that originates in the first sector, and the proportion, $0.267 = \theta_{II} = (1 - \theta_I)$, is accomplished by money originating in the second sector. Of course, $0 < \theta_I, \theta_{II} < 1$ and $\theta_I + \theta_{II} = 1$. The case, $\theta_I = 1$, $\theta_{II} = 0$, is excluded because that would mean that the capital-

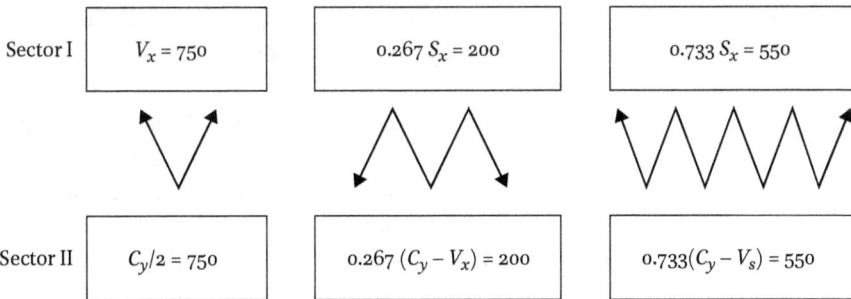

CHART 6.1

ists of the capital-goods sector need not prepare any consumption-fund when the circulation-period opens on the first day of October. The case, $\theta_I = 0$, $\theta_{II} = 1$, is likewise excluded because that would imply that the capitalists of the consumption-goods sector need not possess any money-capital for the purpose of purchasing the means of production.

From the above analysis, it follows that the capital-goods sector must hold money-capital of $M_I + M_3{}^v = 1350$, together with the consumption-fund of $M_3{}^s = 137.5$, and that the consumption-goods sector must hold money-capital of $M_2{}^v + M_3{}^s = 850$, together with the consumption-fund of $M_2{}^s = 225$, at the opening of the circulation-period on the first day of October. Altogether the means of circulation, $M_I + M_2 + M_3$, are enough to realise the entire value of the annual output of the aggregate-social capital. A simple reproduction of capitalist society requires the pre-existence of this much money in the system as means of circulation. For example, consider the following scheme:

	(1487.5)		(600 = M_I)		(750 = $M_3{}^v$)		(137.5 = $M_3{}^s$)
I	4500	=	3000c	+	750v	+	750s,
II	3000	=	1500c	+	750v	+	750s.
	(1075)		(100 = $M_3{}^c$)		(750 = $M_2{}^v$)		(225 = $M_2{}^s$)

For each term in money value, the quantity of money required for circulation is shown inside the parentheses, assuming that $k_1 = 0.2$, $k_2{}^v = 1$, $k_2{}^s = 0.3$, $k_3{}^c = 0.25$, $k_3{}^v = 0.5$, $k_3{}^s = 0.125$, $\theta_I = 0.733$, and $\theta_{II} = 0.263$. All in all, $M_I + M_2 + M_3 = 2562.5$ must be present for the circulation of $U_x + U_y = 7500$ in this case.

(β) In the present context, it must be supposed that only commodity-money, such as gold, is used as the means of circulation. Gold coins in actual circulation, however, tend to be abraded, lost or stolen, so that some annual depletion of the existing stock of the means of circulation cannot be avoided. In that case, even apart from changes in the non-monetary demand for gold, and apart from changes in the turnover-time and structure of capital that affect the proportion of active to idle money, a new production of gold sufficient to recover the depletion of the means of circulation must be envisaged. Monetary gold is produced in the capital-goods sector, together with industrial gold, but it cannot for that reason be treated as means of production proper.

Since monetary gold is neither directly nor productively consumed, it drops out, as it were, from the reproduction system, and is set aside from it. This is not the case with strictly non-monetary gold, which is demanded as a material for either means of production or as articles of consumption inside the system, although many gold-made luxury objects cannot be treated in the same way as, for example, a gold tooth, which is a genuine article of consumption. More on

THE REPRODUCTION-PROCESS OF CAPITAL (ACTUALITY)

this to follow. Because of the need to circulate commodities, the reproduction-process of capital must furnish monetary gold, which cannot be 'consumed' and therefore does not form a part of real economic life. From the point of view of real economic life therefore the production of monetary gold is unquestionably a burden, a cause of *faux frais* or unproductive costs to society. Yet precisely this production of a useless object constitutes the crucial step towards the conversion of a simple reproduction of capitalist society into its expanded reproduction.

Let us denote by m_x and m_y the annual abrasion of monetary gold in the capital-goods sector (or the X-sector), and the consumption-goods sector (or the Y-sector), respectively. The reproduction-process of capital must then produce $m = m_x + n_x = m_x + m_y$ as monetary gold. Accordingly, the reproduction-scheme becomes:

$$\left.\begin{aligned}
U_x &= C_x + V_x + S''_x + m_x + n_x, \\
U_y &= C_y + V_y + S'_y + m_y.
\end{aligned}\right\} \tag{15}$$

This involves two inter-sectoral exchanges:

$$C_y = V_x + S''_x, \quad n_x = m_y. \tag{16}$$

The surplus value, $S_x = S''_x + m$, of the X-sector now consists of means of production proper and monetary gold, m. The means of production must be exchanged for capitalists' consumption-goods contained in C_y as before, but only part of monetary gold, m, corresponding to n_x, can be exchanged for capitalists' consumption-goods consisting of m_y. This m_y is the part of the surplus value, S_y, of the Y-sector which the capitalists of that sector cannot consume, but instead must give up in exchange for monetary gold, n_x. Hence, the capitalists of the X-sector can consume $S'_x = S''_x + n_x$, but not $m_x = S_x - S'_x$; the capitalists of the Y-sector can likewise consume S'_y but not $m_y = n_x = S_y - S'_y$. The annual production, $m = m_x + n_x$, of monetary gold thus causes a deduction from the consumption of surplus value in both sectors. However, this means that:

$$C_y\,(\,= V_x + S''_x) < V_x + S_x, \tag{17}$$

namely, that the basic condition of an expanded reproduction is already fulfilled. If monetary gold is produced at all – even if only to restore the depleted portion of the existing means of circulation (and even if such a depletion occurs only in the X-sector so that $m_y = 0$, or only in the Y-sector so that $m_x = 0$) – the real process of reproduction cannot remain on a simple scale.

For example, let us suppose that the abrasion of monetary gold in the two sectors is $m_x = m_y = 10$. In order for both sectors to replenish their depleted stock of money-capital and consumption-fund, the first sector must produce $m = m_x + n_x = 20$, in addition to the means of production proper. For example, consider the following scheme:

I $4560 = 3040c + 760v + 760s$,
II $3000 = 1500c + 750v + 750s$,
     IIc $= 1500 < 1520 = I(v + s)$.

It indicates that the condition of simple reproduction is violated by the amount of 20 of the production of monetary gold. Of the surplus value (760s, of the first sector), 740 consists of the means of production proper and 20 consists of monetary gold. Half of this monetary gold, $n_x = 10$, together with the means of production proper, may be exchanged for consumption-goods, so that the consumption by the capitalists of the first sector is 750, out of a surplus value of 760. In the second sector, the capitalists must give up $m_y = 10$ in the surplus value of 750s in order to obtain monetary gold, $n_x = 10$, from the first sector, so that they consume 740 out of the surplus value of 750s again assuming that $k_1 = 0.2$, $k_2{}^v = 1$, $k_2{}^s = 0.3$, $k_2{}^c = 0.25$, $k_3{}^v = 0.5$, $k_3{}^s = 0.125$, and $\theta_I = 0.733$, $\theta_{II} = 0.267$, the total quantity of money needed is 2574.4 in order to circulate the commodity-value of 7540 as shown in the following tabulation:

	(1503.6)		(608)		(760)		(135.6)		(m)
I	4540	=	3040c	+	760v	+	740s″	+	20,
II	3000	=	1500c	+	750v	+	740s′	+	10,
	(1070.8)		(98.8)		(750)		(222)		(m_y)

The production of monetary gold by 20 units (m) is separated from that of the means of production proper in the first sector. However, the 10 value units of consumption-goods, corresponding to m_y, must be bought by the first sector in order to increase its consumption of surplus value from 740s″ to 750s′. Each sector then acquires 10 units of newly produced monetary gold to make up for the abrasion of old monetary gold.

The relation (17) implies that the surplus value actually produced, $S_x + S_y$, is already more than sufficient to maintain a tolerable standard of living for the capitalist class. Since $m_x + m_y$ need not be consumed, it can be devoted to the luxury of acquiring unconsumable money. To put it otherwise, unless the capitalist class can at least afford this much 'luxury', the reproduction-process of capital cannot subsist even on a simple scale, given the fact that circulating money tends to be abraded. This proposition suggests that as the productivity of labour rises so as to permit the capitalist class to save its income, the saving will in the first instance take the form of money accumulated outside the system of reproduction. Indeed, if capitalists do contemplate an accumulation of capital, the first step towards it is to hold $m_x + m_y$ in the form of money as accumulation-funds, thereby absorbing the corresponding value of the means of circulation. The ensuing shortage of the means of circulation in the system is felt in much the same way as the physical depletion or abrasion of the existing stock of money and stimulates the production of monetary gold.

It is true that the reproduction-scheme always exhibits an equilibrium situation, in which all goods, including gold, are produced just as much as they are socially needed or desired. However, this does not mean that disequilibrium can never occur; on the contrary, every commodity, including gold, is frequently either over-produced or under-produced by capital. The reproduction-scheme only takes it for granted that no disequilibrium situation permanently reproduces itself because the law of value, working behind the scenes, sees to it that any disequilibrium is eventually corrected. Gold too is produced as anarchically as any other commodity, and it can at any time be over-produced or under-produced. The application of the law of value to the capitalistic production of gold was already discussed in the previous chapter. It is only necessary here to recall that gold is a special commodity, the imputed market price of which fluctuates relatively little under normal circumstances because of considerable flexibility in the demand for it. If gold is over-produced, for whatever reason, the value of gold falls below the quantity of labour actually spent to produce it, and the value of other commodities rises above the quantity of labour so spent to produce them. Hence, in functioning as the measure of value, gold underestimates its own labour-content and overestimates the labour-content of other commodities. For example, suppose that a unit of gold and a unit of another commodity have been actually produced by 7.5 hours of labour. If gold has been over-produced to such an extent that the gold price of the other commodity turns out to be 2 instead of 1, this would mean that gold has measured the socially necessary labour per unit of the other commodity as 10 hours, and the socially necessary labour per unit of itself as 5 hours. To the production of the other commodity, a windfall gain will then accrue as a windfall loss will accrue to the production of gold. Hence, it becomes irrational for gold-producing capitalists to remain in this sector for long, rather than shifting their capital to the production of the other commodity.

When the supply of gold increases, however, the prices of other commodities do not in fact rise 'proportionally' or even 'almost proportionally', as the so-called quantity theory of money insists. This is because not all gold is used, either as means of circulation or even as money in general. The slightest fall in the value of gold can raise the social demand for gold itself, or that of its products, which are kept outside the system of reproduction. The capitalist propensity to 'hoard' gold and gold products is an important preparation for accumulation, since gold and gold products held outside of the reproduction system in effect constitute society's accumulation-funds. The formal distinction between monetary and non-monetary gold is often academic because in reality the former becomes the latter and vice versa, as easily as food-corn can be sown and seed-corn can be eaten. This flexibility of a commodity-money, such as gold, is the essential property of a purely capitalist society. Only when this flexibility is lost – say, with the introduction of inconvertible paper money – does the 'quantity theory phenomenon' arise (see Chapter 2). In an ideal capitalist system, the purchasing power of gold is far more stable than the price of other commodities; that is one of the important attributes of gold as money, particularly in its function as the measure of value.

The accumulation of gold (or any such monetary commodity) as mercantile wealth, outside the sphere of circulation, constitutes a pre-condition of the accumulation of capital. Therefore, 'the reproduction of the money material', which Marx treats in Section XII of *Capital*, Volume II, Chapter XX, forms a vital connection between the theory of a simple reproduction and the theory of an expanded reproduction. In this section, Marx abstracts from foreign trade and translates the flow of 'world money' in and out of the country in response to the changing balance of trade into the expansion and contraction of domestic gold production, in response to the changing demand for the money-commodity. This procedure of *dialectical internalisation* is indispensable to the theoretical exposition of a purely capitalist society as a closed system. The need for such a methodological translation, specifically in the case of gold, also underlines the special quality of the money-commodity, the production of which is sheltered from drastic price fluctuations, because of a large reservoir of gold stock lying outside of the reproduction system. When the reproduction system requires more money, the requisite amount of gold is immediately drawn from the reservoir; when the system possesses redundant money, the reservoir promptly absorbs the excess. Thus, the production of gold need respond, only in the long run, as the capacity of this reservoir changes.

The building of the gold reservoir means that capitalists are saving instead of consuming the whole of their income, which they appropriate as surplus value. Even if gold-producing capitalists do not save, others do so by 'sale without purchase' (in other words, selling, directly or indirectly, consumption-goods to the gold-producing sector, but retaining the gold thereby earned without buying other commodities), which corresponds with 'purchase without sale' (that is, purchasing consumption-goods with money not obtained by the sale of any ordinary commodity) of the gold-producing sector. The saving of surplus-value income by the capitalist class, in the form of accumulated gold or gold products (as accumulation-funds), foreshadows an expanded reproduction.

(γ) Thus, the first condition of the accumulation of capital, or the expansion of the scale of reproduction, is the formation of potential accumulation funds by the capitalist class outside of the reproduction system. Yet the fulfillment of this condition is merely a preparatory phase prior to actual accumulation. In order for accumulation to become actual, it is necessary that accumulation-funds should return to the reproduction system and be converted into productive elements. Hence, the second condition of capital accumulation is the availability, within the system, of additional labour-power and means of production. Only when the second condition is satisfied can the reproduction scheme be converted into:

$$\begin{cases} U_x = C_x + V_x + S_x & (S_x = C'_x + V'_x + S''_x + m'_x + n'_x), \\ \\ U_y = C_y + V_y + S_y & (S_y = C'_y + V'_y + S'_y + m'_y), \end{cases} \tag{18}$$

where C'_x and C'_y are the additional means of production, V'_x and V'_y the additional labour-power, and $m'_x + n'_x$, the extra supply of money. Here the extra supply of money is assumed to be currently produced, rather than withdrawn from the previously accumulated pool of gold. If (18) is rearranged to:

$$\begin{cases} U_x = (C_x + C'_x) + (V_x + V'_x) + S''_x + m'_x + n'_x \\ U_y = (C_y + C'_y) + (V_y + V'_y) + S'_y + m'_y, \\ C_y + C'_y = (V_x + V'_x) + S''_x, \quad m'_y = n'_x, \end{cases} \tag{19}$$

then the circulation of commodities can again be divided into the three operations: (i) the internal circulation, within the X-sector, of $(C_x + C'_x)$; (ii) the internal circulation, within the Y-sector, of $(V_y + V'_y) + S'_y$; and (iii) the intersectoral circulation involving the exchange of $(C_y + C'_y)$ for $(V_x + V'_x) + S''_x$ and the exchange of m'_y for n'_x. The abrasion of the circulating medium is entirely disregarded.

For illustration, let us consider the following scheme, which is the same as (13) above:

I $6000 = 4000c + 1000v + 1000s,$

II $3000 = 1500c + 750v + 750s,$ $\qquad\qquad$ (13)

$II_c = 1500c < 2000 = I(v + s).$

Now, I propose to truncate this scheme by removing from it $S_x - \bar{S}_x = 500$ and $S_y - \bar{S}_y = 0$. It does not matter how the truncation is effected, provided that a scheme of simple reproduction is obtained in consequence. The quantity of money necessary to circulate all the components of the truncated system can be calculated by the method already established. If, in the present case, $k_1 = 0.2$, $k_2{}^v = 1$, $k_2{}^s = 0.3$, $k_3{}^c = 0.25$, $k_3{}^v = 0.5$, $k_3{}^s = 0.125$, and $\theta_I = 0.733$ are assumed, it can be shown by the following:

(1891.6)		(800)		(1000)		(91.6)	
I 5500	$=$	4000c	$+$	1000v	$+$	$500\bar{s}$	
II 3000	$=$	1500c	$+$	750v	$+$	$750\bar{s}$	(20)
(1041.8)		(66.8)		(750)		(225)	

that the money needed for circulation of the commodities worth 8500 is 2933.4. This much money will be assumed to exist prior to accumulation. The question is how the remaining $S_x - \bar{S}_x = 500$ and $S_y - \bar{S}_y = 0$ should be circulated. Let us again consider the problem in three separate phases.

(i) The circulation of $C_x + C'_x$
The circulation of C_x has already been explained in the context of a simple reproduction. The X-sector offers the value, C_x, of the means of production to the market, while it possesses money-capital of $M_1 = k_1 C_x$, which provides enough means to circulate C_x entirely during the circulation-period. However, M_1 does not include the means of circulation necessary to realise the value, C'_x, of the additional means of production. Therefore, if an additional $m_1 = k_1 C'_x$ is needed, this can only come from m'_x. Those capitalists intending to accumulate next year must therefore spend m_1 out of m'_x in circulating C'_x, and so m_1 now becomes the money-capital of the X-sector together with M_1.

(ii) The circulation of $(V_y + V'_y) + S_y$
The circulation of $V_y + \bar{S}_y$ has already been considered in the context of simple reproduction. Hence, there remains only the circulation of $V'_y + (S'_y - \bar{S}_y)$ to be considered. It is immediately apparent that the circulation of V'_y requires $k_2{}^v V'_y$ from out of m'_y. The remainder can be written as:

$$S'_y - \bar{S}_y = S_y - (C'_y + V'_y + m'_y) - \bar{S}_y$$

suggesting that $k_2{}^s (S'_y - \bar{S}_y) = -k_2{}^s (C'_y + V'_y + m'_y + \bar{S}_y - S_y)$ must also be paid out of m'_y.

(iii) The exchange of $(C_y + C'_y)$ for $(V_x + V'_x) + S''_x$
Here $C_y = V_x + \bar{S}_x$ is already explained. Hence, there remains only the exchange of C'_y for $V'_x + S''_x - \bar{S}_x$. It is clear that $k_3{}^v V'_x$ should come from the first sector. The remaining exchange of $C'_y - V'_x$ for $S''_x - \bar{S}_x$ will be so arranged that commodities of the value, $\theta_I (S''_x - S_x) \times 2$, are circulated by money originating in m'_x, and commodities of the value of $\theta_{II} (S'_x - \bar{S}_x) \times 2$ are circulated by money originating in m'_y.

Now the above information can be put together in the following two equations:

$$m'_x = k_1 C'_x + k_3{}^v 2V'_x + k_3{}^s \theta_I 2(S''_x - \bar{S}_x),$$
$$n'_x = m'_y = k_3{}^c \theta_{II} 2(S''_x - \bar{S}_x) + k_2{}^v V'_y \qquad (21)$$
$$- k_2{}^s (C'_y + V'_y + m'_y + \bar{S}_y - S_y).$$

Since $C'_y = V'_x + (S''_x - \bar{S}_x)$ and $V'_x = 0.25C'_x$, $V'_y = 0.5C'_y$, the substitution of known numbers in these equations results in:

$$m'_x = 0.45C'_x + 0.18325(S''_x - 500).$$
$$(21')$$
$$m'_y = 0.141154(S''_x - 500) + 0.009615C'_x.$$

On the other hand, if $\alpha_x = 0.4$ is the rate of accumulation of the first sector, the following relations must hold:

$$S''_x + m'_y = (1 - \alpha_x) S_x = 600,$$
$$(22)$$
$$C'_x + V'_x + m'_x = \alpha_x S_x = 400.$$

In view of (21'), these can alternatively be written as:

$$1.141154 S''_x + 0.009615C'_x = 670.577,$$
$$(22')$$
$$0.18325 S''_x + 1.7C'_x = 491.625.$$

From this one can readily calculate that:

$$S''_x = 585.75, \quad C'_x = 226.05, \quad V'_x = 56.51, \quad m'_x = 117.43,$$
$$S'_y = 522.36, \quad C'_y = 142.24, \quad V'_y = 71.12, \quad m'_y = 14.28.$$

[To obtain the second line, recall that $C'_y = V'_x + S''_x - \overline{S}_x$ and $S'_y = S_y - (C'_y + V'_y + m'_y)$].

The present information clearly enables one to rearrange the original scheme (13) into the following:

(2009)	(845.2)	(1056.5)	(107.3)	(m'_x)	(n'_x)
I 6000 =	4226.1c″ +	1056.5v″ +	585.8s″ +	117.4 +	14.3,
II 3000 =	1642.2c″ +	821.1v″ +	522.4s′ +	14.3.	
(1056)	(78.2)	(821.1)	(156.7)	(m'_y)	

$$(23)$$

The quantities of money needed for the circulation of commodities are calculated with the same k's and θ's as in (20). In comparison, it can be readily confirmed that the quantity of money that the first sector requires for accumulation (2009) is greater than that which is present in the truncated system (20) of simple reproduction (1891.6) by $m'_x = 117.4$. Similarly, the quantity of money that the second sector requires for accumulation (1056) is greater than that which the truncated system (20) already possessed (1041.8) by $m'_y = 14.3$. The possibility of this rearrangement (23) demonstrates that the original scheme (13) actually contains the production of both m'_x and m'_y, which are necessary for the intended expansion of the scale of reproduction.

Accordingly, if in the following 'execution year' of accumulation, $e = 100\%$ is maintained, the scheme grows into:

$$\text{I} \quad 6339.1 = 4226.1c + 1056.5v + 1056.5s,$$
$$\text{II} \quad 3284.4 = 1642.2c + 821.1v + 821.1s, \qquad (24)$$
$$\text{IIc} = 1642.2 < 2113 = \text{I}(v + s).$$

This scheme can now be truncated at $\overline{S}_x = 585.8$ (= S''_x of the previous year) and $\overline{S}_y = 522.5$ (= S'_y of the previous year). The truncated system then already possesses its necessary means of circulation, 3065 (= 2009 + 1056). The additional money required for the circulation of $S_x - \overline{S}_x = 472.7$ and $S_y - \overline{S}_y = 298.7$ can now be calculated as before with the same k's and θ's. Specifically, (21) may be written as:

$$m'_x = 0.45C'_x + 0.18325(S''_x - 585.8),$$

$$m'_y = 0.0096154C'_x + 0.1423(S''_x - 585.8) + 68.9308.$$

(21'')

And, if again $\alpha_x = 0.4$ is assumed, (22) becomes:

$$0.00962C'_x + 1.1423S''_x = 648.3214,$$

$$1.70000C'_x + 0.1833S''_x = 529.9387.$$

(22'')

Hence, the following data can be calculated:

$$S''_x = 565.45, \quad C'_x = 250.76, \quad V'_x = 62.69, \quad m'_x = 109.12,$$
$$S'_y = 689.07, \quad C'_y = 42.39, \quad V'_y = 21.19, \quad m'_y = 68.45.$$

In this light, (24) can now be rearranged to:

$$
\begin{array}{llllll}
(2118.2) & (895.4) & (1119.2) & (103.6) & (m'_x) & (n'_x) \\
\text{I} \quad 6339.1 = & 4476.9c'' + & 1119.2v'' + & 565.5s'' + & 109.1 + & 68.4, \\
\text{II} \quad 3284.4 = & 1684.6c'' + & 842.3v'' + & 689.1s' + & 68.4. & \\
(1124.4) & (75.4) & (842.3) & (206.7) & (m'_y) &
\end{array}
$$

(24')

Again, in comparison with the truncated system, one can conclude as follows. The first sector of (24') possesses the means of circulation of 2118.2, which is greater than the 2009 possessed by the first sector of (23) by $m'_y = 109.1$, and the second sector of (24') possesses the means of circulation of 1124.4, which is greater than 1056 possessed by the second sector of (23) by $m'_y = 68.4$. Thus, in general, whenever an expanding reproduction-scheme requires additions to the means of circulation, they can always be produced within the scheme itself.

It has therefore been established that the reproduction-scheme is free not only from a real disequilibrium, but also from a monetary disequilibrium. That is to say, so long as the money-commodity is capitalistically producible, there cannot in principle be any shortage of the medium of circulation socially needed to circulate use-values as commodities. Although the production of non-monetary commodities must be sacrificed, to some extent, for the provision of unconsumable money, and although the rate of growth of the real economy is somewhat slowed down because of the need to expand the production of the monetary metal, the capitalist reproduction of goods in the form of commodities does not become 'contradictory' simply because money has to mediate

exchanges. However, there is an important reservation to this general statement, for the presence of fixed capital causes certain problems, which have yet
to be discussed.

(c)   The Replacement of Fixed Capital

(α) The presence of fixed capital complicates the total circulation of commodities in the reproduction-scheme. In the case of a simple reproduction,
however, the complications can be easily sorted out. Thus, the fundamental theory, described above, requires only minor modifications. The case of
an expanded reproduction is not so simple. A major problem arises there,
which cannot be satisfactorily settled within the confines of the theory of
reproduction-schemes. It thus becomes necessary that the actual process of
capitalist accumulation should be treated in a more concrete environment. Let
us begin with the less problematic case of a simple reproduction.

For definiteness, it will be assumed in the following that fixed capital is represented by a standard 'machine', which can be used for three years. The value of
this machine will be denoted by H, one-third of which, $h = \tfrac{1}{3} H$, is transferred to
the new product every year. This value, h, also constitutes the annual depreciation of the machine, which leaves no scrap value at the expiry of its life. For the
sake of simplicity, assume no price fluctuations over time, and consider, first,
a single firm, which invests in one 'machine' every year. Table 6.4 below shows
what happens to the firm in the first six years. On the left-hand side of each
column, representing a year, is the existing value of capital: H, in the first year;
($\tfrac{2}{3} H, H$) in the second year; and ($\tfrac{1}{3} H, \tfrac{2}{3} H, H$) from the third year onward. On
the right-hand side is indicated the addition to the depreciation-fund: $D_1 = h$,

TABLE 6.4

Year 1	Year 2	Year 3	Year 4	Year 5	Year 6
$H - h$	$\tfrac{2}{3}H - h$	$\tfrac{1}{3}H - h$			
	$H - h$	$\tfrac{2}{3}H - h$	$\tfrac{1}{3}H - h$		
		$H - h$	$\tfrac{2}{3}H - h$	$\tfrac{1}{3}H - h$	
			$H - h$	$\tfrac{2}{3}H - h$	$\tfrac{1}{3}H - h$
				$H - h$	$\tfrac{2}{3}H - h$
					$H - h$
$h = D_1$	$2h = D_2$	$3h = D_3$ $\;=\;$	$R_4 = D_4$ $\;=\;$	$R_5 = D_5$ $\;=\;$	$R_6 = D_6$

in the first year; $D_2 = 2h$ in the second; and $D_3 = 3h$ in the third year, and onwards. In the fourth year, the replacement, R, of the worn out machine begins. The total depreciation-fund, accumulated up to the third year, is $D_1 + D_2 + D_3 = 6h$; the replacement cost, $R_4 = H$, is equal only to $D_3 = 3h$. Hence, it appears as though the depreciation-fund of $D_1 + D_2 = 3h$ remains with the firm, serving no purpose. The formation of such a fund becomes quite large relative to the value, H, of the machine, if its durability, n, increases, because the magnitude of the fund will be $D^* = (n + 1)H/2$, under the present assumption of the straight-line method of depreciation.

In the case of a simple reproduction, D^*, at first sight, seems to serve no useful purpose. Indeed, it is formed only in the process of net investment or accumulation, that is to say, in the course of building the capital of ($\frac{1}{3} H$, $\frac{2}{3} H, H$) from scratch. The assumption of a social simple reproduction, however, requires that when this firm is making a net investment, another firm is making a corresponding disinvestment, letting ($\frac{1}{3} H, \frac{2}{3} H, H$) contract to ($\frac{1}{3} H, \frac{2}{3} H$) in the first year, and then to $\frac{1}{3} H$ in the second. The two firms taken together contribute $3h$ to D_1 (where h is depreciated by the first firm, and $2h$ by the second), which forms the fund to purchase a new machine, H, in the second year. The two firms together also make $D_2 = 3h$ (where $2h$ is depreciated by the first firm, and h by the second), which is used as the fund to purchase a new machine, H, in the third year. Table 6.5 below shows how the net investment of the first firm is really financed by the corresponding net disinvestment of the second firm, under the assumption of a simple reproduction, so that the newly defined D_1 and D_2 are really absorbed by the system as R_2 and R_3.

TABLE 6.5

Year 0	Year 1	Year 2	Year 3
First firm $H - h$		$\frac{2}{3}H - h$	$\frac{1}{3}H - h$
		$H - h$	$\frac{2}{3}H - h$
			$H - h$

$$D_0 \;=\; R_1 \quad D_1 \;=\; R_2 \quad D_2 \;=\; R_3 \quad D_3$$

$\frac{1}{3}H - h$			Second firm
$\frac{2}{3}H - h$	$\frac{1}{3}H - h$		
$H - h$	$\frac{2}{3}H - h$	$\frac{1}{3}H - h$	

The above analysis can be easily generalised and summarised by the following statement: under a simple reproduction, the net formation of depreciation-fund, D, in society at the end of the year, t, is always equal to the social requirement of funds for the replacement, R, of worn out equipment at the beginning of the year $t + 1$. This proposition might appear to have a very simple consequence for the reproduction-scheme, because if society as a whole maintains a stationary fixed capital structure, such as ($\frac{1}{3}H$, $\frac{2}{3}H$, H), only H has to be produced and circulated as if it were a circulating capital. The circulation of H should have no difficulty, as long as $3h = H$ is successfully monetised by the sale of the commodity produced by ($\frac{1}{3}H$, $\frac{2}{3}H,H$) and other productive elements. However, it is this monetisation of $3h$ that has to be investigated here from the point of view of the reproduction-scheme. Let us therefore examine the internal circulation of C_x within the capital-goods sector. Once this circulation is clarified, the inter-sectoral circulation, involving the exchange of $V_x + S_x$ for C_y, does not pose any new theoretical problem. Moreover, the internal circulation of $V_y + S_y$ in the consumption-goods sector need not be considered here, since it contains no circulation of fixed capital goods.

In the reproduction-scheme, C_x includes the value of the depreciation (H_x) of fixed capital, together with the value of circulating constant capital (Z_x) consumed in the production of the social output of capital goods, the value of which is U_x. If a certain number of standard 'machines', which last for three years, are used in the production of U_x, and if the aggregate value of all these machines annually produced is represented by H_x, then the fixed capital structure of this sector is ($\frac{1}{3}H_x$, $\frac{2}{3}H_x$, H_x). Since the annual depreciation, $3h_x$, is equal to the annual replacement, H_x, as the foregoing example suggests, it is clear that the value of fixed capital, H_x, may be treated in the same way as the value of circulating capital, Z_x in $C_x = H_x + Z_x$, both values being transferred to and preserved in the annual product of value, U_x, of the means of production. The following discussion will be considerably simplified, if it is assumed that fixed capital exists only in the first sector, namely, that $C_x = H_x + Z_x$ and $C_y = Z_y$. The reproduction-scheme can then be written as:

$$U_x = (H_x + Z_x) + V_x + S_x,$$
$$U_y = C_y + V_y + S_y.$$

(25)

Let us consider the following numerical example:

I $720 = (300h + 60z)c + 60v + 300s,$
II $1080 = \quad 360c \quad +120v + 600s,$ (25′)
with $H^* = 900$, $H_x/Z_x = 5$, $C_x/V_x = 6$, $C_y/V_y = 3$, $e = 5$,

where $H^* = 900$ refers to the value of the existing stock of fixed capital, and $H_x = 300h$ is the value of fixed capital currently reproduced. For the sake of simplicity, it may be assumed that one value unit represents one standard machine. In that case, the above implies that 900 machines are always applied to the production of capital goods, but that only 300 are annually worn out and reproduced.

Since the internal circulation of Z_x within the first sector has already been accounted for, let us only consider the circulation of H_x. In the H_x-sphere, it can be imagined that all capitalists produce just one machine each for this sphere. However, if all of them wear out one machine in the same year and must replace it, the problem appears at first sight insoluble. It is true that they all produce exactly one machine to replace one worn out machine with the same fixed capital structure of ($\frac{1}{3} H$, $\frac{2}{3} H$, H). However, since they are producing each machine 'as a commodity', it is impossible for them to circumvent the market by directly installing a machine of their own making in their own plant. It must be supposed, for example, that the capitalist who uses a red machine produces only a yellow machine, and the capitalist who produces a blue machine needs a green machine, and so on. Thus, in any case, they must each sell their machine-product for money in the first instance. The question, then, is: who is able to buy a machine before selling his own machine, and where does he obtain the means of circulation necessary for the purchase? Unless a H is sold first, the $3h$ embodied in it cannot be 'monetised', and hence it cannot generate the purchase fund for any machine.

It is, of course, not usually the case that all firms operate with an identical age-structure of fixed capital, producing individually what they want to use themselves. If such were generally the case, nothing would need to be produced as a commodity. Yet to suppose that only some capitalists, whom Marx in this case calls the 'Section-1' capitalists, are obliged to replace worn out machines this year, while others, whom Marx calls the 'Section-2' capitalists, need not do so,[220] does not solve the problem. For even in that case, the 'Section-1' capitalists must spend money to buy new machines before they have sold their own machine-product for money. Whether the capitalists in 'Section-1', equipped with the means necessary for the circulation of H, refer to specific capitalists or to a segment of every capitalist enterprise, the source of that means of circulation cannot be found in the sales proceeds of newly produced machines. It must be found in the historical past of building the present scale of fixed capital, that is to say, in $D^* = (n+1)H/2$, which has been left out of consideration up to this point.

---

220   Marx 1967, *Capital*, Volume II, p. 461.

If the present scale of simple reproduction presupposes the fixed capital structure of $(\frac{1}{3} H_x, \frac{2}{3} H_x, H_x)$, the latter could not have been built without money. Just as an individual capitalist, in the course of building the present capital of $(\frac{1}{3} H, \frac{2}{3} H, H)$ over three years, formed a depreciation-fund $D_1 + D_2 = 3h$ in the first two years, society as a whole should have done the same. Once D^*_x is thus formed, the part of it that corresponds to $M_1{}^h = k_1 H_x$ must be activated as the means of circulation every year in order to realise the value, H_x, of the annual output of new machines needed for the replacement of the worn out machines in this sector. Since $D^*_x > H_x$ for $n < 3$, it is expected that not all of D^*_x will be needed for the present purpose. It will be shown later how capitalist society makes use of such strictly idle funds as $D^*_x - M_1{}^h$ for productive purposes. In the meantime, if $M_1{}^h$ is first spent by some capitalists to buy a few machines, those who sold the machines can immediately buy an equal number of machines; the string of transactions will then be used to buy the machine output of those who originally spent $M_1{}^h$, circulating all of H_x in the process.

There is, however, no need for k_1 to be the same, whether with respect to Z_x or to H_x. Let us therefore assume that $M_1{}^h = k_1{}^h H_x$ circulates the newly produced machines, and $M_1{}^z = k_1{}^z Z_x (k_1{}^z \neq k_1{}^h)$ circulates the non-machine component of C_x. If $k_1{}^h = 0.25$, $k_1{}^z = 0.2$, $k_2{}^v = 0.2$, $k_3{}^v = 0.5$, $k_3{}^c = k_3{}^s = 0.25$ and $\theta_I = 0.5$, then the quantity of the means of circulation necessary for the scheme (25′) can be readily calculated as in (25″) below. If the circulation of fixed capital in the H_x sector is thus clarified, other circulations involving fixed capital can be similarly understood, at least insofar as the case of a simple reproduction is concerned.

	(222)		(75)		(12)		(60)		(75)	
I	720	=	(300h	+	60z)c	+	60v	+	300s,	(25″)
II	1080	=	360c	+	120v	+	600s.			
	(315)		(75)		(120)		(120)			

(β) In order to examine the circulation of fixed capital under an expanded reproduction, let us revert to the example of a single firm, which invests in the standard machine with a three-year durability. In this case, however, let us first imagine that the firm invests every year in a machine that is somewhat larger than the one purchased the year before, so that the value, H_t, of the machine obtained in year, t is always a little greater than the value, H_{t-1}, of the machine introduced in the previous year. Machines of all sizes, however, are assumed

Table 6.6

Year 1	Year 2	Year 3	Year 4	Year 5	Year 6
$H_1 - h_1$	$\tfrac{2}{3}H_1 - h_1$	$\tfrac{1}{3}H_1 - h_1$			
	$H_2 - h_2$	$\tfrac{2}{3}H_2 - h_2$	$\tfrac{1}{3}H_2 - h_2$		
		$H_3 - h_3$	$\tfrac{2}{3}H_3 - h_3$	$\tfrac{1}{3}H_3 - h_3$	
			$H_4 - h_4$	$\tfrac{2}{3}H_4 - h_4$	$\tfrac{1}{3}H_4 - h_4$
				$H_5 - h_5$	$\tfrac{2}{3}H_5 - h_5$
					$H_6 - h_6$
$\downarrow$	$\downarrow$	$\downarrow$	$\downarrow$	$\downarrow$	$\downarrow$
D_1	D_2	$(H_1)\,D_3$	$(H_2)\,D_4$	$(H_3)\,D_5$	$(H_4)\,D_6$

$$D_3 > R_2 = H_1 \quad D_4 > R_5 = H_2 \quad D_5 > R_6 = H_3 \quad D_6 > R_7 = H_4$$

to last for exactly three years. Let the firm depreciate them by the straight-line method, with no scrap value. Table 6.6 above shows what happens to this firm in the first six years. Here it is apparent that, at time t, the machine value invested three years ago must be replaced with an equal value, $R_t = H_{t-3}$, while the depreciation-funds formed in the previous year are greater than that, $R_t < D_{t-1}$, and the value of the machine currently produced is still greater, $D_{t-1} < H_t$, for any $t \geq 4$. In particular, if it is assumed that $H_t = H_0(1 + g)^t$, with a constant growth rate, g, the following relation must hold:

$$
\left.
\begin{aligned}
D_t &= \tfrac{1}{3} H_0 (1 + g)^{t-1} (3 + 3g + g^2) \\
R_{t+1} &= H_0 (1 + g)^{t-2}
\end{aligned}
\right\}
\tag{26}
$$

so that :　$R_{t+1}/D_t = 3g / [(1 + g)^3 - 1]$

and　　$\lim_{(g \to 0)} [R_{t+1}/D_t] = 1.$

This relation is the same as the formula derived by Domar for the general case, where the durability of fixed capital, here assumed to be 3, is replaced by n.[221] In the Table 6.6, the age-composition of fixed capital after the third year is always $(\tfrac{1}{3} H_{t-2}, \tfrac{2}{3} H_{t-1}, H_t)$ and $H_{t-2} < H_{t-1} < H_t$ so that the replacement value,

---

221　Domar 1957, p. 161.

$R_{t+1} = H_{t-2}$, is always smaller than the value of depreciation, $D_t = (H_{t-2} + H_{t-1} + H_t)/3$. Only under simple reproduction is H_{t-2} equal to $H_{t-1} = H_t = H$.

The age-composition of fixed capital can as well be expressed in terms of the larger or smaller number of the same machines, instead of the larger or smaller machine sizes. Let us therefore suppose that the replacement value of the standard machine is 1, and consider the age-composition of fixed capital in terms of the number of standard machines. These machines always transfer one-third of their original (replacement) value to the new product every year. The three cases are compared in Table 6.7 below.

In *Case I,* the total value of annual depreciation is 300, which is just enough to replace 300 two-year-old machines wearing out this year. Hence, $D_t = R_{t+1}$, and there is no deficit or surplus. Such a structure of capital as this one will be described as 'simple'. In *Case II,* the total value of annual depreciation is 350, which is not enough to buy 450 new machines to replace the same number of two-year-old machines wearing out this year. Hence, $D_t < R_{t+1}$, and there is a deficit of 100 machines (or value units). The structure of a capital such as this will be described as 'backward-weighted'. In *Case III,* the total value of annual depreciation is 350, which is more than enough to buy 300 machines, so as

TABLE 6.7

		Capital structure		*Depreciation*
Case I	(300)	two-year-old machines = R_{t+1}		100
$(R_{t+1} = D_t)$	300	one-year-old machines		100
	300	new machines	↓	100
	900		$\equiv$ $D_t =$	(300)
Case II	(450)	two-year-old machines = R_{t+1}		150
$(R_{t+1} > D_t)$	300	one-year-old machines		100
	300	new machines	↓	100
	1050		$>$ $D_t =$	(350)
Case III	(300)	two-year-old machines = R_{t+1}		100
$(R_{t+1} < D_t)$	300	one-year-old machines		100
	450	new machines	↓	150
	1050		$<$ $D_t =$	(350)

to replace the same number of two-year-old machines wearing out this year. Hence, $D_t > R_{t+i}$, and there is a surplus of 50 machines (or value units). The structure of capital that gives rise to a surplus, as in the present case, will be described as 'forward-weighted'.

It can be readily understood that a simple reproduction is consistent only with a 'simple' age-composition of fixed capital. It is also obvious that an expanded reproduction always presupposes a 'forward-weighted' age-structure of fixed capital, just as a contracting reproduction presupposes a 'backward-weighted' age-structure. The reason why the circulation of fixed capital goods poses no serious problem in the simple reproduction-scheme is that the age-structure (or composition) of fixed capital, in that case, is bound to be 'simple'. In the case of an expanded reproduction, the 'forward-weighted' age-structure of fixed capital causes intricate problems. To see this, let us consider the following scheme of expanded reproduction as of 31 September last year:

$$
\begin{array}{lll}
\text{I} & 855 = (300h + 60z)c + 90v + 405s, \\
\text{II} & 680 = 240c \qquad\quad + 80v + 360s, & (27) \\
& \text{IIc} = 240 < 495 = \text{I}(v + s),
\end{array}
$$

where $H^* = 900$, $H_x/Z_x = 5$, $C_x/V_x = 4$, $C_y/V_y = 3$, $e = 4.5$.

Let us truncate this scheme by removing $S_x - \overline{S}_x = 255$ and $S_y - \overline{S}_y = 0$, and assume the following:

$$
\begin{array}{llll}
k_1^{\,h} = 0.25, & k_2^{\,z} = 0.2, & k_2^{\,v} = 1, & k_2^{\,s} = 0.2, \\
k_3^{\,v} = 0.5, & k_3^{\,c} = 0.25, & k_3^{\,s} = 0.25, & \theta_I = 0.5.
\end{array}
$$

Then, the quantity of money necessary for the circulation of commodities in the truncated system can be calculated as below:

	(214.5)	(75)	(12)	(90)	(37.5)	
I	600	= (300h	+ 60z)c +	90v	+ 150s	(27')
II	680	= 240c	+	80v	+ 360s	
	(189.5)		(37.5)	(80)	(72)	

The presence of this much money (404.0 = 214.5 + 189.5) can be taken for granted.

Suppose that $S_x - \bar{S}_x = 255$ includes new machines of a value of 150. Then the stock of machines, $H^* = 900$, can be increased to $H^* = 1050$, if there is enough money to circulate these 150 new machines. I now assume that the above scheme (27) can be so rearranged that for this year the first sector will operate as:

I. $(+16.7\%)\ 997.5 = (350h + 70z)c + 105v + 472.5s.$

That will then require that the following conditions be met:

$$\alpha_x S_x = 3H'_x + Z'_x + V'_x + m'_x,$$

$$(1 - \alpha_x) S_x = S''_x + n'_x, \tag{28}$$

where:

$$m'_x = k_1^h\, 3H'_x + k_1^z Z'_x + k_3^y 2V'_x + k_3^s \theta_I 2(S''_x - \bar{S}_x),$$

$$n'_x = m'_y = k_3^c \theta_{II}\, 2(S''_x - \bar{S}_x) + k_2^y V'_y - k_2^s(C'_y + V'_y + m'_y + \bar{S}_y - S_y). \tag{29}$$

Since $Z'_x = 0.2H'_x$, $V'_x = 0.3H'_x$, $V'_y = 0.333C'_y$, $C'_y = V''_x + S'_x - \bar{S}_x$, and $\bar{S}_x = 150$, however, (29) can be numerically restated as:

$$m'_x = 1.09H'_x \quad\ + 0.25S''_x \quad\ - 37.5,$$
$$m'_y = 0.01667H'_x + 0.26387S''_x - 39.58.$$

Then, if, specifically, $H'_x = 50$ is assumed, these equations can be further simplified to:

$$m'_x = 0.25S''_x \quad\ + 17,$$

$$m'_y = 0.26387S''_x - 38.74667. \tag{29'}$$

Moreover, since $S_x = 405$, the assumption $H'_x = 50$ enables one to rewrite (28) as:

$$\alpha_x\, 405 = 175 + m'_x,$$
$$(1 - \alpha_x)\, 405 = S''_x + n'_x. \tag{28'}$$

Thus, when (29') is substituted into (28'), the following set of equations can be easily solved for both α_x and S''_x, which will determine all other related variables:

$$\alpha_x 405 \quad = 192 \quad\quad + 0.25S''_x,$$
$$(1-\alpha_x)405 = 1.26387S''_x - 38.74667.$$

Hence, it follows that:

$$\alpha_x = 0.5767, \quad S''_x = 166.29, \quad m'_x = 58.57, \quad m'_y = 5.13,$$
$$C'_y = 31.29, \quad V'_y = 10.43, \quad S'_y = 313.15.$$

In light of this information, one can now conclude that the rearrangement of (27) requires the following disposition of $S_x = 405$ and $S_y = 360$:

$$
\begin{array}{llllll}
& (37.5) & (2) & (15) & (4.07) & (m'_x)\ \ (n'_x) \\
\text{I} & 405s = 150\,(3h') + & 10z' & + \ 15v' & + \ 166.29s'' + & 58.57 + 5.13, \\
\text{II} & 360s = \ 31.29c' + & 10.43v' & + \ 313.15s' & + & 5.13. \\
& (4.07)^* & (10.43) & (-9.37)^{**} & (m'_y) &
\end{array}
$$

(30)

The system already possesses enough money to circulate $\bar{S}_x = 150$. Hence, for the circulation of $S''_x = 166.29$, only 16.29 value units require additional means of circulation. The same number of value units emerge when $V'_x = 15$ is subtracted from $C'_y = 31.29$. Since $\theta_I = 0.5$, $k_3{}^c = k_3{}^s = 0.25$, the amount of money required to circulate these 16.29×2 value units is $(4.07)^* \times 2$, originating equally from the two sectors. The system also possesses enough money to circulate $\bar{S}_y = 360$ by assumption. Hence, for the circulation of $S_y = 313.15$, the money that circulates 46.85 value units becomes redundant. With the assumption of $k_2{}^s = 0.2$, the redundant quantity of money is calculated as $(-9.37)^{**}$. Thus, (30) shows that (27) contains enough money to enable its rearrangement to:

$$
\begin{array}{llllll}
(248.1) & (87.5) & (14) & (105) & (41.6) & (m'_x)\ \ (n_x) \\
\text{I} \quad 755 \ = & (350h'' + 70\,z'')c'' + & 105v'' & + \ 166.29s'' + & 58.57 + 5.13, \\
\text{II} \quad 680 \ = & 271.29c'' + 90.43v'' & + \ 313.15s' + & 5.13, & \\
(194.66) & (41.6) & (90.43) & (62.63) & (m'_y) &
\end{array}
$$

(27'')

$$H^* = 900 + 150 = 1050$$

Since 150 newly produced machines are adequately circulated, society's stock of machines grows from $H^* = 900$ to $H^* = 1050$. Yet only 50 of the newly produced machines (H'_x) are to be depreciated this year, together with one-third of $H^* = 900$ ($H_x = 300$). It is for this reason that the output of the first sector in this rearrangement is smaller by 100 value units than that in (27). The 100 newly produced machines, the value of which will not be transferred to the product this year, are omitted from the first sector of (27″).

In view of the above rearrangement, the scheme grows this year to the following:

$$
\begin{array}{llllll}
 & & (87.5) & (14) & (105) & (41.6) \\
\text{I} & 997.5 & = (350h + 70z)c & + & 105v & + (166.29 + 306.21)\,\text{s}, \\
\text{II} & 768.7 & = 271.29c & + & 90.43v & + (313.15 + 93.79)\,\text{s}. \\
 & & (41.6) & & (90.43) & (62.63)
\end{array}
\qquad (31)
$$

One may now truncate this scheme by removing $S_x - \overline{S}_x = 306.21$ and $S_y - \overline{S}_y = 93.79$. Then, the truncated part already possesses enough money (248.1 in I and 194.66 in II) for the circulation of commodities. This time, however, for the sake of argument let us suppose that $S_x - \overline{S}_x = 306.21$ contains no new machines. In that case, the scheme (31) says that one-third of $H^* = 1050$ has transferred its value to the new product, so that $350(= H_x)$ new machines have been produced just to cover depreciation. However, this does not mean that 350 two-year old machines are currently worn out. In fact, 300 two-year old machines wear out this year. The 50 additional machines currently produced serve to cover the depreciation of the 150 machines, added to the stock of fixed capital, H^*, last year. They are still one-year old and need not be replaced. If these additional 50 machines are actually purchased by the capitalists of the first sector (and they can certainly do so with the money of 87.5 value units in their possession), then the stock of machines will increase this year again from $H^* = 1050$ to $H^* = 1100$ prior to any accumulation. No conversion of surplus value into fixed capital takes place this year, because $S_x - \overline{S}_x = 306.21$ is not supposed to contain any new machines. Yet H^* increases by the value of 50 machines without accumulation, that is to say, without any conversion of surplus value into capital!

The addition of 150 machines last year has transferred the capital structure of the scheme from *Case I* to *Case III*. If no further accumulation occurs, the situation next year should be as in *Case III'* of Table 6.8 on the next page. Yet if the 50 machines are in fact added to the present stock, the situation next

TABLE 6.8

		Capital structure		*Depreciation*
Case III'	(300)	two-year-old machines = R_{t+1}		100
	450	one-year-old machines		150
	300	new machines	↓	100
	1050		⟨	$D_t =$ (350)
Case III''	(300)	two-year-old machines = R_{t+1}		100
	450	one-year-old machines		150
	350	new machines	↓	116.7
	1100		⟨	$D_t =$ (366.7)
Case IV	(350)	two-year-old machines = R_{t+1}		117
	350	one-year-old machines		117
	350	new machines	↓	117
	1050		⊜	$D_t =$ (350)

year will be different, and, as shown in *Case III''* of the same table, this will be the case despite the absence of either accumulation or technical progress. This is quite strange. In Chart 6.2 overleaf, the situations before and after the accumulation of 150 machines are compared. In both cases, the existing stock of machines, H^*, is shown by the area of a large rectangle on the left. The section corresponding to the value of 300 two-year old machines is shaded. The arrow from the bottom of the rectangle shows the formation of depreciation-funds. The arrow returning to the shaded portion of the rectangle indicates the replacement value of the stock of machines. The black circle represents the possible addition to the stock in the absence of further accumulation.

(γ) The Japanese economists who investigated this kind of problem have offered two tentative answers to it. According to one, there is no rational reason for these 50 surplus machines to be purchased. The capitalists of the first-sector wanted to accumulate 150 machines last year, not 200 machines. If this year they contemplate no accumulation, they will replace only the 300 machines wearing out currently, not 350 machines. Consequently, 50 surplus machines have been over-produced and can never be sold. In most cases, the exponents

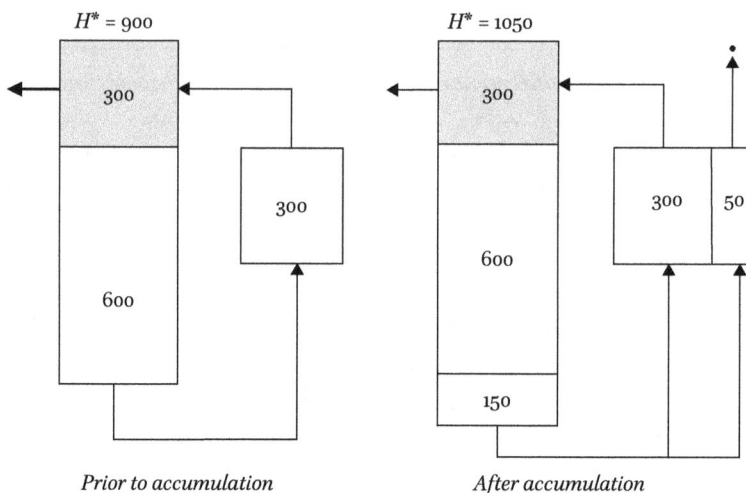

Prior to accumulation   After accumulation

CHART 6.2

of this doctrine are delighted rather than embarrassed because they see in this an easy explanation of 'the contradiction inherent in the capitalist system of reproduction'. Some have gone so far as to produce a theory of periodic crises on the basis of these unrealisable surplus machines.

The reason why 50 surplus machines cannot be bought is that the 150 new machines added last year (ΔH^*) do not have the same age-composition as the pre-existing stock of 900 machines (H^*). If, indeed, ΔH^* was invested last year in 50 'second-hand' two-year-old machines, 50 'second-hand' one-year-old machines, and 50 new machines, the age-composition of fixed capital would have remained 'simple', as in *Case IV* of Table 6.8 above, and there would have been no deficit or surplus machines. It is, however, obvious that only in exceptional cases can capital accumulation occur in such a sophisticated manner. Consequently, although the 150 machines introduced last year have depreciated one-third of their value, they have not physically become the equivalent of 100 new machines. The use-value of 150 machines has been integrally preserved, while one-third of their value has disappeared. Since the capitalists want the use-value of 150 machines, but not the use-value of 200 machines, there can be no conceivable demand for the 50 additional machines according to the first theory.

The other view is to admit that the expansion of the scale of reproduction is possible even in the absence of the conversion of surplus value into capital.

At least those capitalists who sold 150 new machines last year are capable of purchasing 50 additional machines this year, without sacrificing any part of their surplus value. The idea that in a growing economy, depreciation can provide a significant source of investible funds is certainly well founded in experience, and cannot be objected to as contrary to the reality of capitalist society. Since the capitalists lose nothing, but only gain by purchasing the 50 surplus machines and extending the scale of their operation, there is no convincing reason as to why they should be inhibited from doing so. Moreover, the reproduction-scheme presupposes equilibrium, in the sense that nothing can be over-produced unless capitalists make a miscalculation with regard to prospective demand. There is no evidence that they have done so in the present case.

However, if the 50 surplus machines are added to the stock of capital this year, there will be another surplus of 66.7 machines in the following year, as shown in *Case III"*. If these machines are also added to the prevailing stock, there will be a deficit of 61.1 machines in the second year. But suppose that these machines are not replaced. In the third year there will again be a surplus of 18.5 machines. If the capitalists continue in this manner, without converting any more surplus value into constant capital, it can be calculated that after the tenth year the structure of capital will become 'simple' at about $375 = D = R$. In this example, for the sake of argument, all restrictions that might impede such investments are assumed away. The quantity of money available to the system is, of course, considered sufficient to circulate all surplus machines. With the same value composition of the product, 75 additional machines will require the additional variable capital of 22.5 value units, while the labour-power, wage-goods and money necessary to circulate them are all assumed to be present. The conclusion then follows that 75 surplus machines are given to the capitalists permanently as if they were a free bonus, or a gift of nature, in consequence of the once-and-for-all accumulation of 150 machines ten years earlier.

Having recognised the possibility of expanding the scale of reproduction without a conversion of surplus value into constant capital, Shigeto Tsuru and Yoshihiro Takasuka conclude as follows:

> There still remains an important problem. If accumulation funds can be generated from outside of surplus value, and if what is merely a transfer of pre-existing value can serve to promote an expansion of productive powers, it is no longer certain that the value relation remains invariant to a given state of productive technology. This problem which has

not at all been satisfactorily solved in the past controversies over the reproduction-schemes deserves a more systematic investigation.[222]

It is my view that the problem *cannot* be settled within the abstract framework of the reproduction-schemes, since the complication arises from the concrete nature of fixed capital itself, which cannot be wholly considered in that narrow framework. To be more specific, fixed capital has a twofold character. On the one hand, it is a means of production, which must be regularly reproduced. On the other, it is a means of production, which need not be reproduced every year, since it only gradually wears out. In the former aspect, a piece of fixed capital, just as any other commodity, must be strictly distinguished from permanent assets or the forces of nature, which fundamentally cost nothing to society and cannot be produced as commodities. Yet in the latter aspect, a piece of fixed capital shares common elements with permanent assets, which it most closely approaches at the limit, and hence cannot be treated simply like any other commodity.

The following passage shows Marx's awareness of this important fact:

> With the increase of capital, the difference between the capital employed and the capital consumed increases. In other words, there is increase in the value and the material mass of the instruments of labour, such as buildings, machinery, drain-pipes, working cattle, apparatus of every kind that function for a longer or shorter time in processes of production constantly repeated, or that serve for the attainment of particular useful effects, whilst they themselves only gradually wear out, therefore, only lose their value piecemeal, therefore transfer that value to the product only bit by bit. In the same proportion as these instruments of labour serve as product-formers without adding value to the product, i.e., in the same proportion as they are wholly employed but only partly consumed, they perform, as we saw earlier, the same gratuitous service as the natural forces, water, steam, air, electricity, etc. This gratuitous service of past labour, when seized and filled with a soul by living labour, increases with the advancing stages of accumulation.[223]

---

222   Takasuka 1968, p. 242.
223   Marx 1967, *Capital*, Volume II, pp. 607–8.

A similar view is also expressed by Knut Wicksell, as follows:

> Goods of greater durability (such as streets, railways, buildings, etc.) cannot be regarded or treated as capital in the narrower sense, but, once they are there, must be placed, economically speaking, in the same category as landed property itself.[224]

Thus, if 150 machines accumulated in one year can still function as 150 machines in the following year, in which one-third of their value is already transferred to the new product, then 50 machines, which no longer possess value and hence cannot transfer any more value, render a 'gratuitous service' or free productive capacity to society. The lack of proportionality or correspondence between value and use-value (apart from the life expectancy of the machines) observed here suggests that insofar as machines are concerned, the form of value does not quite subsume real economic life. It is true that an item of fixed capital is a commodity, and must be treated as such in the sphere of circulation. Yet it refuses to be consumed in the same manner as ordinary goods are consumed, either directly or productively.

In the reproduction-schemes, in which the reproducibility of capitalist society must be studied from the point of view of the circuit of commodity-capital, fixed capital can be treated only insofar as the commodity-form can subsume it, that is to say, only insofar as it renders no 'gratuitous service', its age-composition remaining 'simple'. It is not the purpose of the reproduction-schemes to consider every concrete detail of the capitalist economy; their purpose is fully served when the reproducibility of all the goods that society needs as commodities is confirmed. To consider the more concrete side of fixed capital, as it functions in the productive sphere, would be to misapprehend the dialectical significance of the theory of the reproduction-schemes, which must not be degraded to a mechanical theory of two-sectoral growth. Such an arbitrary device cannot reasonably account for the actual process of capitalist growth in any case. It must not of course be concluded that the reproduction-schemes cannot exhibit any aspect of capital accumulation. The scale of reproduction expands when circulating (constant) capital is generated from surplus value. The conversion of surplus value into fixed capital, however, involves a problem that must be examined in a more concrete context, namely, in the context of the actual process of capitalist accumulation.

---

224 Wicksell 1954, p. 119.

C   The Actual Process of Capitalist Accumulation (The Unconditioned
       Actuality of Capitalism)

(a)   *The Organic Composition of Capital*

(α) Only the *possibility* of capital accumulation has been studied so far. An
expanded reproduction of the capitalist production-relation becomes an *actuality*, contingent upon the natural growth of the working population. On the
basis of the same contingency, the annual reproduction of commodities can
uniformly expand with the conversion of surplus value into capital, provided
that the age-composition of fixed capital remains 'simple'. However, the actual
process of capitalist accumulation must overcome all contingencies, for otherwise capital could not accomplish its purpose and organise a whole historical
society according to its own principle. To overcome the present restriction,
capital introduces innovations in the technical method of production in its
own peculiar way. It is this fact that establishes capitalism as a historically
significant mode of production that must of necessity advance the productive
powers of labour.

   In the adoption of a new technical method, an individual capitalist is motivated by the pursuit of an *extra surplus value*. Even though the extra surplus
value must disappear as the new method of production is more and more
widely adopted, a gain in the productive powers of labour remains. To the extent that the technical progress contributes to the reduction of the necessary
labour-time, the production of relative surplus value is enhanced. Although
consistent with the general nature of capitalist chrematistics, the pursuit of
extra surplus value must not, however, be supposed to become actual under all
circumstances. The concrete process of capital accumulation exhibits a cluster
of technical innovations during a particular phase of the recurring business
cycle. Extra surplus value is most vigorously pursued in the phase of depression, when the severity of capitalist competition is especially pronounced. The
reason for this fact is explained by the presence of fixed capital, which embodies a technical method of production.

   If an improvement in the method of production bears only on circulating capital – such as raw materials and fuel – and involves no change of fixed
capital, all capitalists will immediately adopt the improved method, unless
the adoption is specifically obstructed by patent and other non-economic restrictions. As already mentioned, such extra-economic practices must be abstracted from in the theory of a purely capitalist society, hence the question
of extra surplus value does not arise, at least not to any significant extent, in
the absence of fixed capital. The introduction of technical progress becomes a

meaningful economic problem only when the new method involves a physical adaptation of fixed capital. Fixed capital, which embodies a particular technology, must be depreciated over a lengthy time span. A typical industrial plant may, for instance, take ten years before it is fully depreciated. In that case, no capitalist enterprise can abandon the existing plant in the first few years of its operation, even if a more efficient method of production has been discovered and is perhaps already being adopted by some new firms. A large part of capital value advanced, which has not been recovered in the form of money, cannot be recklessly sacrificed. Only when the sacrifice is small, relative to the advantage of adopting a new method, will the capitalist consent to scrap the existing plant.

In the phase of depression that follows a crisis, there are two reasons why the adoption of a new method becomes easier. First, many of the existing plants, by this time, have already depreciated much of their value, leaving a relatively small portion of advanced capital value unrecovered. Secondly, the disruption and the contraction of the social reproduction-process destroy both the value and the use-value of the presently advanced capital, whether in the form of commodities or means of production. In such a state of affairs, the un-depreciated value of existing fixed capital has become virtually worthless in any case. For example, an existing machine could be used for another year or so if it continued to be worked at its normal capacity. Yet the market conditions may be such that the machine can only be run at half its capacity, which would not be economical because of the unusually high cost of maintenance. In such a case, both the value and the use-value of the existing machine have already been destroyed.

When the reproduction-process of capitalist society is paralysed under the effect of an economic crisis and subsequent depression, not only functioning productive capital but also commodity-capital loses its value, together with its use-value. The circulation of commodities being generally inactive, the existing stock is difficult to sell. The prevailing prices often do not justify continued production of new commodities, at least not at the normal capacity. Capital value can be maintained only in the form of money, since money alone is the general means of purchase. The reluctance to invest, even in circulating constant capital and variable capital, must accordingly leave the existing plant idle. In the actual process of capital accumulation, periodic disruptions of social reproduction caused by the *absolute excess of capital* cannot be avoided. To explain the excess of capital, however, the concept of the *organic composition of capital* must first be introduced, so that accumulation involving no rise in the composition ('widening' or extensive accumulation) and accumulation involving a rise in the composition ('deepening' or intensive accumulation) may

be distinguished. 'The reproduction on an enlarged scale [is said to be] extensive if the field of production is extended; intensive if the means of production
is made more effective',[225] according to Marx.

(β) 'In this chapter [Chapter xxv of *Capital*, Volume I] we consider the influence of the growth of capital on the lot of the labouring class', says Marx.
'The most important factor in this inquiry is the composition of capital and
the changes it undergoes in the course of the process of accumulation'.[226] After
this prefatory remark we find the following important specifications:

> The composition of capital is to be understood in a twofold sense. On the
> side of value, it is determined by the proportion in which it is divided into
> constant capital or value of the means of production and variable capital
> or value of labour-power, the sum total of wages. On the side of mate-
> rial, as it functions in the process of production, all capital is divided into
> means of production and living labour-power. This latter composition is
> determined by the relation between the mass of the means of production
> employed, on the one hand, and the mass of labour necessary for their
> employment on the other. I call the former the *value-composition* and the
> latter the *technical composition*. Between the two there is a strict correla-
> tion. To express this, I call the value composition of capital, in so far as
> it is determined by its technical composition and mirrors the changes of
> the latter, the *organic composition* of capital. Whenever I refer to the com-
> position of capital, without further qualification, its organic composition
> is always understood.[227]

The technical composition is therefore a concept similar to what is nowadays
called the 'capital-labour ratio'. Yet such a concept would be meaningless unless 'the mass of the means of production employed' were measurable, free
from the index number problem. Since diverse items of the means of production cannot generally be reduced to a homogeneous mass, the concept of the
technical composition cannot be strictly defined. However, it may be taken
to refer to technology or the 'roundaboutness' of the methods of production,
which the value composition of capital more or less expresses. If the rate of
surplus value is given, the value composition of capital in an industry indicates

---

225   Marx 1967, *Capital*, Volume II, p. 172.
226   Marx 1967, *Capital*, Volume I, p. 612.
227   Ibid.

the extent to which the production of its use-value requires labour that produces other use-values. For instance, the spinning of cotton yarn requires, in addition to spinning labour itself, all sorts of other labour, such as labour that makes raw cotton, labour that constructs the spinning machine, and so on. The ratio of the spinning labour to all other forms of labour that indirectly contribute to the spinning of yarn determines the value composition of capital in the cotton-spinning industry, given the rate of surplus value. In other words, it is the indirectness or the *roundaboutness* of the method of production that the value composition of capital reflects, other things being equal. Yet the value composition of the aggregate-social capital can change even when all methods of production remain the same, if the pattern of social demand varies. For example, it may be supposed that the value composition (c/v) is 1 in agriculture, but 2 in manufacture. If the proportion of the output of agricultural goods to the output of manufactured goods changes, then the value composition of the aggregate social capital moves between 1 and 2, even though both agriculture and manufacture continue to employ the same methods of production. The value composition of capital also varies if the rate of surplus value changes, although the technology remains the same. The concept of the organic composition excludes those variations in the value composition of capital that do not originate in a change in the technical method of production.

Although at this point Marx has not introduced the concept of fixed capital, and appears to take constant capital as wholly consisting of circulating capital, he makes it clear that the organic composition reflects a particular level of industrial technology. However, if a given level of industrial technology is embodied in fixed capital, the latter cannot altogether be ignored in the definition of the organic composition. In the presence of fixed capital, the ratio of constant to variable capital advanced (k) differs from the ratio of the constant-capital component to the variable-capital component in the value composition of the product (k^*). (Note that this k has nothing to do with the reciprocal of the velocity of monetary circulation, k, extensively discussed in previous sections of this chapter). If the value of fixed capital advanced is H, and the portion of it transferred to the product is h, it is clear that:

$$k = \frac{(H + Z)}{V} \quad \text{and} \quad k^* = \frac{(h + Z)}{V} \tag{32}$$

where Z stands for circulating constant capital, and V for variable capital. If $H = \gamma Z = nh$, the two ratios are related as:

$$k = \frac{(\gamma + 1)n}{\gamma + n} k^* \tag{33}$$

Hence, only when the stock-to-flow coefficients, γ and n, are constant is the rate of change of k equal to the rate of change of k^*.

In the actual process of capital accumulation, it is not always possible to assume that the speed of value transfer (n) and the proportion of fixed to circulating constant capital (γ) remain constant from year to year. Suppose, for example, that a spinning machine operated by five workers converts 500 tons of raw cotton into 400 tons of cotton yarn per year. If one-tenth of the machine depreciates in the meantime, and if the annual quantity of labour per worker is given, the technology may be represented by (1/10, 500, 5) = (wear and tear of the machine, raw cotton, labour-power). If, however, the scale of reproduction is doubled, without involving a change in technology, 800 tons of cotton yarn must be produced in a year with 2(1/10, 500, 5) = (1/5, 1000, 10). With constant values, the proportion ($h : Z : V$) has not changed, whether the output of cotton yarn is 400 tons or 800 tons, and hence k^* remains the same. Yet there is no compelling reason to believe that the proportion ($H : Z : V$), and hence the ratio, k, is also maintained unchanged.

In the actual process of accumulation, the expansion of output occurs more frequently by wearing out the existing machine twice as fast as before, rather than by introducing another machine, which transfers its value to the product at the same rate as the pre-existing machine. During the prosperity phase of business cycles, it is the case that in addition to the increased employment of workers, overtime work or shift-work is also quite common. Thus, the plant runs day and night, accelerating the depreciation of the existing equipment. No claim is made that all types of fixed capital have to be used more intensively when the output level rises; some new tools and machine parts may indeed be added as the scale of operation expands. Yet if it were possible to adjust the 'plant size' at will, in response to all variations of output, one important reason for paying special attention to fixed capital disappears. The 'fixed' element in the production-process, at least in the short run, implies that some machinery must be used more intensively in the phase of business prosperity. This means that neither n nor γ can be held constant, so that even if k^* is constant, k must change.

Thus, when Marx distinguishes between an extensive accumulation (widening), with the organic composition of capital remaining the same, and an intensive accumulation (deepening), with a rise in the organic composition of capital, it seems appropriate to interpret the meaning of the organic composition in the sense of k^*. Indeed, he writes: 'This law of the progressive increase in constant capital, in proportion to the variable capital, is confirmed at every step by the comparative analysis of the prices of commodities'[228] Elsewhere,

---

228   Marx 1967, *Capital,* Volume I, p. 622.

Marx also comments that he 'always mean[s] by constant capital advanced for the production of value, unless the context is repugnant thereto, the value of the means of production actually consumed in the process, and that value alone'.[229] If accumulation is to take place without involving a change in the technology embodied in the existing plant, the organic composition of capital (k^*) can be maintained constant only because the speed with which the pre-existing value of fixed capital is transferred to the new product is accelerated. The organic composition of capital advanced, in the sense of k, necessarily falls in the course of an 'extensive accumulation'.

This point has not been clearly understood in the traditional analysis of expanded reproduction-schemes. In most cases, n and y are arbitrarily fixed as parameters, and mechanical theories of capital accumulation are proposed assuming no divergence of dk/k from dk^*/k^*. However, the schemes that assume the constancy of these coefficients cannot hope to represent the actual process of capital accumulation. The presence of fixed capital under such stringent restrictions is an unnecessary complicating factor, which adds no new theoretical dimension to the analysis of the schemes. Therefore, I suggest that the only accumulation that can be treated adequately in the abstract context of the reproduction-schemes is an extensive accumulation not involving a change in the organic composition of capital in the sense of k^*. This amounts to claiming that technical changes that accompany the replacement of fixed capital (and that consequently raise the organic composition of capital) are irrelevant to the analysis of the reproduction-schemes.

As already mentioned, two aspects of fixed capital must be distinguished. In one aspect, fixed capital is a reproducible means of production; in the other aspect, it is a temporarily irreproducible means of production, comparable to the gratuitous forces of nature. It is the first of these aspects that must be confirmed in the reproduction-schemes. In the schemes of simple reproduction, the replacement of worn out fixed capital poses no problem, but simple reproduction is a drastic abstraction of capitalist society, which almost never in fact reproduces itself simply. Although the schemes of expanded reproduction are more concrete, in that they allow for capital accumulation, the schematic framework is still much too binding to enable a consideration of the manifold effects of technological changes, without simultaneously obfuscating the dialectical significance of the reproduction-schemes. If technology is unchanged, and if therefore the organic composition, k^*, is to be held constant in the schemes of expanded reproduction, it is surely out of the question to allow for the accumulation of fixed capital that cannot actually occur without a change

229   Marx 1967, *Capital,* Volume I, p. 213.

in k^*. The abstract level at which the schemes should be discussed is simply not adequate to the treatment of the more concrete aspect of fixed capital.

(γ) The presence of fixed capital, as the embodiment of a given level of technology, must be taken seriously in the study of the actual process of capital accumulation. An industrial plant, which typically lasts for ten years or so, cannot be replaced as it wears out. Yet depreciation-funds can be accumulated for its eventual renewal. The value of the plant is therefore unilaterally transferred to the product, and there is no need for the capital-goods sector to annually reproduce the worn out portion of heavy capital equipment. In other words, from the point of view of annual reproduction, the plant of a given size may be taken as if it were a natural gift, except that depreciation-funds must continually drop out of the reproduction-process. The capital-goods sector can therefore concentrate on the production of circulating capital so as to enable the scale of social reproduction to 'widen'. During the prosperity phase of business cycles, new investments in circulating constant capital, rather than in fixed capital, set the pattern of expansion.

'Once given the general basis of the capitalistic system, then, in the course of accumulation, a point is reached at which the development of the productivity of social labour becomes the most powerful lever of accumulation', says Marx.[230] In other words, Marx introduces the accumulation that involves technical changes as typical of a more advanced historical phase of capitalist development, rather than being typical of each depression phase of business cycles. This view is further confirmed by the following statement: 'The accumulation of capital, though originally appearing as its quantitative extension only, is effected, as we have seen, under a progressive qualitative change in its composition'.[231] However, this view constrains his understanding of the law of population as follows: 'The labouring population therefore produces, along with the accumulation of capital produced by it, the means by which itself is made relatively superfluous, is turned into a relative surplus-population; and it does this to an always increasing extent. This is a law of population peculiar to the capitalist mode of production'.[232]

In this way, Marx gives the impression that capitalist accumulation is accompanied by an uninterrupted rise in the organic composition of capital and a secular increase in relative surplus population. If this were true, however, the capitalist mode of production would never have been able to organise a whole

230   Marx 1967, *Capital*, Volume I, p. 621.
231   Marx 1967, *Capital*, Volume I, p. 628.
232   Marx 1967, *Capital*, Volume I, p. 631–2.

society according to its own principle, because of 'an always increasing' mass of capitalistically unemployable workers. Moreover, if productive workers were always available at or near subsistence wage, there would hardly be any reason as to why capitalist accumulation would ever innovate the existing technology and thus go through a cyclical process. It must be understood that the accumulation of capital does not always involve a rise in its organic composition; rather, an extensive accumulation involving no rise in the organic composition is the more normal pattern throughout the prosperity phase of business cycles. Only in the phase of depression is an intensive accumulation, which involves a technological restructuring of the existing plant, forced upon capital.

The alternation of extensive and intensive accumulation in the course of business cycles is that which characterises the actual process of capitalist accumulation. This view is not inconsistent with the following remark of Marx elsewhere in *Capital*:

> The cycle of interconnected turnovers embracing a number of years, in which capital is held fast by its fixed constituent part, furnishes the material basis of the periodic crises. During this cycle business undergoes successive periods of depression, medium activity, precipitancy, crisis. True, periods in which capital is invested differ greatly and far from coincide in time. But a crisis always forms the starting-point of large new investments. Therefore, from the point of view of society as a whole, [it forms] more or less, a new material basis for the next turnover cycle.[233]

The law of population peculiar to capitalism is the other side of the same coin. In the course of an extensive accumulation, the relative surplus population is increasingly absorbed by capitalist industry, raising wages in consequence. 'According to the economists themselves, it is neither the actual extent of social wealth, nor the magnitude of the capital already functioning, that leads to a rise of wages, but only the constant growth of accumulation and the degree of rapidity of that growth'.[234] 'If the quantity of unpaid labour supplied by the working class, and accumulated by the capitalist class increases so rapidly that its conversion into capital requires an extraordinary addition to paid labour, then wages rise, and, all other circumstances remaining equal, the unpaid labour diminishes in proportion'.[235] However, it is not possible simply to assert, without appropriate economic analysis, that 'the very nature of accumulation

233   Marx 1967, *Capital*, Volume I, p. 186.
234   Marx 1967, *Capital*, Volume I, p. 621.
235   Marx 1967, *Capital*, Volume I, p. 620.

excludes every diminution in the degree of exploitation of labour, and every rise in the price of labour, which could seriously imperil the continual reproduction, on an ever-enlarging scale, of the capitalistic relation'.[236]

The shortage of labour-power that translates itself into a sharp rise of wages must cause the excess of capital, the state in which a further accumulation of capital is accompanied by no additional appropriation of surplus value. When that state is reached, capital loses its purpose and ceases to accumulate. The phase of stagnation must therefore set in, from which capital can extricate itself only by a 'rationalisation' of the plant. For when the competition among capitals is particularly intense, in view of the general difficulty of selling commodities, a drastic reduction in the cost of production, due to the adoption of a new technical method, is by far the most dependable way to survive. The pursuit of extra surplus value thus becomes a categorical imperative. Some investments in fixed capital embodying new techniques will therefore occur in a number of industries, and will soon be followed by the majority of capitalists whose old plants by now represent little or no value.

A rise in the organic composition of capital is the consequence of this widespread adoption of new technology. Of course, not all technical progress is 'labour-saving', but the technical progress that is significant from the point of view of the actual process of capital accumulation is the one that makes the technology more 'roundabout', by raising the organic composition of capital, because its rise forms the relative surplus population that will be absorbed in the subsequent phases of recovery and prosperity. Another bout of extensive accumulation can take place on the basis of the presently formed relative surplus population. The following section will show, more rigorously, how the cyclical process of capitalist accumulation must occur.

(b)   The Cyclical Accumulation of Capital

(α) The accumulation of capital means the conversion of surplus value into capital. This conversion, however, cannot be effected unless additional means of production are already available in a suitable form, that is, in a form capable of integrating additional labour-power into variable capital. Let us first consider the case of an extensive accumulation, presupposing the existence of fixed capital that embodies a particular technology. Since the technology is given, additional means of production and additional employment of labour-power must conform to it. The organic composition of capital, in the sense of k^*, remains constant as the scale of reproduction expands. However, any

---

236   Marx 1967, *Capital,* Volume I, p. 621.

increase of output accelerates the turnover of fixed capital, letting the organic composition, in the sense of k, fall.

When accumulation occurs, surplus value, S, in society must include the value to be invested in new constant capital, ΔC, and the value to be invested in new variable capital, ΔV. If it is assumed that a given proportion, α_v, of surplus value is devoted to investment in new variable capital: $\alpha_v = \Delta V/S$; thus, if $e = S/V$ expresses the rate of surplus value, then the desired rate of accumulation of (variable) capital is:

$$\alpha_v e = \frac{\Delta V}{S} \cdot \frac{S}{V} = \frac{\Delta V}{V}, \tag{34}$$

which can also be viewed as the rate of change in the demand for labour-power. This coefficient, α_v, is related to the previously defined rate of accumulation, α, by the formula, $\alpha_v = \alpha(1 + k^*)$, so that α_v falls when the organic composition of capital, in the sense of k^*, rises. However, the natural growth rate of the working population, g, is exogenously determined and cannot agree with $\alpha_v e$, except by mere coincidence. Thus, in general, the two rates of change diverge, as $\alpha_v e$ may be greater or smaller than g. However, if $\alpha_v e < g$ were the case, the unemployment of productive workers would secularly increase, and the capitalist mode of production would never be able to organise a whole society according to its own principle. Such a case must be excluded from the theory of a purely capitalist society. Hence, it must be supposed that $\alpha_v e > g$ in the following discussion.

However, if the demand for labour-power rises faster than the supply of it, it is obvious that sooner or later the market for labour-power will become

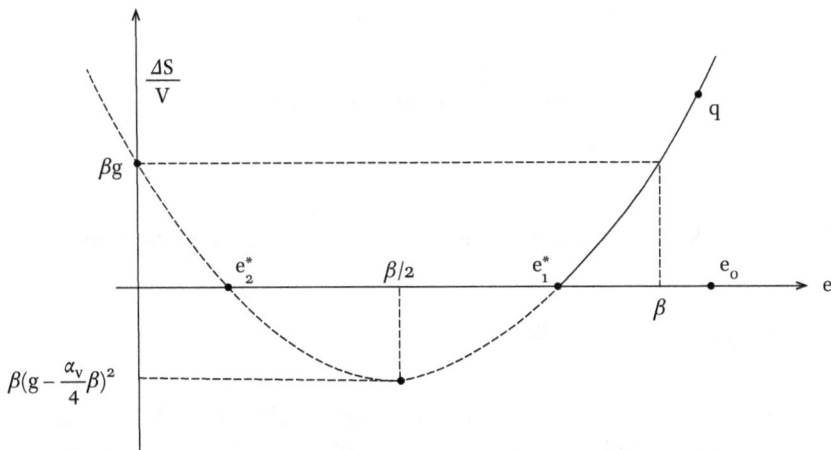

FIGURE 6.1

tight, inducing wages to rise in consequence. Since wages are the price of labour-power, a rise in wages depresses the rate of surplus value, unless the production of absolute surplus value is simultaneously and vigorously pursued, either by the lengthening of the working day or by the intensification of labour. A fall in the rate of surplus value means that surplus value declines relative to variable capital; it does not necessarily imply a retrenchment in the absolute magnitude of surplus value, because the magnitude of variable capital always increases with accumulation. Capital will continue to accumulate so long as ΔS obtainable from ΔV remains positive. To see the limit of capital accumulation, let us introduce a dynamic relation:

$$\Delta e = -\beta(\alpha_v\, e - g), \tag{35}$$

for some speed of adjustment, $\beta > 0$. For example, if the desired rate of accumulation of (variable) capital is 20%, and if the natural growth rate of the working population is 5%, there is a gap of 15%. The speed of adjustment, β, measures the extent to which this gap contributes to the reduction of the rate of surplus value. It is clear that this speed, β, must be neither too small nor too large if the capitalist mode of production is to function reasonably. Indeed, if the rate of surplus value hardly ever changed, despite a considerable gap between the supply of labour and the demand for it, labour-power would not be a commodity. On the other hand, if a minor gap led to a drastic change in the rate of surplus value, the capitalist economy would be unstable. The range within which an appropriate β must fall, in view of the parameters α_v and g, will be made apparent in due course.

From the definition of the rate of surplus value, it follows that:

$$\Delta e = \frac{\Delta SV - S\Delta V}{V^2} = \frac{\Delta S}{V} - \alpha_v\, e^2. \tag{36}$$

Hence, the substitution of (35) for Δe into (36) yields:

$$\frac{\Delta S}{V} = \alpha_v e^2 - \beta(\alpha_v\, e - g), \tag{37}$$

which (with $\Delta S = 0$) is a quadratic equation in e, possessing real roots if and only if:

$$\alpha_v \beta - 4g \geq 0 \quad \text{or} \quad \beta \geq \frac{4g}{\alpha_v}. \tag{38}$$

The capitalist system is considered sufficiently flexible when this condition is satisfied. For example, if $g = 0.05$, $\alpha = 0.4$, $k^* = 4$, and $\alpha_v = 0.08$, then (38) requires that $\beta \geq 2.5$. Thus, if $\beta = 2.5$ and $e = 3.5$, then (35) shows that $\Delta e = -2.5(0.28 - 0.05) = -0.575$. This means that, since the desired rate of accumulation exceeds the rate of growth of the working population by 0.23, the rate of surplus value must at least fall from the present 350% to 292.5%. The capitalist system is expected to possess at least this much flexibility. Now, suppose that β is in fact much higher and is = 4. In that case (37), with $\Delta S = 0$, can be solved for:

$$e_1^* = \frac{\beta}{2} + \sqrt{\left(\frac{\beta}{2}\right)^2 - \frac{\beta g}{\alpha_2}} = 3.2247,$$

$$e_2^* = \frac{\beta}{2} + \sqrt{\left(\frac{\beta}{2}\right)^2 - \frac{\beta g}{\alpha_2}} = 0.7753.$$

Since accumulation is manifestly impossible if $\Delta S / V \leq 0$, it follows that the parabola defined by (37), as depicted in Figure 6.1 on page 407, cannot represent a path of accumulation for any e belonging to the interval, (e_2^*, e_1^*). The same is also true when e is smaller than $\beta / 2 > e_2^*$. This is because the negative slope of the parabola (assuming $\Delta S / S$ to be independent of e) means:

$$\frac{d}{de}\left(\frac{\Delta S}{V}\right) = \frac{d}{de}\left(e \cdot \frac{\Delta S}{S}\right) = \frac{\Delta S}{S} < 0, \tag{39}$$

so that $\Delta S > 0$ would imply $S < 0$, which is, of course, out of the question. Hence, the parabola (37) depicts the path of capital accumulation only for $e > e_1^*$. However, it must be admitted that under a given social and technological condition, the rate of surplus value, e, must be bounded above by some number, $e_0 = \max e$, because beyond that point the reproduction of labour-power becomes an impossible proposition. The actual process of capital accumulation is then compatible only for the rates of surplus value lying in the interval, (e_1^*, e_0).

This interval may be called the feasible range of e. However, when the length of the working day and the intensity of labour are more or less given, the rate of surplus value, e, uniquely corresponds to the length of the necessary labour-time. For example, if the working day is 12 standard hours, and if $e = 100\%$, then the necessary labour-time is 6 hours. Given the technology embodied in the existing plant, a productive worker can produce in 6 hours a definite basket of wage-goods, which define a corresponding 'real wage-rate' per day. Hence, corresponding with the feasible range of the rate of surplus value (e_1^*, e_0), there is a range that is also feasible with regard to real wage-rates (u_{min}, u_{max}). When the rate of surplus value is at its maximum (e_0), the corresponding real wage (u_{min})

may be scarcely better than some biological subsistence level; when the rate of surplus value is at its minimum (e_1), the corresponding real wage (u_{max}) is probably sufficient to pay off past debts. Hence, under the prevailing social and technical condition, some average wage-rate between the two extremes can be taken to represent the reproduction cost of labour-power. When capital introduces a new plant, embodying a particular level of technology, in the recovery phase of business cycles, it is to be expected that there will exist an abundant supply of productive workers employable at a low real wage-rate, rather close to u_{min}, with a high rate of surplus value, close to e_0, corresponding to it. As accumulation proceeds, gradually absorbing the existing supply of labour-power, the rate of surplus value falls in response to the rising trend of wages, as the increment of surplus value, ΔS, per worker declines. In the diagram, a point such as q tends to move along the parabola, steadily approaching the critical point, e^*_r. At this point, capital accumulation yields no more increment to the already available surplus value, and so becomes completely aimless. It is then said that capital is in a *state of absolute excess or superabundance*. No further accumulation can take place, and no further reduction of the rate of surplus value is possible, which also implies that the real wage cannot improve beyond that point.

(β) It is not necessary to imagine that all capitalist firms simultaneously reach the state of the excess of capital. When some firms in various important industries find themselves unable to make new investments, a 'multiplier' process is set off, disrupting the normal operation of society's reproduction. Some additional means of production already produced, envisaging a normal demand, can no longer be sold, and their suppliers are obliged to contract their production and cancel orders for their own means of production, and so on. Since accumulation-funds cease to be spent, a difficulty in monetising the value of newly produced goods will soon be felt everywhere, and a further contraction of the scale of reproduction cannot be avoided. If the reproduction of commodities dwindles, so must the reproduction of the capitalist production-relation. A growing number of productive workers are released from their regular employment, as the climate of depression and stagnation covers the whole economy. Goods already produced, whether as means of production or as articles of consumption, remain unsold, losing their value together with their use-values. The impression of an 'overproduction' therefore pervades capitalist society.

The overproduction of commodities is however a mere manifestation of a more fundamental disequilibrium known as *the excess of capital*. When the scale of social reproduction fails to expand as expected, a cumulative contraction of business is set off, leaving a large number of commodities un-saleable. The process of contraction, often suddenly brought about by an industrial crisis, entails a cessation of productive operations, at the normal capacity at any rate, in many existing plants. For the existing plants, the impossibility to operate at full capacity is a deathblow, because part of the plant, which stands idle, cannot be maintained without incurring a heavy cost. Both the value and the use-value of the existing plant tend to be destroyed in the period of severe depression. Yet it is precisely for this reason that industries can be released from the restriction of the existing technology. As fixed capital loses its value, the technology embodied in it ceases to constrain the capitalist method of production. Those capitals, which have so far accumulated enough depreciation-funds or accumulation-funds, or which are otherwise in possession of readily investible money, can therefore proceed to build new plants.

Of course, not all capitals are in this position. On the contrary, many will find themselves insolvent, and business bankruptcies will be widespread. However, that only means that competition is particularly harsh in the period of general depression. Not all capitalists can be losers in the game; the stronger ones prevail over the weaker, making the 'centralisation' of capital a prominent feature of the period. Centralisation means the annexation of weaker capitals by the stronger. Hence, the winners of the competition can expand the scale of their operation more than is made possible by the 'concentration' of capital through ordinary accumulation. The economies of the larger scale of operation, together with a new industrial technology, enable the winners of the competition to achieve a drastic reduction in the cost of their production. When a phase of recovery arrives, with increasing investments in new fixed capital in various industries, the technological base of the economy will also be renovated.

Investments in new plants that take place in this phase of business cycles generally tend to raise the organic composition of capital. According to Marx,

> The additional capitals formed in the normal course of accumulation serve particularly as vehicles for the exploitation of new inventions and discoveries, and industrial improvements in general. But in time the old capital also reaches the moment of renewal from top to toe, when it sheds its skin and is reborn like the others in a perfected technical form, in which a smaller quantity of labour will suffice to set in motion a larger quantity of machinery and raw materials. The absolute reduction in the demand for labour which necessarily follows from this is obviously so much the greater, the higher the degree in which the capitals undergoing

this process of renewal are already massed together by virtue of the centralisation movement.[237]

Even though 'in the normal course of accumulation', without involving a renewal of the plant, various technical improvements can be adopted by capital, far more significant is the overall renovation of the plant, which proceeds
together with the 'centralisation movement', because this kind of renovation
is more likely to raise the technical and organic composition of capital. The organic composition can be raised only by investments in a new and presumably
heavier class of fixed capital, which embodies a more advanced technology.
Such investments, of course, require a greater concentration of capital. The
centralisation accomplishes, almost overnight, the concentration of capital
that would ordinarily take years to realise, and makes it easier to adopt a more
indirect method of production. In this case, even an 'absolute reduction in the
demand for labour' might occur. However, it is important to understand that
unlike the concentration of capital, which is the necessary consequence of any
accumulation, centralisation depends on contingent factors. Although some
degree of centralisation occurs in every depression period, it is not possible
to theoretically determine how much capital is actually centralised under any
given condition. Moreover, capital, once centralised, may again be split into
parts by such things as 'the division of property within capitalist families'.[238]
It is therefore quite unwarranted to expect that every centralisation of capital
necessarily 'leads to monopoly'.

In the last few decades of the nineteenth-century, the centralisation of
capital did indeed lead to the system of organised monopolies, particularly
in Germany and the United States, eventually atrophying the traditional system of free competition. The reason why the same tendency had not been
manifest prior to that period cannot be explained by the theory of a purely
capitalist society; it can only be explained at the more concrete level of the
stages-theory, in which the use-value aspect of technology is of primary importance. Pure theory must presuppose a technology that is readily manageable
by the commodity-economy, and that therefore does not require an intervention of extra-economic human relations. Such a technology does not lead to
the systematic centralisation of capital of the kind that the development of
the steel industry entailed in the late nineteenth-century. If a particular firm
concentrates capital much more than others, since a more or less uniform concentration of capital by all firms does not make any one of them particularly

---

237   Marx 1967, *Capital,* Volume I, p. 628.
238   Marx 1967, *Capital,* Volume I, p. 625.

monopolistic, technological considerations will act in favour of 'the division of property'. The capitalist market, in the middle of the nineteenth-century, remained freely competitive despite frequent centralisations of capital, because industrial technology generally spurned an oversized business management with the exception perhaps of the cases of the railways and public utilities.

What is important in the present context is not the tendency for capitalism to depart from the freely competitive system, but the ability of industrial capital to automatically improve upon productive technology within the scope of free competition. The above-quoted passage of Marx emphasises the important fact that the rebuilding of fixed capital, which embodies a new technology, is often accompanied by a recognisably enlarged size of the plant of many, not just a few, capitalist firms. The technology appropriate to a large-scale operation, in this sense, is the one that saves the input of labour-power relative to the material means of production, and that consequently raises the organic composition of capital.

(γ) Thus, given the rate of accumulation or the capitalists' propensity to save, the proportion of additional variable capital, ΔV, to surplus value, S, that is to say, the ratio $\alpha_v = \Delta V/S$, is reduced from that which prevailed previously, since $\alpha_v = \alpha/(1 + k^*)$ falls as k^* rises. In the following phase of business prosperity therefore the demand for labour-power, $\Delta V/V = \alpha_v e$, will be lower than previously, for any given rate of surplus value. That will reduce the speed with which additional surplus value per unit of variable capital, $\Delta S/V$, declines with a fall in the rate of surplus value. Figure 6.2 below compares the new path of capital accumulation with the old one. For example, if α_v falls from 0.08 to 0.06, whereas $\beta = 4$ and $g = 0.05$ remain as before. The minimum rate of surplus

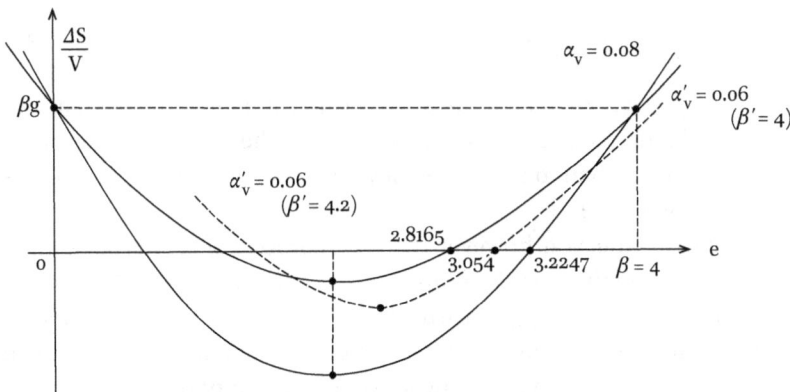

FIGURE 6.2

value, consistent with a meaningful capital accumulation, will be $e^*_1 = 2.8165$, instead of $= 3.2247$. Here, $\beta = 4$ still satisfies the condition (38) under the new $\alpha'_v = 0.06$. Thus, if β is unchanged, the critical rate of surplus value at which capital accumulation ceases is lower than previously.

However, it may be thought that there is no reason why β should remain unchanged when α_v falls. The fact that the condition (38) now requires $\beta \geq 3.33$, rather than ≥ 2.5 as it was previously, might suggest the advisability of allowing for a rise in β. If β rises, the whole parabola, labelled $\alpha_v{}' = 0.06$, shifts to the right, and generally increases the steepness of its slope, with the minimum point of the parabola moving below and to the right of the original position. Hence, the fall in the critical rate of surplus value, $(e_1{}^*)$, brought about by the reduction of α_v can be cancelled by a pronounced simultaneous rise in β. However, a rise in β is not a necessary consequence of technical progress. While as an index of market sensitivity, β may have a long-run tendency to improve, it does not necessarily do so because the organic composition of capital, k^*, has risen. It may therefore be reasonable to suggest that technical progress, which reduces α_v, always leads to a decline in the critical rate of surplus value, e^*_1, even if β may simultaneously improve somewhat. This sets a limit to the improvement of β, relative to the fall in α_v. Specifically, in the present case, with the assumed $g = 0.05$ and fall in α_v from 0.08 to 0.06, one may insist that a new β' should be constrained by the relation, $e^*_1(\beta') < 3.2247 = e^*_1(\beta)$. Together with (38), this relation requires that:

$$3.3333 \leq \beta' \leq 4.3484.$$

So long as the variation of β is kept within this range, e_1 always declines with technical progress. This condition can be stated more generally as:

$$\frac{de^*_1}{d\alpha_v} > 0 \quad \text{or} \quad -\frac{\alpha_v}{\beta} \cdot \frac{d\beta}{d\alpha_v} < \frac{g}{e^*_1 \alpha_v - g} \tag{40}$$

For example, if $\beta' = 4.2$, then $e^*_1 = 3.054$. That is to say, along the new path of capital accumulation (shown by the broken curve), the rate of surplus value falls to 305.4%, rather than to 281.7%, in view of the somewhat improved sensitivity of the capitalist market.

If this is generally the case, however, the actual process of capital accumulation, involving a rise in the organic composition of capital, is not at all inconsistent with a historical rise in u_{max}, since a fall in e^*_1 and an improved technology both tend to increase the quantity of wage-goods per worker. This point will be studied more carefully in the following section. More important in the present context is the implication of the above analysis for the cyclical formation and absorption of relative surplus population. Of course, it is true that 'every labourer belongs to the relative surplus population during the time when he is only partially employed or wholly unemployed'.[239] However, the 'progressive production of a relative surplus population or industrial reserve army'[240] must not imply a cumulative increase in the number of wholly or partially unemployed workers. Marx claims that the 'whole form of the movement of modern industry depends upon the constant transformation of a part of the labouring population into unemployed or half-employed hands',[241] because the long-run trend of capitalist accumulation is to raise the organic composition of capital. However, the real problem here does not lie in a 'progressive' formation of an industrial reserve army that is independent of the cyclical course of capital accumulation. The real economic problem is rather that a relative surplus population 'creates for the changing needs of the self-expansion of capital a mass of human material always ready for exploitation, independently of the limits of the actual increase of population'.[242] This occurs during the cyclical course of capitalist accumulation. Hence, Marx's decision 'not to take into account the great periodically recurring forms that the changing phases of the industrial cycle impress' on the relative surplus population, and only to emphasise that 'it has always three forms, the floating, the latent, the stagnant',[243] is not wholly above reproach from the point of view of the dialectic of capital.

(c)   *The Value of Labour-power*

(α) 'Every special historic mode of production has its own special laws of population, historically valid within its limits alone. An abstract law of population exists for plants and animals only, and only in so far as man has not interfered with them'.[244] The law of population peculiar to capitalist society does not concern itself with the determination of the natural growth rate (g) of the working population. That rate – which is determined by biological, cultural and sociological factors, but which cannot be directly influenced by capital – must be regarded as given from outside the commodity-economic system. The capitalist law of population establishes the manner in which capital adapts to and makes use of the existing population. Capitalist society, in consequence,

---

239   Marx 1967, *Capital,* Volume I, p. 640.
240   Marx 1967, *Capital,* Volume I, p. 628.
241   Marx 1967, *Capital,* Volume I, p. 633.
242   Marx 1967, *Capital,* Volume I, p. 632.
243   Marx 1967, *Capital,* Volume I, p. 640–1.
244   Marx 1967, *Capital,* Volume I, p. 632.

sometimes appears over-populated and sometimes under-populated with productive workers.

A mode of production that never fully employs the existing working population, and that is therefore characterised by a chronic under-employment of direct producers, cannot form a historical society. If productively employed, however, labour-power at least maintains itself with the product of its necessary labour ($g = 0$); more frequently, it grows at some positive rate ($g > 0$), as determined by biological and socio-cultural factors. An economic theory of population takes a non-negative growth rate of the working population as given, and examines the relationship between that rate and the growth rate of economic variables – such as productive capacity, output and employment. A population theory, such as the Malthusian theory, which directly concerns itself with the natural growth rate of population, is of a different sort and must not be confused with what might be called an economic population theory, even if the determining factor of the demographic growth rate (g) is expressly claimed to depend on 'economic' factors (whatever this might mean). The classical doctrine, which considered real wages as the primary regulator of the natural growth rate of population, is a particularly outrageous example of this confusion. Even empirically, it is not true that higher wages always increase the birth rate and diminish the death rate of infants, and vice versa. Even if it were true, the adjustment would require such a long time that in the meantime economic variables would, in any case, necessarily adapt to the current growth rate of population.

Since labour-power is not a product of labour, the supply of labour-power cannot be readily adjusted to the social demand for it by the ordinary functioning of the commodity-economic mechanism. An economic theory of population is therefore justified in treating the natural growth rate of the working population as exogenously or autonomously determined. What the economy can do, given the growth rate of the working population, is the problem that specifically concerns the economic theory of population. It is clearly a general norm of economic life common to all societies that in the absence of technical progress, the scale of social reproduction cannot be expanded faster than the current growth of the working population. As a corollary of this proposition, it follows that every society must have its own method of introducing labour-saving technical devices if it intends to grow faster than the rate at which its population naturally grows. The capitalist law of population exhibits the peculiarly commodity-economic manner in which capitalist society introduces new technology, so as to make the best possible use (from the point of view of capital) of the gradually self-expanding working population.

What is peculiar to capitalist society's production is that it always intends to grow faster than labour-power naturally grows. Hence, sooner or later the demand for labour-power will exceed its supply. Yet the accumulation of capital cannot proceed unless additional productive elements, including labour-power, are readily available as commodities in the market. Since productive elements other than labour-power are capitalistically producible commodities, they can always be made available in the market. Labour-power alone cannot be produced when it is needed. It is for this reason that capital has to maintain the supply pool of labour-power in the form of a *relative surplus population* (which is also called the 'industrial reserve army'). The social reservoir of labour-power however cannot be maintained at a constant level. It is sometimes full and sometimes empty. The law of population explains how capital fills and drains this social reservoir of labour-power.

In the actual process of accumulation, capital forms and absorbs the relative surplus population. It does not unilaterally produce a surplus population that it can never employ. On the contrary, it is only when the excess of capital, caused by the shortage of labour-power, frustrates further accumulation that the formation of a surplus population becomes unavoidable. At this point, capital is compelled to innovate the existing plant, while discarding the obsolete technology embodied in it and introducing the technical progress that constitutes the basis for a new capitalist production-relation. Just as investments in new fixed capital in a cyclical phase of depression form a relative surplus population by raising the technical composition of capital, investments in circulating constant capital, during the ensuing phase of prosperity, absorb the existing supply of labour-power until the strain in the labour market leads to a sharp rise of wages, eventually forcing capital into another stalemate. This does not exclude all improvements in the technical method of production during the prosperity phase of business cycles. However, if such improvements do occur in individual firms during the period in which the capitalist economy by and large sails smoothly, they do not revolutionise the existing technology of society as a whole. The formation of a relative surplus population is a consequence of society-wide technological progress.

The alternate formation and absorption of relative surplus population ensures the durability (or staying power) of the capitalist mode of production, for only by this mechanism can labour-power be contained in the commodity-form. Labour-power is the only commodity that capital cannot directly produce. Yet without labour-power as a commodity, capitalism cannot operate. It is therefore a vital matter for capitalism to assure the availability of labour-power. When the shortage of labour-power develops in the course of an extensive accumulation, the price mechanism of the market cannot stop the persistent rise of wages and the consequent fall of the rate of surplus value. This is not the case with other commodities that capital can directly produce. If the price of any commodity rises, capital automatically responds by producing more of that commodity, and this adjustment will continue until the price rises no further. That is why the law of value asserts itself through the motion of prices, thus determining the real cost to society of the production of ordinary commodities. This mechanism does not apply to labour-power, the value of which must therefore be determined otherwise.

(β) Even though the value of wage-goods for workers' consumption can be determined in the market, what assortment of wage-goods should be deemed 'necessary' for the reproduction of labour-power poses another question, which has not been answered. For this reason, it is often asserted that the living standard of wage-earning workers is rigidly fixed at some subsistence level, although such a thesis is not even consistent with the fallacious idea of the absolute impoverishment of the working class, with which the thesis is often jointly defended, unless, of course, the biological subsistence itself is susceptible of a secular deterioration. It is true that the standard of living cannot be determined by the price mechanism. The market does not determine a 'natural' or an 'equilibrium' wage-rate, because labour-power is not a product of capital. However, that does not imply that the real wage is determined outside of the capitalist system, which contains but does not wholly consist of the price mechanism of the market. Being exogenous to the market does not mean being so to the inner structure of the capitalist system.

In the course of capital accumulation, given the technological base upon which the capitalist production-relation is founded, there is a lower limit below which the rate of surplus value cannot fall without rendering further accumulation meaningless. There is also an upper limit beyond which the rate of surplus value cannot rise without rendering the reproduction of labour-power impossible. The feasible range (e^*, e_o) of the rate of surplus value is a well-defined concept because given the length of the working day and the intensity of labour, the rate of surplus value exactly determines the length of labour-time necessary for the reproduction of labour-power. Since the technology is already given, the output of wage-goods producible during the 'necessary' labour-time is also unambiguously determined. Hence, the determination of the real wage, or the living standard of workers, amounts to identifying a normal rate of surplus value that belongs to the interval (e^*, e_o) in any particular period of capitalist history. Some reasonable formula can always be constructed to select a normal $\bar{e}$ from the range (e^*_l, e_o) in such a way as to let $\bar{e}$ represent the rate of surplus value prevailing in the period of so-called 'average activity'.[245]

Once $\bar{e}$ is selected, the value of labour-power per day, which is equal to the necessary labour-time per day, is immediately given by the formula, $\bar{v} = t/(1+\bar{e})$, where t is the length of the working day. Any collection of wage-goods, which embodies the same value as $\bar{v}$, is the normal real wage-rate, $\bar{u}$, representing the standard of living of the working class. Of course, that $\bar{u}$ falls in the interval, (u_{min}, u_{max}), as explained earlier. Thus, the value of labour-power is not 'exogenously' determined at a subsistence level; it is determined 'endogenously' in the actual process of capital accumulation, and depends on the extent to which capital incorporates the available technology of production. With the development of the capitalist method of production, the minimum feasible rate of surplus value, e^*_l, is expected to fall, but the production of relative surplus value is also furthered so as to raise the maximum feasible rate of surplus value, e. Therefore, the normal rate $\bar{e}$ may not substantially vary over a long period. Yet if technology improves, the same $\bar{v}$ can, of course, produce more wage-goods; the living standard of the working class can therefore easily rise in the course of capital accumulation.

Let $v = t/(1 + e)$, where t = the average length of the working day of an employed worker, be taken as fixed. Let also $u = a(\theta)v$, where u is the index of the physical size of the basket of wage-goods, which an average worker receives as wages, and $a(\theta)$, $a'(\theta) >$, o is the average productivity depending on the technical parameter, θ. Then the relation between real wages and the rate of surplus value can be written as $u = a(\theta) t/(1 + e)$ and may be graphed, as in Figure 6.3 overleaf. On each curve, representing a particular level of technology, a possible selection of a point, $(\bar{e}(\theta), \bar{u}(\theta))$, is shown by a small circle. There is no unique method of selecting such a point. For example, $\bar{e}(\theta) = [e_o(\theta) - e^*_l(\theta)]/2$, is one possible way of obtaining $\bar{e}(\theta)$, although there are presumably many other ways. However, it is quite obvious that a very special selection, such as $\bar{e}(\theta) = e_o(\theta)$, will be necessary to justify the subsistence-wage theory, and that more obvious sophistry is needed to choose $\bar{e}(\theta)$ from the range $[e_o(\theta) - e^*_l(\theta)]$ in such a way as to let the corresponding $\bar{u}(\theta)$ fall with the advance of technology. In the graph, a dotted curve is inserted to show a possible case of $\bar{u}'(\theta) < 0$. However, if $\bar{e}(\theta)$ is so selected as to represent the cyclical phase of average or medium activity, it is clearly impossible for $\bar{u}(\theta)$ to have a negative derivative.

There are some passages in *Capital* that might be interpreted to support the so-called doctrine of absolute impoverishment or immiseration. Even without these passages, Marx's treatment of the progressive or cumulative

---

245   Marx 1967, *Capital*, Volume I, p. 632.

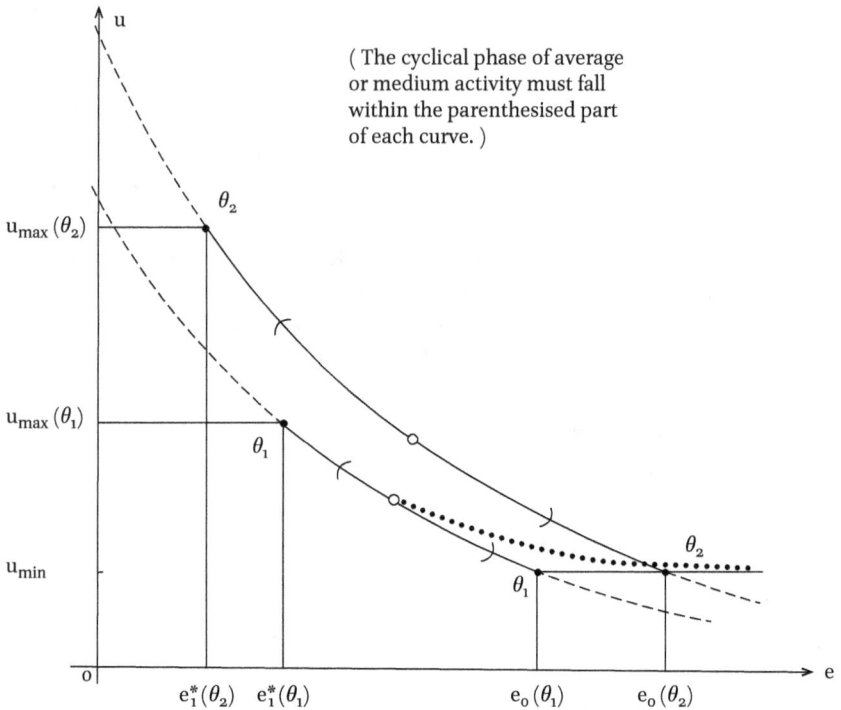

(The cyclical phase of average
or medium activity must fall
within the parenthesised part
of each curve.)

FIGURE 6.3

formation of relative surplus population, or industrial reserve army, can easily
cause the impression that the living standard of the working class is destined
to worsen, as capital accumulation proceeds. Perhaps in the middle of the
nineteenth-century, this impression was widely shared in the light of empirical
evidence. But it is important to realise that there is no theoretical presumption
that absolute impoverishment is always necessary. It is certainly not 'the absolute general law of capitalist accumulation' that 'the greater this reserve army
in proportion to the active labour-army, the greater is the mass of a consolidated surplus-population, whose misery is in direct proportion to the labour
put in', and that 'the more extensive the lazarus-layers of the working class,
and the industrial reserve army, the greater is official pauperism'.[246] These are
mere empirical facts, which by themselves do not explain an economic law.
Empirical phenomena of a particular stage of capitalist development must be
evaluated in the light of the law of population, previously established in the
theory of a purely capitalist society. What the above theory shows is that as

---

246   Marx 1967, *Capital*, Volume I, p. 644.

long as $\bar{e}(\theta)$ is chosen so as to correspond with the workers-versus-capitalists relation in the cyclical phase of average activity, rather than in the trough of business depression, absolute impoverishment is impossible. On the contrary, the standard of living of the working class must be expected to rise as capital accumulates, incorporating more advanced technology.

(γ) Thus, regardless of how $\bar{u}(\theta)$ is selected, the amount of labour socially necessary to produce the basket of wage-goods of that size may be regarded as the value of labour-power, $\bar{v}$. The value of labour-power is indeed 'historically determined', but not in some vague, impressionistic sense; 'historically' here means 'in correspondence with the particular level of technology that capital is under the commodity-economic compulsion to adopt at a given moment of history'. The value of labour-power cannot therefore be determined independently of the commodity-economic necessity that governs the behaviour of capital. The determination of the value of labour-power cannot be exogenous to the capitalist system, if indeed it is a consequence of the capitalist law of population. By virtue of this fact, the only open-endedness remaining in the account of the operation of the law of value, which governs the motion of capital, is now closed. For as long as labour-power remains a commodity, the value of which is well defined, the law of value sees to it that the capitalist mode of production operates safely as the value-formation-and-augmentation process. The law of population therefore supplements the law of value, by defining the value of labour-power, that is, by establishing the ability of the capitalist mode of production to permanently contain labour-power in the form of the commodity.

One important consequence of the law of population is that no productive worker remains permanently unemployed under capitalism, a point that is often overlooked. If, indeed, unemployment of productive workers is observed to exist, it means that the cyclical phase of average activity has not yet been reached, and wages have not yet risen beyond $\bar{u}(\theta)$. Consequently, the excess of capital cannot occur. Nor is a society-wide technical innovation necessary when the reservoir of labour-power can still feed an 'extensive' accumulation of capital. In the cyclical phase of average activity, capitalism always achieves a full employment of productive workers. That is why, in the period of 'precipitancy' following the phase of average (or medium) activity, capitalism in fact mobilises even such workers as would be 'unemployable' under other conditions. As for productive workers, they receive wages well beyond the value of labour-power, and labour-power becomes increasingly uncontrollable as a commodity. This fundamental disequilibrium, however, is allowed to develop only up to the point where the excess of capital forces a remoulding of capitalism. In the ensuing period of depression, a large number of productive workers become unemployed. Yet they have earned enough wages in the period of 'precipitancy' to survive the hard days of depression, unless the depression is inordinately protracted due to contingent factors. A purely capitalist society cannot admit such contingent factors as might have contributed, for example, to the long depression of the 1870s.

In the cyclical course of capital accumulation, wages thus sometimes fall below the value of labour-power, and at other times rise above it. The value of labour-power is revealed by the level of wages that prevails in the period of 'average activity', which is dependent on a particular complex of industrial technology. If wages rise too far above the value of labour-power, the existing technology no longer permits the extensive accumulation to continue, and a society-wide reorganisation of productive technology is forced upon capital. There is, however, no theoretical reason to believe that capital is unable to meet this challenge. On the contrary, it is the ability of capital to resort at this point to an 'intensive' accumulation that explains the extraordinary resilience of the capitalist mode of production. The structural flexibility of capitalism, which enables it to incorporate more and more advanced technology of production, when it conforms to its aim of chrematistics, is that which establishes the historical significance of this institution. If, indeed, such flexibility were absent, capitalism would not have lasted much more than a decade, given that it would have been unable to overcome the excess of capital.

The excess of capital often causes a violent and spasmodic disruption to the normal working of the capitalist economy. Yet the law of population peculiar to capitalism is certain to intervene, restructuring the technological base of capital and generating a *relative surplus population*. Only through the operation of this law is the continued conversion of labour-power into a commodity, the ultimate foundation of capitalism, guaranteed, and the grip over this institution by the law of value confirmed. Thus, the law of population, under which the value of labour-power is determined, establishes a purely capitalist society as a *perpetuum mobile,* a self-sustained motion, or, in other words, as Hegel's 'absolute and unconditioned actuality'. Pure capitalism never collapses or breaks down of its own accord because of the excess of capital. On the contrary, by overcoming the excess of capital, capitalism makes itself what it is, that is to say, what it 'simply and positively is', as Hegel puts it, without depending on any alien principle.

In accomplishing this self-dependence, capital has made no concession; it has unremittingly pursued its one single purpose of value augmentation, thereby turning all possibilities into necessities. The actual process of capital accumulation is the absolute necessity of capital, 'absolute' because it is not constrained by any principle outside it. Precisely for this reason, however, 'the truth of necessity is freedom' (Hegel): capital is now free from self-destruction. Having thus assured itself of its own imperishability, capital can proceed to build its own kingdom, developing its ideological aspirations into the laws of the market. The dialectic of capital accordingly now leaves the sphere of Essence and follows capital into its kingdom of the Notion.

www.ingramcontent.com/pod-product-compliance
Lightning Source LLC
Chambersburg PA
CBHW070859030426
42336CB00014BA/2252